KARL BARTH

KARL BARTH God's Word in Action

Paul S. Chung

CASCADE *Books* • Eugene, Oregon

KARL BARTH
God's Word in Action

Copyright © 2008 Paul S. Chung. All rights reserved. Except for brief quotations in critical publications or reviews, no part of this book may be reproduced in any manner without prior written permission from the publisher. Write: Permissions, Wipf and Stock Publishers, 199 W. 8th Ave., Suite 3, Eugene, OR 97401.

Cascade Books
A Division of Wipf and Stock Publishers
199 W. 8th Ave., Suite 3
Eugene, OR 97401

www.wipfandstock.com

ISBN 13: 978-1-55635-527-1

Cataloging-in-Publication data:

Chung, Sueng Hoon, 1958–

    Karl Barth : God's word in action / Paul S. Chung.

    xvi + 504 p. ; 23 cm. —Includes bibliographical references and index.

    ISBN 13: 978-1-55635-527-1

    1. Barth, Karl, 1886–1968. 2. Barth, Karl, 1886–1968—views on socialism. 3. Christianity and politics. 4. Religious pluralism. I. Titles.

BX4827. B3 C478 2008

Manufactured in the U.S.A.

This volume is dedicated in honor of Professor Dr. Friedrich -W. Marquardt (1928–2002) at the FU of West Berlin, and President and Professor Timothy F. Lull (1943–2003) at Pacific Lutheran Theological Seminary, Berkeley, California.

The fact that God's Word is God's act means first its contingent contemporaneity.... The dogmatician, too, must think and speak in a particular age.... The problem of theology and dogmatics can be seen as wholly set within the framework of the problem of culture.

    Karl Barth, *Church Dogmatics*, I/1:145, 283–84

CONTENTS

Foreword · ix

Acknowledgements · xi

Abbreviations · xiii

Introduction:
Karl Barth in the Context of Competing Interpretations · 1

1. Karl Barth's Theology and Socialism in Safenwil: 1910–1918 · 28
2. Karl Barth and the First Edition of *Romans* (1919) · 114
3. Karl Barth between Hope and Disillusionment: The Tambach Lecture of 1919 · 162
4. Karl Barth and the Second Edition of *Romans* (1922) · 192
5. Karl Barth: Between the Times in Germany · 235
6. Karl Barth and *Theologia Naturalis* · 286
7. Martin Luther in the Theology of Karl Barth · 345
8. Karl Barth as a Theologian who Discovers Judaism for Christian Theology · 377
9. The Liberative Dimensions in Barth's Theology · 419

Conclusion: Karl Barth and an Unfinished Project for Religious Pluralism · 449

Bibliography · 485

Index · 503

FOREWORD

THE FAMOUS WORDS OF OLD BARTH, "GOD FOR THE WORLD, GOD FOR humanity, heaven for the earth," can stand as a motto regarding this very clearly written and engaging book that marks and characterizes the life and theology of Karl Barth. Barth is without comparison as a twentieth-century theologian who has determined a field of theological discussion still present to date. In a knowledgeable and precise analysis, Paul S. Chung proposes the themes in which Barth's theology has emerged, gained its profile, and initiated landmark decisions. In this analysis, Chung states that the churches need to have their orientation for Barth's theology, not only in a national socialist Germany, but also in South Africa or Latin America in their most difficult crises. What is penetrated here in this book stretches from Barth's confrontation with religious socialism (Ragaz) to his subsequent breakthrough of dialectical theology ("Tambach lecture") and to two different editions of *Romans* via the first exciting encounter with Roman Catholicism (Przywara) to the century problem of natural theology (Brunner), and finally to the distinctive themes of *Church Dogmatics* (Christology, the church and Israel) and to openness toward ecumenicity in the face of religious pluralism. At this juncture, the difficult dogmatic problems are understandably discussed with great caution and care whether it is a debate over *analogia entis*, the role of *extra Calvinisticum* or the secret of the person of Christ (*anhypostasis* and *enhypostasis*).

What is most significant for me is that Chung is involved both knowledgeably and with daring evaluation and judgment in present-day scholarly discussions and debates about Karl Barth. Here, different interpretations such as those of Friedrich-Wilhelm Marquardt and Bruce McCormack, as well as the reservations of feminist theologians, are provocatively explicated. Furthermore, his study includes the controversially discussed relationship between Barth and Bonhoeffer and the pigeonholing charge of neo-orthodoxy. Chung's arguments are not only of a historical or dogmatic-confessional nature. They include also the questions and problems of our present time. This makes Chung's project a modern book and a great contribution that explicates the fascination and strength of Karl Barth, above all, articulating his intellectual achievement and profound humanity for our present-day reality in a new and fresh way.

Christian Link
University of Bochum, Germany

ACKNOWLEDGEMENTS

THIS BOOK HAS A TWOFOLD TASK: FIRST, IT INTENDS TO CLARIFY BARTH'S keen interest in social and political realms in his early writings, prior to his dogmatic turn; and second, it seeks to deepen and actualize the political dimension of his dogmatic theology in regard to his theology of Israel and issues of *theologia naturalis* and religious pluralism.

In writing this project, I am indebted to Professor Eberhard Busch and his understanding of Karl Barth's doctrine of Israel. I appreciate that he presented to me with the gift of his illuminating book *Unter dem Bogen des einen Bundes: Karl Barth und die Juden 1933–1945* (1996). My sincere gratitude is likewise extended to Prof. Andreas Pangritz at the University of Bonn, Germany, a former assistant of Helmut Gollwitzer and Friedrich-Wilhelm Marquardt.

Furthermore, I express my gratitude to Prof. Bertold Klappert at Wupertal and Prof. Christian Link at Bochum. They kindly invited me to join the discussion of Barth's theology with them during my research period at the University of Bonn, Germany, in June 2007. My gratitude also goes to Rev. Dr. Hans Ulrich Jäger in Einsiedeln, Switzerland, a Ragaz expert and follower of Ragaz's practical way in the field of ministry, for deepening my understanding of the relation between Karl Barth and religious socialism. Prof. Peter Winzeler at the University of Bern made valuable comments on my understanding of the relation between Martin Luther and Karl Barth and helped me to understand Barth's theology of creation from an ecological perspective. I am thankful to Prof. Raymond Carr for his proofreading and comments. My sincere gratitude is offered to the faculty of Wartburg Theological Seminary. I remain indebted to them for their encouragement and accompaniment of my theological journey, not only as Luther's follower, but also as Barth's student.

I would like to thank T. & T. Clark and the Continuum International Publishing Group for permission to use selected texts from the following: Karl Barth, *Church Dogmatics*, edited Geoffrey W. Bromiley and T. F. Torrance, 1936–1962; *Church Dogmatics* I/1–IV/3, edited by Geoffrey W. Bromiley and T. F. Torrance, first paperback edition, 2004. Used by permission of T. & T. Clark and the Continuum International Publishing Group. I also gratefully acknowledge receipt of the following: From Theologischer Verlag Zurich (Zurich, Switzerland) permission to cite from Karl Barth, *Der Römerbrief* (Erste Fasssung) 1919, edited by Hermann Schmidt, and F.-W. Marquardt, "Erster Bericht über Karl Barths 'Sozialistische Reden'"; and from Oxford University Press (Oxford, England) permission to cite from Karl Barth, *The Epistle to the Romans*, translated by Edwyn C. Hoskyns; and Bruce L. McCormack, *Karl Barth's Critically Realistic Dialectical Theology: Its Genesis and Development, 1909–1936*.

Paul S. Chung
Dubuque, Iowa
Thanksgiving 2007

ABBREVIATIONS

AB	Dietrich Bonhoeffer. *Act and Being: Transcendental Philosophy and Ontology in Systematic Theology*. Edited by Wayne Whitson Floyd Jr. Translated by H. Martin Rumscheidt. DBW 2. Minneapolis: Fortress, 1996.
ADT	*Anfänge der dialektischen Theologie*. Vol. 1, *Karl Barth, Heinrich Barth, Emil Brunner*. Edited by Jürgen Moltmann. Theologische Bücherei; Neudrucke und Berichte aus dem 20. Jahrhundert, Bd. 17. Systematische Theologie. Munich: Kaiser, 1962-1963.
B-B	Karl Barth and Rudolf Bultmann. *Karl Barth-Rudolf Bultmann: Letters 1922-1966*. Edited by Bernard Gaspert. Translated and edited by Geoffrey W. Bromiley. Grand Rapids: Eerdmans. 1981.
BevT	Beiträge zur evangelischen Theologie
BHT	Beiträge zur historischen Theologie
B-Th I	Karl Barth and Edward Thurneysen. *Karl Barth-Edward Thurneysen: Briefwechsel, 1913-1921*. Edited by Edward Thurneysen. Zurich: TVZ, 1973.
B-Th II	*Karl Barth-Eduard Thurneysen: Briefwechsel, 1921-1930*. Zurich: TVZ, 1974.
CD	Karl Barth. *Church Dogmatics*. 4 vols. Translated and edited by Geoffrey W. Bromiey and G. T. Thomson. Edinburgh: T. & T. Clark, 1956-1969. See also *Church Dogmatics*. 4 vols. Translated First paperback edition. Edinburgh: T. & T. Clark, 2004.
CDE	Karl Barth. *Die Christliche Dogmatik im Entwurf.* Bd. 1, *Die Lehre vom Worte Gottes, Prolegomena zur christlichen Dogmatik*. Edited by Gerhard Sauter. Zurich: TVZ, 1982.

DBE	Eberhard Bethge. *Dietrich Bonhoeffer: Man of Vision, Man of Courage*. Translated by Edward Mosbacher et al. Edited by Edwin Robinson. New York: Harper & Row, 1970.
DBW	Eberhard Bethge, et al., editors. *Dietrich Bonhoeffer Werke*. 17 vols. Munich: Kaiser, 1986–1999.
DBW	Geffrey B. Kelly et al., editors. *Dietrich Bonhoeffer Works*. Translated by Daniel W. Bloesch and James H. Burtness. 7 vols. Minneapolis: Fortress, 1996–2001.
E	Dietrich Bonhoeffer. *Ethics*. Edited by Eberhard Bethge. Translated by Neville Horton Smith. The Library of Philosophy and Theology. New York: Macmillan, 1955.
EvT	*Evangelische Theologie*.
EVZ	Evangelischer Verlag Zurich.
FQI	Barth, Karl. *Anselm: Fides quaerens intellectum*. Translated by Ian W. Robertson. London: SCM, 1960.
KD	Karl Barth. *Die kirchliche Dogmatik*. Munich: Kaiser, 1932; Zurich: EVZ, 1938–1965.
KPD	German Communist Party.
LPP	Dietrich Bonhoeffer. *Letters and Papers from Prison*. Edited by Eberhard Bethge. Translated by Reginald H. Fuller, Frank Clarke, John Bowden, et al. New York: Macmillan, 1972.
LW	Helmut T. Lehmann, editor. *Luther's Works*. Volumes 31–55. Philadelphia: Fortress, 1955–1986; Jaroslav Pelikan, editor. *Luther's Works*. Volumes 1–30. St. Louis: Concordia, 1955–1967.
MEW	Institut für Marxismus-Leninismus beim ZK der SED. *Karl Marx, Friedrich Engels Werke*. 37 vols. in 38 bks. Berlin: Dietz, 1956–1989.
NuG	Peter Fraenkel, translator. *Natural Theology: Comprising "Nature and Grace" by Professor Dr. Emil Brunner and the reply "No!" by Dr. Karl Barth*. London: Bles, 1946
R I	Karl Barth. *Der Römerbrief*. Erste Fassung unveränderter Nachdruck der ersten Auflage von 1919. Zurich: EVZ, 1963.
R II	Karl Barth. *The Epistle to the Romans*. Translated by Edwyn C. Hoskyns from the sixth German edition of *Der Römerbrief*. London: Oxford University Press, 1968.
SA	*Sturmabteilung*
SC	Dietrich Bonhoeffer. *Sanctorum Communio: A Theological Study of the Sociology of the Church*. Edited by Clifford J. Green. Translated

	by Reinhard Krauss and Nancy Lukens. DBW 1. Minneapolis: Fortress, 1998.
SPD	Social Democratic Party of Germany.
SPS	Social Democratic Party of Switzerland.
ST	Thomas Aquinas. *Summa Theologica*. Translated by the English Dominican Fathers. 21 vols. New York: Benziger Brothers, 1947.
TC	Karl Barth. *Theology and Church: Shorter Writings, 1920–1928*. Translated by Louise Pettibone Smith. London: SCM, 1962.
TK	Karl Barth. *Die Theologie und die Kirche*. Munich: Kaiser, 1928.
ThSt	Theologische Studien.
TVZ	Theologischer Verlag Zurich
UCR I	Karl Barth. *The Göttingen Dogmatics: Instruction in the Christian Religion*. Vol. 1. Translated by Geoffrey W. Bromiley. Grand Rapids: Eerdmans, 1991.
USPD	Independent German Socialist Party.
WA	*D. Martin Luthers Werke: Kritische Gesamtausgabe*. 61 vols. Weimar: Hermann Böhlaus Nachfolger, 1912–1921.
ZEE	*Zeitschrift für evangelische Ethik*.
ZTK	*Zeitschrift für Theologie und Kirche*.

*In this book two editions of *Church Dogmatics* (in 1956–1969 and 2004) are used in an interchangeable way. Translation and page numbers are different.

INTRODUCTION Karl Barth in the Context of Competing Interpretations

KARL BARTH LIVED INTENSELY. AS A COROLLARY, HIS THEOLOGY CANnot be adequately understood without reference to his life of social commitment. His thought-form is contextual and dynamic, sometimes repulsive. He was keen and open to modification, clarification, and correction in his theological trajectory. Barth, moreover, was not averse to self-critique and turnabout in his theological pilgrimage. Although there are many followers and movements of Barthianism, he remained hesitant and even averse to identifying himself with any form of "ism." In Barth's words we hear: "God is not identical with any ideology, and is not to be confused with such. Hence, conversion to Him is not to be confused with any human decision for rearmament or disarmament in orientation to any ideology" (*CD* IV/4:140). Understanding Barth this way implies an ongoing resistance to any real attempt at a systematization of his theology although, paradoxically, he is the systematic theologian of *Church Dogmatics*.

Barth's expressive style of writing and his point of departure along the lines of "beginning anew at the beginning" aroused many different interpretations and called for variegated dialogues with him. For Barth, "in theological study, continuation always means 'beginning once again at the beginning.'"[1] In this light, for Barth, doing theology means that it must be established through nothing but audacity. His break with established theology invoked such a spirit of audacity. Although different in intention from Franz Overbeck, Barth cited him approvingly for his theological direction. "It was over forty years ago that I read this remark

---

1. Barth, *Evangelical Theology*, 164–65. Cf. *CD* I/2, § 64.2. "The Dogmatic Method."

by Franz Overbeck, 'theology can no longer be established through anything but audacity.' I paid attention to it. The liberal theologians will have to pay attention to it as well." [2]

In his commentary *The Epistle to the Romans* (8:24) Barth states: "If Christianity be not altogether thoroughgoing eschatology, there remains in it no relationship whatever with Christ" (R II:314). Barth's dialectical theology is basically and definitely oriented toward eschatology. Needless to say, Barth's dialectical-organic theology in the 1919 edition of *Romans I*, in fact, assumes an eschatological character and horizon. "Trust in God cannot be separated from eschatology." "Solving the riddle of the world cannot be separated from eschatology" (R I:241, 246). The theology of *Ursprung* associated with the immediacy of God in *Romans I* and the theology of *Krisis* in *Romans II* can be understood first of all in light of God's eschatology, God's in-breaking reality into the world. Here, Barth cross-examines his theological development and exercises a self-criticism, especially in relation to his theological subject matter. When we read Barth from a political perspective, an expectation associated with eschatological longing constitutes his *hurrying* involvement in the political world, but at the same time we see him as a *waiting* theologian, remaining sober and down-to-earth, free from any political fanaticism.

The Grounding Break in Karl Barth

As far as Barth interpretation is concerned, it was Hans Urs von Balthasar who noticed two decisive turning points in the development. The first is the conversion from theological liberalism to Christian radicalism during the First World War, the expression of which we find in Barth's two *Römerbriefe*. The second liberation comes through his reading of Anselm of Canterbury's proof for the existence of God (1931) rather than in the brochure *Nein!* (1934) against Emil Brunner as is commonly assumed.[3] Balthasar's insistence on the second turn, from dialectic to analogy, gained prominence as the catalyst for advancing successive research on the theological unfolding of Barth's thought.

T. F. Torrance, by contrast, marks three developmental stages in Barth's thought as he moved from the new starting point via dialectical

---

2. Jüngel, *Karl Barth: A Theological Legacy*, 54.
3. Balthasar, *Theology of Karl Barth*, 79–80.

thinking to dogmatic thinking. These stages are as follows: (a) In the new starting point of dialectical thinking there occurred a break with liberal theology during the year 1914, a break that reached its climax with the first edition of *Romans* in 1919; (b) the second principal stage began in the 1920s, when the thorough revision of his first *Romans* commentary came out, and the first volume of Barth's projected *Dogmatics* exhibited the influence of Kierkegaard in a dialectical and realistic fashion; (c) the third stage came through Barth's study of St. Anselm when Barth made the really decisive transition from *Christian Dogmatics* (*Christliche Dogmatik im Entwurf* [1927]) to the *Church Dogmatics* (*Kirchliche Dogmatik* [1932]).

Barth's *Christian Dogmatics* met opposition and resistance from his critics. In the Germany of the 1920s, phenomenological, psychological, numinous, and existentialist interpretations of Christian faith were in fashion. Barth realized that he was not able to escape the remnants of existential philosophy in his *Christian Dogmatics*. Eventually, through his study of St. Anselm in the summer of 1930, Barth was able to emancipate himself from a preunderstanding of human existence by purging the language of Kierkegaard from his discourse and by stepping over the eggshells of philosophical systematics.[4] As a result, Barth eventually referred to his *Christian Dogmatics* as a false start (*CD* III/4:xii).

Like Balthasar, Torrance interpreted the turn from dialectical theology to analogy as a radical paradigm shift, marking a new theological development. According to Bruce McCormack, this reigning paradigm—as represented by Balthasar and Torrance—has been influential especially on English-speaking Barth scholarship. Following this paradigm, Hans Frei takes Barth's study of Anselm as representing a revolution in Barth's thought.[5]

In contrast to this standpoint, Eberhard Jüngel, in dealing with the development of Barth's theology, argues for one decisive break in Barth's theological development, that is, Barth's break with theological liberalism during the year 1914. In Jüngel's words we read: "This expression [a theology of the Word of God] is . . . better suited than the alternative 'dialectical theology' to describe the continuity in the path which Barth followed after the break with the theology of his teachers—though it was,

4. Torrance, *Karl Barth: Early Theology, 1910-1931*, 134. Cf. Barth, *How I Changed My Mind*, 42-44.

5 Frei, "Doctrine of Revelation," 194. Cf. McCormack, *Critically Realistic*, 4.

to be sure, a winding path with several turns."[6] According to Jüngel, the theology of the Word of God can be portrayed as a *terminus a quo* (as a starting point) and a *terminus ad quem* (as an aim or terminal point in time), which can be perceived in a shift from Barth's dialectical thinking to his dogmatic theology. Jüngel quotes Barth's own remark about "the inner dialectic of the subject matter [*Sache*]" in the preface to the second edition of *Romans*. With the phrase "the inner dialectic of the subject matter," Barth intended to express the idea that not only speech about the *Sache* but also the *Sache* itself should be conceived of as being dialectical.

However, Barth's turn to dogmatic theology expresses a change in his thought that reveals a turn from the assertive dialectic to a dialectical style of assertion. This dialectical style of assertion undialectically affirms the Word of God. For Jüngel, Barth's turn to an undialectical Word of God becomes possible only by way of "a completely different reorientation of the previous thought-movement."[7] For this reorientation, Barth improves himself through his study of Anselm of Canterbury, whose influence can be already seen in *Christian Dogmatics* (*Die christliche Dogmatik im Entwurf* [1927].) However, Barth's revision of *Christian Dogmatics* did not reach its goal by simply eliminating a basis, a support, or even a mere justification by means of existential philosophy (*CD* I/1:ix). With his move to the undialectical Word of God, Barth began to develop his doctrine of the *analogia fidei*. Therefore, in dealing with Barth's turn to Anselm, Jüngel insists that Barth's theology of analogy increasingly exhibited a hermeneutical circle and established the confessional and narrative character of his dogmatic argumentation. In this regard, analogy becomes the formal foundation and structure of Barth's dogmatic assertions.

Given this fact, Jüngel expresses his agreement with Balthasar and Torrance's high regard for Barth's study of Anselm. Likewise Frei contrasts analogy as "an analytical, technical category" with dialectic as "anti-liberal use of the category and procedure." According to Frei, dialectic in Barth's later development became an important subordinate device and formal category in the service of analogy. Analogy redescribes "conceptually and by means of a series of fluid juxtaposition (of figures, images, events, persons, points of view) the teleological, temporal flow of the divine-human

---

6. Jüngel, "Von der Dialektik zur Analogie," in Jüngel, *Barth-Studien*, 128.

7. Jüngel, "Die theologische Anfänge: Beobachtungen," in ibid., 47.

relation, of which the New Testament depiction of Jesus Christ gives at once the foundation and the aim."⁸

However, unlike Jüngel, Spieckermann has discovered a form of analogy in an earlier phase of dialectical theology (*Romans II*) that would serve as a basis for the *analogia fidei* in Barth's later stage. In her view, the analogy of the cross that can be found in *Romans II* is the original form of the *analogia fidei*.⁹ Close to Spieckermann, Michael Beintker finds evidence of analogical thought in Barth's early writings of 1919 and the 1920s. Barth's reflection on a form of analogy can be traced back to his Tambach lecture (1919). As Beintker says, "the *Denkform* of the *analogia relationis sive proportionalitatis*, which sets forth a correspondence between the God-human relation and the human-human relation, forms a constant in Barth's work from the time of the Tambach lecture onward."¹⁰

Drawing upon Spieckermann and Beintker's studies, Bruce McCormack makes a contribution to understand the theology of Karl Barth in a critical, realistic, and dialectical fashion. For him, talk about a radical turn or shift from dialectics to analogy is out of the question. On the basis of *Realdialektik*, a dialectic in objectively real relations, in *Romans II*, and by viewing the *analogia fidei* as grounded in the dialectic of veiling and unveiling in revelation, McCormack asserts the thesis that "in truth, the *Realdialektik* of veiling and unveiling is the motor which drives Barth's doctrine of analogy and makes it possible."¹¹ As far as Barth remains a dialectical theologian in his *Church Dogmatics*, *Christliche Dogmatik* deserves, for McCormack, a special focus in continuity with *Church Dogmatics* (1932) rather than to be regarded as a false start.

However, concerning the coexistence of dialectics and analogy in Barth's thought,¹² it was Friedrich-Wilhelm Marquardt who, before Spieckermann and Beintker, first perceived and attested to Barth's reflection on a relationship between dialectics and analogy in Barth's earliest

8. Frei, *Types of Christian Theology*, 160.

9. See Spieckermann, *Gotteserkenntnis: Ein Beitrag zur Grundfrage der neuen Theologie Karl Barths*.

10. Beintker, *Dialektik in der 'dialektischen Theologie' Karl Barths*, 261–62. Cf. McCormack, *Critically Realistic*, 10.

11. McCormack, *Critically Realistic*, 18.

12. We also take note of the coexistence of dialectic and analogy in Eberhard Mechels's writing in 1974; cf. Mechels, *Analogie bei Erich Przywara und Karl Barth*.

lecture, "Faith in a Personal God" ("Der Glaube an den persönlichen Gott" [1914]). A material development of analogy comes from the *Ursprung* onwards. At a minimum, Barth's concept of analogy stands materially as well as temporally before the conceptualization of dialectics in *Romans II*. Marquardt argues that analogy and dialectic for Barth can be seen as simultaneously grounded in his thought of *Ursprung*. This formulation is the basis for the *Ursprung* of analogy in 1914. This coexistence comes to the surface in Barth's Tambach lecture in such a way that his reflection on analogy is not merely of scholastic character but of a social-critical and inclusive dimension from the start.[13] In this regard, Marquardt takes Balthasar's model of Barth's turn from dialectic to analogy to be untenable. According to Marquardt, analogy and dialectic for Barth can be grounded co-originally in his thought of *Ursprung*.[14]

When it comes to a radical turning point in Barth's thought, it seems that a significant paradigm change occurred from 1915 to 1916. In his important article "The Humanity of God" (Die Menschlichkeit Gottes"), Barth gives an indication of his meeting with Christoph Blumhardt (April 1915): "Was it—this has played a decisive role for me personally—precisely the failure of the ethics of the modern theology of the time, with the outbreak of the First World War, which caused us to grow puzzled also about its exegesis, its treatment of history, and its dogmatics? Or was it, in a positive sense, the message of Blumhardt concerning the Kingdom of God which, remarkably enough, was only then becoming timely?"[15]

In a letter from April 1947, Barth mentioned his background and his subsequent turning away from it. Here he makes reference to his former position as a middle place between Kant and the young Schleiermacher. From autumn 1908 to autumn 1909, Barth was an assistant editor to Martin Rade at the *Christliche Welt*. After that he came into the church and developed his theological thought not as a half-minded adherent but as a thorough adherent of the school of Marburg. However, seven years later (also in 1916!), Barth made a new discovery, and his relationship with theological liberalism finally came to an end.

Barth's entrance to the Social Democratic Party of Switzerland (SPS) on January 26, 1915, his meeting with Blumhardt in that same month,

---

13. Cf. Marquardt, *Christ in der Gesellschaft*.
14. Marquardt, *Theologie und Sozialismus*, 208–9.
15. Barth, *Humanity of God*, 40–41.

and finally the beginning of the commentary on Romans (1916) mark Barth's break with liberalism between 1915 and 1916. Regarding Barth's correction of his previous position (from his Safenwil period), he deals with mostly in *Romans II*, but not very much in *Romans I*.

Barth's discovery of Reformation theology in 1921 in Göttingen does not revoke his discoveries as expressed in *Romans I* during his Safenwil period but only deepens and radicalizes them. Barth's personal report of 1916 indicates his understanding of *Romans I* as his initial break with his liberal background. Barth stood in the tradition of Blumhardt's message of the kingdom of God and remained faithful to it. Even toward the end of his life, in his *Ethics* fragment *The Christian Life (Das Christliche Leben* [1959–1961]), Barth makes a fundamental affirmation of Blumhardt's message, which was also his position in *Romans I*.[16]

Therefore we cannot ignore the relevance of *Romans I* for Barth's subsequent works, especially for *Romans II* and his dogmatic work. In his *Church Dogmatics* he tries to overcome the limitation of the *Romans II* eschatology in terms of *Romans I*.[17] It is important to point out that Barth himself, in an interview, denied any break between the theology of *Romans* and *Church Dogmatics*, saying that "there are people who say there was a break in my theology between the *Römerbriefe* and now. For me, there was never a break there! In the *Römerbrief* I drew back the bow, took aim at a definite target, and let the arrow fly and the subject-matter which was there in question changed in the process—and afterwards, appeared quite differently."[18]

Barth's eschatological Christology or christological eschatology in *Romans I* has been overlooked and marginalized. As a matter of fact, Barth takes the event of resurrection to be a perfected future of world-consummation (R I:60, 122), or as a present reality of the in-breaking of the coming world-salvation. In this light, the cross is understood as the event of reconciliation with the world and as a fundamental transformation of the relation between God and humans. Therefore, Barth develops an *eschatologia crucis* in terms of an *eschatologia resurrectionis*. This

16. Barth, *Christian Life*.
17. Cf. *CD* I/2:50; II/1. § 31. 3; *CD* IV/3.2 § 71. 4. 6.
18. See "Brechen und Bauen: Diskussion mit Prof. Karl Barth am 5 August 1947." In Barth *"Der Götze wackelt,"* 112. Cf. McCormack, *Critically Realistic*, 452.

eschatological concept of cross and resurrection provides a basis for a universal/inclusive dimension of eschatological Christology in Barth.[19]

Karl Barth and Political Radicalism

As for Barth's social-critical dimension of hermeneutics in the second commentary on Romans, we need to note a fundamental remark: "the historical critics, it seems to me, need to be more critical!" (R II:x). This was Barth's response to his critics' charge that he was a "declared enemy of historical criticism." Barth's response reveals that his approach to hermeneutics constituted a breakthrough to a new relationship to theology, its subject matter, and political relevance. Barth's critics of *Romans I* accused him of eliminating history from his interpretation of Romans. They argued that in place of historical-critical exegesis Barth had applied biblicism and pneumatic exegesis. In the foreword, Barth states that Paul "addressed his contemporaries as a child of his age." But more importantly, "he speaks as a prophet and apostle of the Kingdom of God to people of every age" (R I:v).

According to Barth, Paul's vocation as a prophet and apostle of the kingdom of God to the contemporaries of every age is more far important than Paul's message in the past as a child of his time. Barth's concern about his own time leads him to consider the doctrine of inspiration more important than the historical-critical method for the task of understanding. Barth's hermeneutic in both *Romans* commentaries is to see through the historical to the spirit of the Bible. However, his intent was not to become pneumatic or a declared enemy of historical criticism by rejection of it (R II:xiii). Rather, Barth appears as a social-critical theologian beyond the historical critics. Therefore, we can conclude that Barth does not reject the rightful place of the historical-critical method in biblical investigation.[20]

Barth charged his contemporaries with giving up the task of a serious, respectful understanding and explanation of Paul's Romans for his time, out of respect for history over and against tradition. Historical critics approached the biblical texts on the basis of Ernst Troeltsch's triadic

---

19. Klappert, *Versöhnung und Befreiung*, 330.
20. Barth's letter to Thurneysen on January 1, 1916. In *B-Th I*, 119–22, 121. See also Smart, *Revolutionary Theology*, 36.

formulation: (a) the principle of criticism, (b) the principle of analogy, and (c) the principle of correlation. Under the presupposition that God is God, Barth does not reject this triadic principle; rather he radicalizes it in light of the theological subject matter. For Barth, to see through the historical to the spirit of the Bible is not merely to focus on Paul himself, but it is a task of understanding God as theological *Sache*. The spirit of this *Sache* inspires; thus God speaks to us even in the midst of our sociopolitical upheaval. The kingdom of God as theological subject matter is the in-breaking reality of God into our time. To see through our time to God's in-breaking reality is a more critical and radical approach than the historical-critical method.

When it comes to hermeneutics in Barth's exegesis, Jüngel focuses on an existential relationship between the text and its interpreter. In so doing, he tends to compare Barth to Heidegger. When Barth, for instance, radicalized the oblique intention toward *intentio recta* of theological *Sache*, Jüngel saw a new direct intention, namely a new naiveté that emerges from the energy of self-reflection.[21] Unlike Jüngel's reading of Barth's hermeneutics of simultaneity in a Heideggerian fashion, Marquardt attempts to see Barth's notion "more critically than historical critics" in light of political-social and historical consciousness.[22]

According to Marquardt, a social and political problem is supposed to be the criterion for the meaning of historical criticism in view of Barth's principle of understanding. The primacy of reality can be seen as the key concept in his hermeneutics. Recognizing the primacy of the text's reality before the exegetical method of historical criticism, Barth radicalized the historical-critical method by placing it second to the Bible's addressing sociohistorical and political concerns. This view is, for Barth, an exegetical discipline—in other words, a result of radical critical reflection rather than a postcritical *second naiveté* in the sense of Heidegger or Jüngel.

Obviously Barth does not replace the hermeneutical circle through his *Sachkritik*. Rather he makes this hermeneutical circle the criterion of all historical critique. In radicalizing the historical-critical method, Barth calls into question "text in texts," "the word in words," "the subject matter in the matters of subject," namely the depth of the text, which is the objectivity of the historical critics. Given this fact, Barth's dialectical

21. Jüngel, "Die theologischen Anfänge: Beobachtungen," in Jüngel, *Barth-Studien*, 98.
22. Marquardt, "Exegese und Dogmatik in Karl Barths Theologie," 381–406.

thinking of God's eschatology is explicitly of hermeneutical and social-practical character and horizon.[23]

According to Marquardt, Barth's theology cannot be understood apart from its life-setting in his socialist activity.[24] In the Barth files there is a yet-undeciphered report on Kropotkin and Leninism. The real origin of Barth's theology is, argues Marquardt, "his theological existence in Safenwil," which means "socialist praxis."[25] Marquardt's contribution severely challenges the general neo-orthodox or conservative portrait of Barth.

In dealing with a consequence of Barth's concept of the politics of God for the society, Ulrich Dannemann makes a theological justification of Barth's understanding of society, social structure, and its concrete political forms for his investigation. According to Dannemann, Marquardt's interpretation enables us to see and reconstruct—more clearly and precisely than in existing Barth scholarship—the history of the theological existence of Karl Barth from its genesis, its continuity, and its discontinuity from his early theology of socialism to his dogmatic-theological discourse of Jesus Christ.[26] Apart from Marquardt, Dannemann pursues the connection between theological knowledge and political praxis in Barth primarily through a systematic structure-analysis of Barth's two *Romans* commentaries and his doctrine of reconciliation in *Church Dogmatics*.

In an introduction to the debate about Karl Barth in Germany, George Hunsinger (in a North American context) tries to actualize political radicalism in the theology of Karl Barth. Hunsinger's thesis is that "theology must not be politicized, nor politics theologized. Theology can make its contribution to politics only by remaining theology."[27] In agreement with the basic orientation of Marquardt, Hunsinger tries to clarify and correct what remains obscure and misleading in Marquardt's interpretation. Albeit with a critical reservation against Marquardt, Hunsinger does assent that "the socialist perspective which Marquardt opens up may well be one of his most lasting achievements."[28]

23. Ibid., 396–97.
24. Marquardt, *Theologie und Sozialismus*, 291; cf. Gorringe, *Karl Barth: Against Hegemony*, 16.
25. Hunsinger, *Karl Barth and Radical Politics*, 58.
26. Dannemann, *Theologie und Politik*, 19–20.
27. Hunsinger, *Karl Barth and Radical Politics*, 181.
28. Ibid., 191.

According to Hunsinger, the contributions of Marquardt and Frei lie not only in starting with Barth's earliest writings, but also in paying considerable attention to the first edition of *Romans* (1919), which has been widely neglected. Barth's concept of God (*alles in allem real verändernde Tatsache dass Gott ist* [29]), which is also Marquardt's key concept of Barth's political hermeneutics, is to be understood on the basis of a practical socialist experience, thereby maintaining an intrinsic connection with society and politics. In viewing Barth's political praxis as an analogy or parable of God's kingdom, Hunsinger characterizes a relationship between theology and politics in Barth's mature theology as follows: "formally analogical, materially socialist, and existentially actualist."[30]

Drawing upon Marquardt, Peter Winzeler, and Sabine Plonz, Timothy Gorringe attempts to construct a contextual reading of Barth for the sake of an "affirmation of a remarkable unity in his theological output from 1916 to 1968."[31] In accepting Marquardt's basic thesis—that Barth's methodology is his theological social biography—Gorringe makes a genetic reading of the inextricability of theology and politics in Barth's thought. Barth's own advice to students in his lectures on nineteenth-century Protestant theology—that they "make a synchronous chart for every single year of the period" "for the sake of a mass of connections"—serves as inspiration for Gorringe to engage in a contextual, genetic, and historical-material reading of Barth. For Barth, the "historian should take history seriously as a force outside himself, which had it in its power to contradict him and which spoke to him with authority."[32]

Barth's first *Romans* commentary was written in a highly contextual sense, evident in his dialectical unity between theological *Sachkritik* and political awareness. This unity both illumines and determines Barth's eschatology. However, many scholars tend to abandon Barth's earlier position after his move from Safenwil to Göttingen. In contrast to Marquardt's religious-socialist reading of Barth is the statement of Klaus Scholder, for instance, that "with the turn to biblical theology Barth effectively gave up political engagement. The political world in the narrower sense, the world of political ideas and decisions, no longer formed any fundamen-

29. "The fact that not only sheds new light on, but materially changes, all things and everything in all things is the fact that God is" (*CD* II/1:258).
30. Hunsinger, *Karl Barth and Radical Politics*, 225.
31. Gorringe, *Karl Barth: Against Hegemony*, 13.
32. Barth, *Protestant Theology in the Nineteenth Century*, 58.

tal part of his theological thinking."³³ And in protest against Marquardt, Gerhard Sauter says that Barth had no political theology in any plausible sense of the term.³⁴

Jüngel, in his study on Barth, also takes issue with other interpretations of Barth on two fronts. He challenges the liberal-fascistic interpretation of Barth in the school of Munich, and the religious-socialist interpretation of Barth in the school of West Berlin. Jüngel first calls into question works of Falk Wagner and Friedrich Wilhelm Graf, stating,

> I marvel at the 'reconstruction of the construction' of Barth's theology, which in Germany comes primarily from Munich. They see through Barth's theology and pronounce it to be simply a genuine product of the spirit of its time, even though it was directed against that spirit. In this connection I should also like to expose, as an offense against good taste, the thesis that Barth's theology has a fascist structure. Surely theology can stand as a critic of its time only insofar as it is a child of its time. But in light of the work of Karl Barth this should not even be an issue.³⁵

With this criticism Jüngel has in mind the thesis of Wagner, who argues that "the content and structure of Barth's theology is relevant to not only socialism but also fascism and the making of fascist theory."³⁶

Jüngel's judgment of the Munich school—the thesis of the fascistic structure in Barth's thought as an offense against good taste—is also relevant to Pannenberg's approach to Barth. For instance, when Pannenberg regards the absoluteness of Jesus in Barth's theology as "necessarily totalitarian" in the sense of theological forcing to conformity, he is appropriately associated with Wagner.³⁷ On the other hand, Jüngel also takes issue with the religious-socialist interpretation of Barth by Helmut Gollwitzer and Marquardt in West Berlin: "I truly envy the imagination of the socialist interpretation of Barth (which in Germany comes primarily from West Berlin) and its practical-sounding yet preposterous theorems. In this connection I should like to continue to make a distinction between the artifice of word association and the strenuous task of interpretation

---

33. Scholder, *Churches and the Third Reich*, 45.
34. Sauter, "Soziologische oder Politische Barth-Interpretation?" 176–77.
35. Jüngel, *Karl Barth: A Theological Legacy*, 14.
36. Wagner, "Theologische Gleichschaltung: Zur Christologie bei Barth," 41; cf. Jüngel, *Karl Barth: A Theological Legacy*, 139.
37. Pannenberg, *Systematic Theology* 2:477–78.

and, in case of doubt, to prefer historical and logical argumentation to any sort of undisciplined explanation."[38] Regarding both interpretations as abstraction in which Barth's dogmatic line of argument can be eclipsed, Jüngel applies Barth's own warning "Latet periculum in generalibus" (Danger lurks in generalities) to such interpretations.[39]

Jüngel's entire essay on "Barth's Theological Beginnings" is, by and large, a rejoinder to Marquardt's profound but controversial book *Theologie und Sozialismus: Das Beispiel Karl Barths* (1974). Marquardt's fundamental thesis is that Barth's theology can be understood by way of the correlative interaction between theology and democratic socialistic praxis. In Marquardt's view, Barth's concept of God should be interpreted by way of his social experiences. By contrast, Jüngel's fundamental thesis is that the political is surely a predicate of theology, not the other way around. This remark is essentially correct. His insistence that Barth thoroughly depoliticized the concept of revolution in *Romans II* is directed against Marquardt's position. However, Marquardt's intent is not to make theology a mere predicate of the political, as Jüngel suspects.

Barth, in his letter to Eberhard Bethge (in May 1967) concerning his Dietrich Bonhoeffer biography, articulated his concern and direction for the political praxis that he had silently or only incidentally mentioned to that point: "ethics—co-humanity—servant church—discipleship—socialism—peace movement—and, hand in hand with all that, politics."[40] In this line Gollwitzer, in his article "Reich Gottes und Sozialismus bei Karl Barth" (1972), portrayed Barth's way as starting from a religious-socialist identification between the kingdom of God and socialism toward a distinction between the revolution of God's kingdom as *analogans* and the democratic-socialistic option as *analogatum*.

Although Jüngel is critical of Gollwitzer and Marquardt, he poses an important question regarding one of the tasks of future research. He raises the question of "the extent to which Barth's contemporary experiences ("praxis") helped to shape his knowledge. A reciprocal relationship between knowledge and praxis can be clearly seen in the striking reversals which punctuated his theological development."[41]

---

38. Jüngel, *Karl Barth: A Theological Legacy*, 14.
39. Ibid.
40. Barth, *Briefe 1916–1968*, 404.
41. Jüngel, *Karl Barth-Studien*, 27.

Dialectical Theology and Neo-Orthodox Theology

Bruce McCormack's reading of Barth reveals a reciprocal relationship between theological knowledge and life-praxis in Barth. His treatment of Barth's early period is evaluated highly, and it is unlikely to be superseded for many years in English-speaking countries. McCormack's term, "Karl Barth's critically realistic dialectical theology," plays a decisive role in convincingly interpreting and analyzing the mutual relationship between Barth's contemporary experiences (praxis) and his theological way of knowledge. However, McCormack's "critically realistic dialectical theology" takes issue with the religious-socialist interpretation of Gollwitzer and Marquardt in terms of historical accounts and materials.[42] In addition, McCormack's book challenges a neo-orthodox reading of Barth. McCormack notes that neo-orthodox readings of Barth in the Anglo-American world were propelled and reinforced in the 1950s above all by Balthasar's thesis on Barth's second groundbreaking turn from dialectics (in his commentaries on Romans) to analogy (in his book on Anselm).[43]

However, on closer examination of the social and political situation in which Barth's theology emerged, we must not direct our attention from the fact that his theology was always bound to situational and political spheres. Barth's theology is always time-bound and up-to date rather than timeless and nonpolitical. When we look at the genesis and development of Barth's theology during his pastoral work in Safenwil, his dialectical theology was expressed and articulated in a highly contextual way with respect to World War I, religious socialism, the October Revolution in Russia, and the general strike in Switzerland. In addition, Barth's theology of analogy, which can first be seen explicitly in his Tambach lecture and then in *Romans II*, demonstrate the political relevance of God, society, and human beings from the start.

In view of Barth's dogmatic turn, we do not need to marginalize his keen interest in his cultural situation. The connection between the

---

42. McCormack, *Critically Realistic*, 80, 88, 173, 175, 177, 184, 194.

43. Cf. Heron, *Century of Protestant Theology*. The term *neo-orthodox*, in a pejorative sense, connotes a theology of resorting to a one-sided emphasis on biblical revelation and dogmatic reaffirmation of Christian confessions and dogmas. As a twentieth-century theological movement, neo-orthodox theology is understood as a radical break with the heritage of nineteenth-century liberalism. Karl Barth is counted as one of the most important representatives of the neo-orthodox movement.

theological awareness of *Sache* and the political consciousness of the time is well articulated in the preface of *Church Dogmatics* with respect to German liberation. His dogmatic theology cannot be properly understood apart from its social and critical consciousness. His dogmatic theology includes a social and historical perspective by "beginning always at the beginning" rather than repristinating church doctrines.[44]

Karl Barth and *Theologia Naturalis*

In speaking of a neo-orthodox interpretation of Barth, we need to mention Karl Barth's critique of *theologia naturalis*. An attempt to relate Barth to *theologia naturalis* or *analogia entis* would be complicated, even a conundrum. It was Barth himself who was strongly resistant to such metaphysical discourse for the sake of the God of Abraham, Isaac, and Jacob, and Jesus Christ. However, in the process of breaking new ground in Barth's development, Balthasar perceived that an old doctrine of *extra-Cavinisticum* provides a basis for Barth to preserve and integrate natural theology in his christological inclusivism.

In scrutinizing Barth's Amsterdam lecture on "Church and Culture" (1926), Balthasar affirmed that Barth agreed with Thomas Aquinas's dictum that grace perfects nature rather than destroys it.[45] Balthasar was convinced that "if he [Barth] maintained this position unswervingly, the break with Emil Brunner might have been forestalled, and his debate with Catholicism might have taken a different turn."[46] In Barth's study of St. Anselm, Balthasar notices that "there seems to be room for the analogy of being after all."[47] Of course, Barth eliminates and replaces *analogia entis* through *analogia fidei*, in that all knowledge of God comes only through the revelation of God. God is known only through God. The analogy of faith clearly indicates that Jesus Christ is at the center of God's self-revela-

---

44. According to Barth, a dogmatic theology that understands itself as *theologia viatorum* must necessarily be the reflection of the church and the task of the church that engages itself concretely in its time and always for a particular time (*CD* I/1:281). Christian thinking and discourse must lead to its own responsibility for the present time. Thus, Barth is perplexed when both Ragaz and Tillich look upon their work as dynamic while regarding his as static for no reason (*CD* I/1:74–75).

45. Balthasar, *Theology of Karl Barth*, 82.

46. Ibid., 82–83.

47. Ibid., 148.

tion. Nonetheless, Balthasar argued that "there must be a periphery to this center."⁴⁸ Although *assumptio carnis* (assumption of human flesh) is not identical with the order of creation (in orientation toward the incarnation), "it possesses images, analogies, and dispositions that truly are presuppositions for the Incarnation."⁴⁹

Barth's critique of *theologia naturalis* can also be witnessed in his debate with Emil Brunner. Barth's *Nein!* to Brunner was not merely theologically, but politically, motivated in face of the so-called German Christian support for Nazism. The danger of natural theology lay in domesticating and naturalizing the knowledge of God in the self-revelation of Jesus Christ. In the face of Hilter's rise to power, an attempt was made to domesticate and absorb Christianity into the German nature and culture. The so-called *Deutsche Christen* (German Christians) collaborated and advocated reconciliation with Nazi ideology. In addition, Roman Catholic theologians misapplied St. Thomas Aquinas's dictum (that grace perfects nature rather than destroys it) to provide theological grounds for the concordat between the Vatican and Hitler. In other words, these theologians asserted that grace does not destroy German nature (blood and soil), but perfects and fulfills it. As a result, the essence of the Christian gospel is at stake in Barth's confrontation with the natural and ideological theology of the *Deutsche Christen*. This is why Barth responded to Brunner's mediating pamphlet *Nature and Grace* with an angry and radical "No!"

However, regarding christological inclusivism in Barth's theology, Torrance says that according to Barth, "natural theology (*theologia naturalis*) is included and brought into clear light within the theology of revelation (*theologia revelata*), for in the reality of divine grace there is included the truth of the divine creation." In this sense, "grace does not destroy but completes it."⁵⁰

According to Marquardt, Barth's acceptance of *extra Calvinisticum*⁵¹ provides a universal-inclusive basis for his Christology of *anhypostasis* and *enhypostasis*. This doctrine becomes, for Barth, not only an indication of the remaining majesty of divine Word even in his state of incar-

---

48. Ibid.
49. Ibid.
50. Torrance, *Karl Barth, Biblical and Evangelical Theologian*, 147.
51. Calvin, *Institutes of the Christian Religion*, II.13.4.

nation, but also—in Barth's typical supplementary way—a witness for the divine actuality as well as for the divine universality of the Word.⁵² Marquardt assumes that Barth might revoke his previous radical rejection of *theologia naturalis* through his doctrine of reconciliation (cf. "The Light of Life," CD IV/3.1 §69.2). As evidence for this, Marquardt introduces Barth's own testimony in his interview with *Brüdergemeine* in 1961: "Later I retrieved the *theologia naturalis* via christology again. Today my critique would be: One must say *theologia naturalis* only differently, i.e., just christologically."⁵³

Given this fact, Marquardt's basic thesis is that "the christological establishment of natural theology is identical with the transformation of structure of its inherited form."⁵⁴ What is here to be considered is not a renewal of *theologia naturalis* in affirmation of *logos spermatikos*, but a social and material transformation of its traditional form from a standpoint of a particular-inclusive Christology. Thus Marquardt takes a step further in insisting that within the universal-christological framework of Barth, the content and impulse of *theologia naturalis* is reappropriated, deepened, and transformed socially and materially through *theologia revelationis*. Christ's divinity is to a theology of revelation what his humanity is to the content of *theologia naturalis* because in Jesus Christ the *humanum* of all humans is posited and exalted as such to the unity with God (*CD* IV/2:49). There is no natural realm existing independent of christological effectiveness. This is Marquardt's approach to a material and social transformation of *theologia naturalis* in its inherited and traditional sense from a standpoint of the collectivity of the human species.⁵⁵

To avoid a misunderstanding of a relation of Barth to natural theology in his doctrine of lights, Pangritz introduces an interpretation by Hans-Joachim Kraus: "The so-called 'doctrine of lights' represents the positive pole of the negation of natural theology. . . . Barth presents a

---

52. Marquardt, *Theologie und Sozialismus*, 260. Furthermore, Otto Weber states that the *logos asarkos* can in truth be only a pure boundary concept for Barth. See Weber, *Grundlagen der Dogmatik II*, 143.

53. Quoted in Marquardt, *Theologie und Sozialismus*, 263.

54. Ibid., 264. "Judaism is for Barth a witness to the kernel of truth of the natural theology within the revelation of grace." Marquardt, *Entdeckung des Judentums*, 316.

55. Of the typology of Adam and Christ in Romans chapter 5, Barth emphatically says, "Jesus Christ is the secret and the truth of sinful and mortal humankind and also the secret and the truth of *human nature* as such" (Barth, *Christ and Adam*, 50).

christologically founded counterproposal to the theory of religion that is based in the doctrine of the *logos spermatikos* and was developed within the domain of natural theology."[56]

However, Herman Diem disagrees with Marquardt's thesis that Barth never totally rejected natural theology but denied it on political grounds.[57] Strangely enough, Diem argues that Barth—even on the basis of the *extra Calvinisticum*—"rejected all attempts at a 'mediating' or natural theology."[58] Thus, Diem attacks Marquardt's attempt at imputing the possibility of a natural theology from the perspective of the history of human species. Marquardt's attempt would lead to a conceptual confusion in Barth's Christology.

In a similar vein as Diem, McCormack rejects the possibility of natural theology in Barth. According to McCormack, Barth knew that in Reformed Christianity the Bible is indispensable as the rule of faith and life, but God could speak elsewhere in nature and history. McCormack argues that this has nothing to do with an affirmation of natural theology because revelation in the Bible or in nature and history is actualized by means of the source of revelation.[59]

Barth's confrontation with Przywara concerning the *analogia entis* in Münster did not misrepresent or misinterpret Przywara's concept of *analogia entis* as some scholars insist.[60] As McCorrmack says, "Barth had not finally been satisfied that Przywara's talk of '*von Gott her*' had been sufficient to remove his *anlogia entis* from the sphere of Thomas's realistic reflections. His understanding of the *anlogia entis* would not undergo any significant modification from this point on."[61] However, Balthasar is convinced of a radical christological orientation in Przywara. Beyond the

---

56. Kraus, *Theologische Religionskritik*, 50. Cf. Pangritz, *Karl Barth in the Theology of Dietrich Bonhoeffer*, 137.

57. Diem, "Karl Barth as Socialist," 135.

58. According to Diem, Marquardt's thesis of "expanding and completing the christological anhypostasis through an anthropological enhypostasis" "undercut the Christian *sacramentum* and destroyed it or made it superfluous" (ibid., 131).

59. McCormack, *Critically Realistic*, 306. Barth understands the Reformed rule of *finitum non est capax infiniti* as a way of "rejecting any view which would seek to quantify revelation, making God partly hidden and partly revealed in case of all traditional natural theologies" (ibid., 352).

60. Cf. Balthasar, *Theology of Karl Barth*, 147–50, 227–37. See also Jüngel, *Gott als Geheimnis der Welt*, 385–91.

61. McCormack, *Critically Realistic*, 391.

Thomist-Scotist opposition, Przywara developed his concept of *analogia entis* through a radical christocentric framework.[62]

In dealing with Barth's radical rejection of any form of natural theology and the *analogia entis* in both neo-Protestantism and Roman Catholicism, Han Küng cites the famous foreword to the first volume of *Church Dogmatics*: "I regard the *analogia entis* as the invention of Antichrist and think that because of it one cannot become Catholic. Whereupon I at the same time allow myself to regard all other reasons for not becoming Catholic, as short-sighted and lacking in seriousness" (*CD* I/1:x).

Barth's radical rejection of Brunner's idea of a point of contact for divine revelation was also relevant to Vatican I. According to Barth, Vatican I introduced a cleavage in the idea of one God, which led to a twofold sense of God: a natural and a supernatural God. Instead of the analogy of being, Barth introduced an analogy of faith. However, for Küng, Barth's concept of *analogia fidei* "includes the analogy of being."[63] Moreover, when it comes to the lights, words, and truths of the created world in the doctrine of reconciliation, Küng accused Barth of not publicly admitting his retraction of his former position against natural theology and analogy of being.[64] The following statement convinces Küng of Barth's own correction of his former protest against the natural theology. "Dangerous modern expressions like the 'revelation of creation' or 'primal revelation' might be given a clear and unequivocal sense in this respect" (*CD* IV/3.1:140).

Moltmann goes a step further, regarding natural theology as the goal of Christian theology rather than regarding natural theology merely as the presupposition for Christian theology. Hans-Joachim Iwand becomes a mentor for Moltmann's eschatological understanding of natural theology: "Natural revelation is not that from which we come; it is the light

---

62. Przywara, *Was ist Gott*, 75. Cf. Balthasar, *Theology of Karl Barth*, 249. Balthasar cites the words of Przywara: "The way to God and the image of God is only a shadowy hint of something which is brightly revealed by Christ alone. . . . By his own decision, God is revealed to us nowhere else but in Christ. All the flourishes that present God to the creature are flashed out and explained in Christ. They are features of the one and only real God, who is Father, Son and Holy Spirit. There is no other God beside him, and any other general features of God are merely the foreglow or afterglow of Father, Son and Holy Spirit."

63. Küng, *Does God Exist?* 517.

64. Ibid., 527.

towards which we move. The *lumen naturae* is the reflection of the *lumen gloriae*.... The theme of true religion is the eschatological goal of theology."⁶⁵ At issue for Moltmann is to see that "natural theology is only as yet an advance radiance of the eschatological theology of glory."⁶⁶ Therefore, natural theology can be seen as the advance radiance and promise of the kingdom of glory, not as "a forecourt of revealed theology," but "as a fore-shining of revealed theology's eschatological horizon."⁶⁷ When natural theology is understood as a *theologia viae* concerning the sighing of creation (Romans 8), Moltmann renews natural theology in light of *theologia publica*, which is in turn sensitive to and responsible for the political arena, natural scientific findings, and the life of the earth.

According to Barth, the world is in need of parables and capable of being a parable for the kingdom of God. Under the real promise of God's future, this world becomes transparent to God's invisible presence and potentially a parable in reflection of God's in-breaking reality. In asking whether it might not be that Jer 31:34 is in the process of fulfillment, Barth answers with his public and universal theology.⁶⁸

Karl Barth and Israel

It would be difficult, in fact, to understand Barth without reference to his reflection on Israel. The synagogue and church are called to listen anew to the divine Word and to a completely new decision of responsibility.⁶⁹ When it comes to Barth's doctrine of Israel, Klappert illustrates and illuminates various models. First, he looks at negative models: (a) the model of substitution (or replacement), and (b) the model of integration. This

---

65. Iwand, *Glauben und Wissen*, 290-91. Cf., Moltmann, *Experiences in Theology*, 70.

66. Ibid., 76.

67. Ibid., 72.

68. "It is indeed unfortunate that the question of the truth of talk about God should be handled as a question apart by a special faculty.... Philosophy, history, sociology, psychology, or pedagogy, whether individually or in conjunction, all working within the sphere of the church, might well take up the task of measuring the church's talk about God by its being as the Church, thus making a special theology superfluous.... All sciences might ultimately be theology.... The separate existence of theology signifies an emergency measure on which the Church has had to resolve in view of the actual refusal of the other science in this respect" (*CD* I/1:5.7).

69. Klappert, *Israel und die Kirche*, 11.

model can be called the viewpoint of religious indifference in that it is a way that denies the dependence of Christianity on Judaism or on the election of Israel. In other words, Christianity has no more or less to do with Judaism than with Buddhism or communism.[70] Some elements in Barth's doctrine of Israel are sharply charged with supporting this direction. When it comes to the history and life of Israel, Barth argues that the history of Israel is the history of expectation of their crucified Messiah. According to Barth, the church is the aim and ground of election for the people of Israel. From this comes the view that Israel, as such, is a vessel of dishonor. While Israel is the witness to divine judgment, the church is the witness to honor and divine mercy (*CD* II/2:259–61).

(c) According to the model of typology, Israel is a type of the church and of the salvation that is ultimately represented by the church. It refers to the model of "fore-portrayal pointing to a superior counterpart."[71] Israel and its institutions—their whole history—serve only as figurative types of the church that finally brings God's salvation. Israel's history and institutions are regarded as types of the church and its salvation. This model can be called the viewpoint of inheritance in a way that interprets the history of Israel as the prehistory of Christianity, in that Judaism is perceived as an anachronism. (d) In the model of illustration, Israel is understood as an exemplary negative foil of human existence, whereas the church is the stage that overcomes it. This model can be called the viewpoint of necessary contrast in a sense that understands Christianity in basic contradiction to Judaism and views Jewish existence only as a foil. If the Israelite is symbolized in the figure of the Pharisee, so the Christian is symbolized in the figure of the Good Samaritan.

(e) The model of subsumption speaks about the destruction of the special election and covenant of Israel on the one hand and the subsumation of Israel's special status under generality valid for all on the other hand. According to Käsemann, in contrast to Bultmann's existential-anthropological understanding, Paul's teaching on justification is to be understood in a cosmic framework (on the basis of Rom 1:28–3:20; 5:12–13; 8:18ff). At stake in Paul's teaching on justification is primarily God's reign over the world and concrete individuals.[72] In Käsemann's framework of

---

70. Lapide and Moltmann, *Israel und Kirche*, 16–17.
71. Klappert, *Israel und die Kirche*, 18.
72. Käsemann, "Justification and Salvation History in the Epistle to the Romans," 75.

justification, Israel is subsumed and classified under the universality of justification of the ungodly as its consequence.[73]

In a turn to positive models, several ideas emerge. (a) We first mention the model of complementarity: Israel and the church are understood as people of God who supplement and complement each other in competition, coexistence and pro-existence. This model is practiced for the purpose of dialogue between Jews and Christians, between synagogue and church. In it, Israel and the church can be seen as partners in solidarity and as the coexisting community sharing an eschatological-messianic horizon of hope. (b) In the model of representation, the relation of the church to Israel is understood as that of deputyship. In this understanding the Gentiles enter provisionally in place of Israel, who does not recognize the Messiah. The Israel-remnant is the placeholder for the whole of Israel, and the Gentiles as the latecomers represent placeholders for the synagogue's majority among which the Gentile provisionally participates in Israel's election.[74]

(c) In the christological-eschatological–dependence or participation model, the church is dependent upon the election of Israel, which is proved in Jesus Christ, and the promised fulfillment of this election toward Israel, not only in the past, but also in the future. What is at stake is not the context of a universal eschatology of creation but a particular and universal eschatology of Israel (Mark 13:10, 26–27; Acts 1:16ff; Rom 11:25–26; Eph 2:11–12). The christological-participation model provides a basis for the Gentiles to participate in the history of God's election of Israel.

In dealing with the various models of the relation of the church to Israel, Klappert categorizes Barth's doctrine of Israel as a tension between a christological-eschatological–participation model and an ecclesiological-integration model. Because of this unresolved tension in Barth's thought, Barth expresses his doubt about Jewish-Christian dialogue, while at the same time calling for ecumenical dialogue and rejecting a Christian mission to the Jews (*CD* IV/3.2:877). Although Klappert is aware of Barth's decisive rejection of Christian anti-Semitism, he understands this rejection as a tension, conflict, and impasse in Barth's doctrine of Israel.

---

73. Against Käsemann's anti-Jewish implication in his understanding of justification, see Krister Stendahl, *Paul among Jews and Gentiles*.

74. Marquardt, *Entdeckung des Judentums*, 253. According to Marquardt, Barth retains the significance of biblical idea of the Israel-remnant and its idea of representation.

When it comes to Karl Barth's treatment of Israel in his doctrine of election (*CD* II/2), it was formed between the winter semester of 1939–1940 and the winter semester of 1941–1942. This doctrine of election was comprised at roughly the same time as the Wannsee conference on January 20, 1942, during which time the Final Solution of systematic execution of the Jews was organized and planned. It is unlikely that Barth knew of any details of genocidal activity when he was engaged in his reflection on Israel in *CD* II/2. Although Barth has a positive approach to the Jews—because of some elements of his integration model—he argues that the Jewish form of the community has a different function from the church. Compared with the service of the church for the witness to God's mercy, the distinctive witness of Israel is to the judgment of God and thus to the frailty and death of the passing man.

What Themes will be Organized, Investigated, and Actualized in this Monograph?

Given the debates about political radicalism, *theologia naturalis*, and Israel in Barth's theology, in this monograph I am interested in tracing and analyzing the particular and inclusive dimension of Barth's theology of God's Word in action and how this dimension effects the development of his dialectical theology via analogical theology; I am interested, further, in his dogmatic theology. For this task I will deal with Barth's reflection of God's Word in action with respect to political ethics, Israel, and recognition of religious others.

Barth's concept of God's Word in action for the world was shaped and influenced considerably by his practical-socialist experience and thus is inseparable from society, culture, and politics. However, Barth's profound elaboration of theological *Sache* is not reducible merely to an anthropological experiential-expressive quarter. As Schellong cautions about Marquardt's interpretation, a reading of Barth through his social biography should not fall into reductionism.[75]

Therefore, my concern in this monograph is to show a relation between Barth's theological thinking about current issues in his time (such

---

75. Schellong notices a certain narrowness in Marquardt's presentation, a tendency toward "the restriction to the biographical." However, "this sociological, political, yet non-reductionist approach is what gives Marquardt's book its significance" ("On Reading Karl Barth from the Left," 150, 142).

as political radicalism, Israel, natural theology, and religious others) by examining and analyzing the development of Barth's theology biographically and contextually from his earliest writings on toward his dogmatic theology. Here it is of special importance to scrutinize and reflect on what basic theological factors of God's Word in action interact with Barth's political engagement taking issue with a social, political, and cultural agenda. The relevance of theology to social questions or, in other words, a connection between theology and political involvement, would be formulated and conceptualized in various contextual stages with respect to Barth's attitude of "beginning always at the beginning."

His continual correcting and deepening of God's action of theological *Sache* corresponded with his experience of contemporary social questions. Authentic theology does not fall from the sky or rise from below without reference to what enables, stimulates, and sharpens human experience from below. This is characteristic of the antibourgeois, irregular character of Barth's mode of thought. I agree that Barth would come to a radical understanding of God through his socialist praxis, but socialist praxis should also be reformulated critically in accordance with his radical concept of God's Word in action for the world. As Gollwitzer says rightly about Barth's theology, "his spirit cannot be reduced to a simple or a single formula."[76]

In fact, Barth did not want to be venerated by his followers but to be understood in a genuine sense. This book finds itself, therefore, as a contextual-hermeneutical and historical-genetic reading of Barth especially in light of God's Word in action for the world. To say the least, Barth's theology can be seen as world-affirming in terms of a dialectical and analogical relation in speaking of the mystery of God and the grace of God in Jesus Christ for the world. The former dimension of God's mystery is related to Barth's eschatological proviso while the latter dimension of God's grace actualizes God's radical concern for the world in light of reconciliation in Jesus Christ with the world. This refers to his metaphor of *Theanthropologie*, which I would like to call *cantus firmus* in the polyphonies of Barth's thought-form and motif. This characterizes Barth's theology of God's Word in action in terms of *Keine Weltlosigkeit Gottes*: "The theology which I tried to fashion out of scripture was never a private affair, foreign to the world and humanity. Its object is: God for the world,

---

76. Gollwitzer, "Kingdom of God and Socialism in the Theology of Karl Barth," 100.

God for human beings, heaven for the earth. It followed that my whole theology always had a strong political component, explicit or implicit... this interest in politics accompanies me to the present day."[77]

In the first chapter I will focus on an organic connection of theology to social-political consciousness in Barth's train of thought. Here I will attempt to construe his early writings in Safenwil in light of Barth's intellectual background and his theological development in his social life-setting. Barth's understanding of God's action as the in-breaking reality of God's future will be seen and discussed in relation to his political direction.

Chapter 2 will shed light on the genesis of and social context producing the first edition of Barth's commentary on Romans. In the analysis of *Romans I*, special attention is given to Barth's eschatology in regard to its social and political significance. In *Romans I* we explore how Barth shaped and developed his controversial relation to religious socialism (Leonhard Ragaz), and, furthermore, his confrontation with Leninism will bring to the light a lasting relationship between Barth and Blumhardt's movement in terms of christological eschatology. At this juncture there will be an outline of theology and social questions in Germany, especially a comparison between Friedrich Naumann and Blumhardt.

Chapter 3 will examine Barth's Tambach lecture of 1919. His Tambach lecture shows the unique way and orientation of Barth's development, especially as this development concerns a relation between dialectical theology and parable theology. In fact, it is not a mere middle part, mediating as an intermezzo *Romans I* to *Romans II*. This lecture rather provides an initial and profound insight of Barth in his approach to Blumhardt's message of the kingdom of God in light of parable teaching. Furthermore, it needs to be discussed in relation to his Amsterdam lecture (1926), in which Barth's genuine quest for a relationship between God's kingdom and natural theology resurfaces.

In chapter 4, I will discuss Barth's theology of *Krisis* in *Romans II* from a social and political perspective. It is alleged that Barth turned away from social questions and human praxis unilaterally by focusing on God as *wholly other*. However, his *Romans II* cannot be properly understood without reference to *Romans I*. Therefore, in this chapter his time-eternity dialectics will be examined and discussed in social and political

---

77. Barth, *Letzte Zeugnisse*, 21.

perspective, and I will bring to the fore Barth's confrontation with the postwar situation in Russia.

In chapter 5, I will shed light on Barth's theological development between his time in Germany, namely, in his teaching positions in Göttingen, Münster, and Bonn. An analysis will be given of Barth's developments in political ethics, the Word of God, and dialectical theology. Then I will discuss Barth's confrontation with Erik Peterson. In Münster, Barth's encounter and debate with Roman Catholicism (especially Przywara) regarding the *analogia entis* and the *anlogia fidei* occurred. This problem will be examined in relation to Barth's seminal study of St Anselm. In this context, it is significant to discuss Barth's understanding of Feuerbach.

In chapter 6, I will deal with Barth's political stance towards National Socialism in Germany and his confrontation with Brunner regarding *theologia revelatus* and *theologia naturalis*. I will further discuss the unresolved problem of the *analogia entis* and the *analogia fidei* in Barth's theological structure more broadly, in view of a relation between covenant and creation. In speaking of the *analogia relationis* as a central motif in Barth's theology of analogy, I will evaluate the *analogia relationis* with regard to natural theology, especially in the context of Barth's doctrine of lights.

In chapter 7, there will be a discussion of Martin Luther and Barth regarding Christology in regard to *anhypostasis* and *enhypostasis*. I will explicate the extent to which Barth integrates and expands Luther's theses—"Jesus was born a Jew" and Jesus Christ as "the mirror of the fatherly heart of God"—into his inclusive understanding of *anhypostasis* and *enhypostasis* Christology. At this point I attend to Barth's Christology, admiring its mediating position between the Lutheran *est* and the Reformed *however*. In it, a Lutheran dimension is not excluded, but included, in Barthian thought.

In chapter 8, I will deal with Barth's doctrine of election in the *Church Dogmatics*. In scrutinizing Barth's doctrine of Israel, I will compare Barth's positive assertions of Israel to his critics' analyses. In a discussion of Barth's theology of Israel and reconciliation, it is important to evaluate Barth's legacy after the Shoah in a positive way. In chapter 9, there will be a study of Barth's analysis of alienation and reification. Thus the liberative dimension of Barth's theology will be scrutinized. Attention will be given to Barth's view of democracy and socialism. In conclusion, I will discuss Barth's unfinished project about the mystery of God and religious pluralism. The ecumenical and global relevance of Barth will be brought to the fore in a discussion of his ecumenical legacy, the theocentric direction of his theology, and his contribution toward a Christian perspective on religious pluralism. At this juncture my focus is given to Barth's world-affirming theology in relation to religious pluralism from the perspective of Pure Land Buddhism in reference to Takizawa and Asian minjung theology.

ONE Karl Barth's Theology and Socialism in Safenwil: 1910–1918

Karl Barth's Intellectual Background: A Biographical Sketch

KARL BARTH WAS BORN IN BASEL, SWITZERLAND, ON MAY 10, 1886, where he also died on December 9, in 1968. In 1904 the young Barth began study at the University of Berne "with my father's kind but earnest guidance and advice." "What I owe to those Berne masters, despite everything, is that they taught me to forget any fears I might have had. They gave me such a thorough foundation in the earlier form of the "historical-critical school that the remarks of their later successors could no longer get under my skin or even touch my heart—they only got on my nerves."[1]

In the winter of 1906 (on January 20) Barth delivered a lecture on "Zofingia and the Social Question." Referring to Leonhard Ragaz, a staunch representative of Swiss religious socialism, Barth considered the social question to be "one link in the chain of development, or better *the* problem of mankind, which Jesus once posed to the ancient world." By stopping a "robust gathering round the colours, whose essential national (!) task consists in handing down 'honorable ancient student customs' to posterity in as intact a form as possible," Zofingia should become an association "filled with a new spirit, with the spirit of social responsibility towards the lower strata of society and above all towards ourselves."[2]

---

1. Busch, *Karl Barth: His Life*, 34.
2. Ibid., 37.

As Barth argues, "We have to agree that the rift between Capital and Labour, Mammonism and pauperism, rich and poor . . . grows continually larger."[3] Although little social analysis is found here, Barth was aware of political realities as a task of Christian responsibility on the question of social class. After preliminary examination in Berne, and following his father's advice, Barth went to Berlin, although he wanted to go Marburg. In time, Barth was enthusiastic about going up to Marburg, which he described as "my Zion."[4]

By the early 1890s the theology of Albert Ritschl exercised a dominant influence upon the theological faculties in Germany. Members of Ritschl's school included scholars such as Wilhelm Herrmann, Adolf von Harnack, Ferdinand Kattenbusch, Johannes Gottschick, Julius Kaftan, Friedrich Loofs, Theodore Haering, and Martin Rade. *Die christliche Welt*, the representative journal of the day, powerfully represented the view of the Ritschlian school. Although Ritschl was in conflict with Lutheran orthodoxy during this time, Ritschl found Luther himself to be a great figure to use in combat against Lutherans. It was Ritschl who paved the way for new Luther research in the early twentieth century in pupils such as Karl Holl. Moreover, he represented new historical work and exercised a strong impact upon church historians such as Harnack in view of the history of dogma and Ernst Troeltsch in the study of Christian social ethics.

According to Ritschl, Christianity finds its basis in historical study rather than in immediate religious experience. All theological assertions should be based on the historical life of Jesus; in fact his personal relationship with God, his obedience and trust, and his ethical vocation and fellowship with humankind are personal vehicles of God's self-revelation. Justification and sanctification are the constructive principles underlying Christian doctrine. From the standpoint in which reconciliation involves an ethical commitment to the kingdom of God, the idea of the *unio mystica* has no place at all. Thus, the new relationship with God in reconciliation originates in the community of faith directed toward the kingdom of God.

Finally, the idea of the kingdom of God achieves the needed reconciliation between Christianity and culture. *Lebensführung* (i.e., a reli-

---

3. Barth, *Vorträge und kleinere Arbeiten, 1905–1909*, 74.
4. Busch, *Karl Barth: His Life*, 44.

gious, ethical lifestyle) becomes a main focus for Ritschl in dramatizing justification, sanctification, and the kingdom of God.[5]

Seeing the kingdom realized through Christian vocation in the world, Ritschl moves to identify even Christian morality with the cultural consciousness of his day in Germany. As a theologian of culture, Ritschl has been often accused of becoming a strong representative of "Culture Protestantism," a form of Christendom baptized by bourgeois Prussian society. Cultural Protestantism held that the ethical demands of Jesus and cultural values are in harmony; in cultural Protestantism the true ideal of life led to no potential conflict with social or cultural structures. While uncritical of the political social system in Prussia, Ritschl saw Bismarck's policies as genuine progress, in contradistintion to the aristocratic conservatives and the social revolutionists.

Theologically, as a student of Herrmann, Barth was critical of Ritschl.[6] According to Barth, Ritschl's ideal of the Christian life is regarded as "the very epitome of the national-liberal German bourgeois of the age of Bismarck."[7] In the mid-1890s, Troeltsch had initiated and led the *Religionsgeschichtliche Schule* (history of religions school), focusing on a historical-critical basis that challenged dogmatic assumptions. The belief in the absoluteness of Christianity, which was based on a supernatural conception of revelation and thus at the heart of Ritschlism, became deeply questionable and was challenged by the historical-critical method of Troeltsch. In 1897 a split emerged between the older, dogmatically oriented school of Ritschlians and the younger, historical-critically oriented school of *Religionsgeschichte*.

In editing *Die Christliche Welt* Martin Rade supported younger radical members by accepting their contributions as part of the history of religions school. At the start of the twentieth century, Troeltsch emerged

---

5. For Ritschl "the Christian idea of the kingdom of God denotes the association of mankind—an association both extensively and intensively the most comprehensive possible—through the reciprocal moral action of its members, action which transcends all merely natural and particular considerations" (Niebuhr, *Christ and Culture*, 98).

6. Besides, there was another reason for Barth's ill feeling against Ritschl. During the period of Barth's honorary professorship at Göttingen, Walter Rathenau, the *Reichsminister* for Foreign Affairs, and of Jewish origin, was assassinated. Regarding this event the faculty at Göttingen took no action. As the prototype of the national, liberal German bourgeoisie, Ritschl was, for Barth, "a sturdy, dry, insensitive lump who notices nothing." Cf. Barth to Thurneysen, 28 June 1922, in *B-Th II*, 88–89.

7. Barth, *From Rousseau to Ritschl*, 392.

as the most important figure, exercising profound influence upon the theological situation in Germany. However, it was Herrmann, with his engaging style, who became the counterpart of Troeltsch, helping Barth to overcome relativism and historicism in theology.[8] As a student of Herrmann at Marburg, Barth stated: "The name of Troeltsch, then at the heart of our discussions, signified the limit beyond which I thought I must refuse to follow the dominant theology of the age. In all else I was its resolute disciple"[9]

Karl Barth in Berlin

Characterizing the intellectual surroundings of Barth as a student in Germany was his pursuit and penetration of the poles between Ritschl and Troeltsch. Barth became a student with a high regard for Harnack in Berlin. He had little concern about Reinhold Seeberg. Instead of indulging in cultural life in Berlin, Barth saw and heard Harnack very thoroughly. "I . . . wisely avoided Seeberg, foolishly, alas, took no notice of Holl; and instead went enthusiastically to listen to Harnack (and equally keenly to hear Kaftan and Gunkel)."[10] Harnack's great lecture on the history of dogma touched Barth's heart. According to his recollection, he heard Harnack's argument directly in the classroom that "the dogma of the early period was a self-expression of the Greek spirit in the sphere of the gospel."[11] In Berlin, furthermore, Barth became preoccupied with the *Ethics* of Herrmann (1846–1922). Reflecting on this experience, Barth stated, "Herrmann was *the* theological teacher of my student years. The day twenty years ago in Berlin when I first read his *Ethik* [*Ethics*] I remember as if it were today. If I had the temperament of Klaus Harms, I could speak of Herrmann in the way he spoke of Schleiermacher, or I could say as Stilling did of Herder. 'From this book I received the push into perpetual motion.' With more restraint, but with no less gratitude, I can say that on that day I believe my own deep interest in theology began."[12]

8. McCormack, *Critically Realistic*, 38–41.
9. B-B, 153.
10. Busch, *Karl Barth: His Life*, 38.
11. Ibid., 39.
12. Barth, "Principles of Dogmatics according to Wilhelm Herrmann," 238.

In addition to Immanuel Kant, Schleiermacher became the leading light for Barth during his student time in Berlin. Along with Herrmann's *Ethics*, Barth purchased a copy of Schleiermacher's *Speeches on Religion to its Cultured Despisers*. In the winter semester of 1906–1907 in Berlin Barth was interested in socialism. Incidentally, he participated in a series of lectures by Walter Simons on "Christianity and the Social Question." According to Marquardt, Karl Vorländer's book *The New Kantian Movement in Socialism* (*Die neukantische Bewegung im Sozialismus*) is located in Barth's book shelf with the inscription: "Karl Barth. Cand. theol. Berlin WS 1906/07."[13] Barth would have read it during his time at Berlin. In addition, in 1906 Werner Sombart was a professor in the Department of Economics at Berlin. Sombart's influence on Barth in Safenwil is evident in Barth's 1911 lecture "Jesus and the Social Movement."

In a meeting at the Worker's Association in Küngoldingen (February 1914), Barth recalled his learning of socialism through someone he called "S." "Through S. I was acquainted with socialism and I was driven to more exact reflection and the study of the matter. Since that time, I have considered socialist demands an important part of the application of the gospel. Certainly, I also believe that they cannot be realized without the gospel."[14] Although Barth did not identify "S," Marquardt's assumption that it was Sombart is credible. Notably, Barth had already read Sombart during his semester in Berlin in 1906.

Sombart (1863–1941) actually started his career with a powerful academic critique of capitalism. During his lifetime he was presumably the most influential and prominent social scientist in Germany. While Heidegger provides a counterexample, Sombart's embrace of Nazism relegated to near oblivion his fame as one of the most brilliant and influential scholars.[15] When Sombart was offered an opportunity to become a successor of Max Weber at Heidelberg, he couldn't take the position because of his socialistic orientation, which became uncomfortable for Grand Duke Friedrich II (1857–1928). In 1896 Sombart's first edition of *Sozialismus und soziale Bewegung* distinguished him as a radical so-

---

13. Marquardt, "Erster Bericht über Karl Barths 'Sozialistisches Reden,'" 478.

14. In the edition of "Evangelium und Sozialismus, 1914," "S" is versed as S[afenwil], which is less convincing. Cf. Barth, *Vorträge und kleinere Arbeiten*, 2:731. Cf. Marquardt, "Erster Bericht über Karl Barths 'Sozialistisches Reden,'" 470–88.

15. Grundmann, "Why Is Werner Sombart Not Part of the Core of Classical Sociology?" 257–87.

cialist based on his positive acceptance of Marxist historical materialism. However, Sombart did not share Marx's base-superstructure theorem with which Marx put an excessive emphasis on productive forces influencing and even determining relations between production and the ideological sphere. In Sombart's view, the primacy should rather be placed on superstructure.[16]

Because of his ardent fight for the cause of the socialist movement, Sombart received special attention from Friedrich Engels, who mentioned his name in his supplement to the third volume of *Capital*. According to Engels, Sombart was regarded as giving "an outline of the Marxian system which, taken all in all, is excellent. It is the first time that a German university professor succeeds on the whole in seeing in Marx's writings what Marx really says."[17] Rather than rejecting or transcending Marx, Sombart added a sociopsychological and sociocultural dimension to the analysis of the genesis and the nature of capitalism. Sombart's fame drew many students to his lectures both at Breslau, where he held the chair of economics at the university, and at the *Handelshochschule* in Berlin, where he worked from 1906 to 1917. In 1917 he was appointed a successor of Gustav Schmoller at the University of Berlin.

Karl Barth in Marburg

According to Barth's recollection, he underwent a number of theological and philosophical influences while in Marburg, beginning with his theological foundation under Herrmann and continuing with the philosophical influence of Kant and the neo-Kantians. Barth is explicit about Herrmann's influence:

> I came to Marburg as a convinced 'Marburger.' And when on the day I began my ministry the mail brought me, five minutes before I was to go to the pulpit, the new, forth edition of the *Ethik* as a gift from the author, I accepted this coincidence as a dedication of my whole future. . . . I cannot deny that through the years I have become a somewhat surprising disciple of Herrmann. . . . But I

---

16. In this regard, Parsons said that Sombart has "assimilated the main content of Marx into the framework of historico-idealistic thought." See Parsons, *Structure of Social Action*, 495.

17. Engels, "Supplement to 'Capital Vol. 3,'" 893–94.

could never inwardly agree that I had really turned away from my teacher. Nor can I so agree today.[18]

In addition, Barth encountered the Kantian and neo-Kantian emphasis on practical reason at Marburg through Cohen and Natorp. This philosophical direction would be deeply related to the field of socialistic analysis that would later become manifest in Barth's pastorate at Safenwil. Like Kant, Cohen was interested in establishing the epistemological foundation of modern science. Cohen tried to develop his philosophy on the basis of mathematical physics. Kant's basic insight, the so-called Copernican revolution in philosophy, comes from the fact that objective reality is known only insofar as it conforms to the knowing mind.

The human mind is active in the knowing process. Objects of experience may be known, but things lying behind the realm of experience, or things-in-themselves, are unknowable. Therefore, Kant's epistemology is based on sensible intuition—which Kant often conflates with imagination—and the categories of understanding. The senses furnish raw data, which the mind then organizes and systematizes. Although the faculty of imagination intuits, imagination cannot possess an identity of its own. Empirical data are perceived by intuition and are brought by the categories of understanding to form the objects of knowledge. The faculty of understanding is involved in the processes of classifying and ordering data that is presented to it by means of the faculty of imagination. This means that what we view and how we view are dependent on our idea of reality. The world is actually the way we see it. In Kant's famous dictum: "Thoughts without concepts are empty, intuitions without concepts are blind."[19]

Things are known as they appear to our senses and are formed into objects by the categories of understanding. The thing in itself (*Ding an sich*) is not known to us. Kant distinguishes *phenomena*, namely things as they appear, and *noumena*, namely things as they are in themselves. It is the *noumena* that give rise to our knowing. Generally Kant uses *noumenon* (thing in itself) to refer to an object existing apart from any relation to a knowing subject. All we know are phenomena, as they are present in our experience. Because we cannot gain knowledge of things in themselves, Kant's theory of knowing puts restrictions on transcendental

---

18. Barth, "Principles of Dogmatics according to Wilhelm Herrmann," 238–39.
19. Kant, *Critique of Pure Reason*, 93.

realities (God, the immortal soul, human freedom). Such postulates are to be seen and discussed in other domains of human reason, namely reason in its practical area. The *noumenon* is conceived of as free. Freedom exists apart from the relationship between reason and understanding.

Therefore, practical reason is not freedom itself, but an effect of freedom. This particular relationship between practical reason and freedom is called the moral law. Our relation to the world, according to Kant, is not merely restricted to scientific knowledge; there is a realm of moral value. Kant establishes the moral nature of existence in terms of the universal human moral experience. The fundamental law of pure practical reason is known as the categorical imperative. According to Kant, the command of the categorical imperative is as follows: "act as if the maxim of thy action were to become by thy will a Universal Law of Nature."[20] The human subject must act in accordance with the idea of the moral law.

Cohen takes issue with the precritical and ontological existence of *Ding an sich* in Kant. Thought as such, and not the world of the *noumena*, gives rise to cognition. By taking "being" to be the product of thought, Cohen argues that the real being is generated not by empirical sensation but by the thought itself. The knowing subject is a transcendental, pure and simple consciousness as a mathematical point. Thought has no origin in anything outside itself, because it is self-originating. Sense experience is not a source of the content of knowledge but a basic feature of human experience. Cohen's concept of origin (*Ursprung*) refers to the beginning of cognition in thought itself. As far as the origin, as the logical originator gives rise to its content, *Ursprung* is originative and creative of the objects of its knowledge.

For Cohen, logic, ethics, and aesthetics are valid patterns of cognition, especially in logic where all scientific knowledge is asserted to be valid. The reduction of human knowledge to the three patterns of logic, ethics, and aesthetics raises a question of the whereabouts of religion. Cohen was a pious liberal Jew. He placed religion under the heading of ethics. In agreement with Kant, Cohen maintained that ethics had to be universal. According to Kant, ethics are centered in his categorical imperative. This law has its source in the autonomy of a rational being. The moral law confronts us as an "ought" demanding our will in conformity

---

20. Kant, *Fundamental Principles of the Metaphysics of Morals*, 38.

to the law. Morality requires a belief in the existence of God, freedom, and immortality.

Like Kant, Cohen was convinced that there would be moral progress of the human race in the teleology of history. The interest that the Marburg school aroused among Marxists was less due to its radical apriorism than to its attempt at grounding socialist ethics on Kant's theory of the practical reason. Cohen and Natorp did not regard themselves as Marxists, but as socialists with a conviction that socialism could only be founded in ethical idealism. A striving for the ethical is an endless process toward complete social justice in our world. Because the goal of ethics is to attain universal global justice, we must have hope of attaining that goal. Therefore, Cohen argues that a socialist society would be established through moral progress.

For Cohen, God appears as the idea of the unity of three different patterns: logic, ethics, and aesthetics. The existence of God is not like people's existence. God as *Ursprung* exists only in a logically pure sense, not in a personal-ontological sense. God as *Ursprung* is a mathematical zero point. The idea of God guarantees an eternal world and human capacity of achieving ethical justice. The worldview of the ordered world and voluntary ethics are integrated in the idea of God, which is called the religion of reason. At this point Cohen's Jewish belief in the uniqueness of God becomes manifest. God transcends the physical world but at the same time provides us with the moral imperative to act ethically. Judaism provides a basis for Cohen to take in earnest the religion of reason, in other words, ethical monotheism. Therefore, Cohen's program for ethically established socialism becomes manifest in the following: "Socialism is right, insofar as it is grounded in the idealism of ethics. And the idealism of ethics has grounded the socialism . . . Kant as an ideal politician explicitly based himself on Plato, and he is for the republic . . . he is the true and actual originator of German socialism."[21]

Karl Vorländer (1860–1928), an outstanding representative of the neo-Kantian movement, attempted to combine Marxism and ethics by means of Kant's philosophy of ethics and epistemology in order to support the neo-Kantian socialism that Cohen represented. According to Vorländer, socialism must not marginalize an epistemological-critical

---

21. Cohen, "Kant, 1896," 70.

foundation and ethical enlargement, the aspect lacking in Marxism.[22] In 1921 Vorländer was convinced that he would fight for a synthesis between Marx and Kant. In his interim report on *Die neukantische Bewegung im Sozialismus*, he said that one cannot connect socialism historically with Kant: "I emphasize explicitly that the Königsberg Philosopher has not played a role of 'originator of socialism' historically, and that the development of the socialism in contrast has run into 'under completely other philosophical auspices'. What is at stake is only the possibility of methodical, systematical, logical connection."[23] In Vorländer's view, there would be no contradiction between Kant and Marx; thus Kantian philosophy of morality could be integrated into Marxism without violating the latter's basic assumption. For Vorländer, historical materialism is understood to define consciousness rather than to become an economic determinism that produces social and cultural consciousness. Consequently there is an interaction between the base and the superstructure in which human will plays an important role.

According to Marquardt, in Vorländer's book *The New Kantian Movement in Socialism* (*Die neukantische Bewegung im Sozialismus*), Barth underlined the following sentence: "'What is at stake is not whether Kant possibly already has had the socialistic idea, but whether his ethics can be really the point of departure to a socialistic ethics.'"[24] However, the neo-Kantian way to socialism has been characterized by its idealistic ethical revisionism, in contrast to scientific socialism in a Marxist sense. All in all, during his student period between Berlin and Marburg, Barth's approach to socialism is located between Marxist elements in Sombart and the neo-Kantian ethical socialism in Cohen and Vorländer.

In April 1907 Barth again enrolled in the University of Berne. However, Fritz Barth became tired of his son's wild goings-on and sent his son off to Adolf Schlatter in Tübingen. Dismayed at Schlatter, Barth made acquaintance with Christoph Blumhardt for the first time on December 27, 1907, and then frequently visited him in Bad Boll, "though my eyes were not yet fully open."[25] With his father's final consent, Barth studied under Herrmann and Adolf Julicher in Marburg, and together with Rudolf

---

22. *Marxismsus und Ethik*, eds. Sandkühler and Rafael de la Vega, 17.
23. Ibid.
24. Marquardt, "Erster Bericht über Karl Barths 'Sozialistisches Reden,'" 479.
25. Busch, *Karl Barth: His Life*, 44.

Bultmann later assisted Martin Rade (1857–1940) editing *Die christliche Welt* in 1908. At the Aarau Student Conference before the beginning of the semester at Marburg, Barth had already been able to hear Herrmann's lecture ("God's Revelation to Us") and Ragaz, whose theme was that God was meeting us today in socialism. Incidentally, it was in Marburg where Barth also renewed his acquaintance with Eduard Thurneysen, his lifelong friend from Zofingia. During his stay at Marburg, Herrmann became the great theologian for Barth. In acclaiming his greatness, Barth said, "I soaked Herrmann in through all my pores."[26]

Johann Wilhelm Herrmann

What underlines Herrmann's lifelong concern is the possibility of securing Christian faith from a metaphysical or scientific knowledge of the world. Herrmann distinguished himself from the old liberalism and also from all orthodoxies and all positivistic theology. Herrmann became the leading theologian among the faculty at Marburg (1879–1917) and was regarded as one of the most important systematic theologians of his time. His teaching gained an international reputation by including not only such students as Barth and Bultmann but also American students in pre–World War I Germany.[27] As Barth recalled,

> The air of freedom blew through his auditorium. It was certainly not by chance that for decades every semester a small caravan from Switzerland made the pilgrimage to Marburg and felt especially at home there. Our rebellious minds, repudiating all authority, found satisfaction there. We listened gladly when traditionalism on the right, rationalism on the left, mysticism in the rear were thrown to the refuse dump, and when finally 'positive and liberal dogmatics' were together hurled into the same pit.[28]

In his essay "Why Does our Faith Need Historical Facts?" (1844),[29] Herrmann strove to answer the problem of the relation of faith to history with concentration on the inner life of Jesus, which is the essence of religion for Herrmann. It is the inner life of Jesus on which faith is grounded

---

26. Ibid., 45.
27. Welch, *Protestant Thought*, 2:45.
28. Barth, "Principles of Dogmatics according to Wilhelm Herrmann," 267.
29. Herrmann, "Warum bedarf unser Glaube geschichtlicher Tatsachen?" 214–38.

as historical fact. He banned every trace of metaphysics from theology. His project for the exclusion of metaphysics from theology was not meant to denounce science and morality as unnecessary life-expressions. Rather ethical claims held a special place for him in relation to religion. For Hermann, historically grounded theology meant being grounded in the inner life of Jesus as a historical fact. Historically grounded theology in Troeltsch's sense is also grounded in the communion of the Christian with God, who comes about in history. Besides, Schleiermacher's *Speeches* had a deep influence on Herrmann and helped to improve his mature understanding of religious experience.

Herrmann's deep interest in securing the independence of religion from science and ethics moved him back from Ritschl toward the direction of Schleiermacher. In Barth's recollection, Hermann praised Schleiermacher's *Speeches* as "the most important pieces of writing to have appeared before the public since the closing of the canon of the New Testament."[30]

Herrmann's way to religion is first of all to distinguish religious knowing from all other forms of scientific knowledge. According to Herrmann, God is transcendent and supramundane. Therefore, God is not known through the way science knows the world. In fact, God lies beyond all of what science can prove and have access to. The self-revelation of God offers the basis for the rise of religion; religion lives from revelation. That being the case, the scientific method cannot prove God's reality. Science and philosophy cannot touch the reality of God. The object of Christian faith does not lie within the realm of scientific knowledge of the world. The human situation is too easily marginalized and ignored in Cohen and Natorp. True religion is neither produced by the moral will (Kant), nor identical with it (Cohen). Besides, religion is not the objectless emotion that accompanies the moral will (Natorp). "True religion, which 'carries in itself the energy of the moral purpose' . . . has also its own root and its own life."[31]

In the concluding sentence of *Die Metaphysik*, Herrmann stated: "When we seek to do theological work, we do not clutch at the goals of metaphysics."[32] However, Herrmann's concepts of religion and revelation

---

30. Busch, *Karl Barth: His Life*, 44.
31. Barth, "Principles of Dogmatics according to Wilhelm Herrmann," 245.
32. Quoted in Welch, *Protestant Thought*, 2:45.

are not in opposition to the anti-Christian position of modern philosophy and of natural and historical science. "The real enemy's position is on the right, within Christian theology itself."[33]

Our knowledge of God becomes possible only based on the fact that God has come to us in history. Independent of nature or natural science, Christian faith stands on its own foundation because religion lives from revelation alone. The self-revelation of God on which religion is based is the miracle that occurs beyond the natural and against nature. Schleiermacher's definition of religion as the feeling of absolute dependence in his *Glaubenslehre* stands under a critical reservation because, for Herrmann, religion is not identical with feeling without reservation. Religion is an ability given by God in which humans see and experience God's work in their lives.[34]

As Herrmann defines religion "in relation to empirically demonstrable objects, the decision must be made whether the subject can hold his ground in a life which he has for himself alone, an 'inner life.' The awakening of the individual to a consciousness, based on itself alone, of such a life of his own is religion."[35] Revelation, as the reality of God, confronts us. What stands in opposition to the reality of revelation are traditionalism, rationalism, and mysticism.

According to Herrmann, Troeltsch "was 'just a bit too fastidious' to assume for himself the decoration of 'positive.'"[36] Herrmann stood in opposition to positive confessionalist theology, the liberal-*freisinnig* theology, and the mediating theology. Just as he critiqued metaphysics or mixed theology, he protested orthodox confessionalism. According to Herrmann, religion arises from *Erlebnis* (experience), which is not to be demonstrated or disputed. The religious *Erlebnis* is to be found in the concept of *Vertrauen* (trust) or *Wahrhaftigkeit* (trustfulness): trust in Jesus Christ as the historical fact of the person of Jesus. Religion and ethical demand are inseparably connected with the concept of *Wahrhaftigkeit*. The human being as an inwardly independent being has an inner dependence and a moral autonomy. Keenly aware of Feuerbach's critique of religion as a projection of human wish fulfillment, Herrmann granted for

---

33. Barth, "Principles of Dogmatics according to Wilhelm Herrmann," 248.

34. Herrmann, *Systematic Theology*, 20.

35. Quoted in Barth, "Principles of Dogmatics according to Wilhelm Herrmann," 243.

36. Ibid., 248.

faith a spiritual importance to historical fact: "An honest atheist stands in all circumstances closer to the Christian faith than a representative of a religion of wish, no matter how christianly it is garbed."[37]

The only place where faith is to be located lies in the inner world of human consciousness. The locus of self-certifying faith consists exactly in the *Erlebnis* of "a communion of the soul with the living God through the mediation of Christ."[38] However, what differentiates Herrmann from mysticism is that the latter is unhistorical, seeks God in the depth of the soul, and absorbs the soul into God. What Herrmann aims at doing is Christian *Erlebnis*, which is bound to a historical fact, that is, to the inner life of Jesus. What constitutes our consciousness of God's communion with us consists in the historical fact of the person of Jesus and ethical demand for the moral law. For Herrmann, the historical Jesus is the revelation of God in which faith in God is grounded. The historical Jesus in a Herrmannian sense is not to be equated with the historical Jesus in historical-critical research because a historian deals only with outer or external history. Therefore, it would be devastating to establish the basis of faith by way of historical-critical investigation.

However, for Herrmann, inner or internal history plays a more significant role for establishing faith. The historian as historian has no access to this history of spiritual effects. The inner life of Jesus is present to us as the objective fact rather than as the facticity of Jesus that the church requires. The inner life of Jesus becomes a part of our own sphere of reality. Moreover, Jesus himself becomes a real power to us when he reveals his inner life to us. What the gospel offers as the guiding principle is the inner life of Jesus himself. Revelation is not doctrine: "The inner life of Jesus is the 'saving fact.'"[39] As Herrmann stated, "historical research cannot confront us with the Savior Jesus Christ. It cannot help us to find the historical Christ whom Christians assert to be their salvation. The inner or spiritual life of Jesus which it is necessary for us to see is never in any sense a minimum of the historically demonstrable; it is a fact 'in experiencing which one sees his own existence as bound up with the

---

37. Herrmann, *Ethik*, 107.
38. Herrmann, *Communion of the Christian with God*, 9.
39. Barth, "Principles of Dogmatics according to Wilhelm Herrmann," 249.

Omnipotent."[40] The ground of faith must be in Jesus's inner life in a historical sense that touches human hearts by evoking human trust in God.

Karl Barth's Earliest Writings

In the autumn of 1908 Barth took up a post as an editorial assistant to the *Christliche Welt*, which was published under the editorship of Professor Martin Rade. Working as an assistant editor of *Die Christliche Welt* in *Zeitschrift für Theologie und Kirche* at Marburg, Barth contributed his article titled "Modern Theology and Work for the Kingdom of God" ("Moderne Theologie und Reichgottesarbeit," 1909).[41] It appeared in a section of "theses and antitheses" in the *Zeitschrift*. (Barth's article met opposition from two professors of practical theology, Ernst Christian Achelis at Marburg and Paul Drews at Halle.[42]) Herein Barth observed that his colleagues who were trained under the influence of liberal theology at Marburg and Heidelberg experienced difficulties in the beginning of parish ministry compared with those trained under a more conservative and orthodox influence at Halle and Greifswald. Barth described the reason for this difficulty by way of religious individualism and historical relativism. For Barth, conservative students drew upon authoritative doctrine as normative statements of faith, but modern theological students had no such normative statements of faith. Liberal theology stood for theory while a work for God's kingdom stands for praxis in the form of the pastorate. In Barth's view, liberal theology stood in contrast with the praxis of God's kingdom. Two decisive elements (religious individualism and historical relativism), which Barth detected as the essence of the modern liberal theology, became obstacles when students trained in liberal theology encountered church praxis.[43]

Both the individualism of religion and the relativism of history homogenize and undermine the claim to revealed truth, whereas the concept of God's kingdom and its praxis make a claim for the universal validity of revelation. In the framework of liberal theology, divine revelation is no longer at the center because of human claims for the truth as an

---

40. Ibid., 250.

41. Barth, "Moderne Theologie und Reichgottesarbeit," 317–21.

42. Achelis, "Noch einmal: Moderne Theologie und Reichgottesarbeit," 406–10; Drews, "Zum dritten Mal: Moderne Theologie und Reichgottesarbeit," 475–79.

43. Barth, "Moderne Theologie und Reichgottesarbeit," 317–18.

individual center. Religion is grounded on personal rather than universal validity. As far as the Christian faith does not formulate the universal, responsible, and theological axiom, it strives to explore the content of the truth in terms of the personal ground of religion. Therefore the religious experience comes to the fore, and the relativity of all human knowledge precedes Christian faith, which is grounded in divine revelation.

From this basic principle of liberal theology, Barth anticipated the consequences of pluralism emerging out of the concept of Christian faith in that there takes place a subjective and religious trustfulness. All things are relative. Barth in this regard stood before the problem of value-relativism. The university-educated student of modern theology, equipped with religious individualism and historical relativism, faced a disadvantage in the ministry compared with a student of the more conservative school. The dilemma of theological value-relativism sharpened itself in regard to the problem of church praxis and its theological legitimation.

If the witness of all religious experience is accepted as the criterion of Christian discourse on God, theology must abandon an objectively true and obliging knowledge of God and claims to the truth of universality. How is it possible to come to a responsible church action in the Christian community with respect to forms and contents of various religious experiences? Would every church action and every action of religious trustfulness become legitimate in the same way on the basis of religious individualism and historical relativism? The two primary characteristics on which liberal theology is based suggest an inevitable tension between theory and praxis. In the end, liberal theology makes theologians incapable of praxis.

According to Barth, liberal theology is incapable of creating a bridge between theory and praxis. Because of its confrontation with modern science and modern culture-consciousness, liberal theology neglects the churchly character of theology.[44] In order to make claims for universality in the church, liberal theology needs to be actualized in the context of church praxis and Christian faith. To overcome the limitation and dilemma of liberal theology, that is, the lack of connection between theory and praxis, Barth proposed an idea of coexistence between a more theoretical way of faith and the more practical way of faith. What he noticed in liberal theology was a problem of value-relativism and a problem of

---

44. Barth, "Moderne Theologie und Reichgottesarbeit," 319–21.

the relation between theology and praxis. This perspective remains significant for the development of Barth's theological work.[45]

In his response to the aforementioned two critics of his article, Achelis and Drews, Barth regarded religious individualism to be bound to Jesus Christ as its norm and authority. On the question of how Christ is present to us, Barth found the true objectivity in Christ as the objectivity and norm in Christian religious experience. This is not at human disposal. The presence of Christ lies in "affection," in the sense of Schleiermacher's term. Christ is known in the depths of human consciousness: "The normative, objective, eternal lies only in the 'affection' of this inner experience. Everything which is set forth in thoughts and words belongs itself once again to the relativizing stream of history and is, as that which passes away, only a parable."[46]

Barth was ordained in the Reformed Church in Berne in 1908. In mid-August 1909, Barth left Marburg to begin to work as an associate pastor at the German–speaking congregation of the *église nationale* in Geneva. In Geneva his teaching and preaching reflected his learning from Marburg and from the circle of the *Chrstliche Welt*. His attempt was "to foist all that historicism and individualism on the people in Geneva."[47] In his essay "Der christliche Glaube und die Geschichte" ("The Christian Faith and History," published in 1912),[48] which was delivered to a gathering of pastors at Neuchatel on October 5, 1910, Barth made continuous attempts to develop a theoretical framework for the justification of the praxis of God's kingdom. What was at stake for Christian theology at that time was the problem of the relation of faith and history. It constituted "the indispensable presupposition and theoretical basis" for pastoral praxis.[49]

Faith presupposes the revelation of God in history, but a historical investigation rejects God's historical interventions by showing the im-

---

45. Dannemann, *Theologie und Politik*, 28–29.

46. Barth, "Antwort an D. Achelis und P. Drews," 484; cf. McCormack, *Critically Realistic*, 72.

47. Busch, *Karl Barth: His Life*, 57.

48. Barth, "Der christliche Glaube und die Geschichte," in *Vorträge und kleinere Arbeiten*, 2:149–212. This essay was later revised in light of Ernst Troeltsch's famous lecture, "The Significance of the Historicity of Jesus for Our Faith" and published in the *Schweizerische Theologische Zeitschrift* (1912).

49. Husinger, *Karl Barth and Radical Politics*, 193.

possibility of verifying revelation and miracle in history. Therefore, God disappears from history. The work of historians of religion serves as a "profane propaedeutic"[50] for theological work by clearing the ground of all false objectification of theology. Herein faith is not involved when it comes to talk of scientific knowing, of causes and of effects. Faith, according to Barth, is defined as "experience of God, unmediated consciousness of the presence and reality of the trans-human, trans-worldly and therefore simply superior power of life."[51] Faith itself is the "historical movement par excellence" actualizing and making our cultural consciousness historical. "It stands heterogeneously over against the cognitive apparatus which assesses validity in logic, ethics, and aesthetics. At the point of faith two problems intersect one another which lie on completely different planes . . . the problem of the I, of the individual person, of the individual life, and the problem of law-structured consciousness, human culture, and reason."[52] Through the moment of faith, "the abstract possibility of culture-consciousness is actualized, transformed into concrete reality."[53] Herein the old Kantian-Schleiermacherian opposition between religion and science is overcome; religion does not enter into competition with logic, ethics, and aesthetics; nor yet is it separated from them. Rather it actualizes and transforms culture-consciousness into concrete reality. Scientific consciousness, because of its abstractions from reality, is not competent to establish the connection to reality. As Marquardt rightly comments, "religion with its eschatological vigor can help society to achieve vitality and social-scientific consciousness to establish 'a connection to reality.'"[54]

As far as faith activates and actualizes the culture-consciousness of the individual into a concrete reality, Christian faith has its peculiarity through the personality of Jesus. In the personality of Jesus, the experience of God is somehow historically conditioned and determined and has been present within human society. The historical Jesus becomes the resurrected, living Christ in the community of Christ. From this perspective, the problem of the relation of faith and history has no fundamental

50. McCormack, *Critically Realistic*, 74.
51. Barth, "Der christliche Glaube und die Geschichte," in *Vorträge und kleinere Arbeiten*, 2:161; cf. Gorringe, *Karl Barth: Against Hegemony*, 27.
52. McCormack, *Critically Realistic*, 75.
53. Ibid.
54. Marquardt, "Socialism in the Theology of Karl Barth," 71.

importance. Rather it can become questionable only for those who stand outside of the experience of faith akin to Troeltsch. However, for those who live in the experience of faith, Christ outside of us is equal to Christ in us, and history is equal to faith. Therefore, "faith and the historicity of culture become synonyms."[55] Christ's righteousness becomes my righteousness; Christ's piety becomes my piety. He becomes I.

Revelation becomes historical in that revelation as history becomes effective through faith. Divine revelation in history can be experienced in the present through faith rather than through historical investigation. This coinherence between history and faith provides the basis for Barth to establish a theological connection to reality and to justify theological praxis in it. From this perspective, faith cannot be undermined and threatened by historical investigation. It was Schleiermacher who revealed how faith could be born in the individual. Through Schleiermacher, Luther's meaning becomes obvious. Through Schleiermacher's intuition, justification, and election become a fact "in the feeling brought about by God."[56] The ground of faith is the personal, inner life of Jesus. Faith is, therefore, direct, living contact with the living Lord. As far as the ground of faith is the inner life of Jesus in terms of the inner experience, as far as faith rests on Jesus's own consciousness of God, the work of artists and composers such as Michelangelo, Bach, Mozart, and Beethoven (and including the work of numberless little ones who are bearers of Christ's reality) could be regarded as sources of revelation alongside Paul. "Barth welcomes Luther's 'if you believe, you have' and Melanchthon's exclusive concentration on the 'benefits of Christ', along with the sayings of old Angelus Silesius ('If Christ is born a thousand times in Bethlehem and not in you. . . .')."[57]

In Geneva Barth encountered the real poverty of the industrial working class. He paid visits to the impoverished and spent a great deal of time in relief work with the poor. As Barth says, "I knew as a student the fed-up indifference of bourgeois circles and the poverty in Geneva. I regarded at that time the social misery as a necessary fact of nature, under which faith was not simply to set forth a strong but impractical hope.—Something new was brought to me through Calvin's idea of a city of God on earth, and it led me to the fact that Jesus has portrayed the

---

55. Barth, "Der christliche Glaube und die Geschichte," in *Vorträge und kleinere Arbeiten*, 2:163.

56. Ibid., 186.

57. Busch, *Karl Barth: His Life*, 57.

kingdom of God as a state of complete love of God and brothers."[58] His reading of Calvin's *Institutes* helped Barth to think more deeply about the relation between the kingdom of God and the world. Despite the fact that old orthodoxy was introduced and taught in caricatures at the universities when Barth had studied Calvin, he committed to relearning theology from the basics.[59]

Karl Barth and the Social Question in Safenwill

As Barth noted,

> Although in Geneva I had still lived completely and utterly in the religious atmosphere which I brought with me from Marburg, and especially from the circle of the *Christlcihe Welt* and its friends, when I moved to the industrial village of Safenwil, my interest in theology as such had to step back noticeably into second place (even though it continued to be nourished by my eager reading in the *Christliche Welt*, the *Zeitschrift für Theologie und Kirche*, and even in the works of Troeltsch, etc.) Because of the situation I found in my community, I became passionately involved with socialism and especially with the trade union movement.[60]

Barth's posthumous manuscript, "Socialist Speeches," makes it possible to understand variations in his relation to socialism, particularly in his practical relation to organized socialism and the social democratic party in Switzerland and socialistic International. The "Socialist Speeches" (later so named by Barth himself) is the title of a collection of some forty-three addresses that Barth delivered during his Safenwil period.[61] Barth began his pastorate in Safenwil on May 1, 1911. Four and a half months later he began to give his first socialist speech at the meeting of the Laborers' Society in Safenwil. The Laborers' Society was the official name of the local group of the Social Democratic Party of Switzerland. Barth was not a member of the socialist party yet when he began his "Socialist Speeches." These earliest "Socialist Speeches" were formulated word for

---

58. Barth, "Evangelium und Sozialismus," in *Vorträge und kleinere Arbeiten* 2:730.
59. Barth, *Theology of Schleiermacher*, 264.
60. Ibid., 263.
61. Cf. Vorwort to Barth, *Vorträge und kleinere Arbeiten*, 1:viii. Andreas Pangritz reports that F.-W. Marquardt deciphered and edited Barth's "Socialist Speeches" from 1911 to 1919. Cf. Pangritz, *Friedrich-Wilhelm Marquardt*, 29.

word just like sermons, and they construct comprehensive texts written out in the passion and precision of his proclamation.[62] Half of Barth's pastoral time in Safenwil was the time of World War I and the October Revolution in Russia.

Karl Barth and the Social Movement for Jesus

In 1911 Barth became the pastor in Safenwil, Switzerland, an industrial and agricultural area in the canton of Aargau. The first phase for Barth's socialism can be located from the beginning of his pastoral work till the outbreak of the First World War. Barth himself testified in a speech ("Evangelium und Sozialismus") of his interest in a relation between the gospel and socialism, during a meeting of the Workers' Association in Küngoldingen on February 1, 1914.

> How have I come to combine the gospel with socialism? I was educated to judge human beings not according to their money value, and to take material misery of the others as a serious problem. As a student I came to know the jaded indifference of bourgeois circles and the poverty in Geneva. At that time I still regarded social misery as a necessary fact of nature, to which faith had to provide a strong but impractical hope.—Something new was brought to me by Calvin's idea of 'God's city' on earth, and it led me to the fact that Jesus has portrayed the kingdom of God as a state of complete love of God and love among brothers. –Through S. I was acquainted with socialism and I was driven to more exact reflection and the study of the matter. Since that time, I have considered socialist demands an important part of the application of the gospel. Certainly, I also believe that they cannot be realized without the gospel.[63]

This pastoral context is an indication of the religious-socialist genesis of the socialist Barth. As we have already seen, Barth's keen interest in the social question became visible in his learning of ethical socialism in Marburg. In addition, Barth's acquaintance with S [Sombart] dates

---

62. Barth's minutes from July 1911 until February 20, 1919, remain from when Barth served as secretary on the church board. Marquardt reconstructs Barth's political activity as a pastor at this time in the analysis of these church minutes. See Marquradt, "Aktuar," 93–139.

63. Marquardt, "Erster Bericht über Karl Barths 'Sozialistisches Reden,'" 473.

back to Barth's student days at Berlin, although in Marburg in 1908 Barth had bought a copy of Sombart. Sombart's writings such as *Socialism and Social Movement* (1896) and *Der Moderne Kapitalismus* (1902) were already published.[64] In addition, as we have already seen, Sombart taught in Berlin during Barth's stay there, and Sombart's influence on Barth can be seen in his "Socialist Speeches," for example, in "Jesus Christus und die soziale Bewegung" (1911) and in "Die Arbeiterfrage" (1913/14).[65]

The installation service for Barth took place on Sunday July 9, 1911. Barth's father, Professor Fritz Barth, gave the sermon. One of the confirmands (born in 1896) remembered: "It gave us a huge amount of respect that he came from Geneva to us in Safenwil, to our quiet little village, where most of the people were farmers or worked in the factory."[66] For the next ten years of his life, Barth would live and work here. As Barth began his pastorate in Safenwil, Gustav Hüssy-Zuber was the chairman of the church board who was responsible for the employment of the pastor, the church budget, and the link between the congregation and the community. The Hüssy family was a member of what Barth called the House of Hüssy, a factory dynasty in Safenwil. Their family members owned a weaving establishment, a paint factory, and a sawmill in the area. Barth considered this time to be formative in his theological development: "It was during my time at Safenwil that I changed my mind decisively in a way which also affected the outward form of my future career."[67]

Barth also renewed his friendship with a former friend at Marburg, Eduard Thurneysen, a pastor of a neighboring church in Leutwil. Thurneysen was the person who brought Barth in contact with religious socialism in Switzerland. Through Thurneysen, Barth came into contact with Hermann Kutter, who was then fifty years old (1863–1931). Kutter completely impressed Barth by the "molten lava of his eloquence, like an uncanny volcano." "Amazed at his astonishing intelligence and mental

---

64. McCormack, *Critically Realistic*, 80. McCormack says that "Barth's personal copy of Sombart was not printed until 1908." "It is most likely that Barth only read Sombart after his arrival in Safenwil." With this statement, McCormack critiques Marquardt's conviction that "Barth had already read Sombart during his semester in Berlin in 1906." It appears that McCormack is unaware of Sombart's powerful influence as a professor of economics in Berlin when Barth was a student there.

65. Barth, *Vorträge und kleinere Arbeiten, 1909–1914*, 380–409, 573–689.

66. Marquardt, "Aktuar," 93.

67. Busch, *Karl Barth: His Life*, 61,

power," Barth "learned to speak the great word "God" seriously, responsibly and with a sense of its importance."⁶⁸

Keenly aware of the political responsibility of a Christian in society, Barth preached on many political matters. In addition, Barth was active in *Safenwil Arbeiterverein*.⁶⁹ The Hüssy family, which was highly respected in the church and in the civil community, owned a weaving mill and dye works as well as a sawmill where the workers were paid extremely low wages. They were not organized into a trade union. Barth even introduced Cohen, whom he knew at Marburg and read copiously in Geneva. However, the working people did not understand the academic discussions of socialism.⁷⁰

In his first socialist speech at the meeting of the Laborers' Society in Safenwil Barth dealt with the question of the origin and meaning of the state upon the request of the president of the Society. At the start Barth, however, preferred to give his lecture a different name: "Human Rights and Citizens' Responsibility" (October 15, 1911).⁷¹ Herein Barth discussed human rights and citizens' responsibility in regard to the origin and meaning of the state. "Human rights" is the catchphrase for "revolution" in all times. Revolution represents the demand for freedom in the name of human dignity. However, as long as revolution lies in the demand of a freedom movement for the individual, it is not fruitful for the origin of the state.⁷² In explanation of a relation between a capitalist revolution and human rights Barth—seeing human rights of personal freedom needing to be realized in the economic arena—discussed a clash with the human rights of the proletariat worker.⁷³ Barth did not escape from a socialistic critique of the concept of social class. Here he understood a class struggle from above. "It is completely right, if it is spoken from a socialist side that this struggle has been opened not from the proletariat,

---

68. Ibid., 76.

69. "When I moved to the industrial village of Safenwil, my interest in theology as such had to step back noticeably into second place.... I became passionately involved with socialism and especially with the trade-union movement.... I had to read Sombart and Herkner, I had to read the Swiss trade-union newspaper and the *Textilarbeiter*" (Barth, *Theology of Schleiermacher*, 263).

70. Busch, *Karl Barth*, 56.

71. Barth, "Menschenrecht und Bürgerpflicht" (1911) in *Vorträge und kleinere Arbeiten, 1909–1914*, 361–79.

72. Ibid., 365.

73. Ibid., 366.

but from the employer . . . It was the anarchy from above, to which the anarchy from below was only the answer."⁷⁴ What Barth intended in dealing with the problem of the state in view of a tension between human rights and citizens' responsibility, is to combine two things: morality and politics. "Morality and politics may not be two different things, they are one and the same. A moral which could not be a political moral is no moral at all because the essence of the moral is just the political citizen's responsibility."⁷⁵

Alongside Cohen, Barth argued for the progress of politics and morality not in the dream of an ideal state but in the ethical and political work. "In this progress or let's say more precisely in this progress we set in motion the state-thought, and we operate our civil duty and just with it our human rights."⁷⁶ Cohen's ethical socialism was incorporated into Barth's reflections so that the state-thought must be produced anew "in a tension between human rights and civil duty."⁷⁷ In other words, in the progress from the human rights to civil duty and from the civil duty to human rights, Barth noticed a point of departure regarding the political problem and task.

With ethical socialism in Cohen's sense, Barth noticed that the program of the Swiss Social Democratic Party would solve a relation between capital and labor in terms of a more or less violent expropriation of the means of production on the part of the state.⁷⁸ However, Barth was of a different opinion. Instead of stressing the function of the state he "places his greater hope on the progress of social relations in all classes."⁷⁹ Seeing that organized labor stood against organized capital, Barth asked if this dialectical relation between capital and labor takes place for the civil duty. If so, citing August Bebel's term "rote Kladderadatsch,"⁸⁰ Barth conceived that something unexpected and unfortunate would happen. According to Barth, the Swiss Social Democratic Party raised the concept of class to a definitive form of society in a conservative way. In Barth's

---

74. Ibid.
75. Ibid., 371.
76. Ibid., 374.
77. Ibid.
78. Ibid., 375.
79. Ibid., 376–77.
80. Ibid., 376.

view, "the highest aim of political endeavor cannot be fatherland."[81] What is more important for Barth is to balance political priorities between human rights and civil duty. This is the essence, meaning, and origin of the state.

Barth's speech "Jesus and the Social Question" was the topic chosen by the workers' union. In 1912 the Social Democratic Party of Switzerland (SPS) and the workers' union came to terms with each other for mutual support regarding the agitation of socialism, propaganda, and educational work. Already in 1910 the workers' union emphasized educational work in a series of public lectures for workers. Barth's speech at the local Laborers' Society on the theme "Jesus and the Social Movement" (on December 7, 1911) was extensively reprinted in the *Aargau Free Press* between Christmas and New Year's. In this speech Barth called into question the injustices carried out by the local factory owners, one of whom was a member of his congregation. Barth's lecture "Jesus Christ and the Social Movement" became an indication of Barth's position about the relation between the gospel of Jesus Christ and socialism. Barth argued that Jesus himself was more socialistic than the socialists. "Jesus is the movement for social justice, and the movement for social justice is Jesus in the present. . . . The real contents of the person of Jesus can in fact be summed up by the words: 'movement for social justice.'"[82]

We see in this speech a classic example of the religious-socialist identification of the Laborers' movement with Jesus, and Jesus with the well-being of this movement. The Socialistic Party newspaper printed the complete text of the speech, reporting, "The lecture of Pastor Barth last Sunday here on the theme 'Jesus and Social Question,' given at the request of the local Laborers' Society, was well attended. Women were present too. The theoretical discussion and the comparison with today can be found on page two of this edition."[83]

In Safenwil Barth was introduced for the first time to the real problem of social life. Before his very eyes, class warfare occurred in his parish. This forced him to study factory legislation, insurance, trade-union affairs, and so on. In Safenwil Barth no longer asked about the praxis-relevance of theology in general as we see in his *Moderne Theologie und*

---

81. Ibid., 379.
82. Barth, "Jesus Christ and the Movement for Social Justice," 19–37.
83. Marquardt, "Aktuar," 119.

Reichgottesarbeit. Instead he concretized the question of the practical-political relevance of Christianity. "One might well say that for eighteen hundred years the Christian church, when confronted by social misery, has always referred to the Spirit, to the inner life, to heaven. The church has preached, instructed, and consoled, but she has *not helped*, in the face of social misery she has always commended help as a good work of Christian love, but she has not dared to say that help is *the* good work."[84]

From this assertion we see that, on the one hand, Pastor Barth was deeply disturbed by social misery that brought human life to degradation and moral collapse. On the other hand, he sought a responsible reaction of Christian community toward the material and moral plight of workers. Barth's contact with socialism materialized primarily through his practical confrontation with the real situation of Safenwil workers. It does not ignore his theoretical or social philosophical reflection. Therefore, we need to pay attention to the socialistic influence upon his theological development in the sense of a correlation. For instance, Barth's turning away from the individualism of liberal theology and constructing universalism in his thought shows the primacy of the social/political dimension over the individual/particular dimension in Barth's thought and theology

What is characteristic of Barth's practical concern is articulated in the following: "When I talk about the movement for social justice, I am not talking about what some or all Social Democrats are doing; I am talking about what they *want*. . . . What concerns us, therefore, are not the words and deeds of Bebel or Jaures, of Greulich or Pflüger or Naine, nor even the words and deeds of socialists in Aargau and Safenwil."[85] What Barth intends to demonstrate is "the inner connection" between social democracy or socialism and the eternal Word of God that became flesh in Jesus, namely "the inherent connection between Jesus and socialism."[86] According to Barth, Jesus is not the representative of the Christian church, worldview, or ideas. For the bridge between Jesus and socialism, Barth introduced Jesus's way of life in which "as an atheist, a materialist and a Darwinist, one can be a genuine follower and disciple of Jesus."[87]

---

84. Barth, "Jesus Christ and the Movement for Social Justice," 26.
85. Ibid., 21.
86. Ibid., 22.
87. Ibid.

In Barth's view, what connects socialism with Jesus is a movement from below. If socialism is "a movement from below to above," "the movement of the economically dependent," "the movement of the proletariat" who is "always dependent in his existence upon means and the goodwill of the factory owner," Jesus himself came from the low social class of the Jewish people at that time. Jesus was also a worker, getting along with the poor and the lowly. His message was good news to the poor, to those who were dependent and uneducated. This was the eruption of a volcano from below to above. A liberation theology in Barthian fashion has its foundation in the belief that "the kingdom of God has come to the poor."[88]

Barth did not forget to differentiate between the kingdom of God for social democracy and the kingdom of God for Jesus. In agreement with Sombart (who says "the quintessence of all socialist doctrines of salvation" contained in a poem of Heinrich Heine—"to build the kingdom of heaven even here upon the earth"—), Barth introduced the message of Jesus for the poor. Socialistic passion and praxis for building up the kingdom of heaven on earth need not be diametrically opposed to Jesus's good news of the kingdom of God for the poor. A church's transformation of Jesus' social and material concern into cultivating the inner life and preparing candidates for the kingdom of heaven is "the great, momentous apostasy" from Christ.[89]

The fundamental contention is that God's kingdom comes to us in matter and on earth because the Word became flesh. In light of God's movement from above to below, wholly and completely, the gospel is a movement from below to above. In Jesus there is no dualism between spirit and matter, between heaven and earth. In keeping with Matt 25:32–46, Barth stressed that the spirit having value before God is the social spirit. Jesus opposed material misery and created new people in order to create a new world. "Regarding the goal, social democracy is one with Jesus."[90] Herein Barth cited a famous statement of Oettinger: "The end of the way of God is the affirmation of the body."[91]

Barth's critique of capitalism is along the lines of socialistic critique: "The class contradiction" is "the daily crime of capitalism." Private prop-

88. Ibid., 25.
89. Ibid., 26.
90. Ibid., 28.
91. Ibid., 29.

erty as a means of production belongs to the factory owner. However, in the account of the rich man and the poor Lazarus, Jesus wanted to say that a rich person does not enter into the kingdom of God (Luke 16:19–31). A Marxist theoretician, Joseph Dietzgen, who was a despiser of Christianity, was right in saying that the original sin of the human race is self-seeking. The similarity between Barth's argumentation and that of a more Marxist approach is shaped in his passion for the socialistic spirit of solidarity. In view of *The Communist Manifesto* of 1848, Barth argued that socialism proceeds from solidarity and it emphasizes solidarity "as the source of his power and progress" to the social consciousness of the worker. Furthermore, he argued, "Solidarity is the law and the gospel of socialism." As a socialist, one ceases to be an individualist and thus ceases to think, feel, and act as a private person, so he or she should become a class-conscious worker. "To be a socialist means to be a 'comrade' in consumer's unions, in labor unions, and in political parties" "as a member of the forward-striding, fighting totality."[92]

Dietzgen has argued that "conscious and planned organization of social work is what the longed-for savior of the modern period is called."[93] Therefore, should the socialist call to solidarity and Jesus's gospel stand in contrast to one another? By no means, because there was only "a social God, a God of solidarity" for Jesus. "There was also only a social religion, a religion of solidarity."[94] On the basis of the "awareness of the collective, solidarity, communal, social God" Jesus's call to discipleship, namely, the rule of corresponding action follows. As Barth said passionately and convincingly, "Let him take it in who can, that one must lose one's life in order to find it, that one must cease being something for oneself, that one must be a communal person, a comrade, in order to be a person at all."[95] Jesus is the partisan of the poor. "Real socialism is real Christianity in our time."[96] Certainly the correct socialism for Barth is not that which the socialists now do, but rather what Jesus does—and what the socialists want to do. At a minimum, the demands of the socialists cannot be real-

---

92. Ibid., 33.
93. Ibid.
94. Ibid., 34.
95. Ibid., 35–36. Cf. Schellong, "Karl Barth als Theologe der Neuzeit," 57–58.
96. Barth, "Jesus Christ and the Movement for Social Justice," 36.

ized without the gospel. The kingdom of God was close to the poor, and Jesus identified himself with them.

Be that as it may, Barth would be hesitant in terms of the manner in which socialists act to attain it. Concerning the socialistic manner necessary for attaining the goal, Barth distanced himself from secular socialists because his socialism is theological in light of the gospel of Jesus and the kingdom of God. The socialist's concern is in line with what Jesus wanted to do. "Leave the superficiality and the hatred, the spirit of mammon and the self-seeking, which also exists among your ranks, behind. . . . Let the faithfulness and energy, the sense of community and the courage for sacrifice found in Jesus be effective among you, in your whole life; then you will be true socialists."[97] As a pastor, Barth had to stand in the forefront of the class struggle. These writings reflect a belief that theology and social questions are not in conflict, but complement each other in light of the gospel. Theology and national economy, sermons and politics, are not separated from each other but belong together. Barth's sense of the identification of God's kingdom with true socialism—"real socialism is real Christianity in our time"—does not mean at this time that we can strictly identify our socialism with God's kingdom through our utilization of God to serve human interests or to exploit God for human purposes. Rather we follow the movement of the kingdom of God, serving, believing, and obeying its promise for the poor, alienated and wrecked.[98] "Jesus is more socialist than the socialist." Seen from the divine side, the gospel is "wholly and completely a movement from above to below. It is not that we go to heaven, but that heaven comes to us."[99] For this reason, Barth did not agree with the manner in which socialists acted to attain their goal.

After this socialist speech, Barth was ridiculed and attacked sharply as an ignorant idealist by the manufacturer, Walter Hüssy, a nephew of the Safenwil church board president. His "Open Letter" (February 1, 1912) was printed on February 3 in the *Zofinger Tagblatt*. It declared Barth's lecture to be "a long rabble-rousing speech, garnished with an incredible number of religious quotations," and he heard from it the demand "Private property must fall—not private property in general, but private

---

97. Ibid., 37.

98. Gollwitzer, "Kingdom of God and Socialism in the Theology of Karl Barth," 79–80.

99. Barth, "Jesus Christ and the Movement for Social Justice," 27.

property as a means of production."[100] According to Walter Hüssy, what Barth wants is his ideal of a future state![101]

Barth responded in "Answer to the open letter of Herr W. Hüssy of Aarburg on February 6, 1912," by arguing that Hüssy's response was a fundamental misunderstanding of his speech. Barth would carry on the fight with Hüssy stating, "despite the prevailing coldness, I enter the fray in my shirt sleeves rather than my frock coat and reply with equal clarity."[102] Against the charge that his lecture was "a 'rabble-rousing speech' with the purpose of 'sowing discord between employer and employee,'" Barth clarified that his speech was directed objectively about capitalism as such, and it did not refer to specific capitalists.[103] Barth's response sounds harsh because he regarded Hüssy's protest as "pathetically naïve."[104]

Regarding the problem of private property, Barth's idea was in line with the official program of the Swiss Social Democratic Party even although he was not yet a member. Barth explained that what led him, as a pastor, to the side of socialism lay "in the idea of a socialist state of the future."[105] His concise definition of capitalism reads: "The net profits of the common work of the entrepreneur and the worker now become the private property of the former, because he is the private owner of the means of production. This is the essence of the capitalist economic system."[106] Socialism fights against this economic system on grounds of inequality and dependence. The private profit that Hüssy stands for is opposed to the justice of socialism and the Bible.

Barth also wrote a letter to the father of Mr. Hüssy, Mr. Hüssy-Juri in Safenwil. In it Barth announced that his sharp response was not directed personally to either the father or the son. Barth was seeking to attack the economic system of capitalism objectively, not its particular, individualistic expressions. In the interest of the congregation, Barth hoped that his speech would not cause any disturbance to friendly relations between the pastorate of Safenwil and the house of Hüssy. Barth's official answer

100. Ibid., 37–38.
101. Ibid., 39.
102. Ibid., 40.
103. Ibid., 41.
104. Ibid., 42.
105. Ibid., 43.
106. Ibid., 44.

was one of the clearest texts using Marxist argumentation emerging from a biblical paradigm. In protest of Barth's attitude, the president of the Safenwil church board, Gustav Hüssy-Zuber, who was a cousin of Walter Hüssy, resigned.[107]

A number of attacks poured upon Barth in the *Zofinger Tagblatt*. The first "letter to the editor" (on February 12) was under the polemical headline "Concerning the Red Danger in Safenwil." The writer sought "to catch Barth in the fly of his pants," insulted him as "a Red Doctrinaire," as "a Red Messiah," as "the Messiah from Safenwil," as "a combative little pope," as "Mr. Trade Pastor," and as "an Ivory Tower Wise Man." The second anonymous letter (on February 14) with a more moderate tone was sent to the editors of the *Zofinger Tagblatt*.[108] There was also criticism from Marburg about Barth's lecture as "the superficiality of Barth's theology!"[109] However, Barth did not abandon his conviction that socialistic demands were to be understood as an indispensable part of the gospel and are completely dependent on the gospel for their realization.

Karl Barth and Socialist Activities

Barth's Sunday sermon was attacked by the newspaper (in its edition of July 15, 1912), under the title "Pastoral Agitation: A sermon held this past Sunday in a congregation in our district." The article states, "A certain pastor seeks to bring to life once again the times of the religious upheavals, even though in a modern, social-political dress." "Finally, we would like to ask whether the church is the proper place for the pastor to express his political views. The great majority of our church-goers, free-thinkers

---

107. We read in the minutes of February 13, 1912, that "Mr. Gustav Hüssy-Zuber tendered his resignation as President and member of this authority. Preliminary notice is taken of this fact" (Marquardt, "Aktuar," 121).

108. "The open letters of the two Safenwil gentlemen have brought me great joy. In this way no one needs to lick any more envelopes to close them, and everyone can read the letters. I think the best thing would be for the Pastor to become an Industrialist. With his intelligence and good books, from which he thinks to derive his life experience, he would quickly have a learning experience behind him. Then he could share profit and loss with his workers and see whether they stay with such an arrangement or break away. To Mr. W. Hüssy, the nobleman who knows less of life's needs, we would recommend that he change and become pastor in Safenwil. The spiritual profession would not harm him. After a few years industrialist and Pastor would have come closer together in their view. Yours sincerely." Ibid., 120-1.

109. Busch, *Karl Barth: His Life*, 70.

alongside the social democrats . . . seek on this day, with more reason than their Shepherd demonstrates, an hour of edification and meditation. *That* is true worship, Dear Pastor, and not what you dare to offer us!"[110]

This attack of the *Zofinger Tagblatt* was echoed by the *Aargauer Volksblatt* which was close to the Catholic–conservative People's Party. Under the title "A Terrible Crime" (in the edition of July 16, 1912) it reads: "In the district of Zofingen a reformed Pastor gave a sermon last Sunday, in which he, referring to the Sunday Gospel of the Reformed Lectionary (Matthew 5, about the self-righteousness of the Pharisee), castigated the pharisaic in political life, and illustrated it by pointing to the hollowness, half-heartedness and inconsequentiality of certain people, whose greatest lie is their claim that they are 'free-thinkers.'"[111]

In the spring of 1913 there occurred a conflict with the owner of the textile firm Hochuli and Co. in Safenwil. In the minutes from a meeting on February 6, 1913, we read: "The firm of Hochuli and Co. complains in a letter of Jan. 28 about the scheduling of the confirmation classes in the last three months of the instruction year . . . The secretary is asked to give the Firm Hochuli and Co. written information, with reference to 44 of the Aargau Church Order, which prescribes for the Summer 2-3 hours and for the Winter 3-4 hours per week." However, Hochuli responded that he would no longer accept any more confirmation youth in his factory. Barth proposed, for the sake of peace, that during the final three month, the three hours per week be one and a half hours twice. The church board adopted the provision extending from May to New Year's twice a week an hour-and-a-half session. And the factory was notified of this regulation. We shall deal with this affair in more detail later because this conflict accompanied the whole period of Barth's pastorate.

In a sermon on the cleansing of the temple (January 19, 1913), Barth justified Jesus' anger based on a higher notion of justice than the customary order. What Jesus carried out in the remple was a revolution against the existing order. "There in the Temple, Jesus ignored the customary order with the fullness of the power of the Messiah. . . . Yes, Jesus carried out a revolution—when the divine appears in human form, there must always

---

110. Marquardt, "Aktuar," 109.
111. Ibid.

be a revolution against human order. Let us be drawn into this struggle. ... Oh, if only we would awaken and want to *become* fighters!"[112]

In a sermon of February 23, 1913 Barth stresses Christian solidarity with the suffering of the world: "The misery of the world is your misery, its darkness is your darkness ... We must acquire for ourselves that holy sense of solidarity which bears the suffering of the world in its heart, not in order to sigh and shake our heads over it, but rather to take it in hand so that it will be otherwise."[113] Barth also saw a clear connection between the social question and the question of militarism. Barth had served as the president of Blue Cross (a social service group) ever since January 1912. Under his leadership, the "Blues" sometimes worked together with the "Reds" (i.e., socialists) in Safenwil.

In his "Dissenting View on Military Aircraft" (March 14, 1913),[114] Barth distanced himself from the naïve pacifism of the socialists at that time. Against the patriotic sentiment that any expenditure for military aircraft means especially clear evidence of true love of fatherland, Barth (based on Matt 6:10 and Luke 11:2) regarded war as a criminal offense against humanity.[115] War is War. "Military-expenditures are as such 'horror before God.'"[116] Barth also paid attention to the German Social Democratic Party. "I was well aware of August Bebel and old Liebknecht, and saw the prophetic cloud hovering over the German Social Democrats before it disappeared."[117]

In his Easter sermon (March 23, 1913) Barth encouraged his congregation to become concerned about the battle between the kingdom of God and the kingdom of evil: "The message of Easter leads us to the boundary between two worlds. And on this boundary, a battle is raging. Two gigantic kingdoms are engaged in a war with one another ... The world strives against God. But we cannot and we may not be mere specta-

---

112. Barth's sermon of January 19, 1913 in Barth, *Predigten 1913*, 38; cf. McCormack, *Critically Realistic*, 97–98.

113. Barth's sermon of February 23, 1913 in Barth, *Predigten 1913*, 72.

114. Barth, "Gegenrede betreffend militär-Flugzeuge," in *Vorträge und kleinere Arbieten*, 2:485–93.

115. Ibid., 489.

116. Ibid., 493.

117. Busch, *Karl Barth: His Life*, 71.

tors of this battle of which Easter speaks. We have to become partisan on one side or the other."[118]

Soon after his wedding (on March 27, 1913), Barth prepared a lecture, "Belief in the Personal God" (delivered to the Aargau Pastors' Association at Lenzburg on May 19).[119] In Aargau Barth tried to reconcile his Marburg insights with his new socialist discoveries of the kingdom of God. In addition, in the sermon on May 4, 1913, he recognized the task for the pastor in the prophetic consciousness of Amos: "A prophet is, in all things, precisely the *opposite* of that which most people expect from a pastor these days and of that which most pastors have really been . . . The prophet is the employee of God. For him, it is a matter of indifference what people think of him and what they do to him . . . He knows that if he does his duty, they will be shocked by him and indignant . . . The prophet is the representative of the unaccustomed."[120] The kingdom of God does not stand in contrast to catastrophes and violent storms in revolution; rather they are in the service of it.

The importance of the lecture "Belief in the Personal God" lies in the fact that it demonstrates Barth's early affinity toward the coexistence of dialectical thinking and analogical thinking. For Barth, personality and absoluteness are predicates of God in which religious experience becomes possible. The concept of personality lies between transcendentalism and psychology. In fact, just as transcendentalism refers to the infinite aspect of personality, psychology points to a concrete and finite aspect of personality. When viewed transcendentally, personality does not match with an absolute subject. Likewise if the concept of absoluteness were applied to a personal subject, the concept of personality would dissolve. Therefore absolute personality is nonsense. The only solution is to see two concepts in contradiction. God is an infinite Spirit. The problem of analogy comes out in Barth's consideration of human personality and divine personality.[121]

For Barth, the analogical way of thinking is not based on the process of human ontological abstraction. This being the case, Feuerbach's

118. Barth's sermon on March 23, 1913 in Barth, *Predigten 1913*, 143.

119. Barth, "Glaube an den persönlichen Gott," 21–32, 65–95.

120. Barth's sermon on May 4, 1913 in Barth, *Predigten 1913*, 209.

121. In light of this relation, Balthasar thinks "the first hints of the analogy of faith break through Barth's suggested approach" in this article "Glaube an den persönlichen Gott." See Balthasar, *Theology of Karl Barth*, 178.

thesis—that the concept of God is the result of human projection—critiques religious experience. As Barth said, "We cannot find in the human personality an analogy to the real content of religious faith in God . . . A concept of God that results from projecting human self-awareness into the realm of the transcendent cannot latch on to the reality of God, or describe it exhaustively. Religion's notion of God cannot be a projection from our side; it can only be the reflection of a fact that has been carried into us. This fact is the *life in God* which is granted to us through our *association with history*. This is the real religious experience; in it we possess God, and because of it we can speak of God."[122]

The possibility of speaking of God comes out of the *life in God*, a reflection of a fact that has been created in us. Beginning on the divine side, analogical reflection is given to us through human *association with history*. Herein the anthropological approach to God is denied. Instead, Barth identifies the analogy of faith or the analogy of history for the first time. What is at stake here is that the motives of religious socialism and comprehensive universalism surface for the first time. The *Ursprung* of the analogy makes religious experience with God possible and justifies human speech about God. By way of dialectics and analogy we have God and can speak of God on the basis of them.

This *Ursprung* is formulated, in fact, not merely in a negative way but also in a positive way. The meaning of all negations is, from the start, the gaining of a theological position, namely, of a new beginning and starting point of thought. The intention of positive theology is also the intention of dialectical theology. Barth cites a formulation of Cohen to illustrate his point: "'Non-grounding becomes the ground for grounding of the thought and the willed.'" That is, the critical a priori of Kant becomes a positive-theological *apriori* of God-thought. As Barth said, "to negate the grounding of the actual as such, that is to say, at the same time to affirm it. Negation of space and time is simultaneously master over them . . . It is the truth and validity of apriori which rests in itself, which proves itself here as the positive side of God-thought."[123]

Already in 1914 Barth articulated a positive a priori not only in relation to the grounding of the thought and the willed, but also in relation to the grounding of the actual. In this dialectical framework, the concept

---

122. Barth, "Glaube an den persönlichen Gott," 89; cf. Balthasar, *Theology of Karl Barth*, 178–79.

123. Ibid., 72. Cf. Marquardt, *Theologie und Sozialismus*, 208.

of *Ursprung* is used so that the development of analogy becomes possible. The analogy of *Ursprung* stood before the conceptualization of the dialectics in *Romans II*, materially as well as temporarily. Analogy and dialectics can be co-originally set in the thought of *Ursprung*.

Barth's thought of *Ursprung* by way of dialectics and analogy in 1914 can be seen later as a basis for the development of his socialistic theology in the Tambach lecture of 1919. In November 1913 Barth's *Sozipredigten* (socialist sermons) caused five of six members of the church board to resign. "Newly elected were the Misters Hans Hilfiker, Wagner, Ernst Widmer, Artur Hüssy, Arnold Scheurmann, a moving company proprietor, and Ritschard, Mr. J. Schärer, School Property Administrator, was elected president."[124]

In the sermons of 1913, we notice Barth's strong preference for socialism in light of the kingdom of God. In a sermon dated 16 November, Barth addressed the socialists' decision to retreat from the *Landes* church in Prussia: "The leader of this movement has made a declaration: We are for the religion, but against the state religion. We are for all churches, but against the state churches."[125] The church retreat movement was carried out among Prussian social democrats on October 28, 1913. In all, 1,328 social democrats removed themselves from the Prussian *Landes* church. For Barth, the church as the state church was without a doubt a disadvantage compared with the watchman office of the old prophets. In his sermon of August 31, he even praised August Bebel, the chairman of the German Social Democratic Party (SPD) who had died in Passugs, Switzerland, on August 13, 1913. According to Barth, if we regard a man like Bebel from a Christian standpoint, we must say that he gripped important points about what Jesus wanted much better, and followed Jesus more passionately, than most so-called Christians. Although Bebel made errors, Barth did not hesitate to declare that through him "a voice of God, an announcement of the coming Kingdom of God" could be heard.[126]

Barth continued articulating his conviction about Bebel on September 14, knowing that many in the congregation were saddened at his death. In Barth's view, Bebel was a man who had declared God's Word to his time. The life of Bebel was beautiful, great, and even godly because

---

124. Marquardt, "Aktuar," 121.
125. Barth, *Predigten 1913*, 591.
126. Cf. Barth's sermon on August 31, 1913, in Barth, *Predigten 1913*, 435.

it was dedicated completely to truth and human rights. "I am delighted about it, because he [Bebel] is for me a sign that God is living in humankind, and that a strong resistance is against the power of egoism. I think just definitely that the loving God needs also such people and speaks to us through them."[127]

Several people were offended by Barth's sermon of September 14. There was even some talk of having him removed from his position. Nevertheless, on the edge of social catastrophe Barth still had hope about a gathering of the Socialist International in Basel's Münster Cathedral in November 1912 and of a peace conference between the German and French parliaments in Bern in the summer of 1913.[128] On November 24 and 25, 1912, the International Socialist Congress took place, and there was a demonstration against the impending war that would become World War I. In Basel's Münster Cathedral, the International Socialist congress declared war against war in an internationally unanimous decision. In the summer of 1913, forty-one members of German *Reichstag* had a meeting with 164 French delegates as well as with twenty-one French senators in a conference in Bern in order to advise a communication between Germany and France.

During this time, Barth came in contact with Leonhard Ragaz (1868–1945) who, as one of the most prominent and influential figures among Swiss religious socialists, brought forward his view of the kingdom of God from 1902 onwards during his time as the pastor of Basel cathedral. Starting in 1908, he held a theological chair in Zurich but resigned from it in 1921. As Barth pointed out, "although 'Religious Socialism' was also prompted by the younger Christoph Blumhardt's message of hope, by virtue of its critical and polemical presentation it was already a characteristically Swiss movement."[129] Barth also participated in this movement, read *Neue Wege,* and conversed with prominent representatives of the movement. However, he was hesitant about identifying himself fully with religious socialism. Interested as he was, he kept his distance from it. In Barth's letter to his mother on November 20, 1913, he was preoccupied with a study of social questions. He had to teach a course to a group of workers and youth who came to him every other week Sunday after-

---

127. Ibid., 470.
128. Barth's sermon on September 21, 1913 in Barth, *Predigten 1913*, 478.
129. Busch, *Karl Barth: His Life*, 77.

noon for one and a half hours. Moreover, his wife, Nelly, who was not ashamed to support his work, stated her feelings about the mood of the day: "I am fundamentally fed up with bourgeois society."[130] In connection with his work in the Safenwil Workers' Association during the winter of 1913–1914, Barth produced an extensive dossier on the "Workers Question."[131]

In this "Workers Question," we see Barth's connection with SPS and the workers' union in Safenwil and his effort to provide a more solid theoretical basis for his socialist praxis. Barth lamented, "How stupid that I missed an opportunity to take Wagner's national economy in Berlin."[132] At any rate, in his "Workers Question," Barth made use of writings such as *Die Arbeiterfrage: Eine Einführung* by Heinrich Herkner (1863–1932), who was professor of the national economy at the Königlichen Technischen Hochschule, Berlin.[133]

Here Barth showed his interest in the history of two important industry plants, namely, the firm C. F. Bally in Schönenward and that of the Sulzer Brothers in Winterthur, both of which are still today considered great Swiss enterprises. Through collecting data, Barth became concerned about the life circumstances and conditions of his parishioners and comrades. Barth's "Workers Question" was used already in winter 1913–1914 in Safenwil or in Aargau before his entrance to the party in 1915. We shall deal with Barth's dossier later in more detail. In 1914 Barth spoke on "The Gospel and Socialism" and "The New Factory Act." In a sermon in June 1914 about the Berne Exhibition (published in *Neue Wege*), Barth declared that "the evil of capitalism was the consequence of a world without God." The Christian hope of a new world is to be brought into being by the living God. At the same time, Barth was critical of Friedrich Naumann. (Naumann was an important representative of social democracy in the German Protestant context. Early on, Barth was impressed by Naumann's social activity. However, as Naumann became associated

---

130. Ibid., 576.
131. Cf. Barth, "Arbeiterfrage, (1913/14)," in *Vorträge und kleinere Arbeiten*, 2:573–682.
132. Ibid., 577.
133. Furthermore he utilized the book *Die Gewerbliche Arbeiterfrage* by Werner Sombart (1863–1941), from the collection of Göschen, and the works of Paul Pflüger (1865–1947), who was the pastor in Zurich-Aussersihl from 1911 to 1918 and the national council member of the SPS. Barth, "Arbeiterfrage, (1913/14)," 573.

with the war policy of the German empire, Barth grew dismayed.) In Barth's view, Naumann had made a political compromise and so no longer looked for something better beyond war and capitalism. For Barth, however, the sentence "God is" amounted to a revolution. Socialism was, therefore, a very important and necessary application of the gospel.

Karl Barth and *Die Hilfe*

Before the outbreak of the First World War, Barth reviewed the previous year's publications of *Die Hilfe*, whose editor was Naumann. Naumann was influential and reputable within the German Protestant church. He also began, as a liberal, to be involved in the Inner Mission movement in Hamburg. In his earlier thought he held a view similar to the religious socialist movement. Naumann founded *Die Hilfe* in 1890. However, around 1895–1896 he turned from religious socialism and became a defender of the national state and patriotism. In his statement in *Die Hilfe* he wrote, "Of what use to us is the best social policy when the Cossacks are coming? Whoever wishes to concern himself with domestic issues must first secure people, Fatherland, and borders; he must be concerned with national power. Here is the weakest point in the Social Democracy. We need a socialism which is capable of ruling . . . Such a socialism must be German-national."[134] Thus Naumann became a strong defender of the German military buildup between 1905 and 1914.

With an invitation from Rade, Barth wrote a review of *Die Hilfe* which was published in *Die Christliche Welt*. Barth recognized the great service *Die Hilfe* had provided over the years with respect to practical social progress, unemployment insurance, trade unions, land, and housing reform. However, Barth noticed that Naumann was no longer capable of bringing to the fore the relevance of Christianity for political life.

According to Barth, politics that raises the necessary concessions and compromises to the dignity of generally valid ultimate ideas is different from politics that make concessions and compromises for the sake of immediate goals. What Barth argued for was a politic of hope, full of revolutionary longing for a better way that would come in the midst of the world of relativity. "It is one thing to become accustomed to the world

---

134. See Kupisch, *Zwischen Idealismus und Massendemokratie*; cf. McCormack, *Critically Realistic*, 108.

of relativities, finally becoming completely satisfied and . . . at home in them, as those who have no hope. It is another thing altogether, in the midst of this world of relativities, to be incessantly disquieted and full of longing, fundamentally revolutionary *vis-à-vis* that which exists, longing after the better which will come, after the absolute goal of a human community of life beyond all temporal necessities."[135]

In *Die Hilfe*, Naumann failed to seek this truth of longing against all that exists. In contrast to *Die Hilfe*, the SPS took seriously the political momentousness of the absolute God. Christian hope that takes God seriously in the social political arena means a revolutionary unrest, always moving forward, longing for something better in the future rather than being satisfied with what is offered by the world of relativities. What Barth discerned in socialism was this revolutionary unrest and disquiet revealed in longing for the future. However, Barth was aware of August Bebel's mistake of supporting the military appropriations bill which had been passed by the *Reichstag* in the summer of 1913. This is what Naumann called Bebel's "last will and testament." Such compromises in the Social Democracy did not signify a fundamental change of socialist direction as Naumann had expected. As Barth states, "If the Social Democracy should be transformed into a radical reform party on the soil of capitalism and nationalism as *Die Hilfe* so much expects—we do not believe it—then that would be for us at most a new disappointment, as the politics of *Die Hilfe* is finally a disappointment for us, not, however, a proof that a politics which simply capitulates before certain alleged realities is the only possible, the correct politics. We should expect more from God."[136]

What we discern in Barth's review is a theology of radical socialism. There is a direction that has higher political faith, which is, by no means, satisfied with political and economic relativities. Although concessions and compromises are made, they are done in inner contrast to all temporality. Barth found this direction in International Social Democracy. Taking in earnest the ultimate, namely, God, politically, the Social Democracy sought to rewrite politics. This radical revolutionary socialism was based on the standpoint of the absolute, which is the genuine otherworldliness

---

135. Barth, "Die Hilfe 1913," *Die Christliche Welt* 28 (15 August 1914) 776. Cf. McCormack, *Critically Realistic*, 109.

136. Barth, "Die Hilfe 1913" in *Die Christliche Welt* 28 (15 August 1914) 776; cf. McCormack, *Critically Realistic*, 110.

(*Jenseits*) of all social relativities; it is, in other words, the standpoint of God. This radical socialism that represents the standpoint of God takes a position that is not ready to establish peace with the reality of the present era, with capitalism, nationalism, and militarism.[137]

According to Barth, *Die Hilfe* had no understanding of the inner essence of Social Democracy, that is, of the revolutionary unrest, the radicalism, and the enthusiasm. Although *Die Hilfe* understood the industrial-democratic element, which was the whole reform apparatus in the social-democratic program, it shook its head at their unrealistic ideals. "'Utopia,' 'fantasy,' 'outmoded Marxist dogma,' or even 'agitation talk'—that is the repertoire of their fight against the left." The position of *Die Hilfe* against the left resorted to "placing this utopia and talk into a box, and placing *'Gegenwartarbeit'* ['present work'] arm in arm with decisive liberalism."[138]

In April 1915, in wartime Germany, Barth went to Marburg with Thurneysen for the wedding of his brother Peter who married Rade's daughter, Helene. At the wedding Barth had an opportunity to meet Rade's father-in-law, Naumann. Barth engaged in a passionate discussion with him over the war. Naumann's position on the war became obvious in his description of religion: "All religion is right for us . . . whether it is called the Salvation Army or Islam, provided that it helps us to hold out through the war."[139] Barth's disappointment with him led Barth closer to Blumhardt. Barth's subsequent comparison of Naumann and Blumhardt is evident in their obituary that Barth wrote in the year that the two died. I shall deal with Barth's obituary on Naumann and Blumhardt in a later chapter on the Tambach lecture of 1919.

The radical-revolutionary hope of the working class was not merely political but theological for Barth. He arrived at this position because his concept of radical socialism came from the absolute God. "It is a religious difference, which separates the hope of the proletariat from the hope of the circle of *Die Hilfe*. Naumann does not understand this religious difference, and he levels it off to a mere political difference."[140] However, what is central to Barth's position is well articulated in his understanding of

---

137. Ibid., 778.
138. Ibid.
139. Busch, *Karl Barth: His Life*, 84.
140. Barth, "Die Hilfe, 1913" in *Die Christliche Welt* 28 (15 August 1914) 778.

hope: "in the midst of this world of relativities, to be incessantly disquieted and full of longing. To be fundamentally revolutionary against that which exists. To long after the better which will come, after the absolute goal of a human communal life beyond all temporal necessities."[141]

Barth believed that the one who seeks faith in *Jenseits* of war and capitalism, as *Die Hilfe* does, seeks in vain. The hope and longing for the new and the better has its origin and telos outside *Jenseits* of all temporal necessities because this hope comes from God. Therefore accommodation to an existing reality or the status quo is perpetually challenged and discredited since we should expect more from God. In *Die Hilfe* Barth spoke of God in political relevance and developed his discourse of God in the context of social justice, revolution, socialism, and radicalism. Barth critically supported revolutionary leftist socialism before World War I and interpreted socialistic theory and praxis in light of his understanding of God, who is *Jenseits* of all temporal necessities. Thus Barth integrated socialistic theory and praxis into his theology. In other words, Barth attempted to see the "left" of socialism grounded in the "above" of God because he deepened and actualized God as the radically *Novum* in the context of a radically new society. As Danneman states, "In the bringing-in of the transcendence-thought (God and socialism as the *Jenseits* of the world of capitalism) lies the theology of Barth's radical socialism."[142]

Religious Socialism in Switzerland

Barth's theology cannot be properly understood without reference to his socialistic activity and Swiss religious socialism. His "Socialist Speeches" and activity until the outbreak of World War I—as has been described above—are themselves reflective of liberal theology, especially when dealing with a relation between theology and political praxis. However, after the war he made a new departure by breaking with his liberal background. To further appreciate Barth's theology and social praxis after the war, it is first necessary to look at the movement of religious socialism in Switzerland. For understanding the development of religious socialism in Switzerland, it is worthwhile to take note of a historical event beginning with Christoph F. Blumhardt (1842–1919). Although Blumhardt

---

141. Ibid., 776.
142. Dannemann, *Theologie und Politik*, 37.

is not depicted as a religious socialist in an authentic sense, the movement of religious socialism in Switzerland has one point of departure in him. Representatives of Swiss religious socialism such as Kutter and Ragaz were strongly influenced by Christoph Blumhardt. Blumhardt, properly understood, is both an example and father of religious socialism in Switzerland. Ragaz, in his book *Der Kampf um das Reich Gottes in Blumhardt, Vater und Sohn, und weiter!* is full of honor and respect for Blumhardt.

Blumhardt is spiritually and theologically related to his father, Johann Christoph Blumhardt (1805–1880). In his parish at Moettlingen the elder Blumhardt was involved for two years in a process of healing a woman who suffered a high degree of hysteria as seen from a medical perspective. As she was healed, a voice sounded out: "Jesus is victor." Thus, Jesus's victory became the grounding principle for his healing work in light of the kingdom of God. For him, the kingdom of God had a strong cosmic and apocalyptic dimension rather than being confined to an individualistic and pietistic realm of salvation. The presently real quality of the kingdom of God was bound up with the incarnation of Jesus Christ. However, the reality of the kingdom of God was not restricted to the historical Jesus, but after the ascension the kingdom of God broke into the world in which the healing of a possessed woman was regarded as a sign of God's in-breaking reality. What is important is that hope for the kingdom of God and the voice that said "Jesus is victor" was understood as an immanent concretization of God's kingdom.

According to the elder Blumhardt, the kingdom of God is not shortened or reduced to a spiritual, otherworldly salvation of the soul but is sharpened in concrete-physical and social-material realms. This tendency to integrate the material arena and concrete content into the movement of God's kingdom finds a strong expansion in the younger Blumhardt. In 1852 Johann Blumhardt moved from Moettlingen to the retreat house in Bad Boll.

After the death of his father, Blumbhardt placed a new accent on his father's watchword, "Jesus is victor." Beyond a healing ministry in Bad Boll, Blumbhardt made a radical turn to the world. As Blumbhardt stressed, "The kingdom of God comes to the street where the poorest, the most offended and the most miserable are. There the kingdom of God comes."¹⁴³ For Blumhardt, God is directed toward the world in spite of its sinfulness. With a social turn Blumhardt found the effect of the kingdom of God in the socialist movement in which he sees the life of humans occupying a place of utmost importance. Without falling into replacing the kingdom of God with socialism, Blumbhardt discerned a sign of God's in-breaking reality in the socialist movement for the sake of humanity. "The purpose of God is this-worldly" makes Blumhardt's direction so explicit that God is the starting point and the ground for the redemption of the world, not the other way around. God is related to the this-worldly dimension (that is, to the material realm) so radically that according to Blumhardt, revolution can become a word of God.¹⁴⁴

In 1899 Blumhardt arrived at a practical consequence from his understanding of God's kingdom. In protest against Wilhelm II, he joined the SPD. His entrance into the Social Democratic Party in Germany was not meant to be a sign of his interest in the politics of the party but an expression of his fundamental solidarity with the poor and a practical performance of his idea of the kingdom of God. After Blumhardt's speech in Göppingen (in June 1899), Eugster-Zuest founded the textile union (*Webeverband*) in Apenzell, Switzerland. In December 1900, Blumhardt was elected to the Social Democratic Congress in Württemberg. Then in 1889 Kutter came into contact with Blumhardt and paid visits to Bad Boll.

Hermann Kutter

In December 1902 when Hermann Kutter (1863–1931) published his work *Das Unmittelbare: Eine Menschheitsfrage*, he was a pastor at Neumunster in Zurich (between 1899 and 1926). Under the influence of Blumhardt, his work appeared as a philosophical interpretation of Blumhardt's thought. He characterizes the new life as the living God revealed in Jesus Christ. A turning away from the pure speculative theology to immediacy is identical with a return to the living God or, in the sense of Blumhardt, to the kingdom of God. In this light Kutter noticed in Social Democracy a will to social change, an in-breaking reality of immediacy into an incomplete and deficient society.

143. Lejeune, *Christoph Blumhardt*, 47–48.
144. Ragaz, *Kampf um das Reich Gottes in Blumhardt*, 115.

In his book *Das Unmittelbare*, there is a positive evaluation of the socialistic movement inspired by Blumhardt. The protest of Social Democracy against the old authority, its struggle for a better social order, and its utopia of a new community are, for Kutter, signs of the living God. In a sense, the work of Ragaz was connected to the emergence of Kutter's theology. In April 1903 Ragaz preached a sermon that came to be known as the "Bricklayers' Strike Sermon." In December of the same year, Kutter's prophetic voice was manifest in his book *Sie Müssen! Ein offenes Wort an die christliche Gesellschaft* (*They Must! An Open Word to Christian Society*) (1905).

In September 1906 Ragaz gave his important speech "Das Evangelium und der soziale Kampf der Gegenwart" ("The Gospel and the Current Social Struggle") to a gathering of Swiss pastors. In it Ragaz scrutinized the social class struggle and challenged Christians to get involved in the movement of social justice. In October 1906 the first conference of Swiss religious socialism in Degesheim occurred. Finally, in November of the same year the first issue of *Neue Wege* was released.[145] Given this fact, the religious socialism of Switzerland was developed first of all through the influence of Kutter and Ragaz (1868–1945) in 1906. Their journal *Neue Wege* appeared, bearing the strong influence of Ragaz, its founder and editor. The *Freie Schweitzer Arbeiter*, edited by Gustav Benz and Otto Lautenburg, was the other voice of religious socialism. Although a socially and politically liberal pastor in Basel, Benz rejected Social Democracy, unlike Ragaz, who had already joined the SPS in 1913.

At any rate, the religious socialist movement in Switzerland was greatly indebted to Kutter's books, *Sie Müssen!* (1905) and *Wir Pfarrer* (1907), in which the message of Blumhardt played an important role. Although *Das Unmittelbare* remained—because of philosophical language—without great effect to the readers, Kutter's book *Sie Müssen!* aroused great public attention. He argues that God takes sides with Social Democracy, not with the church. In his analysis of society, Kutter defended the political interest of Social Democracy against charges and attacks from the side of church. What is to be fought against is not Social Democracy but the Christian society that had abetted social injustice and misery. "The Social Democrats are revolutionary, because God is there. They must be forward, because God's kingdom must be forward. They are

---

145. Buess and Mattmüller, *Prophetischer Sozialismus*, 48.

people of revolution, because God is the great over-thrower."[146] The atheism, materialism, and internationalism of Social Democracy are no less than a protest of Christian society and conventions that have fallen into mammonism. The kingdom of God breaks in with the social democrats into the society. "Class struggle is a necessity provoked through mammon . . . The contradiction of classes is such that fighting has become not only necessary, but also the essence of humanity."[147] Social Democracy becomes God's instrument that denies the existing social order. They must. They cannot do otherwise. "The most violent revolutionary is the living God." He is the overthrower without reservation at all.[148]

Be that as it may, Kutter remained a pastor and a prophetic voice throughout his active life. "We must meet ourselves in our life and struggle, in our morality and religion toward God. The Bible starts out of him . . . For the Bible God is the single reality that is taken in earnest."[149] Furthermore, at the center of Kutter's work is the insistence that the Social Democrat carried out the will of God. The atheism that was so frequently blamed by Christian conservatives (such as, for instance, Stoecker and Naumann) bears in it the stamp of the living God.

For Kutter God used Social Democracy as an instrument to awaken the church. It is to be seen as the hammer of God. The socialists must serve God's purpose. What Kutter saw behind the hope of the Social Democrat is an unconscious Christianity. Therefore, the society has no right to complain about revolution. "The salvation becomes, at first, full in the material thing. Sin means a faulty placement of the spirit against the material. On the contrary, the spirit must direct itself again to the material." "God's promise fulfills itself in the Social Democrats: They must!"[150] However, Kutter believed that pastors are confronted with a different kind of work in which they are to shape the conditions for the new society by being faithful to the living God. They are to proclaim a prophetic call to Christians in accordance with a life in immediacy with this living God. Kutter was more restrained about involvement with politics. He did not join the Social Democracy Party. Kutter's prophetic call had more to do

146. Kutter, *Sie Müssen*. 90.
147. Ibid., 85.
148. Ibid., 74.
149. Ibid., 58
150. Ibid., 59, 61.

with theology and the church than with politics. Among his books, *Sie Müssen!* maintained a lasting influence as the founding document of the religious-social movement in Switzerland.

Unlike Blumhardt's entrance to Social Democracy as a sign of solidarity with the poor, Kutter's contribution to the social question meant a new form of preaching. Such an approach gave rise to the following question: to what degree does a Christian take part in the socialist movement in a practical-political way? This question remained an issue of conflict between Kutter and Ragaz. Finally the environment of the general strike in Zurich in 1912 fostered a break between Kutter and Ragaz.

Leonhard Ragaz

Unlike Kutter, Ragaz was a political activist. Ragaz was born on July 28, 1868, in Tamin, a small mountain village in Canton Graubünden in the German-speaking part of Switzerland. He grew up in the democratic atmosphere of a Swiss village and remained a strong believer in democracy all his life. Impressed by the cooperative forms of economic life among Swiss mountain farmers, he was concerned with a decentralized form of socialism. His father was active in a number of offices in the community, and his father's interest in politics passed over to Ragaz. Because his family was constantly surrounded by financial difficulties, Ragaz was well aware of social problems from his personal experience. After graduation from high school in nearby Chur, he decided to study theology, enabled by a scholarship. He enrolled at the University of Basel and spent some time at the universities in Jena and in Berlin. He then returned to Basel.

The theological background that he learned and developed in his years of study was liberalism, especially Hegelianism. (A. E. Biedermann, who made a great impact on Ragaz, was a Swiss Hegelian theologian.) In 1890 Ragaz was ordained as a Reformed pastor and began his ministry in three villages in Canton Graubünden. During his parish work, his main concern was with the intensive study of the Bible and the theology of the priesthood of all believers, encouraging the laity to be more involved in parish life. Between 1893 and 1895 Ragaz served as a language and religion teacher in Chur in part for health reasons, and also in part due to his dissatisfaction with ministry. During this time he was in contact with the writings of Christian socialism, including Carlyle, Kingsley, and Robertson, and German authors such as Naumann.

In 1895 Ragaz returned to the pastorate as a senior pastor in Chur and remained there until 1902. Influenced by the writings of Kierkegaard and Ritschl, he was preoccupied with ethics. In Chur he met Clara Nadig and married her. She remained a supportive companion throughout his difficult life. His experience with social issues was later deepened when, in the pastorate in Chur, Ragaz came into contact with poverty and social problems such as bad housing, poor working conditions, broken families, prostitution, criminality, and alcoholism. Later he wrote about this experience, saying it was "the comprehensive solidarity of guilt".[151] Involved in an educational program for workers and giving talks to worker's groups, Ragaz was given Karl Marx's *Das Kapital* as an expression of gratitude from the laborers' association. In 1902 he received a call from the Münster Cathedral in Basel. During his pastorate in Basel, the kingdom of God became, for him, the central teaching of Christianity. Seeing the kingdom of God as a gift of God, Ragaz called for human participation in the coming of God's kingdom. Wherever people work for justice, peace, and humanity, one will find the signs of God's kingdom. The labor movement was one of the most important signs of God's kingdom for Ragaz.

Ragaz later experienced the great bricklayers' strike in 1903. Troops were called to intervene. In his sermon known as the "Bricklayers' Strike Sermon," Ragaz claimed that Christ was on the side of the oppressed. The social movement, which for him was associated with the "humanization of humans," became a sign of the kingdom of God; therefore, Christians are asked to take part in the struggle for the oppressed: "So the social movement is in its deepest ground a realization of the idea which stands in the middle point of the gospel: Human beings as the children of God and the brotherhood of humans . . . Who understands it, sees, in spite of all wave and storm, the blowing and ruling of the creative Spirit of God."[152]

Shortly after the "Bricklayers' Strike Sermon," Ragaz became acquainted with Pastor Hermann Kutter in Zurich. Together Ragaz and Kutter founded a religious-social movement to join in the struggle for the humanization of humanity, "in the drama of the humanizing of mankind, whose value we do not quite realize yet."[153] Interestingly enough,

---

151. Bock, *Signs of the Kingdom*, xii.

152. Mattmüller, *Leonhard Ragaz*, 2:85.

153. Ragaz, "Gospel and the Current Social Struggle," in Bock, *Signs of the Kingdom*, 14.

Herrmann's concern for the working class echoed in the development of religious socialism. Herrmann's concern for socialism—regardless of his individualist bent—was mediated by Oskar Holtzmann. The thesis of "the social movement as the unconscious bringer of divine will" came out ten years earlier than Kutter's book *Sie Müssen!*, and six years earlier than Blumhardt's entrance to the social democratic party.

Herrmann's thesis reads: "The Christian church has to thank modern socialism that her horizon is expanded, her formation of thought is deepened, in short, her inner life is enriched."[154] It was delivered by Herrmann as an address to the Evangelical Social Congress in 1891. Ragaz accepted Holtzman's reappropriation of Herrmann's socialism as the legitimate child of the Reformation for his development of religious socialism.[155] Kutter's book *Sie Müssen!* also made a significant contribution to the task of theology, especially in Switzerland. In 1906 Ragaz delivered his address "The Gospel and the Current Social Struggle" ("Das Evangelium und der soziale Kampf der Gegenwart") at a pastors' conference in Basel. This is one of the fundamental documents through which Ragaz was able to deepen and actualize religious socialism in terms of his theology of God's kingdom and to bring to the fore its social and political implications. As the second thesis reads, "The Kingdom of God is the central concept of the good news. Jesus teaches the worth of each child of God as well as the brotherhood of men under God. Jesus sees Mammon as the greatest enemy of man."[156]

According to Ragaz, socialism in its basic goals provides "the direction that will lead us out of capitalism to the next higher level in historical development."[157] Ragaz's intent in this regard was not to identify the teachings of Christ with socialism. Rather his "task is simply to determine which *telos* an economic order must have if it is to harmonize with the life-style required by the gospel."[158] When seen in light of the gospel, capitalism, the telos of which "centers on the increase of capital," is condemned "as a means to greater profit."[159] However, in the midst of

---

154. Cf. Jäger, *Ethik und Eschatologie bei Leonhard Ragaz*, 248.
155. Ibid., 246.
156. Bock, *Signs of the Kingdom*, 3–4.
157. Ibid., 6.
158. Ibid.
159. Ibid.

capitalist society, "the social movement reveals itself as the true way to God for our race."¹⁶⁰ The social movements such as the political organization, the labor union, and the cooperative "made workers members of a reputable community and brought them under the discipline of the community."¹⁶¹ The better economic order, that corresponds to the gospel, is the socialistic one because the spirit of socialism is in complete economic solidarity. What Ragaz argued for is "a religious rebirth," "a Spirit-guided community" and "a radical renewal of the spirit."¹⁶²

For Ragaz, social change and religious reform should complement each other rather than contradict each other: "Social change can topple capitalism and with it Mammonism . . . ; it can bring about a fairer distribution of the earth's goods, but still not satisfy the souls of men; it can link people together socially but it will not unite them in the deepest sense."¹⁶³ As far as a deeper unity between the social struggle and spiritual movement is concerned, the telos of religious socialism is "an act in the drama of the humanizing of mankind."¹⁶⁴ In 1907 Ragaz accepted an invitation to address the World Congress of Free Christianity in Boston. While in North America, he was impressed by Walter Rauschenbusch and his Social Gospel. (Rauschenbusch's book *Christianity and the Social Crisis* was later translated by Ragaz's wife, Clara Nadin, into German.) In 1908 he accepted a call to professorship in systematic and practical theology at the University of Zurich. Here Emil Brunner, who later became a founder of dialectical theology, took a different direction than Ragaz. Emil Brunner remembered Ragaz when he stated, "that was a great time, when Ragaz came to Zurich. Then theology was interesting, not as a science, but a proclamation in our time, as encounter with historical reality, with the labor question, with the war issue."¹⁶⁵

In 1909 Ragaz first came into contact with Blumhardt of Bad Boll in Germany. Like Kutter and Barth, Ragaz was greatly influenced by him. Ragaz found in Blumhardt's message of eschatological waiting for the kingdom of God an activist and social dimension. Seeing the sign of the

160. Ibid., 11.
161. Ibid., 12.
162. Ibid.
163. Ibid., 15.
164. Ibid., 14.
165. Ibid., xiv.

coming kingdom in the socialism and labor movements, Blumhardt was deeply engaged in the social struggle from 1899 to 1906. Kutter saw the kingdom only as a movement out from God, whereas Ragaz stressed a task of human participation in the kingdom by distinguishing an absolute hope from a relative hope in the kingdom of God. For Ragaz, relative hope can be seen as a sign pointing to the kingdom and a summons for human participation in the movement for social justice. Absolute hope, by contrast, is based on God's action alone; absolute hope measures and judges relative hope.

Although greatly inspired by Kutter's *Sie Müssen!*, Ragaz was uncomfortable with the social-ethical quietism present in Kutter. Kutter's conviction was that the church must be first renewed before entering into the social struggle. Rather than restricting himself to the sphere of church, Ragaz was active in the labor movement by joining the Social Democrats. The difference between them led to a conflict within the religious-socialist movement in Switzerland. In contrast to Kutter's *von Gott her* (out from God), Ragaz dialectically emphasized the direction *zu Gott hin* (toward God) as the free effectiveness of human praxis, which is grounded on the direction *von Gott her* in a particular way. In Ragaz's letter to Kutter (on May 9, 1907) we read: "The right of this '*zu Gott hin*' I'd like to represent generally. It is one of the differences between you and me. The '*von Gott her*' is certainly right principally and systematically. I also represent it, as far as I can truly represent it."[166]

As Barth characterized the difference between them, "Leonhard Ragaz developed what Kutter meant to be a view of the current situation and an interpretation of the signs of the time." For Ragaz, "the church must regard socialism as a preliminary manifestation of the kingdom of God . . . He made it a true system of 'Religious Socialism.'"[167] The systematic approach of Ragaz was, however, what Barth was hesitant to accept. In seeing the action of God in history, there is a tendency in Ragaz's theology of history to ideologize the kingdom of God totally as socialism.[168]

In 1912 there occurred a general strike in Zurich in which Ragaz was active. Again in this matter Kutter broke with Ragaz and retreated from the religious-social movement. During his participation, Ragaz was

166. Jäger, *Ethik und Eschatologie bei Leonhard Ragaz*, 228.
167. Ibid., 78.
168. Ibid., 226.

shocked by the attack of the military upon workers. His later antimilitarist stance, associated with this experience, became a dominant factor for Ragaz's development of the peace movement. In the same year the Peace Congress of the Socialist International was held at the Münster Cathedral in Basel. Ragaz spoke of God's work in building up God's kingdom with unchurched people. However, World War I became a great obstruction and setback for the religious-social movement. Proving the international element of socialism to be an illusion, workers in each country rallied to fight for their fatherlands. International Workers were not united in solidarity but instead came to fight and kill each other in the war. Unlike Kutter, who hoped for a German victory, Ragaz hoped for a German defeat. After 1913 Ragaz was active in the Swiss Social Democratic Party (SPS). During the war, various options were debated for the future of the Party. Lenin exercised a considerable influence among Swiss leftist socialists. Trotsky came to Switzerland, and Ragaz had a stimulating encounter with him, albeit in his anti-Bolshevist stance. Recalling their encounter Trotsky noted that "the Zurich professor Ragaz, a committed Christian, more a theologian with his education and profession" stood on the most extreme left wing of Swiss socialism. Ragaz represented the most radical fighting method against the war and was for the proletarian revolution.[169]

As Lenin began his socialist activity in Zurich, Bolshevism came into conflict with the religious-social movement. In his article "The Battle against Bolshevism" ("Sozialismus und Gewalt" [1919]), Ragaz saw Bolshevism as a betrayal of socialism. He argued that the socialists must fight against the perversion of socialism.[170] Ragaz's campaign against the entrance of Swiss Socialists into the Communist International was a well-known fact. In Zurich the leftist group of Münzenberg and his *Jungburschen* followed for years the religious-socialist direction that Ragaz had represented. Ragaz's influence on the socialist youth organization had not ebbed, so that the socialist youth were impressed by Ragaz's seriousness and his ethical demand. However, Münzenberg found himself more under the influence of Lenin than under the religious-socialist spirit. Münzenberg was critical of Ragaz's demand to abandon violence,

---

169. Trotsky, *Mein Leben*. 217.
170. Ragaz, "Battle against Bolshevism," in Bock, *Signs of the Kingdom*, 43.

and charged that "he [Ragaz] preached salvation out of political oppression and exploitation through love."[171]

In 1915 much had been discussed about the military and violence. Together with a women's conference in Bern initiated by Clara Zetkin, the International Socialist Youth Conference during Easter of 1915 was regarded as a prelude to the meeting of the International workers' movement in the Zimmerwald. Müntzenberg hoped that the Youth organization would make a contribution to the first International Youth organization after the betrayal and collapse of the Second International during the war. "The Youth organizations became in many countries leaders of the whole proletariat, and avant-garde in the fight against the imperialistic and social democratic betrayal."[172] At the International Youth conference in Bern, Münzenberg came into contact for the first time with Bolshevists. Lenin, who remained at his home in Bern, directed Bolshevists by phone behind the scenes. In this conference the Bolshevist thesis was raised: people must exploit the war for the revolutionization of the masses and must not speak about peace too early.[173] Ragaz and Lenin never talked to each other, but an indirect dialogue occurred between them over the issue of the question of the revolutionary use of violence. The leader of the Youth organization stood on the side of Lenin by turning away from the religious-socialist approach. Münzenberg wrote, "Lenin saves us from religion."[174]

Through *Neue Wege*, Lenin was aware of the antiwar position in the religious-socialist circle. Lenin reported that a pious philistine declared that it was not bad to turn a weapon against the war agitator, whereas famous Social Democrats such as Kautsky justified the chauvinism scientifically: "Whose voice is it? Our citation is extracted from a journal of a petit-bourgeois Christian democrat, whose journal is published in society of the upright cleric in Zurich."[175] Lenin actually began his attack on Ragaz and his religious socialism before Ragaz came to know about Lenin. Ragaz also reported, "I had no relation with Lenin and was not concerned about him. But Lenin was concerned about me and

---

171. Mattmüller, *Leonhard Ragaz*, 2:154.
172. Ibid., 155.
173. Ibid., 156.
174. Ibid., 157.
175. Lenins Werke, 21:82, as cited by Mattmüller, *Leonhard Ragaz*, 2:158.

our movement. Lenin calls us in one Zurich journal 'tearful social clerics' who would keep the workers' association from the use of violence. Obviously we stood in the way for him. The necessity of the violence was for him a dogma."[176] Warning against the danger of Bolshevism as practiced in the Soviet Union, Ragaz himself was confronted with the spirit of Bolshevism. In an article (in *Neue Wege* in November 1918), Ragaz defined Bolshevism as "Lenin's dictatorship of the proletariat as practiced in Russia."[177] Lenin acclaimed that the proletariat must break with the bourgeois dictatorship through the dictatorship of the proletariat.[178] The meaning of the Bolshevist dictatorship of the proletariat lay in taking away the means of production, the state apparatus, and finally the cultural apparatus, especially the press. This was the way of eliminating ruling violence through revolutionary violence. Only then could the whole economic, social, and cultural apparatus serve socialism in a genuine sense.[179]

According to Ragaz, Bolshevism from above and Bolshevism from below were no less than a minority rule over majority by holding "a belief in violence rather than justice, in dictatorship rather than democracy, in absolutism rather than freedom, in matter rather than spirit." For Ragaz, therefore, "Bolshevism is imperialism and militarism in another form."[180] There was only one way to revolution: through a military coup and a military dictatorship evolving from it. But Ragaz did not find the idea of military dictatorship bearable or feasible: "The emergence of socialist militarism after the destruction of capitalistic militarism is one of the saddest surprises that we have witnessed in our time."[181] In order to battle Bolshevism, Ragaz calls for a new orientation in socialism. The kingdom of God must overthrow the kingdom of violence and build up the kingdom of freedom. Therefore, socialism has a task of uniting "a powerful sense of community and a passionate consciousness of freedom."[182] Although Ragaz argued that a certain measure of violence becomes

176. Ragaz, *Mein Weg*, 2:83.
177. Bock, *Signs of the Kingdom*, 43.
178. Ibid., 51
179. Ibid., 52.
180. Ibid.
181. Ibid., 53.
182. Ibid., 55.

inevitable, he denounced every use of violence as a defeat of socialism. Ragaz's ideal was a social revolution without violence, a victory without violence through a spirit of truth toward "an immediate socialism and an immediate democracy."[183]

We cannot underestimate an anarchist element in Ragaz's religious socialism. Anarchism, especially in its communal form, had a strong impact on Ragaz's theory and praxis until his late phase. In 1914/15 when there took place a collapse of the Second International after World War I, Ragaz strove to seek a new orientation and content for socialism. He came into contact with an anarchist circle initiated by a medical doctor, F. Brupbacher, in Zurich. As Ragaz recalled, this period belonged to his "anarchist intermezzo."[184] However, in April 1915, under the influence of Gustav Landauer, Ragaz broke with the Brupbacher circle. In Landauer's concept of idealistic socialism Ragaz saw a point of contact with his theology of God's kingdom-socialism. Socialism as a voluntary attitude and movement is to be realized in a new community. For Ragaz there was a close connection between Landauer's anarchism and his socialism of the kingdom of God. According to Ragaz, Landauer was an anarchist in the sense that he—with or without *Credo*—knew something about a living God and God's kingdom.

The influence of Landhauer upon Ragaz and Ragaz's emotional participation in Landhauer's life and destiny become explicit at this point. On the questions of rejection of the state, the condemnation of the war, and the fundamental demand for violence-free activity, we notice a parallel between Landhauer and Ragaz. Gustav Landauer, an activist of the Bayern revolution, founded the "Socialist Alliance" with Martin Buber in 1908 in the attempt to build up a communal socialism, a community without hierarchy or violence. Early in 1919 he was called by the comrades of the Munich counciliar republic and took part for six days in the Bayern council government. After the collapse of the first council republic in April of 1919, Landauer was put under arrest and slain on the way to prison.

What Landauer defended was a new socialism without enforcement or authority: "The socialist alliance declares as the aim of endeavor anar-

---

183. Ibid., 61, 63.
184. Ragaz, *Mein Weg*, 2:64.

chy in the original sense: Order through alliances of voluntariness."[185] In the alliances there is neither rule nor oppressed, but only the community of equality. Neither class struggle nor proletarian politics can be the aim. With this idea in mind, Landauer turned away from an orthodox and a revisionist Marxism; he also turned from a program of the reformist party in the Second International. To be sure, the central content of Landauer's vision was directed against the dominion of human over other humans and the dictatorship of the proletariat. In Ragaz's emphasis on the community as a sociological form, we see Landauer's idea of *Bünde der Freilligkeit* informing Ragaz. Ragaz found in Landauer's thought a methodologically open anarchism. According to Ragaz, Landauer's anarchism was not doctrine (in fact did not mention dogma) but was a method that he operated in freedom and superiority. From this viewpoint he looked and worked onwards, always remaining in freedom and never becoming slave to his method. Ragaz looked upon Landauer as one of "the greatest socialists of all ages."[186]

Next to Landauer we need to mention Buber and Peter Kropotkin. In connection with Landauer, Buber developed a similar anarchist idea of the community. Buber's concept of community cannot be detached from his concept of religiosity. He was a very important dialogue partner to Ragaz because Buber integrated his anarchist project of socialism into the Jewish tradition of faith in God. Starting from the God of the Bible and God's promised kingdom, Buber and Ragaz shared their own view of transformation of the social relation in this light. In April 1928 Buber and Ragaz organized a convention in Heppenheim under the heading, "Socialism through Faith" ("Sozialimus aus dem Glauben").[187] At stake for them was a shared commonality between the Hebrew prophets and early Christianity. In April 1923 Buber had reviewed Ragaz's book *Weltreich, Religion und Gottesherrschaft* (1923) in the literary section of the *Frankfurter Zeitung*.[188]

The hope of the kingdom of God and communal renewal of the world united a Jew, Buber, with a Christian, Ragaz, beyond religious barriers. Like Ragaz, Buber understood himself as a religious socialist. As

---

185. Harms, *Christentum und Anarchismus*, 104.
186. Böhm, *Gottes Reich und Gesellschaftsveränderung*, 195
187. *Sozialismus aus dem Glauben*.
188. Buber, "Three Theses of a Religious Socialism," 259–60.

Buber states in "Three Theses of a Religious Socialism" (1928), "Religious socialism can only mean that religion and socialism are essentially directed to each other—that each of them needs the covenant with the other for the fulfillment of its own essence . . . Unity with God and community among the creatures belong together. Religion without socialism is disembodied spirit, and therefore, not genuine spirit; socialism without religion is body emptied of spirit and, hence, also not genuine body."[189] Ragaz conceived of Buber as standing much closer to him than many Christian representatives. The anarchist methodology of a cooperative and communal society was accepted and reflected by Ragaz in his social and ecclesiological explication. Ragaz was convinced that an anarchist concept of the cooperative community was the only adequate sociological form of Christianity. Next to the labor union, he believed it must become a necessary and fundamental component of the new political and social construction of society.[190]

In addition, a Russian, Peter Kropotkin, helped Ragaz to overcome the Darwinian concept of evolution. In his book, *Gegenseitige Hilfe in der Tier und Menschenwelt* (1908), Kropotkin, without finally rejecting Darwin's concept of the fight for survival, did not regard this idea as one single motive in the development and progress of nature and humanity. Kropotkin made an attempt to discuss and build an anarchist philosophy on natural scientific grounds. Against the Darwinian idea of struggle for survival, he proposed that the regulation is the mutual aid that gains significance in the process of evolution. According to Kropotkin, there is in nature and history a structure of reciprocal aid and an attitude of solidarity.

Marx and Kropotkin would share a similar social vision of communism, but Marx was skeptical of the immediate establishment of Communism. According to Marx, the attainment of the final stage of Communism goes on ahead of the phase of a raw Communism. Therefore, the dictatorship of the proletariat and the transition from state power monopoly to the revolutionary party appeared to Marx to be unavoidable. However, in a circle of anarchism, the appropriation of the state through the party is not meant to be the negation of the state but only another interpretation of state despotism. According to Kropotkin,

---

189. Ibid., 258. Cf. Gudopp, *Martin Bubers dialogischer Anarchismus*, 95ff.

190. Gudopp, *Martin Bubers dialogischer Anarchismus*, 65–66.

a communist society could be realized without the state.¹⁹¹ The vision of the dominion-free society, the organization of life in community, and an anti-institutional stance made an impact on Ragaz. Ragaz held such an anarchist vision as "the basis of socialism" in a better and more adequate form than Marxist socialism. Furthermore, Ragaz distinguished between a dogma and a methodological principle of anarchism. He rejected anarchism in the form of a total philosophical-theoretical explanation of the world and human race. What attracted Ragaz was a principle of the federative construction of society in terms of small and personal unified social groups from below to above. Opposed to a form of the state, this idea is oriented toward the cooperative and communal essence of society.¹⁹²

Given this fact, anarchism as a principle stands in the line of God's kingdom because the theocracy of God's kingdom means none other than an anarchist order. The anarchism of God's kingdom does not mean disorder or chaos but quite the reverse. Here every human being stands in a direct relation to God and in freely ordered and equally based community to each other. The kingdom of God does not run counter to anarchism, but anarchism comes out of the kingdom of God. Where anarchism stands under the rule of God, there is no master-slave relation in the interpersonal realm. The primary rule of God does not tolerate a secondary dominating form of human over human. Where there is the Sprit of the living God, there occurs a voluntary and domination-free personal community.

In this anarchist principle of a cooperative and federal community Ragaz saw a concrete realization-form within the historical process. Where God rules and is given glory, the traditional structure of dominion and rule can be broken and eliminated. Then a new communal and cooperative order of solidarity must be developed. As Ragaz stresses, "the anarchism of the immediacy under God is the highest form of historical life and of human community."¹⁹³

After 1916 the religious-social movement began to decline, in part due to Ragaz's conflict with Kutter and in part due to his rejection of the dialectical theology of Barth. In his first edition of *Romans* (1919),

---

191. Harms, *Christentum und Anarchismus*, 28–29.
192. Ragaz, *Mein Weg*, 2:70.
193. Ragaz, *Geschichte Israels*, 104.

Barth, speaking on behalf of Social Democracy, expressed his critique that Ragaz's religious socialism had limitations. In 1919 at a religious-socialist conference in Tambach, Barth was invited in place of Ragaz, who was unable to speak because of health reasons. Herein Barth dealt a final blow to any kind of hyphenated Christianity in light of *totaliter aliter* revolution. In the wake of Barth's commentary on Romans (1919, 1922) and the Tambach lecture (1919), many pastors in Germany and Switzerland left their previous alliance with religious socialism in order to become followers of the dialectical theology of Barth. This remained a bitter experience for Ragaz, who attacked dialectical theology as reactionary, quietistic, antihumanistic and antisocial.

Ragaz sensed that Barth, in his *Romans I*, initiated his attack on religious socialism. After the publication of *Romans I*, Ragaz wrote in his diary: "Barth, Römerbrief: That is possibly the strongest attack up to now against me, because it cuts the center. Inspired by Kutter, misusing Blumhardt, full of poison, spitefulness, and arrogance. But so many significant and profound things."[194] Ragaz regarded Barth as turning away from the religious-socialist movement at three levels: 1) the religious-socialist message was theologized, so that it led to a new orthodoxy; 2) it was reduced to a churchly sphere (ecclesiologized) with the consequence of a new clericalism; and 3) it was reduced to Paulinism, that is, in Barth's *Römerbrief*, Paul's epistle to the Romans retained primacy over Jesus's Sermon on the Mount.[195]

In 1921 Ragaz published an anthology of writings of the two Blumhardts with his own commentary, *Der Kampf um das Reich Gottes in Blumhardt, Vater und Sohn—und weiter!* In the same year Ragaz made an important decision to commit to the labor movement. By abandoning his teaching position on the theological faculty in Zurich, he moved into a predominantly working-class section of Zurich, *Aussersihl*, where he built up an educational center for the poor. He spent the rest of his life working at this center and editing the journal *Neue Wege*. In his struggle for peace and against the power of militarism, Ragaz became a pacifist and a supporter of the League of Nations.[196]

---

194. Mattmüller, *Leonhard Ragaz*, 2:251.

195. Ragaz, *Mein Weg*, 2:188.

196. In this regard Ragaz became an admirer and an ardent supporter of Woodrow Wilson and his idea of the League of Nations. However, in Barth's later stage, Ragaz was friendly to Barth's theology. Barth was satisfied with Ragaz's agreement with him. Ragaz

Karl Barth and Eduard Thurneysen in the Midst of the World War I and Socialism

The Situation of Social Democracy in Switzerland

The period of the Second International (1889–1914) cannot be simply identified with the Marxist movement. Many sources of European socialism had influenced the ideology and movement of the socialist parties that belonged to the International. For instance, there was a tradition of Lassalleanism in Germany, Proudhonism and Blanquism in France, and anarchism in Italy. Although Marxism stood out as the dominant ideology of the workers' movement and proletariat, this was not the ideological center of the Second International. This International can be understood as an assemblage of socialist parties from different backgrounds representing the masses and various workers' movements.[197]

The philosophical texts of Karl Marx such as the *Paris Manuscripts* of 1844 and *The Critique of Hegel's Philosophy of Right* remained unpublished until the 1930s. One group, which viewed Marxism as a theory of social development and progress out of capitalistic society and its inevitable and necessary collapse, tried to combine and complement the philosophical ethics of Kant with a historical materialism. This is the classic way of neo-Kantian Marxism dominant in figures such as Cohen, Natorp, and Voländer.

In the socialism of the Second International we notice that there was a struggle against anarchism and revisionism, and a conflict between Social Democrats and left-wing groups after the Russian Revolution of 1905. When Barth joined the Swiss Socialist Party in 1915, this party was still radical in its progressive orientation because it did not split into communist and revisionist wings until the Zimmerwald conference. No doubt the German Social Democracy was dominant in the Second International. Lassalle's party (founded in 1863) gained considerable support among the workers. A new party, the *Sozialdemokratische Arbeiterpartei* was organized in 1869 at Eisenach under the leadership of August Bebel (1840–1913) and Wilhelm Liebknecht (1826–1900).

---

also regarded "Barth's gratitude to be an act of discipleship which casts a glow of reconciliation on the remainder of my earthly days." Busch, *Karl Barth: His Life*, 322.

197. Kolakowski, *Golden Age*, 4.

In 1875 the Lassalle and Eisennach parties were united at Gotha to form the Socialist Worker's party. However, the Gotha Program, which was a compromise between Marxism and Lassalle's revisionist orientation, was severely criticized by Marx himself. In 1878 Bismarck enacted an emergency law prohibiting socialist meetings and publication, under the pretext of forbidding an environment that could cause an attack on the emperor's life. The local party organization was dissolved, and many party leaders were forced to emigrate. The crucial issue in the first phase of the International was controversy with the anarchists. In the early 1880s an anarchist association (the Alliance Internationale Ouvriere) came into being; Kropotkin, Malatesta, and Elisee Reclus were included in this group. According to Marx, socialism would restore human individual life in all its fullness, remove political organisms, and thus replace institutionalized oppressive forms of social organization and community with a direct association of individuals.

However, this vision was based on reorganizing civil society in terms of technique and the organization of labor that was already created in the capitalist world rather than on a liquidation of the existing institutional forms. Marx held that the overthrowing of the state and political authority did not mean the destruction of social and industrial organization. The socialization of property would prevent society from degenerating into an apparatus of violence based on injustice and inequality. However, according to anarchists, the aptitude of human beings for friendly cooperation would prevent all injustice, once the institutions of dictatorship and tyranny were liquidated. In opposition to Darwinism, Kropotkin argued for human aid and cooperation, in that the natural inclinations of individuals would ensure the harmony of society. Therefore, the anarchists made attacks on Marxist socialism as a new form of tyranny to replace bourgeois society.[198]

The last years of the Second International were overwhelmed by the war issue. The question was closely related to nationalism and self-determination. The International had condemned militarism at Brussels in 1891 and at London in 1896. If a war broke out, a large part of the proletariat was to be mobilized and thus fall into the general slaughter. If necessary, they allowed for the possibility of rebellion. However, if the fatherland was attacked, they argued it is the duty of socialists to take part

198. Ibid., 20.

in the defense. The call to strike and rebel was within the reformist policy. The left wing (including Lenin, Rosa Luxemburg, and Karl Liebknecht) put forward a more radical position: In the case of the outbreak of war, no attempt must be made to stop it; rather the war must be used to overthrow the capitalist system. At the Basel Congress in 1912—while the First Balkan War was breaking out—an antiwar resolution was passed. The delegates dispersed with the slogan "war on war" and in the conviction that the socialist movement was strong enough to prevent the danger of the imperialist war.

The collapse of the International occurred in the face of the 1914 war. German social democrats surrendered to the fatherland's call to arms. The great majority of socialists in every country of Europe adopted a patriotic attitude in favor of the war policy. The opponents of war were expelled and in April 1917, the Independent German Socialist party (USPD) was formed. Among their membership was Karl Kautski, Hugo Haase (chairman of the SPD since Bebel's death in 1913), and even revisionists like Eduard Bernstein. In addition, the left wing, which had formed itself into the Spartacus League at the beginning of 1916, joined the USPD.

Although the Swiss Social Democratic Party (SPS) belonged to the First and Second Internationals, the socialist movement in Switzerland underwent a dramatic radicalization at the outbreak of World War I. It was Lenin who exercised the decisive impact on the workers' movement in Switzerland. On September 5, 1914, Lenin arrived with Nadeshda Krupskaja and her mother in Bern and led a discussion with Robert Grimm on the socialist situation in Switzerland. Lenin was on a campaign to win the young workers for the socialist cause as he did later in Zurich. In February 1916 Lenin and Nadeshda Krupskaja moved from Bern to Zurich and remained there until they returned to Russia in April 1917. Zurich was a great place for Lenin to concentrate on scientific socialist writings in the library there; and in addition, people of a leftist orientation gathered there from all other countries. In Zurich Lenin worked on his book *Der Imperialismus als höchstes Stadium des Kapitalismus*.[199]

When the war split the SPS into various fractions, three different groups emerged: the social chauvinists, the left wing of socialists, and the centrists. The social chauvinist group was represented by *Gruetliverein*,

199. Krupskaja, *Biographie*, 116–21.

and its direction was under the leadership of people such as Herman Greulich, Paul Pflüger, Gustav Müller, and Johann Sigg. This right wing supported the unconditional defense of the fatherland and *Burgfrieden*, whereas the left wing struggled against the war and their opponents in Switzerland. Centrists took an opportunistic attitude between the two opposing trends. The left-wing group was represented under the leadership of Münzenberg, Fritz Platten, and people of *Revoluzzer*. Robert Grimm was one of the most important leaders among leading centrists, who were a majority within the socialist workers' movement in Switzerland.

Although the SPS officially sent its delegates to the Zimmerwald Conference (September 5 to 8, 1915), some of its representatives, such as Grimm, Platten, and Naine, also freely participated in the conference. The manifesto of Zimmerwald leftists and their resolution *Weltkrieg und die Aufgaben der Sozialdemokratie* were underwritten by Platten from the Swiss side. Zimmerwald leftists argued that the imperialist war was conditioned by the economic system of capitalism, and the war must be regarded as a necessary result of this economic system. Therefore, Marxism should be further applied and developed toward the stage of late capitalism. Furthermore, the imperialist war must be transformed into a revolutionary civil war through an internationally led class struggle against the bourgeois of all countries. Lenin and Zimmerwald leftists blamed the collapse of the International on treachery and opportunism on the part of the social-democratic leaders. Through this position, Bolshevists and Zimmerwald leftists distanced themselves sharply from all pacifist attempts. In fact, the 1915 Zimmerwald conference paved the way for the foundation of the Third International.

However, a couple months before the Zimerwald conference, a meeting of the Zimmerwald group was held in Bern and Olten. In a meeting of the small Bureau of Zimmerwald union (in winter of 1916) there occurred a sharp contrast between the Grimm-led centrist group and the Bolshevist group. In 1915/16 Zimmerwald leftists in Switzerland penetrated the workers' movement. In addition, Münzenburg, a director of the Swiss Socialist Youth organization, mentioned that Zimmerwald leftists in the SPS had taken action in close connection with Lenin and his Bolshevik group, with whom they had kept close contact since the fall of 1915.[200]

200. Egger, *Entstehung der Kommunistischen Partei*, 71.

According to Münzenberg, the Swiss Socialist Youth followed Lenin's way to revolution. "After we . . . had known Lenin personally, we gained the firm conviction that he was *the* right leader, who could point us to the right way to a good revolutionary activity."[201] That the revolution needed an avant-garde fighter was Lenin's political motto. On the question of revolutionary use of violence, Lenin attacked religious socialists by calling them emotionally tearful social clerics who stood in the way of the working class's use of violence. Ragaz in turn criticized Leninism as an ideology that led to the necessity of violence. In 1917 the Socialist Youth International published Lenin's pamphlet *Militärprogramm der proletarischen Revolution* and Lenin's *Abschiedsbrief an die Schweizer Arbeiter*. In opposition to Christian socialists and the centrists of Robert Grimm, who were afraid of using weapons, Lenin said, "the capitalistic society was and is always a shock without end."[202] In spring 1917, the Youth organization deviated from religious socialism by following the socialist theory of Lenin. Zimmerwald leftists gained the first success in the party assembly of November 20 and 21, 1915, in Aarau in the SPS. The resolution of the party assembly was that "the war can be brought to an end only through the revolutionary action of the working class."[203] This above-mentioned milieu was the situation of the Swiss Socialist Party when Barth joined there.

Karl Barth and Eduard Thurneysen: World War I and Socialism

In his *curriculum vitae*, which Barth formulated in the evangelical faculty at the University of Münster (1927) we read: "First the outbreak of the world war brought a turn." This refers to Barth's turn to theological work in a determined perspective and expectation, that is, from the standpoint of the kingdom of God toward which the two Blumhardts' message of Christian hope was principally oriented.[204] Barth's break with his theological teachers and neo-Protestantism began with the outbreak of World War I. In August 1914, counter to Barth's expectations from Social Democracy in his *Die Hilfe 1913*, socialist representatives in the

201. Mattmüller, *Leonhard Ragaz*, 2:163.
202. Ibid., 163.
203. Ibid., 72.
204. Schellong, "Barth Lessen," 14.

Reichstag voted to support the war policy and grant war credit finances to Chancellor Bethmann-Hollweg. German troops invaded Belgium. Then, to Barth's amazement, ninety-three German intellectuals published a petition in support of Kaiser Wilhelm II's war policies and government. As Barth remembered,

> One day in early August 1914 stands out in my personal memory as a black day. Ninety-three German intellectuals impressed public opinion by their proclamation in support of the war policy of Wilhelm II and his counselors. Among these intellectuals I discovered to my horror almost all of my theological teachers whom I had greatly venerated. In despair over what this indicated about the signs of the time I suddenly realized that I could not any longer follow either their ethics and dogmatics or their understanding of the Bible and of history. For me at least, 19th century theology no longer held any future.[205]

Barth experienced the twilight of the gods as he witnessed Harnack, Herrmann, Rade, Eucken, and the like positioning themselves with respect to the new situation. All his German teachers, with the exception of Rade, were compromised in the face of ideological war. "It was like the twilight of the gods when I saw the reaction of Harnack, Herrmann, Rade, Eucken and company to the new situation, and discovered how religion and scholarship could be changed completely, into intellectual 42cm cannons." "The ethical failure of the liberal theologians in Germany has to do with a failure of their exegetical and dogmatic presupposition." For Barth, "a whole world of exegesis, ethics, dogmatics and preaching," which he regarded "to be essentially trustworthy, was shaken to the foundations, and with it, all the other writings of the German theologians."[206]

Thurneysen was pastor in the Aargau in the congregation of Leutwill from 1913 until 1920. He reported that Barth was preoccupied with the Holy Scripture, erecting the tablets of the Bible before him and reading the books of expositors from Calvin though the Biblicists to the modern critical interpretation of the Bible. On the basis of the Bible, Barth's theological thinking was deeply related to the life of humankind, namely, the wholeness of human existence from the beginning. In Thurneysen's characterization, "Karl Barth as a proclaimer of the biblical Word had

---

205. Barth, *Humanity of God*, 14.
206. Busch, *Karl Barth: His Life*, 81.

also a very vigorous and concrete word to speak to the actual political problems in the sphere of his community and his country and in the context of the world events of those days."[207] Through his open character and by introducing Barth to his large circle of interesting friends and acquaintances, Thurneysen was a stimulus to Barth. Barth came into contact with religious socialist conferences through Thurneysen. Barth's acquaintances with Kutter and Ragaz were also initiated by his lifelong friend, Thurneysen. From 1914 to 1916 Barth corresponded with Ragaz on a regular basis.[208] Thurneysen's writing on Dostoevsky, his work on "Socialism and Christendom,"[209] and his project on new homiletics affected and contributed to the development of Barth's dialectical theology.

In his letter to Thurneysen (September 4, 1914) Barth expressed his opinion against the war. "*Dei providentia—hominum confusion* . . . The manner in which you make the 'wrath of God' positively fruitful is clear. The formula 'God does not will the war' is perhaps misleading. God does not will egotism. But he does will that egotism should reveal itself in war and become itself the judgment . . . I would relate the wrath of God yet more strongly to the 'godless existence' itself and would think of social injustice and war as symptoms or consequences of the latter."[210] In a sermon from August 1914, Barth denounced the war as "unrighteous, sinful, unnecessary, and stemming only from the evil of human nature. The war is not a natural phenomenon like the sun and the rain. It is not inevitable or insurmountable. One may and should expect much more from God. In the war God's punishment has come upon us."[211] Still, Barth was not moved by Christian pacifism.

After finding Herrmann's signature on the war manifesto, Barth expressed his disappointment to him.

> Especially with you, Herr Professor (and through you with the great masters—Luther, Kant, and Schleiermacher), we learned to acknowledge "experience" as the constitutive principle of knowing and doing in the domain of religion. In your school it became clear to us what it means to "experience" God in Jesus. Now however, in answer to our doubts, an "experience" which is completely

207. Smart, *Revolutionary Theology*, 14.
208. Rostig, *Bergpredigt und Politik*, 132.
209. Cf. Thurneysen, "Sozialismus und Christentum," 221–46.
210. Ibid., 27.
211. Schellong "Barth Lessen," 16.

new to us is held out to us by German Christians, an allegedly religious war "experience"; i.e., the fact that German Christians "experience" their war as a holy war is supposed to bring us to silence, if not demand reverence from us. Where do you stand in relation to this argument and to the war theology which lies behind it?[212]

Barth's critique of war theologians, especially Harnack, traces back to Schleiermacher. "He [Schleiermacher] was unmasked. In a decisive way all the theology expressed in the manifesto and everything that followed it (even in the *Christliche Welt*) proved to be founded and governed by him."[213] In addition to his criticism of liberal theology, Barth expressed his bitter disappointment with socialism. Although he expected from Kutter's book *Sie Müssen!* that socialism would serve as "a kind of hammer of God," socialism also swung into line. "In the cathedral in Basel the socialists of all lands had solemnly assured each other and the world that they would be able to offer effective resistance to the outbreak of any new war." Despite the socialist decision of resistance to the outbreak of war, what really happened was "the apostasy of the party," and especially the "failure of German Social Democracy in the face of the ideology of war." The status of neutrality in Switzerland required the Swiss in World War I to develop a high degree of military defense preparation. During wartime one or another of the church board members in Safenwil was absent due to military service. It was recalled that at the mobilization of the Swiss Army, Barth was at the Safenwil Railway Station every morning in order to give his good wishes to those who were called to military duty.[214]

However, despite his criticism of Social Democracy, Barth joined the SPS on January 26, 1915 as a token of his solidarity with it. Barth articulates his intent: "I have now become a member of the Social Democratic Party. Just because I set such emphasis Sunday by Sunday upon the last things, it was no longer possible for me personally to remain suspended in the clouds above the present evil world but rather it had to be demonstrated here and now that faith in the Greatest does not exclude but rather includes within it work and suffering in the realm of the imperfect."[215]

---

212. Karl Barth to Wilhelm Herrmann, 4 Nov. 1914, in Schwoebel, *Karl Barth-Martin Rade*, 115. Cf. McCormack, *Critically Realistic*, 113.

213. Busch, *Karl Barth: His Life*, 82.

214. Marquardt, "Aktuar," 103.

215. Smart, *Revolutionary Theology*, 28.

Pejorative terms such as "the Red pastor of Safenwil" or "Bolshevik" poured down upon Barth. But "the Aargau Workers' Party was hardly a dangerous enclave of the Red International."[216]

As we have already seen in his "Workers Question," Barth would perform his socialistic base work a year prior to his entrance to the party. From several places in the text one can discern that Barth has also formed this writing for an oral lecture. It is uncertain whether he used it already in the winter of 1913/14 in Safenwil or in Aargau. Our knowledge of this occasion is from his letter exchange with Thurneysen on January 1, 1916, in which he states that he has "made full use of" this dossier "with local workers" "every Tuesday" at the end of 1915. "I make it without enthusiasm, simply because it is necessary." This writing on "Workers Question" is an indication of the degree to which Barth understands the worker's question in a socialistic perspective.[217]

Two texts without information on the time of formation consist of data and notices regarding the history of two important industry plants: the firm C. F. Bally in Schönenward, and Sulzer Brothers in Winterthur. Barth was interested in the family history of the firm owners, the technological development of their businesses, the social conditions of their companies, and also the religious self-understanding of these industry owners. It is not clear so far whether what is represented here are excerpts from the present history of the company or independent data collections of Barth. Barth's intended use of the information can certainly be surmised. Through the collection of information Barth is concerned about the life circumstances and living conditions of his parish members and comrades. Because the two enterprises offer examples of the social conscience of certain capitalists, it is also conceivable that these texts could have been materials for the great dossier.

This work is especially interesting because it documents a way of working, namely via empirical analysis. Barth worked with hardly accessible statistical material: wage and price scales, "household [income] calculations of workers," statistics of working hours, paragraphs of labor law in various countries, Youth labor statistics, statistics about profit and receipts, insurance statements, records of bank dividends, a report of occupational hazards (from a tobacco worker), statistics about accidents,

---

216. Busch, *Karl Barth: His Life*, 83.

217. Here I deal with Marquardt's report on Barth's "Socialist Speeches." Cf. Marquardt, "Erster Bericht über Karl Barths 'Sozialistische Reden,'" 475–78.

about women in the labor force (different from Swiss cantons), about money devaluation, about the cost of business middlemen, about age structure in industry, about the housing situation, about overpopulation in living space, and about vacation time. Here we see some discussions important for Barth's holistic perspective, such as his critique of the so-called scientific management, the Taylor system, through which nourishment, motion, and timing of the worker as a human time machine should be regulated solely from the standpoint of economic efficiency.

According to Barth, the current labor conditions included an enormous squandering of resources. Every increase in productivity was also for this reason to be welcomed because promotion of production means also progress for humanity under the given circumstances. The sole question for Barth was whether the economic effectiveness of the system operated at the cost of the humanity of the worker, whether the system displaced the "personality," whether the ideal worker who experienced as few irritants as possible was in fact immeasurably more prone to nervousness and so to workplace accidents, and whether all this was not the quintessence and practical zeal of a through-and-through materialistic worldview. To this, Barth's answer was unequivocal: as long as the economic principle of effectiveness stands in service to "the system," i.e., capitalist production, then rationalization does not serve the general progress but only the monetary gain of the shareholder. At the same time, workers experience moral and political oppression, losing the consciousness of solidarity because of personal isolation and the loss of reflection and feeling. This means a smashing of the worker's stance, of the worker's will to resistance, and of the worker's will to the self-organization of the proletariat.

There is another example: Barth's no to the so-called yellow worker organization, which was promoted as a strike-breaking organization by entrepreneurs, which would create agitation among the workers against the class struggle and would work for peaceful negotiation for the sake of employers. In confrontation with such organizations, Barth argued with the concepts of Marxist political economy and notices:

> But the socialists have not created yet *the class contrast*. It is the product of present economic order: "Free" work contract on the basis of private property to the means of production. Through this order a part of society is made principally dependent and practically exploited. The *class struggle*, i.e. the fight for the power

of the worker class aims at the overcoming of such contradiction, i.e. the peace. There is no other peace than that of the new order of relation for one who is in earnest with the healing of the worker's stance.[218]

Here Barth specifies the concept of worker: "'Worker' in a general sense is every well-behaved human. Herein is it meant: *the worker who stands in service and wage of industrial enterprise*"—also the wage worker. Its special feature Barth defines with the description of its labor relation.

> The worker is without possessions, i.e., for subsistence he is dependent upon *the employer*, who through the labor contract with the worker acquires and pays for labor power. The employer is . . . qualified for this contract as the possessor of the *means* of production (factories, machines, raw material) and therefore of production *profit*. *Labor contract*: An obligation between two opponents with equal rights, seemingly very clear and fair, in reality, a sequence of disadvantage follows *on the part of worker*. (a) The worker is dependent upon the labor contract for his survival, while the employer can live on property, pension, or labor. (Marginal note: "on the one hand a question of life, on the other hand a business interest!")." (b) The worker engages his person in labor contract; the employer engages (and risks) only his belongings. (c) The worker cannot restrict his 'production' (labor supply), without going into the ruin, while every other production can be restricted. If the wage decreases, he must work longer and more intensely. (. . . 'Demand and supply determine the wages here and elsewhere . . . We buy the labor on the cheapest market. If a man is not satisfied with his wage or relations, under which he works, he can leave. Against this nothing can be said).[219]

As Barth comments, the ruling classes

> regard it as a matter of course that the *worker finds himself/herself in his/her place determined by "free" labor contract*. In a misunderstood interpretation of the Christian concept of subordination one mistakes superiority of the employer (which is based on capital possession) for divine order, rebellion against it for "indignation," "overthrowing," etc. The attitude toward strike, therefore, is typical of state and society ('laziness,' disturbance of economic life, exception law). For the worker the most necessary should be

218. Marquardt, "Erster Bericht über Karl Barths 'Sozialistische Reden,'" 477.
219. Ibid., 477.

good enough, while one draws no border line to enrichment of employers. *The welfare of industry* becomes one-sidedly identified with the gain of employer (factory law). The risk of the employer is estimated morally very highly, while the well-being and the risk (crisis, accidents) of the worker stands in the second line at any rate.[220]

In March 1915 a conflict occurred within the church board when a request was made for financial support for a military newspaper, "A Good Defense and Weapon," which was published by an evangelical church organization. When the president of the board moved to approve a sum of 10 francs from the budget, Barth took a position against such a patriotic-military Christianity. According to Barth, there could be no question of patriotic-military Christianity in the church. "Hüssy held, on the contrary, that one needed to put himself in the position of the soldier, and from that vantage point would gladly have such material created for him."[221]

Barth delivered his first lecture ("War, Socialism, and Christianity") as a new party member on February 14, 1915 in Zofingen. In calling for the reformation of Christianity and socialism, Barth argued that "A real Christian must become a socialist (if he is to be in earnest about the reformation of Christianity!). A real socialist must be a Christian if he is in earnest about the reformation of socialism."[222] Barth was asked frequently how he could deal with the external and internal relation of religion and socialism, or church and socialism. To what extent could he serve as a pastor and at the same time as a practicing socialist? In a lecture addressing "Religion and Socialism" in December 1915, Barth clarified the reason for his socialistic cause in a rather confessional tone:

> I have become a socialist in a very simple way, and I live socialism in a very simple way. Because I would like to believe in God and God's kingdom, I place myself at the point where I see something of God's kingdom break through. . . . I think I can see the mistakes of socialism and its proponents very clearly. But much more clearly I see in the grounding thought, in the essential endeavor of socialism, a revelation of God which I must recognize before all and about which I must be delighted. The new society, which

---

220. Ibid.
221. Marquardt, "Aktuar," 105.
222. Busch, *Karl Barth: His Life*, 83.

is based on the foundation of community and justice, instead of capriciousness and the law of the jungle, the new order of work in the sense of common activity of all for all instead of in the sense of exploitation through egotism of the individual, the new connection of humans as humans over the barrier of class and nations . . . finally the way to this goal: the simple brotherhood and solidarity [that appear] first among the poor and underprivileged of all countries—I must recognize all these new [features], which socialism brings it into political and economic life, as something new from God's side. . . . Socialism—despite its imperfections, which people should discuss calmly and openly—is for me one of the most gratifying signs for the fact that God's kingdom does not stand still, that God is at work, and hence I may not and cannot stand against it indifferently. . . . From the sentiment of duty, that tells me: this is where you belong, if you take God in earnest. Through my membership in the Social Democratic Party I believe to confess a very important point in complete plainness to myself and to my parish that God must come to honor. . . . People may cling to religion and still associate themselves with another party or remain without a party. . . . But I cannot find the kingdom of God there, where people again and again make money more important than the human beings, where possession is again and again the scale of all value, where people set the nation over humanity in anxiety and small-mindedness, where people again and again believe more in the present than in the future.[223]

To overcome compromise or accommodation of Christianity and socialism there was a need for a renewal of the so-called Christian morality and so-called socialist politics. In a lecture, "What Does It Mean to Become a Socialist?" on August 16, 1915, Barth expressed his intention to renew socialism regarding the failure of socialists in the Second International and their wrong collaboration with the War policy. According to Barth,

> We would like to become dangerous to the structures, otherwise we may pack up. Hence: "socialist personalities." As Kautski thinks, is the idea of a socialist personality one that changes the conditions, bourgeois ideology? Against this view Barth writes: "Historical materialism in the sense of Marx does not have the form of *merely* economic course, but more so the emerging independent of the living human over against matter. Within the

223. Marqurdt, "Erster Bericht über Karl Barths 'Sozialistische Reden,'" 472–73.

circumstances and transcending them, the human wants to rise up. The relation is that of the interrelation. The ideals may be an illusory bubble of economic development; but the human is the most real and stands above economy. That has been overlooked and there was a lack of depth in socialist praxis (not by the founders of socialism, cf. Engels)." "Not: first better humans, then better situation. Not: first better situation, then better humans. Both of them together and interwoven—we need human beings, grasped by the transcendental power of the socialist truth. Only the redeemed can redeem. The new human being must be created."[224]

Barth's "Socialist Speeches" are evidence of the fact that Barth "eagerly read the writings of Marxist theoreticians from Marx through Kautski to Lenin."[225] Meanwhile, a meeting with Blumhardt became a remarkable event for Barth at this time. Thurneysen introduced Barth to Blumhardt himself at Bad Boll. Of course before Berlin and Marburg, in his Tübingen period, Barth had already visited Bad Boll a couple times. Barth's meeting with Blumhardt this time was different in its significance from his previous one. He stayed in Bad Boll from the tenth to the fifteenth of April 1916. In Blumhardt's message, Barth noticed that "the hurrying and the waiting, the worldly and the divine, the present and the future met and were united, kept supplementing one another, seeking and finding one another." "What is more fundamental is Blumhardt's way of connecting knowledge of God with the Christian hope for the future. God is the radical renewal of the world, and at the same time becomes completely and utterly new." "The new element, the New Testament ele-

---

224. Ibid., 482. In Engels's letter to Joseph Bloch (on 21/22. September 1890): "According to a materialistic interpretation of history, what a moment determines *in the last instance* in the history is the production and reproduction of actual life. More have neither Marx nor I ever insisted . . . The economic situation is the basis, but the various moments of superstructure . . . exercise also the development in the process of historical struggles and decide predominantly in many cases its *form*. It is an interaction of all those moments, in which lastly through the infinite amount of accidents . . . the economic movement asserts itself as the necessary thing" (*MEW* 37:463ff.).

225. Gollwitzer, "Kingdom of God and Socialism in the Theology of Karl Barth," 102. In examining carefully Barth's "Socialist Speeches," this runs counter to McCormack's hunch—"If Barth did study Marxist literature, it was sometimes after 1917, and even then, there is no primary source evidence which would confirm such a hypothesis" (McCormack, *Critically Realistic*, 88, fn. 27).

ment, which appeared again in Boll can be summed up in the one word: hope."[226]

Through appropriating Blumhardt's message, Barth tried to overcome a controversy between Kutter and Ragaz. Kutter put more emphasis on the prophetic knowledge of the living God. Ragaz was more concerned with active discipleship along the lines of the Franciscan ideal of poverty. In the face of the outbreak of the First World War, Kutter was moved with a summons to tranquil reappraisal. But Ragaz responded to the war with an appeal for pacifist action. Kutter never became a Social Democrat, while Ragaz became one in 1913. Barth feels himself more in line with Kutter's radical tranquility without ruling out Ragaz's energetic tackling of social problems.

Barth's position moved toward the eschatological question of Christian hope in the Blumhardtian sense. Thereby Barth took God seriously in quite a different way than either Kutter or Ragaz. "The world is the world. But God is God"—this "but" remains because the world is to be transformed by this "but": Something new is expected from God. As Thurneysen reports, the slogan "The world is the world. But God is God" was accepted and interpreted in Barth's own way; Blumhardt's message of the kingdom of God became an important leitmotif for Barth.[227] This concern about God, which is associated with Barth's understanding of radical socialism, functioned as a critical pole to self-destructive bourgeois society and empirical Social Democracy, which failed with the outbreak of the war. Drawing upon a concept of the kingdom of God, Barth's socialism is characterized by the socially transcendent and critical utopia, in contrast to the existing social order. Barth's emphasis on God as the absolute *Novum*, his skepticism of human self-righteousness, and his practical concern about religious socialism would be the point of departure for Barth in his dialectical theology in distinguishing between God and humans.

On January 1, 1916, Barth reported to Thurneysen on his work in Safenwil: "Imagine! I have the workers here enlisted again in a course on the ordinary practical questions (time of work, women's work and the like), every Tuesday, making full sense of the dossier on these things that

---

226. Gollwitzer, "Kingdom of God and Socialism in the Theology of Karl Barth," 85.

227. Thurneysen, *Karl Barth "Theologie und Sozialismus" in den Briefen seiner Frühzeit*, 9.

I at one time assembled."[228] Although, regarding "the formation of trade unions as one of his chief political concerns," Barth had less interest in Marxist principles and ideology as a worldview than in practical social questions associated with the life of workers. "The aspect of a socialism which interested me most in Safenwil was the problem of the trade union movement. I studied it for years and also helped to form three flourishing trade unions in Safenwil (where there had been none before). They remained when I left. That was my modest involvement in the workers' question and my very limited interest in socialism. For the most part it was only practical."[229]

On January 17, 1916, "a letter from factory-owner Hochuli" arrived. The occasion for it was Barth's sermon of January 16 and his address at the confirmation of youth two days earlier, in which the pastor had taken issue with a celebration hosted by Mr. Hochuli. Mr. Hochuli considered the expressions used in the sermon and in the address to be "slanderous and discrediting." He demanded their retraction within three days. If the pastor refused to take back his remarks, he threatened to file suit. Barth reported to Thurneysen in a letter on January 10: "Our factory Owner Hochli hosted a drinking party for his 500 employees on the occasion of his daughter's wedding, and all of them, including my confirmation youth were totally drunk, and conducted themselves shamefully. So are our people kept as fools, with whips and sugar bread, and are at his beck and call."[230] Unlike Thurneysen, Barth saw the political nature of the drinking party and its connection to the relationship between the ruling class and the people. Barth rejected the accusations of slander and defamation because he defended himself by saying that he did not characterize the textile work as hell and Mr. Hochuli as the Devil.[231] The Hochuli affair tells us the realities of late capitalism. Barth's politically motivated pastorate had its foundation in his experience of the brutality of social relationships within capitalism. Already in the sermons of 1913, Barth

---

228. Smart, *Revolutionary Theology*, 36.

229. Busch, *Karl Barth: His Life*, 103–4.

230. Thurneysen's response is different. "When I observe the signs of enjoyment at my local tavern on Saturday evening, I see the same picture. That Hochuli makes the offer in this case is in so far no basic difference, as the people will have their feast, and take it where they can get it. All of this can only strengthen you in your appeal to the little flock." *B-Th I*, 123.

231. Marquardt, "Aktuar," 134.

condemned child labor and pleaded with parents to endure economic plight rather than deliver their children too early into the world of the factory. However, those sermons were without success. In this situation he came to a radical, revolutionary conviction that reforming and moderating actions can be explained from the objective misery of this place.

On December 8, 1915, Barth wrote to Thurneysen: "Social Democratic Party and cartel of Worker's Union Baden. Thursday December 6, 1915, evening 8 o'clock, in Schulhaussaal. Lecture on 'Are religion and socialism in agreement?' Presenter: Mr. Barth, pastor, Safenwil. Committee of education expects numerous visits."[232] In a religious socialist conference in Pratteln near Basel, Barth was impressed by Hans Bader's lecture in which a distinction between Ragaz and Kutter was made. In his letter to Thurneysen (September 8, 1915) Barth outlined this distinction:

> For Ragaz: it is of importance to consider "experience of social needs and problems." The "Ethical demand" is necessary.
>
> For Kutter: What is central is "experience of God."
>
> For Ragaz: there is an emphasis on "belief in development."
>
> For Kutter: the kingdom of God is understood as promise.
>
> For Ragaz: there is an "optimistic evaluation of Social Democracy" and "opposition to the church."
>
> For Kutter: "the Social Democrats can never understand us." "Religious responsibility" must be taken "in the church in continuity with the pietistic tradition."
>
> Ragaz calls for "Religious-Socialist Party with conferences and new ways," and emphasizes sympathy with workers and other laymen. He is in expectation of martyrdom and in protest against war.
>
> Kutter, however, calls for "circles of friends for spiritual deepening and for work." With concentration primarily on the pastors his concern lies in "the building of dams for a much more distant future."
>
> Conclusion: the religious socialist thing is finished. Our task is to begin with taking God seriously.[233]

232. Thurneysen, *Karl Barth 'Theologie und Sozialismus,'* 29.
233. Smart, *Revolutionary Theology*, 31.

After this, Barth adds his own opinion of Ragaz's effort, that is, to put principles into practice. In his approach to Ragaz and Kutter, Barth places himself closer to Kutter theologically, but without losing the practical concern of Ragaz. As Barth asks, "is it not better to strive toward the point where Kutter's 'No' and Ragaz' 'Yes,' Kutter's radical tranquility and Ragaz' energetic tackling about the problem ring together?"[234]

On May 23, 1916, Barth was elected president of the religious socialist conference at Brugg. However, at this time Barth became alienated from the religious socialists. Barth was not regarded as a committed supporter of either Kutter or Ragaz. In coming to terms with Kutter, however, Barth was concerned more about holding for a period of tranquil growth than having time for organized activities. In addition, there occurred an emotional conflict between Ragaz and Barth. Barth wrote a review of Blumhradt's *Hausandachten* (*House Prayer*) in an issue of *Neue Wege* with the title "Wait for the Kingdom of God." In his review Barth expressed his critique of religious socialists with the following words: "Our dialectic has reached a dead end, and if we want to be healthy and strong we must begin all over again, not with our own actions, but quietly 'waiting' for God's action." Ragaz refused to publish it, regarding it as quietistic. This episode severed any contact between Barth and Ragaz. Barth mused, "Ragaz and I roared past one another like two express trains: he went out of the church, I went in."[235] Although Barth was alienated from religious socialism, he still served as a delegate to the SPS Party Congress in Bern (June 8, 1917).

God as the New World in the Bible

In "The Righteousness of God" ("Die Gerechtigkeit Gottes" [1916]), which was given in the Town Church of Aarau in January 1916, Barth elaborated on the social question in light of God's righteousness. Herein we see Barth's contrast between God's righteousness and human righteousness. The former is based on Christ's way, while the latter depends on the Tower of Babel. What is the deepest and surest fact of life for Barth

---

234. Marquardt, *Theologie und Sozialismus*, 83. In the interpretation of Marquardt, Kutter's living God was philosophically rather than biblically grounded, while Ragaz's kingdom of God arose from political principles rather than from Scripture (ibid., 49).

235. Busch, *Karl Barth: His Life*, 92.

is that God is righteous.[236] Human effort to do righteousness would lead to human construction of the Tower of Babel. *Eritis sicut Deus* ("You will be like God" [Gen 3:5]) would sound in our attempt at taking divine righteousness under our own management.[237] "Apart from God's righteousness, all clever newspaper articles and well-attended conventions are completely insignificant," because "the primary matter is a very decided Yes or No to a whole new world of life."[238] In critically dealing with the righteousness of the state and religious righteousness, Barth determines that the righteousness of the state will fail in touching "the inner character of world-will at any point."[239] The state is dominated by this will and the war stands as a striking illustration. Likewise, Christianity as a religion does its job in its uninterrupted way, "in the midst of capitalism, prostitution, the housing problem, alcoholism, tax evasion, and militarism"[240] Barth's critique of Christianity as a religion sounds so hostile because it is regarded as a comforting illusion and a self-deception. It is a product of a human attitude of "as if," full of pride and despair that come from a Tower of Babel.[241]

However, in wartime, God's righteousness becomes a problem and an issue for discussion. Where the human Tower of Babel falls to pieces we look for righteousness without God and a god without God and against God. However, such a god is not God, and is not righteous. "The god to whom we have built the tower of Babel is not God."[242] This god is a dead idol. According to Barth, the righteousness of God can be found only in a wholly other way. God's will is not a continuation of our own, but God approaches us "as a Wholly Other . . . not a reformation but a re-creation and re-growth."[243] In the presence of God's righteousness what is needed from us is humility and childlike joyfulness, which are called faith in the biblical context. "Where faith is in the midst of the old world of war and money and death, there is born a new spirit out of which grows a new

---

236. Barth, "Righteousness of God," 9.
237. Ibid., 16.
238. Ibid., 17.
239. Ibid., 19.
240. Ibid., 19–20.
241. Ibid., 20.
242. Ibid., 22.
243. Ibid., 24.

world, the world of the righteousness of God."[244] The righteousness of God becomes our possession and our great hope in that the way of Christ as "the inner way of simple faith" shows us the love of God.[245]

In his article "The Strange New World within the Bible" ("Die neue Welt in der Bibel"), which was delivered in the church at Lentwil in the autumn of 1916, Barth finds the Bible to be the canon of theological discourse on God, humans, and the world. In other words, the development of Barth's theology results from the discovery of the new world in the Bible. The Bible is a witness to the new world in which Barth finds the being of God *extra nos* and speaks of the transcendence of God in a theologically positive way. Whoever wants to interpret the Bible must speak of the new world in it. Barth materializes concepts such as the absolute and the new from the standpoint of God in a biblical-theological manner. In the biblical discourse on the new world, Barth defines the *Jenseits* of the existing society as knowledge of God. The Bible qualifies a contrast between the human/relative and the absolute/divine as a verifiable position. The standpoint of God, which is to be shown in the Bible, is not the image of the individual-relative standpoint of humans, but the example toward which an explicit and univocal action of human being must orient itself.

Barth's discovery of the Bible enables him not only to make progress in his theological thought but also to deepen his political thought. In these two articles we see how the Bible for Barth begins to break itself out of the encapsulation of modern, bourgeois thought-forms and opens anew knowledge of God beyond churchly self-understanding, and enters into dispute with social idols.[246] As Thurneysen states, from the message of the biblical witness Barth saw God's intervention as the new world in the Bible in the midst of war and revolution.[247]

Given that Barth understood his lecture activity in connection with his parish work, we notice that Barth arranged the manuscript of a funeral sermon on Safenwil worker Arnold Hunzinker under his "Socialist Speeches." In other words, for Barth, party and parish work belong together. His funeral sermon was published in the *New Free Aargauer* (on

---

244. Ibid., 25–26.
245. Ibid., 26.
246. Barth, "Biblical Questions, Insights, and Vistas," 51–96.
247. Thurneysen, *Karl Barth 'Theologie und Sozialismus,'* 18.

Monday, September 3, 1917), which was the official publication organ of the Aargau Social Democratic Party and of the cartel of workers' unions. This sermon interpreted the socialist understanding of death and resurrection in the workers' particular struggle against capitalism, in light of Barth's theological subject matter. Here Barth accepted and applied the interpretation without contradiction.

> One lives on in one's matter—in the worker's matter—and in the end the mourning congregation is requested to "Take care that you understand and grasp the living that was in our dead comrade, and let go of the transitory, human affairs, that lies now over there. Take care of it, you of his sons and daughters, you of his colleagues and comrades, all of you that have known him—and not known him! Then it does not go backwards from this grave into human sadness and desolation, but forwards to new greater victories of life.[248]

Barth portrayed Arnold Hunziker as an exemplary worker, i.e., as unselfish socialist, not directed by egoistical interest, who has understood "that one cannot live just only for oneself and also only for one's family, that there is a higher duty, which nowadays unswervingly commands the workers to hold together and to vouch for each other." [249] Barth saw divine effectiveness in the life of the worker Arnold Hunziker and all the workers. On the eve of Swiss general strike (from November 12 to 14, 1918), Barth wrote to Thurneysen: "It seems to me that we come just too late with our bit of insight into the world of the New Testament. . . . if only we had been converted to the Bible *earlier* so that we would now have solid ground under our feet! One broods alternately over the newspaper and the New Testament and actually sees fearfully little of the organic connection between the two worlds concerning which one should now be able to give a clear and powerful witness."[250]

---

248. Marquardt, "Erster Bericht über Karl Barths 'Sozialistiche Reden,'" 474.

249. Ibid. "It became clear to him that the worker must be a conscious, not a sleeping person, a fighter and not a coward. . . . Hence he had to become a *Social Democrat*. I say: he *must*. . . . In him there came to light and breakthrough precisely this, which also moves the great masses unconsciously and spinelessly in their innermost hearts: the realization of the deprivation of the people in their dependence upon capital, and the insight of the sole help, which must consist in solidarity, in the willing and unselfish and brave community of the dependent, and finally the hope and will: Things must change, if only the human beings would come to themselves."

250. Smart, *Revolutionary Theology*, 45.

In response (November 14, 1918) Thurneysen affirmed an organic connection between the movement of God and the revolutionary event of the general strike in Switzerland. The root cause of the revolutionary event, which was implanted by God in the hearts of the workers, consisted in a longing for a new world. Because of his bold assertion, Thurneysen was denounced as a Bolshevik pastor.[251] Along the line of Barth, Thurneysen interprets the Bible in terms of the social-historical connection that implies a hermeneutical character. For Thurneysen and Barth a historical-materialistic reflection of understanding process underlies their approach to the organic connection between the world of the Bible and the world of the newspaper.[252]

The significance of Blumhardt and Kutter for Thurneysen lay in their reappropriating the voice of socialism for the repentance and renewal of the church. In other words, against popular misunderstanding they did not fall into a politicization of the church through socialism, or conversely into an idealization of socialism through Christianity. From this standpoint we see that Barth and Thurneysen were attesting to an organic connection between the Bible and political events. The new world in the Bible has material relevance to what happens politically in our world. Barth tried to find in the Bible actual political orientation toward human action in the revolutionary situation of 1918. The connection between the Bible and the newspaper occupies fundamental hermeneutical significance for his exegesis as well as for his understanding of the Word of God. Reading of all sorts of world literatures and, above all, the newspaper, was urgently recommended for understanding Barth's *Romans* commentary.

In the face of the daily newspaper, Romans needed to be understood in a new light. This competence came out of the conversion to the Bible, from inside out, namely, from its own subject matter. Barth's theology of the Bible explicitly retains this social, political interest instead of withdrawing it from biblical interpretation. For Barth, biblical interpretation

---

251. Thurneysen's letter to Barth (January 13, 1919) in *B-Th I*, 309.

252. Later, in his writing on "Socialism and Christendom" (1923), Thurneysen called for the renewal and repentance of Christianity in the face of the challenge of the proletarian brother. Socialism, argues Thurneysen, is not only the cry for a new world and the longing and hope thereof. It is, when seen in its historical development, necessarily a comprehensive countermovement against the ruling powers and tendency that appeared in the culture and economy at that time. Socialism became the single critique and enemy of mammonism and militarism in the second half of nineteenth century by taking seriously these two forces. Thurneysen, "Sozialismus und Christentum," 242.

has to do with reflection on the relation between God and the Bible and social circumstances. The blueprint of theology should be no other than the preparation for a political sermon and social praxis. As Barth further states,

> One day I awakened as president of an eleven-member emergency commission with 6000 francs of cash as capital that was raised by our manufacturers. All at once at the eleventh hour mammon begins to totter on his throne and it is a life or death matter for soup to be prepared in the schoolhouse for everyone. . . . The question is whether such measures can prevent the entry of Bolshevism into Safenwil? . . . The post arrives—again without a newspaper. What is happening in Basel? The cowardly anxiety of the *Basler Nachrichten* is an amusing point in the general world picture. I wonder what Kutter's sermon sounded like yesterday, whether or not, and how, perhaps, he found a way to make a public spectacle of the principalities and powers of this age. What are we going to say this time in the coming period of Advent?[253]

The Bible does not pass by the problem of the political situation. What was at issue is how to articulate adequately the organic connection between the Bible and politics. It was, therefore, of special significance for Barth to identify the organic relevance of the Bible and the political-update event in a theoretical-practical manner. In other words, the Bible is a Word to a theological subject matter as well as a Word to social situation. The primary theme of the Bible and theology is the history of God that renews the world. God who speaks of God's will in this history is by no means a continuation of human will. In contrast, the will of God radically demands a new creation of humans, leading all human morality, culture, and religion to silence. God's deed brings a new world to the fore. The Bible witnesses from the beginning to the end to God's new life of advent, of breaking through. Jesus Christ stands before us as the victor who has overcome the old world. Christ "has become the mediator for the whole world, the redeeming Word, who was in the beginning of all things and is earnestly expected by all things." "He is the redeemer of the growing creation about us." What the Bible announces is "that God must be all in all; and the events of the Bible are the beginning, the glorious beginning of a new *world*."[254]

253. Smart, *Revolutionary Theology*, 45–46.
254. Barth, "Strange New World within the Bible," 49.

Having faith in the God of the Bible means believing in God's breakthrough which is begun in Jesus Christ. This faith leads to believing that a relation between God and the human world must be acknowledged as God's victory. God's condescension in Jesus Christ, the fight and victory of the kingdom of God are, for Barth, political content. The acts of God are not restricted to the private existence of individuals, but are social and universal. No wonder that Barth repeatedly relates the Revelation of John, chapter 21, to the proclaimed revelation of the new world: "Behold the tabernacle of God is with men! The Holy Spirit makes a new heaven and a new earth and, therefore, new men, new families, new relationships, new politics."[255] God makes a new politics. So God's action is political. The unity between knowledge and interest can arrive in this discovery of the Bible when this political interest is brought explicitly to social consciousness and defined in accordance with it. Barth seeks in Bible just such an actual political orientation of human action as in the revolutionary situation of 1918. This is also a hermeneutical aspect for Barth that directs him to knowledge and understanding by putting together the newspaper and the Bible. This social-historical contemporaneity retains a fundamental significance for Barth's hermeneutics regarding exegesis and his understanding of the Word of God. This contemporaneity will become manifest in his commentary on *Romans*. Barth argues for a conversion to the Bible from the inside out, from its own subject matter to what lies beyond.

A new world, namely, the world of God, is in the Bible. It is a spirit in the Bible. God drives us to the primary matter, whether we want it or not. The Holy Scripture interprets itself despite our human limitations. We must dare to follow this urge, spirit, and current in the Bible. Herein Barth conceptualizes a hermeneutical spirit, *"scripturae ipsius interpres,"* in terms of the world-effective reality. The resurrection creates its world-effectiveness through the constitution of a subject of the new, in other words, a "solid subject," in Ernst Bloch's sense. That is the meaning as the new physicality.[256] The new world in the Bible is grounded in the resurrection of Jesus Christ, which is of social and political significance. The resurrection is not to be exchanged for the immanent law of history or as the law of dialectical materialism. However, in the effective realm of

---

255. Ibid., 49–50.
256. Marquardt, *Theologie und Sozialismus*, 108.

the resurrection, God has no spectators, because the resurrection is the constitution of the revolutionary subject. Given this fact, *totaliter aliter* in Barth's view mediates the reality of God and the reality of world, and grounds God's presence in society.

Totaliter aliter is not a metaphysical or distancing concept but a qualified concept with a particularly social content. Henceforth the new world in the Bible, the new world of God, implies the revolutionary overthrowing of the existing bourgeois society. *Totaliter aliter* is originally the new society in the thought of Barth in contradiction to the declining society, and the original in this contradiction is God. As to the concept of *totaliter aliter* Barth reports: "It was Thurneysen who whispered the key phrase to me, half aloud, while we were alone together: 'What we need for preaching, instruction and pastoral care is a "wholly other" theological foundation.'"[257] Human praxis must be shaped in correspondence to the breakthrough of God, which means the new world. Human political action has a task and a duty to participate in God's new creation of the world. From this standpoint, Barth articulates his theopolitical slogan: "waiting for the kingdom of God."[258] This waiting should not be misunderstood as a passive and unpolitical theology, a so-called waiting-room theology; for being just such a theology Ragaz ridiculed it.[259]

By contrast, it is a deeply engaged commitment and a revolutionary stance in expectation of the coming kingdom of God. Barth's theology of expectation is well articulated in his lecture of 1922, "Not und Verheissung der christlichen Verkündigung." Schellong views Barth's theology of waiting for God in light of *veni creator Spiritus*. What is decisive for Schellong's approach to Barth is the sighing call for the coming of the Holy Spirit. "Sighing: *veni creator spiritus!* is now once according to Rom 8 full of hope more than triumph, although one would already have it."[260]

In 1916 Barth began working on his commentary on *Romans*, which was eventually released in 1919. During this period of working on *Romans*, Barth became more critical of the religious socialists as well as liberal theology, although he continued his active involvement in the

257. Busch, *Karl Barth: His Life*, 97.
258. "Auf das Reich Gottes warten," 175–90.
259. Mattmüller, *Leonhard Ragaz*, 2: 222; see n. 23.
260. Schellong, "Barth Lessen," 12.

SPS. At the end of 1917 he ceased his involvement in the religious-socialist movement. Barth and Thurneysen resigned from the committee from the conference in Olten, which had resolved on the reorganization of religious socialism on December 10.[261] When it came to a relation between socialism and Christendom, Thurneysen mentions Blumhardt and Kutter as two men who had heard the command of the time and fulfilled it, although not denying the inspiration of Ragaz.[262] For Thurneysen the whole problem of ethics and its related eschatological question not only would be a question of the art of theological dialectics, but must be rolled up in a completely new way, forced by the real dialectics of life as such.[263]

Likewise, Barth's socialism can be expressed theologically and eschatologically in light of the kingdom of God or the absolute Revolution of God. His socialist praxis, therefore, maintains a theological character and contour. In this regard we notice that Barth would stand closer to Ragaz politically, but with a theological affinity to Kutter. But Barth hesitated with religious socialists in general. The term "Revolution of God" was generally used in the circle of religious socialism. Barth appropriated this term from religious socialism in order to develop, clarify, and radicalize his theological position and political radicalism in his *Romans I and II* in particular. Herein we discern Barth's position "on the most extreme left side" within the SPS. When it comes to Barth's socialist activity within the SPS in Safenwil, he distanced himself from Zimmerwald leftists. But given his friendship with Fritz Lieb (1892–1970), we can assume that Barth's position was in line with left-wing radical socialists within the SPS at this time. Later he would move toward the Second and a half International under the leadership of Robert Grimm, which was formed in protest against the Third International.[264]

Later in his lecture on Schleiermacher, Barth recalled his relationship with Kutter and Ragaz:

> what we needed for preaching, instruction, and pastoral care was a "wholly other" theological foundation. It seemed impossible

---

261. Busch, *Karl Barth: His Life*, 104.
262. Thurneysen, "Sozialismus und Christentum," 241, 243.
263. Ibid., 244.
264. Gollwitzer, "Kingdom of God and Socialism in the Theology of Karl Barth," 112.

to proceed any further on the basis of Schleiermacher . . . But where else could we turn? Kutter was also impossible, because he, like Ragaz later on, would have nothing to do with theology, but only wanted to know and to preach the "living God." He was also impossible for me, because, with all due respect for him and his starting point, his "living God" had become extremely suspicious to me after his wartime book *Reden an die deutsche Nation* [*Speeches to the German Nation*].[265]

---

265. Barth, *Theology of Schleiermacher*, 264.

TWO Karl Barth and the First Edition of *Romans* (1919)

IN A LETTER TO EDUARD THURNEYSEN (JULY 19, 1916), KARL BARTH informed him of his preoccupation with an exegetical investigation of Romans. With great excitement he found in J. T. Beck a guide who led him in this exegetical work. In addition to Beck, Barth was influenced by Pietist writers such as Johannes Bengel, C. H. Rieger, and August Tholuck. On 9 September 1917, Barth came to the passage in Rom 5:12-21.[1]

The first draft of the book *Romans* was completed on June 3, 1918. There immediately followed a period of intensive revision.[2] This manuscript was first printed in December 1918 but only later released, in 1919, by the Bern publisher G. A. Boeschlen. During Barth's work on *Romans*, the revolution in Russia (February 1917) put an end to czarist rule. Then the shock of the October Revolution in Russia swept Switzerland in November of 1917. There had been a lot of local strikes, demonstrations, and riots among the working class and socialists until they reached a climax in the general strike in Switzerland in November 1918. On 8 June 1917, Barth still served as a delegate to the SPS congress in Bern.

---

1. At this time he was entangled in great and decisive events. "Fifty-five women employees in the knitting mill organized themselves last Monday. Now they are threatened with notice of dismissal. In regard to this I talked with the manufacturer this afternoon in his villa, like Moses with Pharaoh, asking him to let the people go out into the wilderness. Polite man's talk in deep easy chairs which unfortunately ended with a flat rejection and declaration of war, during which I had to hear that I am the worst enemy that he has had in his whole life" (Smart, *Revolutionary Theology*, 42).

2. According to his diary, Barth finished his manuscript on August 16, 1918 and was declined by three Swiss publishers. On August 30 Barth sent the revised manuscript to his publishers. Hermann Schmidt, "Vorwort des Herausgebers," in Barth, *Der Römerbrief*, 1919, xiii. Cf. Groll, *Ernst Troeltsch und Karl Barth*, 65-66.

Barth wrote his first edition of *Romans* as he became caught up in the joy of discovery. The task of his exegesis during this time was to hear anew Paul's message in terms of seeing through the historical into the spirit of the Scriptures. As a child of his time, Paul spoke to his contemporaries. But what was more important for Barth's exegesis was to hear from Paul as the prophet and apostle of the kingdom of God who spoke to all people in all ages.[3] Barth's hermeneutical and practical concern in *Romans I* was to see the eternal spirit of the Bible penetrate the historical-critical method. For Barth the historical-critical method has its place in preparation for understanding the biblical text. However, what was more important for Barth was that an understanding of history be continuous, more accurate, and a more penetrating dialogue between the wisdom of yesterday and the wisdom of tomorrow.

Barth's stance toward the historical-critical method was directly related to his disillusionment with the outbreak of the war and the bankruptcy of all liberal theologians in the German universities, who did not view the war critically. In the autumn of 1916, Barth was led to the discovery of the Bible, that is, "the new world within the Bible."[4] When theology and worldview, coupled with their hermeneutical filters and interpretation of the Bible, were shaken to the core, the Bible struck him in a completely new manner; for Barth, the discovery of the Bible was "completely dominated by an interest in the concrete situation in which with all of our contemporaries we found ourselves enmeshed."[5] Social issues, therefore, become indispensable for exegesis. The subject matter that concerns us is an organic connection between the Bible and the world of the newspaper. Keenly aware of the human being's historical existence and its social and economic structure, Barth moves himself toward integrating historical problems and social criticism into his exegesis of Romans. Rather than dwelling on the difference between the times in terms of historical criticism, Barth, along with St. Paul, makes an attempt to articulate a struggle for the new world that the Bible promises.

Exegesis moves in retrospect as well as in prospect toward the future of God, which means, for Barth, a conversation between the wisdom of yesterday and the wisdom of tomorrow. For example, one must consider

3. Vorwort, v. in *Romans I*.
4. Barth, "Strange New World within the Bible," 28–50.
5. Marquardt, "Socialism in the Theology of Karl Barth," 60.

Barth's exegetical study of Rom 8:9–15 and Romans 13 from the angle of his political involvement with social questions: religious socialism in Switzerland and Leninism in Russia, for example. The creation waits in eager anticipation for the revelation of the children of God. God as the coming new reality makes us stand in solidarity with God's fight and thus with God's coming victory. Life in Christ and its nature lie just in the perspective of the future. This perspective of God's future, which is realized in reborn communion with Christ, drives us to be responsible for what God creates and prepares in the world (R I:238).

Blumhardt's message, which articulates the suffering of the oppressed for freedom in God's future, influenced Barth's understanding of the relation between the faithfulness of God and eschatology. The suffering of the oppressed can be "a part of nature history of the Spirit" (R I:240). The renewal of the world begins with the new humanity of the children of God. The real content of apocalyptic eschatology can be seen in its taking sides with the oppressed in the present. In Barth's words, "God is one-sidedly a God of the lower but not a God of the upper, indeed, without reservation, a God of the small (i.e. the totally marginal)" (R I:367). Furthermore, Barth's social criticism can be well articulated from his concise remark in *Romans II* in that the "historical critics, it seems to me, must be more critical" (R I:xviii).

Ursprung as the Eschatology of God

Barth's thesis that the world remains the world but that God is God tells that the world must be transformed by this "but God is God," notwithstanding. Barth is convinced that there must be a fundamental difference between God and the world. The world is not capable of knowing naturally who God is. However, a relation of God and the world is structured in a dialectical and organic way rather than remaining dualistic. According to Barth, the power of God erupts from above, cutting through the world longitudinally or perpendicularly. Barth's eschatology of *senkrecht von Gott aus* is first of all to be seen in light of God's reconciliation with the world in Jesus Christ. In the universal/cosmic reconciliation of God with the world, a turning back of humankind to its origin (*Ursprung*) occurs. God proves God's faithfulness to the world—beyond human sacrilege and injustice—and God's loving power to the world (R I:67). The revelation of

God in Christ is not emptied but is the fulfillment of history, culminating in the law and even to the present.

Therefore history stands in the effecting domain of God in the present. The revelation of the faithfulness of God becomes visible because it is the effecting power in all (R I:69). The world of God is not a purely transcendental world without relation to this world. But in Christ the world turns to its origin and the world of God breaks through this world, achieving a provisional victory (along the lines of Blumhardt's message of "Jesus is victor") in historical events. Therefore the breakthrough of God in history occurs in now-time.

Barth's understanding of reconciliation, which is universally/cosmically set in motion in Jesus Christ, is deeply related to the redemption of the world that religious individualism and liberal theology lack the ability to understand. Although Barth turned away from J. T. Beck,[6] Blumhardt's influence remains compelling in regard to the cosmic perspective in *Romans*. Of Rom 8:19–22 Barth says, in a Blumhardtian fashion: "The actual sonship of God which we do not have yet, but expect is the 'redemption of our body,' the victory of God in the materiality of the whole creation of which our own existence is only particle and example. 'This is our aim and our hope'" (R I:247–48). The solution of the world enigma and eschatology are not separated from each other because the whole creation waits for humanity, that is, the revelation of the children of God. Our hope for the future of God is not mere waiting for an event in the outer world, but "we are called and capable of one day becoming the mediator and helper for the destroyed world, one day to speak the redemptive words as a strange and hostile objectivity and power of destiny" (R I:245). The Spirit as the Spirit of radical transformation pours upon us, so that "we might strongly call for more Spirit to enter the world, for a continuation of the Spirit's outpouring on all flesh" (R I:246).

The kingdom of God has been implanted in history and nature, and like a germ cell will continue to grow until the consummation of the kingdom on earth becomes complete and the entire cosmos is restored. This refers to Barth's understanding of the organic growth or organism of

---

6. For instance, the organic growth of the kingdom is borrowed from J. T. Beck and is a cosmically and naturalistically conceived Christ principle. But for Barth the organic growth is not given naturally or historically, that is, through a nature principle, but grounded and justified at every moment *von Gott aus* (from God outward) in a pneumatological and universal framework.

God's kingdom. Through our reception into the body of Christ, our fellowship with God becomes part of an organism, in that individual parts are completed in this organism and stand in living connection to each other. The kingdom of God as organism embraces the whole cosmos. Nevertheless, God's involvement with the world does not mean mere identification between God and world. Rather, it points to a dialectical and organic relation initiated by God's movement from above. Barth's phrase of "organic growth" does not mean a mechanical construction based on any possibilities existing in this world; rather it refers to the new life's possibility created in Christ. As God becomes living to humans, humans are in turn living in God. In Christian faith, humans enter into the kingdom of the absolute spirit. "Through the disposition which is given to faith by the faithfulness of God, humans are a part from individuality, life stance, and performance, implanted transcendental-organically into the living growth of divine righteousness" (R I:80). This refers to the practical shape of *analogia fidei* which later was in full bloom in Barth's theology.[7]

Speaking of *Sache* (on Rom 1:16-17), Barth states:

> The *Ursprung*, which was always claimed, known, yearned for, and under pain sought after, opened its mouth again. The divine word, "it shall be" is again fulfilled. . . . Nothing historical, rather the precondition of all history. . . . The opening of a new aeon, the beginning of a new world in which God once again has power. This power of God stands behind us. This is our gospel that we announce. This is our *Sache*. (R I:7-8)

What Barth seeks in *Romans I* is to understand the power of God in the resurrection of Jesus Christ which has a universal/cosmic dimension and content. What is behind Barth's concept of *Ursprung* as God's eschatological reality is his theological concept of God's universal reconciliation with the world, in line with Blumhardt's. Through the term *origin* Barth portrays humans in an immediate relation to God. In fact, we could see the whole actuality, namely, the invisible nature of God mirrored in the visible. There is no outside without inside, no phenomena without es-

---

7. Barth's principle that "God is God" goes hand in hand with God as the Origin (*Ursprung*). Barth mentions the *Ursprung* as the source of the *totaliter aliter*, which would become more manifest in regard to the parabolic character of the world in his Tambach lecture (1919). Therefore it is of special significance to view *Ursprung* in *Romans I* in relation to a dialectical analogy of *Ursprung* in the Tambach lecture.

sence, no works without the eternal power and Godhead. Human beings are capable of seeing things as they are and as having their own origin in the eternal power and Godhead. Because the cosmos is produced out of creative reason (logos), and because this creative reason dwells in us, we can say the God-idea is known to humanity, God has made Godself known to us (R I:15). However, the seed of the immediate knowledge of God in us was crushed because of the fall. Although the fall made a secret out of the divine, there is no longer a secret to those who have been born in Christ: "God speaks in Christ and we hear in Christ. The power of God is no more secret to us. It reveals itself more and more as the life of our life" (R I:420).

Through revelation, which means a breakthrough of God's will from heaven to earth, from God's consciousness to human consciousness, the original nature of God, that is, the pristine divine nature, has appeared in humanity. God no longer leads us to war against the world but declares it as God's world, being in solidarity with it (R I:61). Humanity's experience as the children of God is not based on our religious experience but on the Spirit as the object in which our spirit takes part. God is at work in and through humanity as a result of God's universal power (R I:237). When humankind is restored, God's own Spirit steps in to take the place of the flesh (R I:60).

According to Barth, our knowledge of God on the basis of the power of God is realized in Christ. "Our *Sache* is our knowledge which is a realized knowledge of God in Christ; in which God does not become objective, but comes close to us, immediately and creatively; in that we not only see, but are seen, not only understand, but are understood; not only comprehend, but are grasped" (R I:7). We share in the immediacy of the knowledge that God knows Godself because "the concept of God is given us as immediately as our own being" (R I:14). However, this immediacy is not grounded on a human search for God but in God's initiative grasping of human being. In other words, as Hermann Kutter had described it: *von Gott aus*, out from God.

Kutter takes a middle stance between Blumhardt and Barth. The social question in Kutter's thought was anchored in the fundamental theological horizon of preaching. This is performed neither in terms of eschatological and christological-pneumatic proclamation of the kingdom of God (like Blumhardt's) nor in terms of the Ritschlian concept of God's kingdom-idea (like the young Naumann). For Kutter the Bible speaks of the living God. The Bible starts from God onward. This understanding of God is redefined idealistically as immediate life in his early writing, *Das Unmittelbare* (1902). This immediate life, appearing in Jesus Christ, stands against dead and rigid religion. In his writing *Sie Müssen!* the immediate life turns into a concept of the living God. For Kutter, "social democracy belongs to the gospel."[8]

The living God is the redefinition of idealistic "immediacy" so that "God" is not present in the mediation of the Christian doctrine of God, such as ceremony, dogmas, religious consciousness, or religion in general, but present in life, especially in the immediacy of human deeds. Given this fact, social democracy is to be seen from God onward: "The social democrats are revolutionary, because God is revolutionary. They must move forward, because God's kingdom must move forward. They are people who overthrow, because God is the great overthrower."[9] However, such an identity does not mean a strict identification, but an analogy: "Jesus had an eternal, unchangeable must: the must of God's love. In just such a must the social democrats stand . . . What the gospel has in common with social democrats is . . . a great irresistible must, with which they announce a new condition of divine progress against the present age."[10]

An organic relation between identity and analogy in Kutter's thought-complex plays an important role in Barth's understanding of God's kingdom in relation to the world in *Romans I*. However, Barth's way of expressing the immediacy of humanity in relation to God as *Ursprung* is accused of resulting in a pantheistic conception of the God/world relation. In Barth God is "the innermost but disarrayed nature of all things and all men in their height and depth" (R I:34). For humans in Christ the grace of God is natural, not alien. Being in Christ means one is transplanted into the tree of life. Being in Christ means the objective truth of divine love to the world. Being in Christ means the new or rather the most primordial nature of life. It is the natural foundation of all existence, our nature in God (R I:220). Given this statement, Hans Urs von Balthasar sees a platonic and oriental Christian concept of identity

---

8. Kutter, *Sie Müssen!* 196.
9. Ibid., 93.
10. Marquardt, *Theologie und Sozialismus*, 78.

shaping Barth's theology, and from that point the pantheistic concept of nature becomes necessarily dialectical.[11]

However, Barth's standpoint is not inextricably tied to a philosophical unity of idealism but to christological universalism in light of the resurrection of Christ from the dead. The movement of God is not to be understood as a mechanical process or an immanent cultural history, but as the critical, actual, limiting, and justifying principle over the world.[12]

In addition, Barth's concept of analogy is dialectically structured. If we see Barth's idea of *Ursprung* as *totaliter aliter* in his Tambach lecture (1919) as complementary to the idea of *Ursprung* in *Romans I*, then the *Ursprung* is the synthesis from which the antithesis and also, obviously, the thesis comes out (*ADT* 51). This is the Origin that is the condition of position as well as negation; that is, it is an affirmation of revolution as well as its relativization. The organic relation between God and the world is not based on an immanent/dialectical process of Hegelian synthesis. Rather it serves to articulate "the concrete dialectic of society, its thesis and antithesis, its origin (*Ursprung*) in God, its analogical relation to God."[13] The Origin as the synthesis of producing thesis and antithesis is actualized in now-time, not as an identification of God and the world, but as a parable or analogy, mirroring eternity. God's actualizing movement of breakthrough unfolds organically and dialectically in temporal realms. The positive side of dialectics in *Romans I* is dynamic, growing, becoming and organic with respect to a mutual relation between God and the world. There is no equilibrium, but a mirroring of God's breakthrough into history. The socialist movement can then be seen as a reflection of God's kingdom, which is the true Revolution.[14]

---

11. Balthasar, *Theology of Karl Barth*, 51.

12. Already in his article "Faith in a Personal God" ("Der Glaube an den persönlichen Gott" [1914]), Barth states that the total transcendence of the absolute belongs to the construction of a sufficient idea of God, and it must become the idea of pure origin. Denying the founding of actuality at the same time affirms it. This is the affirmative side of the God-idea. In this dialectical relation between affirmation and negation Barth's concept of origin speaks to this positive side of the actual world.

13. Marquardt, *Theologie und Sozialismus*, 219.

14. In light of his Tambach lecture, Barth's dialectics of Origin from the positive side says Yes to a socialist movement as a reflection of God's kingdom, but this movement does not represent the whole of God's kingdom because God's Revolution is superior to any human revolutions. Furthermore, Barth's dialectics on the negative side says No to any human attempt at clericalization or secularization of God.

Through human efforts to establish independence from God (a form of sin), humankind breaks away from direct existence with God. Barth's critique of human "desire to be autonomously over against God" (R I:177) as only one sin was to strip of ideological justification the bourgeois preoccupation with self-realization through acquisition of money and power. Estrangement between God and humans requires a principle of analogy in order to express a dialectical unity between discontinuity and continuity. What makes a *negative* relation of humans to God is the wantonness and injustice of humanity against God. Humans became condemned apart from free fellowship with God. For Barth the relation between God and humans is organic, rather than mechanical, because God grasps us and is comprehended by us.

God's creative love retreats and is withdrawn in the face of human wantonness and injustice. God appears as a "stony guest" (R I:12) by turning God's face to the face of the irritator. The world under the wrath of God is characterized by the wantonness and unrighteousness of human beings. This rebelliousness is the decisive human resistance against God in claiming to take the place of the Original-Eternal and idolize it. It is characterized as *"ein prometheisches Ansichreissen"* (a Promethean breakthrough) in removing the prerogative of God (R I:12). Therefore the relationship between God and humanity and between God and the world stands in negative *Krisis* because of our rebellion against God: "The kingdom of God must go its own positive way; also with the ascetic turning away from the state there would not be much created—as indeed with a premature *Civitas Dei-experiment"*(R I:387). Barth also warns against a revolutionary secularization of God's *Sache*, or a clericalization of human structures for the sake of the *Sache* of God (cf. Tambach lecture). We are not allowed to take in advance "God's world-revolution" individually, but create its presupposition (R I:387).

The message of Blumhardt, "Jesus is victor," echoes that in the death of Christ the struggle (and in his resurrection the victory) of divine reality over the powers of sin and death have been consummated (R I:98). In Christ "God's reality becomes our reality" (R I:313). Barth makes a distinction between so-called history in Adam and actual history in Christ (R I:66–67, 223–25). God's history breaks through into the so-called history of Adam. When this happens, time is fulfilled in the eternal now (R I:86–87). In terms of the divine breakthrough, the kingdom of God as actual history is fulfilled and established in the midst of so-called history. The breakthrough of God's power in Christ is the "uncovering of the never still, necessary reality in the cross section of time" (R I:106).

The organic metaphor that Barth uses is a protest against Protestant individualism. In light of Christ's resurrection, we become "an organic particle of the creation, bound up with the whole, which is now reconciled with God" (R I:171). "We are no longer the same. We are inserted in the process which carries forward from the beyond into the present" (R I:166). Our participation in the organism, the in-breaking movement of God, becomes an integral part of the presently constituting organic eschatology *von Gott aus* in *Romans I*. However, building up the kingdom of God is not on our part because "the breakthrough of the grace of God now organically unfolds itself" (R I:195). The organic unfolding of the grace of God is a movement from above to below, which calls for human movement toward God. "In Jesus the original and new nature of things in God has appeared for us." It breaks through, springs, overflows and desires for everything to be integrated into "the rhythm of the eternal life-movement, *von Gott her, zu Gott hin*" (R I:106).

In this connection, Barth boldly interrelates the deed of the human being organically with the action of God because "the inherent power of grace is the free, good will of human beings which streams out of God and is oriented towards God." Therefore human will, as the creation of God, is free and good. Consequently "there is no distinction between what God does for us and what we must do. Humanity under grace is what they will make of themselves. They are free in God. . . . They have the gift of activity of good will" (R I:169).

With this provocative statement in mind, Barth tries to reappropriate the socialist idea of human self-creation through labor and praxis in order to reclaim the radical idea of grace in the service of the poor. In this way the socialist idea that human beings are what they will make of themselves does not contradict the inherent power of God's grace that implies the free, good will of human being in favor of liberating praxis and solidarity with the poor. As a result, a traditional antithesis of grace and human will is overcome in favor of the inherent power of God's grace.

In addition, for Barth, the movement of the kingdom of God is basically "a one sided movement from below" (R I:367). This movement enables us to seek an analogy of God's movement in the socialist movement from below. It reveals that socialism as an analogy of God's kingdom gains in prominence. We are encouraged to become committed participants in this movement, in expectation of the *novum* of God. However, socialism does not represent the kingdom of God. God is ready at the present moment to leave behind any old and uncertain socialism. The historical time of socialism will expire without bringing the world what it promised. However, what is more important than this dissolution is the historical time when the presently diminishing glow of Marxist dogma will light up anew (R I:332). Barth was motivated by what he has called "the glowing coal in Marxist dogmas." That is, the revolutionary goal of world transformation. Yet, in *Romans I* Barth describes this ember as "unfortunately extinguished." Nevertheless Barth does not lose sight of the hope for "the resurrection of a socialist church in a world become socialist" (R I:332).

The Kingdom of God and its Sociocritical Dimension

Critique of Religious Fetishism

As we have already seen, the kingdom of God that came in Jesus Christ is, according to Barth, interpreted as the hope of the existing society. The past, present, and future of society can be seen as corresponding to the past, present and the future of God and thus holding a sociocritical aspect (R I:218–63). Therefore, theology has the task of illumining the sociopolitical context surrounded and impacted by the world war and revolution (R I:366). In *Romans I* Barth carried out his fundamental critique of liberalism. The fundamental fault of liberalism was not a historical contingency but was the very essence of liberalism. Liberalism is the system of alleged freedom that is randomly proclaimed by humans. That is, the ideology and praxis of "free plays of the powers," which is in radical contradiction to the freedom dawned and opened in Christ (R I:177–78).

Therefore liberalism belongs to the past, which has been overcome by God's acts upon society through Jesus Christ. If theology takes in earnest the hope of a society stamped and imprinted in Jesus Christ, it assumes a form of critique on the political ideology and praxis of liberalism. The political failure of "the liberal culture and social order" (R I:177) is to be analyzed critically in light of the eschatology in Jesus Christ. In *Romans I* Barth considers the relation of human beings to God in terms of predestination: God's original intent toward the world and human beings is election, which is the truth of all history. This election is to be proved and established as its reality in the end (R I:342). By contrast, reprobation of the world and humanity appears for Barth only as incident, disruption, war, and emergency measure. God's work necessarily includes an abolition of this reprobation (R I:342). Therefore condemnation as such is no longer the divine purpose. Rather God's history on the march is so directed that this reprobation must become superfluous, involved in getting rid of its cause (R I:343, 318–19).

The epoch of condemnation has become the past through the inner logic of divine predestination, and in Christ God is determined to carry out God's original decision of election for the world and to fulfill it in the real freedom of the kingdom of God (Romans 11; R I:318–45).

Barth's understanding of predestination in *Romans I* would imply *praedestinatio dialectica* rather than *praedestinatio gemina*. Needless to say, the human fall before God cannot be thought of without divine condemnation (R I:11–17). The absurdity and impossibility of Adam's deed corresponds to God's condemnation. This connection between the fall and condemnation is, in Barth's view, so relevant that human beings take responsibility for themselves in the occurrence and consequence of their negative relationship to God. Resistance against God is the result of humanity's own deeds (R I:12–13). According to Barth, human confusion between God and the world is therefore based on the fall as resistance. It is not permissible for humans to seek God as long as they remain in the state of condemnation. Out of this situation arises confusion, fairytale changes, and malicious misunderstandings in speaking of human beings and God (R I:19). In human consciousness there occurs a blur: "the difference between intransitoriness, originality, and superiority of God and transitoriness, relativity and dependence of the thing" (R I:18). From here human beings reduce God to the level of a thing, that is, to a form of natural and historical life. God is replaced in part through a No-God (R I:18).

Moreover, out of the first step of this confusion or fetishism comes the self-idolization of human beings. Apart from communion with God, human beings take the place of God and thus become God (R I:13). Where humans become God, the world becomes lordless and full of idols (R I:12–13). Alienated from God, human beings find themselves seeking idols because the world of God becomes the world of idols: "Now

God's magnificence makes do with wretched figures of Jupiter and Mars, Isis and Osiris, Kebele and Attis, with derivative magnificence of state and culture and nature, with mammon and personality, art and science, church and virtue in which images of the human beings offer ambiguous veneration"(R I:18).[15] With the help of the category of "possession," Barth relates production of idols to the human position toward God. It is in human attitudes toward God that we always face God. For Barth, religion is described and analyzed in terms of social categories seen predominantly in left-wing Hegelian philosophy. Humanity's stance and its resulting situation is that of its relation to God. It is not only an individual (moral, spiritual, religious) attitude but an objective situation, not only a matter between God and the soul but also a matter of the relation of humans toward one another. Thus, the universality of God is conceived as *a priori* in social terms because we always have God (R I:11).

It is at this point that we can see the special significance of Barth's analysis of the phenomenon of religion as it is connected to his biblically legitimate concept of God.[16] When humans stand in a positive relation, namely, an election-relation to God, they have real communion and fellowship with God. The original and immediate relation of the human being to God proves itself only under God's gracious election. When human beings leave this original communion with God, a religious greed for possession begins the production of idols. God becomes an object to private human desire and the egoistical desire of possession. According to Barth, religion is colored and fashioned in social categories of possession that are bound to the tradition of Marx and Moses Hess. The possession of God has always to do with the law of possession in bourgeois, capitalistic society. Speaking of social and political unrest, Barth deals with the situation of desire and the suffering proletariat from the perspective of religious socialism.[17] Humans take captive the objective truth of God and domesticate God into human subjectivity. In a sluggish and wicked way the human being relates God to his or her own personality. When one should think of God, one thinks of oneself. Thus it is believed that persons are themselves in relation to God only as God stands in relation to themselves (R I:13). Through the private/egoistical attitude of the human

15. Cf. Marquardt, "Religionskritik und Entmythologsierung. Über einen Beitrag Karl Barths zur Entmythologisierungsfrage," 344–45.

16. Marquardt, "Götze wackelt," 409.

17. Ibid., 413–14.

being, the relation to God assumes a character of possession-relation in that God is reduced to an object of human craving for possession (R I:70, 72).[18] By virtue of this human craving for possession, the production of idols begins; humanity's religiously productive force inserts idols between humanity and God. In this possession-relation, the human ruins God's election-relation to God. However, for Barth, God cannot be possessed by humans. God is not at human disposal at all. Once God is possessed, this God is not God in Jesus Christ but an idol.

As Barth analyzes religion from the standpoint of the category of "possession," he also observes the law of possession in bourgeois-capitalist society in this regard. Barth's critique of religion therefore has a parallel to Hess and anticipates the young Marx, whose early writings had not been published at that time. Barth's critique echoes the early writings of Marx par excellence, such as the "Paris Manuscript." A religious process of idol production corresponds to a structure of bourgeois myth production. Religion lies in the fact that the attitude of humankind exists in relation to God in terms of an undying or incessant desire for the divine (R I:12). Religious people who seek God in their undying desire face the barrier of the nondisposal and otherworldly dimension of God. Herein they suffer, and this limitation determines their existence. After all, Barth does not exclude desire, suffering, and a so-called problematical religious *a priori* (in a Troeltschian sense) but recognizes these by making them his point of departure in the analysis of human religiosity. After all, desire, suffering, and a so-called problematical religious *a priori* in a Troeltschian sense are not excluded by Barth, but recognized by making it his point of departure in the analysis of human religiosity. In place of an inviolable desire for the divine Barth discerns in religious people an attempt at mythologizing and idolizing the original/eternal.[19]

In the emergence of the phenomenon of fetishism in which humans stand against God, human autonomy manifests itself as heteronomy: "The production of idols succeeds: Israel *receives* his stormy and craving king, the lost son *receives* his share in fatherly inheritance, Mars *rules* the hour and Venus-Cybele *removes* the throne, which we established for her, Mammon *becomes* world-ruler, we *become* 'personalities', 'the state has us' (Naumann) and the culture *eats* us, art and science and church *become*

---

18. Balthasar, *Theology of Karl Barth*, 74.
19. Marquardt, "Religionskritik und Entmythologiserung," 345–46.

purpose and content for themselves" (R I:19). Given this fact, the service of idols becomes dominant, as if they would be God. This is the reign of lordless powers and violence (R I:19). This is the human's mythologization of the exchange of God for idols.[20] In terms of the production of idols, humans established the world of objects for religious worship and veneration (Jupiter, Mars, state, mammon), which equates to a religious fog for Barth.

Fetishism (R I:17–21) inevitably occurs in the production of such a religious fog (R I:18–19). Fetishism of God implies fetishism of human thought and deed. In religious fetishism idols, as psuedogodly powers, exercise a strong impact on human life. Here humans try to take the place of God. Arbitrary phantasmic absolutization and idolization arise out of the religious productive power of human being (R I:18) and function as God over the human being. Religious fetishism makes humans "slave and match" of relativity, which they have set in place of God (R I:19). In fact in fetishism the process of human thought and action, the nonfreedom, is realized. In other words, humans desire to possess God but end up being possessed and subjugated by idols. This is the result of the co-mingling of time and eternity. An interim kingdom is built up so that it exercises an interim worldly magic. In his analysis of the religious production process, Barth articulates a social dimension of the bourgeoisie's attempt at mythologizing God, at exchanging God for idols, and consequently at separating God from the human being.[21]

Barth's analysis of fetishism is an expression of the estrangement of humans from God and from themselves (R I:14). "I do not do what I want to do, but I do what I hate" (R I:208). Through this corruption of the human relation to God, the human person appears as nothing but a distorted image rather than as one acknowledged and elected by the will of God (R I:208). Because of this distorted image of God human action demonstrates a fundamental vagueness.

> I can acknowledge my products not as my legitimate children, but as they stand against me as strange and hostile in meeting with my own disapproval, regardless of the fact they belong to me, namely to what I know and want . . . I don't understand them, I don't love them, I must deny, but they stare at me like a bad, ugly

---

20. In the Tambach lecture (1919) Barth denounced clericalization and secularization of Jesus Christ for an attempt at making a mythological-religious exchange of God.

21. Marquardt, "Der Götze wackelt," 415.

and misshapen child. Nevertheless, they are no doubt my works and I cannot dispute my authorship of them. (R I:208)

In Barth's analysis, alienation and human fetishism of thought and action can manifest themselves in the mechanisms of economy, state, culture, and religion. These political mechanisms imprison society to its own alienation. It is only the revolution of God that can emancipate human beings from the imprisonment of alienation and fetishism (R I:65, 120). This is a separation of togetherness belonging to God and humans. Here God becomes a class god.[22] In light of the production of idols and fetishism, it is of special significance for Barth to take into account Feuerbach's critique of religion. In *Romans I* Barth transplants his understanding of religion into the fields of politics, economy, and culture. In Barth's analysis of the inner logic of the human negative relation to God, we perceive the extent to which Barth relegates it to a social and political relation imbued with alienation and fetishism. From here we see Barth's critique of liberal theology embedded with an ideologically liberal form of the state, capitalism, and militarism. Let us now turn to Barth's critical approach to this form.

Critique of Ideology: Capitalism, State, and Militarism

Capitalism and the State

In *Romans I* Barth defines the lordless powers of political ideology and praxis of liberalism in the sphere of capitalism, state, and militarism—that is, all vicious "isms" (R I:20). According to Barth, fundamental to the fixation of liberalism's political idols are first of all four catalogs of idols in *Romans I* (cf. R I:"Der Sturz," 18–22). It is now the fetish that humans venerate in place of God. In humanity's dethroning God, human sacrilege and injustice cause ethical and social confusion. Because humans' resistance against God's future encapsulates and misuses the truth, their world becomes the "playground of all possible voidness, place of world war, and house of the fool" (R I:18). In the consciousness of humankind, the difference between the originality and superiority of God is blurred with relativity, and the dependence of things is blurred. In other words, God is reduced to the level of fetish. Humans replace No-God

22. Ibid., 416.

with the god of the self; in other words, they become gods. What humankind offers its veneration are images of state, culture, nature, mammon, science, church, and virtue. God is no longer God, no longer majestic but a desired object of the human experience. To put it more concretely, God becomes a mirror for human experience. From this distorted relation to God, human sacrilege and injustice emerge. In the world without God that paves the way to individual arbitrariness and human injustice, "nature and culture, materialism and churchliness, capitalism and socialism, imperialism and democracy" fight against each other for the seat of power (R I:20).

As a result, political ruling places appear in the form of capital, state, and militarism. For Barth the primary idol of individual desire in liberalism is personality: "personal life is no longer an answer to world war and revolution" (R I:366). Three idols of the ruling mechanism in liberal social order are capitalism, state, and militarism, which are interconnected. Capitalism emerges on the basis of the fetishism of or fixation on the material possession of mammon. This fetishism process converts religious desire for possession into the sphere of economics, labor process, and social-economic order. Human labor, rather than intended to gratify necessary desires of human beings, is for the gain of private material possession. In the organization of labor the character of fetishism-structure emerges in negative relation to God.

From here economic competition arises within an organization between participants in the labor process. Economic order functions according to the principle of the "free game of powers" (R I:177). Economic competition makes the human "struggle for existence, lead it more intensely than animal life" (R I:22). The disorganizing function of economic struggle and competition institutionalizes the differentiation of human beings into the "haves, the have-less, and the have-nots," separating them into the rich and the poor. According to Barth, because of human sin, the freedom in Christ is converted into the freedom of Adam. In fact, Adam's sin was a freedom that is "lordless under the dominion of the sin," "a collapse into the absolute accident and uncertainty of fate" (R I:177).

Liberal culture and social order are based on this ideal of freedom. The whole history of this line is a history of ignored possibility, of missed opportunity, of a "wrong track and cul-de-sac" (R I:177). The "free game of powers" becomes a real issue only in God (R I:177). Outside creative, living unity and truth of God, liberalism becomes sin. As we dissociate ourselves from God, our powers appeal to adversity for meaning, to mutual destruction. Human freedom without God is the worst slavery. The power of God's grace should stand against the battleground of world war, which is caused by the free human game of powers without God. The "free game of powers" without God implies the contrast that rules society, between the high and the low, between the rich and the poor, between the powerful and the powerless. In this contrast we Christians must take a one-sided and decisive stance for the marginalized. "You do not belong to the lord. You cannot be neutral . . . You belong to common people." "Do not mediate on the high standard of life, but put yourself into their low-grade place" (R I:367).

In a capitalist society a violent state is here while seemingly an established church is there. A good society ruled by mammon is here while a dull enigma of the mass there (R I:262). This contrast assumes a form of class conflict between a mammon-ruled society (i.e., bourgeois class society) and the destitute proletarian class (R I:378). Class struggle proceeds on the basis of this class conflict. The economically forced dominion of the bourgeoisie is the class struggle from above, which the proletariat confronts using the instrument of "strike and general strike and street fighting" as well as the weapon of reaction and revolution as preconditions for fighting against this evil as long as protest and embanking take a fundamentally radical political turn (R I:383–84). This is a class struggle from below. Furthermore, God, for Barth, is "a God of the Jew and the Gentiles, but not a God of the high and the low, but onesidedly a God of the low, not a God of the great and the small, but a God of the small without consideration" (R I:367).

As a result, according to Barth, "the movement of God's kingdom inside of social and cultural class is thoroughly not generally and indifferently beginning and proceeding one, but basically and one-sidedly a movement from below" (R I:367). Human politics cannot become an obstacle to the fulfillment of divine promises. Evil is overcome in the good. We Christians are co-workers in the building up of God's world (R I:382). The fetishism process of material possession, in Barth's analysis, eventually leads to an antagonistic class society. Disorganized society fractures into bourgeoisie and proletariat classes through deliberations of free power.

As Barth stresses in a poignant way, "the rich who oppresses you is the poor man. Never respect his mammon at a single moment! Defend yourself against the dominion of his idols! Insist or make a conquest of your freedom! . . . But above all show him, give him, if possible, what he does not have: Your actual freedom from futility, through which he—also he!—can become righteous and lively" (R I:374). In our humble attitude for the poor and the low, which is our solidarity with poor Lazarus, we will—despite all differences—become united into one in the order of the coming world (R I:367). Given the class structure in a capitalistic society, the existence of the state means an obvious phenomenon of humankind's negative relation to its divine *Ursprung* (R I:376). "The state as such is evil;" it is a repulsive distortion of the administration of history through God's righteousness which once was and will be once again. It is at the same time a phenomenon of the wrath of God who punishes humankind (R I:376). For Barth, the function of the state is enslavement of the subjugated (R I:377), even in a parliamentary democracy because "a devilish art of outvoting" here serves this purpose of the state (R I:377). For the execution of its task the state needs a corresponding instrument, thus, the article of the law and machine rifles are invented by the state (R I:383). The state is powerful and violent simply because the state belongs and is connected to class society (R I:262, 377).

Through raising taxes and so-called duties, the rulers oppress the destitute and the honest in a most powerful way. The use of such an economic advantage always favors the elite. In the respect that the elite claim before the law, and in the case of remission and execution, humanity and the right always remain the last motif (R I:389). In short, the state is the instrument of oppression toward the destitute proletarian class by the rich or bourgeois social class (R I:366–67). Through tax policy and legislation, the state secures the economic oppression of the destitute for the possessors with the help of state power (R I:374).

Militarism

Along the lines of his critique of the state, Barth also brings militarism into critical account. The outbreak of World War I was for Barth a pointer to the telos of the liberal social order. Liberalism and its use of violence changed the world into a scene of world war (R I:18). According to Barth, this development could be explained as the interweaving of militarism with the structure of capitalism and the state. Capitalism develops itself into colonialism so that there is a tendency in the capitalist society to encourage a lack of peace in foreign relations (R I:140).

The state as a violent instrument calls for political conflict. The use of powers and violence is likewise grounded in the essence of the state. This causes a rise of militarism in the state and society. The politics of oppression in the inner realm and the politics of war in relations with foreign states complement each other. So "flame thrower, mine dog, gas mask, flying bomb and submarine" (R I:389) are logical tools for the purpose of wreaking havoc; this propensity reveals the telos of capitalistic society. This militarism is therefore a necessary component of the violent state. Moreover, as an element of the violent state, militarism intensifies unlimited use of power and violence. The dominion of militarism drives the capitalistic state violence to war in general. "Arrogant England plays chess with boisterous Germany—and always also inversely!" (R I:376). World War I was, for Barth, a power struggle between violent states that consequently led to politically organized mass homicide. This event documents the self-destruction inherent in political ideology and the praxis of liberalism (R I:177).

Parallel to his critique of the ideology of state, capitalism, and militarism, Barth also deals with the church in critical terms. Although the church has been given Moses, it has turned his inheritance into a codex of letters. Within the church, the Letter to the Romans is dismembered into individual dead pieces, thus reshaping the Truth into doctrine and ethics. Although the church received Luther, it has distorted him as the patron of inwardness—Germanness, evangelical freedom. "Finally they make the cross in a million ways the symbol of highest humanity. They sing the suffering Christ . . . and in all this the Church—not the world—once again crucifies him" (R I:421–22). The kingdom of God enters in place of religious individualism. Against religious individualism Barth set divine universalism in motion. In place of the ethics of religious socialism or the religiously righteous person whom Barth critiques as a Pharisee in the exegesis of Romans chapter 2, the movement of God's grace enters by calling for "each moment a quite specific knowledge of the situation and to which a necessary deed corresponds" (R I:524). "Pacifism and social democracy do not represent the kingdom of God, but the old human kingdom in a new guise" (R I:42). "And because they are not worried by the progress of actual history they feel that much more secure in the exceptional religious/ethical situation within so-called history. They forget how relative this situation is" (R I:46).

Barth and Lenin?

According to Gautschi, a Swiss historian, Lenin stayed three times in Switzerland: a) 1903–1905 in Geneva, b) 1908 in Geneva, and c) 1914–1917 in Bern and Zurich. Although Lenin was critical of the imperialistic economy in Switzerland associated with bank capital and countries of super power, he was quite impressed by the political freedom based on the federative system and maximal realization of democracy within the workers' movement and association. Lenin began to exercise his influence upon the leftists among the SPS after the Zimmerwald conference (1915) and upon the socialistic Youth.[23]

After moving out to Zurich in February 1916, Lenin led a circle of extreme leftists called "Kugelklub," to which the so-called Zimmerwald leftists belonged. As a member of the Social Democratic Party in the city of Zurich, Lenin regularly took part in party congresses. According to his letter to Armand, his girlfriend and comrade, Lennin was working behind the split of the SPS from the winter of 1916 to 1917. His pamphlets, which were typewritten at this time, were circulated among leftists in Zurich; his Bolshevist thesis, which demonstrated proletarian antimilitarism, also carried some weight. Lenin's main opponent was Robert Grimm, a representative of the Zimmerwald centralists. In his *Abschiedsbrief an die Schweizer Arbeiter* (April 8, 1917), Lenin emphasized cooperation between Russian Bolshevists and revolutionary Social Democrats within the SPS.[24] The Social Democrats and workers' movement were extremely attentive to the situation in Russia after the outbreak of the October Revolution. Barth was actively involved in the Workers Association and the struggle for the future direction within the SPS. Barth's first edition of the *Romans* provides a reflection of his theological socialism in confrontation with Leninism and the Russian Revolution. His political slogans in the first edition of the *Romans* commentary, such as, "it is more than Leninism" (R I:381), "social democrats not religious–social," and his posi-

---

23. Cf. Egger, *Entstehung der Kommunistischen Partei*. See Mattmüller, *Leonhard Ragaz*, vol. 2, chap. 4, "Ragaz und Lenin im Kampf um die Sozialistischen Jugend."

24. Cf. *Zur Geschichte der kommunitschen Bewegung in der Schweiz*; Aus dem "Vorwarts" 1968–1980, 310–11.

tion "on the most extreme left" give a clue to Barth's relation to Leninism on the one hand and religious socialism on the other.

What is striking in the first edition of *Romans* is Barth's political exegesis of Rom 12:16–13:10, which he places under the heading of "Superiority." There has been no lack of debate on Barth's theological reflection on Rom 13:1–7 in relation to Lenin's work *State and Revolution*. Following the line of Bastiaan Wielenga, who noticed a parallel between Barth's exegesis and Lenin,[25] Marquardt extended Barth's understanding of the Revolution of God in connection with Lenin's model of state and revolution. An indirect quotation of Lenin's work in Barth's first edition of the *Romans* is that "Your [Christian] state and revolution is in heaven, in the hiddenness of human beings" (R I:380).[26]

According to Marquardt, Lenin's work appeared in German when Barth was preoccupied with the interpretation of Romans 13. Besides, the correspondence with Thurneysen reveals that Barth worked on Rom 9:13 on March 25, 1918. That being the case, it is reasonable to conclude that Barth commented on Romans 13 around the end of 1918 during the November revolution in Germany and the general strike in Switzerland. Lenin's work was completed in August 1917, and its first German version appeared in 1918. The foreword to the second edition is dated 17 December 1918. Barth could have known of Lenin's work in writing the first edition of *Romans* because there were already three different German translations in Berlin and Bern. The excerpts of *State and Revolution* had been published in the socialist press in Germany. Besides, *Pravda* had published the preface and the first chapter of "State and Revolution" in German already on December 17, 1917. Barth's close friend Fritz Lieb, who was active among Zimmerwald leftists, would have been sympa-

---

25. Wielenga, *Lenins Wege zur Revolution*, 433–36.

26. "Ihr Statt und ihre Revolution ist im Himmel." In this sentence Barth's linguistic irregularity in using a singular verb would be a clue to his acquaintance with Lenin's pamphlet *State and Revolution*, which was circulated underground within the radical leftists of the SPS. It seems that Barth had the title of Lenin's *State and Revolution* in mind. In the early twenties even Rudolf Bultmann read Lenin's *State and Revolution* and, surprisingly enough, agreed with him in some ways. On September 9, 1919, Bultmann wrote to a friend: "Shortly if the second and this actual revolution does not come, yet, so everything remains in the old and becomes rather much worse . . . That it will work without a period of 'dictator,' I think not. Since I have read Lenin [!], I am enthusiastic for this personality. I am only afraid that we have no Lenin. One does not have to do death fire so much as in Russia." Cf. Evang, *Rudolf Bultmann in seiner Früzeit*, 81.

thetic to Lenin and his Russian comrades during their exile in Zurich in early 1917.

However, on the basis of Groll's investigation, Eberhard Jüngel argues that Lenin's pamphlet appeared on November 20, 1918 and Barth's manuscript of *Romans* went to the printers in December.[27] As a result, it would be impossible to suggest that Barth read Lenin's *State and Revolution* during the commentary on Romans 13. Bruce McCormack likewise argues that Barth's commentary on Rom 13:1–7 was restricted only to Barth's confrontation with Ragaz and religious socialism rather than Leninism, regardless of the fact that Barth nowhere mentioned Ragaz's name.[28]

In support of Marquardt, however, Ulrich Dannemann pays more attention to the analysis of theoretical and practical relevance between Barth and Lenin rather than assuming a literary dependence of Barth upon Lenin.[29] When we look at Lenin's activity in Switzerland, there is no doubt that Lenin exercised a considerable influence upon the leftists of the SPS. Consequently it is safe to say that Lenin's works and Leninism would have been within Barth's horizon.

Theology of the Revolution of God in *Romans I*

Barth's specific term the "Revolution of God in *Romans I* is first of all relevant to religious socialism in Switzerland. In *Sie Müssen!* Kutter devoted a whole chapter to revolution as effective of the absolute in world history. For him, revolution is the volcano of eternity in history.[30] The apocalyptic turning point of the world that Jesus has proclaimed was the overthrowing of the world. Shyness with regard to violence bound to the revolution should not hold Christians back from revolution. The living God needs violence. That is revolution, but in the revolution God rules.[31] The concept of revolution is handed out by mammon and the fact of revolution becomes a historical necessity because of mammon. The egoistic mode of

---

27. Jüngel, "Die theologische Anfänge: Beobachtungen," in *Barth-Studien*, 26.
28. McCormack, *Critically Realistic*, 173.
29. Dannemann, *Theologie und Politik im Denken Karl Barths*, 78.
30. Kutter, *Sie Müssen!* 70.
31. Ibid., 77.

production is the area in need of revolution. Other than being violent—it seems—the social question cannot be resolved.³²

However, in Blumhardt's letter to Howard Eugster-Zust (written July 7, 1904), he expressed reservation regarding Kutter's identification of God with human revolution: "What should so overthrowing, yet incomplete revolutionary movement that belongs just to world history blow in the highest place of God?"³³ Prior to Barth and Eduard Thurneysen, Blumhardt distinguished an actual overthrowing and a radical Revolution of God from the yet-incomplete revolutionary movement of socialism. Rather than rejecting socialistic revolution, Blumhardt defended himself against the ideologization of human revolution in the highest place of God. In addition, Blumhardt maintained a critical reservation against revolutionary violence: "We must not be bloody over-throwers. . . . But full of quiet and power we go through all developments and bear the final goal of peace in mind. This goal cannot come without a shaking breakthrough."³⁴ Despite disagreement between Kutter and Blumhardt as to the nature of violent revolution and God's relation to revolution, a concept of the "Revolution of God" or "Revolution of the kingdom of God" was used in all religious-socialist circles. From here Barth accepts this term and refines and develops it in his unique theological way. We now turn to Barth's understanding of what the Revolution of God means in his theological framework.

Barth formulates his concept of divine action with the world, society, and human being in terms of "divine world revolution" (R I:380). He identifies this turn of God to the world as an absolute Revolution *von Gott aus* (R I:379), "Revolution coming in Christ" (R I:381). The slogan of "absolute revolution" can be understood as Barth's own version of "absolute hope" in Ragaz, and the revolution *von Gott aus* is Kutter's influence on Ragaz and Barth. Furthermore, Barth viewed the *Ursprung* of God in terms of the revolution of God, in that God is defined as loving in the most free and living movement. Therefore, theology begins anew its way of thinking from the end of its way. God in this way is opposed to us. God as love is not complete but exists "in the most free and living movement" (R I:344). In this movement God enters into us. From this standpoint

---

32. Ibid., 82, 86.
33. Mattmüller, "Einfluss Christoph Blumhardts auf schweizerische," 239.
34. Sauter, *Theologie des Reiches Gottes*, 139.

we notice that Barth's doctrine of God—"The being of God as the One who loves in Freedom" (*CD* II/1. §28)—is grounded in his conception of God's revolution. Therefore, the being of God is in act for the world.

However, what distinguishes Barth's stance from religious socialism is his christological formulation of the Revolution of God, in which God's revolution coming in Christ refers to a connection between Christology and revolution. The motto "the world revolution" would be easily associated with a Leninist idea of world revolution. Consequently, Barth's usage of "Revolution of God" is not to be understood as merely symbolic-metaphorical jargon but as deeply anchored in his social-political context.[35] Eschatology, coupled with God's wrath and judgment, is interpreted as the real history, before human history that is characterized by the wantonness and injustice of humankind. This wantonness, which refers to human desire and yearning to become divine, leads to "ein prometheisches Ansichreissen" [a Promethean breakthrough] (R I:12). In it injustice is evoked as a result of the human attempt to make ourselves the center of history and of the world. "This is the resistance of man under which his whole world suffers: he always seeks God and always finds false gods, he always means to serve God and always serves himself" (R I:13).[36]

All subsequent social problems are grounded in the human Promethean yearning for *eritis sicut Deus* ("You will be like God") in resistance to divine grace: "So the present state, as it has taken the place of the original city of God which is to be renewed in Christ, equates to 'violence' because its pure power and character of coercion is expressed and recognized in contrast to the righteousness and freedom of the city of God" (R I:376). This character of violence and coercion seen in the state and politics is regarded as "a devilish art of outvoting" (R I:501-3); such is true whether they invoke Gustav Adolph, Napoleon, Cromwell, Friedrich the Great, or August Bebel.

Drawing on St. Paul, according to whom our "state and revolution" is in heaven, Barth argues for Christians to have nothing to do with supporting the existing structure and order of the state; therefore, the present state and society must be replaced. Because Christians have their real fatherland in God, they must take into account "the absolute Revolution

---

35. Against this political understanding, Jüngel endorses a metaphorical understanding of God's Revolution, see Jüngel, "Die theologische Anfänge: Beobachtungen," in *Barth-Studien*, 118-19.

36. Cf. Hood, *Contemporary Political Orders and Christ*, 47.

of God," which Barth calls to bring down the present state and society (R I:379). Therefore, Christians must deny the fundamental principle of the use of power and violence. Rather than competing with the state, this Revolution of God denies it and "revolutionizes revolution" (R I:234). What is at issue for Christianity is connected with the political program, "all or nothing" (R I:379).

Barth himself polemicizes this position to be "more than Leninism." "It is more than Leninism! As far as Christianity is concerned it is 'all or nothing' in the sense that the fulfillment it expects is not . . . the goal or result of a development or a gradual 'ascent of man' but the discovery of a new creation or the substance of a new knowledge. *This* program cannot be the object of any ethics" (R I:505–7). There is no doubt that everyone is subject to the state powers. Christians may act and involve themselves in the affairs of the state but must deny them ideological legitimation. A Christian position characterized by the shibboleth "starve them religiously" stands in expectation of the revolutionary dissolution of the present state in light of the Revolution of God. This is not out of respect for the existing social order, but rather out of radical contempt for it. It is not because of opportunism, but rather for the sake of God's *Sache* (R I:380). Barth's political position can be summarized as a countermovement to the existing society and its institutions; Christians act and join in solidarity with those who prepare the way for a new society which will be positively and affirmatively considered in light of the Revolution of God.

It is also important to consider what Barth means by the slogan: "it is more than Leninism." Which group does Barth call opportunism? How should Barth's radicalism be understood in the first edition of *Romans*? In order to answer these questions, we need to look at the historical situation of the SPS in which Barth was still active.

As we have already seen during Lenin's activity in Bern and Zurich from 1915 to 1917, Leninism exercised a strong impact on leftists in the Party such as Münzenberg and Platten. In addition, the leftists of Zimmerwald struggled with the centralists of Zimmerwald such as Robert Grimm and social patriots. The revolution concept within Leninism is to be seen and judged critically and politically in light of Barth's concept of Revolution of God which means world revolution. Barth's acquaintance with Leninism might have been mediated through the leftists of Zimmerwald in the party or even Lenin's own activity and pamphlets in Switzerland. It is true that Lenin's French manuscript had already appeared in 1918 through his colleague in Geneva. As we have already seen in one of Lenin's *Letters from Afar,* his theory of the state and revolution had become known to the socialists who were Barth's contemporaries.

What is characteristic of the Leninist position lies in the mediation between the Scylla of the revisionist affirmation of the state and the Charybdis of leftist radical rejection of the state for the sake of the dictatorship of proletariat.[37] From the perspective of Lenin's concept of revolution, Barth's position falls into the category of anarchism. In Lenin's words: "If the state is the product of the irreconcilability of class antagonism, the liberation of the oppressed class is impossible . . . without the destruction of the apparatus of state power which was created by the ruling class and which is the embodiment of this alienation."[38] But "we are not utopians, we do not 'dream' of dispensing at once with all administration, with all subordination." Lenin continues, "these anarchist dreams, based upon the incomprehension of the tasks of the proletarian dictatorship . . . serve only to postpone the socialist revolution until people are different."[39]

Unlike Lenin's colorization of Social Democrats in Europe, however, Barth's radical position is well expressed:

> That you as Christians have nothing to do with monarchism, capitalism, militarism, patriotism and liberalism is so obvious that I need not to say anything. . . . The cause of divine renewal may not be mixed up with the cause of human progress. The divine may not be politicized and the human not divinized, not even for the sake of democracy and social democracy (R I:381).

Nevertheless, Barth encourages Christians to consider that they give the Kaiser that which belongs to him, and to God what belongs to God. God's revolution, which means the new heaven and the new earth where God's righteousness dwells, may not be bound to a political ideology or religious socialism. "Fulfill your duties without illusion, but no compromising of God! Payment of tax, but no incense to Caesar! Citizens initiative and obedience but no combination of throne and altar, no Christian Patriotism, no democratic crusading. Strike and general strike, and street fighting if needs be, but no religious justification and glorification of it! Military service as soldier or officer if need be but under no circumstances

---

37. Cf. Wielenga, *Lenins Weg zur Revolution,* 370–79.
38. Marx, Engels, and Lenin, *On Historical Materialism,* 377.
39. Ibid., 588.

army chaplain! Social democratic but not religious socialist! The betrayal of the gospel does not belong to the political duties" (R I:390).

On the question of revolutionary method Barth stands within the radical social-democratic way. God's taking sides with the poor encourages Christians to consider that they could hardly place themselves otherwise than "on the most extreme left" (R I:381). Barth's stance on the most extreme left within the Social Democrats would be in parallel with leftist radicalism in Switzerland from 1914 to 1918.[40] Barth's revolutionary stance in light of God's revolution distances him sharply from monarchism, capitalism, militarism, and patriotism. But Barth's radical denial of the existing social order must be seen in relation to his reflection on active political involvement. In addition, Barth's endorsement to "strike and general strike and street fighting, when it must be" should be the absolute opposite of anarchism. It is not utopian dialectic but "dialectical materialism in which the most radical anarchist denial of the State runs together with a highly political participation in the State."[41]

Barth's affinity to the anarchism of Kropotkin and Landauer can be seen in his "Socialist Speeches"; however it should be understood as a method, not as a worldview. Barth comments on the first postwar congress of the Second International that "the International marches again, not in the direction of the social patriots, but in the direction of Eisners, i.e. in the direction toward the zeal of the Munich conciliar republic"[42] in which Landauer participates. In addition, Barth rejects Lenin as an anarchist. In this regard Barth moves dialectically in a radical socialist direction involving the anarchist denial of the state as well as an active participation in building up the conciliar republic, which he regards as the human work of shaping the precondition for God's kingdom. Be that as it may, we should not ignore that Barth's political idea, as seen in accordance with the resolution of the general strike in the Swiss Party, is

---

40. Historically speaking, radicalism was in connection with western Swiss and French anarcho-syndicalism with which the workers' movement in the German-speaking area of Switzerland influenced J. Guillaume and Fritz Brupbacher and Jakob Herzog in the period from 1900 to 1912. Cf. Jost, *Linksradikalismus in der deutschen Schweiz*.

41. Gorringe, *Karl Barth: Against Hegemony*, 46. As a development of the integration of anarchism into Marxism, Karl Korsch, in his 1950 interview, asserted that the future of socialism was in need of a synthesis between Marxism and all other socialisms, particularly anarchism and syndicalism. Korsch's demand was later was accepted by Rudi Dutschke's program of "Neue Linke." Cf. Harms, *Christentum und Anarchismus*, 49–50.

42. Marquardt, "Erster Bericht über Karl Barths 'Sozialistische Reden,'" 485.

a critical counterproposal to Lenin's political model. There is a parallel between Barth's endorsement for general strike without religious justification and the resolution of the SPS in 1913.[43]

God's revolution as world revolution may not be supported by "individual anarchist outbreaks" (R I:380), "because the divine world revolution, the establishment of the city of God is not the cause of the individual. The individual . . . as such can and shall not break away from the imprisonment of this world" (R I:380). Not "every disturbance in Aussersihl or Russia" (R I:364) must be identified with the world revolution. Until the general strike in November of 1918, there were a great deal of uproars and strikes in Aussersihl, a sector of the poor in Zurich. Concerning the process of revolution in Russia, Barth tried to engage in confrontation with Lenin's theory of revolution. In reflecting on the Revolution of God, he elaborates on the possibility of a genuine revolution on the basis of Jesus Christ: "What Christ brings means a real revolution, the dissolution of all dependence" (R I:141).

"The counter-movement for freedom"(R I:159), which is revealed as the greater power of God in Jesus Christ, corresponds to the Revolution of God against the alienation and reification of human existence taking place in the process of revolution. In the final analysis, not moral ethics but the movement of God must correspond to our knowledge and action in every single moment of our lives (R I:392). Indeed, there is a correspondence between God's movement and human praxis in terms of the inherent power of grace, in that there is no distinction between what God does for us and what we must do (R I:169). The radical idea that human beings are what they will make of themselves is unsupportable in Barth's view. A self-reliant view is distinct from Barth's view of the inherent power of grace, which implies the free and good will of human beings for liberating praxis and solidarity with the poor. According to Barth, the movement of the kingdom of God within the social and cultural contradiction is definitely and basically "a one-sided movement from below," in

---

43. On the question of a general strike a discussion occurred in the party with respect to the trade union congress on September 15, 1913. This congress was held in response to the local general strike in Zurich (July 11, 1912). In this resolution the Swiss trade union rejected the so-called revolutionary general strike in a Marxist-Leninist way. However, in the resolution of the third point, a mass strike could be supported as defensive and protest action when the government's measurement threatened common life interest of the working class. In such a case there was no other alternative except for the mass strike (cf. the general strike in November 1918).

that God is "one-sidedly a God of the lower but not a God of the upper, indeed, without reservation, a God of the small [i.e. the totally marginal]" (R I:367). Barth's political slogan—"Social democratic, but not religious socialist!" (R I:390)—challenges both the communism molded by Lenin's idea of revolution and the religious socialism of Ragaz in Zurich.

Let us explore Barth's challenge more carefully. First of all, there appears to be a certain relevance and affinity between Lenin's radical idea of revolution and Barth's Revolution of God. Despite oft-repeated criticism of Lenin, he is, at least, concerned with dismantling the structures of an oppressive society, and thereby liberating the poor from the ruling class in the bourgeois social system. Barth is, nevertheless, critical of Lenin, calling into question the relationship between state and revolution in Lenin's understanding. Barth's unease with Lenin lies in the latter's dangerous concept of proletarian dictatorship. Barth wonders whether the dictatorship of the proletariat amounts necessarily to a dictatorship over the proletariat in postrevolutionary Russia. According to Barth, the Revolution of God does not compete with the state. The Revolution of God, in fact, matters "more than Leninism." God's revolution breaks out "with the aim, not to improve the present state, but to replace it, to dissolve the violence of injustice from top to bottom by the power of justice" (R I:371).

According to Barth, the purpose of revolution consists not in substituting the dictatorship of the proletariat for the state but in dissolving every form of ruling state and class dictatorship in favor of establishing ever-increasing social justice and democracy. At this point Barth's concept of revolution runs counter to Lenin's. The Revolution of God as an ethical criterion breaks through the absolutism that is a by-product of Leninist proletarian dictatorship. Moreover, Barth's concept of God's Revolution relativizes the dictatorship of the proletariat; in other words, it revolutionizes the revolution (R I:234).[44]

Barth's concept of God's revolution points to permanent revolution, in that his dialectical notions of origin (*Ursprung*) and parable (*Gleichnis*) posit an ongoing correspondence between social justice and the coming kingdom of God. This organic but parabolic correspondence preserves

---

44. Accordingly Marquardt argues that Barth could very well have known Lenin's *State and Revolution*. Beyond Lenin's position, Barth moves toward "dialectical materialism in which the most radically anarchist denial of the state runs together with a highly political participation in the state" (Marquardt, *Theologie und Sozialismus*, 135).

the freedom of God and blocks any possibility of idolizing a dictatorship or a distortion of social justice and democratic equality in the process of human revolution. God's Revolution is, according to Barth, more revolutionary and radical than Lenin's revolt. Here Barth's political radicalism becomes dangerous. When the state realizes the danger of these revolutionary methods, then martyrdom becomes a real possibility (R I:522). "Over against everything which wants to be great I must take the standpoint of the small people, with whom God begins, not because they are virtuous but because their righteousness does not stand in the way, or at least, does less so" (R I:490).

Under the term "superiority," Barth deals with the situation of the revolution in Russia. Arbitrariness is not at all the same as superiority. "You cannot represent the reality of God (*Gottes Sache*) arbitrarily" (R I:369). Barth argues that arbitrariness or stubbornness of the revolutionaries in Russia should be ruled out in the light of the revolution of God, which attacks privatization and the privileged particularism visible in the postrevolutionary society. Christianity should not pursue a paticularistic revolution in the manner of the Russian revolution because "your [Christian] *state and revolution is* in heaven concealed from human beings" (R I:380).

Barth thus connects the revolution of God with the world revolution in an eschatological and universalistic sense because "the world Revolution of God," which means the setting up of God's state in human society, "is not an individual business." The individuals as such (for instance, Lenin and Ragaz) cannot break out of the imprisonment of this world. Concerning God's world revolution, it must not be impeded by "individual anarchistic outbreak, or individual bungler" (R I:380). According to Barth, the love of Christ means that we must remain faithful to "the hope, the unquiet, the longing, radical, and permanent revolution" (R I:353). "Because the love of Christ is the communion of the Spirit, in which we stand with him. This communion is but growth in the righteousness of the kingdom of heaven. This is a fighting position against the violence of this aeon" (R I:262). At this moment (1918)—"precisely what we call revolution" (R I:316)—we look forward to when the embers of Marxist dogma are newly kindled and the socialist Church will be resurrected in a socialist world" (R I:444).

Barth's political stance of "more than Leninism" critiques, radicalizes, and revolutionizes an individualistic, anarchistic revolution in Russia or in *Aussersihil* (the poor quarter) by dealing with God's revolution as the permanent world revolution. This stance does not have to do with political utopian anarchy that Lenin describes in his *State and Revolution*. Rather Barth accused Lenin and Ragaz of encouraging an individual anarchistic uprising. The catastrophic upheaval in Zurich's *Aussersihil* or in Russia must not be identical with the world revolution of God. Therefore Barth warns us not to anticipate the world revolution in an individualistic way, but undertakes to shape its preconditions. At this juncture, Barth concedes that "strike and general strike and street fighting" be revolutionary weapons against the existing order "when it must be." However, he rejects the religious justification and glorification of these actions (R I 383–84).

Unlike the anarchist, Barth does not reject a highly political participation in the state but is reminded of Marx's call for permanent revolution, which was still influential among radical Social Democrats. For Barth the love of Christ functioned as "the hope, the unquiet, the longing, the radical and permanent revolution" (R I:353). Barth believed that in the midst of the disillusionment of the contemporary Leninist project of liberation and revolution, humanity expected "the fulfilled historical hour when the now-dying embers of Marxist dogma will flare up anew as world truth, when the socialist Church will rise from the dead in a world become socialist"[45]

In McCormack's view, following Anzinger's interpretation, Barth's vision of divine world revolution can be found in its structural form in the idea of Rosa Luxemburg (1870– or 1871–1919), who was the chief theoretician of left-wing German socialism and a powerful critic of Lenin's concept of a dictatorship of the proletariat.[46] Although Barth knew of

---

45. In *Church Dogmatics* Barth mentioned Marxism in speaking of eschatology "which Karl Marx gave to his followers as the supreme good and as the appropriate driving motive for socialist action on the way to it" (*CD* II/2: 388).

46. McCormack, *Critically Realistic*, 175. Cf. Anzinger, *Glaube und kommunikative Praxis*, 227–28. Luxemburg critiqued Lenin's idea as a mechanical transference of Blanquist principles, i.e., the organization of conspiratorial groups to the social-democratic movement. In Lenin's thought Blanquism plots to destroy the existing order by a coup d'état involving conspiratorial ideology. Luxemburg's principle of spontaneity of the masses would contradict the dictatorship of the proletariat, in which the proletariat is organized by professional functionaries of the revolution. In Luxemburg's view, the dictatorship of the proletariat would be replaced by the dictatorship of a clique.

Luxemburg at the time of his Tambach lecture (1919), Luxemburg did not totally negate resonance of the dictatorship of the proletariat.[47]

Barth's critical reflection on the postrevolutionary social order in Russia plays a decisive role in considering whether or not to participate in the process of realizing world revolution, whereas Lenin's optimistic overestimation of his revolution in Russia signals a possibility of distorting the genuine revolutionary concern and spirit. What is important for Barth is to engage in the praxis of liberation and the struggle for establishing the precondition of the world revolution of God in solidarity with the poor and oppressed in the process of revolution. Barth's political eschatology is not merely future oriented but concretely involves a praxis of liberation that remains faithful to the radical, permanent revolution of God. This divine revolution is constantly in pursuit of new social justice and order in light of the breakthrough of the kingdom of God in the world.

The General Strike in November 1918

As Eberhard Busch reports, in the summer of 1917 Barth was involved in the formation of trade unions.[48] Conflict arose in the village at the end of August. Barth appeared as one of the speakers at a demonstration. Arthur Hüssy said in the minutes: "The Socialists would not have been successful without the help of the pastor. The pastor agitated for them. The result was the cohesion of the Free Thinkers on their side."[49] Near the end of 1917 the Socialists in Safenwil won the political village council election over the free thinkers, and the socialists grew much stronger that year throughout the whole of Switzerland. Furthermore, the economic situation among the working class deteriorated rapidly. In August there were general warning strikes and demonstrations against rising inflation. In the middle of November, after knowledge of the Bolshevik revolution in Russia was spread abroad, there were violent sympathy demonstrations in Zurich. Although the left wing of the party did not take part, representatives of pacifist groups, such as Willi Münzenberg, participated. These demonstrations resulted in the death of four people in Zurich.

47. Geras, *Legacy of Rosa Luxemburg*, 50.
48. Busch, *Karl Barth: His Life*, 103–4.
49. Marquardt, "Aktuar," 126.

In November 1917, when troops intervened in a celebration of the Bolshevik revolution by left-wing socialists in Zurich, the conflict between government and workers in Switzerland intensified. The general strike in Switzerland arose for various reasons. One of the most important reasons was the miserable economic situation of the workers, which was made manifest in their economic demands. In January 1918 the Swiss national parliament drafted a bill to address the difficulty of food supply in which responsible nonmilitary people from sixteen to sixty years old were conscripted into various forms of civil service. As a result, workers could be militarized and forced to accommodate to civil occupations and subjected to the control of martial law. Against this government measure the so-called Olten Action Committee was formed in the small village town of Olten near Basel under the initiative of Robert Grim (February 4, 1918). Here the SPS also joined with leaders of various trade unions. Thereby a committee of seven members, which consisted of three representative of SPS (Robert Grimm, Friedrich Schneider, and Rosa Bloch) and four representatives of trade unions (Karl Duerr, Konrad Ilg, August Huggler, and Franz Reichmann), were organized. In the first meeting they appointed Robert Grimm as the president and Karl Dürr as the secretary.

The Olten Action Committee was thus founded and held authority to decide on a common response about conscription as well as economic and political programs. At the Bern conference (March 1–3, 1918), the Olten Action committee was enlarged to include two more representatives: Ernest-Paul Graber for the SPS and Charles Schürch for the Swiss trade union were elected by voting; and Fritz Platten replaced Rosa Bloch. In addition, the committee decided against the government's prohibitions of "Freie Jugend," and "Jugend-Internationale," and against the government's decision to oust Willi Münzenberg.[50] In July, with consent of a Swiss Workers' Congress, the Committee succeeded in gaining authority to call for a mass strike that included the closing down of trains and newspapers.

Grimm proposed a document that dealt with various phases of the general strike. This so-called "civil-war memorial" includes 1) general agitation and increased demonstrations through the press, pamphlets, flyers, and proclamations; 2) increasing agitation through demonstration

---

50. Schmidt-Ammann. *Wahrheit über den Generalstreik von 1918*, 89.

during the workday; 3) increasing action through a limited general strike and its contingent repetition; and 4) applying the strike in general as an unlimited measure, which would lead to open revolutionary fighting and to the period of open civil war.[51]

Although Grimm described in this memorial document a revolutionary way of overcoming the civil state, the question of a general strike had already been discussed in its various dimensions with the trade union congress on September 15, 1913, which was held in response to the local general strike in Zurich (July 11, 1912). In this resolution the Swiss trade union rejected the so-called revolutionary general strike. However, in relation to the third point above, a mass strike could be supported as a defensive protest action when the government's measures threatened common life interest or the indispensable rights and freedom of the working class. In such cases, they concluded, there was no other alternative except for a mass strike.[52] In 1918 the Olten Action Committee took the third point of the resolution of September 15, 1913, into consideration.

If the general strike were seen in this light, it would move in a social reform effort toward improved living conditions by legislating new economic and social programs rather than by inspiring revolutionary movements to overthrow the government. Strike action taken against a miserable economic situation could not be interpreted as revolutionary action in a Marxist-Leninist sense. The workers' association did not try to use its economic demands as the basic strategy for the sake of fundamental transformation and revolution of the political structure. In addition, it is noteworthy that Platten, one of the important representatives of Leninism in Switzerland, resided in Russia for most of 1918, and Münzenberg was no longer in a position to exercise his influence on the strike action since his imprisonment in November of 1918. In protest of Robert Grimm's leadership, Platten withdrew from the committee on August 28, 1918. Criticizing Grimm, Platten said that he'd rather sink into the International than make such diluted politics together.[53]

---

51. Egger, *Entstehung der Kommunistischen Partei*, 125.

52. Ibid., 93.

53. Ibid., 145. The Olten Action Committee was portrayed as the "hesitation apparatus" by "Volksrecht," and people in leadership such as Ilg condemned the committee members as "petite-bourgeois politicians" and Grimm and Greulich as "opportunists" (ibid., 192).

On October 28, 1918 the leftist members of SPS decided to celebrate the first-year anniversary of the October Revolution in Russia on November 10, and thus call for a revolutionary fight in accordance with Russian proletarian revolution. In a meeting on October 17, Platten declared that all left-wing groups should unite themselves for the union of radical leftists in support of Russia. The end of the war was near, and it was believed that the fight for socialism must be taken seriously. However, against this propaganda, Greulich responded that Bolshevism showed a distorted picture of socialism. This would not be the way of the Swiss working class. Besides, the west Swiss newspaper printed an extract of Lenin's pamphlet on *Die Aufgabe der Linken von Zimmerwald in der Sozialdemokratischen Partei der Sweiz*; therefore it was interpreted that the real plan was for subversion. In this pamphlet, which was written in November 1916, Lenin wrote polemically against Zimmerwald centralist Grimm and represented his famous standpoint on the means of the revolutionary fight.

According to Fritz Brupbacher, who belonged to the Zimmerwald leftists, Lenin's work was regarded as a kind of platform for the SPS. Münzenberg, Platten, and Radek followed in the footsteps of Lenin. Lenin's manuscript, which was given to his friend in Geneva, Henri Guilbeaux, was published in 1918. All Leninist followers opposed the Olten Action Committee. When the political situation became tense in Zurich on November 5, 1918, the government decided to send troops (based on the request of General Wille), possibly in preparation to intervene. The Olten Action Committee appealed to the government to pull back the troops, however, with no avail. The troops' intervention aroused the anger of the working class. Thus the Olten Action Committee made the decision to proclaim a twenty-four-hour protest strike in nineteen cities from November 7 to 9.

On November 10 the Committee called for a nationwide mass strike, presenting a nine-point list of demands. These included 1) the immediate election of a new national parliament; 2) the right of women to vote; 3) the introduction of work; 4) the introduction of a forty-eight-hour working week in all public and private manufactures; 5) the reorganization of the army in the pattern of a people's army; 6) the guarantee of providing foodstuffs for life, in agreement with the agricultural farmers; 7) the introduction of a national old-age– and disability-insurance program; 8) the establishment of a state monopoly for imports and exports; and 9) the declaration of the responsibility of the rich for the state debt.[54]

In response the government refused all demands and called for an immediate cessation of the strike. The strike proceeded for the most part without bloodshed or violence. The general strike lasted from November 12 to 14. Then the general strike arrived at the fourth phase, as we see in Grimm's memorial document, that is, open civil war and removal of the capitalist state. However, the Olten Action Committee did not dare to do that. Mr. Hilfiker gave the following statement in the minutes of the church: "As a result of the day's events [i.e., the general strike, which had to come to its high point in the period of November 11–14] there was a gathering of the free thinkers, out of which Safenwil now had a civil defense group [a bourgeois self-defense group against the threatening revolutionary elements, such as had formed in those days in many places throughout Switzerland]."[55]

On this occasion, Mr. Ernst Hüssy-Senn made the following statement: "One of the worst supporters of socialism is the pastor. He namely, in a private conversation in a family, glorified the Strike, saying that the Swiss government 'let poor children starve,' and that the Strike was necessary because of the 'higher wages' paid by the Swiss National Railroad to its workers."[56] The participation of the railroad workers in the nationwide strike posed a difficult problem for the Olten Committee. The wage and personnel policies of the National Assembly since the beginning of the war made the railroad workers especially angry.[57]

On November 14 the strike action was ended by decision of the Action Committee, regardless of the fact that the government remained stubborn and adamantly refused to meet any demands. The cessation of the strike was due to the fact that the Committee was fearful of violent outbreaks, and control over striking workers was tenuous at best. The Swiss bourgeoisie celebrated the cessation of the strike as a great victory while leftists spoke of capitulation or a betrayal by the Olten Action Committee. Although left-wing socialists had expected more than a mere protest from this event, the goal of the strike was not revolutionary in

---

54. Ibid., 132–33.
55. Marquardt, "Aktuar," 127.
56. Ibid., 128.
57. Schmidt-Ahmman, *Wahrheit über den Generalstreik von 1918*, 128.

conduct or scale. It was a protest against an unjust economic situation in order to alleviate the plight of the workers by introducing and legislating socially and economically better programs by the government.[58]

In regard to the events of November 1918, Thurneysen wrote to Karl Barth: "So where does the journey go from here? Towards world Bolshevism? Only one thing is clear to me: we must think of the kingdom of God consistently as 'other' and keep our hope pure from all democratic and other 'preliminary stages.'"[59] As the strike unfolded, however, Barth complained of missing an organic connection between the two worlds: "If only we had been converted to the Bible *earlier* so that we would now have solid ground under our feet! One broods alternately over the newspaper and the New Testament and sees fearfully little of the organic connection between the two worlds concerning which one should now to be able to give a clear and powerful witness. Or is it different for you?"[60]

In response Thurneysen made it clear, in regard to the deeper meaning of the general strike and revolutionary changes, that there was an organic connection between the movement of God and the revolutionary events in Switzerland, Germany, and Russia. "It is true that this crying of poor, tormented, unfortunate men and women often expresses itself in a stormy and unruly way . . . Such men and women would often like most to shatter the old world and bring in the new by force."[61] Therefore by Thurneysen's interpretation, the root cause of this event lay in a longing for a new world, which had been implanted by God in the hearts of workers. Because of his inflammatory address in his parish, Thurneysen found himself denounced locally as a Bolshevik pastor.[62] However, their longing for a new world through this event became the saddest thing of all by remaining without "fruits of righteousness" [Heb 12:11].[63]

In the years 1917–1919 Barth experienced the revolution in Russia and the general strike in Switzerland and the third International. In the year 1932 Barth presented a book to Fritz Lieb with the inscription: "To

58. Mattmüller, *Leonhard Ragaz und der religiöse Sozialismus*, 2:375.

59. McCormack, *Critically Realistic*, 187–88; cf. Eduard Thurneysen's letter to Karl Barth, October 30, 1918, in *B-Th I*, 299.

60. Karl Barth's letter to Eduard Thurneysen, November 11, 1918, in Smart, *Revolutionary Theology*, 45.

61. McCormack, *Critically Realistic*, 188, cf. Eduard Thurneysen, *Die neue Zeit*, 77.

62. Thurneysen's letter to Barth, January 13, 1919, in *B-Th I*, 309.

63. Thurneysen's letter to Barth, November 14, 1918, in *B-Th I*, 301–2.

the representative of the 3rd International from a representative of 2 ½ International."[64] In connection with the fight for the formation of a Communist International in the year after 1918, there was an international gathering of socialists that was bound to the Communist International in its critique of majority socialism of the Social Democratic Party in Europe. This group rejected Moscow centralism, which was in charge of formulating twenty-one points to build up the Third International. In protest of the twenty-one points, Graber and Grimm opted to participate in the Second International instead. The first summons to this gathering was issued on December 7, 1920 in Berne. Barth placed himself in this line. The adherents of Second International stood on common ground with the communists of the 1915 Zimmerwald Conference, but they were against social patriotism and Moscow centralism. Barth spoke about the problem of violence in this context. Principally, according to Barth, the person who justifies violence is no longer a socialist. One must make every effort to overcome it: "The previous social system is grounded in violence. Principally socialism cannot think of using violence as a means. Admittedly, there are no pure politics, even socialistic politics cannot be pure."

For that reason Barth could only affirm violence in the following cases: "a) if in the defensive against an illegal enemy, b) for a decisive moment of the victory."[65] This last criterion is for Barth illuminating and characteristic. He set this principle against actions of mere revolutionary steam, or revolutionary potency, which he addressed specifically in the second edition of *Romans*, arguing that "demonstration against the red Brother" is not an antirevolutionary action. Rather it is the programmatic criterion of whether a revolution is to be carried out or not. In the "Socialist Speeches," it means: "If radical intention and time are ripe—is there the power toward revolution?" We need "not feeling, but careful practical deliberation." The decision lay in the question of whether the proletariat trusted in will and power for themselves. In this connection Barth critiqued the Swiss general strike since no decision was made in the strike. Therefore, conflict continued. Barth asked, is there "overthrowing

---

64. Gollwitzer, "Kingdom of God and Socialism in the Theology of Karl Barth," in Hunsinger, *Karl Barth and Radical Politics*, 112.

65. Marquardt, "Erster Bericht über Karl Barths 'Sozialistisches Reden,'" 483.

will of the Olten committee? Does not an error about the situation lie in this direction? "⁶⁶

In the midst of the general strike, however, Barth fell ill with influenza and was forced to remain in bed. Shortly after recovering from influenza, Barth "appraised" or explained the general strike as a consequence of the political situation. Consequently a rumor spread around the village that Barth 'praised' the general strike. On February 19, 1919 he resumed his activity in his workers' association by expounding political events "as our workers say of such explanation." On the same day Barth led a discussion in the workers' association about the general strike of November 1918. Barth collected all materials available and concluded that the authorities had reacted to the general strike only with repressive forces. Even the bourgeoisie recognized that the general strike resulted from the political and economic victimization of the workers in society. The class-conscious burgeoisie would only stir up the desire for revolution in the lower classes. Barth was also aware that the neck-breaking aspects of a radical Bolshevist position had become clearly apparent in the course of the strike. Barth's own position, however, stood against Bolshevism and for a radicalized socialism. He spoke about the meeting of the Second International at the beginning of February in Berne and about the conference of the Swiss Socialist Party, which at the time rejected the Second International. Then he spoke about the Russian Revolution, which should be attempted but not imitated.

On May Day (Labor Day) he even marched with his workers behind the red flag to Zofingen. "He was not ashamed of taking the side of the workers."⁶⁷ In a motion, the president of the Free Thinkers, merchant Hans Widmer, read: "The pastor glorifies Spartakism and Bolshevism, deals in socialist propaganda, writes inflammatory articles in Labor's Newspaper, takes part in May Day marches, and on these accounts neglects his office as pastor."⁶⁸ However, it is a lie to claim that Barth glorified Bolshevism and Spartakism because he had done precisely the opposite by warning the workers that this would not be the right way.

> The kingdom of God is the kingdom of God. We cannot conceive of the transition from the analogies of the divine reality to hu-

---

66. Ibid., 483–84.
67. Busch, *Karl Barth: His Life*, 106–7.
68. Marquardt, "Aktuar," 132.

man reality radically enough .... The new Jerusalem has not the least to do with the new Switzerland and the revolutionary state of the future; it comes to earth in God's great freedom, when the time has arrived. Of course this hope does not sap courage and strength. ... for the things of today and of this world, it supplies them.[69]

Social Questions in Germany, the Blumhardt Movement and Karl Barth

In the 1919 obituaries written in commemoration of Friedrich Naumann and Christoph Blumhardt (titled *Vergangenheit und Zukunft*), both of whom died in August of the same year, Barth complained that the Christian socialist, Naumann, together with his friend Stoecker, an enlightened preacher to the imperial court, never arrived at the new great thing as anticipated through the secularization of the evangelical social intentions.

Naumann (1860–1919) was born in Leipzig and studied theology there from 1879 to 1883.[70] He involved himself in activities with John Wichern's place of education, *Rauches Haus*, in Hamburg, whose idea of inner mission proved a formative influence upon Naumann. As a pastor in an industrial community in Saxony, Naumann came into contact firsthand with the social problems of workers. As an industrial chaplain in Frankfurt, he was interested in the program of Social Democracy and began to read the New Testament in relation to the social questions of the poor. In this study he discovered a message of the New Testament so radical and so revolutionary that it aimed at the transformation of the world (*ADT* 39; Robinson, *Beginnings*, 36).

Taking leadership of inner mission in 1880, Naumann engaged in a fundamental renewal of Protestantism. He became a major representative of a liberal-minded group in the Evangelical-Social Congress in that he was opposed to the political conservatism of Adolf Stoecker. In Naumann's view, the charitable work of the inner mission was not competent to deal with social problems adequately. He began to take a different stance toward the Social Democrats than Stoecker did. For Naumann, the Social Democrats, wedded to a social concern for Christianity, posed a serious

---

69. Busch, *Karl Barth: His Life*, 109.
70. Welch, *Protestant Thought*, 2:242–44.

challenge to Christianity. He studied the writings of Marx, Lassalle, and Liebknecht, thus considering socialism to be a theoretical basis for improving the religious-moral narrowness of the inner mission. This spirit is represented in the words of Barth: "Is it possible that the godless Social Democrats (they were fighting against the church!) understood God better than the church did? Was it possible that the church needed to repent and turn to the God of the godless?" (*ADT* 40; Robinson, *Beginnings*, 37).

In 1889 Naumann brought a workers' catechism to the world with a program for social reform in which we see restrictions on free capital accumulation, extension of social security benefits for the workers, the due right to work, limitation of women's hard work, protection of Sabbath vacation, and the like. For him Jesus was a man of the people and appears as a friend of the poor with religious openness to the world. What Naumann envisaged was a new social Christianity with an introduction of the "social Jesus," "the Jesus of the poor and oppressed according to the picture of St. Francis of Assisi" (*ADT*: 40; Robinson, *Beginnings* 37) and in favor of social programs by reform in economic and political realms. With this idea Naumann became a major leader in shaping the direction of the Evangelical Social Congress in the 1890s. Naumann's concern in his numerous lectures and articles was "the relation of Christianity to the social question" and contrasting "the false socialism with the true socialism" (*ADT* 40; Robinson, *Beginnings*, 37).

However, gradually a strong concern for a Christian social program for reform was left behind. Instead, national inspiration of German imperialism began to forge a direction toward "a religious veneration of nature and of modern culture" (*ADT* 40; Robinson, *Beginnings*, 37). Thus Naumann became involved in forming the National-Social Party in 1896. He regarded imperial Germany as the best political form for the worker.

Eventually Naumann gave up his conviction of dealing with social questions in terms of Jesus' message. He came to regard Francis of Assisi as "a good, noble fool, who has nothing to teach us in the age of the telegraph and express trains" (*ADT* 41; Robinson, *Beginnings*, 38). His program for Christian socialism gave way to a national socialism. In 1917 he supported the resolution of the Democratic (middle-leftist liberal) parties in the *Reichstag* for peace of communication, and founded a state city school (*Hochschule* for politics, founded in 1920). The following year he became a cofounder of the *Deutsche Demokratische Partei*. For the sake of "the new trinity of democracy, industry, and world power" (*ADT* 41; Robinson, *Beginnings*, 38) Naumann turned to the world of conservative politics.

In his obituary for Naumann, Barth mentioned his first knowledge of the subtitle of the newspaper *Die Hilfe* as a schoolboy when he saw it on his father's desk. The strong words—"Help for God, help for one's brother, help for the state, help for oneself" (*ADT* 40; Robinson, *Beginnings* 37)—made an impression on him, although he did not understand them at the time. In July 1914 Barth, in a lecture as well as a contribution to the *Christliche Welt*, criticized Naumann. Because of his compromise, Naumann was insignificant in relation to war and capitalism. In his "Socialist Speeches," Barth determined his political and theological place in opposition to Naumann (July 1914).

Barth asked: "is, according to Naumann, the idea still to fight? Is the existing or the ought-to-be important? Are the compromises grasped and treated as something provisional? Which is greater, the unrest, the desire for an absolute future, or the enjoyment of the relativities of the present? Is the idea related to the reality, otherwise is the idea reversed?" According to Barth, in Naumann there is at last pleasure in the "aesthetically transfigured reality that is greater than the pleasure of the idea. As reality one tolerates in an unexamined manner: (a) Bourgeois-capitalistic economic development, (b) the national state, (c) the war." At this point Barth blames Naumann for completely abandoning the protest against this "reality" and instead giving the strongest weight to proclaiming relative realities. Naumann lacked enthusiasm and faith for overcoming the world, which he relegated quietly into personal feeling. He approved the endeavor of social democracy only inside the existing order.

Barth rejected Naumann for his "uncomprehending opposition to all social democratic radicalism." For Naumann, capital, technology, the workers' movement, racial differences, competition, and war were still only objects of moral will, and he discussed in general only disconnected ethical demands instead of going along with the question of God. Barth characterizes this fact as Naumann's "moral misunderstanding of Christianity." For Barth it is not the practical question but the God-question that is of utmost importance. We expect more from God, place ourselves therefore more critically before the real, and make the ideal therefore prevail in a more lively way. From this text (July 21, 1914), we notice that Barth critiqued any socialism that wanted to work only within the existing order.

In April 1915 Barth and Thurneysen went to Marburg during wartime where his brother Peter wedded Martin Rade's daughter. Barth engaged in a passionate argument with him, but was only frustrated by him. In the words of Naumann: "all religion is now right for us, whether it is called the Salvation Army or Islam, if it only helps us to hold out through the war" (*ADT* 42; Robinson, *Beginnings* 39). Naumann failed to make a distinction between a Christian social goal and a national social goal. By lacking such a distinction, Naumann and the other religious socialists betrayed the New Testament. According to Barth, Naumann had in essence turned away from the God who instigates the renewal of the whole world, the transformation of life.

In all of this a pathetic attempt was made to find meaning in the nonsense of life under the given conditions. The church advocated in its teaching the maintenance and establishment of equilibrium, together with the social reform that is a "careful protection of capitalism, democratization with deep respect for the Kaiser and the military, development of personality, but preferably only in the realm of German inwardness" (*ADT* 41; Robinson, *Beginnings* 38). Barth accused Naumann of dedicating his life to this value as the highest and the ultimate in his life. As Barth complains, "Naumann was back where he had started—with the God who acts inscrutably, with the religion of the soul which may seek comfort and power in the world, but does not seek victory *over* the world" (*ADT* 43; Robinson, *Beginnings* 39). As the spiritual leader of left-wing German liberalism after Bismarck, Naumann became a famous speaker in parliament. Although he had an interest in the movements for trade unions and cooperatives, Naumann was no longer able to "understand the heart, the spirit, of socialism." Rather he proclaimed and advocated to the Social Democrats "reason, moderation, and opportunism" (*ADT* 43; Robinson, *Beginnings* 39). The consequence of the secularization of Christian social principles among most German religious socialists led to the support of the German state and Kaiser Wilhelm's war policy of 1914. Thus, "[Naumann's] figure is the embodiment of the tragic greatness, guilt, and shame, not only of his people, but of our whole age" (*ADT* 43; Robinson, *Beginnings* 40).

If for Stoecker and Naumann pietism fell in the gray zone of German nationalism, then Blumhardt ushered pietism into a more radical and prophetic direction. Blumhardt made a prophetic witness in relating the kingdom of God dynamically to the world.

According to Blumhardt (1842–1919), we Christians are called to become participants in the progress for the kingdom of God. Our progress comes from God outward. The in-breaking reality of God's kingdom includes a developmental progress of God's kingdom in the world; however it does not mean confusion or conflation of the divine with the human. The life of God is not from humans but from God onward. In coming from God, history is integrated by virtue of the incarnation and the resurrection. As Barth states, "Blumhardt had a fine, keen ear for the sighing for redemption which runs through all of creation and mankind" (*ADT* 46; Robinson, *Beginnings*, 42).

In Blumhardt's thought there is a tension between the present and future realization of God's kingdom. The reality of God that has not yet arrived on earth can be found in the continuous incarnation of Christ in creation and in history. We participate in God's fight in creation and history and stand in hope of the final victory of God. This is a resistance of hope against the darkness of the present moment, and at the same time a confession of hope in expectation of God's consummation.

In seeing Jesus as the incarnate presence of God in the world and the cross as a symbol calling for responsibility and solidarity between human beings, Blumhardt relativized all that exists, whether Christian or non-Christian, in light of the reality of the in-breaking kingdom of God. God speaks and manifests God's will to the heathen as well as to the Christian. An involvement with people of the world comes to the fore for the sake of the kingdom.[71] Blumhardt's theology of God's kingdom is of universal scope, including both Christians and the heathen. Furthermore, missions as a way of Europeanizing or Christianizing becomes meaningless because God's presence can be found in other cultures and languages. In Barth's words, "he also saw more clearly the light of the promise and the faith into which *all* men, *all* relationships and movements, particularly of the "worldly" life are brought by the gospel; as a result, he focused his attention on a variety of spheres and areas of life to which his father's eyes had not been fully opened" (*ADT* 46; Robinson, *Beginnings*, 42).[72]

---

71. Blumhardt, *Reden* 1:151. "'Blumhardt is involved with unbelievers!' Yes, dear people, I am freely involved with unbelievers; I am involved with the entire world much more than you know. And I hope to have much more to do with the world!"

72. Blumhardt's remark becomes obvious: "My father once wrote to me that I should

Blumhardt's turn to the world for the sake of the poor, abused and miserable occurred in his political years from 1899 to 1906. Joining the German Social Democratic Party (SPD), he wrestled with the social structure of injustice, violence, suffering, and predicament in which he understood his involvement as a new service of God in the world.

He spent six years in the *Landestag* until retiring from political work in 1906. Blumhardt's confession to conversion to socialism is not ideologically colored and biased; it is rather a way of expressing and deepening his concern for service of God's in-breaking reality in the world. As Barth says, "because he believed in God, he also believed in man, and because he believed in man, he also believed in the renewal of the world" (*ADT* 46; Robinson, *Beginnings*, 43). Although he expressed his agreement with socialism's political efforts and social concerns, he was hesitant to identify socialism with the kingdom of God.

Rather than being driven by socialist theory, Blumhardt saw the SPD as an instrument of protest against nationalism, religious individualism, and the dark side of industrial capitalism. Thus Blumhardt recognized the parabolic character of SPD for the sake of God's kingdom. Blumhardt, like Naumann, had a keen interest in modern technology and evolution and became a great friend of nature and of natural science; he learned from nature "the joyous message of the inexhaustibility of the possibilities of life," that is "a parable of the resurrection" (*ADT* 47; Robinson, *Beginnings* 43). His reflection upon every human movement and cultural achievement in light of parable or preparation kept him from indulging into one-sided admiration of human beings and their achievements. For Blumhardt, "all that is perishable is but a parable, but still a parable of the *imperishable*" (*ADT* 47; Robinson, *Beginnings*, 43).

With this idea Blumhardt distanced himself from the Christian and national socialist movement of Stoecker and Naumann. "The social movement must become a human movement, not a bourgeois and national movement . . . It must be a loud protest against the spilling of blood, against everything that means oppression."[73] In comparison with an attempt to blend the Christian gospel with German patriotism from

---

make it a rule for myself at all times to view everyone as a believer, never to doubt it, and never to talk to a person in any other way. This found an echo in my own soul. If a Mohammedan comes, I call him a believer, I never accept that anyone is an unbeliever . . . Every human being believes, because God believes" (*Reden* 1:133).

73. Ibid., 255.

Wichern via Stoeker to Naumann, we notice Blumhardt's prophetic vision on social questions in light of God's kingdom in that we see the great divine "Forward!" as a driving force, characterizing Blumhardt's prophetic socialism (*ADT* 46; Robinson, *Beginnings*, 43).

In 1907 Blumhardt left the political world. Despite his retreat from the political world, he did not abandon his passion for connecting the in-breaking reality of God and the betterment of social progress for humanity. Rather, in 1910 he wrote to Ragaz, who was at this time a leading religious socialist in Switzerland: "A movement of the Spirit of Christ proceeds through the times."[74] In condemning the war as contrary to the essence of Christ, Blumhardt made this radical statement: "Here there is neither Jew nor Greek, neither British nor French; here is the kingdom of God, in the view of Christ the living one."[75] He never compromised his stance against nationalism, chauvinism, and the war. His eschatological hope never extinguished at its heart.

According to Barth, the controlling passion in Blumhardt's movement was to bear witness to the living God. He characterizes what shaped Blumhardt's dynamic dialectics between hurrying and waiting in terms of "hope—hope for a visible and tangible appearing of the lordship of God over the world . . . hope for radical help and deliverance from the former state of the world . . . hope for all, for mankind . . . hope for the physical side of life as well as for the spiritual" (*ADT* 48–49; Robinson, *Beginnings*, 41–42). For Blumhardt, with this hope in mind, belief in God meant to take in earnest this all-embracing hope for the world. Blumhardt considered and dealt with everything in light of this great hope by placing one's self and one's life in the great light of this hope.

In contrast to Naumann, Blumhardt did not intend to secularize the universalism of the New Testament or to Christianize social democracy. Rather "Blumhardt's secret was his endless movement between hurrying and waiting, between the lively participation in the fullness of what is and astonished inner waiting for that which occurs through the power from on high. In his relation to God, he achieved also a vital relation to his own time. No world war and no revolution could make him a liar" (*ADT* 48; Robinson, *Beginnings*, 44). Blumhardt's sense of eschatological hope provided Barth with a path for his own dialectical theology in

---

74. Ibid., 272.
75. *Reden* 3:183–84.

a parabolic-analogical sense in light of eschatology. We see in Barth's speech on "the Christian's place in Society" at the Tambach conference his dialectical theology in accordance with Blumhardt's spirit. Barth is indebted to Blumhardt for his future direction in dialectical encounter and supplementation between "the hurrying and the waiting, the worldly and the divine, the present and the coming, again and again met, were united . . . sought and found one another" (*ADT* 49; Robinson, *Beginnings*, 45). Barth's reflection on analogy and parable also was shaped and motivated in accordance with the great hope of God's kingdom and the political radicalism that could be found in Blumhardt. At least Blumhardt remained a significant figure for Barth in his theological development as a witness to "the victory of the future over the past" (*ADT* 49; Robinson, *Beginnings*, 45).[76]

---

76. Later in *Church Dogmatics* IV/3 (§69.3. "Jesus Is Victor"), Barth discussed Blumhardt's message in light of the prophetic work of Jesus Christ. Furthermore, in his posthumously published writing on "Ethics as a Task of the Doctrine of Reconciliation," Barth related Blumhardt's message to the struggle for social justice. *KD* IV/4 [Nachlass], 425.

THREE Karl Barth between Hope and Disillusionment: The Tambach Lecture of 1919

The Political Situation in Germany and Switzerland

AS ONE SHOULD HAVE SURMISED BY NOW, TO TRULY APPRECIATE KARL Barth's theology as a theology of the action of God for the world, one has to be open to the political situation that forms the crucible for his thought. Groundbreaking events form the background for Barth's revolutionary theology. Such is the case when one considers Barth's Tambach lecture. On December 22, 1917 there was a formal negotiation for a treaty of peace held at Brest-Litovsk between Russia and Germany. Then on March 3, 1918 the Treaty of Brest-Litovsk was signed. Lenin reflectively wrote in an article, "A Hard but Necessary Lesson," in *Pravda*, that the Treaty of Brest-Litovsk would "appear as one of the greatest historical turning points in the history of the Russian, and international, revolution."[1]

The German political situation in the aftermath of the revolution of November 1918 was extremely complex. As we have already seen, the German Social Democratic Party (SPD) came out in support of the national war policy in August 1914 by seeking "to capture and use the state, not to overthrow it."[2] In 1919 "the Wilsonian program of liberal democracy, national self-determination and a League of Nations as the custodian of peace" made a serious appeal to the Social Democrats. Comrades on the extreme left separated from the Social Democrats in 1917 over the renewal of war credits. As a result, some important mem-

---

1. Quoted in Carr, *Bolshevik Revolution: 1917–1923, vol. 3*, 60.
2. Carr, *German-Soviet Relations*, 5.

bers left to form a new party, the Independent Socialist Party (USPD).³ It retained socialist intellectuals and the Spartacus League in professing a revolutionary Marxist program. The Spartacus League was formed early in 1916 under the leadership of Rosa Luxemburg and Karl Liebknecht, and became the nucleus of the future German Communist Party (KPD). In 1917 the League, while remaining a separate body, joined the left wing of the Social Democrats that had formed the USPD.

Apart from the Spartacus League, which was famous for its revolutionary propaganda, most of the Independent Social Democrats were more pacifist than revolutionary. Once the war was over, the USPD dissolved, then its members joined either the KPD or the reconstituted SPD. After the war, however, most of people in Germany were ready to hear the Wilsonian program of peace through democracy. The Independent Social Democratic leaders such Karl Kautski, Hilferding, and Haase were the most persistent critics of the Bolshevik Revolution. In addition, in Wilson's note of October 23, 1916, we perceive that he did not want to negotiate with William II: "If it [the government of the United States] is likely to have to deal with them later in regard to the international obligations of the German Empire, it must demand, not peace negotiations, but surrender."⁴ However, on October 2,8 the revolution from below in Germany started with the sailors' revolt in Kiel, which was precipitated by the ill-conceived decision to battle against the English by mobilizing eighty thousand soldiers. On October 29, the stockers went out on strike, on the very day when the fleet was scheduled to leave. When passive resistance turned into mutiny, the red flag flew from every ship. And when the success of the sailors' mutiny began to fan other sparks into flames, the leaders of Social Democrats demanded the emperor's abdication. Revolution spread throughout Germany.

A republic was proclaimed in Munich on November 8, 1918. The next morning the kaiser abdicated the throne, and the Social Democrats told Prince Max that they were ready to take over the government. Prince Max passed on to Friedrich Ebert (the chairman of the SPD) the office of imperial chancellor. Philipp Scheidemann (the second-ranking member of the party) thus proclaimed the birth of the German republic from

3. For Barth's sympathy to USPD, see Barth's letter to Thurneysen (June 13, 1921), in *B-Th I*, 495–96. For the understanding of the Second and a half International, see Egger, *Entstehung der Kommunistischen Partei*, 205–6.

4. Quoted in Eyck, *History of the Weimar Republic*, 37.

the steps of the *Reichstag*. In regard to the Spartacus League, Ebert was worried about the possibility of a Bolshevik-style revolution in Germany. What was at stake as the first duty of the government was for Ebert to proclaim "peace, security, and order."[5]

During the upheaval of 1918, the Spartacus League transformed itself into the German Communist Party, whose two outstanding leaders were Rosa Luxemburg and Karl Liebknecht. In 1916 the Imperial Military Court gave Liebknecht a four-year sentence for joining a street demonstration. In October 1918 Prince Max's cabinet set him free. Rosa Luxemburg was also set free due to the German revolution in November 1918. When the situation in Berlin became unbearable, Gustav Noske, who had played the role of imperial commissioner in Kiel at the time of the sailors' revolt, was appointed by Ebert as supreme commander to undertake the mission of normalizing order and restoring peace. On the night of January 5, 1919, the Spartacists launched an attempt to seize power by capturing the center of Berlin. The rebellion, however, was crushed. On the night of January 15-16 1919, after street fighting in Berlin, Liebknecht and Luxemburg were arrested by the police and murdered by reactionary freebooters.[6]

As E. H. Carr characterizes the situation in 1919, all roads in Germany led to Russia: "The extremists of the Left look upon her as the realization of their own political ideas; the pan-Germans look upon her as providing the only possible outlet for surplus population and compensation for the loss of colonies."[7] When the German revolution started in November 1918, the Bolsheviks were jubilant. The revolution, however, ended in disappointment for them and went in favor of the parliamentary constitution of the Weimar Republic. After the subjugation of the Spartacus uprising, the Republic exercised brutal repression on the League in Berlin and on the attempts to establish a Soviet republic in Munich. In February 1919 Karl Radek was arrested. (He had been the Soviet delegate at the founding congress of the German Communist Party.) In Weimar the central government had set its meeting on February 6, 1919. The Republic's first parliamentary cabinet was known as Weimar Coalition. President

---

5. Ibid., 50.

6. Frölich, *Rosa Luxemburg: Gedanke und Tat*, 325, 356-74; cf. Malanowski, *November-Revolution 1918*

7. Carr, *German-Soviet Relations*, 13.

Ebert selected his former colleague, Philip Scheidemann, as chancellor. Gustav Noske assumed leadership of the *Reichswehr*.

The general strike in November 1918 occurred in Switzerland. On October 1, 1918, before the general strike, bank workers in Zurich were striking. The workers' union organized in support of a local general strike. During this time (on June 13, 1919) there was a proclamation for international solidarity in Zurich with Rosa Luxemburg. The trade unions in Zurich and Basel intended to initiate a further comprehensive strike movement. The local general strike occurred in August 1919 in Basel. As a result of these events, the year 1919 saw a heated debate in the history of Swiss socialism regarding entrance of the SPS into the Third International. In mid-July the executive committee of the party voted to join the Comintern (120–10). On August 16–17 in Basel an extraordinary party congress meeting voted 318–147 for their entrance.

According to Marquardt's report on Barth's "Socialist Speeches," in the decisive years of 1917 and 1919, Barth lectured in his party many times, reporting on the world political situation with topics such as the peace outlook in 1917, the Swiss general strike in 1918, and the progress of Bolshevist Revolution in 1919. On one occasion Barth interpreted and commented on the first Soviet constitution, "The Declaration on the Rights of the Working and Exploited People." This lecture was a paragraph-by-paragraph analysis of the constitution over a period of several weeks to a Safenwil audience. As a consequence, Barth was confronted with the bourgeois rejection of this revolution. He also analyzed and commented on bill drafts (e.g., for a new Swiss factory law), in very arduous, detailed judicial work, and interpreted literature (e.g., under the headline "Conscience" a Tolstoy drama) and under the headline "The higher rights," and from the party newspaper, a story that belonged to the genre of light fiction.[8]

In February of 1919 Barth was active in the workers' association and made an evaluation in retrospect of the general strike. When Jacques Schmidt (1882–1960) argued against the dictatorship of the proletariat in resistance to Fritz Platten,[9] Barth took it into account, and Thurneysen was in agreement with Schmidt's position. Platten's program for the Third International was based on the militarism of the proletariat. However, it

8. Marquardt, "Erster Bericht über Karl Barths 'Sozialistische Reden,'" 471–72.

9. Schimdt, "Am Scheideweg. Schweitzerischer Parteitag und internationale Konferenz," in *Neuer Freier Aargauer* Nr. 34, (11.2. 1919).

led to a bloodbath. The democratic tradition in Switzerland was different from that of Russia, which called for a dictatorship until people could be trained for democracy. In Schmidt's view, the true revolution did not need the method of violent revolution.[10] Coupled with the communists, the adherents of the Third International were not completely against the dictatorship of the proletariat. However, Barth deviated in this decisive point from his like-minded comrades. On April 16, 1919, he spoke about this theme under the heading "Democracy or Dictator."

> *No judgment* about the Russian Party. The Principal significance of its attempt, let alone its historical attainment. Imitation is something else. How do we locate ourselves with respect to the deviation of our program in the Russian sense?—The Soviet constitution is another story, one to be considered seriously. Our democracy must be better adjusted to the realities of life. What is at stake is the issue of dictatorship, the character of minority rule, exclusivity, and violent overthrow [of the government]. Would we like to [follow the Soviet example] or not? If it happens without us, it is not an unjust retaliation, and I speak as a person, who suffers together with the others: the bourgeois have misused their position. Democracy and church have not proven themselves worthwhile. Violence calls for violence, but the question is whether we want that to happen.[11]

According to Barth, the principle of retaliation must be excluded because it is immature and unfruitful. Otherwise, it remains an upside-down world caught in an old solution. That being the case, the previous protest and the endeavor of Lenin's revoluiton would be untrue.

> The power of socialism bases itself on the fact that socialists were earnest in their demands . . . (a) The violent overthrow. In that case the new society is established on an old foundation. Hence, success does not justify the means . . . History calls for such violent eruptions—the goal is not achieved—concessions to human weakness should not to be made into a principle.—Possibility for us?! (b) Minority rule. The acknowledged errors of democracy are not remedied by abolishing democracy. Who protects us from the errors of the workers' leaders . . . ? . . . The minority should rule through its intellect, i.e., become a majority. (c) The exclusivity of

---

10. For an introduction to Schmidt's argument, see McCormack, *Critically Realistic*, 191–92.

11. Marquardt, "Erster Bericht über Karl Barths 'Sozialistische Reden,'" 484.

the working class . . . and the goal for the abolition of class? How about spiritual values? Thus: No, on the contrary make use of the present situation through political work, more of a co-operative system, more social formation![12] (my translation)

This is the position that Barth had called "more than Leninism" in his *Romans I*, and it is the reason he rejected Lenin as an anarchist. Barth preoccupied himself with Kropotkin in detail and reported on his socialist ideas in Safenwil. Barth's comment on the first postwar congress of the Second International, in which he took part as an observer, expresses his satisfaction: "The International marches again, not in the direction of social patriot, but in direction of Eisners, i.e. in direction toward the zeal of Munich council republic."[13] As we have already described in the relation between Ragaz and Landhauer, Landhauer's idea of socialism was without hierarchy or violence. When the German revolution broke out in late 1918, Landhauer was in Bavaria with his friend Kurt Eisner, who was leading the revolutionary movement. Rather than following Eisner's idea of a left-wing version of Social Democracy, Landhauer wanted an out-and-out workers council. In the early part of 1919, he participated in the Bavarian Workers Council. He was in charge of information when the council took over Munich. His idea of a "Socialist Alliance" in solidarity with Martin Buber would aim at forming a socialism of communality without enforcement and authority.

Landhauer's vision critiqued orthodox, or revisionist, Marxism and the socialistic party of the Second International. He was against the dominion of human beings over other human beings and the dictatorship of the proletariat. Barth was more concerned with a radical version of Social Democracy in the sense of Kurt Eisner, i.e., that the proletariat takes part in the holy fight representatively for other humans and is the bringer of renewal. Barth had at this time still affirmed and approved the Soviet constitution, "The Rights of Working and Exploited People" as "fight reprimand for the sake of previous socialistic confrontation regarding the claim of the Moscow centralism."

In the wake of Schmidt's article in the *Neuer Freier Aagauer*, Barth explained the Russian Revolution "as an attempt which had to be made but was not to be imitated." The revolution in Russia would become a dic-

---

12. Ibid., 484–85.
13. Ibid., 485.

tatorship rather than lead to a classless society. "The acknowledged shortcomings of democracy are not improved by its abolition."[14] In a "Word to the Citizens of Aargau" (July 10, 1919), Barth wrote an open letter to the Aargau bourgeoisie in face of the defeat of a moderate Social Democratic candidate by a bourgeois candidate. Barth asked, "Is it really necessary that things followed the same course with us that they are following in Russia and Germany; that the socialist movement is not taken seriously for so long until the day comes that it denies its roots and becomes a disastrous conflagration?"[15]

In the article "What Should Not Happen," Barth critiques Bolshevism as a brilliant deception. "The revolution envisioned by socialism is no more and no less than a conversion of the entire world, a conversion of the whole of humanity. Less is nothing."[16] "Bolshevism belongs to the old and not to the new being for which humanity longs . . . Socialism may not simply become the counterpart of capitalism, the proletariat an all-too similar successor of the bourgeoisie, the class struggle a mere fight of one beast against another. Bolshevism has no future. In the knowledge of that which does have a future, we cannot become Bolshevists."[17]

In addition to socialism in Russia, Barth cast a critical eye on the Weimar Republic in Germany, which was a watered-down version of socialism. For Barth, in the case of Bolshevism the right goal is envisioned in theory at a minimum but becomes bourgeois in its methodology and praxis. In the case of Weimar, the socialist goal is surrendered to the revisionists who stand in favor of a modified state capitalism. At any rate, in both cases the spirit of true socialism is betrayed.[18] The Swiss should not

---

14. Busch, *Karl Barth: His Life*, 106.

15. Barth, "Wort an das aargauische Bürgertum!" in *Neuer Freier Aargauer: Sozialdemokratisches Tagblatt*, July 10, 1919, 1. Quoted in McCormack, *Critically Realistic*, 192–93.

16. Barth, "Das was nicht geschehen soll," in *Neuer Freier Aargauer: Sozial demokratisches Tagblatt*, August 15, 1919, 1.Quoted in McCormack, *Critically Realistic*, 193.

17. Quoted in McCormack, *Critically Realistic*, 194.

18. McCormack's identification of Barth's position in the Tambach lecture with the watered-down socialism in the Weimar government is less convincing because Barth never regarded it as the best hope for Germany in the present reality of 1919. Cf. McCormack, *Critically Realistic*, 200. Rather Barth in one of his "Socialist Speeches" ("Democracy or Dictatorship") emphasized the direction of International toward the zeal of the Munich conciliar republic.

follow either example if it seeks true socialism. Barth warned the Socialist Party against joining the Third International, which was completely under the control of the Soviet Union.

The Tambach Lecture: The Christian Place in Society

Amid postrevolutionary confusion in Germany, there were pastors and theologians in Germany looking for something new in the church's life. A new journal called *Der Christliche Demokrat: Wochenblatt für das evangelische Haus* published its first issue on April 6, 1919, under the direction of Otto Herpel and George Fleming. Two pastors from Hessen, Herpel and Heinrich Schultheis, arranged a conference for religious socialists from September 22 to 25 at Tannenberg, a sanatorium in Tambach, Thuringia. The political views of the participants were diverse, but they were desperate for a new direction in the midst of the confusion of postwar Germany, and so took interest in religious socialism.[19] Those who attended the conference "were deeply concerned about the revolution which had taken place in recent years and now as Christians were on the look-out for new ways in political and church life."[20] Because the religious social movement in Switzerland was older and more prominent than in Germany, conference planners looked to the Swiss for speakers. Ragaz was the first choice as speaker, but he declined because of his active campaign against the Swiss party's entrance to the Third International. He also declined because of his poor physical health. Barth, who was almost unknown in Germany, was asked to give a lecture in Ragaz's place because Barth was regarded as one of Ragaz's followers. Conference planners gave Barth the lecture title "The Christian Place in Society." In his letter to Thurneysen, Barth wrote: "Here I send you what I have written for Tambach in uninterrupted day and nights shifts [a preliminary draft of "The Christian in Society"]. As you see, it has become a rather complicated kind of machine that runs backwards and forwards and shoots in all directions with no lack of both visible and hidden joints."[21] Although Barth's Tambach lecture is located between *Romans I* and *Romans II* in a

19. For historical background and a full account of the Tambach lecture, see Marquardt, *Christ in der Gesellschaft*, 7–24.
20. Busch, *Karl Barth: His Life*, 110.
21. Barth's letter to Thurneysen September 11, 1919, in Smart, *Revolutionary Theology*, 47.

chronological sense, it reveals important meaning for the development of Barth's thought, especially in regard to theology and politics, coexistence of dialectical method and analogy, and theology and culture. It is not merely an indication of a theological station in between *Romans I* and *Romans II*. Let's turn to examine and analyze Barth's lecture in Tambach.

The Present Situation of Society between Hope and Confusion

In the first section of his lecture, Barth discusses the Christian's political position in society. Rather than provide social ethical reflection or church politics in regard to the present society, he introduces and defines society's situation as one of conflict and contrast. Barth is concerned with the promise of God in the midst of social confusion: "We should like to be out of this society—and in another" ("Christian's Place in Society," 273).[22] We cannot turn away from life and society in suspicion and disillusionment. In spite of all transformation and overthrowing, however, everything remains as it was in the old thing. How do we then formulate and elaborate the Christian's place in society toward the great promise of God? In the midst of confusion surrounding us, Christians have something to offer. However, this is not the work of the noblest and most devoted Christians. Rather it is the work of Christ. "The Christian is *the Christ*. The Christian is that within us which is not ourselves but Christ in us" ("Christian's Place in Society," 273). "Christ in us," in the Pauline perspective, is meant to be "a presupposition of life" including "over us," "behind us," "beyond us." In light of Christ the Lord of all reality, namely, Christ in us, in Pauline perspective, the Christian and the society cannot be separated from one another.

Therefore, there should be no apartheid, no erecting of fences between Jews and Gentiles, the politically correct and the others, or between so-called Christians and so-called non-Christians. All are in Christ. As Barth remarks, "the community of Christ is a house open on every side; for Christ is always for the other, and he died even for those who are outside. There is in us, over us, behind us, beyond us—a consideration of the meaning of life, a reminder of the origin of human being, a turning to the Lord of the world, a critical no and a creative Yes in regard to all the

---

22. See the English translation in *Word of God and the Word of Man*, 273.

content of our consciousness, a facing away from the old and toward the new aeon. Its mark and fulfillment [is] the cross!"[23]

The Augustinian confession ("Thou wouldst not seek Me hadst thou not already found Me!") becomes a foundation for our real possession of Christ, in that "we acknowledge Christ, his present, and his future" ("Christian's Place in Society," 274). Barth's intent is to relate the Augustinian dictum to the social existence of humans in unrest: "We can no longer find rest apart from the kingdom of God" because "it is the Beyond itself that is the chief cause of our unrest" ("Christian's Place in Society," 317). If Christ is in us, society cannot be abandoned by God in spite of its wrong ways. However, this inclusiveness does not mean Christianizing all human actions and institutions in the society, or secularizing Christ in terms of a hyphenated Christianity: "The relation between "Christ in us" and the world is not merely a matter of opening the sluices and allowing the ready water to stream over the thirsty land" ("Christian's Place in Society," 276).

As Barth argues, all combinations like "social-Christian, social-evangelical, social-religious . . . and the like" are immediately handy, but the question is highly worth considering whether "the hyphens that we draw with such intellectual courage do not really make dangerous short circuits ("Christian's Place in Society," 276). Barth's decisive objection to every form of hyphenated Christianity would be later seen in his rejection of "Deutsche Christen" during National Socialism in Germany. It has nothing to do with an abstract *totaliter aliter* principle against the world of culture, society, and history. Rather it stands in great service to an anti-apartheid movement. What is at stake in the Tambach lecture is a protest against every form of apartheid at a logical, theological level but also at a practical-churchly and political-social level.[24]

In this regard, Barth does not allow theoretical and practical dualisms in his theological understanding of God. Following in the footsteps of Blumhardt, Barth agrees that to believe in God is also to believe in humanity, and believing in humanity leads to believing in the real renewal of our world. "The paradox that God's service is or must become service to humankind is very ingenuous" ("Christian's Place in Society," 276). In this regard Barth identifies the society with life. There is no un-

23. *ADT* 4 (my translation)
24. Marquardt, *Christ in der Gesellschaft*, 54, 57.

social life, or any realization of life outside of the society. Life is *a priori* social. People cannot disengage themselves from life and society. Married life, civilization, the economic order, art and science, and the like take their course "in accordance with the laws of their own logical workings" and are "modified by another factor full of promise" ("Christian's Place in Society," 272).

Be this as it may, the idea of the autonomy of culture, the state, and economic life was exploited exhaustively before the war ("Christian's Place in Society," 272, 279). As a matter of fact, society as the totality and universality from which people cannot escape is really ruled by its own logos. That is, "a whole pantheon of its own hypostases and powers" ("Christian's Place in Society," 280). This society has its own center that may rule the life of society. However, society had fallen into a catastrophe that determines the present situation in which we stand. The reality of this situation had become shockingly clear to those conscious of the state of society around them. At issue was the society of Switzerland and Germany in September of 1919, which stood in the sign of revolutionary times. Barth writes, "Today for the sake of social democracy, or pacifism, or the youth movement, or something of the sort—as yesterday it would have been for the sake of liberal culture or our countries, Switzerland or Germany—we may very well succeed, if the worst comes to the worst, in *secularizing* Christ" ("Christian's Place in Society," 277).

This is what Barth speaks of as the basic mark for the historical situation of the present society. The basic moment of social life that proceeds in the time of revolution as its own legitimization is not removed, but belongs to the identity of this society—present in its contemporary catastrophe. Barth quips, "Use the thought-forms of Jesus as the law for every economic, racial, national, and international order!" ("Christian's Place in Society," 279). He argues that on the one hand there was the transfiguring optimism of Richard Rothe. However, we could not go back in that direction. On the other hand, there is the way forward to the liberalism of Naumann. We could not go forward in that direction either. The society of 1919 in its revolutionary phase existed also under the historical law, that is, the brutal fact that such forwarding legitimization of social life was not removed but survived without ruin. "Our serious use of 'the thought-forms of Jesus' is prevented at the very start by the brutal fact that the autonomy of social life is by no means done away by our having become thoroughly tired of it" ("Christian's Place in Society," 279).

The destructive autonomy and legitimization of culture, state, and economic life lead to idolatry, the recognition of "a whole pantheon of its own hypostases and powers" ("Christian's Place in Society," 280). The power of the demonic over our life is not yet broken. This is a society of principal brokenness from which we are tempted to retreat in deep suspicion of and disappointment with life. However, Barth names the desire for a new, different society in the midst of all the old that is filled with misdirection and lies. This new society must be "a righteousness in the midst of a sea of unrighteousness" ("Christian's Place in Society," 273). Barth's was an attempt to seek unity in the complete brokenness of society and the origin of corruption. This was "a spirituality within all our crass materialistic tendencies, a formative life-energy within all our weak, tottering movements of thought, a unity in a time which is out of joint" ("Christian's Place in Society," 273).

What Barth tries to do in the Tambach lecture is to seek a different society where righteousness exists amid unrighteousness and the new under the old. However, through his previous knowledge of historical relativism, Barth was well aware of the fact that there is no absolute in nature or the world. If this stance is understood to indicate that in the night of world history all cats are gray, then Barth's eschatology against the existing order could easily be misunderstood. Barth makes a concerted attempt to clarify the relation between the old and the new social order. Theologically and politically, he views the new in the old, justice in injustice, and unity in brokenness. Historical relativity stands under hope, rather than under necessity. Full of hope, Barth analyzed the current situation. Therefore, Barth did not give his consent to the mood of disillusionment in the German revolution—for example, Hans Hartmann's program of June 1919—that possibly influenced quite a few of participants in Tambach conference. The German revolution did not deliver what it promised. Instead of appropriation of the revolution for renewal, all that was seen was compromise, anxiety and cowardice. Barth encouraged Christians toward social renewal by helping them to see themselves as unique centers of potential for revolution. "Let us establish a new church with democratic manners and socialistic motives!"("Christian's Place in Society," 280).

In fact, Barth was aware that the Social Democracy had turned into a radical reformist party, drawing upon capitalism and nationalism, just as Naumann's newspaper *Die Hilfe* had expected. In the Tambach lecture Barth without a doubt expresses inevitable disillusionment with this Social Democracy. But Barth does not tolerate such frustration with the revolution; rather he replaces disillusionment with hope for a better society. In fact, frustration and disillusionment threatened to flood over participants in the Tambach conference.[25] Barth argued, in spite of this, that Christ, who is one with God, rules out this frustration and disillusionment: "The divine is something whole, complete in itself, a kind of new and different something in contrast to the world. It does not permit of being applied, stuck on, and fitted in. It does not permit of being divided and distributed" just because "it is more than religion. It does not passively permit itself to be used: it overthrows and builds up as it wills. It is complete or it is nothing" ("Christian's Place in Society," 277). Therefore, to secularize Christ or to clericalize society is an attempt that will end in failure. Religious socialism assumed that God belonged to a special religious domain. This assumption led to the position of Naumann, who had come to terms with the Lutheran two-kingdoms theology. Barth argued, in opposition, that the meaning and the power of the living God create a new world. "There is only a solution, and that is in God himself" ("Christian's Place in Society," 282). Therefore we Christians are called to "*priestly agitation* of this hope and this need, by means of which the way to the solution, which is in God, may be made clearer to us" ("Christian's Place in Society," 282). This is what Barth takes as his point of departure in his Tambach lecture.

Given this fact, we perceive that Barth conceptualizes an ethical concern of practical reason in a Kantian sense in light of God the Origin, namely the living God. Knowledge of God is related to the logos of society because society is the practical arena. What makes Barth interested in critical idealism is not a question of epistemology but a question of social existence; not dialectics of thought, being, history, and nature but "the concrete dialectics of society, its thesis and antithesis, its origin in God, its analogous relation to God."[26]

Our Standpoint: Movement

In the second section of the Tambach lecture, Barth develops his theological reflection on the breakthrough of God's history into world his-

---

25. Ibid., 45.
26. Marquardt, *Theologie und Sozialismus*, 219.

tory, so that he makes a social-political reflection on a possible and hopeful development in the present situation. These two aspects—God's breakthrough into history and its hopeful consequence for the current situation—are conceptualized by the term "movement." First of all, Barth expresses his position not in terms of a static standpoint, but in terms of an attempt to catch "the bird in flight," that is, a moment of movement. What is truly important in this movement is not socialistic or religious-social or Christian movement in general. This is "the movement of God," so to speak, perpendicularly from above (*senkrecht von oben her*) "which transcends and yet penetrates all these movements and gives them their inner meaning and motive" ("Christian's Place in Society," 283).

This movement is "the movement whose power and import are revealed in the resurrection of Jesus Christ from the dead" ("Christian's Place in Society," 283). According to Barth, this is the movement of God's history, the power and significance of which is revealed in the resurrection of Jesus from the dead. "The new life revealed in Jesus Christ is not a new form of godliness" ("Christian's Place in Society," 285). The world of God breaks through and appears in secular life—that means "the bodily resurrection of Christ from the dead" ("Christian's Place in Society," 287). This movement cannot be identified with religion as such. Rather it uncovers the hidden sense and motivation behind all human movements and establishments, cutting through them regardless of whether a socialist movement or a religious movement. What is at stake is to bear witness to the reality of the living God and to set ourselves into the power of the Origin, into the reality of God. We are moved by the bodily resurrection of Christ from the dead. We take part in its meaning and power. The new must come from above (*von oben her*), which is the history of God. Essentially the knowledge of God fights against all secularization, all accommodation, all hyphenated combinations. Eschatology is fulfilled and concretized perpendicularly from above in the history of Jesus Christ, his cross and resurrection.

Barth's Christology is construed in this regard with an eschatological and universal scope. His proposal of *omnia instaurare in Christo* (to restore all things in Christ) is an act that stands in solidarity with society ("Christian's Place in Society," 281). Barth perceives that the power of the new already becomes effective amid the old society, and that the old society was fused within the new society in an apocalyptic and eschatological manner. Although we do not ignore "the brutal prerequisites of social life—the state and the economic system, art and science, and even the more primitive necessities of eating, drinking, sleeping, and growing old" ("Christian's Place in Society," 289), we can no longer, according to Barth, succumb to these laws as ultimate independent authorities because our souls have awakened to the immediacy of God by virtue of the power of resurrection of Jesus Christ.[27] "This awakening of the soul is the vivifying movement of God into history or into consciousness, the movement of Life into life." "All independent life aside from Life is not life but death" ("Christian's Place in Society," 290).

This social contradiction does not result in a mere suspicion of or resignation from political involvement. In light of the movement of life, it must stand full of hope. Barth designated movements in his current situation (such as the anti-authoritative youth movement, modern expressionist art, the Spartacists or communist movement, the antichurch movement, among others) under which the church stood socially and politically after the revolution of 1918. In that we see "our contemporaries from Naumann to Blumhardt, from Wilson to Lenin" move "in all the different stages of the one movement" ("Christian's Place in Society," 294). For Barth it is of special significance to understand "the raw primordial elements of motives and motion" lying in all movements of our time and in their signs

Distancing himself from the religious socialism of Ragaz, Barth spoke of revolutionary upheaval that came explicitly out of a theological context from Spartacist Rosa Luxemburg.[28] In view of the biblically oriented "moment of God's history," which is the moment whose power and significance is revealed in the resurrection of Jesus Christ from the dead ("Christian's Place in Society," 282), Barth understands the Spartacus

27. This immediacy, which is associated with Hermann Kutter's philosophical category of immediacy (*Unmittelbarkeit*) is hidden in *Romans I* (pages 7, 9, 14) and is in his Tambach lecture no longer conceived of in an ontological-immanent manner, but in an analogical-dialectical manner under the eschatological proviso.

28. Rosa Luxemburg, in her tactical propaganda pamphlet *Kirche und Sozialismus*, in the year of the revolution of 1905, called for discipleship to the Crucified One from the church. In 1919, in the program of the Spartacus League, she identified the revolutionary proletariat with the Crucified One of Golgotha. Luxemburg identified the material determination and the meaning of the discipleship of Jesus with "the gospel of brotherhood and equality" among the oppressed for the sake of the gospel. She pushed the church to practical solidarity in the struggle for liberation from material misery as well as in struggle for the resurrection of the people. See Luxemburg, *Kirche und Sozialismus*, 20.

praxis as the struggle against politics that would create a socially unjust economic structure. "The Wholly Other in God drives us with compelling power to look for a basic, ultimate original correlation between our life and that wholly other life" ("Christian's Place in Society," 288). The movement of God is the revolution of life against the power of death that holds it fast. In God, who is "the Origin of origin," we can come to a positive position. In God we live and move and have our being. In search of God we should look at the resurrection itself by participating in it. We should not be discouraged by "the negative appearances of disintegration in ourselves and in the world" ("Christian's Place in Society," 295).

Barth had already articulated the idea of "Placing ourselves into under the power of Origin" (*ADT* 41) in his "Faith in a Personal God" ("Der Glaube an den persönlichen Gott" [1914]). The total transcendence of the absolute had to become an idea of "pure Origin." "The foundation of the actual as such" at the same time affirms it. Dialectical sublation (*Aufhebung*) of space and time is at the same time dominion of them. It is the resting truth and validity in itself of an *a priori* that proves itself here as the positive side of God-thought.[29]

From this statement we come to know that the meaning of negation was from the beginning the gaining of a theological position: namely, one of new beginnings and a point of departure for Barth's further thought. This positive theology in a predialectical stage is already indicative of the intent of the dialectical way. "No grounding—in a phrase of Herman Cohen—becomes a ground of grounding of thought and will."[30] In the face of the power of death, we are not uncommitted observers. We are moved by and are conscious of God. God in history lives in us and around us. "We do share in the resurrection movement: with or without the accompaniment of religious feeling we *are* actuated by it" ("Christian's Place in Society," 296). In this regard we notice Blumhardt's echo in Barth: "It is the light of victory into which our hope and our need have entered. The hope rather than the need is the decisive, the supreme moment . . .

---

29. Marquardt, *Theologie und Sozialismus*, 208.

30. Ibid. In other words, a critical a priori of Kant becomes a positive-theological a priori of the God-idea. In relating the positive a priori to the founding of the actual, Barth implies a possible discourse on analogy. That "*Aufhebung* of space and time" is dialectically conceptualized, including an idea of overcoming them—refers to the origin of Barth's analogy. Therefore we cannot insist on "a shift from dialectics to analogy" in Barth's theological development (Balthasar, *Theology of Karl Barth*, 79–80).

God applies the lever to lift the world. And the world is being lifted by the lever that he has applied. God in history is *a priori* victory in history" ("Christian's Place in Society," 296–97). In his Tambach lecture, this was the theological and political banner with which Barth encouraged all participants to march through skepticism, disillusion, and disintegration in the wake of revolution in Germany and Russia. The last word means the kingdom of God in that creation, redemption, and the consummation of the world have become possible through God and in God.

The advancing glory of God has overcome a barrier between God and the human being in that we have our hope and our need pulsing and stirring within us. So we live in transition as those with such a hope "from death to life, from the unrighteousness of humans to the righteousness of God, from the old to the new creation" ("Christian's Place in Society," 297). We are participants in the service of the kingdom of God by fighting against negative appearances and forms of disintegration in our society. Therefore, the message of the epistle to the Colossians came to mind for Barth: "By him were all things created that are in heaven, and that are in earth, visible and invisible, whether they be thrones, or principalities, or powers: all things were created by him, and for him" (Col 1:16). How does Barth relate the Pauline message of the cosmic Christ to the kingdom of God and our participation in it?

Regnum Naturae: *Created by Him and for Him*

In the third section of the Tambach lecture, Barth deals with Paul's statement "all things were created by him and for him" in light of the resurrection, which thoroughly affects the relation between God and the world. It is the great proclamation of the epistle to the Colossians that the relation between God and the world is moved through the resurrection in a fundamental and comprehensive way. Thus a protest against a particular social order in society becomes "an integral moment in the kingdom of God." However, we are not supposed to identify our hopes of the social revolution with the kingdom of God since "the kingdom of God does not begin with our movements of protest" ("Christian's Place in Society," 299). Given this fact, Barth's concern becomes manifest in his special way of radicalizing the idea of God's revolution in the face of the October Revolution in Russia and the revolutions in Germany and the general strike in Switzerland. According to Barth, the kingdom of God does not begin with human protest movements. It is the Revolution that is before all revolutions, as it is before the whole prevailing existing order of things. It is out of this that both thesis and antithesis arise.

Naturally we shall be led first not to a denial but to an affirmation of the world as it is. "As we find ourselves in God, we find ourselves committed also to the task of affirming Him in the world as it is and not in a false transcendent dream world." Only out of such an affirmation can the real, radical denial (of the world) then take place, which is apparently and manifestly "the meaning of our movements of protest" ("Christian's Place in Society," 299). The God who is the Revolution is at work in all reality. Nevertheless God's Revolution must not be intermingled with the immanence of the socialist world revolution. According to Barth, "eating, drinking, sleeping, growing old" all belong to "the most brutal presupposition of the society," which is called *regnum naturae*. Genuine eschatology casts a light that shines not only forward but also backward; therefore the concept of creation is from the beginning an eschatological thought: in other words, the meaning and significance of *regnum naturae* is to be gained only from the perspective of the *regnum gratiae*. "Even the *regnum naturae* is the kingdom of God with the addition of—and in spite of—the veil" that now lies over this glory of God ("Christian's Place in Society," 300).

The eschatological critique of all that exists is a connecting point to religious-socialist thought and remained the point of departure from which Barth accessed the idea of creation. His idea of analogy is applied to the area of creation. In other words, the creation must be seen critically in the interest of eschatological renewal *per analogiam*. Consequently for Barth, not the kingdom of creation, but the creation of the kingdom of God gains prominence. As Barth says, there is an objectivity to our thinking, (i.e., discourse) and deeds within the existing social relation and in the consciousness of imprisonment, but this world also can be qualified as containing the promise ("Christian's Place in Society," 308). At this point Barth pays special attention to the work of the human being and to the human being as worker. The daily work done within the old world stands as a sign of promise for the new world. In honest work the *regnum naturae* encounters the coming new. Creator is and remains the Creator even in our fallen world.

According to Barth, there is a correlation between the kingdom of God and the world. Those who see it have "a penchant for *objectivity*"

("Christian's Place in Society," 307). Out of such correlation comes the consciousness of responsible solidarity. An organic relation between God and the world can be genuinely conceived of in terms of a coexistence between dialectics of the concrete and social analogy. Because God is Creator, the *regnum naturae* belongs to God. The affirmation of *regnum naturae* can be found in Jesus's parables. "Through [Christ] and to [Christ]" can false world-denial be overcome. Likewise, unconditional certainty about the society proves to be wrong as all false world affirmation. We meet here, for the first time, Barth's reflection on the social-parable character of the kingdom of God, in which the divine stands in analogous relation to the worldly.

This proves to be a point of departure in Barth's teaching of analogy in his early stage. Barth's approach to the idea of creation is based on a synthetic inclusion of the synoptic parables. The genre "parable" can be understood as a vehicle for the thought of an analogy—bound to a social and political content and scope. Thus the reality of the world is dealt with as an eschatological parable. As far as Barth's teaching about the analogy and parable of the kingdom of God through analogy is concerned, it is anchored in the concrete social-political relation between the kingdom of God and society.[31]

In Barth's words: "We *cannot* rest content with seeing in things transitory *only* a likeness of something else. There is an element in analogy that demands continuity" ("Christian's Place in Society," 317). During the revolutionary period after World War I, socialism was still portrayed as opposing the old order, which was an analogy that demanded continuity for the sake of the kingdom of God. In Barth's argumentation, the place of Christians in society should be "as hope-sharing and guilt-sharing comrades" within social democracy. It is "in this field that which we must work out the problem of opposition to the old order [and] discover the likeness of the kingdom of God" for our time ("Christian's Place in Society," 319). So understood, at the crucial point, Barth gives in to the protest that "socialism, with concentrated weight" makes "against the whole structure of society, intellectual and material" ("Christian's Place

---

31. The world revolution and analogy (*Gleichnis*) must be taken literally and seriously. The social and political realms stand in need of and capable of becoming analogy for the kingdom of God, not mere identification between social affairs and kingdom of God, but that which is capable of reflecting the kingdom of God "indirectly as a mirror-image." (Gollwitzer, "Kingdom of God and Socialism in the Theology of Karl Barth," 98).

in Society," 315). However, this socialism is not identical with the Social Democrats' watered-down version in the Weimar government, which Barth allegedly seemed to regard "as the best hope for Germany in the present."[32]

The socialism that Barth has in mind here is a protest movement (as an analogy of God's kingdom) against the existing social democrats in Germany. It points to a radical socialist position "on the most extreme left" (R I:381). For Barth, God as *totaliter aliter* is originally and basically the new society that stands in contradiction to the collapsing society. A socialism that corresponds to God as the *totaliter aliter* points to radical socialists, namely, "hope-sharing and guilt-sharing comrades" involved in renewing the degeneration of social democracy. The eschatological point of departure can be discussed in the following ways: 1) The *extra nos* of God's effect stands over the content of consciousness and faith. If faith is against secularization, namely, if it does not support the protest against the existing order, we rather perceive God in the protest movement. Therefore, God and God's kingdom lie in our protest movement and hold a critical position. 2) From this eschatological superiority we find original grace in all social relations that are to be affirmed, and in the order of creation through which we find ourselves. Politically speaking, eschatological radicality means awakening revolutionary comrades and calling them to discipleship in the revolution of God in history. If we refer to our endurance as an inquiry of its relation to God, this endurance is not only positive but critical.

What Kutter grasped as the inner necessity or as the "must" of the proletariat is again found in the daily normality of parable. For Barth, a new biblical interpretation emerges in the form of parable. All earthly realms point beyond themselves analogically in advance to the picture or image of the coming *Novum*. "So much synthetically the idea of creation is added to an eschatological idea, so much so that one must raise the function of analogy-thought analytically from the thought of origin. It functions just as the thought of dialectics, as the instrument to the thought of origin."[33] Everything impermanent is only parable. The original can be found in its heavenly analogy. Jesus uses this meaning of parable (Matt 13:10–17; Mark 4:10–12). The children of this world are much wiser,

32. McCormack, *Critically Realistic*, 200.
33. Marquardt, *Theologie und Sozialismus*, 114.

and they defend their interests better than the children of light do. In the Tambach lecture, as in *Romans I*, Barth repeats that Christians have a duty to give to the kaiser what belongs to him. But they give to God something different that belongs to God. Without becoming the servant of idols. we have a joyful freedom in and out of the house of mammon by recognizing the state as the beast from the bottomless pit. The analogy of the kingdom of God has an anti-ideological function as long as ideology (as the "superstructure") is the establishment from a superior standpoint in control over the process of daily life. On the basis of the Life of God as the Origin of human life, we affirm real life. Therefore, *regnum naturae*—the great penultimate that frames every thought, speech and action—can always become *regnum Dei*, as long as we are in the kingdom of God and the kingdom of God is in us ("Christian's Place in Society," 310). This is the truth in Christ fundamental to a biblical knowledge of life.

Regnum Gratiae

There is "a victorious struggle with darkness" moving "from the *regnum naturae* into *regnum gloriae*" where the problem of life becomes serious and full of promise in Christ. Therefore, in the *regnum gratiae* "*we* live more deeply in the No than in the Yes, more deeply in criticism and protest than in naïveté, more deeply in longing for the future than in the participation in the present. *We* can honor the Creator of original world only by crying out to the Redeemer of the present one" ("Christian's Place in Society," 312). However, in the move from *regnum naturae* toward *regnum gratiae* we see God, "who hath delivered us from the power of darkness, and hath translated us into the kingdom of his dear Son" (Col 1:13, KJV). As society becomes a mirror of the original thought of God, it becomes the mirror of our need and our hope. So the kingdom of God directs itself as an attack on society. The parable is promise and promise want fulfillment.

In place of collaboration with the existing society, radical opposition has entered against society's fundamental basis. Through criticizing, protesting, reforming, organizing, democratizing, socializing, and revolutionizing we strive to witness to the kingdom of God on earth. That is, to establish marks of God's kingdom in our midst. Be that as it may, "there is no continuity leading from analogy over into divine reality" ("Christian's Place in Society," 321). The kingdom of God, which makes all transitory things capable of becoming parable, is "an order of things which is not to be comprehended in the category of time and contingency" ("Christian's Place in Society," 322). The synthesis that we find as the final solution is only in God. "If in *this* life only we have hope in Christ, we are of all men and most miserable" (1 Cor 15:19, KJV). Creation and salvation have their truth in that God is *God* and that divine immanence means at the same time divine transcendence: "The power of the otherworldly is the power of this worldly" (Ernst Troeltsch). In other words, for Barth, this is the power of affirmation and also the power of denial and negation concerning all that exists ("Christian's Place in Society," 322).

In the power of resurrection, naïveté and critique ground their possibilities, their warranty, and their necessity. The resurrection of Jesus Christ from the dead is the world-moving power that also moves us because "it is the appearance in our corporeality of a *totaliter aliter* constituted corporeality" ("Christian's Place in Society," 323). It is of special significance to observe a revelation-oriented approach from which God's revolution as examined in *Romans I* assumes a more christological character in Barth's Tambach lecture. In Jesus Christ human kind becomes aware of its direct relationship with God. The resurrection is given a theological and a political function. The individual who is rendered the first moved by the resurrection is thought of in terms of as a subject of society. The resurrection brings the individual into action and knowledge in society. At this point, it is important to note a sequence. Social knowledge follows social action. The resurrection, which is the forgiveness of sins and liberation from the old world, accompanies one's social role and one's personal identity in the new predication to the individual. This is Easter: God's movement from above to below points to the last thing, the eschaton, the synthesis that means the radical breaking out of everything ultimate, rather than referring to a continuation, result, or consequence of the previous thing. God as the radical intervener stands always near to that which moves us, but God is always incomprehensible, discomforting, almost threatening beyond human comprehension. In this God as *totaliter aliter*, we are in expectation of a wholly other society, namely, a new heaven and a new earth. In accordance with this new heaven and new earth Barth and his listeners were to involve themselves in the "making of a new Switzerland and a new Germany" ("Christian's Place in Society," 323). Here we meet Barth's affirmation of Blumhardt's eschatological spirit moving "perpendicularly from heaven," based on Zündel's commentary on Blumhardt ("Christian's Place in Society," 323).

Regnum Gloriae

Using Calvin's metaphor, Barth elaborates on the attitude of Christians in society, who live from the standpoint of *spes futurae vitae*. A theological standpoint of *spes futurae vitae* has practical consequences for Christians in its assertion that the resurrection has something to do with renewing and transforming society, and in so doing, manifesting God's No and Yes to society as well as to us in society. *Regnum gloriae* will redeem and renew the world and society. Out of this redemption and renewal appear a consciousness of predestination and a power of determining life for the honor of God. The view from creation and salvation to consummation, the view of the "wholly other" of the *regnum gloriae*, means practically that our naïve and critical position in society, or our yes and no is set into the right relation with God. Our view of *regnum gloriae* distances us from shortcuts to absolutism on the right or the left ("Christian's Place in Society," 324–25). In the light of *regnum gloriae*, Barth assumes a way of dialectical theology that allows the freedom of saying yes and no to the right and the left. This perspective leads Christians into society to follow what God is doing. Given this fact, the Tambach lecture implies Barth's farewell to religious socialism. At that time, Ragaz attacked the form of Barth's dialectic as "double sided (*doppleseitig*),"[34] because it would undermine the religious socialist movement.

Karl Barth and a Socially Engaged Theology of Analogy

Barth's theology of social analogy does not contradict his theology of the revolution of God in *Romans I*, which tends to emphasize an organic relation between God and the world without a sufficient eschatological proviso. Here Barth had observed a kind of dialectical relationship between divine action and human action in the historical unfolding of God's kingdom. On the basis of Christ's resurrection, we live and grow into an organism stemming from him. Through an organic participation in God's movement, human existence is an immediacy, a direct relation-

---

34. Kupisch, *Karl Barth in Selbstzeugnissen und Bilddokumenten*, 45.

ship or a direct unity with God. Humanity becomes a particle of God's universal power. The divine in me, the pristine divine nature in humanity, makes humanity a divine race by establishing an ultimate identity between God and humanity. It is God who is at work in and through us (R I:207, 61, 237, 194). The concept of God is given to us immediately in our own being. Humans are not separated from their Origin but accompany it as the home, the central place of their striving, and as a presupposition and telos of their way in all their thought, will, and feeling (R I:14).[35]

For Barth there is no objective transition from the one to the other. We seek the synthesis in God alone. The synthesis is meant in the thesis and sought in the antithesis. Dialectical movement in Barthian fashion is not content with the unity of thesis and antithesis in the Russian Revolution but must be set in motion dynamically toward the revolution of God, which is "more than" the Titanism of Leninism or liberal religious socialism. These tend to seek a unity between socialism and kingdom of God in a historical context. What Barth wanted to do in terms of a parable of God's kingdom in the Tambach lecture was to radicalize his idea of God's revolution, which is superlative to all revolutions. The idea of Origin fulfills itself in a dialectical relation between its position and negation. Position and negation should be conceived of simultaneously as rooted in the common Origin: "From the original synthesis the antithesis comes, but above all the thesis itself comes" (*ADT* 51, my translation). The power of thesis and the power of antithesis are anchored in the original, absolute-producing power of synthesis. Only from the thesis can the genuine antithesis emerge, namely, the genuine (i.e., originally synthesis-producing) antithesis (*ADT* 51). Only from the standpoint of antithesis, which is rooted in the synthesis, can one accept the thesis quietly.

Unlike the Hegelian dialectical method, where a mutual mediation of all positions and negations appears as the synthesis in a historical immanent process, Barth conceives that synthesis as Origin is not identical

---

35. Barth's concept of immediacy and organism caused a serious argument for Balthasar in that "the pantheistic concept of nature necessarily becomes dialectical" (Balthasar, *Theology of Karl Barth*, 51). However, Barth's idea of Origin works as a joint, so to speak, between his conception of immediacy and objectivity in God. In the face of the socialist situation in the Weimar Republic as well as the Russian Revolution, "the grotesque physiognomy of a police state" is exposed (Balthasar, *Theology of Karl Barth*, 51). Barth begins by assuming more strict dialectical lines, breaking with his earlier organic or process-developmental eschatology (Balthasar, *Theology of Karl Barth*, 51). See further Frei, "Doctrine of Revelation in the Thought of Karl Barth," 588.

with the dialectical movement in thesis and negation. Rather, Origin is the condition of the possibility as well as the realizing, creative reality of Yes and No. Thesis and antithesis in no way produce each other in an immanent process, but they are related to each other by virtue of their analogical affinity to the Origin that produces these two. Therefore, there is no mechanical-methodical relation, but only an organic and dialectical relation between the two in light of God's future as the Origin. Therefore for Barth, revolution does not stand in contradiction to analogy (*Gleichnis*). Rather revolution is seen as a fundamental transformation, and Barth takes Reformation theology of justification and rebirth to be revolutionary and transforming in a literal and serious sense. At a minimum for Barth, the Reformation doctrine of grace assumes a radical image of revolution and transformation with respect to its social dimension rather than remaining confined to an individualistic-anthropological sense.[36]

Prior to Barth, the religious-socialist tradition appropriated the Blumhardtian message of the kingdom of God (in the case of Ragaz) or radicalized it to critique the encapsulation of eschatology for the individual renewal in pietism (in the case of Kutter). Under the influence of the religious socialists, on the one hand, and through his involvement in the movement of radical socialists within SPS, on the other, Barth set in motion his theology of analogy in theological, universal, and social-critical terms. So Barth relates the eschatological promise to "God's victory in the materiality of the whole creation" (R I:248; Rom 8:19–22). In the reconciliation between human being and nature, the redemption of both belongs to bodily glory.

Therefore, there is no need to look at the external world with strange and hostile objectivity and destiny. "We are called and enabled one day to become the mediators and aides of the world destroyed by us, one day to speak the redemptive words and to do the liberating deeds which nature expects from her Creator" (R I:245, 247). So Barth continues this concern in the Tambach lecture; in priestly agitation of this hope, we take part in the movement of God as committed workers. "*Today* there is a call for

---

36. Already during the Geneva period, Barth discovered the Reformation theology of John Calvin alongside his discovery of socialism and social questions. Barth brought the radicality of the Reformer's doctrine of grace, which means the transformation of the individual, into connection with social questions within a social-critical and universal horizon.

large-hearted, far-sighted, character conduct toward *democracy*—no, not *toward* it, as irresponsible onlookers and critics, but within it, as hope-sharing and guilt-sharing comrades" ("Christian's Place in Society," 319). But in the Tambach lecture, the organic way in *Romans I* assumes a more dialectical-analogical way. Dialectical method, for Barth, serves freedom for God's sake, in that we also may enjoy a positive and critical stance to any human movements.

During the last years at Safenwil, Barth was preoccupied with revising his first edition of *Romans* in light of world events: the news from Russia and involvement with struggles over the direction of the SPS about the Third International. His disillusionment with the violent postrevolutionary process in Russia and his confrontation with Ragaz made him realize that there would be danger in his daring organic identification of the kingdom of God and socialism in *Romans I*. In light of world events Barth found that an attempt to identify socialism with God's kingdom resulted in a new enslavement of humanity rather than a revolution. An equation of human praxis with God's action must be avoided. Barth attacked and denounced, in analogical terms, the differentiating of God from humans, an attempt at reversing identity of both for the sake of utilizing and exploiting God to serve human interests and purposes. First in Tambach and then in *Romans II* this is branded as "brazen identification."[37]

However, this warning against "brazen identification" in *Romans II* must be seen in light of Barth's social-critical concept of analogy in mirroring God's kingdom. In the Tambach lecture, Barth takes a road to an earthly analogy in expectation of God's eschatology. The Marxists in the Western European revolution failed. The Socialist Party lost its influence and declined. The Soviet way in the postrevolutionary period had become questionable and skeptical, even betraying revolution in its inceptive stage. "It is the original and spontaneously productive energy of the synthesis from which the energy of the thesis and the energy of the antithesis both derive" ("Christian's Place in Society," 321).

God in the dialectical Yes and No to us allows us to have freedom in saying yes and no to the existing order in the right-wing movement as well as to the order of the left-wing movement. Barth's reflection on social analogy in light of the kingdom of God deepens and extends his dialectical theology in *Romans II*. Behind his dialectical theology in *Romans II*

---

37. Gollwitzer, "Kingdom of God and Socialism in the Theology of Karl Barth," 80.

one must note that his theology of analogy plays a part in shaping the relation of eternity-time to the social political arena. Social realms are in need of and capable of analogy. Barth's thesis in the Tambach lecture provides a foundation for his political ethics[38] as well as for his theology of culture.

As for a cultural dimension of Barth's theology, the centurion of Capernaum is portrayed as "a parable for the order of the messianic kingdom." In the parables there does not occur "dilettantism, halfwayness, jerry-building" ("Christian's Place in Society," 307). Barth takes into account an element of analogy in demanding continuity. This continuity is taken as eternity in the human heart, which is the synthesis of Jesus Christ. In search of this eternity in the human heart, "the children of this world are wise; judged by their own standards they do their work well—better than the children of light judged by theirs—and the Lord praises them for it" ("Christian's Place in Society," 307). This remains a fundamental biblical statement for Barth, which he continues and expands further in his theology of social analogy in his Amsterdam lecture (1926)[39] and later in the so-called doctrine of lights of reconciliation (CD IV/3.1. § 69).[40]

---

38. As far as Barth's political ethics regarding church and state is concerned, Barth, in his seminal article "Christengemeinde und Bürgergemeinde" (1946), discusses and deepens the fifth thesis of the Theological Delcaration of Barmen in terms of the direction and line of the gospel, not in terms of the so-called natural-right (thesis 11). The state as the civil community is not grounded in discovery and practice of true natural rights but in the kingdom of Christ. The direction and line of Christian political differentiation, judgment, or choosing is related to the capacity of the *parable* (*Gleichnis*fähigkeit) and desirability of the *parable* (*Gleichnis*bedürftigkeit) of political essence. From a Christian perspective, the civil community has justification of its existence as the parable, as correspondence and analogy in relation to the kingdom of God, which the Christian community is to believe and proclaim. The civil community is capable of reflecting the kingdom of God indirectly, in a mirror image. Therefore it is of utmost importance for Barth to build up the civil community in accordance with the parable of the kingdom of God and to have the fulfillment of its justice as the zeal and content. See Barth, "Christengemeinde und Bürgergemeinde" in *ThSt*, 104 (Zurich: TVZ, 1984), 67.

39. Barth, "Church and Culture," 334-54.

40. In his interview that gave an account of his so-called doctrine of lights, Barth affirmed that there would be a *Mitbrüder* inherited from the kingdom of God outside the walls of Christianity. He reminded his readers that he came from the religious socialism of his earlier period at Safenwil, in that he was in deep solidarity with the children of this world in light of the kingdom of God. See Barth, *Gespräche 1964-1968*, 401.

In thesis 4 of his Amsterdam lecture, Barth states: "Seen from the point of view of creation, the kingdom of nature (*regnum naturae*), culture is the promise originally given to man of what is to become" (TC:341). As far as the Word of God as a word of grace in its content is a word of reconciliation, the broken original relationship between God and humans can be restored "by virtue of the new unbroken tie of reconciliation" (TC:341). As a consequence, the kingdom of Christ, which is not merely confined to the incarnation, has an effective domain outside the visible reality of the church. When it comes to God's speaking to humans in Jesus Christ, humans are capable of joining this promise in terms of God's claim on humans in Jesus Christ. In this regard, Barth interprets culture to imply this promise to humans. Rather than being rejected by the gospel, culture as the promise is confirmed by the gospel. The work of culture in light of the eternal Logos who became flesh and yet lord in the whole domain of culture can be a reflection, a witness to the promise given from the beginning. However, this promise does not exist apart from divine act in reconciliation.

In the realm of nature, the kingdom of the Logos holds its validity and effectiveness as God's claim. Human and cultural activity, under the shadow of all cultural achievements, can be blessed in Christ and carry within itself a spark of the seminal Logos (*TC*:351). At this point, *theologia naturalis* is included and brought into new light through *theologia revelatus*. In other words, the truth of creation is included in the reality of God's grace. Therefore, Barth agrees with Thomas Aquinas's principle that "grace does not destroy nature but perfects it" (*gratia non tollit naturam sed perficit*) (*TC*:342). Christological inclusivism, based on Christ's kingdom, provides for Barth a way to take seriously what *theologia naturalis* intends to express with respect to culture and nature. In this regard, Barth criticizes the independence of culture from the church as an impossible phenomenon and a picture of idols. Humankind cannot establish the kingdom of God or reconciliation with God by virtue of the achievement of culture, although the gospel includes the task of culture. It is only possible through and in the grace of the forgiveness of sin. "In practice the Church can abandon it to society or to 'experts'; but not in principle" (*TC*:343–44). "The Church will not see the coming of the kingdom of God in any human cultural achievement, but it will be alert for the signs which, perhaps in many cultural achievements, announce that the kingdom approaches"(*TC*:344).

Given this fact, the Word of reconciliation does not abolish but establishes the law. As far as the Word of God is the Word of redemption, in principle *regnum gloriae* is in a newly created world. *Sub specie aeternitatis* (in the light of eternity) cultural achievement is not undervalued, but all cultural activity can be seen in it striving for "the highest possible evaluation of the goal" (*TC*:349). Throughout its whole course, the church in fact swims along in the stream of culture (*TC*:351). Christian praxis is a work of culture under an eschatological reservation, The work of cultural tasks takes place among the earthly signs, seen not only as promise or law, but as event or formed reality and real form in the process of becoming under the eschatological anticipation (*TC*:348-49). Therefore Barth stressed that the church, with the highest possible evaluation rather than an undervaluation of cultural achievement, sees all cultural activity striving for the goal of culture. Understood this way, the church stands humanly in profound solidarity with society and human culture. This relationship can be seen as an affirmation of what had been said in the Tambach lecture.

Barth calls for prophetic objectivity rather than methodological objectivity (*TC*:353). In Barth's definition, "the culture is the task set through the Word of God for achieving the destined condition of man in unity of soul and body" (*TC*:337). When we see the task of culture as a definition of humankind realized in the unity of soul and body, a prophetic objectivity lies in overcoming the dualism between spirit and nature, soul and body, internal ream and external realm. This approach points to Barth's third way to a prophetic-ethical understanding of culture in light of eschatology, in contrast to liberal or Cultural Protestantism.[41] Therefore it is of special significance to note Barth's concern about the actualization of an eschatological dimension of Christian faith in regard to human cultural activity, for all Christendom and its relation to culture depend entirely on the hope of Christ who is to come again with his "I make all things new" (*TC*:354).[42]

41. Cf. Winzeler, *Widerstehende Theologie: Karl Barth 1920-35.* 341-42. According to Barth, "it is sheer nonsense to talk of criticizing culture in this regard, for in the last resort attention to Holy Scripture might be called an element of culture or education . . . The problem of culture is the problem of being human, which undoubtedly exists for the theologian too, since theology is a specific activity of humanity. The problem of theology and dogmatics can also be seen as wholly set within the framework of the problem of culture" (*CD* I/1:284).

42. In *Church Dogmatics* (1932) Barth thinks of a relation between God and the

Barth's theological way from God to us is essentially inclusive and integrative of human social, cultural activity and achievements. Again, in Barth's words: "Culture *can* be a witness to the promise which was given man in the beginning. 'It *can*', I say. In Christ, it *is*. Reconciliation in Christ is the restoration of the lost promise. It renews the status of the creation with its great 'Yes' to man, with its reasonableness of reason. It gives man again insight into the meaning of his activity. It gives him the courage to understand even the broken relation in which he stands and acts towards God as still a relation and to take it seriously" (*TC*:343). In H. Richard Niebuhr's typology of "Christ and culture,"[43] Barth would find "Christ transformer of culture" to be meaningful for the sake of culture under the promise of God's kingdom, and at the same time "Christ, recognizer of culture" to be meaningful in light of God's reconciliation, but "Christ, relativizer of culture" for the sake of the future of God. So understood, Barth would agree with a typology of "Christ standing for the culture," on the side of the poor and God's revolution.

---

world in light of his so-called irregular dogmatics, namely, his reflection on God's strange voice outside the walls of Christianity (*CD* I/1). His irregular dogmatic is not a side issue. Rather it penetrates his entire regular dogmatic/dialectical way of thinking, in that his dogmatics do not fall into the gray zone of a positivistic, bourgeois, and modernistic character.

43. Cf. Niebuhr, *Christ and Culture*, 230.

FOUR   Karl Barth and the Second Edition of *Romans* (1922)

The Political Situation in Russia

THE TREATY OF BREST-LITOVSK, WHICH WAS CALLED A "SHAMEFUL peace,"[1] was carried out at Lenin's instigation. The Russian nation had been plunged deeper and deeper into civil war. However, there was no real prospect of the revolution spreading over to Europe. Rather than permanent revolution, the aim was limited to a consolidation of socialism in one country. General Kornilov, a charismatic figure and a hero for the right-wing members in Russia and for the Volunteer Army, commanded the Volunteer Army while General Alexeev was placed in charge of political and financial matters. Alexeev was the chief of staff in the imperial army. Along with Kornilov he became the founder of the White movement in south Russia. As an army of Russian officers, the Volunteers were always in conflict with their Cossack hosts. Unlike the older Cossacks, the younger Cossacks were reluctant to fight for the Whites. The Ice March, an action in which the Volunteers retreated from the river Don to the Kuban, was the heroic epic of the Russian Civil War. The Ice March left a trail of blood. During the civil war—because of a moral collapse—the White Terror reached its climax in the worst pogroms against Jews, whom many of the Whites blamed for the Russian Revolution. However, in the act of the White Terror against peasants, the class resentment and hatred in the act of Red Terror was repeated. The Whites, who had suffered at the hands of the revolution, sought vengeance, not only against the de-

---

1. Figes, *People's Tragedy*, 548.

spised peasantry, but against the Bolsheviks. Most of the officers among the Whites were landowners' sons who had lost their inheritance to the peasantry during the revolution.

After the death of General Kornilov in the Ekaterinodar battle, General Deniken assumed command. The Whites believed that they could win the civil war without the support of the peasantry. This was the main reason for their failure and defeat in the civil war. After the Treaty of Brest-Litovsk, the allies recognized Deniken as the main leader of the White armed forces in south Russia between 1918 and 1920, and promised him material support. The Allies were on the Whites' side and expected them to march triumphantly on Moscow. Such optimism was further strengthened by the rise of Admiral Kolchak on the eastern front. Kolschak was the main White leader in east Russia. Based on his connection with the Allies, Kolschak was recognized as the nominal head of the whole White movement. In the summer of 1918, the Reds faced defeat on all sides. The Soviet Republic declared a "single military camp" against the White movement.[2]

Fanny Kaplan's assassination attempt on Lenin marked the start of the Lenin cult and gave rise to Red Terror. Despite his serous wound, Lenin's quick recovery was designated as a miracle by the Bolsheviks, who promoted Lenin as the people's czar. The deputy head of the Cheka denounced Kaplan's shooting as an attack on the working class, and vowed to crush the forces of any counterrevolution by way of mass terror. These events signaled the start of the Red Terror campaign that caused protests in all areas of society.

Condemning the violence and climate of fear, Patriarch Tikhon cited the prophecy of St Matthew: "All who take up the sword shall perish with the sword" (Matt 26:52). The famous anarchist philosopher Kropotkin denounced the Terror in a letter to Lenin on September 17, 1918: "To throw the country into a red terror, even more so to arrest hostages, in order to protect the lives of its leaders is not worthy of a Party calling itself socialist and disgraceful for its leaders. Workers also condemned the bloody terror perpetrated in their name. 'Enough blood! Down with Terror!' proclaimed the All-Urkrainian Trade Union Council in September. 'Red is the color of truth and justice,' declared the railway workers of Kozlov. 'But under the Bolsheviks it has become the color of

---

2. Ibid., 594.

blood."³ However, in the winter of 1919–1920, the civil war in Russia took a decisive turn in favor of the Bolsheviks. General Wrangel, who led the last White campaign in the Crimea, made a last-ditch effort at resistance against the Bolsheviks, but in April 1920 the Whites were finally defeated.

In Germany a general named Von Luettwitz and a civilian named Kapp organized a revolt—the so-called Kapp putsch—against the Social Democratic government in Berlin. On March 13, 1920, a right-wing nationalist government under Kapp was proclaimed in Berlin.

In Switzerland Jacob Herzog and his group tried to further the action toward Communism. Retreating from the SPS, Herzog founded the Communist Party on October 6, 1918. The members of this party were later described as "old communists" in comparison with "new communists," who were established as the left wing of the SPS. The Social Democratic Party began its work with a revolutionary program, and the Communist group, even before the constitution of Swiss organization, took part in the foundation of the Third International through Leonie Kascher from March 2 through 6 1919 in Moscow. Fritz Platten joined as the representative of SPS. In July the executive committee of the Socialist Party in Switzerland voted 120–10 to join the Third International. An extraordinary Party Congress meeting on August 16–17 in Basel voted 318–147 for entrance into the Communist International. Through the month of August, a host of pamphlets and newspaper articles in Switzerland warned of the consequences of the Bolshevization of the Party.

In addition, the hard-liners in the congress of the Communist International in Moscow demanded twenty-one conditions for the acceptance of any socialist party into the Third International. These conditions included the total breaking away of all reformists and centralists from the Swiss Social Democratic Party and the exclusion of social patriotism and social pacifism. They kept on hold the whole agitation and propaganda for the real Communist character, the reorganization of the party along Soviet Communist lines, the renaming of the party as the Communist Party and unlimited support of all Soviet republics in their battle against the counterrevolutionary forces, and international yellow trade among others.⁴ On November 20, 1920, the "Berner Tagwacht" argued against

---

3. Ibid., 647–48.

4. Cf. Egger, *Entstehung der Kommunistischen Partei*, 202–3 (my translation). Cf. Mattmüller, *Leonhard Ragaz*, 2:530.

the twenty-one conditions saying, "The leitmotif of the *Communist Manifesto* of Karl Marx says: Proletariat of all countries united themselves! The leitmotif of the Communist Manifesto of Moscow says: Proletariat of all countries separated themselves from each other!"[5]

When the extraordinary assembly met in Bern from December 10 through 12, 1920, for a final decision on the issue, Robert Grimm and Graber spoke out against the entrance to the Third International, while Dr. Welti and Humbert-Droz stood for it in acceptance of the twenty-one conditions. However, the proposal was rejected by a vote of 350–213. The rejection of the Third International was equated with the rejection of the existence and the grounding principle of the Third International and revolutionary Communism in Swiss socialism. At that point 209 delegates marched out of the hall and reconvened in the Hotel Dupont to found the Communist Party of Switzerland. The decision of SPS against the Third International was affirmed by the referendum in January 1921 in a vote of 25,475 to 8,777.[6] After the Party meeting in December of 1920, the new Communists and the old Communists together founded the Communist Party of Switzerland.

In his correspondence to Thurneysen (December 11, 1920), Barth, who was present at the Party congress in Bern, mentioned that he was in the midst of a battlefield. The leftists were untrustworthy and aggressive toward the centralists' position against the Third International. Entrance to the Communist International was rejected with a vote of 350–213. Barth wrote to Thurneysen: "The conflict is perfect."[7] Fritz Lieb, a close friend of Karl Barth, was on the side of the leftists in support of the Third International. Later in a letter (on June 13, 1921) Barth wrote regarding a meeting with a young fellow in Basel, W. H., who was a committee member at the center of the Swiss Communist Party. Barth said that W. H., in spite of his deep contempt for the Second-and-a-Half International, did not regard Barth as unacceptable clergy.[8] The issue on the entrance of SPS to the Third International was decisively rejected on December 20, 1920 in Bern. In reaction, a minority group split off from the SPS and formed the Communist Party. In the words of Barth: "I was also in the

---

5. Egger, *Die Entstehung der Kommunistischen Partei*, 204 (my translation).
6. Ibid., 218–19.
7. *B-Th. I.*, 454.
8. Ibid., 496.

audience and present as an eyewitness when there was a sharp split at the Swiss Social Democrat Party conference of 1920 between the Second and the Third-Muscovite-Internationals. The supporters of the Third International, finding themselves in the minority, left the hall in protest by singing 'Peoples hear the signal for the last affray.'"[9]

As mentioned already, in an article ("What Should Not Happen") Barth critiqued Bolshevism as a brilliant deception. In addition to socialism in Russia, Barth cast a critical eye on the Weimar Republic in Germany, which he considered a betrayed version of socialism. In the case of Bolshevism, the goal was envisioned only in theory at a minimum but became bourgeois in its method and practice. In the case of Weimar, the socialist goal was surrendered to the revisionism that stood in support of a distorted, state-controlled capitalism. At any rate, he was skeptical of the spirit of true socialism in both cases. Barth believed the Swiss should not follow either example if they sought true socialism in the future. Barth's warning to the Socialist Party against joining the Third International should not be understood as sympathy for the "watered-down" social democracy in Germany at that time.

Preliminary Observations on the Second Edition of *Romans*

When we see the postrevolutionary process characterized by fear of the terror in Russia it is understandable that Barth's disappointment over the outcome of the Russian Revolution led him to a "sensational anti-revolutionary turn" that amounted to a radicalization of his critique of all that exists.[10] Rather than reprinting the first edition of *Romans* with a German publisher, Barth decided to reform it thoroughly.[11] Barth revised and rewrote it as a man staggering between desk, dinner table, and bed like a drunken man. Barth's friend Fritz Lieb took his place as pastor in Safenwil in May and June 1921 Subsequently, Barth received a letter from Johann Adam Heilmann, the pastor of the Reformed Church in Göttingen, who asked if Barth would apply for the new position of an honorary professorship in Reformed theology at the University of Göttingen. In the meantime, Barth's Tambach lecture had made him famous in Germany.

9. Barth identified Fritz Lieb as one of the most resolute promoters of the Third International, among this group. Cf. Busch, *Karl Barth: His Life*, 107.

10. Marquardt, *Theologie und Sozialismus*, 142.

11. Barth to Thurneysen, October 27, 1920, in *B-Th I*, 435–36.

The first edition of his *Romans* was also being read widely in German theological circles. When Barth paid a visit to E. F. K. Mueller in Erlangen after interviewing in Göttingen, Mueller published news of Barth's visit; this publication of this news caused a stir.[12]

In the preface to the second edition of *Romans*, Barth addressed what led him to "further movement and a change of fronts." These influences were: a) a more extensive study of Paul; b) the posthumous writings of Franz Overbeck; c) learning the real orientation of the thought of Plato and Kant, which he owed to the writings of his brother, Heinrich Barth; d) Karl Barth's increased understanding of the New Testament from the perspectives of Kierkegaard and Dostoevsky; and e) finally Barth's correcting himself in light of the critical review of the first edition of *Romans* (R II:vii).

Heinrich Barth's lecture given at the Aarau Student Conference in March 1919 was entitled "Gotteserkenntnis," and his inauguration lecture ("Das Problem des Ursprungs in der platonischen Philosophie") at the University of Basel was given in November 1920.[13] Impressed by these two lectures, Karl Barth wrote to Thurneysen: "Heiner's lecture has become for me an impetus to keep much more powerfully in view the *totaliter aliter* of the kingdom of God."[14] Heinrich's category of *Ursprungsphilosphie*, which refers to a more radically transcendent conception of God, constitutes a powerful rejection of all natural knowledge of God.

Although this insight had already begun to play an important part in his Tambach lecture, Barth's understanding of God as the eternal and the pure *Ursprung* of all that exists comes to the fore in his famous preface to the second edition of *Romans*: "If I have a 'system,' it consists in that which Kierkegaard has called the 'infinite qualitative distinction' between time and eternity... 'God is in heaven and you are on earth.' The relation-

---

12. "When at the end of the winter semester 1920/1, it became known that Barth was going to spend a few hours at my house on the next day, no less than twenty-eight people appeared without invitation—and this at a time when the majority of the students had already departed. There is a Barth-*Gemeinde* among our theological youth, especially among those students, male and female, who have breathed the modern spirit and are seeking something deeper." Cited from McCormack, *Karl Barth's Critically Realistic*, 243; cited from E. F. K. Mueller, "Karl Barths Römerbrief," in *Reformierte Kirchenzeitung; Organ des reformierten Bundes für Deutschland* 71 (1921) 103.

13. Heinrich Barth, "Gotteserkenntnis" In *ADT* 1:22–55. Cf. Heinrich Barth, *Problem des Ursprungs in der platonischen Philosophie*.

14. December 28, 1920, in *B-Th I*, 456.

ship of *this* God to this human, the relationship of this human to this God is for me the theme of the Bible and the sum of philosophy in one. The philosophers call this crisis of human knowing the *Ursprung*. The Bible sees at the same time crossroads of Jesus Christ." (R II:viii) In his inaugural lecture at the University of Basel in November 1920, Heinrich spoke of the term *crisis:* "*Jenseits* [the Otherwordly] means the crisis of *Dieseits* [this worldly]."[15]

In addition to *Ursprung*, it was Overbeck (1837-1905) who attracted Barth's further development. On January 5, 1920, Barth spoke of Overbeck to Thurneysen: "Our Melchizedek is probably—Overbeck. Perhaps I will write something about him in the *Neue Werke*."[16] According to Overbeck, there is an unbridgeable and irreconcilable chasm between *Urchristentum* (super-Christendom) and all subsequent periods of church history. Barth took his hermeneutical concern about keeping Overbeck's idea of *Urgeschichte* (superhistory) in line with Blumhardt's eschatology. Albeit very different in disposition, terminology, and experience, Overbeck and Blumhardt essentially stand close together (*TC:*56). Barth utilizes Overbeck's idea of *Urgeschichte* to combat Troeltsch's idea of historic Christianity: "The only possible abode of Christianity lies, so far as the past is concerned, not in history, but in the history before history, the Super-history [*Urgeschichte*]" (*TC:*62). According to Overbeck, a presentation attempting to establish Christianity historically would be out of the question. What is at issue is nonhistorical Christianity (*TC:*72).

As a *geschichtsphilosophische* category,[17] *Urgeschichte,* which serves to demonstrate hermeneutical limitation (unlike Schleiermacher's dictum: "The reader can understand better than the author"), is appropriated by Barth to deepen his eschatological concept. In Barth's view, *Urgeschichte* as protology is identical with eschatology in content: "*We know too much about all things, even about those most hidden and unattainable, about the things of which we can actually know nothing at all, the last things*"

---

15. Heinrich Barth, *Problem des Ursprungs*, 21. At this point we see a parallel between Heinrich Barth and Ernst Troeltsch concerning *Ursprung* as *totaliter aliter* since "the force of the *Jenseits* is the force of the *Diesseits*."

16. January 5, 1920, in *B-Th I*, 364. Cf. Barth's writing about Overbeck is entitled "Unsettled Questions for Theology Today" (1920) (*Unerledigte Anfragen an die heutige Theologie*), in *TK*:1-25; *TC*:55-73.

17. Ruschke, *Entstehung und Ausführung der Diastasentheologie in Karl Barths zweiten Römerbrief,* 39.

(*TC*:58). However, in accepting Overbeck's impetus, Barth does not remain radically skeptical; rather he provides it with the eschatological vigor of early Christianity in favor of a radical transcendental eschatology. To do theology in Barth's sense, there is no other way than to take into account the principle that "theology cannot be re-established except with audacity" (*TC*:72). Barth henceforth became a theologian of audacity. His eschatology in the second edition of *Romans* is articulated in the following way: "A Christianity which is not eschatology, completely and without remainder, has absolutely nothing to do with Christ" (R II:298). However, Barth's reception of Overbeck's *Urgeschichte* should not be understood as an antihistorical attitude.[18]

Barth's understanding of eschatology in the second edition of *Romans* does not abandon social questions but rather radicalizes them in light of the kingdom of God. In his lecture to the Aarau Student conference in March 1920, Bath stated, "We are within and not without. . . . within the knowledge of God, within the knowledge of the last things of which the Bible speaks. That is the presupposition from which we come. But all men and women have 'forgotten' this, their 'Origin' . . . In the death of death which takes place in the cross. 'Out of death comes life! From thence comes the knowledge of God, as of the Father, the Origin, the Maker of heaven and earth.'"[19] Besides, Barth never rejected historical-critical study in theological exegesis of the Bible.[20] What he distanced himself from in historical criticism was the idea that the meaning of the text is supposed to be reduced to its historical setting-in-life.

According to Eberhard Jüngel, Barth's development in the twenties can be best understood in relation to his engagement with Kierkegaard. Kierkegaard's "dialectic of existence" gained prominence among all the dialectical theologians such as Barth, Brunner, Bultmann, and Gogarten. However, Barth never saw the "dialectic of existence" as the point of departure in order to explicate a relation between human existence and revelation. In the relation of God to humans, Barth's theological dialectics

---

18. Barth took no pleasure in Oswald Spengler's book *Der Untergang des Abendlandes.* July 4, 1920, in *B-Th I*, 404.

19. Barth, "Biblische Fragen, Einsichten und Ausblicke," in Barth, *Das Wort Gottes und die Theologie*, 71, 89.

20. See questions 2, 3, 14 ("Fifteen Answers to Professor Von Harnack," 167–70 and "An Answer to Professor Von Harnack's Open Letter," in Robinson, *Beginnings of Dialectic Theology*, 176–77.

assumes a way of an analogy of faith, in that the dialectical movement in Barth's fashion gives precedence to God in bearing witness to Godself in and through humans.[21]

Barth's reception of Kierkegaard's dialectic of contradiction and antithesis needs to be seen against the background of Barth's reception of the idea of *Ursprung* in *Romans I* and the Tambach lecture. What Kierkegaard brought to sharpest expression is his anti-Hegelian dialectic of the absolute Spirit, where, according to Hegel, the contradiction of finite and infinite is overcome in higher synthesis through the dialectic of self-consciousness. Against this Hegelian synthesis of reconciliation, Kierkegaard was concerned about establishing the authentic existence of the individual through a dialectic of existence. Kierkegaard's dialectic of "how" to become a Christian is associated with his critique of a Hegelianized culture-Christianity, and it makes him turn to subjectivity.

As far as how to become a Christian, Kierkegaard defines truth in light of the human subjectivity. As long as the question of the truth is posed subjectively, subjectivity or the existential individual becomes crucial in relation to the truth of religion. The question of *how* rather than *what* becomes decisive for religion. The question of *how* as it is associated with subjectivity would later become the war front between Barth and Brunner regarding a human point of contact with the redeeming grace of God. Christian subjectivity is directed toward the God-man. On the basis of a qualitative dialectic, the antithetical nature of God-man, eternity and time come into paradox. When the absolute paradox of the God-man becomes the pattern, Christianity comes into existence. That God becomes man, that eternity becomes time, is for Kierkegaard of paradoxical character. As Kierkegaard states, "The thing of being a Christian is not determined by the what of Christianity but by the how of the Christian. This how can only correspond with one thing, the absolute paradox."[22]

In his attack on Christendom, Kierkegaard introduces the concept of Christianity in the following way: "Christendom has done away with Christianity, without being quite aware of it. The consequence is that, if

---

21. *B-Th I*, 395. Barth reported about his preoccupation with Kierkegaard around 1919. In his letter to Thurneysen (on June 28, 1919) Barth wrote about "Kierkegaard's protest against the world of Christendom" in relation to Tertullian. In 1920 Barth wrote that "the writing often begins with small private morning devotions from Kierkegaard."

22. Barth, *Theology of Schleiermacher*. See also Kierkegaard, *Concluding Unscientific Postscript*, 540.

anything is to be done, one must try again to introduce Christianity into Christendom."²³ Criticizing Christendom as a hypocrisy, a betrayal and a mockery of God, Kierkegaard grounded his attack upon the Christianity of the New Testament, especially that of the Synoptic Gospels. To become a Christian means for Kierkegaard contemporaneity with Christ—which means at the same time a confrontation with the lowliness of God in this man. The God-man in the antithesis is in the paradox. Hegel's error, according to Kierkegaard, was in abolishing the dialectic of contradiction by introducing an aspect of "becoming" (*Werden*) into the dialectical logic of being, becoming, and nonbeing. Christianity requires a human being to restore a qualitative dialectic in recognizing the real qualitative distinctions, in contrast to Hegel's principle of dialectic in which everything different is labeled as logical monism.²⁴ Therefore in a framework of the qualitative dialectic of contradiction, the eternal truth remains in an absolute paradox; in other words, it remains independent of historical proof.²⁵

Following in the footsteps of Kierkegaard, Barth understands Jesus Christ only as paradox, as the end of history (R II:29). Within historical reality, Christ is presented only as problem or myth. In *Romans II* Barth appropriates the Kierkegaardian dialectic of the infinite difference between God and the world for the sake of God's aseity against the sinful condition of humans.²⁶ However, after Erik Perterson's attack on Barth's Kierkegaardian dialectics, Barth's theological subject matter of God appears as a mystery in a nondialectical way. In agreement with Peterson, Barth interprets revelation as being neither nondialectical nor paradoxical.²⁷

23. Kierkegaard, *Training in Christianity*, 39.

24. Kierkegaard, *On Authority and Revelation*, 165.

25. Ibid., 58. As Kierkegaard states, "It is important above all that there be fixed and unshakable qualitative difference between *the historical element in Christianity* (the paradox that the eternal came into existence once in time) and *the history of Christianity*, the history of its followers, etc." "The fact that the eternal once came into existence in time is not something which has to be tested in time, not something which *men are to test*, but is the paradox by which *men are to be tested*" (ibid., 58)

26. See the following references for Barth's term in the fashion of Kierkegaard: Christ as the paradox (R II:20, 25, 27), the problem of contemporaneity with Christ (R II:56–60), the infinite distinction (R II:124), the incarnation as the divine incognito (R II:112), and the impossibility of direct communication (R II:121–28).

27. In chapter 6, "Karl Barth: Between the Times in Germany," I will overview

Eschatology and the Social Question in the Second Edition of Romans

The Cross and Resurrection of Jesus Christ

In *Romans II* Barth attempted to demonstrate his understanding that God was in fact the No-God of this world. The true God would be sought in the Origin of the crisis. The God who is not the completely free, unique, superior, victorious God is the No-God, the God of this world (R II:82). "The true God, Himself removed from all concretion, is the Origin of the crisis of every concrete thing, the Judge, the negation of this world in which is included also the god of human logic" (R II:82). The human relationship to God becomes ungodly by confusing the temporal with God's eternity and permanence, and "in our drunken blurring of the distance which separates us from God, in our investing of men with the form of God" (R II: 168). God is not acknowledged as God, and what is called God is described by Barth as the "No-God of this world which we have created for ourselves" (R II:168).

Therefore as pure negation, God is transcendent over all this-worldly polarities. Furthermore, God as the one beyond the *Diesseits* and *Jenseits* stands over the dualism between nature and spirit, body and soul, or finite and infinite. God is not the Infinite but the Eternal. Therefore, God is the Creator of things, visible and invisible. God is beyond the line of death. Barth's dialectics of infinite qualitative distinction between eternity and time is not a metaphysical dualism, but a dialectical one. Therefore, "the Gospel of the Unknown God does not enter into competition with known divinities, such as Mithras or Isis or Kybles, to whom the sphere of religious phenomena belongs" (R II:192–93). God is always beyond the grasp of humankind. An affirmation and understanding of God comes about as the impossible, the miracle, where the paradox occurs.

Nevertheless, if God is beyond our grasp, how can God as *totaliter aliter* be known to us? God can only be known through God. The possibility of knowledge of God and faith lies in God alone. The dualism of Adam and Christ is not metaphysical but dialectical. The crisis of death and resurrection and the crisis of faith are a turning from God's "No" to God's "Yes." In spite of our inadequacy, we recognize the veritable possibility of divine action in Jesus Christ in whom we find "the sharply defined, final

---

the debate between Barth and Peterson with special attention given to the dialectic of Kierkegaard.

interpretation of the Word of the faithfulness of God to which the Law and the Prophets bore witness" (R II:97). God remains God even in divine revelation, and thus God remains God after the revelation. Jesus Christ is the medium of revelation, not the revelation as such. In Jesus Christ God reveals Godself relentlessly as the hidden, only indirectly-to-be-known God. Here God veils Godself definitively in order to be revealed only to faith. The revelation is the most complete veiling of divine incomprehensibility. "In Jesus, God becomes veritably a secret: He is made known as the Unknown, speaking in eternal silence" (R II:98). Faith in Jesus is the radical Nevertheless, "call[ing] upon God in His incomprehensibility and hiddenness" (R II:99). Barth's dialectic calls to mind the question of the degree to which he accepts the Calvinistic doctrine of *extra Calvinisticum* since his Christology in *Romans II* addresses Christ as the wholly other in Jesus.[28]

However, Barth's understanding of Jesus Christ in as paradox seems to be more inclined to Luther's reflection on *theologia crucis* than to Calvinistic doctrine of the *munus triplex* (R II:159). The *Deus absconditus* as such is Jesus Christ, *Deus revelatus*. Thus, Christ's life is known only through his resurrection. For Barth the life of Christ, which is his *oboedientia passiva*, must be seen from his death on the cross. To be sure, the Calvinistic doctrine of the *munus triplex* is insufficient and incomplete because it obscures and weakens the death of Christ in the New Testament (R II: 159). The content of *Romans*, of theology, and of God's Word is that the subject (*Deus absconditus*) has a predicate (the *Deus revelatus*). Therefore, knowledge of God is, according to Barth, based on the resurrection of the crucified. The resurrection of the crucified, which is the basis for *theologia crucis* in Barth's *Romans II*, makes God the Unintuitable one in terms of God's grace. God becomes intuitable only *sub specie mortis*, thus the event of the cross is the locus where the *Deus absconditus* becomes *Deus revelatus*. For Barth God as *Deus absconditus* is the one who raised Jesus from the dead. This oneness of *Deus absconditus* and *Deus revelatus* is our hope that "is summed up and manifested in all its invisibility and inaudibility in the Cross of Christ" (R II:394).[29]

28. Cf. Ruschke, *Entstehung und Ausführung der Diastasentheologie*, 41.
29. As Barth emphasizes in his *theologia crucis*: "Now the life of Christ is His *obedientia passiva*, His death on the cross. It is completely and solely and exclusively His death on the cross. The doctrine of the *munus triplex* obscures and weakens the New Testament concentration upon the death of Christ . . . Neither the personality of Jesus, nor the

The passion of Christ only becomes a parable of the kingdom of God in the event of revelation. Barth's dialectic of time and eternity, or the Kierkegaardian principle of dialectic, cannot be properly understood without taking into account Barth's *theologia crucis* in light of the resurrection of the crucified. "The Kingdom of God has its beginning on the other side of the Cross" (R II:159). As everything shines in the light of his death, so the kingdom of God has its beginning on the other side of the cross. The crisis for humankind is the fact that God reveals Godself in Jesus Christ; because of this fact, all human life undergoes a critical transvaluation. All creaturely reality in God's absolute crisis is for Barth in *Romans II* based on the self-revelation of God in the cross and the resurrection, which overcomes the *diastasis* between God and humankind. In the resurrection impossibility becomes possibility: "By this radical conception of death the autonomy of the power of resurrection is guaranteed as independent of the life which is on this side of the line of death" (R II:195).

To what extent does Barth express Jesus' death as God-abandonment on the cross? Would the death of Jesus be found as a model of the Father's abandonment of the Son? Or would the death of Jesus be found in the Father's full presence, even in solidarity with Christ in hell?[30] Jesus's death in God-abandonment, including the Father's self-giving, becomes the clue to uncover the veil of God. The veiling and unveiling event of *Deus absconditus* occurs in the cross and the resurrection. God is revealed as the God who shows God's faithfulness and grace to the human race even to the point of swallowing death itself in the self-negation of God. As far as the event of the cross becomes the parable of the kingdom, the king-

---

'Christ-idea' . . . nor his demand for repentance, nor His message of forgiveness . . . nor His call to poverty and discipleship; neither the implications of His Gospel for social life or for the life of the individual, nor the eschatological or the immediate aspects of His teaching concerning the Kingdom of God—none of these things exist in their own right. Everything shines in the light of His death, and is illuminated by it" (R II:159).

30. "*My God, my God, why hast thou forsaken me?*" Nevertheless, precisely in this negation He is the fulfillment of every possibility of human progress as the Prophets and the Law conceive of progress and evolution because He sacrifices to the incomparably Greater, and to the invisibly Other every claim to genius and every human heroic or aesthetic or psychic possibility because there is no conceivable human possibility of which He did not rid Himself. Herein He is recognized as the Christ; . . . In Him we behold the faithfulness of God in the depths of Hell. The Messiah is the end of mankind, and here also God is found faithful. On the day when mankind is dissolved the new era of the righteousness of God will be inaugurated" (R II:97).

dom of God can be understood as the eschatology of the resurrection of the crucified, in light of which everything temporal becomes parabolic in character and possibility. Thus all existing things can be thought of as being in the same nearness to the eschaton.[31]

For Barth *theologia crucis* is of eschatological character. It is also inclusive because it is a vicarious sacrifice, *satisfactio vicaria*, for all. Because of Christ's death, nobody and nothing can separate us "from the wholly incomprehensible love of God which is in Christ Jesus" (R II:329). Barth relates his idea of cross even to the earnest expectation of all creatures. All living creatures live in the time of the divine now, and bear the eternal, living, unborn future. "In every creature St. Paul, with his sharp, discerning, apostolic eye, perceived the holy and beloved Cross" [Luther] (R II:307). From the whole creation in groaning and travail, "this hopeful distress and this distress-ful hope are linked in one all-pervading unity" (R II:310). This is the secret of all secrets because the creature, in sighing, refers to the truth that is revealed in Christ by characterizing our temporal life as standing in this present time as well as in the opportunity of eternity.[32]

Does Barth's idea of eschatology in *Romans II* abandon totally his former eschatology of an organic-critical relation between God and human being in the first edition of *Romans*? Would the eschatology in organic growth toward God be in opposition to the eschatology in analogy? It is appropriate to say that from the time of the Tambach lecture, Barth deepened and actualized his organic-critical relation between God and the human being (in *Romans I*) in terms of analogy as the parabolic reality toward God in a negative-dialectical sense. From a critical-negative dialectical point of view, the world and human history have meaning as a parable of a wholly other world by bearing witness to a wholly other history. "They are, in fact, a parable, a witness, and a reminiscence, of God" (R II:107). However, apart from their subjection to the crisis of God, they are meaningless and incomprehensible. In his *Römerbrief* Barth's reflection on analogy or parable is already central to his reflection of *theologia crucis* in relation to the kingdom of God.

---

31. Kreck, *Zukunft des Gekommenen*, 40–50.
32. As Barth cites Luther: "No human intelligence or human wisdom can thus think and believe it ... The eyes capable of beholding this glory in the creature must be veritably apostolic and spiritual (Luther)" (R II:311).

The original form of the analogy of the cross can become a foundation for an analogy of faith. In this world it is impossible to be a human in union with God. In the paradox of faith, which we can never escape nor remove, "the cross is the bridge which creates a chasm and the promise which sounds a warning" (R II:112). From the vantage point of the cross, a human being is not able to stand before God in his or her own capacity, but rather in the divine attribute in which Christ stood before God through his God-abandonment. What is at stake is to proceed from the cross. His death becomes the only parable of the kingdom of God.

Starting from the cross refers to the positive significance of time-eternity dialectics because the analogy of the cross cannot be adequately understood without the resurrection as divine act. The death of Jesus is seen properly from the resurrection in the power of the Holy Spirit. The power of the resurrection, which is really the power of the Holy Spirit, is the key, and the cross over the threshold is the opening door (R II:188).[33] In the resurrection, the new world of the Holy Spirit touches the old world of the flesh as a tangent touches a circle without touching it. The resurrection of Jesus for Barth is bodily, corporeal, and personal: "The bodily resurrection of Christ stands over against His bodily crucifixion" (R II:205). In light of time-eternity dialectics, the resurrection took place in history but was not subjected to the time of history. "The resurrection is the non-historical (iv.17b) relating of the whole historical life of Jesus to its origin in God" (R II:195). Therefore *futurum resurrectionis* is "a parable of our eternity" and "our true and positive conformity to Jesus" (R II:196).[34]

In the name of Jesus Christ, two worlds encounter and are separated from each other. The intersection between the unhistorical event and historical time is a real and dialectic one. In the resurrection, Barth says, the new world of the Holy Spirit touches the old world of the flesh (R II:30). The resurrection as the point of intersection between God and the world becomes known and graspable in the event of the cross by way

---

33. "The Resurrection is the revelation: the disclosing of Jesus as the Christ, the appearing of God, and the apprehending of God in Jesus. The Resurrection is the emergence of the necessity of giving glory to God: the reckoning with what is unknown and unobservable in Jesus, the recognition of Him as Paradox, Victor, and Primal History" (R II:30).

34. In light of conformity to Christ, Barth took baptism to be "the visible fellowship with God in the bearing of His cross" (R II: 196).

of God's grace. "'Grace is opposed to sin, and devours it' (Luther)" (R II:190). Grace is incommensurable with sin. Sin is to grace what impossibility is to possibility. Grace as the act of God makes our negative human existence without conformity with Jesus "filled with hope by the positive and secret power of the resurrection" (R II:197). "The totality of our human will and intelligence, future as well as past, has been superseded by the pre-eminent, ineffable, and invisible power of our eternal future existence—*futurm aeternum*—the future of the non-concrete possibility of God. This is grace" (R II:191). In this regard Barth interprets grace as the power of the resurrection.

In Barth's dialectical understanding of revelation and resurrection, Christ intersects vertically from above, so that the resurrection is the revelation. "The Resurrection from the dead is, however, the transformation: the establishing or *declaration* of that point from above, and the corresponding discerning of it from below" (R II:30). Insofar as God is the power of the resurrection, we recognize ourselves as the subject of the *futurm resurrectionis*. "The pressure of the power of the Resurrection into my existence, which of necessity involves a real walking in newness of life, cannot be an event among other events in my present, past, or future life" (R II:195). Given the cross and resurrection of Jesus Christ, Barth's eschatology is christologcally structured so that his eschatology of the infinite qualitative distinction between God and humanity is conceptualized in a negative-dialectical-parabolic sense, not in a metaphysical-separatist sense.[35]

Negative Dialectics from a Sociopolitical Point of View

Barth's assertion that the critical historian needs to be more critical (R II:8) implies that Barth is not a bitter enemy of historical criticism. What Barth perceives as the inner dialectic of the subject matter has nothing to do with "the word 'God'" as "the value of a clearly defined, metaphysical entity" (R II:484). For the exegesis in *Romans II*, Barth calls for the necessity of the world of contemporaneity: "A wide reading of contemporary secular literature—especially of newspapers!—is therefore recommended to any one desirous of understanding the Epistle to the Romans" (R

---

35. However, Barth later made a correction regarding his eschatological position in *Romans II* which he came to see as statics and non-relevance to the history. CD II/1: 636.

II:425). It is of special significance to realize that Barth's negative dialectic cannot be properly understood without serious consideration of its sociopolitical contemporaneity. Barth writes in his exegesis of Romans 8:24; "*By hope we are saved*—inasmuch as in Jesus Christ the wholly Other, unapproachable, unknown, *eternal power and divinity* (i.20) of God has entered into our world . . . *for hope that is seen is not hope*. Direct communication from God is no divine communication. If Christianity be not altogether thoroughgoing eschatology, there remains in it no relationship whatever with Christ" (R II:314).

In *Romans I* as well as in *Romans II*, human society stands under God's judgment. But in *Romans I* God's "Yes" is concealed in God's "No" that was revealed in Christ. In experiencing God's "No" in Christ, humankind comes to know God directly as an impossible possibility. When humanity was seized by Christ humanity was put into a position to acknowledge God's "Yes." Otherwise, in *Romans II* the believer—with Job— loves the God who is only to be feared in God's unsearchable eminence or prominence. With Luther, the believer loves the *Deus absconditus*. The wrath of God is "the protest pronounced always and everywhere against the course of the world in so far as we do not accept the protest as our own" (R II:42). Apart from faith in the resurrection, and without Christ, God is a final consequence of divine wrath. God comes to humankind as the crisis of human experience, and as crisis God comes as "the new world which is set at the barrier of this world" (R II:65).

In *Romans I* a praxis of human being is oftentimes interrelated with the inherent power of God's grace so that it was not clear yet if God was understood as the subject who makes the old relation anew (R I:169).[36] Other than in *Romans I*, Barth proclaimed the right of individual, that is, the infinite value of the single individual, in accordance with Kierkegaard. God's relation to the world and human beings is existentialized in *Romans II* as opposed to in *Romans I*, which conceptualizes the human being as a member of a divine-world organism (R I:202). The subject of crisis under which the world of the human being is placed is God. It is God as

---

36. Barth, later in his doctrine of baptism, sharpens his early idea of human praxis under grace (R I:169), through which the irreconcilability between human self-determination and God's grace is overcome. God effects the word and the transformed situation by the Word. The creative action of God and humanity is reversed. Even a Marxist idea of human self-creation (the human is what one will make out of oneself) is conceived of as the idea of grace. Marquardt, *Theologie und Sozialismus*, 282. Cf. *KD* IV/4: 45–49.

wholly other who put humans into the crisis. Barth's theology of crisis, as a result, becomes critical of all that exists. God, who is the subject behind the crisis, is the completely different (*ganz Ändernde*), who establishes infinite qualitative difference from the world. Barth's conception of the inner dialectic of the subject matter in the actual words of the text is of special significance for understanding Barth's negative dialectics. Barth himself relegates his inner dialectic to Kierkegaard's conception of the infinite qualitative distinction between time and eternity. This has negative as well as positive significance (R II:10). God is in heaven, and humans are on earth. This is called the crisis of human perception—*Ursprung* (R II:10).

Negatively speaking, God's power unto salvation is "so new, so unheard of, so unexpected in this world," revealing that God enters into the world as contradiction (R II:38). This refers to the dialectic of contradiction; God affirms Godself as God denies the world and human being. The true God is the Origin of the crisis of every concrete thing, who is removed from all concretion and becomes the Judge of the world (R II:82). "In the place of the Holy God there then appear Fate, Matter, the Universe, Chance, Ananke. Indeed, a certain perception is betrayed when we begin to avoid giving the name 'God' to the 'No-God' of unbelief (i.17)" (R II:43).

Positively speaking, the crisis in which the old human beings find themselves is the turning from divine "No" to divine "Yes." Therefore the contrast between God and human being is not of metaphysical character, but dialectical. Furthermore, Barth's dialectic is that of the movement. This is the negation of negation, which means *Jenseits* for the *Dieseits* and vice versa. The resurrection of Jesus Christ overcomes the negative sense of human existence. It means the synthesis of God and human being, the new world and the old world. The dualism between Adam and Christ, between the old and the new, "exists only in so far as it dissolves itself." "It is a dualism of one movement, of one apprehension, of one road from here to there" (R II:177). It is not "an equilibrium resulting from two equal forces operating in opposite directions." "The KRISIS of death and resurrection, the KRISIS of faith, is a turning from the divine 'No' to the divine 'Yes'" (R II:177).

Therefore humans have only the possibility of faith. In the prophet's no, we encounter the faithfulness of God. We meet the faith of humans "in the awe of those who affirm the 'No' and are ready to accept the void and to move and tarry in negation" (R II:42). As the human moves and tarries in negation, human history is comprehended in its relation to God. Because of the fact that the new and the better are yet to come, the human being remains in the negation in expectation of the radical *Jenseits* (other side) of this world. How and to what extent do we discern in this dialectic of negation a social political dimension? As long as there is hope for the new and the better in expectation of the radical *Jenseits* of this world, the negative dialectic is of anti-ideological character. In other words, it retains an ideologically critical function in protest against the wrong consciousness of this world.

Given this fact, I am convinced that a parallel can be found between Barth's negative dialectics and Adorno's negative dialectics.[37] In his critique of identity and the positivism of pure immediacy in the cognitive and epistemological act, Adorno reappropriates the Marxist critique of a society under the domination of exchange value, in that individuals are reduced to the same level as things. For Adorno, anyone who is enslaved to the identity principle—that is, uncritical and positivist acceptance of society dominated by the reified relation of exchange value—is ignorant of qualitative differences. At this juncture Adorno's negative dialectics retain a critical function with regard to ideology in the way that the mechanism of bourgeois society associated with the domination of the exchange-value relation reduces all qualitative differences to the common basis of reification.

In a similar vein, in the context of judgment, Barth said that God becomes ideology at the point where the human being assumes and appropriates the standpoint of God without God. When human beings adopt God's point of view or do something in cooperation with God, God becomes an ideology, i.e., a notion (R II:74). In this process the consciousness of the human being is misplaced. Thus theology has a task to

---

37. According to Adorno, Western philosophy has always drifted into the search for an absolute starting point, namely, an identity in a metaphysical and epistemological realm. A philosophy of negative dialectics is the destructive resistance to and the constant negation of any attempt at perpetuating an authoritative form of domination and reducing the human subject to reified forms for the sake of the identity principle. Dialectics is not merely an investigation of contradiction for a higher solution of it, i.e., synthesis. Rather it is an act of repeated protest and opposition to all methods claiming universality and identity. "Total contradiction is nothing but the manifested untruth of total identification." Negative dialectics is basically an anti-system. Cf. Adorno, *Negative Dialectics*, 6.

uncover and bring to the light the false consciousness in which confusion between God and the human being, and the divine and the human being, occurred. An attempt to produce idols and the reification related to idol production is strongly challenged. In other words, as theology assumes the standpoint of God, God remains moving in the negation. Here theology is able to eschew the fetish is of this world in producing idols.

> We assume that He *needs something*: and so we assume that we are able to arrange our relation to Him as we arrange our other relationships. We press ourselves into proximity with Him. . . . We dare to deck ourselves out as His companions, patrons, advisers, and commissioners. We confound time with eternity . . . . In 'believing' on Him, we justify, enjoy, and adore ourselves. Our devotion consists in a solemn affirmation of ourselves and of the world and in a pious setting aside of the contradiction. Under the banners of humanity and emotion we rise in rebellion against God (R II:44).

In setting God upon the throne of the world, Barth argues, humankind takes the place of God. In the wake of this, the appearance of idols becomes an inevitable reality. When our relation to God exists apart from and without Christ, what is called God is, in fact, man. "By living to ourselves, we serve the 'No-God'" (R II:44). An illusion of the reality of human life takes place to point out the contrast between ideology and reality. History is the locus where the discrepancy between ideology and praxis of alienated humans takes place. According to Barth, history is defined as "the display of the supposed advantage of power and intelligence which some men possess over others" (R II:77). In other words, this is the display of "the struggle for existence hypocritically described by ideologists as a struggle for justice and freedom, of the ebb and flow of old and new forms of human righteousness, each vying with the rest in solemnity and triviality"(R II:77).

As human beings struggle for their rights and freedom, they in fact practice the opposite. They add wrongdoing and oppression. They are taken captive by the dictatorships they create. Such is the consequence of lordless powers under which false consciousness consolidates and perpetuates a false praxis. The judgment of God is the end of history, and by God's doing away with it God is recognized as the judge. "The redeemer is also the Creator." Under God's judgment, "a transformation is effected so radical that time and eternity, here and there, the righteousness of men and the righteousness of God, are indissolubly linked together" (R II:77). Seen under the judgment of God, human dignitaries forfeit their excellence and importance. Even the noblest of human moral and spiritual achievements are proved to be natural, profane, and materialistic. Therefore, in accordance with God as the eternal, pure Origin of all things, a negative dialectic forces human beings to assume a critical position against all that exists. Therefore the negative dialectic appears as the negation of the false consciousness. When ethics are possible in this regard, they exist only as a critique of every ethos that engages in protest against the ideology and praxis by calling into question the crisis of human being and society.[38]

Political praxis in a positive sense corresponds to the divine negation of the world as a politics of protest against the existing social order. The critique of ideology that is performed in light of the negative dialectic is to be seen against the social dimension of reification and fetishism. Human beings make their political thoughts and deeds the instruments in order to avoid the crisis into which God places them. The critique of religion for Barth retains a critique of fetishim, in which "the 'No-God' is set up, idols are erected, and God, who dwells beyond all this and that, is 'given up'" (R II:50-51). Human conduct is governed and ruled by what humans desire. Human beings become slaves and puppets of things, of nature and of civilization. "Deified nature and deified spirits of men are, in truth, very gods; like Jupiter and Mars, Isis and Osiris, Cybele and Attis, they come to be the very breath of our life" (R II:51).

Barth's critique of religion is supposed to be seen against the background of a critique of ideology. Feuerbach is the person who helps Barth to see clearly that sinful passion is set in motion with the intrusion of the possibility of religion. As Barth states, "In religion the supreme competence of human possibility attains its consummation and final realization . . . ; for in the end human passion derives its living energy from that

---

38. "Once again, then, we are confronted by the problem of the 'This-sideness' of the whole course of our concrete existence. Once again—and now quite unavoidably—our life and will and acts are brought in question. For the freedom of God, the 'Other-sideness' of His mercies, means that there is a relationship between God and man, that there is a dissolution of human 'This-sideness', and that a radical assault is made upon every contrasted, second, other, things. . . . If, therefore, the Church is to be a place of exhortation, it must be a Church altogether aware of its final and indissoluble solidarity with this world of 'dry bones'; it must be a Church which has set its hope upon God only" (R II:427-28).

passionate desire: *Eritis sicut Deus!* In religion this final passion becomes conscious and recognizable as experience and event" (R II:236). Sounding similar to Marx's critique of religion as an opiate, Barth argues that instead of counteracting human illusions, religion acts upon humans "like a drug which has been extremely skillfully administered" by introducing "an alternative condition of pleasurable emotion." The possibility of religions amounts to "bringing forth a rich and most conspicuous harvest of *fruit unto death* (R II:236). In critically examining the human process of making God as a thing in itself, Barth sees in the Marxist critique of religion justification for the revolt of Prometheus against Zeus—"'No-God'—has been exalted to the throne of God" (R II:48).

Barth's point of departure *von Gott aus* functions as a critique of religion for the sake of the right of the individual: "It is precisely we who proclaim the right of the individual, the eternal worth of each single one [Kierkegaard!], by announcing that his soul is lost before God and, in Him, is dissolved—and saved" (R II:116). "The frontier of religion is the line of death which separates flesh from spirit, time from eternity, human possibility from the possibility of God" (R II:238). Our concrete status in the world of time lies under the shadow of death. What is most characteristic of religious piety is the expectation of life in which the human being is attached to religion "with a bourgeois tenacity." "But religion must die. In God we are rid of it" (R II:238). In critiquing religion as ideology, Barth analyzed and questioned the existence of the "bourgeois man." The bourgeois person is the current form of the conservative human. This one legitimizes the existing social order and identifies him- or herself with it, without reservation. This person also confesses allegiance to the great positions of state, rights, church, and society. Barth characterizes the bourgeois person in terms of the satisfied bourgeois of affirmation who becomes the reactionary. In Barth's view, the bourgeois person is seen and analyzed in association with the reactionary, the counterrevolutionary, the legitimist, or the conservative person.

The political praxis of the bourgeois person is seen in her/his active part in the social struggle for existence. Under the struggle for existence, Barth sees that the final vacuity and disintegration happens. As chaos finds itself in disintegration, human reason becomes irrational. As the world is full of personal caprice and social unrighteousness, the true nature of our unbroken existence is unrolled before us. So our ungodliness and unrighteousness stand under the wrath of God (R II:53). Barth understands the struggle for existence as the human urge toward consumption, possession, success, knowing, power, and right. The social existence of the bourgeois person consists of the struggle for his/her own life which he/she forces through against the life-demand and right-demand of the co-fellow. The co-fellow becomes an enemy, in other words, the class enemy, because the struggle for existence is the struggle for preference and privilege, which, in the end, leads to class struggle (R II:51).[39]

Seen in light of God's measurement, even the highest, the most noble and spiritual contrasts among humans appear in their natural, inner-worldly, profane, materialistic significance (R II:56). Human righteousness, as such, is an illusion. People are engaged hypocritically in establishing things in order to guarantee themselves against the riddle of their own existence by claiming to "possess a higher right over their fellows." Even the supreme democratic majority "assumes that a quite fortuitous contract or arrangement should be regarded as superior to the solid organization of the struggle for existence" (R II:479).[40] Human righteousness produces a class society in which human beings exhibit wrongdoing and oppression toward one another. Given this fact, Barth's theological dialectic—"all that exists is as such evil" (R II:480)—is related to his critique of the struggle for existence as a false political praxis in bourgeois society. For Barth, revolution is born out of perceiving that evil lies in the very existence of the existing government. Social order, which is stamped by class society, is not in a position to create rights, freedom, and peace for human beings. The revolutionary makes an attempt to remove the evil in battling and overthrowing it. This one begins by "simply harboring a certain secret poisonous resentment against the existing order" (R II:480).

In light of the resurrection, Barth is not hesitant to back up the cause of socialism for the poor and revolution. Barth's negative dialectics does not say that all cows are black at night. Rather it seeks a politics of protest that would more readily correspond with the kingdom of God because there is a certain inclination and affinity in the God of the gospel to take

---

39. Barth's analysis of history in terms of historical materialism. R II:51, 61, 260, 295–96.

40. At this juncture, Barth is critical of the form of theocracy in Calvin. "If for example, the Church of Calvin were to be reformed and broadened out to be the Church of the League of Nations; this doing of the supreme right would then become the supreme wrong-doing" (R II:479).

sides with those who are "immature, sullen, and depressed"; and with those who "'come off badly' and are . . . ready for revolution." To what extent does Barth in *Romans II* view the cause of revolution in Russia in light of negative dialectics?

> Christianity does not set its mind on *high things*. It is uneasy when it hears men speaking loudly and with confidence about 'creative evolution'; . . . Christianity is unhappy when men boast of the glories of marriage and of family life, of Church and State, and of Society. Christianity does not busy itself to support and underpin,—individualism, collectivism, nationalism, internationalism, humanitarianism, ecclesiasticism. . . . It sees the rich man, not of course actually dead, but still in the torment of Hades. Finding truth more in 'No' than in 'Yes', Christianity recommends men to *condescend to things that are lowly*. . . . Christianity displays a certain inclination to side with those who are immature, sullen, and depressed, with those who 'come off badly' and are, in consequence, ready for revolution. There is, for this reason, much in the cause of socialism which evokes Christian approval. Christianity beholds Lazarus—that is, the poor man as such—not, of course, *with God,* but, nevertheless, in Abraham's bosom. It sees in the lowly at least a parable of life. This is because it cannot forget the meaning of resurrection. (R II:462–63)

Barth's Critique of the Revolutionary Process in Russia

Following *Romans I* Barth makes use of his theological term the "revolution of God" as a criterion to judge human revolutions. In *Romans II* Barth's term "revolution of God" is associated with his principle of the dialectic of the infinite qualitative difference between God and humans in accepting the Reformation doctrine of grace. The discourse of the revolution of God is monopolized by God, that is to say, only God's act is revolutionary. The revolution of God that takes place against us occurs for us, but no longer with us and in us as it is seen in *Romans I*. It takes place basically against us. We are no longer co-workers in participation in the revolution of God, as we are in *Romans I*. As Marquardt suggests, so far as in *Romans I* Barth thinks of God from the perspective of "revolution," he now furthers his efforts in *Romans II* to think of revolution from the perspective of "God."[41]

In *Romans I* Barth was entangled in political complexity and upheavals in view of the Russian revolution, as he stood in parallel with revolutionary upheavals in Germany and general strikes in Switzerland. The first Romans commentary was written in view of the revolution question in a revolutionary situation and filled with profound and hope-carrying participation and involvement. However, the years of 1918 to 1922 bore witness to the disillusionment of many socialist intellectuals in Europe, who experienced the failure of revolutions in Germany and the distortion of the revolutionary cause in Russia. This disillusionment marked Barth's political stance in *Romans II*. Barth makes his way on the most extreme left, turning away from religious socialism to Social Democracy in *Romans I*. Barth's model of the revolution of God is more than Leninism. In *Romans II*, however, Barth takes a road of anti-authoritative demonstration and protest politics in criticizing the Bolshevist-revolution model in light of God as the *totaliter aliter*, a revolution monopolized only by God.

An attempt to monopolize the revolution for God's sake does not intend to weaken but to radicalize the turning from the old world to the new world. Following in the footsteps of Barth, Gollwitzer distinguishes reformism from revolution in saying that reformism occurs in the constant of the system, while revolution is the transcendence of the system. To be sure, a revolutionary attitude ascends toward the qualitatively new, out of which all that exists appears as something to be overcome or to be worthy of overcoming. Therefore "reformism and revolution no longer stand in exclusive opposition."[42] Likewise, Barth says that God wants to be acknowledged as the Victor over the wrongdoing of existence. Along the lines of Blumhardt's message of "Jesus is Victor," Barth's concept of *theologia crucis* gives a christological dynamism to his term "revolution of God" by critically engaging in the problem of revolution and the revolutionary in Russia (cf. "Negative Possibilities," [Rom 7:16–20]; "The Great Negative Possibility" [Rom 7:21—8:7]).

> The revolutionary has made mistakes. He wanted *the* revolution, which is the impossible possibility, i.e., the forgiveness of sin and the resurrection of the dead. This is the answer to the

---

41. Marquardt, *Theologie und Sozialismus*, 143.
42. Gollwitzer, "Kingdom of God and Socialism in the Theology of Karl Barth," 84.

insult, which lies in the existing as such. *Jesus* is victor! But he [the revolutionary] has made the *other* revolution, i.e., the possible possibility of the dissatisfaction, the hatred, the insubordination, the upheaval and the destruction. This is not better, but worse than its opposite, i.e., contentment, satisfaction, safety and presumption, for by dissatisfaction God is far better understood, but far worse misused. He [the revolutionary] wants *the* revolution, which means the establishment of the true order, and makes the *other* revolution which is the true reaction. (The legitimist, on the other hand, himself also overcome of evil, aims at *the* Legitimism which means inauguration of the true Revolution; but he defends *another* legitimism which is, in fact, revolt!) (R II:481)

According to Barth, the occurrence of the revolutionary figure is the consequence of fundamental political antagonism located in a class oriented society. In other words, the conservative or bourgeois stimulates the uprising of the revolutionary. From the perception of evil that lies at the existence of the existing government, revolution is born: "The revolutionary seeks to be rid of the evil by bestirring himself to battle with it and to overthrow it" (R II:480). In the knowledge of the evil in the social order, the revolutionary is born so as to get rid of the existing order as the embodiment of wrongdoing. Thus revolutionaries seek to establish the new and the right in place of injustice. It is the main task for them to deconstruct the existing world through political praxis. This radical negation that the revolutionary attempts is a plausible plan that we cannot refuse. "He [the revolutionary] too is claiming what no man can claim. He too is making of the right a thing. He too confronts other men with his supposed right. He too usurps a position which is not due to him, a legality which is fundamentally illegal, an authority which—as we have grimly experienced in Bolshevism, but also in the behavior of far more delicate-minded innovators!—soon displays its essential tyranny" (R II:480).

Nevertheless Barth presses beyond the critique of the revolution in *Romans I* and now in *Romans II* arrives remarkably at the rejection of the revolutionary way. The revolutionary becomes far worse than the conservative or bourgeois. No doubt that the praxis of the revolutionary comes closer to the truth than the reactionary, because we find divine negation and destruction of the existing in the revolutionary ethos. As the revolutionaries, with their no to the existing order, place themselves uncannily close to the divine No, they hold a special focus of theology for themselves: "Far more than the conservative, the revolutionary is *overcome of evil*, because with his 'No' he stands so strangely near to God. This is the tragedy of revolution" (R II:480). The revolutionary has a preference for the negation of the organization of the struggle for existence that is hypocritically veiled through the ideology of right and freedom: in other words, the class society. For this reason, Barth takes more account of the revolutionary than the reactionary. Barth is, in his own words, "most anxious about the man who embarks upon revolution," whereas he has no material interest in the principle of Legitimism (R II:477).

Nevertheless, Barth's concern does not lie in the revolution as such, but in speaking of the particular existing ordinances of human social life for the sake of demonstration. In fact, the great demonstration to the coming world's order must break through (R II:476). Revolution should not lead to disorder and violence; rather social order and ordinances can retain eschatological quality as the order of the coming world. Barth's anti-Leninist position of demonstration points to a third possibility of reform politics in which revolutionary tactics, the counterrevolutionary strategy, and the legitimist way are all rejected. Therefore Barth's critical revision reached the pseudolevel of high objectivity, which consists in "the great positions of Church and State, of Law and Society" (R II:477). Barth's radical critique of existence plays a decisive role in his pursuit of anti-authoritative and anti-Leninist demonstration for the glory of God. Barth asks what the existing order means.[43]

Barth's position in *Romans II*—what exists is evil as such (R II:480)—is not meant to be a confirmation of the counterrevolutionary way. Therefore, Barth's negative dialectics retain the idea of critical utopia in transcending the actual world, but this transcendence has, in principle, no definite content or form of identity principle at the present time. According to Barth's analysis, the revolutionaries who have been lost must take seriously their revolutionary program and political praxis in correspondence to the revolution of God for the purpose of self-critique. What Barth proposes for this work is to take account of the politics of patient reform work inside the existing structure rather than to point to the

---

43. "The invectives that have been hurled against 'Governments' from the days of the Revelation of John to the fulminations of Nietzsche, from the Anabaptists to the Anarchists, have not been directed against defects in government but against the right of governments to exist at all" (R II:479).

counterrevolution. With this intent in mind, Barth engages in a confrontation with the Red Brothers in Russia, the Bolshevists.[44] The disquiet, the questioning, the negation, the emphatic insistence upon the parable of death, to which Christianity is definitely committed (R II:xii, 16) may be so misunderstood as to be transformed into a positive method of human behavior, into a means of justification, indeed, into the titanism of revolt and upheaval and renovation. The revolutionary titan is far more godless, far more dangerous, than his reactionary counterpart—because he is so much nearer to the truth. To us, at least, the reactionary presents little danger; with his Red brother it is far otherwise. With this danger we are vitally concerned. "For the honor of God we have to bring the revolutionary within the orbit of sacrifice; and his sacrifice is a sacrifice of quite peculiar dignity!" (R II:478).

Barth's analysis of the process of revolution is concretely related to the postrevolutionary violence process in Russia. In this regard, Barth reflects critically on the tyranny of Bolshevism. In *Romans II* Barth casts a critical eye on the social political situation in Russia, a nation threatened by the terror of the Red army in the postwar revolutionary process in Russia. Besides, Barth is aware of the White Russian counter-revolution (in 1920 led by Denikin and Koltchak). "The action of the White Guard" (R II:486), which is in support of the existing order by opposing all revolutionary movements, according to Barth, is intolerable to God. "Behind the existing order—which may itself be new!—stands God. He is the Judge, and He is the Right. Insubordination—and there is also a conservative insubordination!—is insubordination against Him" (R II:486). A principal negation of revolution in a Barthian fashion has little to do with what the counterrevolution represents at the time.

With the terror and violence of postrevolutionary Russia in mind, Barth continues his confrontation with Leninism that had begun in *Romans I*. Barth's critique of the existing sociopolitical structure is radicalized to a critique of the existing structure through the revolution. In contrast to *Romans I*, which was written in the purview of the process of revolution in 1917 and 1918, Barth's critique of nonradical revolution is applied to the Bolshevist revolution in the inceptive stage of its realization and its own existence (1919–1922). The revolutionary order, which had become status quo, had replaced the existing order. It is noteworthy

---

44. Cf. Thurneysen, "Unser roten Brüder," in *Die Glocke* 22 (1914), Nr.8.

that Barth's critique and rejection of the Red Brothers as well as White Guard is carried out from the perspective of the radical socialist position on the most extreme left.[45]

For Barth in *Romans II*, the gospel of Jesus Christ is always calling for the countermovement of God, which points, at a minimum, to a reform politics inside the system, but that tends to transcend the system itself. Therefore it stands as partisanship for the weak against the encroaching form of the strong. Politically speaking, Christianity finds itself as the one on the leftist side against the representative of social disorder. The Russian revolutionaries fell disastrously into a vicious circle because they were not the subject to that free being for which they thirsted. They were not architects of the new order. The revolutionary that had been grimly experienced in Bolshevism "is not the Christ who stands before the Grand Inquisitor, but is, contrariwise, the Grand Inquisitor encountered by the Christ" (R II:480).

The titanism of revolt is Promethean arrogance. Revolution and order belong together only if they are not the product of the existing order; they must be the work of God, because God as God is the New. The new world of God will be revolution and order in one. The revolution and order of God cannot be found but always only sought. They are not at the disposal of the human being. The true revolution of God reveals the alleged revolution of the revolutionary as a mere revolt, in that the existing order will never be removed.

> Even the most radical revolution can do no more than set what *exists* against what *exists*. Even the most radical revolution—and this is so even when it is called a "spiritual" or "peaceful" revolution—can be no more than a revolt; that is to say, it is in itself simply a justification and confirmation of what already exists. For the whole relative right of what exists is established only by the

---

45. In his Tambach lecture (1919), Barth's "hope-sharing and guilt-sharing comrades" within the social democracy mark Barth's opposition to Communism in Russia. Barth's political stance at this time might be heard from "Democracy or Dictatorship" (on April 16 of 1919). The International marches again in the direction of Eisners, namely in the direction toward the zeal of the Munich councilor republic. Kurt Eisner was leading the revolutionary movement in Bavaria when revolution broke out in late 1918. Einsner represented a left-wing version of Social Democracy along the line of Landauer's idea of the workers' council. The Workers' Republic in Munich was of short duration; as a right-wing offensive it led the Communists to take over. The Communist Republic was soon crushed by the proto-Nazi freebooters.

relative wrong of revolution in its victory; whereas the relative right of revolution in its victory is in no way established by the relative wrong of the existing order. (R II:482)

The resisting power of the existing order is not broken through the victorious attack of revolution but is only compromised and forced into another form and thus becomes dangerous. The revolutionary becomes counterrevolutionary because the victory of the revolution is the victory of one part of the existing order. The revolutionary who becomes conservative appeals to the use of violence because the newly established social order is determined through the struggle for existence and class society. The revolutionary becomes the new power elite, who, by veiling the class dictatorship with the help of the ideology of rights and freedom, rules the remaining society: "The more successfully the good and the right assume concrete form, the more they become evil and wrong—*summum jus, summa injuria*" (R II:479).

The true revolution comes from God, and besides God's revolution there is only human rebellion. In deepening and contrasting God's revolution as the critique and transcendence of Bolshevist revolution, Barth understood his reflection on the revolution of God as a contribution to the world-historical theme of revolution. It functions as the prejudgment not for the existing ordinances but against the revolution because the Bolshevist revolution is not capable or competent to produce the eschatological reality envisioned in the Christian message, namely, the real and social content of the forgiveness of sin and the resurrection from the dead. In his witness to the glory of God, Barth included socialist eschatology into his theological reflection.

Moreover, a function of his critique is the mediation of the theological aspect with the world-historical content of forgiveness of sin and the resurrection from the dead. This is the counterpart to the one-sided exclusion of a theological aspect through the Bolshevists, and also of the world-historical content through the Christian bourgeois counterrevolutionary. The negative dialectic is therefore to reverse the *revolution* of God into *God's* revolution. Understood in this sense, society and theology no longer stand like question and answer in the apologetic sense. Rather theological discourse on God, as such, is through and through reflective of social and political character and contour. God's negation is not the operation and effect of a denying Spirit, but the Spirit of justice and righteousness. God is a breakthrough, springing out from inside, and is therefore the relativization of evil. In relation to God everything appears to be different, completely different. God's relativization of evil in a revolutionary way as well as in the reactionary way means an introduction into a new horizon, namely the demonstration of God's glory.

Barth is aware of the relative possibility of good in the midst of evil. The parabolic and analogical notion of the kingdom of God is relevant to radical, eschatological, and revolutionary theology with respect to the creaturely realms, in that God is not supposed to be replaced by the world-historical movement. As Barth had already stated in his Tambach lecture, the movement of God does not begin with our protest movement. In seeing God function as the relativization of the evil within the existing society, Barth relativizes, demythologizes, and humanizes the Promethean arrogance of the revolutionary in the direction of self-critique and self-renewal. In *Romans II* God's revolution means the relativization of evil as well as the relativization of the revolutionary: "It is most improbable that any one will be won over to the cause of reaction—as a result of reading the Epistle to the Romans!" (R II:478). Barth's discourse on God in relation to the world historical revolution has little to do with metaphysical givenness. God is and becomes God in *God's* revolution; in other words, in God's predestination of love and freedom.

When it comes to the problem of ethics, Barth's negative dialectics is in search of God's action, which is deeply embedded in the world of the newspaper. The whole person "must share in the tension of human life, in its crisis-cross lines, and in its kaleidoscopic movements" (R II:425), which means the whole context of human life and reality stand under crisis. Human thought and life must not be detached from their context; such detachment leads to superficiality. Although Barth describes God's relational action with the world in terms of the dialectical method, this method in itself is not enough, because genuine thought must always be broken thought. In other words, dialectical method is also under the eschatological proviso. "Break off your thinking that it may be a thinking of God; break off your dialectic, that it may be indeed dialectic" (R II:426). In doing so, the wholesome disturbance and interruption of God's preparation in the revelation of Jesus Christ calls for humans to come back home to the peace of God's kingdom.

Christian Ethics under Eschatological Reservation

Barth's eschatological perspective of Christian ethics is contextually relevant to the contemporary world of secular literature rather than assuming a postmodern-deontological direction. A postmodern reading of Barth's negative dialectics in the fashion of Derrida (in his critique of metaphysics of presence and binary oppositional thinking)[46] would be skewed to the point that it completely ignores Barth's sensitivity to the hermeneutics of contemporaneity. Detached from Barth's life-setting, such a reading would be in opposition to what Barth really tried to do in *Romans II*: "A wide reading of contemporary secular literature—especially of newspaper!—is therefore recommended to any one desirous of understanding the Epistle to the Romans" (R II:425).

Despite Barth's preference for dialectical thinking, it is not elevated as a theological principle in place of God's standpoint. God's self-revelation is not at the disposal of human capacity when it comes to humans' speaking of God. Therefore, we cannot speak of God even in a dialectical way. According to Barth, the possibility of theology arises only where God speaks. Theology as possibility is not human, but divine, possibility. In spite of this eschatological proviso, the Word of God makes human language significant and capable of bearing witness to it. In accordance with this subject matter, human language is of analogical and parabolic relation between similarity and dissimilarity when it speaks of God. In *Romans II* Barth had already mentioned that the dialectical method is also under the eschatological proviso. In order for dialectics to be genuine thinking, in speaking of God we must break off our dialectic so that it may be indeed dialectic (R II:426). Genuine dialectics, which is broken and wounded under the eschatological reservation, is complemented and supplemented by Barth's teaching of analogy based on God's possibility.

In political demonstration for the glory of God, God as the unknown and hidden God is not a metaphysical dualistic principle but the One whom Barth bears witness to in a dialectical way of sharpening and concretization. The dialectics in Barth's thought results from the combination of, on the one hand, a horizontal God-human relation and, on the other hand, a vertical and christological revealing of God's hiddenness. God retreats from God's hiddenness in order to come to humans. Barth's

---

46. Lowe, *Theology and Difference*.

dialectics of revelation implies a social-historical event. Thus his idea of demonstration possesses social and critical content and contour. It aims at active political praxis as the protest against the existing social order, and in so doing calls for the breakdown of the revolutionary way for taking into account reform work. The politics of the protest, in other words, the tendency to protest—because of an absence of confusion between human protest and divine negation—retains positive and ethical significance in relation to human being and acts. How does human ethical action become possible in light of Barth's negative dialectics?

In *Romans II* Barth states that "the problem of ethics is identical with the problem of dogmatics" (R II:431). As far as the problem of ethics is related to the truth of God, it is in no way actually present or apprehended in a human act of thinking. In agreement with Luther, Barth argues that God's grace means the exposition of the validity of grace, which "involves a perception of the pre-supposition of grace in all concrete phenomena" (R II: 428). "*In medio inimicorum regnum Christi est* (Luther)" (R II:429). Barth's radical understanding of the Reformation principle of God's grace, which must be the content of the church's exhortation, is the basis for the church's final and indissoluble solidarity with this world (R II:427). The mercy of God, i.e., God's crisis, is involved in the movement from death to life, which is the only hope for human beings. In this light, a relation between humans and God carries the compelling demand of an absolute ethic. In other words, "the ethical problem possesses an eschatological tension; otherwise it is not ethical" (R II:430).

"Grace means divine impatience, discontent, dissatisfaction: it means that the whole is required. Grace is the enemy of every thing, even of the most indispensable 'Interim-Ethics.' Grace is the axe laid at the root of the good conscience which the politician and the civil servant always wish to enjoy" (R II:430). Thus ethical and moral ideals are not realizable in this world; rather, ethical behavior rests upon a critical negation of all such ends and purposes and possessions, namely, the forgiveness of sins. If the problem of human ethics is identical with the problem of God, a demonstration is demanded by God for God's glory. The principle of *Soli Deo Gloria* makes it clear that God remains God under every circumstance. In a correlative sense, human freedom under grace "is founded upon the good pleasure of God." "It is the freedom of the will of God in men . . . Free in God, ye are imprisoned in Him. This is the categorical imperative of grace and the existential belonging-to-God . . . Men must not be permitted to remain spectators, otherwise they will be unable to apprehend the conversion which God effects" (R II:220). As a matter of fact, grace displays and operates itself as grace precisely, penetrating and effecting the dissolution of the dualism between sin and grace, so that we no longer stand within the power of evil but in radical opposition to it (R II:220, 222).

Although in the sphere of morality heaven and earth do not mix, human beings under grace are socially and politically active. They are committed people, witnessing to and demonstrating God's glory that is revealed in the forgiveness of sin and the resurrection from the dead in the event of Jesus Christ. Barth's criticism of "brazen" identification between God and the world rejects any attempt at seeing the kingdom of God as a growing organism, or as a growing building from below. In the final analysis, such attempts will lead to the Tower of Babel. What shall we do in this situation? Bath's demonstration for God's glory reads: "We can act only so as to provide significant signposts and witnesses to the glory of God" (R II:432). Although reform work is the denial of the revolutionary transformation of the existing social order, and enters into the place of revolutionary struggle, it is done to acknowledge the relative possibility of the good amid evil and to take in earnest the action of God as a picture describing the contour of the opposite. Therefore as reform work stands in support of the relative possibility in the existing social order, it bears witness to the true and qualitative change of the existing order as coming from God. This is the ethics of witness in demonstration of God's honor.

The ethics in *Romans II* has nothing to do with a bourgeois, utilitarian way of thinking. The truth of ethics should be shaped in accordance with God, who is the subject of crisis in the negation of all human achievements and goals, and the subject of the *novum* in the proclamation of the forgiveness of sin and the resurrection from the dead. Therefore, the criterion and task of this ethics lie in showing its witness to the reconciling work of God in Jesus Christ. Human praxis as a parable or a token of the action of God stands under the eschatological proviso because the action of God cannot occur in time, but only in eternity (R II:435). Human thinking about the idea of eternity is full of promise, and it is the *Krisis* of all other human thoughts. "God is God: this is the pre-supposition of ethics" (R II:439). The solidarity of the Christian with those who are the oppressed and lowly refers to the protest against the dictator of social authority in which we see a pronounced anti-authoritative ethics in *Romans II*. Only God has authority for the human being. Every inner worldly authority is identical with the lordless powers, which isolate humanity from God and the co-fellow. For the sake of individuality, all titanism, all mounting of *high places* is excluded (R II:444). Christianity has little to do with supporting ideas such as "individualism, collectivism, nationalism, internationalism, humanitarianism, ecclesiasticism" (R II:462). Christianity loves the poor and the oppressed, the sorrowful, the hungry, and the thirsty. It sees in the lowly a parable of life. The Bavarian peasant is not nearer the kingdom of God than the Russian man. "The Proletariat may have become blunderingly and coarsely dogmatic" (R II:464).

All ethical action has the character of protest because the ethics of grace is the axe laid at the root of haphazard human conceit. "Opposing what is *high*, it befriends what is lowly; loaning men certitude, it permits them, for the honor of God, no securitas; measuring our time by the eternity of God, it allows us no established rights, gives us no rest, and preserves no strict continuity in its own action " (R II:465). The authorities become dictators that rule the world of human being. Christianity is tempered by the fact that political praxis cannot sufficiently negate the negative dimension of the existing order. This insight leads Christians to give up the blue flower of all revolutionary romanticism (R II:484) and to seek a possible countermovement against great wrongdoing in terms of a self-critical consideration between relatively greater and relatively smaller wrongdoing. This countermovement can be mobilized in the form of protest against the dictatorship of particular social authority and against the method of social oppression.

Given this fact, "no-revolution" in *Romans II* is not the end in itself, but the best preparation for the true revolution of God (R II:483). Barth was aware that the history of revolutionaries was the history of their disillusionment. Reform work witnesses to the judgment of God in protest against the existing order of the conservative/bourgeois and the revolutionary/Bolshevist. In either acceptance of the present order or denial of it, we do wrong. Therefore, everything human is relative.

Be that as it may, the demonstration of reform work, in Barth's view, is still radical and revolutionary in destroying and transcending all systems that exist. In Barth's understanding, there is no more energetic undermining of the existing order than that which is here recommended as acceptance of the existing order as being valid without illusion: "State,

Church, Society, Positive Right, Family, Organized research, &c., &c., live of the credulity of those who have been nurtured upon vigorous sermons-delivered-on-the-field-of-battle and upon other suchlike solemn humbug" (R II:483). Take away pathos from all that exists, and you starve out the most secure. Christians should take up an attitude of fundamental distrust of all things set on high, and exercise a certain biased preference for the oppressed, the immature, the sorrowful, and those caught up in revolution. Christiniaty must turn away from the "high" things and turn towards the "lowly."

In *Romans II*, Christian politics, which is a demonstration, witness and parable of the eschatology of God as *totaliter aliter*, becomes meaningful in light of God's gracious action in Jesus Christ. Theological radicalism of eschatological vigor as seen in christological exclusiveness leans toward an anarchism in its sociopolitical application. Real revolution comes from God, not from human revolt. We have a hope that is the coming world, where revolution and order are one. For Barth, God's grace is the sign that has the significance of the absolute, the categorical imperative. Barth's negative dialectics cannot be adequately understood without the principle of the great positive possibility, which is the truly revolutionary action of love.[47] Love sets up no idol, and it is the good work by which one overcomes evil. As the denial and demolition of all that exists, love is the inversion of all concrete happening. "Love is the destruction of everything that is—*like God*: the end of all hierarchies and authorities and intermediaries" (R II:496).

The Theology of Karl Barth in Universal Scope and Horizon

Barth's eschatology moves in a universal direction. Theological subjects such as law, predestination, and even the possibility of salvation open up for people outside the walls of Christianity and are strikingly relevant to the universal tendency in Barth's thought. In this section it is of special significance to pay attention to his early reflection on law, Israel, and the

---

47. "We define *love* as the 'Great Positive Possibility', because in it there is brought to light the revolutionary aspect of all ethical behavior, and because it is veritably concerned with the denial and breaking up of the existing order. It is love that places the reactionary also finally in the wrong, despite the wrongness of the revolutionary. Inasmuch as we love one another we cannot wish to uphold the present order as such, for by love we do the 'new' by which the 'old' is overthrown" (R II:493).

Gentiles, which will be later discussed and deepened in light of Barth's christological concentration and irregular dogmatics. In *Romans I* Barth's theological method assumes an organic-critical character. On the basis of the power of resurrection, Barth made a provocative attempt to do transvaluation of all values regarding law and the Gentiles.[48] The power of the resurrection that appears in Christ reveals that God is not only of the Jews but also of the Gentiles. The resurrection is the breaking-in of the divine power "in cosmic depth," and "in spatial distance and temporal width" (R I:35).

If the power of the resurrection proves to be effective, and if the ungodly and the immoral seek God and cry for their lost home, then Paul's remark ("Gentiles which have not the law, do the things of the law") gives witness to the resurrection in a remarkable way. Even people outside Christianity do what the law prescribes. That being the case, Christians have no priority over nonbelievers, because the difference between the mountain and valley becomes meaningless if the sun shines the light upon both of them. This is made possible not through human reason or capacity, but through the power of the resurrection which is the principle of the transvaluation of all values (R I:35).

Barth's eschatology *von Gott aus* as seen in light of the resurrection of Christ is not merely relevant and effective for the human soul but to all inside the church as well as outside the church's wall *auf Gott hin* (R I:36). As Barth says emphatically, "It [the power of resurrection] is just the decisive new thing of my gospel. That works effectively and becomes important, and now something more certain than religion and morality in the world. Now the arm of God enters the whole humanity into the movement" (R I:36). This is the divine mission in which the people of God are supposed to call all people to Zion. In Barth's view, if God does not find another way to reach out to the Gentiles, then God's preference for the elect would become through the play of ideology a first-rate shaming of God (R I:39). Relativism is inevitable outside the kingdom of God, which breaks in through the power of the resurrection. The preference given to the pious is no more an entitlement. Therefore those who are pardoned by God, the worker and fighter, stand for God's kingdom. Here we find a transvaluation of all values, where God does not recognize

---

48. See "Umwertung aller Werte," R I:33–42.

the righteousness of humans, but despite human unrighteousness, God makes God's righteousness happen among the ungodly.

There are even people who are hidden Jews: circumcised, doers of the law and thus righteous before God. The new people of God do not belong to the history that wants to be portrayed by psychology. Rather, they belong to the history of history to which the criterion of God applies:

> And now there is a "circumcision," a purification and separation and special preservation for the purpose of the kingdom of God which is no step of the knowledge beside the other, but the absolute step to the knowledge of God, the carrying out and coming into effect of the new objective world, the again-appearing *Ursprung*, the lost nature of the spirit, in which the human appearance fulfills itself with divine Being. Whoever takes part in this belongs to the ultimate Israel of God. This is the trans-valuation that performs now itself through the power of resurrection. (R I:42)

Barth's understanding of the resurrection of Christ in cosmic depth, which functions to relativize all in light of God and to transvalue the relation between Christian and Jew, between Christian and non-Christian, plays a key part in shaping Barth's eschatology in accordance with his current happenings and the in-breaking eschatology *hic et nunc*. However, in *Romans II*, Barth made use of negative dialectics. His dialectical method assumes a parabolic character. God, who is distinguished qualitatively, is the living God in light of which "all human thought and action and possession are no more than a parable" (R II:333). No union between God and humans is possible in this world. Systematic theology, in speaking about God, is "a parable of the indivisible unity of the Truth" (R II:333).

In the light of this crisis, all law, the whole course of this world, all human action and being are "a sign-post, a parable, a possibility, an expectation" (R II:114). However, this principle of analogy or parable makes it possible to co-relate all things to God as the Primal Origin under the eschatological proviso. In the light of the crisis, each individual is not destroyed but realized in relating to their true meaning, thus "established by the deep disturbance of this 'Not Yet' and this 'No further'" (R II:114). A theological dialectic expressed through "God, the 'Yes' in our 'No' and the 'No' in our 'Yes'" (R II:331) asserts a negative, critical tone in favor of divine affirmation. As far as the fatal prattle of systematic theology is a parable of the indivisible unity of the truth, human language appears to be a medium for expressing the Truth as "a parable of the absolute miracle of the Spirit" (R II:333). Therefore no justification is possible except through the utter radicalism of the divine "and yet." In this divine eschatology, Judaism cannot be removed except for Pharisaism, because God does not belong merely to the church. According to Barth, God as the hope of the church lies in the truth that the identity of the God of wrath is also the God of mercy (R II:393).

This being the case, we see that the Troeltschian triad of analogy, criticism, and correlation could be recognized and developed in Barthian eschatological fashion rather than excluding and rejecting it. Unlike Troeltsch, however, for Barth, the christological foundation of the *Krisis* of God is the midpoint in approach to the unknown God; although Barth's Christology in *Romans II* is not fully developed and treated in relation to law, predestination, and the Gentiles. Barth's understanding of Jesus Christ centers on Christ as the righteousness of Godself in which Christ is "the point at which is perceived the crimson thread which runs through all history" (R II:96). The faithfulness of God confirms Jesus Christ. What constitutes the hidden authority of the law and the prophets is the Christ whom we meet in Jesus. Christ who meets us in Jesus is the Word of the faithfulness of God witnessed by the law and the prophets. In Christ's death the faithfulness of God becomes manifest in the depths of hell. In Christ as the end of humankind, God is found faithful.

Barth's *theologia crucis* attests that Christ's suffering is meaningful in terms of the faithfulness of God. The revelation of Jesus Christ, which is a paradox of the revelation of the righteousness of God, "must be the most complete veiling of his incomprehensibility" (R II:98). When one is justified freely by grace, "grace is and remains always the power of God (i.16), the promise of a new man, of a new nature, of a new world: it is the promise of the Kingdom of God" (R II:103). What takes place in Jesus Christ? This is "the dissolution of history in history, the destruction of the structure of events within their known structure, the end of time in the order of time" (R II:103). Jesus's sacrificial atonement can be seen by the fact that Jesus has been appointed from eternity as the place of propitiation above which God dwells and from which God speaks (R II:105). By his death, which is the absolute scandal of the cross, Jesus becomes "the herald of the kingdom of God" and thus declares the impossible possibility of redemption (R II:105).

As far as God's reconciliation in Jesus Christ with the world is concerned, Barth's model of sacrificial atonement by blood comes closer to Luther than to Calvin; Barth's quotation of Luther in this regard is significant: "'Therefore we must nestle under the wings of this motherhen, and not rashly fly away trusting in the powers of our own faith, lest the hawk speedily tear us in pieces and devour us' (Luther)" (R II:106). Barth's understanding of double predestination in a universal trend is clearly recognizable. Double predestination belongs to the proclamation of the radicalism of the gospel. By the free grace of God, by God's calling and election, Israel is, without exception, the children of God in Christ. What is at issue, however, is not the question of becoming the seed of Israel. Rather, the seed of Israel are seen under a double predestination. They belong to the church of Jacob or to the church of Esau. The doctrine of double predestination includes an incomprehensible reality of God in reprobation as well as in God's gracious election. In Barth's view, the contrast between election and rejection leads to a serious misunderstanding of God. Independent of the distinction between two personalities of the elect and the reprobate, the meaning of this doctrine can be sought only in the freedom of God for the sake of the invisible glory of God. There is incommensurability between God's election in freedom and human ignorance (R II:356).

By way of "dialectical dualism" (R II:358), we are to comprehend the God of Jacob in eternity and at the same time the God of Esau in every moment of time. If the man Esau endures the wrath of God only in a representative capacity so as to pave the road for the man Jacob, Barth's question moves toward an inclusive gracious election of God in relation to the reprobates: "What if the existence of vessels of wrath—which we all are in time!—should declare the divine endurance and forbearance (iii.26), should be the veil of the long-suffering of God (ii.4), behind which the *vessels of mercy*—which we all are in Eternity!—are not lost, but merely hidden?" (R II:359). A christological threshold of the doctrine of double predestination, which was later to be conceptualized in his doctrine of election in *Church Dogmatics*, can be seen already in favor of solidarity in his commentary on Rom 9:1–5, 24–29.[49]

49. "The process of revelation in Christ is decisive. In Time, we are *vessels of wrath*: in Eternity, we are not merely something more, but something utterly different; we are—*vessels of mercy*. . . . When in the eternal 'Moment' the Church of Jacob dawns in Christ, the fences are broken down, and the Gentile Esau enters the service of God and

When it comes to the law, Barth formulates its parabolic character in terms of eschatology. In the light of the "coming Kingdom of God where all things will be new" (R II:78), law has "a parabolic possibility," something which is offered to men as an open road to their deepest perception (R II:79). "Where there is law, there is a word of the faithfulness of God" (R II:80). Notwithstanding, Jews and Greeks, including the sons of God and the natural children of the world, are children of wrath. The true God who can be sought in the Origin of the crisis is the judge of every concrete thing, that is the negation of this world. Although the Jews are placed under indictment by the law and are pronounced to be sinners in God's sight, attention is directed towards God through the law. In the light of ultimate and all-embracing crisis, God is known to be God. In it there is the peculiarity of the Jew and the meaning of circumcision. This aspect of the crisis assumes a universal character in dealing with the law and (par excellence) with the ungodly; because God as the unknown God justified the ungodly, quickened the dead and called *"the things that are not, as though they were (iv.17), on whom men can only in hope believe against hope (iv.18)"* (R II:91).

What does it mean to say that Gentiles without the law do the things of the law? The lives of the Gentiles, according to Barth, are only a parable, "but perhaps so perfect a parable that they are thereby justified" (R II:66–67). Although the Gentile world lies in wickedness, "the mercy of God seems closer and more credible than where the 'kingdom of God' is displayed in full bloom" (R II:67). At this point, we see that there is a remarkable parallel between Barth and Troeltsch on the question of the absoluteness of Christianity.[50]

This is a Barthian way of integrating religious *a priori* in light of God as all-embracing reality. Barth's idea of the universalism of grace must not

---

participates in the divine promise. And with Essau enter the hosts of those who stand outside. Then what is without becomes within, what is afar off becomes nigh at hand, what is not beloved becomes beloved, and the place of rejection becomes the place of acceptation (Hos. ii.23, ii.1)" (R II:360).

50. Barth states this in a provocative way: "But those who *have the law*—even if it be the Gospel!—have no occasion to regard such men merely as objects of missionary enterprise, or to speak of them in superior fashion as people possessed of 'elementary forms of religion'. Such men may long have been in possession of impressions of God quite different from those which we ever have had or shall have. And if it were a matter of religion and of experience, these—which are in any case trivial—God can, and does, give to the Gentiles" (R II:67).

be confused with some "rationalistic general religious *a priori*" or with a "universal religion of reason" (R II:382). Nevertheless, "the Gospel of the unknown God is competent to understand the mystery religions better than they do themselves, and avoiding their dangers, is free to gather up the sense in their non-sense" (R II:193). Barth's thesis that "by the Gospel the whole concrete world is dissolved and established" (R II:35), stands in refusal of immediacy and romantic direct communication (R II:41, 50); along the lines of Kierkegaard's thesis that "to be known directly is the characteristic mark of the idol" (R II:38).

However, Barth's negative dialectic does not contradict or exclude the fact that the invisible things of God since the creation of the world are clearly seen, being perceived through the things that are made (R II:45). Our memory of God—an idea reminiscent of Plato—would be a sign that behind the visible creaturely things lies the Origin of all concrete things (R II:46).[51] In a similar vein, Barth in his Tambach lecture (1919) had quoted Eccl 3:11: that God has set eternity in the hearts of human beings, without which it is impossible to find out the work of God from the beginning to the end. Human capacity of finding eternity is the synthesis on the basis of Jesus Christ. Analogy, which stands in demand of continuity, namely, eternity in the human heart, convinces Barth to take into account a biblical statement that the children of this world are better than the children of light ("Christian's Place in Society," 307).

If such is the case, then naturally in *Romans II* "the invisibility of God," for Barth is seen in this context as being "in precise and strict agreement with the gospel of the resurrection" (R II:46–47). In other words, there is "the archetypal, unobservable, undiscoverable Majesty of God," which is mirrored in the world of appearance. "The speech of God can always be heard out of the whirlwind . . . The insecurity of our whole existence, the vanity and utter questionableness of all that is and of what we are, lie as in a text-book open before us" (R II:46).

This refers to an important aspect of Barth's theological idea of analogy and parable, which is a basis for his so-called irregular dogmatics. "Itself the final venture of men, it is bound to perceive that every human adventure can be no more than a demonstration and a parable. Nevertheless, as this final hazard, *as ministering the gospel of God*, theol-

---

51. Barth's affirmation of human memory in light of resurrection does not mean his affirmation of a general revelation without qualification. Cf. Walter Lowe, *Theology and Difference*, 39.

ogy is what it is . . . Theology owes its existence in history and its place in the *universitas litterarum* only to this essential, final, necessary, venture, and to its abnormal, irregular, revolutionary attack" (R II:531). In an irregular and revolutionary manner, the theology of revelation relativizes, sharpens, and transforms an aspect of natural theology, even theology of religions, by radicalizing the wholly other dimension of God as *totaliter aliter* in view of God's possibility (*Gott kann*). Barth's understanding of salvation is more positively articulated when he says: "Every criticism which men exercise upon the ungodly and every busy attempt to convert them become of trivial importance. Beyond human good and evil the arm of God is extended in power; and men are advised to beware of too great daring" (R II:70). Barth's critique of "god" as ideology is not merely of social-political relevance; it is also directed in an immanent and critical way to those who are attached to the absolute claim of Christianity. Barth even attacked the God of the pious people—as far as "they adopt the point of view of God" (R II:73)—by caricaturizing them as no more than examples of Potemkin's village. Given this fact, "the claim to absolute superiority over others falls to the ground" (R II:74). In this regard, for Barth, human righteousness is in itself an illusion (R II:75).

FIVE   Karl Barth: Between the Times in Germany

IN 1921 WHEN BARTH LEFT SAFENWIL TO ACCEPT THE CALL TO Göttingen, the floodgates opened and hateful polemics as well as grateful defenses volleyed about him from the press. An example in the *Zofinger Daily News* reads:

> Barely out of his university studies, without any experience of practical life, and blinded by an almost socialistic revolutionary spirit, he rubbed everyone in this rural area the wrong way.... Only the local socialistic party found him the wished for protector and agitator.... Although comrade Barth was a clever preacher and an intellectual person of great stature, many church members stepped away from worship. In social areas he achieved a number of improvements and could have achieved more in the congregation and the community if his ivory-tower socialism had not prevented him from working together with the bourgeoisie.[1]

---

1. Even worse was circulated in the *Zurzach Daily News*: "So, since he was no good as a pastor, he became a professor in order to make other incapable pastors. Ragaz the second. And this call can be explained no doubt as simply an act of protection by some socialistic friend in his bosom in the kingdom, where such people now rule the higher schools." However, some people saw it differently: "The most meaningful period for our congregation comes to an end. With the appearance of pastor Barth a small group of owners lost their strong influence over the large majority of the population, and this influence can... never be taken back." In another place it was said: "Pastor Barth practiced his office inspired by the principles of a genuine social effectiveness. He cared nothing about his reputation or his position. He taught a genuine Christianity.... When Pastor Barth now leaves our village, threatened by the donkey kicks of this caste, a great part of the population is nevertheless genuinely saddened at his leaving and remembers with gratitude his sacrificial care for the poor and the oppressed. We wish him all the best for his future effectiveness" (Marquardt, "Aktuar," 137–38).

The move from Safenwil to Göttingen was for Barth a remarkably decisive event for the development of his dialectical theology. With the Versailles Treaty (on June 28, 1919), the German situation drastically changed and deteriorated. "The republic was born in defeat, lived in turmoil, and died in disaster."[2] In the face of economic catastrophe, Germany was stripped of all its colonies. Allied troops were occupied with perpetuating the demilitarization of the German army. The Germans were urged to take sole responsibility for causing the war. This situation demanded the financial compensation to Allied powers for what they lost and suffered during the war. The Weimar Republic was nearly two years underway in Germany at the time when Barth took a teaching position as the honorary professor of Reformed theology at Göttingen in 1921. The Ruhr occupation further intensified the debased German mindset to which Barth felt sympathetic. Barth's theology during this time can be understood against this cultural and intellectual background as well as against these political trends.

In August 1922, Barth, Thurneysen, and Gogarten founded the theological journal *Zwischen den Zeiten*. The aim of the journal was to oppose the dominant liberal theology. Barth held three chairs in succession during his time in Germany: at Göttingen (1921 to 1925), Münster (October 1925 to 1930), and Bonn (March 1930 until his expulsion to Switzerland in June 1935). The faculty at Göttingen was strongly Lutheran. Among the Lutheran faculty members, Ritschl was in blessed remembrance as "the founder of the fame of our Göttingen theological faculty."[3]

It was Emmanuel Hirsch at Göttingen who was a full professor (although two years Barth's junior) with highly intellectual erudition among the faculty members. As a "learned and acute man" with "a profound knowledge of Luther and Fichte," he was a thorn in Barth's side.[4] In addition, Erik Peterson, who was an expert in patristic theology, was also an academically competent colleague who overwhelmed Barth intellectu-

---

2. Gay, *Weimar Culture*, 1.

3. Busch, *Karl Barth: His Life*, 133.

4. Busch, *Karl Barth: His Life*, 134. Hirsch was a former student of Karl Holl who initiated the modern interpretation of Luther. As a representative of the so-called Luther renaissance, he later turned to National Socialism and became adviser to *Reichsbishop* Ludwig Müller. Hirsch's academic learning and priority made Barth eradicate his theological ignorance through intensive study.

ally. His critique of Barth's dialectical method led to a confrontation in 1925.

Karl Barth's time (which he refers to as *between the times*) in Germany continues to be regarded today as representative of neo-orthodox Barthianism, in which it is claimed that dialectical theology has no material relevance to the contemporary social and political situation. The political world, in other words, the world of political ideas and phenomena, forms no fundamental component in shaping Barth's theological thought during this period. Barth still did not lose his political position "on the most extreme left" in his *Romans* during his time in Göttingen. Although Barth in fact wanted to say "the same things as were said in Safenwil,"[5] he had to maintain politically inactive partly because of his concentration on theological work and partly because of his status as a foreign (Swiss) worker in Germany. "Now I was happily resolved to get down to theological research and teaching—in grim earnest, in my own way and in my own style. Ragaz and Kutter thoroughly disapproved. Of course I had only a little of the equipment I needed."[6]

As a result, in order to see Barth's continued development we will trace Barth's theological development *between the times* especially in regard to Barth's shift in emphasis from dialectical to analogical theology. Also of interest is Barth's reflection on the relation between political ethics and dogmatics. Then we will discuss Barth's confrontation with Catholic teaching of *analogia entis* in light of Barth's study of Anselm and *analogia fidei*.

Karl Barth and Political Ethics

Barth's political interest was aroused in the case of the murder of Walther Rathenau, which Göttingen faculty members condoned due to his Jewish background. In addition, Barth's colleague Otto Piper was accused of an act of national disgrace by the newspaper because he entertained French students at his home, helping them speak about the work of the Christian League of Reconciliation in France.[7] Barth was in an unfortunate position in relation to the political cause in general because as a *Gastarbeiter*

5. Barth's letter to Thurneysen (November 18, 1921) in *B-Th. II*, 8.
6. Busch, *Karl Barth: His Life*, 126–27. For the political theology of Karl Barth between the times, cf. Winzeler, *Widerstehende Theologie*.
7. McCormack, *Critically Realistic*, 301.

(foreign professor) at Göttingen, he had to restrain himself from political involvement as much as possible. However, Barth made an attempt to deepen his political and theological awareness by appropriating the theology of John Calvin, on which he lectured in the summer semester of 1922.[8]

During his years in Geneva (1909–1911), where he had taken a position as an auxiliary pastor to a German congregation, he lectured on the 1559 *Institutes* of John Calvin. In the summer of 1909 the great commemoration of Calvin's birth (in 1509) was held there. Barth's interest in Calvin continued under the Basel professor Paul Wernle. In fact, this intensive preoccupation with Calvin helped Barth teach the classical theology of Reformation to his students in the summer of 1922 at Göttingen.[9] For Barth, "Calvin is a waterfall, a primitive forest, something demonic, coming down direct from the Himalayas, absolutely Chinese, wonderful, mythological. I lack the organs, the suction cups to take in this phenomenon not to mention presenting it rightly. What I take in is only a thin stream, and what I give out still thinner. I could cheerfully sit down and spend the rest of my life with Calvin."[10]

Of special interest to Barth were Calvin's practical, political concern and the realization that Calvin could speak to the present as a contemporary. "We cannot keep Calvin to what he once said as though he had nothing more or new to say today!" For Barth, the crux of the matter was to make our own response to what he says. However, Barth found that dialogue with Calvin was not easy. Rather it was like trying "to steer a golden path between this Scylla and Charybdis."[11]

No doubt Barth wanted to uncover Calvin's new spirit and work in his own postwar present situation. In dealing with Calvin's ethics in relation to political government, Barth stressed Calvin as "a man of the world" rather than a monk coming from the cloister. Calvin investigated the questions of public life and participated all his life in high politics: "Today we might well imagine Calvin as a most industrious reader of newspapers and writer for them and modern politicians of all parties and countries

---

8. Barth's first experience of the theology of Calvin occurred while he was a young student in his father's lectures at Bern in the winter of 1904/5.
9. Barth, *Theology of John Calvin*, xiii–xiv, 131.
10. B-Th II, 80. Busch, *Karl Barth: His Life*, 138.
11. Barth, *Theology of John Calvin*, 6–7.

would probably learn something from him."¹² In matters such as politics and social economic life, Calvin was by no means "an unworldly idealist," rather "he was supremely practical" and "an aristocratic republican."¹³ As Max Weber says, Calvin may be called and regarded as "a father, if not *the* father, of the political and economic ideal of Western European liberal democracy."¹⁴ Contrary to popular opinion about Calvin's political ideas, Barth argues that Calvin was not a strong believer in theocracy because a link between eschatology and ethics holds high significance in Calvin's thought. Barth applied his favorite citation of Troeltsch ("The power of the next world becomes the power of this world") to Calvin's political thought. (Barth quotes Troeltsch's slogan in his Tambach lecture and then also does it in his book on Calvin.)¹⁵

Barth's idea of eschatological reservation (that "God is still God, and we are still human") is also relevant to Calvin. At a minimum, Calvin expressed and emphasized this antithesis, according to Barth, "much more sharply than Luther." Luther's thesis is that "there can be no fleeing from his [God's] presence to another world."¹⁶ According to Barth, Calvin's idea of the world's state of affairs in light of eschatology needs to be interpreted in a parabolic sense: "In a parabolic sense, not directly, but indirectly, not as it stands but in its relation, as a temporal image of the eternal righteousness of God, to what is thus its meaning and origin."¹⁷ Barth's political understanding of parable and analogy that he had pursued in his Tambach lecture paralleled his approach to Calvin's political ethics; with the thesis that "relation is relativity," Barth gave full credit to Calvin's rejection of medieval radicals, who were echoed in modern liberal theology. "We do not have to wait for Christian freedom because it is itself the great waiting for God."¹⁸

Calvin gains prominence for Barth when it comes to a connection between theology and ethics. It is more important to see that Barth's idea of *totaliter aliter*, which is associated with eschatological proviso and

12. Ibid., 202–3.
13. Ibid., 203.
14. Ibid., 204; cf. Weber, *Protestant Ethic and the Spirit of Capitalism*, 43ff.
15. Ibid., 127.
16. Barth, *Theology of John Calvin*, 205.
17. Ibid., 221.
18. Ibid.

political significance, is deepened and extended theologically through Barth's interpreting Calvin for the sake of his own hermeneutical concern. On the basis of his notion that divine sovereignty relativizes all human rights, Calvin could have agreed with Barth's dialectical Yes and No to both conservatism and liberal radicalism.

> In Switzerland at least it has been our experience that Ragaz and Wernle thought they could appeal with equal enthusiasm to Calvin, the one for revolution, the other for reaction. The last word of the *Institutes* is neither the one nor the other but Christ, Christian liberty, and the celestial country in light of which training—serious, relevant, zealous training, yet no more—is the proper term for what we ourselves ought to be doing.[19]

Barth's further development of ethics in relation to his political direction is of special significance as is seen in a lecture he delivered at Wiesbaden, i.e., "The Problem of Ethics Today" (delivered on September 25, 1922).[20] Akin to his point in *Romans I*, theory must arise out of praxis in that "nothing can come of our facing the ethical question from the viewpoint of spectators." "We are compelled to conceive ourselves as living doers."[21] What Barth had to do was to address the problem of Christian ethics for his day in the face of his current situation: French colonial troops on the Rhine, the Russian revolution and dethronement of the czar, inflation in Germany, and the collapse of the whole vision of the Weimar republic. Of this current situation, Barth notes: "We face it in a more perplexed, embarrassed, and uncertain way than the generation of 1914 did."[22]

Our time is a now an eternity "between the ages" (*zwischen den Zeiten*),[23] from which nobody can escape as spectators of the problem in this reality. The question of what to do in the midst of the perplexity, embarrassment, and uncertainty is the question "regarding the truth about truth."[24] So understood, the ethical question is the theological

---

19. Ibid., 226; cf. Mattmüller, *Leonhard Ragaz und der religiöse Sozialismus*, 2:80, 430–31, 425–26.
20. Barth, "Problem of Ethics Today," 136–82.
21. Ibid., 137.
22. Ibid., 144.
23. Ibid., 143.
24. Ibid., 137.

problem of regarding human life from the viewpoint of eternity.[25] Rather than logical or theoretical investigation, Barth analyzes the problem of the good, which constitutes and "*forms* of human conduct and, all temporal *happenings* in the history both of the individual and of society."[26] In other words, life is the object of theological ethics. However, we live in the midst of crisis and relationship: "The crisis in our lives continues, and with the crisis, our relationship to God. We *live* in this relationship. Let us look well to our responsibilities in it!"[27]

From this standpoint, the ethical responses of Ritschl and Troeltsch are no longer valid because they are attenuated with the previous era. Human relationships are not based on the so-called religious experience. Ritschl's ethics were "the ethics of the bourgeoisie growing prosperous in the time of the consolidation of the Bismarkian empire,"[28] while Troeltsch's ethics were the ethics of the new German economic civilization whose prophet was Naumann. In seeing the ethical problem in the crisis of human being, Barth tried to articulate it in terms of his dialectical theology of crisis. Crisis is understood as a dialectical concept that not only allows for negation but also returns the negation to its original value. The argument against human beings is also an argument for them.[29] Kant is for Barth the most important figure who grounds the conception of the moral personality on the idea of the autonomous will. Good will that moves beyond all finite goals orients itself toward the final goal, which means the categorical imperative of duty in Kant's moral philosophy. According to Barth, in Kant's philosophical framework, the idea of the postulates of God and freedom or a final unity between the kingdom of freedom and the kingdom of nature must take in earnest "an act of faith."[30]

Nevertheless, an act of faith is not supposed to be in opposition to a conception of the millennium, which plays its part in Kant. This idea cannot be eschewed by anybody who takes the ethical question seriously. Barth deals with the socialist idea of chiliasm associated with utopia from the perspective of religious socialism. The ethical question is not merely

25. Ibid., 140.
26. Ibid., 139.
27. Ibid., 141.
28. Ibid., 145.
29. Ibid., 151.
30. Ibid., 156.

about the individual, but it is concerned about "the universally applicable law of humanity."³¹ The ethical goal as the goal of earthly history must be realized not outside of history but with it. For Barth, the ethical question cannot be separated from a teleological idea associated with the goal of earthly history: "Ethics can no more exist without millenarianism, without at least some minute degree of it, than without the idea of a moral personality."³² The idea of a totality of good conduct is really denoted by the idea of the millennium and its derivatives.

At this point Barth stresses that anyone who takes the ethical question seriously must learn from religious socialists in Switzerland. This hope is at the center in shaping and directing Christian ethics in relation to sociopolitical problems. This hope is not merely confined to the sphere of the individual but affects the social and cultural arena in which humans live in an eschatological light.³³ In this regard, Barth shared the practical and revolutionary concerns of Ragaz, who, unlike Barth, resigned his chair at the University of Zurich for the sake of solidarity with the socialist movement in the poor quarter of Zurich.

In addition, Barth's confrontation with Paul Althaus centered on basic questions of Christian social ethics.³⁴ This confrontation was played out in his critical response to Althaus's *Religiöser Sozialismus: Grundfragen der christlichen Sozialethik*. Despite his critical reservation against the liberal theology of religious socialism modeled by Ragaz, Barth defended the cause of religious socialism in his confrontation with Althaus. Althaus argued for "the organic, aristocratic ideal of the State"³⁵—that is "deeply rooted in German history and in the thinking of the German classes"—against religious socialism, criticizing it of "dilettantism, absolutism, and monism." Against religious-socialist programs Althaus spoke about "the very elementary necessity of law and the State."³⁶

Althaus consequently depicted the war as "a mighty self-measuring of the nations for leadership and for the future" rather than denounc-

---

31. Ibid., 157.

32. Ibid., 158.

33. In R I, Barth encouraged Christians to remain firm and faithful to "the hope, the unquiet, the longing, the radical and permanent revolution" (R I:353).

34. *ADT* 152–65; Robinson, *Beginnings* 46–57.

35. *ADT* 154; Robinson, *Beginnings* 48.

36. *ADT* 159; Robinson, *Beginnings* 52.

ing the war as murder.³⁷ Barth, however, attacked the god whom Althaus recommended because if Christian faith is based on the resurrection of Christ, then it is essential to pay disrespectful disbelief to this god.³⁸ For Barth, to believe means to affirm the love of God "as the only conceivable structure of the world."³⁹ In showing his deep mistrust of the sinister connection between Lutheran inwardness and its worldliness in Althaus's thought, Barth argued that Althaus, in removing eschatology from ethics, intended to make eschatology harmless and meaningless in relation to ethics, which is in turn removed from "the threatening shadow" of the eschatology "*ad majorem gloriam hominis.*"⁴⁰ Indeed, for Barth Christian ethics has to do with the goal: not a daydream but a task, not the termination of the ethical struggle. "The enthusiastic, idealistic, communistic, anarchistic, and, it is well to remember (all true Lutheran doctrine to the contrary notwithstanding), even *Christian* hope envisages reality here on earth."⁴¹ The crux of matter in Christian ethics is, "let freedom in love and love in freedom be the pure and direct motive of social life, and a community of righteousness its direct objective!"⁴²

This love is expressed in the overcoming and cessation of paternalism (in other words, by overcoming the exploitation and oppression of humans by humans) and by overcoming class conflict and national divisions brought by war, violence, and unrestrained power. Humans must let the Spirit enter in place of a civilization of things—humanity in place of objectivity and property values, and fraternity in place of hostility. According to Barth, this refers completely to a socialist program for social struggle by retrieving the concept of chiliasm, which has something to do with the idea of a God who loves in freedom as well as with God's existence as a principle that truly transforms everything. Barth's reading of Kant's moral philosophy about the unity of the kingdom of freedom and the kingdom of nature is designed to deepen the socialistic program in view of the categorical imperative of human praxis.⁴³

---

37. *ADT* 161; Robinson, *Beginnings* 53.
38. *ADT* 162; Robinson, *Beginnings* 54.
39. *ADT* 159; Robinson, *Beginnings* 52.
40. *ADT* 163; Robinson, *Beginnings* 56.
41. Barth, "Problem of Ethics Today," 160.
42. Ibid.
43. A great exodus out of the 'kingdom of necessity' into the 'kingdom of freedom' lies at the center of Karl Marx himself, in that the complete emancipation out of the

For Barth this socialist program refers to two lines—morality and history—that meet here in our time. There is no promise of heaven and inward experience that can ever be a sufficient substitute. "Happy therefore is the man who, for all the remoteness, acquires and maintains a sure and single eye for the reality of the millennium."[44] Furthermore, the service of the kingdom of God is supposed to be something more than the millennium. Barth's keen interest in eschatology is considered in terms of the dialectics of God-thought.[45] In stressing God's way, dialectical theology helps us avoid the Scylla of liberal individualistic quietism and the Charybdis of high audacious titanism regarding the ethical question. Nevertheless, "there is no way from us to God—not even a *via negativa*—not even a *via dialectica* nor *paradoxa*."[46] The mystery of God cannot be reduced to any "mere play of words." Human possibility in talking of God may fall short of what is meant to be. What we count on is God's grace, upon which everything hinges. We do not bring God's grace into being by any magic turn of our dialectics. "[God] *is* and he *remains free*: else he were not God."[47]

In this regard Barth's reflection of God's grace is remarkably striking in that the forgiveness of sin does not lead to a cheap quietism but to struggle for human social and political goals: "The new creation of man, the renewal of the unrenewable old man is a *justificatio forensis*, a *justificatio impii*, a surpassing paradox; and also is the positive relation of God's will to man's conduct."[48] The grace of God does not block human action or civilization but makes them "a *witness*, a quite earthly *reflection*, of a lost and hidden order."[49] Regarding the relation between God and

---

process of fetishism in the capitalistic society gives shape and direction to the socialist idea of praxis and liberation. Sounding similar to Kant's categorical imperative for humanity, Marx said: "The human is the highest nature for humans, also with *the categorical imperative* (Italics mine), to overthrow all circumstances in which the human being is humiliated, enslaved, abandoned and despised." Karl Marx, "Zur Kritik der Hegelschen Rechtsphilosophie: Einleitung," (1844) in Marx, *Frühe Schriften*, I:497.

44. Barth, "Problem of Ethics Today," 162.
45. Ibid., 167.
46. Ibid., 177.
47. Ibid., 178.
48. Ibid., 170. Barth contrasted Lutheranism's position, old and new, to the hierarchy of so-called offices for the sake of Luther's radical understanding of *justificatio forensis*. Ibid., 171.
49. Ibid., 173.

humans, Barth brings Jesus Christ to the center: Jesus Christ, who leads the way from God to man, is "God who becomes man, the creator of all things" lying "as a babe in the manger" (Luther).[50] Barth's christological approach to Christian ethics for today does not exclude a socialist ideal of chiliasm associated with Kant's moral philosophy; rather it sharpens and concretizes it in light of God's eschatology in Jesus Christ. In this grace of God, God gives a corrective to the audacious titanism of Russian Leninism.

As we have outlined Barth's reflection of political ethics, his acceptance of the endowed chair of Reformed theology at the University of Göttingen should not be regarded as a break with his previous political activity in Safenwil as if his actions and positions were all a regrettable mistake. Expounding Luther and Calvin, Barth was committed to Jeremiah and Paul against liberal modernism. The focus of Barth's time in Göttingen was to find and lay a solid theological foundation for Christian theology and ethical praxis. A political commitment without a firm theological foundation, as in the case of the liberal theology or religious socialism (especially Ragaz) was, for Barth, "a way of losing everything through a lack of substance,"[51] which he discerned in a liberal theology of religious socialism such as Ragaz's.

The Word of God and Dialectical Theology

For an understanding of Barth's dialectical theology at this time, it is of special significance to mention his lecture "The Word of God and the Task of the Ministry" delivered at Elgersburg (October 3, 1922).[52] Here we see his methodology in concentrated form. This method should be noted when Barth says, "as theologians we ought to speak of God. We are, however, humans and, as such, cannot speak of God. We should recognize both our ought and our cannot and thus by that recognition give only God the glory."[53] This situation is for Barth a perplexity in which theologians as well as ministers stand. That "we ought to speak of God" is decisive for dealing with the object and the method of theological science.

50. Ibid., 181.
51. Gollwitzer, "Kingdom of God and Socialism in the Theology of Karl Barth," 81.
52. Barth, "Word of God and the Task," 183–217.
53. *ADT:* 199; (my translation).

The theologian is no magician who has managed to find a special key to a special door. Now Barth intends to bring up the relation between the Word of God and dialectical methodology without giving up academic theology as science.[54]

When it comes to a theological way of speaking of God, Barth mentions the following three ways: the dogmatic way, the critical way, and the dialectical way. However, these three methods are not fully sufficient to speak of God, because human beings are not capable of speaking of God. If God "must *be* the fulfillment of the promise, the satisfaction of the hungry, the opening of the eyes of the blind and of the ears of the deaf," then theology as a human discourse is no substitute for God ("Word of God and the Task," 199), The perplexity which Barth mentions is related to "people of our times stand[ing] in anxiety and need *before* the closed wall of death" ("Biblical Questions," 85). Barth's manner in expressing God as the *totaliter aliter* is deeply connected to the social, political situation: "For the sake of the suffering of the millions, for the sake of the blood shed for many that cries against us all, for the sake of the fear of God, let us not be *so* sure! Such sureness is only a synonym for smugness" ("Biblical Questions," 85).[55]

Barth's genuine intention in this lecture is to give God alone the glory because "if any utterance at all is in need of substantiation, attestation, and demonstration in corresponding moral, social, and political action, it is the Biblical utterance that death is swallowed up in victory" ("Biblical Questions," 85–86). Therefore "the perplexity of our task is only a token of the perplexity of all human tasks. . . . Giving up the ministry would be as sensible as taking one's life; . . . . We should be *aware* of both the necessity and the impossibility of our task" ("Word of God and the Task," 213–14).

As for the first way, dogmatism taken by theological orthodoxy begins with the incarnation and from this derives necessary dogmas such as Christology, Trinity, soteriology, and eschatology. On the basis of theological objectivity, the first way constructs positive statements about God. In reflection of the incarnation of God (God becoming human) rather than the divinization of humankind (humans becoming God), a

---

54. Kutter protested Barth's attempt at constructing an academic theology. *B-Th. II*: 313ff.

55. Cf. For Barth's Aarau Student Conference (in April, 1920) see Barth, "Biblical Questions, Insights, and Vistas," 51–96.

theologian on this way acquires "a taste of the objectivity." ("Word of God and the Task," 201). According to Barth, the strength of the dogmatic way lies in the so-called supernaturalistic content of the Bible and its dogmas. However, its weakness lies in that it does not recognize its incapability of speaking of God even in terms of the most powerfully conceptualized supernaturalism. God could also act otherwise from whom the dogmatist believes. "The God who reveals himself is God. The God who becomes man is God. And the dogmatist does not speak of this God" ("Word of God and the Task," 202–3).

In contrast to the dogmatic way, the second way is the self-critical method. This is taken and pursued by mysticism and—also in a different way—by idealism in that God is identical with "pure being, without quality, filling all things obstructed only by the particular individuality of man ("Word of God and the Task," 203). From this comes the idea that human being is attacked and negated in the most serious way when it comes to speaking of God: "By it a man places himself under judgment and negatives himself, because it shows so clearly that what must be overcome is man as man" ("Word of God and the Task," 203). However, the critical way is not competent to speak of God by negating humanity. The mystical way becomes the strongest where the dogmatic way becomes the weakest. But the mystics cannot speak of God who stands as the "No" before them, namely, as the darkness to which they surrender themselves. "The cross of Christ does not need to be erected by us!" ("Word of God and the Task," 205). "God may be spoken of only (in that objectivity which orthodoxy knows only too much) when God *himself* becomes man and enters with his *fullness* into our emptiness, with His *Yes* into our No. But neither the mystics nor we speak of that God" ("Word of God and the Task," 206).

The third approach is the dialectical one, which Barth regards as "by far the best" ("Word of God and the Task," 206). In looking to the unnamable living truth, the dialectician is competent to find the proper meaning and significance of dogmatic affirmation and critical negation in a dialectical way. The great truths of the dogmatist and the self-criticism of the mystic are presupposed dialectically without negating them. The living truth may not be named, but it lies between dogmatism and self-criticism and offers to both their meaning and interpretation. That God (but really God!) becomes human (but really human!) is the living truth that is the determining content of a real speaking of God. However, the genuine dialectician knows that this center is inconceivable and incomprehensible. As a result, a direct communication with the living truth is impossible, whether through a dogmatic approach or critical approach. The best alternative is to take a dialectical way between dogmatic affirmation and self-critical negation that is, from the positive to the negative and from the negative to the positive rather than falling into a fixed Yes or No.[56] In this regard Barth illustrates dialectical method using Luther's teaching of *justificatio impii* and the dialectic of the master and the slave in a Christian life.

God's self-revelation is not at the disposal of human capacity to speak for God. Therefore we cannot speak of God even in a dialectical way. Although a dialectician focuses on the presupposition of the living truth in the center, a dialectical statement does not establish this presupposition. How are we capable of bearing witness to the living truth? According to Barth, the possibility of theology arises only where God speaks. It is not because of what the dialectician can do, but because the reality of God, which is the living truth in the center, spoke itself. Theology as possibility is not human but divine possibility. "This possibility, the possibility that God *himself* speaks when he is spoken of, is not part of the dialectic way as such; it arises rather at the point where this way *comes to an end*" ("Word of God and the Task," 211). Given this fact, the dialectician is no better than the dogmatist and the mystic. God may speak for Godself independently of dogmatism, self-criticism, and dialecticism.[57]

The dialectical method—despite its limitation—makes human speaking of God more compelling and more necessary when compared to the two other methods. The genuine possibility that God speaks—that is, an inconceivable and incomprehensible possibility—is neither a humanly attainable goal nor dependent on the dialectical way. In spite of this critical proviso, it is the subject matter, the Word of God, that makes human language significant and capable of bearing witness to it. In accordance with this subject, human language is of an analogical and parabolic relation between similarity and dissimilarity when it speaks of

---

56. "Word of God and the Task," 206–7.

57. In this regard we are reminded of Barth's important aspect of "Gott kann" in the doctrine of the Word of God in *Church Dogmatics*: "God may speak to us through Russian communism, through flute concerto, blossoming shrub, or a dead dog" (*CD* I/1: 55).

God. In recognizing both our obligation and our inability to speak, we give God the glory. Theology as divine possibility enables human capacity—regardless of its inadequacy—to bear witness to the Word of God, which otherwise we cannot speak of. Therefore a dialectical method does not need to be replaced by the parabolic character of human language. In speaking of theological subject matter, Barth construes and appropriates the dialectical method and analogical language in a constructive way.

Finally Barth asks: "Can theology, should theology, pass beyond *prolegomena* to Christology?" As far as the living truth is beyond Yes and No, and the reality of God is beyond the dialectic method, the Word of God (*Deus dixit*), of which we cannot speak, must be dealt with in the *prolegomena* before Christology. Therefore, "it may be that everything is said in the prolegomena" ("Word of God and the Task," 217). Barth's theological program aims at speaking of God who is actually and really God: "Not their existence, but otherworldly of their existence, God's existence stands in question, if they (the people) come to us for help" ("Word of God and the Task," 189). This is at once the task and at the same time the perplexity about God that Barth puts before listeners to his lecture. Other cultural, social and patriotic tasks are child's play. The actual and real God sets religion and ideology in crisis.

God is not a religious god. The real and actual God means for Barth "the fulfillment of the promise, the satisfaction of the hungry, the opening of the eyes of the blind and of the ears of the deaf" ("Word of God and the Task," 199). Barth's discourse about God retains an ideology-critical implication and sociopolitical direction.[58] Barth's break with liberal theology and ideology manifested itself in his turn to the parish and the community, in which a new consciousness and self-consciousness had to be formed against the false gods of the world. As Barth writes concerning the situation, this is

> rather an omen, of a perplexity which extends over the whole range of human endeavor, present and future. It is a perplexity felt by man simply by virtue of his being a man, and has nothing to do with his being moral or immoral, spiritual or worldly, godly or ungodly. However conscious or unconscious of his situation he may be, man cannot escape his humanity, and humanity means limitation, finitude, creaturehood, separation from God ("Word of God and the Task," 189-90).

58. Cf. Winzeler, *Widerstehende Theologie*, 195–206.

In this social, cultural, and human condition "man as man cries for God" ("Word of God and the Task," 190). Humans do not cry for religion and philosophy, but for God, who is the answer to this perplexity. This is the One who became human in Jesus Christ. This is the One who makes all things new.[59] Acknowledging this truth turns our perplexity into our promise. The theology of the Word of God is theology under the cross. That is the special thing in the proclamation of the Word of God that takes place not in the sign of religion but in the sign of the cross—namely, in the middle of world history.

In a recent study of Barth, his dialectical theology and the mystery as the center of the living truth gives rise to a postmodern constructive reading of him. In light of Barth's lecture on "The Word of God and the Task of Ministry, William Stacy Johnson pays special attention to the term of affliction (*Bedrängnis*). "As theologians we ought to speak of God. We are, however, human beings and as such cannot speak of God. We ought to recognize both our obligation and our inability—and precisely in that recognition, give God the glory. This is our affliction. Everything else is mere child's play."[60] According to Johnson, when one tries to speak of God, one inevitably speaks falsely.

> The significance for constructive theology of Barth's theocentric countermelody has not been adequately appreciated. If God is ultimate mystery, then theology remains but a fragile, provisional and broken venture. No claims to infallibility or self-evident certainty can prevail, and no theologian can seek to have the final word against the intractableness of this mystery. . . . Instead, the theologian must continually resolve to wipe the slate clean and be willing, regarding each theological topic, to "begin again at the beginning."[61]

This postmodern reading of Barth would be more possible and more convincing if it had in view the mystery of God in relation to Barth's deliberation on God's Word in action. Furthermore, Barth's theology describes the profound interrelation between dialectics and analogy and their relationship to sociopolitical reality.

---

59. Barth, "Biblical Questions, Insights, and Vistas," 80.
60. Johnson, *Mystery of God*, 1.
61. Ibid., 2.

Barth's Way from Dialectics to Analogy: Karl Barth and Erik Peterson

In July 1925 Erik Peterson, Barth's colleague at Göttingen, published his pamphlet under the title *What is Theology?*[62] in which he made his highly critical assessment of Barth's dialectical theology and in particular of Barth's 1922 Elgersburg lecture, "The Word of God and the Task of Ministry."[63] Unlike Harnack, who critiqued Barth in terms of the historical-critical method,[64] Peterson confronted Barth's theological dialectic. Could one suitably give the glory to God using the dialectical method? Barth's thesis in his Elgersburg lecture reads: "we ought to speak of God. We are, however, humans and as such cannot speak of God. We should recognize both "our ought" and "our cannot" and thus by that recognition give God the glory" (*ADT* 199, my translation) This thesis, according to Peterson, refers to the theology that is the plight-signal of predicament in which humans as humans simply find themselves.

The passion and seriousness that Barth elaborated in his *Romans II* is insufficient for Peterson. "God is just appearance as the dialectical question is appearance, and the answer of the dialectician is also appearance. Likewise, God himself in this dialectic is only a dialectical possibility."[65] In Peterson's view, it is a dialectical possibility to take in earnest God in the way of Abraham's sacrificing Isaac. What the dialectician takes in

---

62. Peterson, "Was ist Theologie?" 9–43.

63. Eberhard Jüngel makes a great contribution in clarifying the significance of Peterson's critique for the development of Karl Barth from Kierkegaard to Anselm of Canterbury. Jüngel, "Von der Dialektik," 127–79.

64. Although Barth's *Romans II* finds agreement from some theologically like-minded colleagues (e.g., Brunner, Gogarten, Bultmann, and Tillich), the first sharp critique came from his former teacher, Adolf von Harnack. The open debate between them took place through publishing in *Die Christliche Welt*. Harnack's "fifteen questions" and Barth's countering "fifteen answers." See Robinson, *Beginnings of Dialectic Theology* 165–87. Running counter to Harnack's scientific theology, Barth locates the scientific character of theology in the fact that the object of theology has existed and must always exist prior to the human method. What determines the content of the gospel for Barth is the gospel itself through the acting and speaking of God rather than historical knowledge. In sounding like his dialectical-analogical method in the Tambach lecture, Barth maintains that "a dialectic relationship . . . points to an *identity* which cannot be carried out and therefore also is not to be asserted. Therefore, the pointers visible on the stages of life's way are to be ascribed value only as *parables*," All "becoming can be parable, only parable" (Robinson, *Beginnings* 183). Here we see Barth's continued development of his dialectical theology in terms of parabolic language.

65. Peterson, "Was ist Theologie?" 13 (my translation).

earnest is only about the Being of God as such. "It is the *nemesis* of where the dialectician arrives, so that he does not come to the seriousness [of theological subject-matter] in spite of his [dialectical] seriousness."[66] All dialectics lead to no higher seriousness than to possible dialectical seriousness. Because God is exalted beyond all human dialectics, the dialectician is not competent to speak in earnest of who God is.

Of course Barth was aware of the fact that God's speaking of Godself does not lie in a dialectical way as such. Rather God's self-speaking begins when the dialectical method comes to an end. Barth's intention was to safeguard the freedom of God so that God should not be bound to any human discourse.

When the dialectic has turned everything into appearance and possibility, God's revelation is made appearance. In this regard, Peterson cites Ambrosius: "*Non in dialectica complacuit Deo salvum facere populum suum*" ("It did not please God to save his people by dialectic,).[67] According to Peterson, it is a confusion to make St. Paul or Luther dialecticians. Kierkegaard was not a theologian but a writer. In distinction from makers of myth or literature, it is essential for theologians to notice that there are revelation, faith, and obedience.[68] Therefore theology is only possible on the basis of revelation, faith, and obedience. In contrast to myth, theology finds that the fundamental principle is that actual epistemology is possible—although it is limited—within the presupposition that there are revelation, faith, and obedience.

The reason that Peterson is critical of Barth's dialectics is due to the fact that Barth explains the incarnation only in a pure paradox. In *Romans II*, Barth understood Jesus as Christ only in terms of paradox (R II:5). Therefore, Jesus Christ can be understood only as problem, only as myth inside of historical clarity (R II:6). Speaking of the incarnation as dialectical possibility means never speaking of it truly. According to Peterson, when Barth says that the impossibility as such becomes possibility, death becomes life, eternity becomes time, God becomes human being, Barth says—although in various turns—always only about the same; in other words, he says nothing at all.[69] Thesis and antithesis are summarized in

66. Ibid.
67. Ibid., 14.
68. Ibid., 15.
69. Ibid., 16.

formal and empty synthesis in which all but nothing is said. Peterson's sharp critique of Barth is centered on the concept of paradox in *Romans II*, in which Barth formulates the paradox of the person of God who became human. This is the most vulnerable point of dialectical theology. According to Peterson, "only under the presupposition that God has become human and has thereby enabled for us to have a participation in the *scientia divina*, only under this presupposition it is meaningful to talk about a real—though only analogous—knowledge of God in theology."[70] Three presuppositions of all theology—revelation, faith and obedience—are involved in a participation in divine Logos anyhow.[71]

For Peterson, participation in the *scientia divina* becomes possible in actuality only in the event of the incarnation in that here analogous knowledge of God also becomes possible. Therefore, there is no theology in the Jew or in the Gentiles. There is theology only in Christianity and only under the presupposition that the incarnated Word of God has spoken.[72] In this light, Barth's reduction of all theology to mere *prolegomena* toward Christology appears absurd. That the incarnated Word of God has spoken must be taken seriously in the act of theological knowledge. This is a critical challenge of Peterson against the dialectical theology that he saw represented in Barth's writings. For Peterson, as far as revelation is a paradox there is neither theology nor revelation. Revelation includes a relative knowability within itself. Peterson argues that Barth deals with revelation in terms of a timeless, abstract, dialectical possibility, so that God is the provider of the synthesis of our thesis and antithesis.

With analogous knowledge of God Peterson points to a matter of special significance for Barth's theological concept. What is at stake for Peterson is that the realistic character of theological knowledge is bound to the real character of revelation.[73] Under this presupposition, an analogous knowing of God can be required. According to Peterson, theology has to take in earnest the incarnation in the act of analogous knowing.

---

70. Ibid., 16.
71. Ibid., 18.
72. Ibid., 26–27.
73. Ibid., 16. As Jüngel says, the issue is about a metaphysical model—Platonic-Thomistic rule—about *participatio entis*, namely, about the participation of the visible world in the being of the idea that is exalted endlessly over it. Although it is done in christological reduction, this model becomes helpful in order to overcome the paradoxical structure of the unity between eternity and time. See Jüngel, *Barth-Studien*, 132.

Barth's reduction of theology to mere prolegomena evaporates revelation into the indefinite. In his Elgersburg lecture, Barth once concluded, "Can theology, should theology, proceed beyond the *prolegomena* to Christology? It could be that everything is said in the prolegomena."[74] Peterson argues that Barth's reduction of theology to prolegomena is not competent in taking into account Christology proper. Theology is rather a sequel of what formulates the logos-revelation into dogma. Therefore, dogma is the objective and concrete expression of the fact that God in the incarnation approaches the human being. Consequently theology, for Peterson, lies in the "Elongatur [prolongation] of Logos-revelation,"[75] in that the Logos-revelation expresses itself into dogma.

Barth's reaction to Peterson is more articulate and nuanced than the thinking of his colleagues in the circle of dialectical theology. As Barth writes, "For long time have I read nothing that would stimulate and irritate me as this glittering and, in every respect, imprudent pamphlet."[76] By responding to Peterson, Barth in his lecture "Kirche und Theologie" (delivered first in Göttingen, October 7, 1925) discerned that Peterson's presentation is "equally brilliant, enigmatic, and lofty" (*TC*:286). Barth regarded Peterson's thesis to be "Roman Catholic and in more than one section super-Catholic."[77] A catholicizing phenomenology of Peterson must be rejected when measured by the Reformation. However, if we accept Schleiermacher without blushing, then Thomas Aquinas is equally acceptable. Both are equally apart from Luther and Calvin (*TC*:288). Although, for Barth, revelation is neither dialectical nor paradoxical, there is dialectic "when theology begins, when we think, speak, or write, or argue on the basis of the revelation" (*TC*:299).

Be all this as it may, the revelation of which theology speaks is neither dialectical nor paradoxical: "Theology is in contrast to mythology and to a dialectical theology related to mythology, the obedient realization of the possibility of knowledge, truly unparadoxical knowledge of God" (*TC*:286). Barth's Godward-oriented articulation that Christ is the Paradox (R II:5–6) is modified by his discovery of ancient Christology. Already before Peterson's attack, Barth was preoccupied with the dog-

---

74. Barth, "Word of God and the Task," 217.

75. Peterson, "Was is Theologie?," 28.

76. Brief von Barth an Bultmann vom 25. September 1925: In B-B: 53–54; cf. Jüngel, *Barth-Studien*, 133.

77. Barth, "Church and Theology," (1925) in *TC*: 287.

matic tradition. Barth reported in his foreword to the new edition of a compendium of *Dogmatik der evangelisch-reformierten Kirche* his interest in Heinrich Heppe through Ernst Bizer (1935).[78]

Barth found in the old orthodoxy a dogmatic oriented toward the central indication of the biblical testimony of revelation. This is a dogmatic that made "worthy continuation of the doctrinal constructions of the ancient church" and maintained the continuity with the ecclesiastical science of the Middle Ages in clinging to the great concern of Reformation. Barth said: "I found myself visibly in the realm of the Church."[79] What Barth here discovered was a respectable theological science leaving room for the church. However, Barth's devotion to confessionalism did not mean a repristination of the older Reformed dogmatics, or succumbing to the patristic and Scholastic ontology, as Bultmann charges.[80]

Already in his response to Peterson's affirmation that "Theology lives from dogma," Barth articulates his Protestant position. "We Protestants must be content to recognize the objective givenness of a 'Kairos' (to use Tillich's word) as necessary for all theological work; that is, we must recognize the definite command of each moment. This command is written in no document, but its authority is binding; although the theologian cannot by reason or rule differentiate it from the equally indispensable illumination of the individual worker which is immediate through Word and Spirit" (*TC*:291). When it comes to a relation between revelation and the history of dogma, "history can indeed become a predicate of revelation, but never possibly can revelation become the predicate of history" (*TC*:292). Barth's return to this orthodoxy was an attempt at deepening

---

78. Barth, "Zum Geleit," in Heppe, *Dogmatik der evangelisch-reformierten Kirche*, iii: "I shall never forget the spring vacation of 1924. I sat in my study in Göttingen, faced with the task of giving lectures on dogmatics for the first time . . . It was at that time that, along with the parallel Lutheran work of H. Schmidt, Heppe's volume, which today is newly edited, fell into my hands; . . . I read, I studied, I reflected, and found that I was rewarded by the discovery that I found myself, here at any rate, in an atmosphere in which the way through the Reformers to Holy Scripture was more meaningful and natural than in the atmosphere of the theological literature which had been stamped by Schleiermacher and Ritschl . . ."

79. Ibid., iv.

80. B-B, 38. "At each moment, in each historical situation, the church has a word to speak. . . . Dogmatics must not ignore the present, the moment. . . . Naturally, what it has to relate to is not just the political, intellectual, or economic situation but the word which is hidden beneath this surface—the word which the church speaks, or sought to speak." *UCR* I:295.

his theological journey in engaging a critical dialogue with church confessions and doctrines. [81]

In accepting and reworking Peterson's challenge, Barth concluded that theology must be understood not as prolegomena but ratification and continuation of Christology. In fact, he explained two years later that it was not his intent to say that his existing work was a corrective to his previous theology. He would feel himself neither justified nor responsible to remain in the gesture of prophets, in the attitude of breakthrough (*CDE*:ix). In the foreword to the second edition of *Romans* (xiii), Barth described his task as one that brought to the agenda "the inner dialectic of the *Sache*" of Paul's letter. With this dialectical turn, Barth suggests that not only the talk about the *Sache* but the *Sache* itself should be dialectical. The dialectics of human knowledge corresponds to a dialectics of being that is to be known. Being that is to be known is dialectical. However, in *Christian Dogmatics*, Barth no longer establishes a "dialectic in the being to be known." Rather he says that "revelation is set above dialectic of our existence" (*CDE*:188). In this way, existential thinking can be avoided.

For Barth, God means an undialectical Word. The theology of the Word of God is undialectical theology. This is the simple and decisive ground for the exclusive possibility of dialectical theology (*CDE*:459). In this light, Barth asserts: Dogmatics is a process of dialogue, of question-and-answer, answer-and-question. Only through this continuing process do we gain understanding. It is using thesis and antithesis to reach a synthesis. It is, in short, dialectical thinking. In agreeing with Peterson's statement that "theology consists essentially *in the concrete obedience to concrete authority*," Barth says:

> Theology is the continuing service to God's revelation, performed by specific men, in the form of conceptual thinking in a specific here and now. . . . Revelation is the content of theology—that is of an ectypal (*ektupos*) theology, a "theology of wayfarers' (*theologia viatorum*) as the ancients called it in contrast to the archetypal (*arketupos*) theology of God himself to the comprehending theology (*theologia comprehensorum*) of the angels and saints in heaven . . . And the revelation is the gift of God's grace. To the specific position on earth corresponds the specific form of both

---

81. In the so-called *Göttingen Dogmatics*, Barth managed to prepare himself—in view of themes such as *Deus Dixit*, Trinity, election, incarnation, Christology of *anhypostasis* and *enhypostasis*—on the way to his later dogmatic theology in *Church Dogmatics*.

the revelation and the theology which serves it, the form of both the authority and the obedience. (*TC*:289)

Although Barth still refers to dialectical theology, he insists that the theological *Sache*, unlike in his *Romans II*, is undialectical. In *Romans II*, Kierkegaardian dialectics of infinite qualitative difference between God and the world is set for the sake of the aseity of God by highlighting the sinfulness of the creature. Barth's theological dialectics reveal human beings as sinners, totally estranged from a God who says "No" to them. In light of the divine "No," the world has a parabolic character. World as parable serves as a signpost paving the way for the kingdom of God. It points beyond itself to the inexpressible mystery of God, who, nevertheless, affirms human life (cf. the Tambach lecture).

For Barth, God is not paradox but mystery. In view of God's mystery the dialectical method can be applied to dogmatic thinking because "the prototype for everything, the thing that makes dogmatics necessarily dialectical, is the reality of God and man in the person of Jesus Christ. Only those who take away this 'and,' only those who picture one thing when they say God-man and can replace 'Jesus Christ' with one name, only they can afford to be *nondialectical* theologians" (*CDE*:456–57). This is why Barth does not hesitate to think of his christological model of incarnation in terms of a strong dialectical unity between the divinity and humanity in the one person of Jesus Christ (*CDE*:301).

Already in his response to Peterson Barth had differentiated revelation, of which theology speaks, from human ways of thinking: "Revelation itself can alone finally determine the real nature of theology" (*TC*:289). When theology arises, dialectics are the real form of our deed and performance. "This very being. . . . 'in the prolongation of the Logos-revelation', is carried on in the forms of human sinful thinking, speaking and writing." As far as theology is conceived of as a "concretion of the Logos," the way of the Logos to earth is from Bethlehem to Golgotha (*TC*:299).

The theology of dialectics is the theology of the wanderer, that is, *theologia viatorum*, not *theologia beatorum ac visionis*. That theology is "on the way" makes theology, as such, dialectical. The radical necessity of supplementation belongs to theology, that is, the principal openness of all sentences and propositions. *Dialegestai* is construction of principally incomplete thought and propositions under which every answer is also again a question, and that beyond themselves point to "the fulfillment in the inexpressible reality of the divine speaking" (*TC*:300).

However, Peterson attacked Barth's dialectical theology by quoting from Ambrose: "it did not please God to save his people by dialectic." According to Peterson, Barth's dialectical method cannot attain the seriousness of God. Running counter to this critique, Barth reaffirms his previous position and way of thinking in his "The Word of God and the Task of Ministry." "We must speak of the 'ought' and the 'cannot' rooted in the subject itself, under which he stands" (*TC*:300). "To take the revelation seriously in the sphere of conceptual thinking means to walk with entire definiteness and determination on the double path marked out for us by the necessity we are under to speak as *men*, but about *God*" (*TC*: 300). In regard to speaking of God's judgment and God's grace, Barth does not abandon his Kierkegaardian dialectics: "The infinite qualitative difference between God and man with which a theology of sinners . . . has to deal in presenting the communion of God and man" (*TC*:301).

In agreement with Peterson, however, Barth takes revelation to be neither dialectical nor paradoxical. God says an undialectical word. He says Amen. Although every theology is in need of dialectical and radical supplementation, the incarnation of God comes to the fore. This calls for thought-movement characterized in Barth's study of St Anselm. God's name (*id quo maius cogitari nequit*) proves Godself as self-existing, not in the sense of dialectics. Dialectics, which serve as a signpost toward something that can never be fully grasped, encounter God's aseity in an analogical fashion. Who God is can be known only by what God speaks of Godself. Barth's starting point as "a mathematical point on which one cannot stand"[82] assumes a way of analogy in finding the form of expression and thought for the sake of God's aseity and theology as science.

Kierkegaard interpreted the Christian message of the incarnation that God became human and the infinite became finite by virtue of human existence. In so doing, the God-man is not differentiated from other humans and thus is understood as a paradox that can be grasped and verified in faith.[83] God is here absorbed thoroughly into the dialectics of human existence. Accordingly, the paradox becomes a philosophical-theological style of thought and discourse in speaking of the incarnation,

---

82. Cf. Balthasar, *Theology of Karl Barth*, 70.
83. Cf. Jüngel, *Barth-Studien*, 178.

which is inherited by the dialectical theology. In making a dogmatic turn, Barth sees in the God of the incarnation that the Word of God fulfils the concept of the paradox in a strange way (*KD* I/1:172). In place of a thought-and-discourse-style paradox enters a hermeneutical model of correspondence; that is, analogy.[84]

Karl Barth in Münster

In July 1925 Barth was appointed professor of dogmatics and New Testament exegesis in Münster (1925–1930). Unlike during his time at Göttingen, now Barth held German citizenship. In Münster Barth came in increasing contact with Roman Catholicism rather than with liberal Protestantism. Barth's seminar on Anselm's *Cur Deus homo?* (in the summer semester of 1926) and the first part of Thomas Aquinas's *Summa Theologiae* (winter semester of 1928/9) exhibited his ongoing concern with Catholicism.

In his lecture "Roman Catholicism: A Question to the Protestant Church" (on March 9, 1928, in Bremen, on March 15 in Osnabrück, on April 10 in Düsseldorf), we see Barth's appraisal of Roman Catholicism and the Protestant church concerning ecclesiology, in favor of the former. Although the substance of the church may be distorted and perverted in Roman Catholicism, it is not lost. In neo-Presatntism, however, it is completely threatened. Despite his sharp critique of the divine I of the church in relation to human surrogates in the office of the papacy, Barth agued that "here is church substance" (*TC*:315).

According to Barth, Catholicism is "a forcible and sharp reminder" to the Protestant church that the Reformation of the sixteenth century had the clear purpose of *reformation;* in other words, "the rebuilding of the church." Therefore "it is neither destruction of the church nor its transformation into a wholly different structure" (*TC*:312). What was at issue in the Reformation was not to "proclaim a new, a second beginning, but the discovery of the old, the only, origin of the Church." "Protestantism protested not *against* but *for* the church. Reformation does not mean rev-

---

84. In contrast to Peterson's attack, Barth's dogmatic turn impacted his *Prolegomena* to *Christian Dogmatics*, namely, *Die christliche Dogmatik im Entwurf* (1927). Barth was attentive to the fact that readers inevitably bring presuppositions to their readings of texts. Barth later declared it to be "comical" to imagine a presuppositonless reading (*CD* I/2:468).

olution" (*TC*:312). However, against the first Reformation, the character of the second reformation which was prepared by the humanists and the visionaries of the sixteenth century "would not in the-re-establishment, but in a relinquishment of the substance of the Church" (*TC*:313).

In the historical development of the Reformation and in a kind of second reformation in the eighteenth and early nineteenth centuries, Barth pays attention to "the confusion of men and the Providence of God" (*hominum confusione et dei providentia*), which plays an important role. Roman Catholicism poses a question to the Protestant church: What constitutes the substance of the church? Barth makes it clear that this is a central question of Catholicism "because in its presuppositions for the church, in spite of all contradictions, it is closer to the Reformers than is the Church of the Reformation so far as that has actually and finally become the new Protestantism."[85]

At this point Barth's ecumenical concern sounds striking: "We cannot deny that we feel more at home in the world of Catholicism and among its believers than in a world and among believers where the reality about which the Reformation centered has become an unknown or almost unknown entity" (*TC*:314). "If I today became convinced that the interpretation of the Reformation on the line taken by Schleiermacher—Ritschl—Troeltsch (or even by Seeberg or Holl) was correct . . . I should have to withdraw from the evangelical Church. And if I were forced to make a choice between the two evils, I should, in fact, prefer the Catholic."[86] For Barth, the Reformation protest against Roman Catholicism should be seen as asserting the presence and action of God in a purer, more compelling form. It must not be understood as if it were intended to cast doubt on the presence and action of God in the Roman Catholic Church (*TC*:316).

In 1926 Erich Przywara's book *Religionsphilosophie* was published. In that text he indicates the *analogia entis* as origin, truth-ground, content, and circumference of natural knowledge of God. Barth is involved in confrontation with this Catholic theology and in consciously distancing himself from it by developing his own doctrine of analogy. Barth's conversation with Catholicism was highlighted by his invitation

---

85. *TC*:314.
86. *TC*:314, n. 1.

to Erich Przywara to give a lecture in Münster in 1929.[87] Barth's response to Przywara can be seen in his lecture "Fate and Idea in Theology"[88] (delivered in February and March 1929 in Dortmund). Barth deals with the concept of an *analogia entis*. The term *analogia entis* is not coined by Przywara but can historically be dated back to Cajetan. According to realism, Barth argues, God is real and has an objective existence independent of and prior to human knowledge of it. How God is known begins with knowledge of directly experienced reality rather than the simple affirmation of God's existence. According to Barth, realists seek God in the givenness of human experience or creaturely reality as it is. They ground their knowledge of God on what Barth calls a "basic orientation that does not permit itself to be further grounded."[89] In fact, God must not be conceived of being given—apart from God's revealing event in Jesus Christ.

In what sense and to what extent does directly experienced reality become possible in relation to the knowledge of God?

> "God is"—what else could that mean than that God participates in being? Certainly, the next statement which is immediately added is that He is Himself being, the Origin, and Perfection of all that exists. And the first statement, together with its corollary, is founded, in turn, (in its classical form, as conceived by Thomas Aquinas) upon a third statement (which can just as well be thought of as their consequence): that everything existing as such participates in God. In that everything existing is conceived as creature, it exists in a relation of the greatest dissimilarity to the Creator. Yet, in that it too has being, it exists in a relation of the greatest similarity to the Creator (*analogia entis*)."[90]

In Barth's view, Thomas provides theological ground for human knowledge of God in the *similitudo Dei* in which human beings are accessible to God by virtue of their creatureliness. Herein Barth sees a danger of realism in its pure form, namely *Deus sive natura*, who is identical with fate rather than the self-revealing of God in God's Word.[91] An attempt at grounding the possibility of the knowledge of God in terms of an analogy

---

87. His excitement is expressed in a letter to Thurneysen (February 9, 1929). *B-Th.II*: 652.
88. Barth, "Fate and Idea in Theology," 25–61.
89. Ibid., 62.
90. Ibid., 33.
91. Ibid., 42.

based on human creatureliness becomes questionable because it makes superfluous God's self-revelation. The revelation—which is something new and beyond creation—does not happen by virtue of some intrinsic capacity of creatures.

But it is a gracious act of God as such. "God not only unveils Himself but also veils Himself in revelation because it is revelation and not revealedness." "Under the act–character of the reality of God . . . the *similitudo Dei* must be given to us in every moment as something new from heaven."[92] Here we notice Barth's confrontation with Thomas's *analogia entis* and Schleiermacher's feeling of absolute dependence. For Barth revelation itself is a revealing event and not a state of being revealed or given.

In contrast to realism's naive conviction, idealism is oriented toward the question that is superior to the given. Idealism is critical thinking by calling the truth into question. It searches for unconditional truth as the ground for providing the ontic and noetic presupposition of the conditional: "It reminds us of God's non-objectivity and therefore of the inadequacy of all human thinking and speaking of God. Idealism guards the object of theology from confusion with all other objects. Idealism directs theological thinking and speaking to the God who, only in His genuine otherness [*Jenseitigkeit*], is really God."[93] In starting from the nongivenness of God, idealists secure the dissimilarity of God to the world at the expense of similarity between them: *Similitudo Dei and major dissimilitudo*.[94]

As far as the criterion of truth is to be given with revelation, idealism—albeit its critical thinking—offers no alternative to its counterpart of realism: "The equation *Deus sive ratio* is just as intolerable for theology as the equation *Deus sive natura*." [95] Steering a course between realism and idealism, Barth's way of thinking is still dialectical in considering the interplay between the given and the nongiven. His dialectic is not that of Hegel. Hegel's idealist method consists in resolving by sublation (*Aufhebung*) the contradictions between the binary oppositions. Nor is it that of Derrida, because Barth does not put the theological subject

92. Ibid., 40–41.
93. Ibid., 47.
94. Ibid., 46.
95. Ibid., 50.

matter under erasure (*sous rature*). In his confrontation with Erikson and Przywara, Barth's concentration on theological subject matter is not merely operating in the sense of Derrida's deconstruction of binary opposites,[96] but performs on the basis of *Deus dixit* in Jesus Christ, which constitutes for Barth the ectypal theology, namely, *theologia viatorum* (theology on the way). It would be called Barth's resistance to the ontotheological tradition. [97]

In his series of lectures on *The History of Protestant Theology since Schleiermacher* for his second semester in Münster (1926), we notice that the subject of history plays an important, constructive role—rather than a hostile, destructive one—for Barth. He often wondered if "in a second life he might not turn completely to history, for which he has a secret passion."[98] In describing the history of the nineteenth century in regard to a series of typical theologians of this time, Schleiermacher (1768–1834) and Feuerbach (1804–1872) are perhaps two crucial figures for Barth.[99] At this point my focus will be given to Barth's struggle with Feuerbach.[100]

---

96. Cf. Johnson, *Mystery of God*, 29–30.

97. Barth's radical attack on *analogia entis* emerged in his lecture at Elberfeld (in October 9, 1929), *The Holy Ghost and the Christian Life*. As he argues, "as long as we do not root Augustinianism completely out of the doctrine of grace, we will never have a Protestant theology" (Barth, *Holy Ghost and the Christian Life*, 14–15).

98. Busch, *Karl Barth: His Life*, 169.

99. Barth's ill feeling toward Schleiermacher has much earlier roots in the manifesto of ninety-three German intellectuals in support of the war policy of Wilhelm II and Bethmann-Hollweg. Behind the theology of this time, Barth sensed the influence of Schleiermacher in the theology of this time. Barth's commitment to Schleiermacher can be seen in his lectures at Göttingen in winter semester of 1923/24 and his two articles during this time. When Brunner's book on Schleiermacher (*Die Mystik und das Wort*, 1924) came out, Barth did not regard Brunner's term, "mysticism," as an adequate designation of Schleiermacher's intentions. According to Barth, Schleiermacher does not remain a negative mystic but a positive thinker with a vital philosophy. Barth dialogued with Schleiermacher until the end of his life. As late as 1968, Barth did not believe that Schleiermacher would have joined in the manifesto of World War I. However, Barth's criticism of Schleiermacher lies in the fact that the latter made human self-consciousness the subject of theology and Christ the predicate. Barth's conversation with Schleiermacher leads finally to a need for a deliberation of a theology of the third article, in other words, "a theology predominantly and decisively of the Holy Spirit." Cf. Barth, *Theology of Schleiermacher*, 278, 266. See further, Barth, "Schleiermacher" (1926), in *TC*: 77, 199.

100. Barth, "Ludwig Feuerbach." *TC*:217–37.

Karl Barth and Feuerbach

Feuerbach was to Barth a philosopher in earnest confrontation with the theology and religion of his time.[101] Feuerbach's critique of religion relies on his concept of the species-consciousness of the human. Religion is the first, namely, indirect self-consciousness of humans. Religion is the childish essence of humankind. When the human individual becomes aware of individual finitude and limitation, he or she has consciousness of what is greater, what is more comprehensive (that is, of the human species, of what characterizes humans as a species in contrast to animals). The individual beauty is neither infinite nor immortal. That is why the cause as well as the object of religion is anchored in this essence of humans. "Religion is the consciousness of the infinite."[102]

Feuerbach's so-called theory of projection cannot be adequately understood without his concept of the human species. To the degree that the divine essence is no less than human essence, theology becomes anthropology. Therefore, the consciousness of God is the self-consciousness of the human, and the knowledge of God is the self-knowledge of the human. The direct unity of species and individuality is just the highest principle, namely, the God of Christendom.[103] God as the embodiment of all realities or perfection is no other than the embodiment of the human species, which realizes itself in the course of world history. God becomes my hidden, certain existence as a member of the human species. To the degree that God becomes human, the human person is the true Christ in the consciousness of the species.[104]

Barth recognizes Feuerbach's critique of Christendom by making Feuerbach a component of his own polemic against the humanization of God in neo-Protestant theology. To what extent have religion, revelation,

---

101. Barth's concern about Feuerbach can be dated back to his article "Faith in a Personal God" ("Der Glaube an den persönlichen Gott" [1914]), in which Barth quotes Feuerbach's lecture *The Essence of Christianity* to critique an attempt at conceiving of God in terms of an analogy to human personality. In his *Romans II*, Barth argues with Feuerbach against Hieler's interpretation of prayer (R II:316). In "the frontier of religion," Barth agreed with Feuerbach's critique of religion (In R II, see the commentary on Romans 7:1–6). See R II:236.

102. Feuerbach, *Wesen des Christentums*, 2.

103. Ibid., 207. See also Chung, *Karl Barth und die Hegelsche Linke*, 135.

104. Barth, "Feuerbach," in Barth, *Die protestantische Theologie im 19. Jahrhundert*, 485. See also the introductory essay by Karl Barth in Feuerbach, *Essence of Christianity*.

and God's relation with humanity in modern Protestant theology become a predicate of humans? God who revealed Godself in Jesus Christ, whom Barth recognizes as wholly other, can be immune from Feuerbach's theory of projection. Rather than becoming Feuerbach's student, Barth uses Feuerbach to combat a definite tendency in religion, theology, and church toward humanizing the divine. Critique of religion—to the degree that it becomes deconstruction of idolatrous images—stands in service of the God of the Bible. Feuerbach's critique of religion is accepted by Barth as one of the most important tasks of theology.

In this regard, according to Barth, the position of Feuerbach as antitheologian was "more theological than that of many theologians."[105] Barth does not feel that there is a reason to disagree with Feuerbach. The summons of Feuerbach was to turn away from lies to truth, "to turn from God to the world and man, from faith to love, from heaven to earth, from Christ to ourselves, from the bodiless ghosts of supernaturalism to real life."[106] Feuerbach's real concern was to help humans since "the secret of immediate knowing is sensation."[107] The principle of his new philosophy is the body in its totality, the actual and complete being of man rather than the *I* of Kant and Fichte, the absolute identity of Schelling, or the absolute Mind of Hegel. So Feurbach regarded Kant, Fichte, and Hegel as supernaturalists who sought the divine essence in reason apart from the human.[108]

For Feuerbach, the concept of the object is no other than the concept of objective and concrete I, namely, you. The consciousness of the world and my own consciousness are mediated through your consciousness. This mediation is of a sensuous nature. The secret of existence is the secret of love in the most comprehensive sense of the word. From this principle head, heart, and stomach seek and find as a goal a common object. With this presupposition, Feuerbach wants to make theologians into anthropologists.[109] This is Feuerbach's way from religion to humanity, in which his critique of religion can be formulated as positive atheism

---

105. *TC*:217.
106. Ibid., 219.
107. Ibid., 220.
108. Ibid., 484.
109. Ibid., 485

or a religious atheism.[110] What is true and real is the human, the most real being. According to Feuerbach, the right of the stomach to have its say in high, even in the highest, matters is not to be denied. Fuerbach's determined antispiritualism becomes meaningful and positive for Barth in purifying and healing a traditional limitation of theology and church in the field of social and economic questions. Feuerbach's fundamental thesis—theology became anthropology—is especially valid for Luther, who made a special attention from God *in se* to God *for us*.[111]

The special significance of Feuerbach for Barth lies in the former's critical relevance to Lutheran Christology and its doctrine of the Lord's Supper, which are based on the idiomatic communion in the majestic nature (*genus majestaticum*); God must be found in the *man* Jesus, so in the Eucharist the communicant partakes of the nature of the risen Christ. In Barth's view, this line of Lutheran orthodoxy refers explicitly to a possibility of reversing above and below, of heaven and earth, of God and man by forgetting the eschatological reservation.[112]

According to Barth, Luther's limitation in his doctrine of the Eucharist lies in his affirmation of real presence without a divine *But*. "To eat body of Christ in the bread is not a *mere symbol* of our union with him; it is the experiencing of the union signified by the symbol. The sought becomes the found, the promised becomes possession, the likeness becomes identity" (*TC*:99). "He [Luther] will contend sharply neither against the doctrine of transubstantiation nor for the so-called consubstantiation doctrine; but only *against* those who make out of the former, 'a necessary article of faith and law'; and *for* the real presence of the body in the bread" (*TC*:103).

Lutheran orthodoxy fixated the God-humanity of Christ in the dogma of the *communicatio idiomatum*, in *genere majestatico*, in which the predicate of divine glory, omnipotence, omnipresence, eternity, and the like are attributed to the humanity of Jesus as such and *in abstracto*. This was called the apotheosis of the humanity of Christ by the orthodox Lutherans.[113] Luther, Hegel (as a good Lutheran), and the Old Lutherans faced Feuerbach's attack. To resist his critique of religion, Barth argues

---

110. Jan M. Lochman, "Von der Religion zum Menschen," in Barth, *Antwort*, 599–600.
111. *TC*:226.
112. *TC*:230.
113. Barth, "Feuerbach," in *Die protestantische Theologie im 19. Jahrhundert*, 487.

that the human relation with God in every respect must become an irreversible one. In this regard, Barth argues that the Calvinist doctrine of *finitum non capax infiniti* (the finite is incapable of the infinite) retains a certain truth as a corrective to the Lutheran position (*finitum capax infiniti*).

"Feuerbach is concerned with the reality, the whole reality of man (heart and stomach!). There can be real talk of God only where the concern is with that reality of man. His interest lay (whether or not with complete consistency is another question) in man's actual existence and situation (*Dasein* and *Sosein*), in the apparently quite uninteresting and obvious life of human beings—in neither man's spiritual nor his physical life by itself, but both together in the unity in which alone the existence of man is possible."[114] Feuerbach's challenge would not be met and countered until the theology of Christian hope (in the case of both Blumhardts) along the lines of "the radical Easter faith of the Eastern Church.[115]

For Barth, the resurrection of Jesus Christ is the grounding revelation of God on which his Christology is anchored. The assumption of all flesh and the reception of the entire natural and spiritual human race into communion with God becomes visible and knowable in the resurrection. In terms of *assumptio carnis*, in which Barth conceives of the incarnation in the Feuerbachian sense of the "human species," Barth would affirm that not only the religious world of phenomena but the world and the human race as such (i.e., the *humanitas*), real and substantial humanness are accepted and assumed into the *assumptio carnis*. As Marquardt says, "the collective human race is assumed into the communion with God and the human race is assumed in the concrete collectives."[116]

In addition, Feuerbach's contribution lies in its affinity with the ideology of scientific socialism exemplified in Engels and Marx[117] in contrast to utopian socialism. Feuerbach's attempt at humanizing religions forms an integral part in motivating "a struggle for emancipation," "a fight for

---

114. *TC*:231.

115. *TC*:232.

116. Marquardt, "Religionskritik und Entmythologisierung," 359.

117. In this context, Barth's remarks on Karl Marx are striking: "If only the Church had been compelled before Marx to show in word and action, and had been able to show, that it is just the knowledge of God which automatically and inevitably includes within itself liberation from all hypostases and idols, which of itself can achieve liberation!" *TC*: 234.

freedom which was initiated as well as limited by the Revolution."[118] In light of Feuerbach's contribution, Barth asks, "Does the guilt of the Church also show itself here in its lack of prophetic insight into the signs of the times?"[119]

> If the atheism of Social Democracy is a warning, a *mene tekel*, for the Church, before which the Church should not be pharisaically outraged but should rather do penance, then the convincing power of Feuerbach's teaching in comparison with the theology of *this* Church is no riddle, even though the core of his teaching is superlatively banal. The Church will be free of Feuerbach's question only when its ethics have been radically separated from both the ancient and the modern hypostases. Then the Church will again win belief that its God is no illusion—but never until then.[120]

However, Barth does not agree with Feuerbach's attempt at reducing theology into the anthropology and glorifying the apotheosis of humans. The essence of humans (the consciousness of species, which Feuerbach makes the measure of all things) amounts to the identification between God and humans. However, for Barth the identification of the essence of God with humans who are characterized by evil and death is the greatest of all illusions. Against Feuerbach's apotheosis of humans, Barth later deepens his christological thinking in terms of the exaltation of humans into unity with God.[121]

Barth's idea of cohumanity has a parallel with Feuerbach's idea of societal relation in which the unity of humans with cohumans becomes the highest and last principle of the new philosophy. Barth's way from religion to Christ surmounts and utilizes Feuerbach's critique of religion. From van Til or Budeus until Ritschl and Troeltsch, religion was not from revelation, but revelation was to be understood from religion (*KD* I/2: 316). Barth's theological program moves in the direction from all reli-

---

118. *TC*:233.
119. Ibid.
120. *TC*:234.
121. Cf. *KD* IV/2:130. Barth's retrieval of Feuerbach facilitates his theological development in conversation with Lutheran Christology. Feuerbach's discovery of "you" coupled with Confucius and Buber has a theological echo in Barth's anthropology (KD III/2:333–35). In Barth's turn to the humanity of God and christological concentration in *Church Dogmatics*, we notice Barth's attempt to raise humanity up to fellowship with God, although it does not mean self-apotheosis. Cf. Glasse, "Barth zu Feuerbach," 474–75.

gious abstraction to the concrete reality of the biblically witnessed work of God, to God's covenant with Israel, to Jesus Christ. This program is a way from religion to Christ.[122] Therefore there is a way from Christology to anthropology, but no way from the anthropology to Christology.

Anselm and the *Analogia Fidei*

When Barth moved from Münster to Bonn (1930), the theological split among dialectical theologians became inevitable. Barth's dissatisfaction with his colleagues such as Gogarten and Bultmann consisted in his conflict with their specific Lutheranism. In addition, Barth's turn to dogmatics for the hermeneutical retrieval of the old doctrine of Christology seemed to arouse skepticism in the eyes of Georg Metz, who was, in fact, opposed to the publication of *Die chrstliche Dogmatik im Entwurf.*

Nevertheless, Barth's dedication to *Christian Dogmatics* must be understood as his concrete prophetic concern—"being feet on the ground"—to be faithful to the life of the church concerning the social-political structure of Germany: "Both before and after my commentary on Romans I have gone my way, and again gone my way, *on the earth.* That means for me concretely . . . that I have no choice but to take up Christian Dogmatics" (*CDE*:8).[123]

In view of Peterson's attack, Barth's dogmatic turn was fruitful in that it resulted in his prolegomena to *Christian Dogmatics,* namely, *Die christliche Dogmatik im Entwurf* (1927).[124] Barth published the first section of lectures in Münster under the title of *Prolegomena zur christlichen Dogmatik,* which was done during the winter semester of 1926/27. However, *Christian Dogmatics* is a revised and expanded version of his former Göttingen lecture *Unterricht in der christlichen Religion: Prolegomena.*[125] The *Prolegomena* appears in a thoroughly new form.

122. J. M. Lochman, "Von der Religion zum Menschen," in *Antwort,* 604.

123. Cf. Gorringe, *Karl Barth: Against Hegemony,* 96.

124. Already Barth had delivered lectures on dogmatics from the summer semester 1924 to the summer semester 1925 under the title of *Unterricht in der christlichen Religion* at Göttingen. And then in Münster, Barth delivered lectures on dogmatics—especially the eschatology in the winter semester 1927/28—and continued dogmatic lectures further from the winter semester 1926/27 to the winter semester 1927/28. Since 1931 Barth gave the dogmatic lectures in Bonn and Basel until the publication of his monumental *Church Dogmatics* in 1932.

125. *CDE*:xi.

Against the position of other dialectical theologians, in which Barth discerned an immanentist tendency associated with the analysis of human existence, Barth emphasized his dogmatic concern about the Trinity.[126]

Later, however, Barth portrayed this dogmatic attempt as a "false start" (*CD* III/4:xii.) because he had not yet managed to clear out the last residues of the existential-philosophical basis—or in other words, the protection or justification of theology (*CD* I/1:xiii). Indeed, reflecting on these years Barth surmised that he "had to rid myself [himself] of the last remnants of a philosophical, i.e. anthropological . . . foundation and exposition of Christian doctrine. The real document of this farewell is, in truth, . . . the book about the evidence for God of Anselm of Canterbury which appeared in 1931."[127]

Barth was most satisfied with this book among all his books. He characterized his development in terms of needing to overcome the "eggshells of philosophical systematics." In retrospect, Barth regretted paragraphs 5 and 6 in *Christian Dogmatics* more than any other part, and he fully eliminated those sections in the *Church Dogmatics*.[128] In following Barth's remarks, Balthasar marked the decisive turning point with his parole "breaking new ground" in regard to the shift from dialectic to analogy in Barth's study of Anselm.[129]

In a transition period between the *Prolegomena* (1927) and *Church Dogmatics* I/1 (1932), Barth also made an essential contribution to deepening the relationship between dialectical theology and analogical theol-

---

126. Barth, already in his lecture "The Principles of Dogmatics according to Wilhelm Herrmann" (1925), paid special attention to the doctrine of the Trinity in Herrmann's dogmatics: "If one has thought that God is eternally subject and never object, that he determines himself and is knowable exclusively through himself in 'pure act' (*actus purissimus*) of his Triune Personality—then one has thought it and must continue to think it. The thought cannot afterwards be put in brackets as just a 'reflection of faith'" (*TC*:256).

127. Barth, *How I Changed My Mind*, 42-44.

128. On the difference between *Christian Dogmatics* and *Church Dogmatics*, see Gorringe, *Karl Barth: Against Hegemony*, 100-8.

129. Balthasar, *Theology of Karl Barth*, 79. Barth himself credits Balthasar, who noticed his interest in Anselm. Balthasar saw the importance of the Anselm book rather than making it a side issue for Barth's theology. Barth wrote that "Hans Urs von Balthasar . . . realized how much it has influenced me or been absorbed into my own line of thinking. Most of them have completely failed to see that in this book on Anselm I am working with a vital key, if not the key, to an understanding of that whole process of thought that has impressed me more and more in my *Church Dogmatics* as the only one proper to theology." *FQI*:11.

ogy through the study of Anselm of Canterbury. Barth ran a seminar on Anselm in 1926, and then in 1930, stimulated by his Münster friend Heinrich Scholz. Scholz produced in Barth a compelling urge to discuss Anselm differently from his previous understanding and to establish and clarify Barth's position in speaking of Anselm's theological method (*FQI*:7).

Already in the *Prolegomena* (1927), Barth pointed emphatically to the significance of Anselm (*CDE*:16, 21, 131–36, 139, 147, 191, 305ff, 371, 487) in registering him as an advocate for correcting the problem of neo-Protestantism. As Barth says, "But of course my love for Anselm goes back much further than that. In my 'Prolegomena' to the *Dogmatics* I made vigorous reference to him and as a result was promptly accused of Roman Catholicism and of Schleiermacherism."[130] The reality of the Word of God rests entirely in itself rather than belonging to Cartesian epistemology. We who are caught in the subject-object schema know the reality of the Word of God in that we are known by it (*CDE*: 109).

For Anselm in his *Proslogion,* the human being can understand God only on the basis of faith, which is connected with the prayer of faith (*CDE*:131). This aspect leads to *credo ut intelligam*. Nevertheless, God remains unknown in human knowing. *Intelligere* as human activity takes place based on a prior act of God. Therefore, "knowledge here means fundamentally acknowledgement. Thinking means thinking-after" (*CDE*: 136). This mode of thought had been a controlling principle to Barth's dialectical theology in *Romans*.

In his treatment of Anselm, Barth made an attempt to further explicate what had remained unsatisfactory in his first treatment of Anselm's theological method in *Christian Dogmatics*. Barth's engagement with the Anselm of *Proslogion* 2–4 was a major reason for him to delay his continuous work of *Church Dogamtics*. As we have already seen in the preface to the second edition of his book on Anselm, Barth asserts that people have to deal with his study of Anselm as the important key to understanding his thought-movement, which is closer to *Church Dogmatics*. What was important for Barth in the study of Anselm was not to provide a full account of Anselm, but to discuss Anselm's proof of the existence of God in the context of Barth's theological program.[131] Although Anselm's theol-

---

130. Cf. *FQI*:7.

131. Barth further explicates Anselm's theological method in his *Church Dogmatics* 1/1 ("The Speech of God as the Mystery of God" [*CD* I/1:162–87], and "The Word of God

ogy was instructive and edifying, Barth did not identify himself with the views of Anselm, and especially not with Anselm's proof of the existence of God (*FQI*:9).

Anselm is distinguished from the "liberal" theologians of his time, in that his *intelligere* is really intended to be no more than a deepened form of *legere*. But—and this distinguishes him just as definitely from the "positivists," the traditionalists of his day—it does involve a deepened *legere*, an *intus legere*, a reflecting upon (*FQI*:41). Anselm is the one who enables Barth to pursue what "faith seeking understanding" meant rather than remaining a dialectician in an irrational or paradoxical fashion. According to Barth, since Aquinas, Anselm had been misunderstood in his historical context. Barth's concern was to update the theology of the Scholastics and make it fruitful for his contemporary situation. Barth

> deems Anselm's Proof of the Existence of God in the context of his theological scheme a model piece of good, penetrating and neat theology, which at every step I have found instructive and edifying, though I would not and could not identify myself completely with the views of its author (*FQI*:9).

Barth attempted to confine his analysis to the most problematic part of Anselm's book, namely, the ontological proof of God—which is the content of *Proslogion* 2-4. Barth presents the theological program of Anselm in terms of the ontological proof of God's existence in the following sections: 1) the necessity for theology, 2) the possibility of theology, and 3) the condition of theology.

As far as the necessity for theology is concerned, Barth was concerned first of all with the necessity for theology on the ground (in practical situations), where Anselm's *intelligere* becomes problematic. It is not the polemical-apologetic proof but the *intelligere* that reflects the Christian faith claim. When the *intelligere* is carried out, it gives rise to joy. Proof and joy can be, at best, a by-product of the performing thought. What is at stake is not about a requirement of faith for the proof of joy: "The necessity of Anselm's *intelligere* does not lie in the desirability of these, its two results. And it is only by virtue of its necessity on a higher level that these, its results, are possible and desirable. Anselm's concern. . . . is theology, the *intellectus fidei*. *Fides quaerens intellectum*—that was the original title of the *Proslogion*" (*FQI*:16). So *credo ut intelligam* is a

---

and Faith," especially *CD* I/1:230).

legitimate Christian proposition because human reason is in the service of and offers praise to God, who revealed Godself in the revelation of Jesus Christ. Revelation is not merely believed at the cost of sacrificing human reason but is to be acknowledged.

The effect of *intelligere* (proof and joy) cannot seize the question of God's existence for faith. A theological inquirer does not ask for the sake of the existence of his or her faith. The inquirer is so sure about *gratia Dei praeveniente* to faith, although he or she cannot understand what he or she believes absolutely with reason alone. "The *rei veritas* remains fixed whatever its relation to the *intellectus ad eam capiendam*. It is presupposition of all theological inquiry that faith as such remains undisturbed by the vagaries of theological 'yes' and 'no.' If *intelligere* does not reach its goal, . . . then in place of the joy of knowing there remains reverence before Truth itself"(*FQI*:18). It is also not about the existence of faith, but about the nature of faith that desires and calls for knowledge.

Therefore *credo ut intelligam* means: my faith itself and as such is a summons for me to knowledge. Faith in God demands and calls for the knowledge of God. "He is the God in whom *intelligentia* and *veritas* are identical" (*FQI*:18). According to Anselm, faith is primarily a movement of the will. Consequently, a relation between faith and will can be understood as the basis for Anselm's psychology. The effective primacy of the will is in correspondence with the original primacy of knowledge. For Anselm faith is impossible without *novum* encountering human beings and happening to them from outside. The seed to be received is the proclaimed and heard Word of God. That it comes to us and we accept it is grace. In faith the potentiality of image (or similarity) of God is actualized. This is *vestigia trinitatis* in distinction of human from animal. That *intelligere* becomes necessary out of faith is "on the way," namely, of eschatological character. "There can be absolutely no question at all of *intelligere* breaking through the barrier between the *regnum gratiae* and the *regnum gloriae*. On the contrary, it is in its very *quaerere* and *invenire* that *intellectus* comes up against the inexorable limitations of humanity in a way that faith, as such, does not" (*FQI*:20). According to Anselm, knowledge stands in the middle between faith and vision—like a mountain standing between one looking at it from the valley and one from the sun. The *intelligere* can be understood as the attainable but limited first step and possibility in the direction of blessed vision which is, in turn, the eschatological counterpart of faith. Therefore, the intellectual—although in all its limitations—is an attainable preparatory stage toward a vision that corresponds eschatologically to faith. So understood, "*Intellectus* is also involved in actualizing the *imago Dei* as this occurs in faith" (*FQI*: 21). This implies what *anlogia fidei* means.

As far as the possibility of theology is concerned, faith is also, for Anselm, in no sense something illogical or irrational. Faith is the right action of will, which is demanded by God and bound up with blessed experience as long as it is faith in God. This means the right faith. Faith comes from hearing, and hearing comes from preaching. Faith is related to the Word of Christ and acknowledged and affirmed by it. If faith is not reception, namely, knowing and affirming the Word of Christ, then it is not faith. The Word of Christ is identical with the word of human beings that legitimately proclaims and represents the Word of Christ. To what extent the Word of human beings represents the Word of Christ in a legitimate way is not, for Anselm, to be established univocally. To it belong the Bible and confession of the ancient church in accordance with its wording. Although not as source, the writings of Catholic fathers, and especially those of Augustine, are emphatically designated as the norms for Anselm. That the church emerges is obvious. "Anselm's subjective *Credo* has an objective *Credo* of the Church as its unimpeachable point of reference—that is, a number of propositions formulated in human words (including, of course, the Bible and the Symbols of the Early Church as basic documents of the Catholic Church's faith)" (*FQI*:24). Faith seeking understanding, therefore, is thinking after or reflecting upon what has already been said in the *Credo* of the Church (*FQI*:40).

That being the case, the subjective *Credo* of Anselm has an objective *Credo* of the church. The Bible and symbols of the ancient church that are basic writings of faith in the Catholic Church belong to the objective *Credo*. Out of this relation between subjective *Credo* and objective *Credo* a possibility of theology happens. Given this fact, *intelligere* comes into being through thinking-after the *Credo*, so *credere* is the presupposition of *intelligere*. In this regard, the *intelligere* is a soluble problem, so that theology is a feasible task. In *intelligere*'s relation to the *Credo*, we talk about theological science as the science of the *Credo* positively (*FQI*: 26). To what extent can the Christian then move and rise from *credere* to *intelligere*?

Where faith seeks understanding, there is a midline to be walked between information and affirmation of what has taken place in the church.

Therefore, this *intelligere*, namely, theology, becomes a possible task. Anselm has found the resolution of his problem in terms of the objective rationality of church authority on the part of Christian believers. *Credo ut intelligam* is not like a fanatic appeal to heaven that means *sacrificum intellectus* (*FQI*:26). The objective *Credo* leads to Christian humility before *ratio veritatis*, which is presupposed in all human knowledge of divine attributes. For *ratio veritatis* the revelation of God as such is peculiar. This revelation enables and establishes the theology as theological science. This is the convulsion-free peculiarity of Anselm's approach to theology.

The condition of theology emerges out of necessity, and it enables the *intelligere* through faith. Theological science can have, as science of *Credo*, a positive character in its relation to the *Credo*. The *intelligere* becomes possible through "thinking-after" the *Credo*, which has been already spoken and affirmed. However, theological questions cannot go back behind the dogma of the Trinity of God or the incarnation. "*Intelligere* will not go beyond the limit of the inner necessity of the articles of the *Credo*, beyond the limit of faith's essential nature which corresponds to these articles" (*FQI*:28). Therefore, every theological assertion is inadequate to express its object. The Word of Christ that was said to us, as such, is not inadequate for us, but to paraphrase this Word in thought or in speech is humanly inadequate: "Strictly speaking, it is only God himself who has a conception of God" (*FQI*:29).

Therefore God breaks away from syllogisms: "Every one of the categories known to us by which we attempt to conceive him is, in the last analysis, not really one of his categories at all" (*FQI*:29). Theology cannot escape this condition. On account of theology's relativity, theological assertions are challenged by the sheer incomparability of their object. According to Anselm, the task of theology, the quest for *intelligere* in the narrow sense, begins where the Bible quotation ends. It is an interim statement in expectation of better instruction (*FQI*:31).

For Anselm there is a fundamental and necessary progress of theological science: "We are therefore justified in ascribing to Anselm the explicit notion of progress in theology, in so far as he thought of the scientific process as an ascent from one *ratio* to an ever higher *ratio*" (*FQI*:32). Still, this progress is not based on the arbitrariness of the theologian, but conditioned by the wisdom of God. "The merely scientific certainty and the perfectibility of its language, is this—while the best of its statements can find human approval, it is not possible for the final criterion of this approval to be demonstrated or appealed to" (*FQI*:33).

Although one concrete criterion for all theological statements is hidden in view of the ultimate sense that God Godself is Truth, there is also a concrete criterion of all theological assertions residing in the text of Holy Scripture. If a proposition is in agreement with the actual wording of Scripture or is a direct consequence from it, it is valid with absolute certainty. But the agreement of a proposition with Scripture is itself not peculiarly a theological proposition. Another condition of *intelligere* is the reality of *credere* as such. It is decisive for knowledge that the right thing should be rightly believed. Where this is not the right faith, the right knowledge is not possible. "Where this right faith is absence there can be no right knowledge" (*FQI*:34).

In this case, the scientific character of theology can be questioned. What is required for right faith is open and childlike obedience, a life in the Spirit, a rich nourishment from Holy Scripture. "Where faith is really faith, that is to say obedience.... For only in faith could this connection between the obedience of faith and the faith of the Church be experienced and only in experience could it be understood" (*FQI*:35).

The condition of *intelligere* that conditions and relativizes all others is prayer. As the title *Proslogion* means, an address to God, prayer is necessary for the sake of qualified *intelligere*. Every right quest—it is grace—does not help, unless God shows Godself. What it depends on is not only that God gives the theologian the grace to think of God rightly, but also that God comes to surface as the object of this reflection. In so doing, right thinking is qualified. According to Anselm, right knowledge is conditioned by the prevenient and co-operating grace of God.

> This general consideration and also the fact that this grace must ever be sought by prayer already imply that the ultimate and decisive capacity for the *intellectus fidei* does not belong to human reason acting on its own but has always to be bestowed on human reason as surely as *intelligere* is a *voluntarius effectus*. (*FQI*:37)

A Critical Assessment

When we look at the theological apologetics of Schleiermacher wouldn't we expect him to turn the desire of faith for proof into the desire for joy?

Would not this desire of faith for joy, according to Schleiermacher, lead to the highest unity of intuition and feeling, or the feeling of absolute dependence? Wouldn't this attempt be responsible for an anthropocentric encapsulation of divine truth and a marginalizing attitude toward the Bible in later developments of Protestantism? No wonder this is the horizon in which Barth represents his thought-form under the shadow of Anselm's theological method. Barth defends himself against making a decision of faith on the basis of "anthropological places" (*KD* I/1:211–12), whether it is reason, feeling, or conscience, etc. The principle that faith as such remains undisturbed by the vagaries of a theological yes and no is and remains, according to Barth, a presupposition of all theologies. In this regard Barth sharpens his critique of a postulated "religious *a priori*" (Troeltsch). As in *Romans*, actualization of the image (or similarity) of God takes place in the act of faith (*KD* I/1:284–85).

Theology has the task that stands between the times: that moves and carries itself out in the hazardous enterprise of faith. Therefore, it is always *theologia viatorum*, namely it has by no means archetypal character, but is ectypal (*KD* I/1:284–85). It is *theologia viatorum*. Every *intelligere* stands under the eschatological proviso. The interim character of theology defends it against rationalists and against Schleiermacher who turned piety into gnosis.[132]

What Barth pursued was a theology daring to be a theology that in a secret sense was not anthropology—a theology. In contrast to anthropology, Barth's theology is grounded and justified on the miracle of revelation and sees its possibility in talking about God in the appearance of Jesus Christ. It is Barth's path seasoned with a spirit of audacity through which one overcomes Cartesianism. So theology is the most difficult and the most dangerous among all sciences.[133]

---

132. Barth, *Die protestantische Theolologie im 19. Jahrhundert*, 385.

133. In contrast, Gogarten and Brunner insist that the decisive task of theology is the development of an anthropology that offers a basis for analyzing the existential alienation of modern individuals from God in order to bring them into contact with the church. Bultmann saw—in terms of Heideggerian existential-ontological method and conceptuality—a new possibility of making the kerygma of the New Testament relevant to the contemporary individual. Tillich undertakes attempts to secure theology in a distinguished place among the culture sciences. However, Barth distanced himself sharply from existential analysis, vis-à-vis Bultmann, and from an attempt to seek a point of contact, vis-à-vis Gogarten and Brunner (*Nein!* in 1934).

In his shift from *Christian Dogmatics* to *Church Dogmatics*, Barth mentions: "I have eliminated in this second version of the book everything I possibly could which might appear to seek a grounding, support or even only a justification of theology in existential philosophy" (*CD* I/1: xiii). In granting existential dialectic a new force and perspective, Barth is not exempt from existentialism as a precondition. His so-called *extra Calvinisticum* provides a correlate for natural theology.[134]

In response to Theodore Siegfried, who argued that Barth's *Christian Dogmatics* was built on an existential-philosophical basis, Barth found it superfluous and dangerous to provide an existential-philosophical grounding of theology in terms of an existential analysis of the situation of the preacher and hearer of the Word of God (*CD* 1/1:126). Barth had to concede that he left room for such existential analysis: "I was paying homage to false gods, even if only after the manner of the *libellatici* of the Decian persecution" (*CD* I/1:127). In fact, the preacher and the hearer have their ground in the Word itself. Barth expresses his astonishment at what he had said in *Christian Dogmatics*: "The hearing human is included in the concept of the Word of God just as much as the speaking God. He is 'co-posited' in it, as Schleiermacher's God is in the feeling of absolute dependence" (*CDE*:148). Now Barth corrects this statement, stating that it is God's free grace that the human being is co-posited in the Word of God with factual necessity (*CD* I/1:140).

Barth's sensitivity to his previous theological program points to his final way to *Church Dogmatics*. As Barth made a shift from *Christian Dogmatics* to *Church Dogmatics*,[135] his thought-form became bound up with the church. In his famous definition: "As a theological discipline

---

134. "It thus becomes evident that the Word of reconciliation is also the Word of creation, and that the latter is renewed and confirmed by the former. The realm of nature is also the kingdom of the Son, not just the realm of grace. In the realm of nature, as the Word of creation, the Son is not yet the incarnate one . . . the *logos asarkos*, however, is not a secondary (although primary), natural, partial revelation. There is only one total Revelation, through the *logos ensarkos*, but the preexistent Logos, as the creator's Word, is the necessary antecedent of it" (CDE:271).

135. McCormack chides Barth for his exaggeration in portraying *Christian Dogmatics* as a false start in relation to *Church Dogmatics*. Be that as it may, Barth's turn to *Church Dogmatics* would not be merely regarded as the second edition of *Christian Dogmatics*, like the first edition of *Romans* (1919) to the second edition (1922). Barth's dependence on existential philosophical concepts associated with *theologia naturalis* is in opposition to his theological method on the basis of Anselm study. Cf. McCormack, *Critically Realistic*, 442–48.

dogmatics is the scientific self-examination of the Christian Church with respect to the content of its distinctive talk about God" (*CD* I/1:1). As far as dogmatics is the scientific, critical self-examination of the Christian church concerning the content of its peculiar speech about God, the church stands in need of self-examination and correction and criticism again and again. Therefore, theology is not in the defensive as to secular questions for defending the church in an apologetic manner. Rather, theology is ready for the acceptance of such questions with the zeal to church repentance and conversion to the *Ursprung*. In this regard Barth asks whether the ungodliness that brought Jesus Christ to the cross and that he refuted in his resurrection is not the theoretical godlessness of atheists but the practical godlessness of the pious, the representative of Christian civilization.[136]

Barth, moreover, did not want his *Church Dogmatics* to "be hailed as the dogmatics of dialectical theology." He made sure that he had written it for the community of church, "not a community of theological endeavour" (*CD* I/1:xiv–xv.): "In substituting the word Church for Christian in the title, I have tried to set a good example of restraint in the lighthearted use of the great word 'Christian,' against which I have protested" (*CD* 1/1:xiii). However, Barth's turn to the church is an attempt to radicalize, integrate, and explicate secular questions in light of his daring way toward the name of Jesus Christ as the reality of the revelation. As a result, Barth formulated his concern and critical questions concerning the Christian character of theology from those outside the church. Therefore, the ghost of orthodoxy or neo-orthodoxy does not fit the radical, questioning character of Barth's theology. Barth did not overlook it in his study of Anselm.

According to Barth, Anselm was probably able to speak about Christian faith in no sense other than as he addresses the sinner as non-sinner, non-Christian as Christian, unbeliever as believer. For him, "the unbeliever's quest is not simply taken up in any causal fashion and incorporated into the theological task but . . . it is in fact treated as identical with the quest of the believer himself." (*FQI*:67).[137]

---

136. Barth, "Christlichen Kirchen und die heutige Wirklichkeit," 213. Cf. Gollwitzer, "Die Bedeutung der Theologischen Arbeit Karl Barths," in Gollwitzer, *Auch das Denken darf dienen*, 1:419.

137. For the significance of Anselm to the outsider of Christian faith, cf. *FQI*:64–75. In this regard we talk about Barth's concern about secular humanism and solidarity be-

In this regard theology as science is not a contradiction, but on track with what has been said since the second edition of *Romans*; that is, an aspect of the irregular dogmatic makes Barth's theological science eschew becoming "an ordinary, bourgeois possibility of consideration" (R II:514–15). So in the teaching of the Word of God in *Church Dogmatics*, Barth did not marginalize his irregular dogmatics, which refers to the strange voice of God outside the walls of Christianity. If theology is satisfied merely with interpreting the creed and dogma of the church, it would fall into the gray zone of positive and bourgeois science.

God's movement toward us is dialectic, and a human participation and encounter with God is in correspondence with the movement of God's kingdom. Having an echo of the socialistic claim for proving this-worldliness of human thinking in praxis, Barth's argument for Anselm's method is basically of a practical direction rather than remaining a purely scholastic question.[138] Barth states that "where faith is really faith, that is to say obedience. . . . For only in faith could this connection between the obedience of faith and the faith of the Church be experienced and only in experience could it be understood" (*FQI*:35).

How then would Barth overcome Peterson's critique for the sake of the freedom-making, undialectical act of God in his revelation (incarnation) that is to precede all human knowledge? Against the priority of the order of knowledge before the order of being—as it is seen in subject-and consciousness-oriented idealism—Barth formulates the priority of the order of being before the order of knowledge drawing upon Anselm, i.e., "The noetic *ratio* (the reason of the inquirer) leads to the discovery of the ontic *ratio* (the rationality of the object), as far as the it follows after it. In so doing, other remaining articles of *credo* depict the way in which the noetic *ratio* precedes the ontic *ratio* and the ontic *ratio* has to follow to discover it."[139]

We notice that there is a priority of the ontic necessity and rationality before the noetic necessity and rationality in conformity to it. "Strictly understood, the *ratio veritatis* is identical with the *ratio summae naturae*; that is, with the divine Word consubstantial to the Father" (*FQI*:45). The

---

tween the theologian and the children of the world in terms of philanthropia (Tit 3:4), namely the humanity of God. Cf. Gollwitzer, "Die Bedeutung der Theologischen Arbeit Karl Barths," in Gollwitzer, *Auch das Denken darf dienen*, 1:412.

138. Plonz, *Herrenlose Gewalten*, 252–53, 344.

139. *FQI*:53.

ratio veritatis as the Word itself is distinguished from the *ratio fidei*, but in relation to it. In other words, the ontic reason presupposes the noetic reason, which is to be in conformity to the *ratio veritatis* still hidden in the Credo or the Scripture.[140]

Given this fact, there is no strict identification between *ratio fidei* (the *Credo*) and the *ratio veritatis* (the Word). Revealed truth functions as an inner text in texts. The outward text should be understood in accordance with it. It is of utmost importance to notice that the ontic *ratio* presupposes and grounds the noetic *ratio*. "Obviously we cannot believe in God without his becoming the Author of a *vera cogitatio*—that is, faith in him also demands knowledge of Him" (*FQI*:19). This is the God whom Christian faith confesses. The ontic *ratio* is not merely what is sought, but gives rise to the search. For Barth—unlike Anselm who sees the *ratio fidei* as being identical with the *ratio veritatis* without question[141]—the Bible as the written Word of God is not identical with Jesus Christ as the revealed Word of God without further ado.

In addition, Barth interpreted the speech of God as the act of God in which he insisted that the speech as the divine act is not affected by the *sic et non* of dialectic (*CD* I/1:157). The mystery of God denotes God's revelation in a hidden, namely, in a nonapparent manner. For Barth, that God is in the act means that God is *a se*. Therefore, Barth's dialectic of veiling and unveiling is occasioned by the secularity of the Word and points to *theologia crucis* (*CD* I/1:179). For Barth, the speech of God as the act of God assumes concrete and contingent contemporaneity, in which a specific *illic et tunc* of the Word of God becomes a specific *hic et nunc*. The contingent contemporaneity as the act or event of God's Word accentuates that there is always a contingent *illic et tunc* from the standpoint of the speaking God. Correspondingly, there is a contingent *hic et nunc* from the standpoint of hearing person (*CD* I/1:149).[142]

---

140. *FQI*:47. "Fundamentally, the *ratio* either as ontic or noetic is never higher than the truth but truth is itself the master of all *rationes* beyond the contrast between ontic and noetic . . . In so far as the *ratio* of the object of faith and the use which man makes of his capacity to think and judge conform to Truth (by virtue of Truth's own decision) its true rationality is determined and the intellectus that is sought occurs"(*FQI*: 47).

141. *FQI*: 47.

142. It is Barth's counterthesis to Lessing's dictum "the ugly, wide ditch" between the Scripture and us. In it Lessing tried to fill the gap between revelation and history in terms of immanence. The inner truth of revelation is accessible and apprehensible in terms of human feeling and experience in which no difficulty would occur in interpreting rev-

Barth's idea of contemporaneity, which is based on the sovereignty of God's Word, has to claim the world, history, and society as the place where Christ was born and died and rose again. In the light of grace, there is no self-enclosed and no protected secular sphere. Namely, the world does not exist in isolation from revelation (*CD* I/1:155). Barth made a move from this standpoint toward the speech of God that is conceptualized as the mystery of God. According to Barth, "only God conceives of Himself, even in His Word" (*CD* I/1:164). This theocentric direction characterizes his theology as a penultimate de-assuring of theology, which is based on God's revelation in a hidden and a nonapparent manner.[143]

Therefore Barth's dialectics of veiling and unveiling does not violate the mystery or freedom of God in Godself. Or the mystery of God as the basis for a penultimate de-assuring of theology is not subsumed into any human dogmatic method or thinking. Rather, it is based on God's movement in Godself in virtue of distinguishing God as the first objectivity and the second objectivity in the Trinitarian life.[144]

Barth argued that the Roman Catholic and Protestant *theologia gloriae* failed to recognize this aspect of the mystery of God's Word. In fact, by abandoning "the indirectness of the knowledge of God," they abandoned "true faith and the real Word of God as well" (*CD* I/1:178). The revealed Word of God as the *ratio vertitatis* precedes and grounds the written Word of God and the proclaimed Word of God. Already in Barth's doctrine of the Word of God in a threefold way, Jesus Christ as the revealed Word has priority before the written and proclaimed word. Jesus Christ who is at the center of understanding the threefold sense of the Word of God is not merely reduced to the written and proclaimed

---

elation as history, and vice versa (*CD* I/1:147). This interpretation, according to Barth, shows a lack of contemporaneity.

143. Drawing upon Luther's idea of *larva Dei*, Barth articulated the dialectical movement of God's veiling and unveiling with respect to the twofold indirectness of God's self-communication. The creature's knowledge of God is indirect partly due to creatureliness and partly due to the creature's sinfulness (*CD* I/1:167).

144. According to Gogarten, God in isolation forms a point of departure for Barth, in that God is the not-yet-revealed God. God's being is in and for itself in Barth's framework, so argues Gogarten. Barth agreed with Gogarten that "theology cannot speak of man in himself, in isolation from God." However, Barth reversed this statement, stating that, "it [theology] must speak of God in Himself, in isolation from man" (*CD* I/1:172). This conception is why, for Barth, the Trinity must be the presupposition of Christology. He argues that God *in se* is *terminus a quo* while God for us is the *teriminus ad quem*.

Word. In that, Barth already forecasted God's strange voice, namely, the Word of God outside ecclesial walls (*CD* I/1:74). God as *ganz anders* can speak to us in a totally different way from our expectation: For instance, in the Old Testament, blessing Abraham through Melchizedek and Israel through Balaam, and redeeming Israel through Cyrus. That God speaks to us in strange, profane forms encourages the Christian church to stay in the attitude of humility and openness (*CD* I/1:54).

One finds that Barth's reflection on irregular dogmatics follows Kutter's prophetic activity.[145] Kutter looked upon the realm of God as greater than the realm of church so that God could stand against church through the forms and events of profane world occurrences. (*CD* I/1:74). God's speech through a pagan or an atheist has to do with Barth's reflection of Anselm's solidarity with the worldly.

Barth's reflection of *ratio veritatis* in regard to the noetic *ratio* and the ontic *ratio* may have led to a confrontation with Tillich's theology of culture. In Barth's view, Tillich replaced socialism with secular culture in general and defended it against the church as a systematic principle, so that he runs the risk of removing the antithesis between reality and symbol (*CD* I/1:64, 74). However, Barth critiqued "the pseudo-eschatological situation" which systematically molded Tillich's theological program (*CD* I/1:75). According to Barth, the provisional distinction between church and world is a symptom in light of God's future rather than "the human cleavage between sacramental daemonism and secular exorcism" (*CD* I/1:48).[146]

Furthermore, Barth distinctly took *ratio veritatis* or *ultima ratio* of the Word of God to be the theonomy. Theonomy would become an

---

145. For the distinction between the ordinary and extraordinary dogmatic way see *KD* I/1:292ff, *KD* I/2:942–43, *KD* IV/3:147ff, 1026ff.

146. Although not ignoring God's speech to the human situation, against it, and for it, Tillich's method of correlation, which is located between an existential question and a theological answer, refers to the mutual dependence of both realms. For Tillich, theonomy is used for the state of culture under the influence of the Spiritual Presence that makes the man Jesus of Nazareth into the Christ. The Spiritual Presence is present in the whole history of revelation and salvation among world religions, before and after the appearance of Jesus Christ. Theonomous culture as a symbol of the theonomy is Spirit-determined and -directed culture. Heteronomy and autonomy are elements within theonomy. Theonomy as the inner aim of the history appears in religion fragmentarily. Its fulfillment is eschatological in relation to autonomous culture and heteronymous culture. Tillich, *Systematic Theology*, 2:13–16. Cf. Tillich, *Christianity and the Encounter of World Religions*, 75–79.

empty idea without a relative concrete form of autonomy. Likewise autonomy can be understood properly only in correspondence and correlation with theonomy. The Word of God as the theonomy has a first form in revelation and a second in Scripture, and a third form in proclamation. Theonomy has a definite and relative form in the sphere of human thinking and speaking of the church that is not the direct counterpart of human autonomy. Human autonomy in the sense of the noetic and the ontic *ratio* stands in as a correlative to theonomy. The heteronomy to which Christian proclamation and its dogmatics are subject implies theonomy. The indication of theonomy calls for "a recognition of the indicative, declaratory and symbolic form" of heteronomy (*CD* I/2:815). However, this symbolic heteronomy (as a second authority besides that of the Word of God) emerges out of a consideration to speak of and set up an absolute heteronomy in view of the authority of the Word of God (*CD* I/2:816).

Autonomy has the concrete and relative form of theonomy in the free human decision, namely, obedience to theonomy and daring in which human free decision comes into play in dogmatic work. Therefore dogmatic method should consist of recognizing, unfolding, and presenting God's act in the revelation, to which human autonomy of obedience and daring corresponds in a responsible way. Therefore all is to be dealt with respect to God in revelation. (*Omnia tractare sub ratione Dei*) (*CD* I/2:871). If dogmatic work begins with *Deus dixit, Ursprung,* or a beginning, then a dogmatic system is not possible for Barth because God speaks in all directions like the periphery of a circle (*CD* I/2:869). God's act of self-revelation must dictate dogmatic method, and this divine action makes an eschatological systematization of dogmatics an illuminating and tempting possibility (*CD* I/2:876). Therefore dogma or dogmatic work assumes an eschatological path inspired by theonomy, namely, the *ultima ratio* of the Word of God.

The sheer incomparability of God—an assumption with which Anselm works—is something of "that which nothing greater can be conceived" (*id quo maius nihil cogitari nequit*). From this there follows that "there is a solidarity between the theologian and the worldling, . . . because the theologian is determined to address the wordling as one with whom he has at least this in common—theology" (*FQI*:68). Therefore, Barth portrays Anselm as the one who "did not really remain standing on this side of the gulf between the believer and non-believer, but crossed it" (*FQI*:71). All theological statements are under eschatological proviso because they are incomplete, broken, and inadequate expressions of the *ratio veritatis*. Therefore, we need to talk about the inexpressible God "*per analogiam*" (*FQI*:117), "*per aliquam similitudinem aut imaginem*" (*FQI*:29), not *per proprietatem* (FQI:80). This is Anselm's great contribution to Karl Barth's dynamic, socially engaged theology of analogy.

SIX   Karl Barth and *Theologia Naturalis*

The Political Situation in Bonn

BARTH'S MOVE TO BONN IN MARCH 1930 IS INFUSED WITH BOTH POLITIcal and theological connotations. From 1929-1931 Germany experienced political and economic difficulty along with growing unemployment. In retrospect, Barth reproached himself for not having been more critical with regard to the threat of National Socialism.[1]

When Barth was moving to Bonn, the cabinet of the Great Coalition (constituted in 1928), led by SPD chancellor Hermann Müller, resigned on March 27, 1930. A new government was formed under Heinrich Brünig of the Catholic Centre Party, who was committed to radical fiscal reform. When this was rejected by the *Reichstag*, Brünig dissolved the *Reichstag*, calling for new parliamentary elections (on September 14) for the sake of Article 48 of the Weimar constitution. In this election, however, the Nazis became the real beneficiaries, holding the second strongest party in Germany behind SPD. The republic came to an end in July 1930. Hitler's *Sturmabteilung* (the SA) took a leading part in street violence against socialists and Communists and then against Jews.

Barth informed Thurneysen that he had voted for the socialist party in the 1929 election.[2] However, in the aftermath of the September 1930

---

1. Barth, "Zwischenzeit," *Kirchenblatt für die reformierte Schweiz*, 118 (1962), 38; quoted in McCormack, *Critically Realistic*, 413: "I was thoroughly wrong at that time in not perceiving danger in National Socialism, which had already begun its ascent. From the very beginning, its ideas and methods and its leading figures all seemed to me to be quite absurd."

2. *B-Th II*: 607.

elections, he began to recognize the danger National Socialism posed to the republic. Explaining the reason for his entrance to SPD (on May 1, 1931), Barth wrote: "After moving to Germany, I imposed upon myself a political interlude which lasted nearly ten years. But early last year, in view of the fact that right-wing terror was gaining the upper hand, I thought it right to make it clear with whom I would like to be imprisoned and hanged."[3] Barth refused to leave the SPD in the summer of 1933 when SPD was completely prohibited and disbanded. When Barth was asked by the rector of the University of Bonn about his relationship with the SPD, Barth said: "I have arranged things with the Minister himself. So perhaps I was in fact the last member of the SDP [sic] in the Third Reich."[4] In his letter to Karl Heim in 1931, Barth understood his entrance to SPD as his obedience to his baptism, "and at the same time as a step parallel to baptism across the Rubicon which separates bourgeois parties from the workers movement."[5]

The collapse of all interim governments helped Hitler become chancellor in January 1933. By banning the Communist Party and the SPD, the National Socialist Party became the only political party in Germany. The idea of unifying the church with the German soul, as articulated by Hirsch and Althaus, found solid academic support among "German Christians." On the day after Hitler's seizure of power, Barth witnessed Gogarten's support of Wilhelm Stapel's dictum that the law of God is identical with the law of the German people. Thus Gogarten entered the ranks of the "German Christians." Because of increasing disagreement among colleagues in *Between the Times (Zwischen den Zeiten)* on the one hand, and because of Gogarten's entrance to German Christians in collaboration with National Socialism (1933) on the other, it became necessary for dialectical theologians to disband and the journal *Between the Times* to be discontinued. "I regarded Gogarten as one of those responsible for the ideology of National Socialism because of utterances like the speech on authority that he made during the 1920s. Then in 1933, I saw him appearing among the so called Young Reformers and for a while even among the 'German Christians.'"[6]

---

3. Karl Barth to Hans Asmussen, January 14, 1932, copy in Karl Barth-Archiv, Basel, Switzerland; cf. McCormack, *Critically Realistic*, 414.

4. Busch, *Karl Barth: His Life*, 225.

5. Gollwitzer, "Kingdom of God and Socialism in the Theology of Karl Barth," 105.

6. Busch, *Karl Barth: His Life*, 223–24. Barth did not hesitate to compose his "Farewell

In addition to Gogarten's compromise, the affair of Günter Dehn took place in Halle in 1931. Because of his critique of Germany's role in the First World War, Dehn was attacked by nationalists and theologians such as Hirsch. Barth published a response to this affair in the *Frankfurter Zeitung* (titled "Why Not Attack along the Whole Line?" in February 1932). A Nazi rally prior to the election of July 1932 left seventeen dead and many wounded after a conflict with the Communists. In protest against this event, the local church arranged an emergency church service under the chairmanship of the Lutheran Hans Asmusen.

However, in 1932 the German Christians founded their own newspaper in October: *Evangelium im Dritten Reich*. Hitler concluded a concordat with the Catholic Church in September 1933. In April 1933 Hitler made a proposal to establish an Evangelical *Reich* Church and appointed the naval chaplain Ludwig Müller to coordinate affairs. The National synod elected Ludwig Müller as *Reich* bishop in Wittenberg on September 27, 1933. This event provoked Barth's pamphlet series *Theological Existence Today* (*Theologische Existenz Heute!*) in June 1933. Martin Niemöller recognized clearly why the German Christians were attracted to the Nazis. German Christians found their ideal in Hitler's propaganda of German nationalism, which corresponded to traditional Lutheran teaching of two kingdoms; such teaching said that the church as the "right" kingdom of God must serve the state, God's "left" kingdom. To run counter to this movement, he helped found the Pastoral Emergency Alliance in response to the Prussian Church's adoption of the "pernicious Aryan Paragraph."[7] However, in 1933 when the Nazi "Aryan clause" became official policy among the German Christians, anti-Semitism became the threatening reality for Jewish life in Europe.

---

to *Zwischen den Zeiten*" (on October 18, 1933). "I read in *Deutsche Volkstum* Gogarten's acceptance of Stapel's theological dictum that for us the law of God is identical with the law of the German people.... In his remarks Gogarten had taken over the fundamental principle of the German Christians.... I cannot see anything in German Christianity but the last, fullest and worst monstrosity of Neo-Protestantism ... I regard Stapel's maxim about the Law of God as being an utter betrayal of the gospel" (ibid., 229–30).

7. In 1928 Barth had already expounded on his position about the "Jewish question," exhorting the Protestant church to stand firmly against cultural anti-Semitism: "We are persuaded that the Anti-semitic movement, which in the aftermath of the world war has had so mighty a boom, is irreconcilable with the Christian point of view and is incompatible with our debt of gratitude to the cradle of Christianity." Cited in Gutteridge, *German Evangelical Church and the Jews*, 58.

As Barth introduced in the first issue of *Theological Existence Today*, what he tried to say regarding the social problem of his current situation was to do theology as though nothing had happened. In order to proclaim the word to the situation, it was of special importance for Barth to take seriously what the word of the theological subject matter meant in the present-day situation.[8] According to Gollwitzer, Barth wrote a long manuscript and one evening read it to Charlotte von Kirschbaum and Helmut Traub. It was "a completely political and unprecedentedly sharp manifesto,"[9] impossible to be published for the political fallout.

However, against Gollwitzer, Stoevesandt reconstructed the history of the genesis of the draft under the indication that Barth's several politically dangerous sentences had been eliminated. According to Stoevesandt, Barth's passage that "the entire Hitler-regime was condemned corrosively and recklessly" is not meant entirely to be a political manifesto. Besides, the original version was titled "From the church politics to the church!"[10] Be that as it may, Barth's way from church politics to the church marked his way of the confessing church toward Barmen (1934), Dahlem (October 1934), and Darmstadt (1947).[11] This refers to Barth's means of church resistance with strong political orientation.

Furthermore, in the foreword of the first volume of *Church Dogmatics* (1932), Barth already connected the relevance of theology to the political field as his programmatic postulate of his dogmatics (*CD* I/1:xi–xii). *Church Dogmatics*, as dogmatics as well as ethics, should make a contribution to "the clarification, especially in the broad field of

8. *Theologische Existenz heute!* Nr. 2 von Z.Z Munich, 1933, 3. See Barth, *How I Changed My Mind*, 46: "I did not have anything new to say in that first issue of *Theological Existence Today* apart from what I had always endeavoured to say: that we could have no other gods than God, that holy scripture was enough to guide the church into all truth, that the grace of Jesus Christ was enough to forgive our sins and to order our life. . . . Without any conscious intention or endeavour on my part, it took on the character of an appeal, a challenge, a battle-cry, a confession. . . . As I repeated this doctrine consistently in this new room, at the same time it took on a new depth and became a practical matter, for decision and action."

9. Gollwitzer, "Kingdom of God and Socialism in the Theology of Karl Barth," 113. This manifesto, although it does not exist any longer, tells of Barth's original political intent in drafting his *Theologische Existenz heute*: "There you have your 'politically coordinated' [*gleichgeschaltete*] theological existence!"

10. Cf. Stoevesandt, "Von der Kirchenpolitik zur Kirche!"

11. In "Darmstädter Wort," we see Barth's concern of deepening his article on Feuerbach (1926) in relation to economic materialism (Thesis 5).

politics which are necessary today and to which theology might have a word to say" (*CD* I/1:xi). With this demand for such clarification, Barth was convinced that his *Church Dogmatics* had the task of clarifying the political situation. In so doing, *Church Dogmatics* does not have to be read as wrestling dilettantishly with strange work alienated from social questions, but as engaged and able to contribute to social questions by participation in the political arena.

Therefore, *Church Dogmatics* has to be understood as a more profound contribution to coping with the political situation and its problems. "A better church dogmatics (even apart from all ethical utility) might actually make a more important and weightier contribution, even to questions and tasks such as German liberation, than most of the well-intended material which so many, even theologians, think they can and should produce when they dilettantishly take up such questions and tasks" (*CD* I/1:xiii).

It is certain that dogmatic thought in its entirety does not lead to a theologically and politically competent *Wort zur Lage* (word in the context or situation) of society. As Dannemann rightly says, "Dogmatics earns rather the competence and quality of the right *Wort zur Lage* of society as the function of the right *Wort zur Sache* of theology."[12] Therefore, "those comprehensive clarifications in theology and about theology itself with which we should be concerned here" constitute for Barth the primary presupposition for clarification in the broad field of politics.

As far as dogmatics' having a political consequence, the question about politics becomes the indispensable theme of dogmatics as such. This connection between *Wort zur Sache* of theology and *Wort zur Lage* of society is articulated in his famous slogan: "Theological Existence Today." What is valid in *Wort zur Sache* is theological *existence* and what is indispensable in *Wort zur Lage* is *today*. With respect to the church-political situation for "German Christians," Barth calls for the theological *Sache*.

As though nothing had happened, means, for Barth, that doing theology is implicitly a political attitude. The task of theology is to reveal the dialectical connection between *Wort zur Sache* and *Wort zur Lage*. First saying *Wort zur Sache* in the sphere of theological vocation, and this saying leads to "the presupposition, which it is necessary every day to

---

12. Dannemann, *Theologie und Politik im Denken Karl Barths*, 123.

say *zur Sache.*" If Barth's political attitude is implicated in his theological work, a theological-political motivation is mediated not only in a dogmatic sense but also in a historical-political sense. As Gollwitzer reports, Barth countered the opinion that the German workers would not tolerate the destruction of their union after hearing Hitler's radio broadcast, the "Tempelhof Field speech," on the evening of May 1, 1933: "You forget the enormous power of a totalitarian state—and you forget that they are German workers. They will gladly fall in line!"[13]

On October 31, 1933 in Berlin Barth stated: "If I now became a preacher, I should make clear about the news every Sunday: I have to proclaim the testimonied Word of God in the Holy Scripture and in my text, not my view of the third *Reich.* And because I am not convinced to speak in the name of God, but only to serve his Word, so I myself would become modest, concretely, and very restrained, so restrained and so abstract that it is possibly again tremendously concrete."[14]

As "German Christians" pondered the consequences of the social cultural situation for Christianity, they made the sociocultural situation their lord. However, Barth's slogan, "as though nothing had happened," first of all questioned the theological *Sache* (the gospel) and then its consequence for the sociocultural situation. In other words, Barth's intent was to integrate a social concept into the dogmatic realm in a historical-socially and systematic manner. His intention did not leave room for justifying the neglect of social analysis from the field of dogmatics.[15]

The "German Christians" misused theological *Sache* by degrading it to the mere instance of legitimation for a fixed political decision. Because of this degradation, they unequivocally identified the National-Socialistic interpretation of social reality with the Christian interpretation of it. In praising the victory of National Socialism over the Weimar Republic as an expression of divine will, they replaced the theological interpretation of social reality through a National-Socialistic ideology of life, history, and the state, including the theory of race, blood and land, *Volk* and state.

---

13. Gollwitzer, "Kingdom of God and Socialism in the Theology of Karl Barth," 113.

14. Cf. Marquardt, "Theologische und Politische Motivationen Karl Barths im Kirchenkampf," in Marquardt, *Verwegenheiten,* 441.

15. Gollwitzer, *Zuspruch und Anspruch. Neue Folge,* 233; cf. Marquardt, "Theologische und Politische Motivationen Karl Barths im Kirchenkampf," in Marquardt, *Verwegenheiten,* 469.

Given this fact, Barth publicly opposed a conflation of Nazi ideology with the church. Barth argued that the community of the church is defined not through blood, race, and land but through the Holy Spirit and through baptism. As for the German Christians and their exclusion of Jewish Christians, they ceased to be the Christian church.

At the celebration of Reformation on October 30, 1933, Barth traveled to Berlin to deliver an address on "the Reformation as Decision."[16] For him, the Reformation is a decision to recognize the rule of God as absolute: "Anyone who wants to celebrate Luther today must have a sword in his hand."[17] The real characteristic of the Reformer lay in his decision to stand on the foundation of Jesus Christ. Barth condemned the supposition that "the dominant movement in the church today" is "the last, most vital, most consummate form of the great neo-Protestant infidelity to the Reformation."[18] Strengthened by the Reformation teaching, he argued that those who have not succumbed to the movement of the state, to the *Volkstum*, or to German Christians must offer resistance. "Smite their spears, for they are hollow!" "They are hollow!"[19] became a watchword for the Confessing Church. Barth's exclamation of "Resistance!" aroused a tremendous response from the audience, forcing Barth pause his speech for several minutes.

In April 1937, Barth talked about his intention in the struggle for the church: "I am reminded still today how I had to deliver a lecture in Berlin at that time, at the climax of this lecture I had spoken—supposedly without intent—this sole word resistance! And this word found, completely against my expectation, a tremendous echo so that I had to stop my speech for some minutes. Resistance!"[20] This word *resistance*, in fact, belonged to the text of "Reformation as Decision." Those who do not credit the neo-Protestant unfaithfulness to the Reformation "have to make *resistance*, strengthened by what the Reformation just today must say to us."[21] The Confessing Church meant a decision, a church in an act of decision, joyously resisting as expressed in the cry: "Smite their spears,

16. Cf. Barth, *Reformation als Entscheidung*.
17. Busch, *Karl Barth: His Life*, 231.
18. Ibid., 231.
19. Barth, *Reformation als Entscheidung*, 24.
20. Cf. Marquardt, "Theologische und politische Motivationen Karl Barths im Kirchenkampf," in Marquardt, *Verwegenheiten*, 446.
21. Barth, *Reformation als Entscheidung*, 23.

for they are hollow!" "They are hollow!"—this cry of resistance makes reference to the battle of Sempach, which was the origin of this expression. In May of 1934, the Confessing Church met at the Synod of Barmen in order to speak out against the heresy of the German Christians.

The Barmen Declaration, which was composed mainly by Barth, was a key moment in the church struggle and remains a landmark example of churchly political opposition. However, there were theological differences between members of the Confessing Church over matters of the relation of the church to the state. Be that as it may, the Barmen Declaration, as the basic text of Barth's theology, stands as the most important ecclesiastical expression of Barth's christological concentration. The first article reads: "Jesus Christ, as he is attested to us in Holy Scripture, is the one Word of God whom we have to hear and which we have to trust and obey in life and in death."[22] The historical genesis of the Barmen Theological Declaration was the first common faith testimony of evangelical Christians in Germany since the more divided period following the Reformation. In this regard, Barmen does not merely remain in the past, but must be understood as "a call forward" in our ecumenical, global context.[23]

Moreover, in the fifth thesis we see a critique of the false theory of the state and a responsibility of the church for righteousness and peace. The mandate of the church, on which its freedom is grounded, consists in proclaiming the message of the free grace of God to the state and all people as well as in service of its own word and work through preaching and sacrament. The Barmen Declaration signers rejected false doctrine that the church in human self-righteousness could set the word and the work of the Lord in the service of any kind of arbitrarily chosen wish, purpose and plan.[24]

The thesis rejects as false the theory according to which the state, beyond its special commission, should become the sole and total order of human life and also fulfill the determination of the church. Furthermore, according to this false thesis, the church should accommodate itself,

---

22. Cochrane, *Church's Confession under Hitler*, 239. For the political significance of the Barmen Declaration for today, see Hunsinger, "Barth, Barmen, and the Confessing Church Today," 60–88.

23. Bergsmüller and Weth, *Barmer Theologische Erklärung. Einführung und Dokumentationen*, 26.

24. Ibid., 39.

beyond its special commission, to the nature of the state, its task and dignity. Thus, the church can become the organ of the state. Against this, in obedience to the power of God's Word, the church is reminded of the kingdom of God, God's commandment and justice for the world. Therefore, we need to extend the significance of the fifth thesis of Barmen after the Holocaust in light of "Darmstädter Wort."[25]

Although Barth himself admitted that the Confessing Church at Barmen failed to produce a statement of solidarity with the Jews,[26] we read in his letter to Steffens on January 10, 1934 that "anyone who believes in Christ . . . simply cannot be involved in the contempt for Jews and in the ill-treatment of them which is now the order of the day."[27] In this period of church resistance, Barth was in fact deeply involved in the theological significance of the Jewish persecution.

In his sermon in December of 1933 in Bonn Castle church, Barth stated,

> It is not self-evident that we belong to Jesus Christ and he to us. Christ belongs to the people Israel. The blood of this people was in his veins the blood of the Son of God. This people's form he adopted, while he adopted the being of man. . . . Jesus Christ was a Jew, but in taking up and taking away the sins of the Jews, the sins of the whole world and even our own, the salvation of the Jews has come also to us. How can we, each time we think about this, not be obliged to think above all of the Jews?[28]

For Barth, the Jewishness of Jesus is an essential article of faith, so that both Jews and Christians become children of the living God.

Historical-political motivation is not excluded for Barth, but it is integrated and mediated in a theological-dogmatic way. Barth himself explained to Brunner that it was "a legend without historical reason," when the formulation "as though nothing had happened" was misunderstood as Barth's appeal to passive indifference in Germany.[29] Barth's theological *Sache* stands in correlation with the social, cultural, and political *Lage*.

---

25. See chapter 9 in this volume, "Liberative Dimensions in Barth's Theology."

26. Barth, *Letters 1961–1968*, 250.

27. Barth's letter to E. Steffens, January 10, 1934. Cf. Haynes, *Reluctant Witnesses*, 195.

28. Quoted in Haynes, *Reluctant Witnesses*, 67.

29. Ibid., 441–42.

His way of differentiating the theological from the political did not necessarily mean separating these two realms from each other. Rather, a way of differentiating is made primarily against any attempt at identification between *Sache* and *Lage*.

Against the blending of Christendom and Nazi ideology Barth wrote in his letter to Georg Merz in April 1933: "The assumption that one could be in agreement with the preamble of the 'German Christians' (in their affirmation of the Nazi state), and then later, have a pure church in opposition to them. . . . will prove to be one of the most deceptive illusions of an era replete with such illusions. Let us leave out the preamble, completely and sincerely, and then we will speak further about that which follows."[30] As a matter of fact, it was essential and fundamental for Barth to speak out against anti-Semitism in support of the Jews.

In the myth-revelation of the German Christians, the theological significance of the Jews is severely distorted. As Barth states,

> It *can* be that one must sometimes say yes. But, is the same church ready to say something to what takes place in our concentration camps? Who has done this? Who says something to what one has done against the Jews? Or what is one to say, if the word of "total state" is heard? And what has happened at the fire of *Reichstag*? And what will be on 12 November? Is it a true election or a cunning maneuver? A stance would have to truly mean, namely, a stance on *these* things."[31]

Theology had the definite stance of speaking out against the Nazi ideology of the total state and its political consequence of the concentration camp as well. Barth publicly opposed the Nazi ideology in matters of anti-Semitism: "The community of those belonging to the church is defined not through blood and therefore also not through race, but through the Holy Spirit and through baptism. If the German Evangelical Church excludes the Jewish Christians, or if they are treated as second class citizens, they will have stopped being the Christian church."[32]

---

30. Cf. Koch, "Barths erste Auseinandersetzung mit dem Dritten Reich," in Bandis, *Richte unsere Füsse*, 501.

31. Cf. Marquardt, "Theologische und politische Motivationen Karl Barths im Kirchenkampf," in Marquardt, *Verwegenheiten*, 445.

32. Haynes, *Reluctant Witnesses*, 66.

For Barth, the first commandment is concrete, so that it must be interpreted politically in the given situation. Barth's resistance against the identification of theology and politics in the year 1933 retained a critical posture toward ideology designed to block political surrender to Hitler and to challenge the church's submission to the National Socialist ideology of anti-Semitism. In his letter of 1934 to Rabbi Emile Cohen, Barth said with great disappointment in view of what was happening to the Jewish community: "We are also in agreement on the fact that the terror which befalls your people today in Germany—As a Christian I can think about it only in shame and horror—is so terrible because in this, known or unknown, the final mysteries of divine grace are touched upon and because with it the Synagogue just as well as the church is called to an entirely new hearing of the divine word and an entirely new responsible decision."[33]

For Barth, doing theology in the years 1933 and 1934 was in no way a timeless, noncontextual, metaphysical reality. In contrast, theology is correlative to the social situation and reality for the sake of explication of the political implications of theology. A relation of theological matters to the concrete political reality must be sought and explicated in accordance with a correlation between *Sache* and *Lage*. Since 1933 Barth had tried to replace the reduction of the political to the theological—as had happened in 1933—through the explication of the theological to the political. The God of revelation in relation to which Jesus Christ was a Jew was the counterreality to the God of the history and myth of German Christians.

In 1933 membership in the SPD was prohibited. When Hindenburg died in August 1934, Hitler became both chancellor and president and required an oath of allegiance from all state officials. Barth was suspended from his teaching duty in Bonn on November 26, 1934 for refusing to give an unqualified oath of loyalty to Adolf Hitler. After being formally dismissed by the minister of cultural affairs in Berlin on June 22, 1935, he was offered a chair in theology at the University of Basel, Switzerland. As Busch reports, the Berlin statement in October 1933 that Barth addressed in his first meeting with the Emergency Pastoral Alliance (*Pfarrernotbund*) led politically to Barth's dismissal from the university and his expulsion from Germany. "What does the church have to say about what is happen-

---

33. Klappert, *Israel und die Kirche*, 39.

ing in the concentration camps?" "Or about the treatment of the Jews." "The one whose duty it is to proclaim the Word of God must address such events with what the Word of God declares."[34]

Karl Barth and Emil Brunner in a Pamphlet War: *Theologia Revelatus* vs. *Theologia Naturalis*

In his *Habilitationsschrift* (1922) at the University of Zurich, Emil Brunner turned to dialectical theology in his confrontation with Schleiermacher. In his 1924 book, *Die Mystik und das Wort*, Brunner made his critical front against Schleiermacher. Brunner argued that what was at stake in his confrontation with Schleiermacher was an either-or attitude: either remaining faithful to the biblical-Reformation faith on the basis of the Word of God or indulging in the pious experience of neo-Protestantism. Although his thinking shared similarities with the dialectical theology of Barth, Brunner sought the relevance of the biblical message to the existential situation of contemporary individuals. His concern was with establishing propaedeutic dogmatics in terms of a relation between law and gospel. A knowledge of God could be acquired through revelation in creation, which stands independent of the revelation in Jesus Christ. For this task Brunner drew on subjectivity in a Kierkegaardian sense. He discerned in Kierkegaard's dialectics of existence a feasible approach to Reformation theology. He called this existential approach "eristics" in his dogmatics.[35] This was the other task of Brunner's eristic theology as a counterproposal to Barth's theology. Kierkegaard was, for Brunner, the greatest *Eristiker*, and his dialectic of existence is the most appropriate way to relate a biblical message to the existence of contemporary individuals.

In the years 1933/34, at the forefront of discussions was the German Christians' position in speaking of a second source of revelation. The entrance of Gogarten to the "German Christians" in the late summer of 1933 motivated Barth to wrestle with an attempt at giving an anthropo-

---

34. Busch, *Reformationstag 1933*, 69–70, 106. From 1935 onwards Barth conceptualized and stressed more explicitly the relevance of theology to politics. We mention Barth's understanding of "Gospel and Law" (1935), his christological-covenantal approach to the state in "Justification and Right" (1938), as well as his famous letter to J. L. Hromadka (1938) for which Hans Asmussen accused Barth of betraying the church to politics.

35. Brunner, "Andere Aufgabe der Theologie," 255–56.

logical direction to theology. This is the so-called problem of natural theology in neo–Protestantism. According to Barth, "German Christians" with whom Gogarten was associated were the last, the most complete, and the worst monstrous product of the neo-Protestant essence.[36] This is characteristic of the situation in which Barth formulated the Barmen Theological Declaration in Hotel "Basler Hof" in Frankfurt on May 16, 1934.[37] The famous first thesis is formulated in a christocentric discourse. But at the same time, Brunner's pamphlet *Natur und Gnade* was introduced to the world as a word of opposition to Barth. A pamphlet war between Brunner and Barth became inevitable, and the interplay occurred in a highly political situation. Their argument centered on the relation between natural revelation in creation and historical revelation in Jesus Christ. Although Brunner knew about Barth's theological approach to culture from his Amsterdam lecture ("Kirche und Kultur"; NuG:19), the former's concern was to construct eristic theology based on the natural knowledge of God, a so-called "point of contact." For the task of the eristic theology, Brunner introduced the twofold sense of *imago Dei*: one formal and one material (NuG:23).

As a matter of fact, Brunner did not hesitate to agree with Barth regarding the original image of God in the human being, namely, that the *justitia originalis* has been destroyed and lost (NuG:22). However, the image of God in a formal sense, in which Brunner discerns a superior position for humans over and against other creatures, is not entirely abolished by sin. What Brunner notices from this perspective is a human capacity for words and that our capacity for of responsibility. In other words, God speaks, and humans respond in a responsible way (NuG:23). This formal side, according to Brunner, does not stand in the way of the material side of *justitia originalis*, regardless of the fact that this *justitia originalis* is completely lost and abolished (NuG:24). Therefore, Brunner's basic contention goes like this: humans are—no matter how sinful—subject and responsible on the basis of the image of God in a formal sense, whereas they are sinners because the image of God is totally and completely lost and depraved. As Brunner says, "This *quid* of personality is negated through sin, whereas the *quod* of personality constitutes the humanum of every man, also that of the sinner" (NuG:24).

36. *ADT*:317.

37. "Die Barmer theologische Erklärung von 1934," in: Steubing, et al., *Bekenntnisse der Kirche*, 300.

Brunner's thesis has not merely existential and anthropological relevance but also pneumatological direction. As far as the world is created by God the Creator, the Spirit of the Creator works and is recognizable in the life of creatures in some ways. As far as God leaves divine imprint upon what God created, the creation of the world is a revelation and a self-communication of God (NuG:25). This notion becomes manifest in the concept of "the consciousness of responsibility" (NuG:25). At this point Brunner boldly affirms that "responsibility of the sinner and knowledge of the will of God as the source of law (the knowledge also being derived from the law) are one and the same thing" (NuG:25). This being the case, how did Brunner respond to two kinds of revelation? For him the answer must be found in a dialectical interconnection between revelation in creation and revelation in Jesus Christ. In Brunner's view, "the revelation in creation is not sufficient in order to know God in such a way that this knowledge brings salvation" (NuG:26).

Nevertheless, drawing upon the revelation in Jesus Christ, we are not to eschew speaking of a double revelation, namely, of one in creation. To what extent does Brunner understand nature in this context? The term "nature" is defined by Brunner in an objective-divine and subjective-human-sinful sense. God has bestowed the traces and imprint of God's nature upon God's works in creation. No matter that the knowledge of God is conditioned by the sinful world, humans can have access to the knowledge of God in terms of the image of God, which is "indestructible, yet always obscured by sin" (NuG:27). Does Brunner confuse the two sources of revelation in terms of his *theologia naturalis*? It would be much safer to say that for Brunner "only the Christian, i.e., the man who stands within the revelation in Christ, has the true natural knowledge of God" (NuG:27). To counterbalance natural revelation in creation with historical revelation in Jesus Christ, Brunner introduces the concept of preserving grace. Only in light of the revelation in Jesus Christ does Brunner speak of the grace of preservation. God's preserving grace, in other words, God's general grace, refers to God's blessing on "the whole sphere of natural life and its goods" (NuG:28). Before the saving grace of Jesus Christ had come, humanity had lived by the preserving grace of God unconsciously and unknowingly.

Therefore human life is not separable from the two realms of natural life and historical life because God does not entirely retreat, or withdraw the grace of preservation from the life of creatures—in spite of sin. From the grace of preservation a Christian teaching of civil and secular office comes into existence. In this regard it is of special significance to speak of all ordinances that underlie historical and social life and form a basic part of all ethical problems such as matrimony and the state (NuG:29). The so-called ordinances of creation and preservation offer a basis for a Christian *theologia naturalis* in accounting for the phenomenon of natural life (NuG:30).

Given what has been discussed, Brunner introduces his famous concept of a "point of contact," which means for him the formal *imago Dei*: namely, human "capacity for words and responsibility" (NuG:31). A human capacity of being receptive to words in the formal sense and not in the material sense is the receptivity that means "the purely formal possibility of his being addressed. This possibility of his being addressed is also the presupposition of man's responsibility" (NuG:31). What necessarily constitutes and presupposes an understanding of the divine message of grace is human knowledge of sin.

Therefore, according to Brunner, the Word of God does not have to create a human capacity for words because human capacity is the presupposition to hear the Word of God. Nevertheless, the Word of God creates a human capacity for believing the Word of God. If there is no more *imago Dei* materially, it is intact formally. The doctrine of *sola gratia* is not in opposition to the point of contact. The possibility in which humans are to be addressed includes the natural knowledge of God. Thus this possibility does not remain in the sphere of the *humanum* in the narrower sense. This possibility is "the necessary, indispensable point of contact for divine grace" (NuG:33). In fact, the contrast between the gospel and natural knowledge of God is not at stake for Brunner. The image of the new creation in the biblical context is always mentioned in regard to the image of *reparatio*, of restoration at the same time (NuG:34).

Brunner's concern about constructing eristic theology within natural theology runs counter to Barth's theology of *sola gratia*. According to Brunner's summing up of Barth's position, the image of God in a human being is entirely obliterated without remnant. Because the revelation in Jesus Christ is the sole norm of our knowledge of God and the sole source of salvation, Barth categorically rejects every attempt at insisting on a general revelation of God in nature, in the human conscience, and in history. Since there is complete revelation in Jesus Christ, it is absurd to talk of two kinds of revelation: one general and one special. Acknowledging

Jesus Christ as the sole saving grace of God, Barth renders other aspects of God's grace such as grace of creation and preservation meaningless. Because of Barth's attachment to the oneness of the grace of Jesus Christ, he recognizes a *lex naturae* of God's ordinances of preservation deriving from creation only as "*per nefas*, as a pagan thought" (NuG:21). Therefore Brunner argues that for Barth to speak of the point of contact with respect to the saving action of God is beyond the scope of his presentation and not a consideration.

In terms of the sole activity of the saving grace of Jesus Christ, Barth takes the new creation to come into being "exclusively through destruction of the old." That is a replacement of the old human being by the new. Therefore, Thomas's dictum—*gratia non tollit naturam sed perficit* ("grace does not destroy nature but perfects it")—is an arch-heresy (NuG:21). Against Barth's position, Brunner emphasized the significance of *theologia naturalis* in his Christian ethics. Christian social ethics can be sought in terms of the redeeming grace of Jesus Christ as well as the concept of the divine grace of creation and preservation. The divine institution of the latter retains a social and ethical function in society. As far as the laws of creation can be known to those who know God in Jesus Christ regardless of sin, "we have to acknowledge divinely appointed objective limits to our freedom and objective guides to the ordering of our society" (NuG:52). In Luther's distinction between church and state in the theory of two kingdoms, the law—whether the written or the *lex naturae*—"is the form in which the divine will is revealed, which only through the Holy Spirit becomes a concrete divine commandment, governing my existence here and now" (NuG:53). Therefore *theologia naturalis* becomes significant and compelling not only for Christian ethics with respect to the human capacity for words and responsibility but also for Christian dogmatics in dealing with a relation between general revelation and special revelation.

In addition, Brunner stresses the practical ecclesiastical significance of *theologia naturalis* regarding the task of the church as the proclamation of its message. For this task, he seeks human words in correspondence with the divine Word in terms of proclamation of the Word of God. As far as the grounds on which humanity has "the possibility of speaking of God and of proclaiming his Word at all" (NuG:56), Brunner is convinced of the human undestroyed likeness to God: the remnant of the *imago Dei*. This is what Brunner articulates as the point of contact, the capacity for words and responsibility. The fundamental significance of *theologia naturalis* for the area of education, ecclesiology, dogmatics, and proclamation (among others) leads Brunner to take in earnest the question of *how*. The *what* is guarded by faith, whereas the *how* has to be guarded by love (NuG:58).

"Faith active in love" is understood by Brunner as the point where the *how* of love with respect to nonbelievers—rather than the *what* of faith—must be prepared intellectually in service of the proclamation of the message theologically. Conceptual and intellectual work of preparation for how to relate love to the world, culture, and creation precedes the *what* of Christian content, namely, faith. Therefore the center of *theologia naturalis* lies in the doctrine of the *imago Dei* and especially in responsibility as a cooperating partner with the redeeming grace of Jesus Christ. A human being, who is inherently capable of being addressed and responsible, has his or her own independent rights and qualifications apart from the grace of Jesus Christ. Concerning a central tenet and a subject of Brunner's theology of eristics, a theory of analogy and ontological correspondence from below comes into the picture by revitalizing the encounter between the human and God, while the revealing grace of Jesus Christ waits for non-Christians in the world to come to Jesus Christ through Brunner's point of contact. In other words, does the revealing and redeeming grace of Jesus Christ need supplementary help from Brunner's eristic theology? Wouldn't Brunner's point of contact be dangerous, even possibly misused by "German Christians" during the Hitler regime? How does Brunner recognize the God of Israel and of Jesus Christ by being so convinced of a natural God?

Although he was aware of Barth's language of analogy, Brunner extended Barth's position to the quarter of Occam's nominalism (NuG:54). Barth's principle of analogy and parable is centered on the kingdom of God without losing christological significance. Furthermore, Barth's language of analogy, formed in a sociocultural context in which the language of analogy based on similarity and dissimilarity, developed a dialectical character in social, cultural, and natural arenas. However, according to Brunner, if the Word of God is a rational and not an irrational event in the Barthian sense (NuG:54; cf. *CD* 1/1:152), then human reason as divine creation is "more suitable for a definition of the nature of God than stocks or stones" (NuG:54). From here Brunner draws quite a strange conclusion that "the whole Barthian theology rests *de facto* upon the doctrine of the formal *imago Dei*, which he so much dislikes" (NuG:55). In Brunner's view, Barth's nominalism supports an existential and ontological point of contact with the redeeming grace of Jesus Christ. "Without knowing it, and without wishing it, Barth himself argues in favor of *theologia naturalis* and of its fundamental significance in theology" (NuG:55).

How did Barth respond to Brunner's challenge and attempt at reconstructing *theologia naturalis* within (or apart from) the sphere of historical revelation in Jesus Christ? Barth's angry "No" to Brunner is justifiable in response to the *Deutsche Pfarrerblatt (German Pastor's Journal)*, in which Brunner's pamphlet is called "a mine of treasure, a veritable gold-mine" (NuG:72). In his introduction, Barth agrees that he practiced repeatedly "true *theologia naturalis*" in the essay "Church and Culture" ("Kirche und Kultur" [1927]) and in some passages of his "Prolegomena" in the same year (NuG:70). Barth noticed that Brunner had been making an attempt to bring "the other task of theology" or the "point of contact" to the agenda since 1929.

Against Brunner, Barth states firmly where he really stands: "Every attempt to assert a general revelation has to be rejected. There is no grace of creation and preservation. There are no recognizable ordinances of preservation. There is no point of contact for the redeeming action of God. The new creation is in no sense the perfection of the old but rather the replacement of the old man by the new" (NuG:74). How did Barth then understand and define natural theology? For Barth natural theology refers to every positive or negative "*formulation of a system*" that claims to interpret divine revelation, whose *subject*, however, differs fundamentally from the revelation in Jesus Christ and whose *method* therefore differs equally from the exposition of Holy Scripture" (NuG:74–75).

In the field of natural theology, according to Barth, something strange is represented in terms of abstract speculation, in that it is not identical with the revelation of God in Jesus Christ (NuG:75). What Barth represents now, in contrast to Brunner's theological eristic of natural theology, is in fact "the real theology" based on revelation in Jesus Christ. In rejecting natural theology, this "real theology" refuses to identify nature as a separate problem. It is for Barth a hermeneutical problem of how to distinguish revealed theology and natural theology and integrate the latter into the former.

Barth's antithesis against Brunner lies primarily in the way that "natural theology usually deals with its *soi-disant* data derived from reason, nature and history, i.e., as if one had them pocketed, as if one had the knowledge of them below one instead of always behind and in front" (NuG:77). Therefore Barth maintains that the proclamation of the church does not have two sources and norms, such as revelation *and* reason or the Word of God *and* history. If Brunner's favorite terms such as "capacity for revelation" or "capacity for words" or "receptivity for words" or "possibility of being addressed" come to the fore apart from or independently of revelation in Jesus Christ, Barth asks how we understand and formulate what the meaning is of the "sovereign, freely electing grace of God" (NuG:79).

To what extent is the capacity for revelation possible and available without reference to the redeeming grace of Jesus Christ? In Barth's view, Brunner's statement that the human undestroyed formal likeness to God is the objective possibility of the revelation of God. Thus the original image of God in this formal sense is not abolished or destroyed by sin. This position becomes questionable, according to Barth. How does it become meaningful to talk about a tension, even a logical contradiction, between a material image of God and a formal image of God in Brunner's project? Furthermore, when Brunner says that the creation of the world is at the same time revelation, self-communication of God, why does Brunner affirm that "sin makes man blind for what is visibly set before our eyes" (NuG:80)?

Given this contradiction, Barth states that according to Brunner, "real knowledge of God through creation does take place without revelation, though only 'somehow' and 'not in all its magnitude'" (NuG:81). Does Brunner conceive that a natural knowledge of God is identical with the one true God, the triune God? For Barth, Brunner moves in this direction: "It is he who is *de facto* known by all men without Christ, without the Holy Spirit, though knowledge of him is distorted and dimmed and darkened by sin, though he is 'misrepresented' and 'turned into idols'" (NuG:81–82).

When Brunner wishes to express the true God from God's creation without Christ and the Holy Spirit, what real meaning does his idea of a materially destroyed image of God retain in this regard? When it comes to the preserving grace, what does Brunner mean in saying that general grace precedes the grace of Jesus Christ? Must not the preserving grace of God be seen and taken into account in light of one revelation of Jesus Christ in the Old and New Testaments? When God preserves God's creation in the midst of corruption and sin, all human activities and institutions such as state and marriage are seen in terms of activity within the preserving grace. However, Brunner does not speak of the one justifying and sanctifying grace of Jesus Christ, but only of a special preserving grace (NuG:85).

From this separate perspective of God's preserving grace, Brunner deals with "the ordinances," "the constant factors of historical and social life" in which he gives higher dignity and a more special place to matrimony as an ordinance of creation rather than of the state. This being the case, divine ordinances of creation are built on the basis of human instinct and reason. When Brunner asserts that "these ordinances of creation are not only known but also respected and 'to some extent realized' by men who do not know the God revealed in Christ" (NuG:87), where is the demarcation between the formal *imago* and material *imago*? Brunner's fundamental thesis—there is a point of contact for redeeming grace—presupposes a capacity for God's revelation in creation anterior to historical revelation. Why couldn't God, whom Brunner believes and confesses, speak to us without the aid of a point of contact?

If God reaches humans with God's Word apart from the formal possibility of the human beings and their *humanitas*, has not Brunner dropped the concept of a human capacity for God? According to Barth, if there is an encounter and communion between God and humanity, it is God who "must have created for it conditions that are not in the least supplied (not even 'somehow,' not even 'to some extent!') by the existence of the formal factor" (NuG:89). Brunner is not capable of adhering to the Reformation principle of *sola fide/sola gratia*. Is it meaningful to distinguish Brunner in his basic conviction from a Thomist or Neo-Protestant?

What forms and presupposes a point of contact in Barth's view is God in Jesus Christ by the Spirit. "The Holy Ghost, who proceeds from the Father and the Son and is therefore revealed and believed to be God, does not stand in need of any point of contact but that which he himself creates. Only in retrospect is it possible to reflect on the way in which he 'makes contact' with humans, and this retrospect will ever be a retrospect upon a *miracle*" (NuG:119). This God has no need of reparation; nor is there a question of a capacity for repair on the part of humans. The *reparatio* in a biblical sense consists in a divine miracle signifying a new creature. As Barth states, "all the comfort, all the power, all the truth of the revelation of God depends on the fact that it is God who is thus revealed to us. And all understanding of this fact of revelation depends on its identity with God being understood, on all possibilities except that of God being excluded" (NuG:117–18).

What is at stake in the controversy between Barth and Brunner consists not in excluding the effectiveness of God's grace in Jesus Christ upon all humans (and even including the domain of nature), but a contrast between the theological *what* and the eristic method of *how*. Brunner attempts to find "the significance of *theologia naturalis* for theology and the church." Therefore, the decisive question for Brunner is "*how* is it to be done?" There is a question concerning language and human existence in that Brunner treats the questions of method, language. and form separately from the content and revelation in Jesus Christ.

However, what shapes Barth's concern decisively is the question, what has to be done? This question constitutes an indispensable form of Barth's real theology regarding content and revelation and faith (NuG:122–23). Barth asks "But what of the How? . . . Could we even for a moment seek the How outside the What? Could it, even for a moment, become a 'decisive' question for us?" (NuG:126). With excessive emphasis on the other task of theology, Brunner goes on the road that he has taken in his eristic way of separating grace from nature independently. Barth's angry "No" to Brunner should not be misunderstood as his total rejection of the natural-historical reality. Rather Barth prefers to see sociocultural and even natural domains in light of one particular-inclusive grace of God's revelation in Jesus Christ by the Spirit. In Barth's words, "the best way of dealing with 'unbelievers' and modern youth is not try to bring out their 'capacity for revelation,' but to treat them quietly, simply (remembering that Christ has died and risen also from them), as if their rejection of 'Christianity' was not to be taken seriously. . . . on the ground of justification by faith alone" (NuG:127).

At this point we discern how Barth's understanding of justification in a forensic sense assumes an inclusive character in dealing with people outside the sphere of Christianity. For Barth, humans have to be overcome by the Word and the Spirit of God, and they must be reconciled to God, justified and sanctified, comforted and ruled and finally saved by God (NuG:126). Therefore the question of *how* that is raised by Brunner must be included and preserved in the question of *what* that Barth takes seriously, rather than by conveying a natural knowledge of God in an independent way.

Barth's genuine concern about natural theology becomes obvious in his poignant, even provocative statement:

> No doubt the question "How?" will always be constituted by man, by human nature, language and form. It will certainly be preserved. The creation and preserving patience of God will see to it that this little monster in me and in others and in our whole common sphere is not deprived of its rights. Does this mean that the question 'How?' can and may be heard independently, as conveying a 'natural knowledge of God'? What has man that he has not received? Are not both he and the question "How?" included and preserved in the "What?" which alone is decisive: in the fact that Christ has died and risen for man? (NuG:126–27).

How do we understand this christological inclusivity with respect to Barth's harsh assertion against *theologia naturalis*? "If you really reject natural theology you do not stare at the serpent, with the result that it stares back at you, hypnotizes you, and is ultimately certain to bite you, but you hit it and kill it as soon as you see it! . . . Real rejection of natural theology can come about only in the fear of God and hence only be a complete *lack* of interest in this matter" (NuG:76). "Hence it has to be rejected *a limine*—right at the outset. Only the theology and the church of the antichrist can profit from it. The Evangelical Church and Evangelical theology would only sicken and die of it" (NuG:128). Barth's statements such as: "real rejection of natural theology," "right at the outset," "a complete *lack* of interest in this matter" and "only the theology and the church of antichrist" would be misleading in comparison with his positive alternative to *theologia naturalis* in terms of statements such as "the creation and preserving patience of God not deprived of its rights," or "the question How? included and preserved in the What? (NuG:126–27)"

Given the tension between the particularity and inclusivity of Jesus Christ, it would be hard to charge Barth with being a hard-line accuser of *theologia naturalis* without qualification. Barth's concern of real theology, unlike Brunner's ersitic theology, rejects an independent manner in dealing with two different approaches separately to the knowledge of God in creation and revelation. However, the real theology that has been taken by Barth is more open and inclusive of the rejection of Christianity on the part of unbelievers and modern youth rather than bringing out their capacity for revelation apart from the inclusive, revealed grace of Jesus

Christ. At this juncture, for Barth "a 'true' *theologia naturalis* can exist only where man's eyes have been opened by Christ" (NuG:97).

As we have already described Barth's genuine concern about *theologia naturalis* in light of God's eschatology (in his *Romans*, 1919, 1922) or in light of parabolic analogy (in the Tambach lecture, 1919) or christological universalism based on so-called *extra Calvinisticum* (in the Amsterdam lecture, 1927) or irregular dogmatics (*Göttingen Dogmatics* and *Church Dogmatics*, 1932), Barth never abandoned his real concern about social and political problems in the natural-material realm and people outside the walls of Christianity. These aspects will be finally qualified and elaborated in his doctrine of lights.

Analogia Entis and *Analogia Fidei* Reexamined in the Context of Covenant and Creation

In an analogy, a correspondence between the concept and its divine referent takes place. According to Barth, revelation is the revelation of God in God's Word, in which God's nature can be revealed *per similitudinem*, *per analogiam*, as far as God reveals Godself in it *de facto*. With this knowledge of God the church realizes a possibility of humans speaking of God, of which they themselves, however, can make no use factually due to their fall. What is important is Barth's combination of the analogous knowledge of God with the revelation. According to Barth, "Revelation is neither creation nor the continuation of creation. It is a mysterious new work of God upon creation" (*CD* I/1:431).

In other words, the analogy is not *analogia entis*, which is peculiar to the creaturely being. Rather it is defined theologically as *analogia fidei* by indicating clearly God's self-revelation in Jesus Christ. God "can" (the possibility determined only through God's free decision or eternal election) reveal Godself in the world without a human perception of it. But a human being is obviously in the act of faith for God in that ontic and noetic necessity and rationality enter analogously in relation to each other. Of course, at this point the ontic priority that is placed on the incarnation is strongly affirmed. Barth, in his *Church Dogmatics*, elaborates and develops this concept of analogy. But by leaving sufficient conceptual clarification, an insistence comes from Roman Catholic theologians that

Barth's *analogia fidei* includes *analogia entis*.[38] Let's turn to this complicated issue in regard to a relation between *analogia fidei* and *analogia entis* and, further, between covenant and creation.

Analogia Fidei *and* Analogia Entis *in Roman Catholicism*

According to Przywara, *analogia entis* is the form of principle demanded from metaphysics in general. So *analogia entis* must be understood as a general principle as such. As far as *analogia entis* is understood as the principle of all creature-measuring metaphysics, this principle sees all creatures move toward God as their origin, meaning, and purpose. This *analogia entis* does not conceptualize all creatures *von Gott aus*, but it experiences the move of all creatures toward God in terms of their ontological disposition and openness, which can go beyond themselves.[39]

Barth sees a contrast between *analogia fidei* and *analogia entis* as the primary front in the controversy between Catholic theology and Protestant theology. In a harsh attack upon *analogia entis* as the invention of the antichrist, Barth also disallows any claims of his *Church Dogmatics* as the dogmatics of dialectical theology. What is at issue here is the community of the church: "There is within the church an Evangelical theology, which is to be affirmed and a heretical non-theology which is to be resolutely denied" (*CD* I/1:xv). *Analogia entis* penetrates as a metaphysical principle into all Catholic thought, while for Barth *analogia fidei* as a theological principle determines fundamentally the thought-form and achievement in his *Church Dogmatics*.

Basically the position of the First Vatican Council (1870) affirmed that certainty comes from reason: "If anyone says that the one true God, our Creator and Lord, cannot be known with certainty by the natural light of reason from created things, he is to be condemned."[40]

In the name of God the wholly other—and also for a political reason—Barth protests strongly against natural theology in the form of liberal neo-Protestantism on the one hand in that optimistic and cultured Protestantism was thoroughly compromised in its liberal theology. On

---

38. Balthasar, *Theology of Karl Barth*, 147–50.
39. Przywara, *Analogia Entis*, 3:19–210. Cf. Jüngel, *Barth-Studien*, 210.
40. First Vatican Council (1869–1870) section 3: Dogmatic Constitution on the Catholic Faith, http://www.ewtn.com/library/COUNCILS/V1.htm; cf. Küng, *Does God Exist?* 510.

the other hand, Barth sees a similarity in the form of Roman Catholicism, which followed in the footsteps of the First Vatican Council. These two forms of Christianity, according to Barth, came to terms with the prevailing political structure and system in adoption of an uncritical stance and conformism first to imperial Germany and later to National Socialism. Under these circumstances it is not surprising that Barth rejected harshly any form of natural theology associated with *analogia entis*: "I regard the *analogia entis* as the invention of Antichrist, and I believe that because of it it is impossible ever to become a Roman Catholic" (*CD* I/1:xiii.).

According to Barth, the teaching of Vatican I is exposed to a cleavage in the idea of one God, dividing God into the natural and the supernatural God. Against such a cleavage Barth says: "Of this God and His truth we have said that He is knowable only by the truth, i.e. only by His own grace and mercy." "But its procedure in the noetic question is different from in the ontological. To that extent it certainly intends to make a provisional division or partition in regard to the knowability of God, and this will inevitably lead to a partitioning of the one God as well" (*CD* II/1:79).

The teaching of Vatican I threatens the gracious work and action of God for the sake of abstracting from God beings in general. God is supposed to be ontologically reduced into commonality with all beings that exist. Given this fact, "the God referred to is engaged in a work and activity with man, which is for man a matter of life and death, of blessedness and damnation, nay more, which is for God a matter of His honor and therefore of the miracle of His love, and from which we cannot abstract for a single moment when it is a matter of the relationship of God and man and in particular of the knowability of God. Apparently Roman Catholic doctrine can and must make this abstraction" (*CD* II/1:81).

Barth opposes *analogia entis* with *anlogia fidei*:

> If there is a real analogy between God and man—an analogy which is a true analogy of being on both sides, an analogy in and with which the knowledge of God will in fact be given—what other analogy can it be than the analogy of being which is posited and created by the work and action of God Himself, the analogy which has its actuality from God and from God alone, and therefore in faith and in faith alone. (*CD* II/1:83)

If the analogy of being "is posited and created" by the gracious action of God, if the analogy of being has its actuality from God alone and in faith alone, Barth's concept of *analogia fidei* is all-encompassing and comprehensive *von Gott her*. According to Barth, we have to understand the knowledge of the Word of God in faith, namely, as the possibility given in faith. In so far as a human being has actual experience with the Word of God in faith, it has to do with *finitum non capax infiniti*. In fact, *peccator non capax verbi divini* (*CD* I/1:238). *Analogia fidei* is in no sense related to the capacity of the human, but to the human under the presupposition of his or her total incapacity.

Nevertheless, in Christian faith a common thing occurs between the speaking God and the hearing human as an analogy, a similarity, in spite of the difference and dissimilarity between them. Here Barth allows himself to speak about "a point of contact" (i.e., faith) between God and a human. The image of God (Gen 1:27) is so interpreted by Brunner that humanity and personality remain a point of contact with God, albeit in the sinful human being. However, Barth rejects any idea that the humanity and personality of a sinful human can mean a point of contact for the Word of God. What the image of God remains and is reserved for in the human is the *recta natura* in which *rectitudo* cannot be attributed to *potentialiter*. The image of God in a human being, which constitutes and forms the actual point of contact for the Word of God is a newly created *rectitudo* as the possibility of the human for the Word of God. This possibility is awakened and restored from the actual death to new life through Jesus Christ. Therefore the reconciliation of humans with God in Christ includes the image of God in itself and begins with setting anew the lost point of contact. This "point of contact" is not outside faith, but only in faith (*CD* I/1:238–39).

Barth felt, in this regard, to stand in proximity to the Roman Catholic teaching of *analogia entis*. Nevertheless, Barth did not intend to speak of his concept of analogy from the standpoint of being, which aims at establishing an ontological commonality between the Creator and the creature despite their dissimilarity. Barth's concept of analogy becomes possible only in faith that is similar to the decision of grace in spite of all dissimilarity. Barth is aware of the fact that Roman Catholic teachings of analogy deal with similarity inside the great dissimilarity.

Likewise with the concept of *analogia fidei*, Barth defends himself against the idea of identity in inequality, in which the deification of the human comes to the surface. Although he rejects the Thomistic idea of *analogia entis*, Barth is not hesitant to accept another dimension of a Thomist idea. As Barth argued, "One might discern the content of truth in even the so-called *analogia entis*" (*CD* I/1:239). According to Thomas Aquinas, "the Christian faith instructs humanity about God. . . . Hence there occurs in human beings something like a similarity with the divine wisdom" (*CD* I/1:239). If Christian faith remains at the center in a Thomistic perspective, Barth associates himself with Luther's teaching of justification by faith: "The faith exalts the heart of human being and carries it beyond it as such to God, that from the heart and God a sole spirit comes." Through faith the human comes to God (*fide homo fit Deus*).[41]

From the point of view of *analogia fidei*, Barth blocked a possibility of deification in the sense of transformation of the human essence into the divine essence in the grace of justification as did Augustine and Luther. At this point, Barth invokes Luther's controversial formulation that becomes an ecumenical focus regarding justification and deification: "In faith Christ is present (*In ipsa fide Christus adest*)" (*CD* I/1:242). In interpreting Luther's formulation of *apprehensio Christi*, or *habitatio Christi in nobis* or *unio hominis cum Christo* (Gal 2:20), not through the ontological deification, but through justifying grace in a forensic sense, Barth stated that faith means union with the believed, namely, Jesus Christ. This *analogia* concept is based on *analogia tes pisteus* (Rom 12:6), that is, the correspondence of the known in the knowing, of the object in the thinking, of the Word of God in the thought and spoken human word. This *analogia fidei* in a Pauline perspective, provides a basis for Barth to take into account the fact that human ontological capacity reverses God's grace. Humans have not created faith for themselves, but the Word has created it.

In seeing faith as the gift of God, not as human works, Barth utilizes the Reformation principle of Luther. Although Barth does not fully define a concept of *analogia entis*, we can know from his assertions that *analogia entis* implies an ontological assertion. God and creature are similar in their being. Seen in the noetic assertion: God can be known in a natural knowledge of God on the basis of a similarity of being. Therefore, God-world relations can be reversed by continual disrespect for God's self-

---

41. *CD* I/1:239.

revelation. From here we can think of the way of human beings toward God in independence of or without revelation in Jesus Christ. It would refer to a creature's attempt at self-apotheosis. From here arises the dangerous consequence that by reducing God into the being-structure and by misusing God's grace for human interest, humans can place God at their disposal.

If we follow a concept of *anlogia entis* in this light, the question of to what extent a Catholic concept of *analogia entis* (such as that of Pryzwara, Söhngen, and Balthasar) remains open and can be seen as identical with *analogia entis* rejected by Barth.[42] Barth's analysis of Gottlieb Söhngen's idea of *anlaogia entis* (*CD* II/1 § 26, the knowledge of God) becomes significant in our context. Against the teaching of Vatican I, Barth affirmed his position as follows: God can be known only through God, namely, in the occurrence of a divine encroachment of his self-revelation. In the prolegomena, Barth deals with the Trinity in its revelation as Christian hermeneutics in speaking of God. Barth's discussion of the Trinity is of a hermeneutical character. However, in Roman Catholic teaching, God is knowable—knowable also without revelation. *Analogia entis* is a way of recognizing and justifying a point of contact with the knowability of God outside divine revelation.

However, Söhngen would subordinate the knowledge of being to the knowledge of God's deeds. Hence, *analogia entis* is subordinated to *analogia fidei*, not the other way around: *operari sequitur esse* [deed follows being]. Deed is valid in the order of being. But for Barth, knowledge of God goes in the reversed way: *Esse sequitur operari* [the knowledge of being follows the knowledge of activity] (*CD* II/1:82).

According to Söhngen, from the *analogia* and *participatio entis* an *analogia participatio in* divine nature cannot be developed or opened. The self-opening up of God can be known only in a divine self-opening. Hence in order to make *analogia entis* visible, "there has to be an assumptio of the *analogia entis* by the *analogia fidei*—"*Analogia fidei is sanans et elevans analogiam entis*"—namely, through Jesus Christ (*CD* II/1:82). Therefore *analogia fidei* is to heal and elevate *analogia entis* through the grace of Jesus Christ. Along the lines of 1 Cor 15:12–13, Söhngen asked, if since it is now proclaimed that the Word takes part actually in our

---

42. Cf. Balthasar, *Theology of Karl Barth*, 237–47; Küng, *Does God Exist?* 509–14, 518–22.

humanity, how can some say that there would be no actual participation of being with him and in him for us (but a naked Word-and-hearing participation)? If we do not really participate in Jesus Christ, Christ has not really participated in our humanity. God's calling makes us really God's children. *Participatio fidei* cannot also stand merely against *participatio entis*. It is rather the participation of being.

Given the relation between *analogia fidei* and *analogia entis* in Söhngen, Barth stated that "if this is the Roman Catholic doctrine of *analogia entis* . . . I must withdraw my earlier statement that I regard the *analogia entis* as "the invention of Antichrist" " (*CD* II/1:82). However, Barth remained uncertain whether Söhngen's position of *analogia entis* represented the official Roman Catholic position.

According to Barth, there is no Word of God without a physical event. Preaching and sacrament is a reminder of this. Approving of F. C. Oetinger's thesis ("corporeality is the end of all the ways of God" [*CD* I/1:134]), Barth insisted that the Word of God binds itself to the spirituality as well as to the corporeality of the creature. What is striking at this point is Barth's affirmation of the doctrine of Eastern Orthodoxy. That is, "eschatological redemption includes within it the most comprehensive sense the cosmos, the creature, as well" (*CD* I/1:134). Barth's spirituality of the Word of God lies primarily in God's speaking, then in human faith of hearing, understanding, and obeying in correlation to this divine speaking. This aspect of divine action and human response in faith distinguishes Barth's from a Roman Catholic teaching of spirituality as well as from Rudolf Otto's idea of the holy which is related to human experience of the numinous (*CD* I/1:135).[43]

Be that as it may, representatives of *Nouvelle théologie* in France made a significant attempt at overcoming the cleavage between the natural and the supernatural spheres as seen in the First Vatican Council. Along the lines of Henri De Lubac, Balthasar argues that the authentic Catholic teaching of the analogy of being is encompassed by the analogy of faith. This was especially the view held by Söhngen in the early

---

43. Barth argues in this regard that the numinous as the irrational cannot be differented from an absolutised natural force. Barth's idea of the wholly other is exclusively bound to the Word of God, while Otto's idea of the wholly other to *mysterium tremendum et fascinans* in religious experience of the numinous, albeit without giving it clear conceptual expression. Cf. Otto, *Idea of the Holy*, 25–26, 30.

thirties against Barth.[44] Given this fact, Küng argues that "the analogy of being—as Balthasar's answer to Barth has shown—does not mean the assimilation of God and man on the same plane and is not the real point of controversy between Catholics and Protestants."[45] Nevertheless, the *act-structure of analogia fidei*, which can be articulated in Barth's Trinity, can be in no way identical with the Catholic teaching of *anlaogia entis* as it is represented by Balthasar.

A misunderstanding of *analogia fidei* from a Roman Catholic perspective would be related to Barth's further use of *analogia relationis* in his doctrine of creation (*CD* III/2). But the point of departure for the *analogia relationis* is the inner Trinitarian being of God. God is in relation with divine others. God corresponds to Godself. Likewise the election of Jesus Christ is in relation with God the Father. From here the relation of God to creature is determined as an analogous relation. Like God in relation, human beings as God's creatures are in relation (I—thou, man–woman). Based on the humanity of Jesus as the image of God, Barth affirmed a correspondence and similarity between God and human beings.

As long as *analogia entis* concerns a correspondence and similarity in comparison to the being of God, Barth rather utilized *analogia relationis* for the sake of the relationship of Trinitarian life as well as God's economic relation to the human being. A relationship between God and creature is set up by the truine God, who exists in freedom to be as Father, Son, and Holy Spirit. God's love in the Trinitarian fellowship is addressed by the humanity of Jesus to the human. Jesus's fellow humanity and his being for the human, which is the direct correlative of his existence for God, is the basis for revealing and attesting to this correspondence and similarity (*CD* III/2:220). Therefore the being of humanity in an encounter with a fellow human is a being in correspondence to God. In it we notice a three-dimensional movement of correspondence grounded 1) in the inner Trinitarian being of God, 2) in the relation between God and human being, and 3) in the human being among fellows. From here Barth attempted to conceptualize the method of *analogia relationis*. An original relation of the Father and the Son, which Barth characterized as "the inner divine co-existence, co-inherence and reciprocity" (*CD* III/2:221) is reflected in the man Jesus.

44. Küng, *Does God Exist?* 518–22.
45. Ibid., 522.

Therefore, the *analogia relationis* or the *imago Dei* can be properly and adequately spoken of in christological terms. This relationship is not affected even by human sin, and therefore persists in the sinful human (*CD* III/2:221). The humanity of Jesus Christ becomes the foundation for including the *humanitas* of all races and elevating it in a disposition toward sociality. The humanity of Christ makes human beings truly human, each in his or her *humanitas*. In terms of *analogia proportionalitatis*, the analogical art that describes a relation between relations, Barth discussed and deepened *analogia fidei* in relation to the correspondence between the being of God and human being. God's relation to Godself is analogous to God's relation to a human being; from here it follows that God's relation to a human being is analogous to a human relation to God. Therefore God's relation to human being or a human relation to God is analogous to a human relation to co-fellows. God as the origin of all correspondence, and the analogical principle must be concretized especially with respect to humans' social and political context as well as to creation.

However, Barth used an analogy of correlation in a very limited sense, holding it valid only for Jesus Christ rather than for all human beings. Given this fact, theological anthropology, namely, a genuine knowledge of human being in general, must be based on Christology, namely, the particular knowledge of the man Jesus Christ. However, Catholic theologians want to discern at this juncture a correspondence adequate to being. So understood, a concept emerges: *analogia fidei seu relationis*. For this reason, Barth's concept of *analogia fidei seu relationis* caused Catholic theologians to maintain that it implies *analogia entis*. But the *analogia relationis* (human being to human being) for Barth is ontically and noetically mediated through the first relation (God *in se*) and the second one (God—God/Man Jesus Christ) without leaving sure ground of the structure of *analogia fidei*.

In light of Jesus Christ, who is the essence of every human, Barth saw a possibility of theological anthropology. The humanity of Jesus is repetition and reproduction of God because the humanity of Jesus is the picture of God, the *imago Dei*, no more or no less (*CD* III/2:219). So understood, the being of the man Jesus is the being- and knowledge-ground of all analogies.[46] In light of this humanity of the man Jesus, Barth deals with the being of humans in being together with other humans. Therefore, *analogia relationis* cannot be properly understood without reference to the humanity of Jesus.

As far as the humanity of Jesus is the repetition and reproduction of God and is thus the image of God, all analogies have to do with essentially godly correspondence and similarity between Jesus for God and his being for fellow humans (*CD* III/2:220). In this analogy a repetition of being takes place that, as such, is an event and, as an event, is relation. The second analogy (Jesus for humans) follows the first analogy (God in relation). His being for humans corresponds to Jesus for God. The humanity of Jesus, his cohumanity, and his being for humans are immediate correlates with his being for God (*CD* III/2:221). Thus, humans in general take part in God's image of the man Jesus.

Analogia Relationis *and Feminist Critique*

Accordingly, Barth pursued further an analogy of order in view of the soul and body of Jesus. Jesus is not only his soul but also his body in an ordered oneness and wholeness. His being is orderly in such a way that he himself is both the higher and the lower, the first and the second, the dominant and the dominated (*CD* III/2:332). As an analogy to the primal contrast of Creator and creatures shows itself as heaven and earth in the structure of the cosmos, so soul and body come in the structure of a human being. Like in the relation between the Creator and creatures, what is important in the relation between soul and body is an order of 'above' and 'below' in a nonreversible manner (*CD* III/2:427). Now in analogical discourse, nature and grace enter into relation to each other. With this analogy in mind, Barth allowed for seeing the human as the preceding soul of the succeeding body, in that a relation between man and woman is conceptualized in a hierarchical manner (*CD* III/2:427).[47] At this juncture, Barth's ethics of sexuality anticipates a feminist critique. First of all, Moltmann argues that "Barth's one-sided, monarchical image

---

46. Jüngel, "Die Moglichkeit Theologischer Anthropologie auf dem Grunde der Analogie," in Jüngel, *Barth-Studien*, 210–232 at 212.

47. Cf. Moltmann's critique of Barth's anthropology as patriarchal in structure. See Moltmann, *History and the Triune God*, 135–38; and Moltmann, *Trinity and the Kingdom*, 148–50.

of the order of soul and body" must be given up on behalf of using "the image of mutual interrelationship, namely the perichoresis of body and soul."[48]

For Barth, however, the reciprocal subordination between man and woman is preserved and established. Genuine responsibility happens in an asymmetrical turn to the other. This interrelatedness and dependence between the sexes stands in protest to an understanding of womenhood as something independent of men. Barth did not see how this question could be resolved apart from the male/female relationship. Rather he denounced the emancipatory tendency of the feminist circle as a worldly affair of the bourgeois movement. Similarly, the socialist labor movement demanded the subordination of the woman-question to class solidarity.

Already in his article on Feuerbach, Barth had expressed his agreement with Feuerbach's philosophy of anthropological realism. This realism includes the whole reality of the human being (heart and stomach). According to Barth, Feuerbach had made more important and effective progress than had modern theology. Feuerbach seemed to perceive that whereas Adam and Eve in their nakedness were the beginning of theology, the resurrection of the flesh is the beginning and the end of theology. Barth understood the resurrection to take place not merely in the spiritual realm but also in the realm of the mortal flesh-body. In other words, the resurrection is an event in the material, bodily being of the human race (*CD* III/2:489–90).

In integrating this realistic idea of a human being, Barth critiqued the position of the church. "Has it not made a point of teaching the immortality of the soul instead of attesting to society, with its proclamation of the resurrection of the dead, that the judgment and promise of God compass the whole man, and therefore cannot be affirmed and believed apart from material and economic reality, or be denied or pushed aside as ideology in contrast to material and economic reality?"(*CD* III/2: 389–90).

In responding critically to a Marxist view of the world, Barth made an energetic effort to revise and alter theological anthropology in the light of an eschatology of the resurrection. At this point, Barth utilized socialistic sociocritique as an indispensable part in his critique of the church's teaching of anthropology. Barth questioned: Has the church not always

---

48. Cf. Moltmann, *History and the Triune God*, 136.

been on the side of "the ruling classes"? Has its faith not been denounced as a "relic of capitalism"? Has it not always been the surest guarantee of the existence and continuance of an order of classes that technically can be understood merely as the order of superiority of the economically strong? Has it not with its doctrine of soul and body brought to the agenda a culpable indifference towards the problems of material, of bodily life, and also of economics? (*CD* III/2:389).

In this way Barth's anthroplogy regarding a human being as the soul of the body cannot be properly understood without a human being as the body of the soul (*CD* III/2:432). Against crude materialism, spiritualism, and Greek anthropological presuppositions, Barth's theological anthropology is called "realistic," in that a human being is understood as a besouled body or as a bodily soul (*CD* III/2:434–35). According to Barth, the concept of subordination and superiority is grounded primarily and actually in Jesus Christ, the crucified Jew, who in his liberating obedience to God stands uncomparatively deeper than the woman under the man and urges the man to subordinate himself to the woman.

Therefore, man and woman exist as "fellow heirs of the grace of life" (*CD* III/4:172). Hence for Barth super- and subordination are primarily and truly grounded and justified in Jesus Christ. Christ stands as the quintessence of all subordination incomparably deeper than the woman. Therefore "this subordination of woman is primarily and essentially to the Lord and only secondarily and unessentially to man" (*CD* III/4:172). For Barth, superordination and subordination are primarily and properly in Jesus Christ, who is "the sum of all humility before God." Jesus Christ as the sum of all subordination stands much lower than woman under man (*CD* III/2:311).

In this way, Barth's reflection of the order of creation between man and woman does not describe an ontological-patriarchal range and orientation. Barth is critical of any understanding that presupposes or assumes that man stands in the same relationship with the woman as Christ does with him and God does with Christ. Surely, a woman does not stand in indirect relationship with Christ vis-à-vis man. The basic order of the human established in God's creation is grounded in the divinity and humanity of Christ, his lordship and service, so that "there can be no occasion either for the exaltation of man or the oppression of women" (*CD* III/2:312).

Seen in this light, *analogia fidei* and *analogia relationis* maintain self-critical reservation and hermeneutical suspicion, refusing to accept the traditional Western ontology of *analogia entis*. *Analogia relationis* associated with humanity results in asymmetrical equality among the unequal (*CD* III/2, § 45.2/3). The exaltation of man and the oppression of woman are radically excluded in the community of Jesus Christ. The man-woman relationship is to be seen in light of the relationship between Christ and community. At this point Barth rejected patriarchalism for the sake of mutual subordination in respect before Jesus Christ, "mutual subordination in full reciprocity" (*CD* III/2:313).

Woman's subordination to man becomes only meaningful in terms of the subordination of the church to Christ. It is not to be misconceptualized in the sense of an androcracy or gynocracy. Barth's conception of cohumanity as the basic form of humanity excludes the possibility of a human in isolation, or all androcracy and gynocracy (*CD* III/2:315, 292). Barth's understanding of cohumanity contradicts the formal logic of market exchange, which materially covers and hides unequal exchange.

Barth's reflection on *natus ex virgine* (the supernatural miracle of the incarnation of God) rejects the natural law of patriarchalism and instead posits the ontological priority of paternity. In so doing, the materiality of the virgin retains a theological preference in the election of the Jewish liberator Jesus. The human redeemer of the nothingness (*Das Nichtige*) is conceived as the Jewish man in the Spirit, born from Mary; also through and in relation to this new Eve, who in service of liberation precedes a work of the man. The woman, not the man, illustrates the reality of community in relation to Christ through her subordination. In a qualified sense, the woman is the community. It is the woman, not the man, who hears Christ and the apostles' exhortation. "She is the type of the community listening to Christ and the apostolic admonition" (*CD* III/2:314). "As woman, she is precisely non-everything: "non-willing, non-achieving, non-creative, non-sovereign," as opposed to man who is willing, achieving and disobedient" (*CD* I/2:188). For Barth, woman's role is accepted as the prototype of humanity in relation to God.

This is why Schleiermacher's bizarre wish to become a woman would not be simply meaningless to Barth. Thus it is of special significance to notice Barth's positive acceptance of Schliermacher's view on the woman. Confronting himself with the *particular veri* of Schliermacher's idea of the woman, Barth writes: "As a living member of the church, man and all other superiors and subordinates in the community have no option but to follow the example of woman, occupying in relation to Jesus Christ the precise position which she must occupy and maintain in relation to man" (*CD* III/4:175).

In that a Jewish man forms the community as the physical body of the resurrected Christ, Barth's ecclesiological preference is definitely for woman, whom Jesus represents. The whole construction of sexual difference is oriented in the form of fellowship and participation, so that "both the superiority and also the subordination in question first take place in Christ himself" (*CD* III/4:173). For this reason, the nothingness of reciprocal privation or castration and groundless sexual jealousy (such as penis envy) are excluded. Whereas the history of theology, natural science, politics, and economy are dominated by the history of man, a woman becomes an attorney of nature. This is clear in Barth's insistence of *natus ex virgine*. The woman, in other words, characterizes human nature whereas the man characterizes human history. Viewing the woman as a helpmate in Gen 2:18, Barth rejects the idea that the male becomes lord of the woman. Rather the super-and subordination are not the order of creation, but divine ordinance in the sphere of the fall (*CD* I/2:194).

When the Word of God calls humans into their proper beings *ex nihilo*, it does so by means of female-receptive attributes, thus allowing human beings to become partners with God in the action of covenant. The woman enters as an attorney of the earth and of the man. The woman, as counterpartner of the man, forms and reflects the partnership of the earth with heaven, Israel and Yahweh, and lastly of the human race and God. Hence it is out of the question to speak of a "man-becoming" of the Word of God in the event of incarnation. Because the woman represents the body of Christ, Barth rejected the construction that the man is the same for the woman as Christ is for the man as an absurd interpretation (*CD* III/2:311).

Barth's idea of *assumptio carnis* points to the humanity of God assuming the humanity of all rather than becoming a "man." Rejecting the understanding of the "man-becoming" of the Word of God in the event of the incarnation, Barth distinguished man's questionable mastery of nature—in terms of patriarchal *dominum terrae*—from the relational *imago Dei* between man and woman (*KD* III/1:210, 220). The freedom and *imago Dei* are revealed in the co-relation and a mutually dependable being between man and woman. Moreover, a human dominion over the animal world in an unqualified sense is rejected in this context because the dominion of humans over animals is an internally and externally limited dominion.

Barth's rejection of the association between *dominum terrae* and *imago Dei* allows *analogia relationis* to be expanded in a human relation with creatures. In this new relation, we may notice that human beings take on the responsibility of care-taking in the creation. In fact, from a Barthian perspective, the project of partnership based on the mandate of dominion through care-taking would become meaningful and compelling.[49]

Barth was aware of the significance of a question of woman's liberation in the socialist and French feminist circles. He argued, in regard to the social condition of women, (particularly as they are explicated by Simone de Beauvoir) that man generally, and Christian theologians specifically, should take feminism into account (*CD* III/4:161f).

> For if Simone de Beauvoir unmasks the myth of the woman and makes no use of the idealistic myth of the androgyne, it is plain that she proclaims another new myth so much the more powerfully and unreservedly—that of the human individual who in the achievement of freedom overcomes his masculinity or her femininity, mastering it from a superior plane, so that sexuality is only a condition by which he is not finally conditioned, with which he can dispense and whose operation he can in any case control. Even in the masculine form presupposed by Simone de Beauvoir, is not this individual a product of wishful thinking rather than a reality? Is he not more a man-God or God-man than a real human figure? . . . Why is it that the whole emancipation programme of this woman, who in her way fights so valiantly and skillfully, is still oriented on man, and particularly on this highly unreal man? (*CD* III/4:162).

Barth's concern is interesting: Is the woman, in her way toward emancipation, competent to avoid and overcome the real limitations of what the man has practiced and ruled? Is not the woman in her fight for *être humain* still directed toward the man? By her principle—"On ne naît pas femme, on le devient"—the feminine must be regarded as only

---

49. Cf. Welker, *Creation and Reality*. See especially Welker's idea of "The Mandate of Dominion: Obligation to Hierarchically Ordered Partnership with Animals and to Dominion through Care taking," ibid., 70–73.

provisional and not essential. Sexual differentiation for her becomes superfluous, disappearing as a secondary reality in comparison with the human act of freedom. Sartre's metaphor gains prominence as the controlling principle in Simone de Beauvoir's idea of *Le Deuxième Sexe*. That is, "l'existence précède l'essence" (*CD* III/4:162). However, "the category of flight from one's own sex" would be vulnerable and incompetent in recognizing the difference as the different. In other words, the man is not the woman as, conversely, the woman is not the man. Despite all equality and dignity of man and woman before God, difference between two sexes must be preserved; the sexes must not be commensurate with each other.

Seen in this light, Barth's reflection on man and woman—regardless of the creaturely inequality between them (*CD* III/4:171)—retains a principal equality of all human beings in a genuine sense (*CD* III/2:301–16). Male and female, in their relation to one another, can be understood as a cohumanity of equality that is established by God. Although Barth conceded that the relationship between man and woman is hierarchical, he claimed that the man is supposed to transform his own position of superordination into a primacy of service, while the woman's position of subordination gains primacy as participation in Jesus Christ's own subordination. (*CD* III/4:170, 172).

Barth's focus in this regard is on "mutual adaptation and co-ordination" (*CD* III/4:172). Jesus Christ, then, is the prototype for a relationship between man and woman in that he is both the higher and the lower, the first and the second, the dominant and the dominated. It is the male's task to follow Jesus by placing himself in lower, second, and dominated service.[50] Therefore "the divine command permits man and woman continually and particularly to discover their specific sexual nature, and to be faithful to it in this form which is true before God, without being enslaved to any preconceived opinions" (*CD* III/4:153). Barth argued that the question of gender "ought certainly to be posed in each particular case

---

50. Barth's logic of super- and subordination is reflected in his reflection on the soul and body in their particular order. His theological anthropology in which a human being, as a preceding soul of his succeeding body, stands in critical relation to the Greek picture of human being. Rather, it is of a realistic and biblical character, because it follows Jesus as the whole man. At this point a human being is fully human in the unity and differentiation of the soul and the body (*CD* III/2:434, 332. 419).

as it arises, not in the light of traditional preconceptions, but honestly in relation to what is aimed at in the future"(*CD* III/4:155).

Analogia Relationis *in the Context of Covenant and Creation*

Given the correspondence of a relation between God *in se* and the man Jesus, between the man Jesus and fellow humans, and between soul and body in the human structure, Barth called such a correspondence *analogia relationis*. Barth extended his use of analogy further in order to flesh out the relation of creation to covenant, nature and grace. In viewing the relation between creation and covenant in terms of *analogia relationis*, Barth himself, Balthasar has argued, described the relation between God and creatures in the classical formulation of *analogia entis*. According to Balthsar, "since the order of creation is oriented towards the Incarnation, it possesses images, analogies, and dispositions that truly are presuppositions for the Incarnation . . . Barth had no difficulty in accepting and approving the analogy of being, in this form, within the context of an all-embracing analogy of faith."[51] Likewise Söhngen insists that for Barth there is no *analogia fidei* without external ground of *analogia entis*.

However, Barth obviously saw the sharpest contradiction between *analogia fidei* and *analogia entis* at a point where Balthasar asserts that *analogia fidei* includes *analogia entis*. As Barth says, "this is not a correspondence and similarity of being, an *analogia entis*" (*CD* III/2:220). The question of the correspondence between the definition of the human as covenant partner and one's creatureliness encompasses the question of the relation between covenant and creation.

In Barth's famous definition we read: As the creation is the external ground of covenant, so the covenant is the internal ground of creation. This differentiation between external and internal ground is accounted for by Barth's assignment of each. Barth theologically discussed creation-relevant concepts such as nature and grace, condition and history, being-structure and event, continuity and contingency. Surely, creation cannot condition the covenant. Nevertheless, it is the external ground for it. In other words, the covenant cannot come into existence without creation: the creation is its external grounds. In Barth's words:

---

51. Balthasar, *Theology of Karl Barth*, 149; cf. *CD* II/1:89-90.

> How could grace come to man as grace if it were coincidental with nature, if nature as such were grace? In reality, grace is a mystery. It is the hidden meaning of nature. When grace reveals itself, nature does not cease to be. How could it cease to be since God does not cease to be its creator? But now there is something more within nature. Now nature itself becomes the showplace of grace. Now the freedom of grace and its mastery over nature becomes visible. (CD II/1:572)

As Barth defined it, the assignment of the exterior (creation) and the interior ground (covenant) is understood such that the interior ground presupposes for itself the exterior ground. The nature of creation is in preparation for grace. Creation is also the possibility made through the covenant. The interior ground makes possible the exterior ground so that creation becomes a possibility for the interior ground. Nature itself becomes the showplace of grace. As Balthasar says, "the new arrangement, culminating in Christ, does not erase the natural arrangement. It presupposes a pristine natural arrangement. The new divine arrangement stands out against the natural backdrop, superseding it and confirming it as the same time."[52] Therefore, "creation is a unique symbol of the Covenant, a true sacrament."[53]

According to Barth, creation and covenant are deeply related to each other. The interrelationship between creation (as the external ground of covenant) and covenant (as the internal ground of creation) is not easy to understand. Creation cannot condition the covenant; nevertheless, it is the external ground for it. The covenant cannot be without the creation; nevertheless, it is the internal ground for it. If the covenant enables the creation, the covenant, as the internal ground, makes creation the presupposition for it. Therefore, the creation becomes the possibility for covenant, a possiblity enabled by the covenant.

Barth presupposes that the covenant belongs to the creation in his doctrine of creation. Revelation, for Barth, is the new, special work—more than nature and more than creation, preservation, and rule. The creation is the way to the covenant, and thus the covenant is the zeal of creation. Creation as presupposition for the covenant is not supposed to be understood as an inherently given existing quality. Barth called grace "the meaning of the nature hidden to us" (KD II/1:572).

52. Ibid., 111.
53. CD III/1:262–63; cf. Balthasar, *Theology of Karl Barth*, 112.

Barth speaks of the creation as having exemplary character, by placing the creaturely world under the sign of the future of God that is yet hidden. The creation is, therefore, to become the space of the future history, namely, an indication of the eschaton of God. Creation, which is the indication and preparation for the covenant, will realize itself in its movement to the eschatological goal. This creation, according to Barth, belongs to history, namely, the space of revelation, a scene of grace. Barth's "No" to Brunner is not supposed to be regarded as Barth's rejection of any attempt at constructing a theology of nature in an ecological perspective. Rather Barth's rejection of Brunner's natural theology is grounded on a rejection of fundamental-ontological *analogia entis*, from which a formal-natural being of *imago Dei* is derived independent of revelation. This "No" to natural theology, in other words, protested the tidal wave of National Socialism that enslaved the German Christians to a temple of German nature and history-myth. The issue was about the human ontological capacity for possessing a point of contact with redeeming grace apart from the revelation in Jesus Christ.

When it comes to dialectical theology seen from the perspective of analogy, Barth took the christological concentration seriously not to block the mystery and freedom of God. God's Trinitarian sociality is, according to Barth, the ground for the sociality of human beings. God exists in Godself above all in God's action toward the outer sphere (creation) and in relation and fellowship. The existence of God is the inner divine "being together," "co-being with each other" and "for being with each other" (*KD* III/2:263). The relation of God in Trinitarian fellowship is further discussed in accordance with the relation to human beings. Here a human being can become a repetition of God's form of life, its copy and reflection, and thus a covenant partner with God (*CD* III/1:185).

The sociality of human beings is a consequence of the sociality of God. As God refuses to be without human beings, so human beings should not be without their fellows. According to Barth, a human being can be only a human being as far as one is and works together with a fellow human being. The human society occurs through this working together, namely, "a free co-existence and co-operation, an open confrontation and reciprocity" (*CD* III/1:185), so the social character of a human being is the basis for the genesis of human sociality and their coordination in society (KD IV/2:845–847). [54]

In his reflection on a Trinitarian understanding of covenantal theology, in other words "theo-anthropology," Barth takes seriously the encounter between the action of God and the action of a human being in terms of *analogia relationis*. From here the relation between God and a human being is acted out and takes place within the history of creation, reconciliation, and redemption. To the creaturely relation in fellowship Barth counts, above all, the relation between man and woman, the existence of people, the reverence for life and the protection of life, as well as the active life of a human being (*CD* III/4:116–648). What is at stake in the relation of fellowship lies in the affirmation of human freedom, namely, freedom in communion and freedom for life.

Barth's critique of neo-orthodox theism, including the philosophies of naturalism, idealism, and existentialism (*CD* III/2:§44. 2, 75–132) does not mean that we don't need to learn from the secular sources and wisdoms. Rather, through them "one can arrive at a non-theological but genuine knowledge of the phenomena of the human" (*CD* III/2:198–99). Theistic anthropology can be useful in telling about humanity's fitness for a theonomous existence in opposition to an autonomous one (*CD* III/2: 198–202). However, Barth's definition of Jesus Christ as both a human being for God (*CD* III/2:§44. 1) and a human being for others (*CD* III/2: §45.1)—in which we see a parallel with Jesus Christ as both the electing God and the elect man—becomes the fundamental basis for him to approach the basic form of creaturely existence. The basic form of existence consists in our own cohumanity. In contrast to capitalist individualism and fascist reductionism of others, genuine cohumanity makes a claim for mutuality, reciprocity, and recognition that "I am as thou art" (*CD* III/2:248).

---

54. For Barth's idea of special ethics, an encounter of the acting God with the acting human does not take place in an empty space but in a historically articulated form. In this historical event of an encounter between God and humans, "it is always a question of God in His articulated and differentiated action, and of man in his correspondingly articulated and differentiated being in relation to this God" (*CD* III/4:28–29). In this event, God and the human are historically articulated figures.

Although Barth rejected the image of God as a capacity or as a supposed moral uprightness (*rectitudio*), God's image for Barth is still regarded as humanity's *recta natura*, or proper nature (*CD* III/2:238). "Humanity would not be humanity if it were not the image of God" (*CD* III/1:184). In fact, Barth's rejection of a concept of an image of God as a point of contact refers only to intrinsic faculty or neutral condition in a human being inherently apart from the grace of Jesus Christ. The rejection of *analogia entis* in the Barthian sense leads to a consequence of his theological concept of the doctrine of creation. God's action of creation is analogical. That God proves God's inner essence toward the external in the creation means that God says yes not only to Godself but also to humanity.

According to Barth, creaturely participation in the being of God is not based on *analogia entis* but on the grace of God's revelation. If *analogia entis* compares creaturely being with other creaturely being, *analogia fidei* refers to the correspondence with God who precedes the creaturely being and calls it into the divine Yes. An analogy of relation does compare relation with relations: *analogia proportionalitatis*.

Although Söhngen stresses the formal agreement between Barth's *anlogia relationis* and the *similitudo proportionalitatis* of Aquinas, the difference remains profound. Barth's *analogia relationis* is a correspondence of relations based on God's Yes to creation or God's love in freedom for the world. The triune God speaks to Godself and then to God's creatures; in God's so doing, a correspondence is created. If *analogia entis* is defined as a relation of God to creatures in a way that creatures through their own disposition are related to God as their innermost and constant *principium* and *finis*,[55] *analogia entis* has, methodologically speaking, no room in Barth's *analogia relationis* in a christocentric fashion. *Analogia relationis* can be seen in light of God's secret, namely, God's election of Jesus Christ. Jesus Christ is himself God's election of grace and therefore God's Word, decision, and beginning (*KD* II/2:102). That God chooses condemnation for Godself in the election of the man Jesus includes God's Yes to the world. This Word as the mediation stance between God and humans makes possible *analogia relationis*. God's freedom and love are identical with the election of Jesus Christ, because Jesus Christ is the

---

55. Cf. Przywara, *Analogia Entis*, 1:95.

electing God and the elect man. *Analogia relationis* is grounded in the election of Jesus Christ.

Furthermore, that the complement of election is faith means that Barth's concept of *analogia relationis* can only be understood in the sense of *analogia fidei*. Barth makes use of the concept of *analogia tou einai*, which is distinguished strictly from *analogia tou ontos*. The *analogia tou einai* refers to a correspondence as *verbum externum*, which precedes all creaturely beings and calls for them into divine being. As Jüngel says, "if *analogia relationis* is grounded in the election of Jesus Christ, if the election of faith corresponds, the analogy grounded in the election becomes knowable not through *lumen naturale* of *ratio*, but through *fides quaerens intellectum*."[56] The possibility of knowledge in *fides quaerens intellectum* is based exclusively on God's self-communication and revelation (*KD* III/1: 400). This act-structure in *analogia fidei* in no way softens the being-structure in *analogia entis*. But the two-edged nature of divine election cannot be adequately understood without the aspect of solidarity with the world. "The vocation of God's chosen one is precisely this: In his election and his mission, the process of divine reconciliation is integrated into the world and becomes a real happening there. The closed circle of election involving Christ and his community is opened out to the world" (*CD* II/2:461).

If we see the doctrine of election as the *summa evangelii* in a Barthian sense, the challenge of Söhngen and Balthasar cannot be simply rejected, but must be discussed in a new perspective. Catholic theology in no way describes the univocal teaching of *analogia entis*. There is a strong tendency within modern Catholic theology (Balthasar, Küng, and Rahner) toward a remarkable affinity to their evangelical counterparts. Barth himself expressed his approval of them with ecumenical passion and solidarity. In a later interview, Barth corrected his attack on *analogia entis* as the invention of the antichrist. He even went so far as to say, "it is no longer necessary to discuss this theory. . . . We are in unity about what can be meant by it."[57]

In this statement, we ask whether Barth stands in contradiction to what he had defended decisively for the sake of *anlalogia fidei*. My question and answer would be Barth's reiteration of his former positive

---

56. Jüngel, "Die Möglichkeit theologischer Anthropologie auf dem Grunde der Analogie," in *Barth-Studien*, 227–28.

57. Barth, *Gespräche, IV, 1964–1968*, 337.

response to *analogia entis* in light of his *analogia fidei*. Barth agreed with Söhngen's proposal on *assumptio* of *analogia entis* through Jesus Christ (*KD* II/1:89). From the start *analogia fidei* has had an inclusive dimension associated with covenantal theology for the world rather than being reduced to an individualist understanding of faith. [58]

Karl Barth's Doctrine of Lights and Theologia Naturalis

In the horizon of the doctrine of reconciliation (*CD* IV/3.1. § 69) Barth remarkably emphasized the independence of creaturely realms. Besides Jesus Christ as the one light of life, there are words of creatures that, as such, have their own lights and truths, languages, and words. Although these truths and words are not identical with God's Word of reconciliation, they are valued as independent frameworks of creaturely beings, namely, as constants in cosmos.

Barth's teaching about secular parables in this regard provides a theological basis for not excluding *analogia entis*, but including, renewing, and transforming it socially and materially in light of *prophetia et revelatio Jesu Christi universalis*. Barth's doctrine of election moves inevitably toward "universal" reconciliation in solidarity with the world. His reflection of analogy and parable in this context is expanded hermeneutically and christologically in recognition of people of other faiths and cultures. Barth's inclusive understanding of *analogia fidei* and *relationis* associated with a "universal" reconciliation of Jesus Christ moves even in affirmation of openly pagan worldliness. In so doing, however, Barth does not appeal to the sorry hypothesis of a so-called natural theology (*CD* IV/3.1:117).

Barth reiterates the first thesis of the Barmen Declaration: "Jesus Christ as attested to us in Holy Scripture is the one Word of God whom we must hear and whom we must trust and obey in life and in death" (*CD* IV/3.1:3). Without leaving the sure ground of Christology, Barth

---

58. In order to avoid a challenge to Barth—in it *analoigia relationis* includes *analogia entis*—Jüngel proposes that *analogia fidei* is to be understood as "form of language of faith." Jüngel's fundamental thesis explains: "God 'spricht'—the humans 'entspricht.'" Jüngel's attempt to construct a theological anthropology is made by adding Barth's concept of *analogia relationis seu fidei* to Heidegger's philosophy. Jüngel, "Moglichkeit Theologischer Anthropologie auf dem Grunde der Analogie," in Jüngel, *Barth-Studien*, 210-32. However, Barth himself, in an interview, does not find the hermeneutics of ontology (Ernst Fuchs) compelling in its interpretation of his theology.

emphatically said, "In the world reconciled by God in Jesus Christ there is no secular sphere abandoned by him .. , even where ... it seems to approximate dangerously to the pure and absolute form of utter godlessness." In light of the resurrection of Jesus Christ, we must "be prepared at any time for true words even from what seems to be the darkest places" (*CD* IV/3.1:119).

With renewed emphasis on *solus Christus* in the Barmen declaration, Barth takes into account true words and parables of the kingdom of a very different kind outside the church. The sovereignty of Jesus Christ that is revealed in his resurrection is not restricted to the churchly sphere (*CD* IV/3.1:117–18). Secular creaturely realms are to be accepted as true parables of God's reign.

In dealing with the *creatura*, the creaturely world, Barth indicates that there is also "a theatre and setting for God's being, activity and speech, and therefore for this history of drama" (*CD* IV/3.1:136). The *theatrum gloriae Dei* is the external basis of the covenant that conversely is its internal basis (*CD* III/1.§41). For Barth, creaturely *esse* and *nosse* are related and conditioned mutually. Even human sin cannot shake the constancy and the essence in the life of cosmos. *Creatura*, the creaturely world, exists as the sphere and place of sin and also as the sphere and place of reconciliation. The persistence and constancy of the creaturely world corresponds to the faithfulness of God the Creator to the creation. In consideration of the relation between Jesus Christ as the one Word of God and the lights of the creaturely word, Barth stated, "The creaturely world, the cosmos, the nature given to man in his sphere and the nature of this sphere, has also such its own lights and truths and therefore its own speech and words" (*CD* IV/3.1:139).

Thanks to the faithfulness of God the Creator, the persistence, self-witness, and lights are not extinguished by the corruption of the relationship between God and humans. Therefore we do not ignore that there are lights, words, and truths of the created cosmos. The created lights exist in distinction from the light of the self-revelation of God in Jesus Christ and again before, during, and after the epiphany of Jesus Christ. Nevertheless, these lights do not exist apart from and independent of the epiphany of Jesus Christ. "As the divine work of reconciliation does not negate the divine work of creation, nor deprive it of meaning, so it does not take from it its lights and language, nor tear asunder the original connecion between creaturely *esse* and creature *nosse*" (*CD* IV/3.1:139).

In order to avoid misunderstanding or confusion of created lights in the cosmos with God's self-revelation, Barth speaks of them as "the luminosity of the creaturely world." In this way Barth is able to speak positively of the persistent luminosity of the world. In the *theartum gloriae Dei* there is a luminosity of the creaturely world, which means the lights of its own words and truths. In this perspective, Barth boldly affirms that "dangerous modern expressions like the revelation of creation or primal revelation might be given a clear and unequivocal sense . . . They are its own revelation, i.e., those of the *creatura* or *ktiais* itself" (*CD* IV/3.1: 140).

The distinctiveness of the cosmos not merely *in re* but also *in intellectu* is known and knows, is seen and sees, and is apprehended and apprehends:

> In relation to man as *pars pro toto* we may say that the world created by God has truth in *intellectu* as well as in reality . . . the world created by God is also (although not merely) a text which may be read and understood, and at the same time its own reader and expositor . . . These do not light up the world with the same brightness as God does in His Word . . . But they bring illumination. They prevent the world from being merely dark, or being plunged into absolute gloom by the sin of man. (*CD* IV/3.1:141).

If there is still a measure of brightness in its relativity, and in so far as the terrestrial truths and words—albeit all its limitation—are actually spoken and heard, they are not, they are "at least an obstacle to the onrush of chaos into the terrestrial life" (*CD* IV/3.1:141).

For this reason it would be foolish and absurd to despise, ignore, and deny them because we cannot live without them. Rather we are to be grateful for them. The intelligibility and intelligence of the divinely created world and cosmos makes itself known to humans and actually comes to know and be known to humans to the extent that it addresses its reason to the grasping of these lines, continuities, and constants. "What is thus bright and audible and true, is always the one in the many, the general in the particular, the steadfast in change, the recurrent in alteration, the identical in the different" (*CD* IV/3.1:142). The objective and the subjective reason of the cosmos assume a multiform, including "the many, the particular, the change, the alteration and diversity" (*CD* IV/3.1:142) rather than assuming reduction and exhaustion into mathematical or other rational patterns or laws. The only thing excluded is chaos.

Although Barth took into consideration the guaranteeing lights of the cosmos, he refrains from speaking of them as "revelation" because no faith is required to grasp them in conversing between the world and itself. What is needed to grasp them is "only the application of the good but limited gift of common sense" because it is not a covenant of God with humans, but "a kind of divinely ordained concordat between the world and itself" (*CD* IV/3.1:143). Although the world as such cannot produce parables of God's kingdom, it remains something because "its result is merely the peace immanent to the world as such in and in spite of every contradiction and conflict" (*CD* IV/3.1:143). Therefore we Christians must be grateful to the world for the fact that the cosmos "maintains the immanent peace and displays it as a created light of its created stability" (*CD* IV/3.1:143).

Barth now characterizes the existence of the cosmos as existence for one another, which is the basic form of what is lasting, persistent, and constant in the creaturely world. The existence in the form of existence for one another in the intelligible and the intelligent cosmos is not a static but a dynamic reality "impregnable, unalterable and indestructible" within its limits. The multiform cosmos has a definite rhythm involving constant repetition, the recurrence of the encounter, the continual resumption of the converse. In the persistent and constant endurance of the creaturely world and cosmos there is "always beginning, cessation and new beginning," "constant discovery, concealment and rediscovery, continual coming and going, no becoming without perishing, but no perishing without new becoming" (*CD* IV/3.1:144).

God does not take away freedom and movement and the process of evolutionary-ecological existence in one another and for one another in the realm of creation. In the natural and cosmic existence of interrelationships, "the general divides off into the particular and the particular is subordinated to the general. The whole is only in the part, yet the part, too, is only in the whole" (*CD* IV/3.1:144). Barth's idea of whole/part system in the interrelationship of intelligible and intelligent cosmos points to the biblical idea of dynamic rhythm "in the course of an unbroken and never-ceasing cycle" (Gen 8:22) (*CD* IV/3.1:144). However, Barth refrains from unreservedly equating the life of God with the rhythm of a terrestrial being in and with time. God is not bound to, compared to, or measured by the evolutionary rhythm of terrestrial being. What moves in this rhythm is the intelligible and intelligent world to which this dynamic rhythm is given as constant and sure existence of the world by God.

The rhythm of the cosmos has definite accents appearing with a certain inner contrariety in the first creation story. The contrariety is intra-terrestrial and therefore relative, appearing as the inner peace of creation. His idea leads Barth to speak of natural and spiritual laws in matters of a part of the cosmic existence, namely, the "existence of creaturely being in certain specific sections and circles" (*CD* IV/3.1:146). In an encounter and converse between the intelligible and the intelligent cosmos, "there are disclosed and discovered and revealed and established certain processes, sequences, courses, connections and relationships of known being and its knowledge." "Laws are formulae for the relative necessity of certain objective and subjective processes and sequences" (*CD* IV/3.1:146). The laws of natural science regarding the encounter and converse between intelligible and intelligent cosmos are valid formulae in their relative validity. In this regard Barth addresses the findings of natural science and technology in a clear and positive way (*CD* IV/3.1:147).

The self-shining lights of the creaturely world embrace the laws of the natural world and intellectual world, empirical science, yes, even technology. Barth argues:

> The so-called exact sciences built on empirical observation and investigation on the one side and mathematical logic on the other, are constituted in virtue of the knowability and in the knowledge of laws. And human technics in the narrower modern sense consist in the application of laws. We do not live only, but we do live also, by and with the fact that there are knowledge and technics in this sense, namely, that there are, as relatively tenable and usable working hypothesis, these formulae which have partial and formal validity within the world as descriptions of relative necessities, and which really count, and may be counted upon, when they are defined in this way" (*CD* IV/3.1:147).

For Barth, natural science and technology can be indications that God is the Creator of the world and Lord of all natural laws. In his volume of posthumous work Barth had written: "[The universe] in its ... movement—from the so-called celestial body into the red and white blood corpuscle in our vein hallows ... the name of God infinitely more seriously than all what can come into consideration as his sanctification under and through us humans."[59]

Barth's reflection on scientific theology calls for, beyond the limitation of *theologia naturalis*, a new paradigm of theology of nature in a way that "all sciences might ultimately be theology." In addition, Barth's definition of God as the all-encompassing, changing, and transforming reality (*Der ganz Ändernde*) makes theological statements analogical, scientific, and critical. The theological concept of God's future and its wholeness is not yet fully present but articulates the eschatological act of God's coming in the future. However, Barth's root metaphor of the "revolution of God" functions rather as an art of hermeneutics of suspicion in critically and realistically calling into question the ideological bias of the science/power nexus which is oftentimes dangerous in the hands of the powerful in the scientific community. As long as Jesus Christ is expressed as the partisan of the poor, or as long as God as the *ganz Ändernde* is on the side of the poor, Barth would be more concerned about unveiling hidden motives and interests behind the human project of scientific rationality. This said, metaphorical discourse in the relation of theology and science remain challenged but not eradicate by Barth's root metaphor of the revolution of God, redirecting them for the sake of social justice.

As far as the observation and investigation of natural science discovered in its partial validity the dynamic rhythm and life-circle of the numinosity of the creaturely world, they are not excluded but included and integrated into theological discourse on divine action with the world. In other words, Barth's reflection on the created cosmos, which may be a form of secular parables of God's kingdom, does not contradict the project of theology of nature, in which interdisciplinary discussion, dialogue, and integration accepts and actualizes the findings of natural science, in its relative validity in matters of the intelligible and the intelligent cosmos. For Barth, theology has no right to ignore, despise, or deny scientific laws and observations out of an encounter and conversation between the intelligible and intelligent world and itself.

Given these facts, for Barth there are lights and riddles in the creation. To the extent that the creature has its own existence, rhythm, contrariety, regularity, and freedom, so it has its own mystery (*CD*

---

59. Barth, *Das christliche Leben*, 189 (*KD* IV/4 [Nachlass]).

IV/3.1:149). We are grateful to the shining of the creaturely lights because they are a truth to be counted upon. Therefore, the creaturely world as the *theatrum gloriae Dei* functions as "the sphere or location, of the event and revelation of reconciliation" that is the triumph of God's glory (*CD* IV/3.1:151). Barth's main concern in this regard is to articulate these creaturely realms in light of the self-witness of the messianic prophet, Jesus Christ, because the self-declaration of God in the prophecy of Jesus Christ does not end up excluding the self-attestations of the creaturely world but rather encompassing the quest for a positive understanding of them (*CD* IV/3.1:152).

Barth's dialectical approach to the relation between the *gloria Dei* and its *theartum*, namely, the lights of this *theatrum*, assumes the way of relativization, institution, and integration. God in God's self-attestation challenges and critically relativizes the shining lights of the universe, but institutes and integrates them positively up into the light of God's self-attestation in Jesus Christ. In other words, they are integrated and taken up and invested with the limited power of creaturely self-witness by the eternal Word of God.

The lights in creation as a conscription to the service of God's glory can be true words in speaking of the goodness of original creation. Such lights of creatures, in witnessing to the prophecy of Jesus Christ, can be the rhythm of creation from the night to the day. Barth could hear such lights in the music of Mozart, which implies the peace of the creation, or conversely its profound enigmatic character and the call for thankfulness. Therefore Barth calls for plural forms of lights, words, and truths. In so doing, Barth encourages us to attentively and constantly listen to them in the creaturely sphere and look for them in every direction. The character of the riddle of creaturely lights cannot be reduced to a single form, but the voices uttered and heard in creation take manifold forms (*CD* IV/3.1:158). These lights and truths can be called the world logoi, which are relativized yet instituted and integrated by the eternal Logos of God. For Barth, listening to the polyphony of the creaturely universe, which is the external basis of the covenant, meant listening to the symphony that God alone elected, determined, and evoked from eternity (*CD* IV/3.1:159).

According to Barth, creaturely realms have their own place and sphere of action within the continuing self-converse of creation. If this dialogue leads to lights, words, and truths as the emergence of constants of intelligible and intelligent cosmic being, it can offer foundations and materials for the continuation of the dialogue, the end of which is not yet in sight because of eschatological reservation (*CD* IV/3.1:163). The dialectical relation between covenant and creation lies in the former relativizing the latter on behalf of institution and integration. In so doing, a creaturely dimension of *theologia naturalis* is not excluded, despised, or destroyed, but is to be included, established, and glorified as the theatre of God's glory in light of the prophecy of Jesus Christ.

In this context and in harmony with God's Word, the truths and the words of the creature acquire a similar final force, value, and significance. "The Heavens declare the glory of God; the firmament sheweth his handywork" (Ps 19:1, KJV). In the power of God's integration, the words and truths in the creaturely realms are instituted, installed, and ordained to the *ministerium Verbi Divini*. As service to the Word of God, they reflect the eternal light of God and correspond to God's truth. We hear Barth's strong concern for the natural world in the following statement: "They speak of the meaning and determination of the creaturely world for what God is and does for man and what he may be and do for God. In the mirror of this final self-declaration of theirs we have a reflection of the final self-declaration of their Creator in His great act of peace" (*CD* IV/3.1: 164).

However, Barth does not intend to provide examples of such true words outside the church (*CD* IV/3.1:135). He would be hesitant to canonize or give dogmatic status to such extraordinary ways and free communications of Jesus Christ (*CD* IV/3.1:133f). Nevertheless, he offers criteria by dubbing "the fruits which such true words seems to hear in the outside world" as supplementary and auxiliary criterion (*CD* IV/3.1:127–28). Barth's hesitation of giving dogmatic status to true words in the outside world is by and large due to his analogical reflection on the secular parables of creaturely realms. Extraordinary and free communications of Jesus Christ in the outside world as *ministerium Verbi Divini* are not meant to be identical unreservedly with the Word of God, or in dissimilar relation to it. They are grasped as parables of the reign of God, of which natural theology, as such, is not competent to understand and clarify.

According to Barth, God speaks of Godself in creation. The creation is a revelation of God's divinity. This makes it possible to interpret a relation between God and creature in terms of an analogy between divine primeval picture (*Urbild*) and a creaturely image (*Abbild*). This position is in contrast to the insistence of the Erlangen school (that included those such as Paul Althaus), which understood that the creation as such is the subject of divine revelation on the basis of the inherently creaturely quality given by God the Creator. Rather, Barth's concept of "creation revelation" (*Schöpfungoffenbarung* (*KD* III/1:426) retains, as the true Word of God, God's silence, No, and judgment (*CD* III/1:372).

The self-authenticating Word of God is not dependent upon or found in an immediate experience with the reality of our life. In this regard Barth's language of creation history as saga points to his hermeneutical concern, in contrast to a historical-critical consciousness and method.[60] Thus scientific language and concepts are relativized in view of God's creation and the resurrection of Jesus Christ. Creation becomes a pure prehistory in which a language of saga points basically to a forwarding aspect, namely, to the time of hope and expectation. Therefore Barth breaks through the narrow horizon of the historical-critical consciousness by the fact that creation as prehistory is a preparation, way, and means toward the covenant.

When *analogia entis* or *theologia naturalis* is to be seen, included, and transformed in terms of the divine initiative action of grace, then, like Calvin, Barth says, "the knowledge of God in Christ includes a real knowledge of the true God in creation" (NuG:108). When we see the interconnection between the material and the formal *imago* in light of God's reconciliation in Jesus Christ with the world, Barth's discourse of secular parables provides a counterproposal to the negative side of *theologia naturalis*. This negative side refers to *theologia naturalis vulgaris*, which is vulnerable to the threatening danger of nothingness. If "through the gift of revelation and faith, human as a rational creature is together with his world miraculously included in these," there is no need of "proclaiming the *analogia entis* as a common 'basis' of Christian and pagan theology"(NuG:104).

As Barth asks, "How can one speak of these things unless the one revelation of Christ in the Old and New Testaments is taken into ac-

---

60. As far as saga is understood as an intuitive, poetically designed picture-language in expressing the temporally and spatially restricted prehistorical reality of history (*CD* III/1:81), Barth utilized his thesis in *Romans II*—"the historical critics, it seems to me, need to be more critical!" (R II:x)—in the context of creation for illustrating and mobilizing his critique of nothingness in a social-historical area

count? Does not the Bible relate all that Brunner calls a special 'preserving grace' to prophecy and fulfillment, to law and gospel, to the covenant and the Messiah, to Israel and to the Church, to the children of God and their future redemption?" (NuG:84). If the creaturely world as the *theatrum gloriae Dei* receives its lights, words, and truths from its Creator, "dangerous modern expressions like 'revelation of creation' or 'primal revelation' might be given a clear and unequivocal sense in this respect" (*CD* IV/3.1:140). However, regarding this statement Küng accused Barth of correcting his previous position without publicly admitting it, unlike Augustine in his *Retrtactions*.[61]

In fact, in his early stage Barth never marginalized the possibility of God's speaking to the world outside the walls of Christianity. This aspect gives a critical and transforming shape and contour to Barth's dogmatic theology in a universal sense. Theology *von Gott her* refers to God's concern about the world from the beginning. If *analogia fidei* associated with *Deus dixit* and *von Gott her* relativizes and integrates the ontological dimension of *analogia entis*, it means that Barth's christological concentration deepens and actualizes God's way to the world in light of the resurrection and God's reconciliation in Jesus Christ. Hence, *analogia fidei* institutes, sharpens, and directs *analogia entis* toward the grace of God in Jesus Christ for the world. So understood, *analogia entis* is not replaced by an ontological form of language (as in the case of Jüngel) but rather established and integrated, transformed materially and socially by way of the inclusive Christology. That is a christological *assumptio* of *analogia entis* in transformation of its traditional and metaphysical structure toward eschatological consummation.

For Barth, the world has a parabolic character in pointing to the kingdom of God that is coming. Not *analogia entis* but *analogia fidei* has interest in such parables in a critical view of what is really happening to the world. *Theologia naturalis* associated with *analogia entis* would be vulnerable—because of individualistic/bourgeois encapsulation of God—to the lordless powers of nothingness in the social, cultural domain. What is in need of parable must be subjected to the criterion of the Word of God and be in correspondence with the kingdom of God.

At this point, Moltmann argues that the inclusive sense of reconciliation in Barth's thought-form "constitutes the ontological connection

---

61. Küng, *Does God Exist?* 527.

between Christ and all human beings." Thus Barth would be in sympathy with Tertullian's concept of "the naturally Christian soul" (*anima naturaliter christiana*).[62] Therefore "the truth of God shines out in history, the lights and truths of the created world are lit up also." In this regard Moltmann seeks to reconcile the contradiction between *analogia entis* and *anlogia fidei* in favor of a dialectical play of reciprocal knowing—*analogia entis* in *analogia fidei*.[63]

However, this dialectical interplay must not be understood as reaching the point where Barth allows room for *analogia entis* without reservation. What *analogia entis* truly wants to express can become possible only when *analogia fidei* and *relationis* are taken seriously with respect to covenant, creation, and reconciliation. As Barth stressed, his concern about *theologia naturalis* in his confrontation with Brunner was that "A 'true' *theologia naturalis* can exist only where man's eyes have been opened by Christ" (NuG:97). In this framework, we notice in Barth's rejection of natural theology his simultaneous affirmation of the creatures in Barth's own way.[64]

In reflection on the known and unknown God in his posthumously released ethics of reconciliation,[65] Barth stated that God is known and at the same time unknown for us all. God is not absent in God's hiddenness but is present: not concealed but revealed. God has a holy name—and so becomes known. However, this God is not completely known: "O that you would tear open the heavens and come down, so that the mountains would quake at your presence" (Isa 64:1, NRSV). The Christian petition of "hallowed be thy name" calls for God's glory in the world, in the church, and first and above all, in one's own heart and life. At this point, Barth remarkably discusses an objective knowledge of God in the field of the world, namely, God's creaturely world in its entirety. As far as we recognize and confess God as the almighty God who is the Creator of heaven and earth, the glory of God is great in this realm. In the universe in its animated and nonanimated movement, we discern a glory of God. "For the creation waits with eager longing for the revealing of the children of God" (Rom 8:19, NRSV).

62. Moltmann, *Experiences in Theology*, 75–76.

63. Ibid.,78.

64. For this insight I am indebted to Peter Winzeler's article "Verneinte Nature der bejahten Kreatur," 309–26.

65. *CD* IV/4:115–53.

In this regard, a Christian petition of "hallowed be thy name" has a practical-existential form in view of hallowing God's name in natural history as well as in world history. If God is made known through God's free grace, if God determines and orients human nature and human essence for and toward Godself, Barth is convinced— surprisingly enough—of the objective knowledge of God as the Creator of human nature. However, this objective possibility of knowing God in the natural world, world history and human nature is not based on the fact that the human is capable of knowing God in accordance with human natural capacity. If God's objective knowledge does not correspond to human subjective capacity of knowing God, it is not God but humanity who is at fault.[66] In a Barthian way of relativization and integration of *theologia naturalis* in light of a Christian petition on "hollowed be thy name," we perceive that Barth deepens the insight of the religious socialist Kutter and his *Sie Müssen!*[67]

God's objective knowledge is much stronger and more effective than human unfaithfulness and ignorance. God's openness for the world is much stronger than God's closedness against it. "These impressions should not be generalized and systematized along the lines of natural theology, but when they lay hold of us with serious force they cannot not be denied."[68] Barth's concern about relativizing, instituting, and integrating socially and materially *theologia naturalis* from his time in Safenwil onwards becomes obvious in his special attention to the passage of Luke 16:8: "And his master commended the dishonest manager because he had acted shrewdly; for the children of this age are more shrewd in dealing with their own generation than are the children of light" (NRSV). This is the basis for Barth's reflection on parables of heaven's kingdom that becomes manifest and obvious in Jesus's use of profane processes and relations to describe it. Barth's so-called doctrine of lights may be understood as his counterproposal to natural theology, a dimension of which is not rejected or excluded without qualification but embraced, recognized, and transformed in terms of an objective knowledge of God in the natural world.

66. Ibid., 121.
67. *CD* IV/4:121–22.
68. *CD* IV/4:122.

At this point we see Barth's theological-ecological concerns in light of God's gracious covenant with all living creatures in creation. The covenant of grace is what is prefigured in the natural life (*CD* III/1:144). All living creatures together with humans are invited and welcomed to the table of the Lord (*CD* III/1:208). Thus Barth does not regard a biblical idea of *dominum terrae* (Gen 1:26) as the authentic definition granted to humans. Rather he rejected an unlimited mastery of human technology over the earth (*CD* III/1:205). Barth's ecological direction is in opposition to the modernistic view of nature without history, in which *Homo faber* as calculating observer put the earth under human disposal for its own sake.

Barth's concepts of preservation, accompaniment, and rule articulates his expression of God's faithfulness to the creaturely world on the basis of God's gracious election instead of on the basis of the assumption of *creatio continuata*. If creation is under the sway of divine providence, this does not repeat or continue creation. Rather it corresponds to it in the continued life and history of the creature. God's lordship, which refers to the lordship of God's being in love and freedom, knows no necessity. It is more than necessary. God's freedom is to transcend all that is other than God, as well as to be immanent within it. Therefore Barth interprets God's providence not as *continuata creatio* but as a *continuatio creationis* (*CD* III/3:8). If the meaning of creation is God's gracious covenant, the necessary relevance to God's freedom tells that God's gracious election is God's gracious covenant. At this point, we must not lose sight of the *manifesatatio gratiae*, i.e., Jesus Christ as its ontic ground (*CD* III/3:73). Just as God desires God's complete transcendence, so God desires to be completely immanent to God's creatures.

Furthermore, Barth's concept of divine providence points to a biblical text of eschatological panentheism—that God will be all in all (1 Cor 15:28). This text means for Barth that God in the final revelation will come to God's zeal within the creatures without ceasing to be God as the Creator, different from God's creature (*KD* III/3:98). This reveals Barth's idea of God as transcendent in God's immanence. God is immanently transcendent and transcendently immanent. In this light, Barth makes a counterthesis to a pantheistic or panentheistic alteration between God and the world.

However, God can do even more than this. God's immanence indwells the other by not taking away this creaturely life. God's relation to the world is not bound to the quantum and quale of a certain mode of action that uniformly proceeds from God (*CD* II/1:315). The eschatological indwelling and rest with God's people and all living creatures is already projected in the protological sense of God's Sabbath. Sabbath is the crown of God's work of creation (*CD* III/3:8). Creation, which is under the rule of God's providence, corresponds to it in the continued life and history of the creature, rather than repeating or continuing creation. God the Creator is not a world principle developing in an infinite series of productions (*CD* III/3: 7).

Barth's idea of Sabbath distinguishes his thinking from a Whiteheadian philosophy of process. In God's rest, God's freedom is revealed. In God's self-limitation through the Sabbath, we make note of God's love in freedom. In God's rest, God does not cease to be the Creator. In the Sabbath rest, God does not continue God's work of creation. In other words, God completed it at the creation of the world and human beings. God's freedom revealed in God's rest is characteristic of the true divinity of the Creator. In God's rest, God reveals God's love. A world principle without such limitation of the Creator's activity would be a substance without love, in contrast to God's rest. God's rest distinguishes God "from a world-principle self-developing and self-evolving in infinite sequence" (*CD* III/1:215). God who loves in freedom is God in the rest of Sabbath.

God does not create the seventh day. Divine cessation is at the same time divine perfection of creation. Here Barth understood divine action of the seventh day as *creatio continua* or *continuatio creationis*, which is "the sign of the continuation of this work on very different lines." In it God wholly identifies Godself with the world and humanity, "willing to be fully immanent even in His transcendence" (*CD* III/3:8). Sabbath, which is regarded as God's celebrating accession to the throne against the created world, as inauguration of divine rule over it, belongs to the essence and continued existence of creatures and hence to the creation of the world. God's *menuha* (God's final rest) consists rather in God's being and in this regard is not created (*CD* III/1:220).

Not in the sense of deism but in terms of God's own rest God is relational to and active for the world, analogously speaking. In completing and crowning all creation, "God ... made Himself temporal and human, i.e., He linked Himself in a temporal act with the being and purpose and course of the world, with the history of man" (*CD* III/1:216). According to Barth, the Sabbath refers to the Creator's immanent presence in God's creaturely world. Therefore Barth expresses the Sabbath as God's world-immanence, an event of anticipation of revelation in Jesus Christ, furthermore as the crown of creation. As far as the Sabbath is the divine presence in the world, God's Yes to all living creatures in highlighting of the Sabbath justifies the *regnum* of all nature. The Sabbath of God from the beginning presupposes the Sabbath of the final rest which is promised in Heb 4:9–10: "So then, a Sabbath rest still remains for the people of God; for those who enter God's rest also cease from their labors as God did from his" (NRSV).

The Sabbath of God stands in messianic hope, and what looks toward the promise of God is not the law but the gospel from the beginning. Thus, Barth's fundamental thesis that creation is the external ground of covenant needs to be understood in a way that God's love is not anthropocentric, but it is to deepen God's universal grace toward natural life of all creatures in the ecological realm. As far as the Sabbath of creation points to the immanence of God the Creator in the world as God's creation, Barth does not hesitate to stress God's radical indwelling in the world. Barth accepts creation as "the mask of God," in the fine phrase of Luther, to the degree that the history of creation is the history of God's glory. The history of God's glory takes place in, with, and under that of creation (*CD* III/3:19).

Consequently in his posthumously released lecture—reminiscent of Luther's metaphor of creation as *larvae Dei* (*WA* 17 II:192, 28–31)—Barth boldly affirmed the thesis that God is objectively known from creation's side. A theology of correlation in a Barthian fashion may serve to include, integrate, and transform creaturely realms into a mask of God—witnessing to the coming future of God.

> God's name, then, is already holy in the world that he created good long before Christianity begins to pray for its hallowing or to be zealous for the honor of God. Is not his name holy in every blade of grass and every snowflake? Apart from us and even in spite of us, it is holy in every breath we draw, in every thought we think, in every effort of man, undertaken and executed well or badly . . . to subdue the earth to himself both in practice and in theory (Gen 1:28).[69]

---

69. Ibid., 121.

SEVEN   Martin Luther in the Theology of Karl Barth

ACCORDING TO BARTH, A CHURCH DOGMATICS MUST BE DEFINED BY Christology and decidedly and wholly christological. The revealed Word of God is identical with Jesus Christ who is witnessed to in the Scripture and proclaimed in the church. The identification of the Word of God with Jesus Christ leads to a christological thought-form in which the exclusivity of Jesus Christ should reach out, at the maximum, to the christological inclusivity of the world and people outside Christianity. Jesus Christ, who is the objective reality of revelation and the objective possibility of revelation (*CD* I/2:25), is identical with the reality of God's revelation in history. Therefore dogmatics, which is christologically justified, takes Jesus Christ as *vere Deus et vere homo* as its primary task. He was the Word or the Son of God as the man who was Jesus of Nazareth. This man Jesus of Nazareth was the Word of God, or God's Son.

By emphasizing Jesus Christ as the center of the new covenant between God and human beings, Barth's theology functions as a dialectical analogy in terms of theo-anthropology. It describes a theology interested in emphasizing the covenantal relationship between God and humans.[1] This theo-anthropology is concretized in light of Jesus Christ as the substance of election in which God's covenant with Israel—as the natural environment of Jesus—retains a positive significance.

Barth's christological development was propelled by his discovery of ancient Christology, namely, the relationship of *anhypostasis* and *en-*

---

1. As Barth says, "'theology' in the literal sense, means the science and doctrine of God. A very precise definition of the Christian endeavor in this respect would really require the more complex term theo-anthropology. For an abstract doctrine of God has no place in the Christian realm, only a 'doctrine of God and of man,' a doctrine of the commerce and communion between God and man." (Barth, *Humanity of God*, 11).

hypostasis with respect to the Reformed doctrine of *extra Calvinisticum*. The union of the eternal Logos with human nature, in other words the humanity of Christ, exists before its union with the Logos. The human nature of Christ has no personality of its own; it is *anhypostatos*. Or positively speaking, it is *enhypostatos*; it has personality, subsistence, and reality only in its union with the Logos of God (*UCR* I:157). In keeping with the Reformed position, Barth understands the concept of the hypostatic union (*unio personalis*) of the Logos with human nature to be the immediate union. In discerning a Nestorian separation of the divine and human natures in the *extra Calvinisticum*, however, Barth, along the lines of the Lutheran position, is critical of something unsatisfactory about the Reformed theory, which has amounted to a "fatal speculation about the being and work of the *logos asarkos*" (*CD* IV/1:181).

In contrast to the Reformed position, the Lutheran position is more interested in the communion of natures (the so-called *communicatio idiomatum*), in which the hypostatic union is seen as a consequence of this communion. The participation of the human Jesus in the divine attributes (such as omnipresence, omnipotence, and the like) underscores the Lutheran doctrine of the ubiquity of Christ's human nature. Regarding the concept of *communicatio idiomatum*, Barth doubted whether we have here a kind of reciprocal relation: revealedness instead of revelation, a state instead of an event (*CD* I/2:164). For Barth, the event of the *unio hypostatica* has to be understood not only as a *completed* event but also as a completed *event*.

Of interest in this chapter is an analysis of Barth's thought in Christology and an evaluation of his contribution to improving the ecumenical controversy between Reformed theology and Lutheran theology regarding *assumptio carnis* in light of a model of *anhypostasis and enhypostasis*.

Karl Barth and *Enhypostasis/Anhypostasis*

Along the lines of the Nicene-Constantinopolitian creed, Barth interprets the preexistence of Jesus Christ as the act of God who works for us in incarnation, revelation, and reconciliation. The confession of the preexistence of Jesus Christ implies that the time and history of sinful creatures are integrated and assumed into the intradivine life of the triune God. However, in favoring *anhypostasis* and *enhypostasis*, Barth rejects *logos asarkos* together with *logoi spermatikoi* (a formless Christ or a Christ principle) as an abstraction. It is helpful at this point to consider the ancient debate on Christology before explicating Barth's inclusive dimension of Christology.

In the Christology of the ancient church, the main problem centered on how God is related to Jesus, in other words, the relationship of the divine nature of Jesus to the human nature. At Chalcedon (451), christological dogma was formulated as two natures, divine and human, in the one person of Jesus Christ. Avoiding extremes such as the Nestorian (the unity of the person) and the Eutychean (absorbing the human into the divine), the creed affirmed that there was no division or separation (against Nestorianism) and at the same time that there was no confusion or change (against Eutycheanism) between the two natures. At the fifth ecumenical council in Constantinople (553), the purpose was to interpret the Chalcedonian creed in such a way as to relieve Nestorian objections.

In the ninth century John Grammaticus articulated the hypostatic unity to the point that the human nature of Jesus cannot be separated from the divine hypostasis at any single moment. This articulation is the so-called doctrine of the *enhypostasis* of human nature (Jesus) in the divine nature of Christ. Leontius of Byzantium, who was one of the neo-Chalcedonian representatives, affirmed the unity of the man Jesus with the Son of God in the formula of the *enhypostasis* of Jesus in the eternal Logos. The man Jesus has the ground of his human existence not in humanity but "in" an impersonal humanity of Christ. The designation "en"-hypostasis expressed Jesus's human nature in unification with the Logos from the beginning.[2]

This teaching of *enhypostasis* cannot be adequately understood apart from the doctrine of the *anhypostasis*. *Anhypostasis* as a negation of the true humanity is inseparably connected with *enhypostasis*, meaning that Jesus Christ has personal existence but only in and through the eternal Logos. If the Word is incarnated in the man Jesus Christ, his humanity is not abolished but fulfilled in union with the person, *the hypostasis*, of the Word of God. In terms of this doctrine, Leontius was able to hold that the humanity of Christ always exists in unity with his divinity, that is, in the eternal Logos. The positive side of this doctrine is called *enhyposta-*

---

2. Andresen, et al., *Lehrentwicklung im Rahmen der Katholizität*, 277–78; cf. *CD* IV/2: 49–50, 90–91.

sis (existence in the Logos). The negative side is called *anhypostasis* (no other independent mode of existence apart from the eternal Logos). The incarnated Word is always the preexistent eternal Word, Son of God who became man (*enhypostasis*). Jesus the man is always none other than the eternal Son of God (*anhypostasis*).

To what extent does Barth understand *assumptio carnis*, namely, the incarnation of the eternal Son in terms of the *enhypostasis* and *anhypostasis* pattern in his *Church Dogmatics*? In what way does Barth discuss the ancient dogma of Christology, namely, the *anhypostasis* and *enhypostasis* of the human nature of Christ, for explicating the mystery of incarnation? How does Barth explicate hypostatic union (*unio personalis*) in light of *anhypostasis/enhypostasis* Christology?

For him, the divine nature was not made flesh; rather the second person of the Trinity was made flesh. Although *unio personalis* or *unio hypostatica* is to be understood exclusively as the Person of the Logos, (the Reformed understanding of *unio hypostatica* as an immediate union, in a genuine sense of the union of God and humanity in Christ), the union of the natures was understood as a mediated and indirect form. This is why the contrast between God (the infinite) and humanity (the finite) is still preserved in the Reformed framework. If the divine person and not the divine nature assumed human flesh, there would be a sharp differentiation and superordination of the *unio hypostatica* (a Reformed position) vis-à-vis the *communio naturarum* (a Lutheran position).

In the doctrine of incarnation (CDE:229, 257; CD I/2:132–71), Barth furthers his reflection of the incarnation by way of the relation between *anhypostasis* and *enhypostasis* (CDE:263f; CD I/2:163ff).[3] When it comes to the *extra Calvinisticum*, so argues Barth, Luther also indicated an *extra* in due and proper form. Likewise Reformed theology along with the *extra* asserted the *intra* with seriousness. It did not want the reality of the *logos asarkos* abolished in the reality of the *logos ensarkos* (*CD* I/2:169). In arguing that the second person of the Trinity became flesh in a completed event, Barth dealt with the Lutheran-Reformed controversy regarding the art of the unity between divinity and humanity in the one person of Jesus Christ for the sake of the so-called *extra Calvinisticum*, or

---

3. At a minimum, we notice a continuity of his christological concern from his so-called *Göttingen Dogmatics* via his *Die Christliche Dogmatik im Entwurf* (1927) to, finally, his *Church Dogmatics* (I/1 and I/2), although with different emphases and nuances.

"in the framework of the superior orderliness of a theology of the divine action" (*CD* I/2:171).

For Barth, the event of the *unio hypostatica* has to be understood as a dialectial unity between a *completed* event and a completed *event*. In the event of the incarnation, the Word is to be sought in God's complete transcendence, freedom, majesty, and glory (*CD* I/2:165, 168). This core of christological thinking remains central in a positive and critical sense in the christological development of Barth's *Church Dogmatics*.

That God revealed Godself and that the Word became flesh meant for Barth that "God has time for us" (*CD* I/2:45–50) and therefore "the Word became time" (*CD* I/2:50). As God becomes the subject in the event of revelation, the revelation should not be understood as a predicate of time. Rather, God's time for us is constituted by God's becoming present to us in Jesus Christ, namely, *Deus praesens* (*CD* I/2:50).[4]

In view of the christological construction of John 1:14 ("the Word became flesh"), Barth accepted a dogma of the ancient church, the doctrine of two natures in Jesus Christ, in which Barth names "very God and very Man" (*CD* I/2:§15.2). Noticing a monophysite tendency (a complete confusion of the attributes of the divine and human natures as in Eutychianism) in Lutheran Christology (associated with the *communicatio idiomatum* of two natures [*CD* I/2:161, 164]) and in its consequent teaching of ubiquity (*CD* I/2:166), Barth stressed the incarnation as the free act of God in Godself, whether or not God excludes or accepts enfleshment. God cannot cease to be God (*CD* I/2:160).

Unlike in his *Göttingen Dogmatics*, however, Barth no longer followed the consequence of Reformed Christology, which would have threatened to separate the eternal Word from the Word who became flesh (a tendency toward total separation of the attributes of the divine and human natures, as in Nestorianism) (*CD* I/2:161–62). For Barth, the Reformed *totus intra et extra* offers as many difficulties as the Lutheran *totus intra* (*CD* I/2:170).

In the reception of the doctrine of *anhypostasis* and *enhypostasis* of the human nature of Christ, Barth defended himself against the docetic tendency as well as the ebionic (*CD* I/2:163). God and the human in Jesus

---

4. In Barth's judgment, God's eternity includes a past, a present, and a future. Even the eternal God does not live without time. God is supremely temporal. As far as God's eternity is authentic temporality, God is the source of all time. Certainly we assume that in becoming flesh, the Logos has become time.

Christ are so deeply related that Jesus Christ exists as the man only in so far as he exists as God, namely, in the mode of being of the eternal Word of God. In connection with the tradition of the ancient church, Barth defines *anhypostasis* to imply the negative. As the human nature of Christ is subsistent in relationship to the being of God, namely, in the *Seinsweise* (hypostasis, person) of the Word by virtue of the assumption of human flesh, Christ has no independent being apart from his concrete being in God, that is, in the event of union. This is *anhypostatis*, in that the human nature of Jesus does not possess its own instantiation or existence.

However, *enhypostasis* means the positive. The human nature of Christ is subsistent in relationship to the being of God by virtue of the assumption, namely, in the *Seinsweise* (hypostasis, person) of the Word. This divine *Seinsweise* renders human nature subsistent in the event of union; thus it has a concrete, independent existence of its own. It is *enhypostatos* in that the human nature of Jesus has its own instantiation or existence only in the divine Son or Logos (*CD* I/2:163).

Barth often referred to this teaching (*KD* III/2:81f; IV/2:52–53, 100–101) and defended it against modern misunderstandings of it (*KD* I/2:180; IV/2:53). According to the Lutheran position, emphasis is placed on a static-ontic interest of Christology (*CD* I/2:170) by interpreting the hypostatic union as the *complete* event, in that emphasis on condescension threatens the freedom and majesty of God. In contrast, the Reformed position represents a dynamic-noetic interest of Christology (*CD* I/2:170–71), where the hypostatic union is understood as a complete *event*. In the Lutheran-Reformed debate on Christology, Barth moves closer to Reformed Christology with the assertion that the Word who became flesh exists outside (*extra*!) the flesh.[5]

The Reformed tradition does not want to relinquish the actuality of *logos asarkos* and thus wishes to comply with the actuality of *logos asarkos*. The Reformed theologians took seriously the need to understand the *logos asarkos* as *terminus a quo* (point of departure), and the *logos ensarkos* as *terminus ad quem* (aim) for the incarnation (*CD* I/2: 169). However, Barth did not ignore an assumption that *logos asarkos* endangers the hypostatic union, leading to a dual concept of Christ.

---

5. As Barth notes, this so-called *extra Calvinisticum* does not refer to a Calvinistic renewal but represents the ancient church tradition against the Lutheran exclusivity of *logos ensarkos*. In this matter, Athanasius, Cyril of Alexandria, and Hilary of Poitiers anticipate Calvin's thought (*CD* IV/1:181).

Reformed Christology in this regard has no more efficacy than Lutheran Christology in safeguarding the hypostatic union. In addition, when we look at Barth's sharp critique of the doctrine of abstract *logos asarkos* in the later christological development in *Church Dogmatics*, unlike in *CDE*,[6] it would be less convincing to arrange Barth's Christology one sidedly into the Reformed position.[7]

What is characteristic of Barth's understanding of salvation is the stressed perfect tense: "it is complete!" The understanding of the incarnation as *complete* event moves Barth closer to Lutheran Christology than to Reformed Christology. What interests Barth, however, is not to synthesize two different Christologies but to affirm the double christological line of thought already represented in the New Testament: the Pauline-Johanine Christology and the Synoptic Christology. In the debate, the Lutheran position represents "faith-*requirement*" (Glaubens-*bedürfnis*) while the Reformed position represents "faith *necessity*" (Glaubens*notwendigkeit*) (*CD* I/2:171). In the Lutheran excessive emphasis on faith-*requirement* Barth notices that the Lutheran position would be vulnerable to the critique of religion initiated by Feuerbach.[8] Barth's concern is safeguarding the sovereign act of God in the incarnation and ensuring the dynamic relationship between *vere Deus* and *vere Homo* in the hypostatic union through the doctrine of *anhypostasis* and *enhypostasis*.

Barth's Reception of Martin Luther and *Theologia Crucis*

What is more surprising in Barth's thought, however, is his full acceptance of the Lutheran teaching of reciprocity and *perichoresis* between God and the humanity of Jesus (*CD* IV/2:70) by including and integrating the man Jesus into the *perichoresis* of the Trinity (*CD* III/2:65–66). As the Son of God, engaged in the inner Trinitarian life, this man Jesus is exclusively the Jesus in the Gospel of John. The mystery of participation in the circle of the inner life of the Godhead is the very foundation of Jesus's true hu-

---

6. *CDE*:269, 271, cf. Barth, "Church and Culture," 334–54.

7. McCormack, *Critically Realistic*, 358–67. In his interpretation of the incarnation of God in the theology of Barth, McCormack reduces and narrows down Barth's adoption of the anhypostatic/enhypostatic model of Christology only for the sake of the Reformed position. McCormack uses Christology to prove his methodology of *Realdialektik* of God's veiling and unveiling.

8. Barth, "Ludwig Feuerbach," 217–37.

manity (*CD* II/2:66). At vital points, Barth retrieved Luther against Calvin and the Reformed tradition. Barth's retrieval of *theologia crucis* becomes manifest in his attempt to combine the doctrine of the two natures with the doctrine of humiliation and exaltation of the incarnated Son of God in the orthodox Protestant dogmatics of the seventeenth century.

Along the lines of Luther, Barth developed his theology of the cross in the context of his doctrine of reconciliation by giving a new interpretation to ancient Christology, i.e., the dogma of two natures and the doctrine of the two states of humiliation and exaltation of Jesus Christ in the dogmatics of post-Reformation theology. As the *promissio* is central for Luther, so the messianic, inclusive, and dynamic history of Christ in the cross and resurrection is central for Barth. For Barth, a *theologia gloriae* in the resurrection can have no meaning without including a *theologia crucis* within it. Barth expressed the theology of the cross with respect to "Jesus Christ the Lord as Servant" (*CD* IV/1:157–642) and "Jesus Christ the Servant as Lord" (*CD* IV/2:3–613) in his doctrine of reconciliation.

Thus Barth carries out the modification and dynamization of the ancient dogma of two natures and the doctrine of two states within the framework of orthodox Lutheran dogmatics. Unlike his early period of dialectical theology in which Barth put a strong emphasis on the qualitative difference between God and the human being (R II), in his late lecture in 1956 Barth amended his Christology in light of the God of Abraham, Isaac, and Jacob.[9] In Jesus Christ, God chose not to be against human beings. Therefore, Barth changed his own provocative expression of "God everything, human being nothing," which he referred to as not only "a terrible simplification, but rather complete nonsense" (*CD* IV/1:89).

To develop his Christology, Barth is cautious about using the classic categories of the two natures, albeit recognizing the importance of the Chalcedonian formulation of *vere Deus* and *vere homo*. In giving a christological basis to reconciliation, he deals with important aspects of 1) the incarnation ("The Son of God went to the far country"), 2) the cross ("The judge becomes judged in our place"), and 3) the resurrection ("The judgment of the Father"), as the humiliation of the Son of God is the theme of *CD* IV/1. The exaltation of the Son of Man is the theme of *CD* IV/2. In this framework, Barth deals with Calvin's threefold understand-

---

9. Cf. Barth, *Humanity of God*, 44–45.

ing of Christology: i.e., the priestly office in *CD* IV/1, the kingly office in *CD* IV/2, and the prophetic office in *CD* IV/3.

Under the heading of "Jesus Christ the Lord as Servant" (*CD* IV/1: 157–642), Barth uses the metaphor of the prodigal son going into the far country. God chose freely to reconcile Godself with human beings in Jesus Christ. The obedience of Jesus Christ is described in various ways in the New Testament such as by God's "emptying himself or becoming a servant" (Phil 2:7), by "humbling himself," by "going to the cross" (Phil 2:8), or by suffering (Heb 5:8). However, this witness must be seen in relation to Jesus Christ as a Jewish man. Otherwise Docetism would result. That Jesus Christ reveals himself in the flesh means to be sinful and therefore under the wrath of God. Barth characterized this fact in terms of the deity of Christ, in which God remains God and does not stop God's sovereignty even in God's humiliation.

As a matter of fact, God has taken unto Godself in the intradivine life, the conditions of the historical person and life of Jesus through the incarnation. In so doing, "God gives Himself, but He does not give Himself away. He does not give up being God in becoming a creature, in becoming man. He does not cease to be God. He does not come into conflict with Himself" (*CD* IV/1:185).

Albeit distancing himself from kenotic Christology in this paradox, Barth also surpasses what Calvin had said about the exemption of Christ's divinity from the suffering of the cross, and therefore comes close to Luther's understanding. In reflecting on the self-humiliation occurring in the death of the Son of God, Barth amplified the divine potentiality of suffering on the cross. In setting the self-humiliation of God on the cross as the self-revelation of God, Barth defended the divine potentiality of suffering in relation to the self-humiliation of Jesus Christ on the cross: "His death on the cross was and is the fulfillment of . . . the humiliation of the Son of God and exaltation of the Son of man." "It is only then—not before—that there did and does take place the realization of the final depth of humiliation, the descent into hell of Jesus Christ the Son of God, but also his supreme exaltation, the triumphant coronation of Jesus Christ the Son of man" (*CD* IV/2:140–41).

The humiliation of the Son of God does not take place apart from the exaltation of the Son of man, but always in and with it. In terms of "his dialectical strategy of juxtaposition," Barth takes the humiliation of the Son of God to be the basis for the exaltation. Simultaneously he regards the exaltation as the *telos* of the humiliation.¹⁰ This aspect is an integral part of constituting a *theologia crucis* for Barth. As Klappert states, "In Barth, the rejection of paradox in Christology has the function and intention of thinking through the *theologia crucis* consistently to the point of taking the cross up into the concept of God. This shows a theology which depicts God who has a primary place on the cross, that is, on earth."¹¹ Therefore the divine potentiality is the consequent concretization stemming from of the *theologia crucis*. Although God is in contradiction to everything finite, to all human suffering, God participates truly in the humanity of Jesus Christ. What is at stake is that Barth's insistence on the divine potentiality of suffering on the cross as the self-revelation of God is central to his *theologia crucis* and his theology of reconciliation.¹²

The obedience of Jesus is seen in light of God's judgment. For Barth, the coming of the Judge means basically the coming of the Redeemer and Savior. Jesus Christ takes our place as judge and our place as the judged as well. He also takes our judgment through his suffering, crucifixion, and death (*CD* IV/1:244-56). It is in the passion, suffering, and death of Jesus Christ that we encounter the act of God for us. In the suffering and death of Jesus, God-become-man says yes to the world and human beings. This *pro nobis* of his death includes God's terrible *contra nos*, because without the terrible "against us," it would not be divine and holy. The priestly Son of God, who went into the far country of sin and death, suffered our punishment and therefore blocked the source of our destruction: "He has removed the accusation and condemnation and perdition which had passed upon us[,] . . . he has saved us from destruction and rescued us from eternal death" (*CD* IV/1:254).

Just as the first part of Barth's Christology deals with Jesus Christ as the priestly Son of God in whom the condescension and humiliation of God are seen in relation to his taking upon himself human sin, so the second part of it, deals with Jesus Christ as the royal (messianic) Son of Man who is exalted in his homecoming. True fellowship with God comes through his kenotic obedience, even to the point of enduring death. Jesus Christ is to the reconciling God what he is to reconciled humanity. Here Barth, other than in *CD* I/2, does not merely ground his thinking in the

10. Cf. Hunsinger, *Disruptive Grace*, 141-42.
11. Klappert, *Aufweckung des Gekreuzigten*, 180.
12. For the potentiality of humiliation of the Son of God on the cross, cf. *CD* IV/1: 180-92.

Christology of the ancient or medieval church, in which a static, unhistorical ontology prevailed.

For Barth the reconciling God and the reconciled man are taken as a double movement (*CD* IV/3.1:4), that is, from God to humanity and then, with the same seriousness, from humanity to God. This double movement is the one single event of Jesus Christ as complete in divinity and complete in humanity. This refers to "the inner dialectic of the Christian doctrine of reconciliation" (*CD* III/1:5).

The contradiction and unity is fulfilled by Jesus Christ, who exists in his totality as both person and work. The integration of person and work in the one Jesus Christ, which is grounded within the unifying framework between Christology and reconciliation, refers to the acting person and the personal work of the one Jesus Christ. Reconciliation is the history of Jesus Christ himself. Therefore neither can reconciliation be separated from Christology, nor soteriology from Christology: "Revelation takes place in and with reconciliation . . . as the revelation of reconciliation" (*CD* IV/3.1:8). The ancient church dogmas of the two natures, the two states, and the incarnation are modified and integrated into the dialectical unity of the Lord-servant being of Jesus Christ (the reconciling God and the reconciled man of the one Jesus Christ as complete in divinity and complete in humanity).[13]

From this aspect of the unity between person and work, which is related to the dialectic between the reconciling God and the reconciled man, Barth sheds light on Jesus Christ as truly God and truly man. This unity with the double movement between the reconciling God and the reconciled man implies, according Barth, the unity between *vere Deus* and *vere Homo* in Jesus Christ. Therefore the God who reconciles Godself in Jesus Christ is truly God, and the man who is reconciled in Jesus Christ is truly man. The unity between the reconciling God and the reconciled man in the one Jesus Christ means the unity of God and man in Jesus Christ. Therefore, Barth's Christology is anchored in the event of the reconciliation. The doctrine of the two natures is an implication of the doctrine of reconciliation in orientation toward the cross. At this point, Barth gives dynamic character to his theology of the cross.

Thus, Barth did not conceive his own Christology on the basis of the incarnation, but rather began with the unity of the person and the

---

13. Cf. Chung, *Karl Barth und die Hegelsche Linke*, 89.

work of the one Jesus Christ in the doctrine of reconciliation. In addition, the double movement between the reconciling God and the reconciled man implies the humiliation of the Son of God (*status exinanitionis*) and the exaltation of man (*status exaltationis*). The covenant between God and human beings is renewed and reconstituted in terms of exchange between the *exinanitio* (the abasement of God) and the *exaltatio* (the exaltation of Man). God, who went into the far country, is the man who returned home. It is in the one Jesus Christ that both took place. In his human existence Jesus Christ suffered and acted as the man in which an exaltation of our humanity took place. Exaltation does not destroy his humanity or abolish his likeness with us: "It means the history of the placing of the humanity common to Him and us on a higher level, on which it becomes and is completely unlike ours even in its complete likeness" (*CD* IV/2:28).

The basis of Christ's *humanitas* consists in: 1) God's eternal decision to reconcile Godself with human beings in Jesus Christ before creation, 2) the historical incarnation, and 3) the true humanity revealed in the resurrection and ascension of Jesus Christ. God's decision to be humiliated in going into the far country means that Jesus Christ as the Son of God became the Son of man through the incarnation. In the incarnation this man is exalted, and this exaltation cannot be separated from God's humiliation in Jesus Christ. As the reconciling God, Jesus Christ is *vere Deus* (i.e., God of self-humiliation [*status exinanitionis*], so Jesus Christ as the reconciled man is *vere homo* (i.e. the man of the exaltation [*status exaltationis*]). With respect to the *humanitas* of Jesus Christ, Barth took the idea of the *unio immediata* to include a *communio naturarum*, yet it "does not remove or alter either the divine essence of the Logos or the human essence existing by Him and in Him," which is "properly and primarily and centrally the divine-human actuality" of Jesus Christ (*CD* IV/2:51).

Barth's View of Luther's Theses: Jesus Christ was Born a Jew, and Jesus Christ as the Mirror of the Fatherly Heart of God

Under the subtitle "The Way of the Son of God into the Far Country" (*CD* IV/1:§59.1), Barth established his theology of Israel in confrontation with Bultmann by reflecting systematically on Luther's provocative thesis that "Jesus was born a Jew" (1523) (*CD* IV/1:167). Confirming Luther's theology as the general rule of all knowledge of God (*CD* II/1:18), Barth explains theologically that the man Jesus is "the mirror of the fatherly heart of God" (*CD* IV/2:249). Along the lines of Luther, Barth says that the existence, the person, and the history of Jesus Christ are the grounds for knowing the Godhead and for knowing God as Father. In his writing *The Humanity of God*, Barth elaborates Luther's formulation this way: in the mirror of the humanity of Jesus Christ, God reveals Godself as Godhead. Jesus is God. Herein we notice Barth's reception of Luther's Christology. In the excursus of *CD* IV/1:§59.1 (166–67), Barth combined and deepened Luther's provocative thesis (Jesus was born a Jew) with Luther's epistemological formulation of the man Jesus as the mirror of the fatherly heart of God. Luther's Christological insight is fundamental for the development of Barth's theological reflection on Israel. As Barth states, "[The Word] became Jewish flesh" (*CD* IV/1: 166). The Christian kerygma "concerns, therefore, the existence of a man of Israel, an Israelite" Jesus "who has come as the Messiah of Israel has come into the world as the Savior of the world" (*CD* IV/1:167). According to Barth, the Jewishness of Jesus of Nazareth is meant to be the mirror of the Godhead of God, of the covenant of God, and of the incarnation of God. Jesus, born as a Jew, is the God of Israel. If Jesus as the born Jew is the mirror of the fatherly heart of God, Luther's Christology of unification and his theology of double covenant need to be rearticulated anew and positively in regard to the thesis that the Jewishness of Jesus of Nazareth is the mirror of the Godhead of the God of Israel. The incarnation of Jesus Christ becomes concrete when it is spoken of as the Israel-becoming of God (John 1:14). The Jewishness of Jesus and the Israel-becoming of the God of Israel belong to each other in a reciprocal relationship.

According to Barth, Luther states, based on the Christ principle in the whole of Scripture, that "the New Testament should really be only the living Word corporeally, and not Scripture" (*CD* I/2:76–77). Luther even advocated that the holy fathers had all of Scripture in the proverbs. We cannot abstract from Scripture, but integrate ourselves into that new world of the Scripture.[14] Luther's concern about the law of God becomes explicit in his insistence that faithful people in the Old Testament had faith in Christ as we have. The patriarchal fathers become paradigmatic examples for Christian faith. Abraham was justified in his faith in the

---

14. WA 24:390, 27.

Word of God and God's promise, just as we are justified by faith in Jesus Christ. For Luther, Abraham is the *summum exemplum evangelicae vitae*.[15]

In the sight of God, the faith of Abraham is accepted like our own faith. According to Luther, the words "when we first believed" should be related to faith in the promise to Abraham, "in thy name shall all the nations in the earth be blessed" (*CD* I/2:76). For Luther, the New Testament is no other than an opening and revealing of the Old Testament. The Old and New Testaments are related as the written Word on the one hand and as the Word preached on the other. Therefore, the books of Moses and the prophets are also gospel. The gospel should not really be written but proclaimed in a living voice (*CD* I/1:122-23).

According to Barth, Luther's concern is to ground the New Testament in the Old, where the promise of Christ resides. Barth integrates Luther's deliberation of three forms of the Word of God into his theology of the Word of God. Regarding the unity of the Word of God Luther contends that the truth is revealed in three ways: through Scripture, word, and thought: in other words, through Scripture by books, through word by proclamation, and through thought by the heart. One cannot understand the truth of the Word of God except for proclamation (mouth), illumination of the Spirit (heart), and the Scripture. Barth credits Luther with the three forms of the Word of God, which include the eschatological character of the Word of God the Father in *se ipso*, such that Barth accurately perceives and describes Luther's theology of the Word of God (*CD* 1/1:122).

For Luther, faith is the same from the beginning of the world to the end. Therefore "the faith is all the same, so all the fathers just like ourselves were justified by the Word and faith and also died therein" (*CD* I/2:77). In the Old and New Testaments there is one way of salvation, one promise, one covenant, and one faith—all accomplished in Christ; this said, the revelation of Christ was also proclaimed in the time of the Old Testament. The fathers entered bliss by the grace of Jesus Christ (*CD* I/2:78).[16] What is important in the Old Testament, according to Luther, is not only a future but also a perfected time, which is the foundation for every past, present, and future. Barth's position is associated with Luther's

---

15. *WA* 57 III:236, 4-5 (A Lecture on Hebrews, 1518).

16. For Luther's influence on Barth's understanding of Scripture as the Word of God, see *CD* I/1:120-24; I/2:520-21.

exegesis. As Barth says, "Luther's comment on this passage [1 Cor 10:1–4] is exegetically sound, that no 'allegory or spiritual interpretation' must be admitted: 'for 'twas not a figure but a plain seriousness, God's Word, that maketh alive and the right faith was there, thus it befell them in no appearance, but 'tis the fact itself was there'"(*CD* I/2:74).

As Barth says,

> According to Luther, "tis all apostles' and evangelists' idea in the whole New Testament, that they hunt and pursue us into the Old Testament, which alone they also call Holy Writ; for the New Testament should really be only the living Word corporeally, and not Scripture. . . . We have 'to know that all the apostles taught and wrote they drew from the Old Testament; for in the same is all proclaimed that was to befall in Christ coming and to be preached, as St. Paul in Rom.1 saith, that God promised the Gospel of His Son Christ through the prophets in Holy Writ: therefore base they also all their preaching on the Old Testament, and there is no word in the New Testament that looketh not behind itself into the Old, in which 'twas proclaimed previously . . . for the New Testament is not more than a revelation of the Old.'" (*CD* I/2:76–77)

For Barth, the covenant is the presupposition of reconciliation (*CD* IV/1:§57, 2), and reconciliation is the fulfillment of the broken covenant (*CD* IV/1:§57, 3). As the promise of the renewed covenant (Jer 31:31–34, 35–37) cannot be separated from God's reconciliation with the world (2 Cor 5:19), so reconciliation cannot remain without its presupposition, namely, the permanence of Israel's covenant. This covenant is understood, strengthened, and interpreted in the framework of reconciliation. Barth expounded on Jeremiah 31 in light of the strongest emphasis on the imperishable nature of Israel's covenant. There is no way to break up or bring cessation to this covenant. There is no speaking of a replacement of the first covenant by the new and eternal covenant of the last days (Jer 31–32). The main passage, Jer 31:31–34 and 35–37, stresses the imperishable nature of the covenant with Israel. Far from being destroyed, "there is a no question of a dissolution but rather of a revelation of the real purpose and nature of that first covenant" (*CD* IV/1:32).

Barth distanced himself at this point from Luther, who had noticed in Jeremiah 31 another new covenant, a new Torah, namely, the church. Likewise Barth distanced himself from Bultmann, who was skeptical whether the covenant in Jeremiah (31:31ff) and Ezekiel (37:26ff) could be understood in an eschatological sense as one covenant with a future, empirical people of Israel. Therefore Barth understood the covenant in Jeremiah 31 as the same renewed Israel-covenant, the same Torah, and the same people of Israel. The eschatologioal *novum* of the imperishable Israel-covenant is the complete change in the form of the covenant in which God will bring the new humans of Israel to the forefront. They will do and hear the covenant and Torah through the Spirit of God (*CD* IV/1:33).

In this way, God will break the opposition of God's people, creating and giving a new heart to God's people. Despite the disobedience and corruption of Israel, God faithfully relates Godself to God's people even though they oppose the faithfulness of God. The *novum* of the imperishable covenant with Abraham and the exodus lies in the faith that God will create a new heart in God's people in order to enable the people to hold onto the Torah in the covenant of election. At this point, Barth affirmed the thesis that Jesus Christ, with his word and action, belongs to the history of Israel. For Barth, the history of Israel does not find its own end in the event of Jesus Christ.[17] Rather, the old form of the covenant made questionable by the unfaithfulness of Israel, God's covenant partner, was replaced by the renewed covenant according to the promise of Jeremiah. Therefore it is not the end of the history of Israel, but the end of the old form of an imperishable Israel-covenant that is promised by Jeremiah and presupposed in the New Testament. The history of Israel in the old form of the covenant (as long as it stood under the sign of Israel's sin and the divine reaction against it—namely the old form of the imperishable Israel covenant) itself comes to an end in order to make a place for its true and peculiar form (*CD* IV/1:33).

According to Barth, this statement is not supposed to discredit the covenant of Israel or regard it as invalid. God negates Israel's unfaithfulness by God's own faithfulness, or God's covenant will toward this people: "What God will do in accordance with this prophecy will be a revelation and confirmation of what He had always willed and indeed done in the covenant with Israel" (*CD* IV/1:34). From the start, the divine covenant with Israel had been substantive. From an eschatological perspective, this covenant will be "the covenant of the free but effective grace of God" "which does not exclude the human race as a whole from the gracious

---

17. Rendtorff, "Die jüdische Bibel und die antijüdische Auslegung," 99–116.

will of God towards it" (*CD* IV/1:34). To defend the dignity of the Jews theologically is Barth's intent in speaking of Jeremiah's promise in the renewed sense when it comes to the end of the old form of the imperishableness of the Israel-covenant. With this fundamental thesis in mind, Barth stated that German National Socialism must fail in its aggression toward the Jews.[18]

By using reconciliation to reveal the efficacy of God's covenant with Israel (2 Cor 5:19), Barth also took the event of God's reconciliation with the world in Christ to be in reciprocal relationship to Jer 31:31ff. Therefore Barth understood reconciliation as the confirmation and fulfillment of the permanent covenant of Israel. In Barth's sentence, we read that the reconciliation as the fulfillment of the broken covenant "speaks of the confirmation or restoration of a fellowship which did exist but had been threatened with disruption and dissolution" (*CD* IV/1:67). According to Barth, God's reconciliation with the world did not happen in an abstract way by eradicating the particularity of Israel's election and covenant. To the contrary, he understood the reconciliation of all humans with God as resulting from the confirmation of election and thus portrays it as God's covenant with Israel coming to fulfillment in Jesus. In the worldwide event of reconciliation in the cross of Jesus Christ, Israel's election does not get lost or disappear; neither is it paganized.

By contrast, God's reconciliation with the world is first of all to be understood as an event of the faithfulness of the God of Israel to God's people. In reciprocal interaction between the permanent election of Israel (Jeremiah 31) and God's reconciliation with the world (2 Cor 5:19), Barth's double thesis is more strongly affirmed: the covenant is the presupposition of reconciliation, and reconciliation is the fulfillment of the broken covenant. The history of Jesus Christ does not separate the God of Israel from God's people but reveals and amplifies God's own zeal for covenantal relationship. As God in Christ (2 Cor 5:19), this one was and is promised and expected in God's covenant with Israel.[19]

Barth secured the particularity of God's election of Israel against attempts in Protestant theology to dissolve the specialty or particularity of the Israel-election into a universal covenant with all humans. Above all, in the Word of God's becoming flesh we must not forget God's covenantal

---

18. Barth, *Schweitzer Stimme*, 322.
19. Barth, *Einführung in die evangelische Theologie*, 30–31.

Word to Israel. Reconciliation as the fulfillment of the permanent Israel-covenant is also God's event of faithfulness to God's people of Israel. God reconciles Godself to Israel in Christ. In the reconciling work of God to Israel, such an act speaks to all people of all times. In other words, God's primary election of Israel becomes manifest and confirmed in the event of reconciliation in which God determines Israel as the witness to the world of all Gentile people. Therefore God comes to the world in Israel though Jesus Christ. The permanence of Israel's covenant presupposes God's reconciliation with the world. The Jeremiah-promise comes in this process of reconciliation as the confirmation of its meaning and to its zeal. Therefore Jesus Christ is the "Yes" and "Amen" to the promise of God toward God's people of Israel.[20]

Barth understood John 1:14 ("the Word become flesh"), to describe the Israel-becoming God. In other words, God went into the far country. Herein Barth came back not only to Luther's writing about Israel in 1523 but also to his grounding epistemological thesis that considered the Godhead in light of the concrete humanity of the man Jesus. Luther's epistemological statement that Jesus Christ is "the mirror of the fatherly heart of God" helped Barth with the particularity of God becoming human in the event of God's incarnation. From this standpoint from below Barth reflected on God as immanent Trinity and God's way into the far country. In Jesus Christ as the mirror, it is knowable that he is God, and his existence is in Jewish flesh (CD IV/1:171).

The Word did not just become flesh (humbled, suffering humanity in a general sense), but the Word became Jewish flesh (CD IV/1:166) in God's history with Israel. As a concrete Israelite man, Jesus stands in the realm of Israel's election. As a Jewish man, Jesus is the culmination of God's history with the people of Israel, namely, the fulfiller of God's covenant with God's people. In Jesus Christ as the mirror of the fatherly heart of God, we know that the self-limitation and self-humiliation of God stand in continuity with the God of the Old Testament who restricts and humiliates Godself as the Father of the Son of Israel (Exod 3:7–8).[21]

---

20. Correspondingly, Gollwitzer actualizes Barth's thesis about people of Israel being the mediator of all peoples, as Gollwitzer states his central christological concern: "the central place of Jesus for the whole human race grows out of ... the central function of Jewish people for the whole human race" (Gollwitzer, *Befreiung zur Solidarität*, 68).

21. Klappert, *Miterben der Verheissung*, 164.

God's becoming Israel in the Jew Jesus means in this sense self-restriction and thus self-humiliation of God.

Barth qualified Luther's provocative thesis that Jesus was born a Jew together with Luther's epistemological understanding of Jesus Christ as the mirror of the fatherly heart of God. Thus the Jewishness of Jesus stands in continuity with God's election of Israel and extends to Jesus's way into the far country from baptism to the cross in respect to the covenantal history of Israel. Furthermore, through Luther's theological epistemology, Barth deepened his reflection on God's becoming Israel in the mirror of the concrete Jewish man, Jesus of Nazareth.[22]

Barth's Christology and Its Political Consequences

Since Martin Chemnitz, Lutheran orthodoxy has distinguished between Christ in *status exinanitionis* and Christ in *status exaltationis*, and it has remained faithful to the *communicatio idiomatum*. The third form of *genus maiestaticum* (formulated by Chemnitz) refers to the fact that the human nature of Christ, even in *status exinanitionis*, is entitled to take part in the divine attributes of majesty; but he relinquished them with his own will (kenosis). In the Lutheran tradition, the doctrine of the two states was incorporated into the fixed theme of the *communicatio idiomatum*, including the *genus maiestaticum*. Human nature is conceived to have the power of the *unio personalis* to participate in the divine attributes. In coming close to Luther's christological thought, we understand Barth's principle of Christology in the following way: Jesus, the man for God, exists as he is for the human being. The reciprocity refers to the mutual being of the man Jesus for God and for human beings in the event of God's revelation in God's creation, specifically in this man Jesus. This man is essentially for God because he is essentially *von Gott her* and in God. Therefore Barth posits the doctrines of the *communicatio gratiae* (communication of grace, CD IV/2:84ff) and the *communicatio operationum* (communication of operation) to safeguard Jesus's specific, singular personhood, in spite of his rejecting both the *communicatio idiomatum*

---

22. Ibid., 170. In agreement with Barth's basic intention, Klappert takes John 1:14 to imply that the Word became a Jewish man and pitched a tent among us (as in the Old Testament God takes the indwelling place in the tent of meeting) and we behold his glory (*KEBOD JHWH*) as the glory of the begotten messianic Son of the Father, full of covenant-faithfulness and covenant-homage (*CHESED we EMET*).

(the communication of proper qualities between the two natures) and the *genus majestaticum* (the communication of glory).[23]

Barth was not so concerned about Christ's divine nature as such but about securing the subject of the communication of properties as the Son of God in the assumption of human nature. Barth questioned whether Lutheran Christology could eschew either the Hegelian way of the escalating apotheosis of human spirit in dialectical progress toward the Spirit of God, or Feuerbach's way of identifying divine nature with human essence. If the finite and infinite do not exclude each other, the former is capable of the latter. To what extent could Lutheran Christology avoid the irreversibility of the relationship between God and human being? (*CD* IV/2:83). Against the Greek conception of God influencing overmuch the Christian discourse about God, Barth criticized this conception of God as "the prisoner of His own Godhead" (*CD* IV/2:85).

Reflecting on the Godhead in biblical terms, Barth insisted that the effective confrontation of the divine with the human, and also of the human with the divine, takes place in Jesus Christ without altering either essence, rather than in direct or indirect identification between them. This mutual and effective confrontation has to be answered within the framework of mutual participation (*CD* IV/2:87). It refers to the *communicatio gratiae*, which means the mutual participation of divine and human essence taking place and resulting from the union of the two in the one Jesus Christ. On the one hand, God, as the acting subject, exists in God's mode of being as the Son in substantial unity with the Father and the Holy Spirit. God first elected and determined Godself. On the other hand, in God's eternal counsel and then in God's execution in time, the Son of God gives God's own existence and actuality by becoming and being the Son of man. He elected and determined Himself for humiliation (*CD* IV/2:84).

In Barth's view, Christ's human nature is determined completely in terms of God's electing grace. It means "the total and exclusive determination of the human nature of Jesus Christ by the grace of God" (*CD* IV/2:88). This is what the *communicatio gratiarum* means. The doctrine of the *communicatio gratiarum* articulates, according to Barth, "the

---

23. The divine attributes are transferred to the human nature by virtue of the personal union. However, the communication occurs in strictly one direction, i.e., beneficently from God to man. Certainly the human nature of Jesus Christ is in full possession of and participates in the full glory of the divine. Cf. *CD* IV/1:182, *CD* IV/2:77-78, 82-83.

concrete filling out of the concept of the *communicatio idiomatum*, and more deeply of the *communio naturarum*, and more deeply still of the *unio hypostatica*" (*CD* IV/2:88). Therefore any work or action of Christ's divine nature is simultaneously the work of his human nature and vice versa. This is what *communicatio operationum* means. It is called the *communicatio apotelesmatum*, or the *genus apotelesmaticum*, namely, "the co-operation of the two natures to specific ends and results" (*CD* IV/2:104).

In it there is the Reformed emphasis on "the basis of this concord in the unity of the person of the Son of God and Son of Man as the subject of the two natures co-operating even in their distinctiveness" (*CD* IV/2:104). For the atonement, Barth follows the Reformed emphasis on Jesus Christ, who exists in the union of two natures, for the atonement. Lutherans concluded that the atonement is the *apotelesma*, while regardless of its logical possibility, Reformed insisted that the union of the divine and human nature is the *apotelesma* of the person of the one Jesus Christ active in and through both natures. This is why the Reformed preferred to speak of a *communicatio operationum* instead of a *communicatio idiomatum* (*CD* IV/2:105).

However, Barth demurred at the barrier between the Lutheran position and the Reformed position concerning the *apotelesma* of the atonement as a splitting of hairs. Although Barth utilized the Reformed position as the departure for the decisive concept of the *unio hypostatica*, he left even Reformed Christology far behind (*CD* IV/2:106). In Barth's view, the unity between *vere Deus* and *vere homo* refers to the *communicatio gratiarum* and the *operationum*, which correspond to the doctrine of the hypostatic union by offering a dynamic character to it. In this light, Pannenberg notices that Barth's concept of *communicatio gratiarum* is not really different from the orthodox Lutheran doctrine of *communicatio idiomatum* in terms of the *genus majestaticum*, albeit eschewing its limitation.[24] Although reflecting on the christological controversy between the Giessen party and Tübingen party, Barth shows his sympathy for the Tübingen party and J. Gerhard; Barth stated that the Tübingen party as well as the Giessen party "succeeded only in calling into question that

---

24. Pannenberg, *Jesus—God and Man*, 303. Similarly Jüngel states that Barth's doctrine of *communicatio gratiarum* (communication of graces) includes the proper concern of the *communicatio idiomatum* (communication of properties). Cf. Jüngel, *God's Being Is in Becoming*, 97, fn. 91.

'God was in Christ' and in that way damaging the nerve of a Christology oriented by the Old and the New Testaments" (*CD* IV/1:183).

In integrating the doctrine of two natures and two states into the reconciling God and the reconciled man of the one Jesus Christ, Barth deepened the gracious act of God that bridges the distance between Creator and creature. According to Barth, the unity between *vere Deus* and *vere homo* means both the *communicatio gratiarum* and the *operationum*, which correspond to the doctrine of the effects of the hypostatic union by providing a dynamic character to the *unio personalis* (cf. *CD* IV/2:51–60). Both the humiliation of the divine and the exaltation of the human are a single event taking place within the one Jesus Christ. Against the excesses of Alexandrian theology (for the sake of *vere Deus*), this unity affects all of human nature in such a way that "He in His divine essence takes part in human essence—so radical and total a part that He causes his existence to become and be also the existence of the man Jesus of Nazareth" (*CD* IV/2:65).

Against the excesses of Antiochian theology (for the sake of the *vere homo*), no element of human essence is unaffected or excluded by this unity because "He gives [Himself] to the human essence as the eternal Son who is co-equal with the Father and the Holy Spirit" (*CD* IV/2:65). Therefore Barth's Christology is characterized by a dynamic dialectic between "from above to below" and "from below to above," in which the messianic history of Jesus Christ stands in correlation with the entire covenantal history of Israel. Rather than eschewing the limitation of Lutheran orthodoxy, but by radicalizing and overcoming it, Barth provided his own Christology in the affirmation of Israel from the perspective of a dynamic dialectic between Christology from above and Christology from below.

Barth related the movement of the humiliation/exaltation theme to the resurrection and the ascension. As in his death on the cross, the exaltation of this man occurs in his unity with the Son of God. To reconcile Godself with the world, the death of Jesus Christ (the obedience of the Son on the cross) stands in connection with the resurrection of Jesus Christ (the grace of the Father in the resurrection of the Son). The concept of the teleological connection between the cross and the resurrection is related to the historical actualization of the humiliation and exaltation of Jesus Christ (*CD* IV/2:145). To stress the political significance of his Christology, Barth deepened the aspect of God's solidarity with the poor under the royal man Jesus Christ (corresponding to the kingly office of the Calvinist threefold doctrine of Jesus Christ). The way of Jesus Christ "is all the more revolutionary, as the One who breaks all bonds asunder, in new historical developments and situations" (*CD* IV/2:173). The man Jesus as the royal man calls all programs and principles into question: "In fellowship and conformity with this God who is poor in the world the royal man Jesus is also poor, and fulfills this transvaluation of all value" (*CD* IV/2:169).

In Barth's reflection of Jesus as the royal man in light of the kingly office, the radical nature of Christ becomes explicit in his ignoring of the rich and the high and mighty for the sake of the poor, the lowly, and the humiliated in light of the revolution of the kingdom of God. The royal man Jesus "as the poorest of the poor" (*CD* IV/2:167) is characterized by Barth as "the pronouncedly revolutionary character of His relationship to the orders of life and value current in the world around him" (*CD* IV/2:171).

Even though Jesus Christ did not hesitate to accept various institutions of his day such as the temple, the law, the family, and even existing political institutions (Barth calls this the "passive conservatism" of Jesus Christ), Jesus was always superior to all these things. In Barth's view, the revolution of God in Jesus Christ does not eradicate Jesus's Jewish surroundings. Jesus might be called "the figure of a representative of a reformed and deepened Judaism" (*CD* IV/2:174). Not expatriating the Jewish establishment of his time but radicalizing it in light of God's kingdom, Jesus and his passive conservatism are to be seen in respect to "the radical and indissoluble antithesis of the kingdom of God to all human kingdoms"(*CD* IV/2:177).

Jesus did not cease to call into question human order and the social and political institutions in light of the kingdom of God in an eschatological sense.[25] In fact, as "the One whose will is that it should be totally changed and renewed," Jesus Christ is depicted by Barth in a provocative manner as the partisan of the poor (*CD* IV/2:180). Jesus, as the mirror of the fatherly heart of God and the self-representation of God's kingdom, stands "in His corresponding partisanship of those who are lowly in this world; in the revolutionary character of His relationship to the established

---

25. Cf. Barth's political interpretation of the beatitudes, *CD* IV/2:177, 189–90.

orders; in His positive turning to man as he exists and is oppressed in this world" (*CD* IV/2:249).

Above all, in the history of struggle and victory of Jesus Christ in the framework of the prophetic work of Jesus, Barth expresses his political theology of Christology in light of God's eschatology par excellence. Barth's modification and dynamization of the incarnation and ancient Christologyis carried out historically and politically from the perspective of Jesus's Jewishness in correlation with the messianic history of Israel. At this point, the offices of the high priest and king (associated with the humiliated servant and exalted royal man Jesus Christ) mean also that Jesus Christ is the prophet, herald, and proclaimer of the kingdom of God that had already come and begun in him (*CD* IV/3.1:165). Barth related the prophetic work of Jesus Christ to Blumhard's slogan "Jesus is Victor" for actualizing history of struggle and conflict of the living Jesus Christ. It is not "the triumph of grace" (Berkouwer), but the history of victory of the living Jesus Christ.

As long as the revelation of the reconciliation of Jesus Christ has its specific historical character, it points to a not-yet-redeemed and not-yet-consummated stage in expectation of the final, definite, and universal revelation by the coming of Jesus Christ in glory (*CD* IV/3.1:186). The prophetic history of Jesus Christ is a history of fighting and conflict under the sign *Christus victor*. Hence, "Salvation history is the history of the *totus Christus*, of the Head with the body and all the members. This *totus Christus* is *Christus victor*" (*CD* IV/3.1:216). As a history of struggle and conflict, the prophetic activity of Jesus Christ means "a remarkable stroke in a strange and remarkable war," the "attack of the grace of God" resisting elements of human life and the world. In it, "there is proclaimed and indicated a decisive, radical and universal alteration of the whole situation and constitution of the world" (*CD* IV/3.1:240).

This refers to the revolution of God in the prophetic history of struggle and victory of Jesus Christ in which the world should experience "a total and radical and universal transformation" (*CD* IV/3.1:241). As Barth argued, "What are all intellectual, moral, artistic, social or political revolutions, all wars and world wars, but limited, particular and passing domestic squabblings compared with the revolution and conflict which are here accomplished and proclaimed in all quietness and friendliness, yet for all the friendliness with a final radicalness and universality?"(*CD* IV/3.1:242).

In respect to the establishment of God's lordship in Jesus Christ on earth, there is no place for us to remain neutral, nonparticipants or merely spectators toward others and ourselves. In protest and opposition to the unreconciled world and the reality of nothingness, we are called to be living participants in the prophetic history of Jesus Christ. Human beings under the grace of reconciliation are free "to live in contact, solidarity and fellowship" with God as well as with the reconciled world. Therefore we live "as companions in the partnership of reconciliation, as brothers and sisters in the fulfilled covenant of God." Human beings under the glad tidings of reconciliation can live and work "in contact, solidarity and fellowship both vertically and horizontally" (*CD* IV/3.1:248).

In fact, it is impossible to have the attitude of an ostrich, burying one's head in the sand. This prophetic history of Jesus Christ can be depicted and understood eschatologically as the supratemporal, transcendent future that has not yet arrived but has begun with Jesus Christ. In other words, a biblical and eschatological perspective tells us about the present irruption of God's future, or the advent of the new human being here and now, or the present passing of the old reality, the disruptive truth of the new and true reality (*CD* IV/3.1:249, 253). The kingdom of God that is coming and has already come is the new life in expectation of eternity, the viewing of time in light of eternity, in which we discern that "the bow of reconciliation, of the victory of Christ and therefore of hope arches peacefully over the whole" (*CD* IV/3.1:258).

Given the reconciliation of the cross, Barth developed a theology of the cross in terms of the actualization and the dynamization of the dogma of the two natures and two states. In it, the double movement between the reconciling God and the reconciled man becomes a controlling principle for his Christology. Barth's doctrine of reconciliation is not an interpretation of the history of the incarnation, or a radicalization of the classic theology of the incarnation. Rather it is the unity between the person and the work in the one Jesus Christ occurring as the reconciliation event on the cross, which is Barth's hermeneutical *modus operandi* in accepting, modifying, and overcoming the classic theology and Luther's Christology. Therefore Barth's Christology of reconciliation is oriented toward the theology of the cross, which has a conspicuously political profile and significance.[26]

An Inclusive Dimension of *Assumptio Carnis*

According to Barth, the eternal divine Logos is the man Jesus, and this man Jesus is the One who was with God in the beginning. With this formulation of the preexistence of Jesus Christ, Barth defended himself against a speculative idea of *logos asarkos* in Reformed Christology. By including the man Jesus in the inner Trinitarian life of perichoresis, God had in Godself the man for Godself before time, and elected him as the partner of God's covenant. The man Jesus came into the flesh by becoming an actual man. The christological principle of *assumptio carnis* becomes valid in eternity and leads Barth to take into account the high priestly office of Jesus Christ who is engaged in eternity for us on the right hand of the Father. Jesus Christ exists eternally for us and in this eternity, he exists for all time.

With this idea in mind, Barth provided predestination with an actual and universal character. The core teaching of divine gracious election is that God made a decision for human beings already before God's work in creation, reconciliation, and redemption before all time in Jesus Christ. Therefore, the eternal Son in his unity with humanity became the elect man (*CD* II/2:102–3) so that Jesus Christ is the inner ground of all works of God toward creation, reconciliation, and redemption. He is the beginning of all divine works. This is what I would like to call Barth's Trinitarian theology of election, in distinction from Moltmann's Trinitarian theology of the cross.[27]

As we have already seen, Barth did not lose sight of the importance of *theologia crucis*. Barth developed his theology of the cross in the context of his doctrine of reconciliation by giving a new meaning to ancient

---

26. Klappert states properly: "the cross of the resurrected in its integral meaning, and self-humiliation of the Son of God on the cross in its necessary character are the ground axiom of Christology, the center of theological argumentation of Karl Barth" (Klappert, *Die Aufweckung des Gekreuzigten*, 170).

27. Moltmann is critical of Barth's theology of the cross due to its lack of Trinitarian understanding. However, Barth's theology of the Trinity is primarily grounded on God's eternal election of the Son in the fellowship of the Holy Spirit and so is theologically prior to Moltmann's Trinitarian understanding of the cross in time. Cf. Moltman, *Crucified God*, 239–40).

Christology, i.e., the dogma of the two natures and the doctrine of two states of humiliation and exaltation. God has taken unto Godself in the intradivine life the conditions of the historical person and life of Jesus in terms of the incarnation. In so doing, God "does not come into conflict with himself" (*CD* IV/1:185). The preexistence of the man Jesus—preceding the inner and primary ground of creation as well as reconciliation—is identical with divine eternal predestination with his election, in the election of Israel, the election of the church, and finally in the election of all (*CD* III/2:582). The divine election in eternity is an act of the self-determination of God in a particular relation to humanity: "Before God seeks and creates fellowship with us, He wills and completes this fellowship in Himself. In Himself, He does not will to exist for Himself, to exist alone. On the contrary, He is Father, Son, and Spirit and therefore alive in His unique being with and for and in another . . . Therefore, what He seeks and creates between Himself and us is in fact nothing else but what He wills and completes and therefore is in Himself" (*CD* III/2:275).

In order to avoid monophysite and docetic tendencies in his understanding of the preexistence of the man Jesus in the divine *perichoresis*, Barth returned to his understanding of *anhypostasis* and *enhypostasis* (*CD* III/2:70 with explicit relevance to *CD* I/2:163–64). In this man, in his being and in his history, God is actually and truly for creatures, and the creatures are for God. Against Calvin, but with Athanasius, Barth highlights the understanding that the election of the man Jesus and our election are based on the eternity of God's Word. The concrete actuality of Jesus Christ exists with God's present taking place and carrying itself out in creation, in and with the existence of Jesus Christ, who "is essentially for God because he is essentially from God and in God" (*CD* III/2:71).

If Jesus Christ, the actual man as God, exists in God as the helper of all creation and every human being, we may talk about the history of covenant and redemption for all. Barth's teaching of *anhypostasis* and *enhypostasis* underlines this uniqueness and universality of Jesus Christ. For the sake of the particularity and inclusivity of the humanity of Jesus Christ, Barth stated the universal range and scope of *assumptio carnis expressis verbis* against a Chalcedonian limitation (*CD* IV/2:48ff, 63–64) on the one hand and against a charge of docetism bound to *anhypostasis* teaching on the other (*CD* I/2:161–65). Would the doctrine of the two natures in traditional Chalcedonian Christology be capable of articulating the universal significance and range of incarnation on the basis of dialectics between distinction and unity of divinity and humanity in the one person of Jesus Christ?

What is remarkably striking in Barth's renewed understanding of *anhypostasis* and *enhypostasis* is his articulation of the universal range and significance of Jesus Christ for all human beings whether Christian or non-Christian. As Barth argued, "In Jesus Christ it is not merely one man, but the *humanum* of all men, which is posited and exalted as such to unity with God" (*CD* IV/2:49). A great contribution that Barth makes through his Christology is to deepen and actualize a Trinitarian concept of *assumptio carnis* in solidarity with suffering humanity outside the walls of Christianity. If the humanity of Jesus Christ exists in actuality 'enhypostatically' in his divine being, our humanity exists again actually and truly 'enhypostatically' in his humanity through the mediation of this God-Man, Jesus Christ. Therefore, what the eternal Word of God has assumed is for Barth not merely a man, but *humanum*, human being and essence, human nature and kind, "which is that of all men, which characterizes them all as men, and distinguishes them from other creatures" (*KD* IV/2:52; *CD* IV/2:48). For Barth, "flesh" does not imply a man, but "human essence and existence, human kind and nature, humanity, humanitas, that which makes a man man" (*CD* I/2:149).

However, this universal aspect is not to shorten or even deny the concrete, individual and once-and-for-all being of the man Jesus. Rather, Barth's emphasis is more nuanced in favor of inclusivity; Jesus Christ is not only a man, rather the *humanum* of all human beings as such transferred and exalted into unity with God (*KD* IV/2:52; *CD* IV/2:49). In explicating the comprehensive character of the humanity of Jesus Christ as the *totus Christus*, Barth again affirms that "the human nature elected by Him and assumed into unity with His existence is implicitly that of all men. In His being as man God has implicitly assumed the human being of all men. In Him not only we all as *homines*, but our *humanitas* as such—for it is both His and ours—exists in and with God Himself" (*CD* IV/2:59).

Regarding continuity between Barth's earlier concepts, such as the Revolution of God or the living God, and his later dogmatic development of Christology, Marquardt asks, "does this christological focus imply a theological break, or is it to be linked up with the previous cluster of ideas? . . . The Biblical Jesus Christ as exposited in church dogma assumes the function that revolution, life, resurrection, and praxis had previously exercised in relation to God and human society, as well as to theological thinking; he is meant to be understood in this function."[28]

In a similar way Barth, in his discussion of Israel, distinguished the historical environment from the natural environment of Jesus Christ. For Barth, Israel as people of God and as Jewish people provide the natural environment in the election of Jesus Christ, *assumptio carnis* of the Word became Jewish flesh (*CD* IV/1:166). In the statement of Barth we read representative inclusivity of Jesus for Israel. "The Son of God in His unity with the Israelite Jesus exists in direct and unlimited solidarity with the representatively and manifestly sinful humanity of Israel. . . . He accepts personal responsibility for all the unfaithfulness, the deceit, the rebellion of this people and its priests and kings. And that is infinitely more than when Israel itself . . . comes under this accusation" (*CD* IV/1:172). God's covenantal relationship with the people of Israel qualifies the nature of all as a preparation for the grace of Jesus Christ. Israel as the natural environment of Jesus Christ as a Jew makes Barth speculate concerning "the possibility of a renewed liberal theology" which seemed to be biblically legitimate. As Barth said about Martin Buber, "to be anthropocentric need not mean to be egocentric . . . At this point, taking as his starting point the unequivocal I-Thou theology of the Old Testament prophets, Martin Buber made his breakthrough. . . . Liberal theology might well find new possibilities within the framework of such a pre-Messianic Judaism."[29]

In view of Barth's theological anthropology, special attention is paid to the relevance between Barth and Buber.[30] Barth's thesis—the cohumanity of human being is the grounding form of humanity (*CD* III/2:§45.2)—corresponds to Buber's thesis that the fundamental fact of human existence is the human with the other human.[31] In seeing human-

---

28. Marquardt, *Theologie und Sozialismus*, 24.

29. Barth, "Liberal Theology: Some Alternatives," 217–18. I am convinced that Pangritz's thesis—the possibility of a renewed liberal theology in biblical legitimating—stands in parallel with Barth's presentation of "a christologically founded counter-proposal to the theory of religion." Cf. Pangritz, *Karl Barth in the Theology of Dietrich Bonhoeffer*, 137, 146.

30. Gollwitzer, "Martin Bubers Bedeutung," 53.

31. Gollwitzer, "Martin Bubers Bedeutung." Buber, in his afterword to *Schriften über das dialogische Prinzip* (1954), concluded with a beautiful wish: "But I would, I could show Karl Barth here, in Jerusalem how Chassidim dances with the freedom of conscience toward the co-fellow."

ity from the perspective of the other (e.g., from the perspective of the atheist Feuerbach, of the pagan Confucius, and of the Jew Buber)—those who depict the idea of humanity in a way akin to Christian anthropology (*CD* III/2:277)—Barth makes a christological projection by grounding the knowledge of the man Jesus in the decision to grasp the freedom of conscience for cohumanity as the root and crown of the humanity-concept.

According to his Jewish flesh Jesus Christ retains Israel as the natural people of Abraham's offspring. In Barth's view, the natural dimension in the Jewish people should not be mystified in an anti-Semitic sense or spiritualized in an ecclesiastical sense. As Barth writes, "It is true enough that the *humanum* exists always in the form of actual man. This existence is not denied to the man Jesus, but ascribed to Him with the positive concept of the *enhypostasis*." What is at stake for Barth is to affirm "no less than the unity in which as man He is the Son of God, and as the Son of God man; and finally no less than the universal relevance and significance of His existence for all other man" (*CD* IV/2:49).

In differentiating *homo* from *humanitas*, Barth took Feuerbach's side in his understanding of humanity. It is of special significance to notice an affinity between Barth's idea of Jesus as the Son of Man who is the representative of the entire human race and Feuerbach's idea of the human species. According to Barth, the *humanum* characterizes all people as humanity by being "the concrete possibility of the existence of one man in a specific form" (*CD* IV/2:48). Herein, Barth's theology gains a sociopolitical prominence in terms of actualizing a universal relevance between Jesus Christ and the social essence of the human species. If the *assumptio carnis* is seen in light of *assumptio humanum*, would not Jesus Christ as the partisan of the poor, or as the revolutionary (*CD* IV/2:180) include "enhypostatically" the suffering humanity under sociopolitical mechanisms of injustice and violence? Might this christological aspect be reread as a form of theology after Auschwitz, or a liberation theology that stands in solidarity with world-weary people? [32]

Luther seems to project a conflict with divine life, that is, God's wrath and God's love onto God's life in the immanent Trinity: "There God enters into conflict with God [da streitet Gott mit Gott]" (WA:45:370, 35). In reflection on Golgotha and the passion and dereliction of Jesus Christ

---

32. In this light, Barth is not hesitant to affirm divine passibility, in agreement with Luther but against Calvin and Zwingli. Calvin, *Institutes* 4:17.30.

on the cross, Gollwitzer brings Luther's formulation to the fore: "Vere derelictus est per omnia" (WA:5:605) (Truly he is forsaken by everybody). Herein Gollwitzer sees also a cleavage going through God proper, that is, the paradox of all paradoxes. In the words of Gollwitzer: "The cleavage goes through not only Jesus, it goes through God proper. God himself is forsaken by God, God himself rejects himself."[33]

Although Barth rejected God's giving up of himself kenotically, he did not ignore divine suffering in Christ the servant, and he even emphasized that God dared to be "God against God" without falling into a contradiction of his being (*CD* IV/1:184).[34] In this regard Barth formulated the possibility of God even in theopaschite terms. God is moved and stirred in God's free power, open and ready to incline to compassion with another's suffering. In affirmation of a particular truth in early patripassian theology, Barth says, "No, there is a *particular veri* in the teaching of the early patripassian. This is that primarily it is God the Father who suffers in the offering and sending of His Son, in His abasement . . . He does suffer it in the humiliation of His Son with a depth with which it never was or will be suffered by any man. . . . The fatherly fellow-suffering of God is the mystery, the basis, of the humiliation of His Son; the truth of that which takes place historically in His crucifixion" (*CD* IV/2:357).[35]

Given this fact, Barth retrieved Luther hermeneutically in order to expand divine possibility in relation to his Trinitarian concept of election and his universal concept of reconciliation in that Barth accepts, modifies, and radicalizes Luther's insight in his own framework. For Barth, *logos asarkos* in the old *extra Calvinisticum* (with its Nestorian tendency) needs to be corrected and renewed in affirmation of a Lutheran exclusive understanding of *logos ensarkos*. Reformed Christology would presuppose that there would be another *logos* next to the Word who became flesh and thus leading to the hidden God, another form of the eternal Word of God next to Jesus Christ.[36]

---

33. Gollwitzer, *Krummes Holz-Aufrechter Gang*, 258.

34. Cf. Barth's appraisal of the kenotic controversy, *CD* IV/1:181–83.

35. In regard to Barth's statement, Moltmann reproaches Barth for his use of a simple concept of God without trinitarian differentiation. However, Barth's concept of God's fatherly fellow-suffering must be seen primarily in terms of the innertrinitarian election of God. Cf. Moltmann, *Crucified God*, 203.

36. Barth discerns this dangerous intimation from Calvin's teaching of predestination. As Barth argues, "It cannot be denied that Calvin himself (and with particularly

Nevertheless, in the *assumptio carnis* God remains God in God's humiliation. *Anhypostasis* and *enhypostasis* help Barth safeguard the majesty and freedom of God from a Lutheran tendency toward limiting God's divinity. Instead of pursuing Reformed Christology, however, Barth concretized the eternal preexistence of the man Jesus in terms of God's covenant of grace with human beings through this man. In the divine free act of gracious election, the Son of the Father is no mere eternal Logos, but as the true God in eternity, he is true man who assumed the *humanum* of all human beings. As Barth modified and corrected Reformed Christology, namely its tendency to double Christ through a Lutheran insight of *logos ensarkos*, so Barth extended and expanded Lutheran Christology with emphasis on God's free act of grace toward an inclusive significance of *assumptio carnis* for all human beings. In applying the term *human nature* to the humanity of Jesus Christ, Barth stated that in Jesus Christ the *humanum* of all men is posited and exalted as such to unity with God (*CD* IV/2:49).

---

serious consequences in his doctrine of predestination) does go a good way towards trying to reckon with this 'other' god" (*CD* IV/1:181).

EIGHT   Karl Barth as a Theologian Who Discovers Judaism for Christian Theology

Karl Barth and Israel in the Doctrine of Election in *Church Dogmatics*

KARL BARTH WROTE OF ISRAEL IN HIS DOCTRINE OF ELECTION IN APproximately 1940. He discussed Israel deliberately and in detail in three different places within the *Church Dogmatics*. In the doctrine of election, Barth spoke of the eternal grounding of the history of Israel in terms of the election of God. The central place of Barth's doctrine of Israel is located in paragraph 34 of *Church Dogmatics* II/2. Herein Barth developed his theology of Israel in connection with his teaching of predestination under the title: "The Election of the Community" (*CD* II/2:195–305). St Paul becomes the key figure for Barth in his question about the relationship between Israel and the church.[1]

Barth's christological understanding of Israel and reprobation is furthermore to be seen in relation to God's historical reign, namely, in the doctrine of providence (*CD* III/3:210–26). Because God's primeval election is the foundation for the whole drama of divine providence, the doctrine of providence can be seen as a part of the doctrine of election in a more comprehensive way. Herein Israel is understood as people who reject Christ, but at the same time, as the elect people of God. Israel, which rejects Christ, is proof of God's existence. This is because Barth reflects dialectically on a Christ-rejecting Israel but at the same time on a

---

1. For Barth, Paul is a Jew and a Christian in whom unity between Jew and Gentile was realized and became possible in an apostle. Therefore the church came to Israel, not the other way around (*CD* II/2:275).

God-witnessing Judaism, namely, Israel *post Christum natum*. Therefore, Barth affirmed that the history of the Jews holds providential significance. Furthermore, in the doctrine of reconciliation, the prophecy of the history of Israel is described as a prefiguration of the prophecy of Jesus Christ. Let's discuss, first of all, Barth's understanding of Israel in light of election and rejection in reference to God's providence over it.

Israel in Election and Rejection

When Israel is viewed from the perspective of the church, Barth takes Romans 9–11 to be the *locus classicus* for understanding the relationship between Israel and the church. Barth dealt with Israel from the perspective of the doctrine of election and significantly took into account the inner connection between predestination and Israel. This understanding points to a perspective of seeing Israel and the church under the rainbow of the one covenant that arches over the whole (*CD* II/2:200).[2]

According to Barth, the doctrine of predestination is "a regulative principle" that "stands at the beginning of and behind all Christian thinking."[3] He sought a closeness of the church to Israel whenever possible—regardless of the external contradiction between them. His way of dealing with Israel and the church in light of such solidarity remained unbroken so that a dialectical relationship between them could be rooted in and actualized under the arch of God's one covenant. Israel does not stand as an enemy but as a helper and a partner for the church.[4]

As far as Israel and the church stand under the rainbow of the one covenant, there occurs a possibility for Christians to participate in the covenantal life of Israel given by God. Because Israel is an indispensable part of Christian faith, Christian faith cannot abandon seeking a relationship with Israel. Thus "in the Logos, who speaks to faith, the *dabar* [God's Word] of Israel speaks to it together."[5] Therefore Christian faith hears

---

2. Busch, *Unter dem Bogen des einen Bundes*.

3. Barth, *Gottes Gnadenwahl*, 35.

4. In the first edition of *Romans* we have already read that "Israel is conscious of its own *Sache* as being distant and hostile. Israel, the hearer and guardian of the Word of God has placed itself outside and beside Christ. The church has crucified Jesus Christ. The way of Christ and the way of the church are, from now on, two separated ways" (R I:269).

5. Marquardt, *Die Entdeckung des Judentums*, 110.

both words: the *logos* in the Greek Bible as well as the *dabar* of Israel in the Hebrew Bible. Christian faith is *dia-logical* from the beginning.

The unity of Christian faith with Israel has a special significance for the knowledge of Israel *post Christum natum*. Israel stands in the hidden reign of God in general world history rather than remaining in the churchly sphere of Jesus Christ. Barth's understanding of the enigmatic existence of the Jews in world history showed his interest of viewing it in light of the providential significance of the history of Israel (*CD* III/3: 212f).

In his approach to the history of the Jews, Barth did not take a point of departure through historical relativism or the self-understanding of the Jews or the interpretation of philo-Semitism or anti-Semitism. Rather, he associated himself with the standpoint of the Christian message, which means God in Jesus Christ (*CD* III/3:216–7). The Jews are "the librarians of the Church," (Augustine, quoted in *CD* III/3:212), and the Old Testament is ultimately the book of their books, and originally their sacred canon without which even the church cannot ultimately live (*CD* III/3:212). Barth, in his doctrine of providence, saw a trace of the divine world governance in the special history of the Jews. They are not "antique-dealers," but God's partner in the covenant, upon whose fulfillment the church is founded. Therefore, they are a constantly self-renewed actualization and demonstration of the human being in virtue of their sacred canon. As Barth states, "His appointment and constitution of Israel as the bearer of light and salvation to all nations is actualized in the death and revealed in the resurrection of the One who is the remnant of the Jewish remnant of Israel, and who definitely died and rose again on behalf of this remnant, indeed of Israel as a whole" (*CD* III/3: 217). Therefore it is natural to say that Barth's perspective on the history of the Jews and their covenantal significance is based on God's faithfulness to them through the cross and resurrection of Jesus Christ as their Messiah.

However, in his doctrine of election, Barth tended to confuse, to some extent, a christological embrace of the Jews with an ecclesiological integration of them. A theological knowledge of Judaism can be seen and judged only from one central place onwards, that is, the church. The church believes in God's mercy, and therefore it perceives the light that shines in the history of Israel. Facing this factual knowledge of revelation, knowledge of Israel and Judaism is therefore a "becoming" knowledge under God's promise in which we meet the mysterious persistence of the

Jews (*CD* III/3:215). The becoming knowledge in Barth's sense is based on God's gracious faithfulness to the covenant with God's unfaithful people.

When Israel is viewed from the Jewish Christian and apostolic perspective—and from the viewpoint of the church—Barth's discussion of the relationship between Israel and the church in terms of their union can be seen explicitly in the example of St Paul as the unity of the Jewish and Gentile apostle (*CD* II/2:268–69). Barth makes an attempt to bring Paul into Jewish-Christian dialogue in view of his three chapters concerning Israel (Romans 9–11) (cf. *CD* II/2:202–5, 240–49, 267–305). Barth's view depicts the Jewish-Christian position as a point of departure and a relational point to the whole doctrine of Israel. In writing his doctrine of predestination, Barth was attentive to the destiny, the right, and the significance of Jewish Christians who disappeared and who became nonexistent and meaningless. From the perspective of Jewish Christians, the church lives with Israel or Israel dies in the arms of the church. In fact, the life or death of Israel in the arms of the church (tolerance or exclusion of Jewish Christians in the community) was the field of confrontation during the year of Barth's church struggle.

In view of the life of the Apostle Paul, Barth states that the position of Jewish Christians becomes at the same time the apostolic position (*CD* II/2:252–53, 269). In the life and mission of the Apostle Paul, Israel lives in the church and the church lives from Israel onwards.[6] According to Barth, Paul exercised his apostleship in the name and for the sake of the church and Israel (*CD* II/2:202). St Paul is an apostle of the church and also—in the sense of the Old Testament—a prophet of Israel. He belongs to those who become Israel from Israel (*CD* II/2:214–15). As a former persecutor of Christians, he is one of those who is saved from fire, namely, like "the plucking of a brand from the burning" (*CD* II/2:232), an Israelite who participated in Israel's wrong step. In his current state, he becomes a direct reminder of the resurrection of Jesus from the dead. He becomes especially a sign of grace. In Paul's evident pain for his people, Barth asks who could become more an Israelite than this apostle (*CD* II/2:202).

---

6. "An anti-Semitism which mistakes and disputes Israel's election from outside can have nothing to do with this zeal.... The Church cannot yield even a hair's breadth to it. The church leads no life of its own beside and against Israel. It draws its life from Israel, and Israel itself lives in it. It is the realization of the life of the community which is Israel's own destiny...The praise of the Church is for the God who is the God of all (Rom 3:29) and therefore over all, the God of the community which embraces Israel and the Church, and the Church and Israel" (*CD* II/2:205).

The unity of a salvation history and an apostolic authority provides a basis for Barth to adopt the Jewish Christian position in dealing with the relationship of the church to Israel. Based on the type of salvation history of St Paul, Barth argued that the existence of Jewish Christians was to be understood as a sign of an inviolable and inextricable continuity of God's way for Israel. "In his own person as the bearer of the apostolic office Paul does indeed see his people, Israel, associated not only passively but actively in the saving events in the presence and work of the risen Jesus Christ"(*CD* II/2:268). The apostle Paul represents this fulfillment as a Jewish person as well as an apostle of the Gentiles. Therefore, Barth regards him as the key figure for the interpretation of the history of Israel.

As a preaching apostle of the old revelation of God in which Israel also takes part, Paul is not "the bringer of a strange revelation" but the interpreter and witness to the words of prophets, which are truly known to the synagogue (*CD* II/2:253). In the figure of the Apostle Paul, it becomes manifest that the church is not only the aim of the election of Israel but is especially the aim of the synagogue. Even though the incomprehensible calling and conversion of the Gentiles to the church, and therefore to Israel, has taken place, the comprehensible conversion of Israel has not yet taken place. It is still a future event. Consequently, the future of Israel and the synagogue will be merged into the church (*CD* II/2:229). A christological-eschatological integration of Israel would be announced in the example of St Paul in a preexemplifying manner.[7] In Barth's description, we see Israel as a vessel of dishonor, a witness to God's judgment, whereas the church becomes a vessel of honor, a witness of God's mercy.

Within the one community of God, Israel serves as the representation of divine judgment, and the church as the representation of the divine mercy. Within the one elected community of God, Israel takes a passing form while the church takes the form of becoming (*CD* II/2:195). In Barth's speaking of the preexistence of the church in Israel (*CD* II/2:212), Israel's mission is "a preparation for the Church" (*CD* II/2:233), thus the church is "in fact the first and final determination of Israel" (*CD* II/2:266).

---

7. "Israel is foreordained to be the Church, and finally to be revealed as the Church, with the revelation of its Messiah, being merged in the Church as its proper and final form" (*CD* II/2:298). At this point, Bertold Klappert notices an ecclesiological integration model anchored in Barth's concept of Israel. Klappert, *Israel und die Kirche*, 39–40.

Barth's doctrine of Israel is located in and moves in a Pauline perspective, not only on the basis of Paul's doctrine, but also in light of his life and his understanding of salvation history. Israel stands always under the viewpoint of God's promise, and also under its fulfillment. For Paul, what empowers life, mission, and the apostolic office is the Word of God, who is Jesus Christ, the Son of the God of Abraham, Isaac and Jacob. Election is focused on Jesus Christ, in whom the indissoluble unity of the one community in its two forms (Israel and the church) is based.

Accordingly, it is important to note that some ecclesiological elements in Barth's doctrine of election need to be seen in reference to eschatological-messianic time (*CD* II/2:298). As the foundation of election, the promise of God, which is given to the people of Israel, is unshakable. The word "beloved" is not the first, but definitely the last word. Barth saw the future of Israel—even including the present state of the unbelieving Jews—as well as the future of the church from the eschatological perspective of God's gracious love (*CD* II/2:303). Israel will not be dissolved into the church, but rather both of them will together participate in God's promise and blessing in the future.

What makes Christian anti-Semitism impossible for Barth is "the relegation of the Jewish question into the realm of eschatology" (*CD* II/2:305). "That Israel's hope is really the hope of Israel and the Church, and is therefore future, makes no difference to the fact that in relation to Israel the responsibility of the church, which itself lives by God's mercy, is already a wholly present reality" (*CD* II/2:305).[8] The eschatological expectation of unity between the church and Israel is described by the Jew Franz Werfel: "How much longer will this Hell reign here on Earth / with blind hate in the South, West, East and North? / Until the Jews becomes Christians/ and until the Christians have become Jews."[9]

Jesus Christ is the ontic ground of the election of Israel in history, In the apostolic mission, Christ fulfils the history of Israel. Therefore, the apostolic office and mission define both Israel's history and promise of renewal through Christ. The life of Israel has already become life from

---

8. In this regard it would be absurd to criticize Barth for not taking into account the relationship between the doctrine of election and eschatology in the concept of time. For this critique cf. Pannenberg, *Systematic Theology*, 3:453.

9. "Delphiches Orakel," in F. Werfel, *Das lyrische Werk*, ed. A. D. Klarmann (Frankfurt, 1967), 527. Cited in Busch, "Covenant of Grace Fulfilled in Christ," 21–22. [With permission of the author]

the dead, in other words, the life of resurrection. At this point, Barth rejected the Christian fanaticism of carrying on a mission towards the Jews, because the true Jewish mission is "the Gentile mission and the existence of the church of Jews." Therefore, the hardening of the rest of the people in Israel does not imply that God has abandoned Israel. The church understands its own origin and goal only in its unity with Israel (*CD* II/2:284). The free grace of God's mercy moves into the center of all Barth's reflections on Israel.

In its interpretative character, Barth's concept of the dissolution of Israel and the synagogue into the church does not necessarily mean a negation of Israel, but its actual revival. As far as the people of Israel is "the librarians of the church," confessing Jesus Christ means confessing the fulfillment of God's promise given first to Israel, which is "the substance of all the hope of the fathers, of all the exhortations and threats of Moses and the prophets, of all the sacrifice in the tabernacle and the temple, of every letter in the sacred books of Israel" (*CD* II/2:204). The church does not lead a life of its own beside and against Israel. It draws its life from Israel and Israel itself lives in it. The God of the community embraces Israel and the church, and the church and Israel (*CD* II/2:205). The fundamental thesis signifies that Jesus Christ is both the crucified Messiah of and for Israel, and the secret Lord of the church (*CD* II/2:198, 207). Israel and church can be defined as the entire environment of the man Jesus.

Like St Paul, Israel is snatched from the fire. In the Christian Jew, the history of Israel is expressed as an experience of survival in a new existence. God's mercy is life from the dead. This is an evangelical knowledge of Israel based on divine graciousness that overcomes Israel's unfaithfulness. "It is not a case of Israel coming to the Church, but of the Church coming to Israel" (*CD* II/2:275). "God needed the Jews for the sake of the Gentiles" (*CD* II/2:279). Herein Barth understands the direction of Israel's hope eschatologically.[10]

Although the synagogue "has aroused the hatred and envy of every kind of Gentile arrogance, yet also been the subject of its own dilettante dreaming" (*CD* II/2:204), Barth argues that the church must *not* embrace

---

10. However, Barth did not conceptualize a dialectical relation between Israel's way to the church and the church's way to Israel, because of his christological concept of salvation history. Nevertheless Barth did not ignore that Christians are called among the Gentiles and move toward Israel, so that they remain guests in the house of Israel, that is, "only transplanted aliens" (*CD* II/2:288).

anti-Judaism to dispute it, but rather assert and teach God's eternal election of Israel in response to it. According to Barth, "confessing Jesus Christ, it confesses the fulfillment of everything that is pledged to Israel as promise, the substance of all the hope of the fathers, of all the exhortations and threats of Moses and the prophets, of all the sacrifice in the tabernacle and the temple, of every letter in the sacred books of Israel" (*CD* II/2:204). Therefore in harmony with the Old Testament prophets, the church "contests the vaunting lie, the national-legalistic Messiah-dream of the Synagogue," because Barth illustrates this fact in accordance with the life of St Paul.[11]

When Israel is seen in the perspective of predestination, Jesus Christ, the Son of the God of Abraham, Isaac, and Jacob is the substance of election. In Barth's doctrine of the election, Jesus Christ is not only the elected man but also the electing God. Election of human beings is grounded in this event in which Jesus Christ is not only noetically but also ontically the ground and the substance of the election. This implies that rejection happens only to Jesus, and thus as the single Man he gives the glory to God. A Trinitarian understanding of predestination speaks out against a *decretum absolutum*. Predestination is neither condemnation nor nonrejection of human beings (*CD* II/2:167, cf. 158–59).

Barth's doctrine of predestination based on the particularity and the uniqueness of Jesus Christ provides a framework for his teaching on Israel. As Barth subordinated the doctrine of election to the doctrine of God, the election in Jesus Christ becames the modus of divine effect toward the outside world in general (*CD* II/2:190–91). Because Jesus Christ as the electing God and the elected man is one, the election of humankind actually takes place in God. In Barth's view, Israel's election participates in Jesus Christ who is the substance of election, and stands under the actuality of the promise of the election in Christ.

From a christological standpoint, Barth described the function of the church in terms of faith, hope, and love, whereas the function of the synagogue is grasped on an unspiritual and negative level with regard to its empirical and historical realm. Barth's negative description of synagogue, associated with a description of the negative role of Israel,

11. Barth's negative selection of the synagogue as representing Jewish obstinacy, melancholy, crankiness, fantasy, conservatism, and an antique certainly speaks against this selection. In his theological-dogmatic understanding of Judaism, Barth differentiates Jews from Christians.

becomes controversial, albeit within the positive significance of his overall teaching concerning Israel. The service of the church is to witness to God's mercy and to proclaim new life through the grace of God's election in Jesus Christ for all. But the service of Israel is linked to the judgment of God and thus to the frailty and death of the passing people. There is something unfortunate sounding in his guiding sentence: "In its form as Israel it is determined for hearing, and in its form as the Church for believing the promise sent forth to man. To the one elected community of God is given in the one case its passing, and in the other its coming form" (*CD* II/2:195).[12]

Israel should come to faith and come into the church, "to the fulfillment of the purpose for which it was determined in accordance with its election" (*CD* II/2:261). The life of Israel appears to be unreal life because "it must be the personification of a half-venerable, half-gruesome relic, of a miraculously preserved antique, of human whimsicality" (*CD* II/2:263). According to Barth, Israel's unbelief would hardly be different from the gruesome godlessness of others, because the elect "will recognize the rejected in the godlessness of others": "in all the blatant and refined examples of dreadful corruption; in the brutality and sophistry, the stupidity and lack of character, the self-will and frivolity, the superstition, heresy and unbelief by which they see themselves surrounded on every hand in ever widening circles" (*CD* II/2:452).[13]

Nevertheless, Barth's thesis of Jesus Christ as the substance of election is formulated polemically against a traditional Reformed understanding of the predestination associated with *decretum absolutum*. This refers to a decree to elect a fixed number of people and to reprobate a fixed number of others. Before God sent his eternal Son, there was God's hidden de-

---

12. Barth's idea of the christological integration of Israel into the church seems to become manifest in that as the passing form of the community, Israel makes room for the church as its coming form: "Where Israel apprehends and believes its own election in Jesus Christ it lives on in the church and is maintained in it as its secret origin and as the hidden substance" (*CD* II/2:201).

13. In challenging Barth's model of Israel's witness to God negatively, Marquardt argues, "If one regards the deepest secret of serious atheism as an intellectual, spiritual and practical way of keeping open the wound of the imperfect, the as yet incomplete world, the human being not yet human, the still to be experienced 'Behold, the tabernacle of God is among the people' and 'God with us,' then every serious atheism has its biblical justification in the Jewish No. More precisely, in the Jewish No, it can become serious." See Marquardt, "Feinde um unsretwillen," in Marquardt, *Verwegenheiten*, 336.

cree. This is God's absolute decree, which means the doctrine of double predestination (*praedestinatio gemina*). Against "the idolatrous concept of a *decretum absolutum*" (*CD* II/2:143), Barth made a new version of the doctrine of double predestination. For Barth, the thesis regarding *homo labilis* must be conceptualized and improved in a christological direction. In confrontation with the controversy between Supralapsarians and Infralapsarians, Barth attempted to overcome limitations of the two parties, that is, the divine disposition with respect to *homo creatus et lapsus* in the Infralapsarian framework and the divine disposition with respect to *homo creabilis et labilis* in the supralapsarian framework.[14]

According to Barth, before choosing or rejecting human beings beforehand and eternally, God determined Godself to be for them as Creator, Reconciler, and Redeemer. "This one person, Jesus Christ, was there with God in the beginning. Predestination is precisely this" (*CD* II/2:157).[15] If predestination is, first of all, God's determination of Godself before it becomes the determination of human beings, then election is two-edged. A universal predestination already would be happening in Christ. In him "God in His free grace determines Himself for sinful man and sinful man for Himself. He therefore takes upon Himself the rejection of man with all its consequences, and elects man to participation in his own glory" (*CD* II/2:94ff). Because this divine self-determination has taken place, this predestination can be seen in a modified sense of the old supralapsarian idea. In the christological framework of double predestination, the crucified Christ becomes sin and curse for us, but the resurrected Christ indicates that the rejection on the cross is overcome by the election.

From the perspective of the resurrection, Barth argued that God has both cancelled the finis of the Jewish rejection of Christ and, against the will of Israel, acknowledged God's own will with Israel. Through the

---

14. These two parties seek God's primal and basic purpose in the context of election and reprobation of the individual by establishing certain fixed numbers in eternity. They centered exclusively upon the individuals as such rather than God's free grace in Jesus Christ for all (*CD* II/2:133). For this reason, they do not "proclaim the free grace of God as glad tidings" (*CD* II/2:134).

15. Furthermore, "we cannot arrive at this assertion until we venture to take a big step, until we admit that the same person, Jesus Christ, stands on both sides of the equation describing divine predestination. One side of the equation (the subject or the object of predestination) is always lost in our musings and usually both are. But we cannot allow that to happen any longer" (*CD* II/2:158–59).

resurrection, God cancelled the definitive rejection by the Jews of Jesus Christ. Therefore Barth thought that the Jewish rejection of Jesus Christ was to be answered positively in light of the resurrection (*CD* II/2:291).

So Barth's christological understanding of election is by no means oriented against the rejection of Israel and Judaism but grounds and justifies the actuality of their election in Christ.[16] Barth's predestinational understanding of Israel's election in light of Jesus Christ presupposes a confirmation of a forward-oriented divine plan rather than falling backwards into the historical-speculative realm. The election of Jesus Christ was his election of suffering and death for himself, in other words, in representation of the sinners who rejected him. Jesus Christ experienced their rejection and is proved as the elected man in his resurrection. All humankind is in Christ "objectively" reconciled because Christ has borne the whole rejection of the cross upon himself, regardless of whether they know it or not.[17] If Christ is the substance of the election of Israel, Israel's rejection cannot be separated from his election. God kills only to make alive. God does not let Godself be dismayed by the typical unfaithfulness and ingratitude of Israel (*CD* II/2:263–64).

Therefore Judaism is christologically relevant not only in a negative sense but also in a positive sense. According to Barth, as we know God only in Jesus Christ, so we know God along with the man Jesus of Nazareth and his people represented by him. God without this man and without his people would be a strange God, an other (*CD* II/2:6). The election of Jesus Christ is directed toward this model. God is no other than God who is in care of this man and united with his people in him and through him.

Four moments (christological, ecclesiological, predestinational and eschatological) characterize Barth's framework and structure in the doctrine of election. Through the Holy Spirit, an individual becomes a recipient of revelation and then becomes one of the special people of Israel in the Old Testament, and the church in the New Testament. This subjective

---

16. "What is decided in Jesus Christ from all eternity and in the midst of time is also and primarily decided about Israel—even about disobedient Israel. Old things have passed away. All things are become new. Thus the result of Jewish unbelief . . . is not to be sought outside but only within the results of the divine mercy" (*CD* II/2:262–63).

17. The basic concept of the doctrine of universal election in Jesus Christ can be found in Blumhardt, *Ansprachen, Predigten, Reden, Briefe: 1865–1917*, 134–35. Cf. Moltmann, *Coming of God*, 249.

reality is based on the incarnation of the eternal Word. The *assumptio carnis* of the Word of God is the assumption of all flesh, of human nature through the Word. This implies a christological/soteriological embrace in the sense of the representation of all flesh in the flesh of Jesus of Nazareth. This christologically representative model makes the divine history affect and integrate humanity into the testimony of God's mercy. In other words, the theologically legitimate ground for the election of natural Israel lies in the incarnation of Jesus Christ.

This refers to a comprehensive election in which Barth conceived of all others in togetherness being elected in Christ. Christ's function is his election of suffering and death for the sin of the world. Barth's concept of the comprehensive election marks the representational and justifying act of Jesus Christ. In other words, the exclusive election of Jesus Christ, which is eternally grounded in God's free election in love, is not merely narrowed down into the parochial realm of the church but is fundamentally open and inclusive of people outside the sphere of the church. With the idea of the environment of Jesus Christ, Barth expresses a primary object of another election, which means the election of human beings correspondingly set into motion through the election of Jesus Christ. The election of Jesus Christ "is the original and all-inclusive election" (*CD* II/2:117). The natural and historical environment of Jesus Christ (*CD* II/2:196) is comprehensive and inclusive of the people of Israel in a natural sense and of the church, as well as of the Jew and the Gentile in a historical sense.

Israel, as the natural environment of Jesus Christ, has a christological structure. In his knowledge of himself and of his election, the man Jesus is both the go-between and the center of his natural and historical environment. Herein Barth's concept of the rainbow of the one covenant is imprinted secured by arching over the whole. Therefore the Jews are the only natural proof for the existence of God. For the concept of christological substance, the God of Israel is the One who does not exist without God's people of Israel. What arches over the church and Israel is not, therefore, an explicitly theological concept, but the secret of God's will of the covenant revealed in Jesus Christ. The relationship between Israel and church, which is characterized by the bow of the covenant, is realized and fulfilled in Christ. In a relationship between Israel and church God's will of covenant is realized in dialectical yes and no.

The Positive Meaning of Israel in God's Election

Although Barth depicts Judas as the archetypal figure of rejection and as representative of Israel as such, Judas himself stands paradoxically in the closest proximity to the church. Like Jesus "Judas alone belongs to the tribe of Judah, the seed of David" (*CD* II/2:459). He was genuinely elected, although rejected at the same time (*CD* II/2:459). But Barth distances himself from identifying Judas exclusively with Israel, because "Jesus was handed over . . . from within the Church." "The Church stands and acts in identity with the Israel which rejected itself Messiah, together with the heathen world which allied itself with this Israel, and made itself a partner in its guilt" (*CD* II/2:460).

But the betrayal of Judas is devoured in the victory of God on the cross. God wants to act towards Godself, as Judas acts towards Jesus. This is the first and positive divine handing over. In the decree of the eternal love of God, the divine positive *paradounai* is included (*CD* II/2:475, 480). As far as Judas's rejection of Jesus is grounded in the eternal election, God, in the performance of God's will, could be related to this point of rejection. The actual betrayal of Judas becomes God's actual point of contact. The work of Judas is done within the church. Likewise "the apostles—plural!—have to share the guilt of Israel and the Gentile world" (*CD* II/2:461). Here one significantly notes that Barth is far from viewing the church in an idealistic manner. Barth does not ascribe guilt for Jesus's death exclusively to Judas or Israel. Although Jews were not totally innocent of the death of Jesus, the church is indicted with the same charge. Barth insists that "the basic flaw was revealed in Judas. . . . It was that of the apostolate as a whole" (*CD* II/2:471–72, 475).

Barth observed an enigmatic double existence of Israel as Isaac and Ishmael, as Jacob and Esau, as Moses and Pharaoh, as church and synagogue (*CD* II/2:240), and speaks of the double realization of the election of Israel. The Gentiles were—without claim, or without merit—accepted into the righteousness of God through God's mercy. What is important for Barth is to retain Israel's calling and hope in one's mind and to carry them in one's heart. In view of Judaism, it is of special significance to acknowledge Israel in Israel, the elect among the elected. The history of Israel stands in closest relation to the essence of God, who, in God's unconditional and incomprehensible freedom, will renew, prove, and glorify God's being as the future Being; God's mercy as the future mercy: "[God] renews, establishes and glorifies Himself by His own future . . . by His future mercy, His compassion by His future compassion" (*CD* II/2:218). God grounds the history of Israel as the order of God's righteousness. Although Israel is defined as a vessel of God's wrath, in view of God's future, God's wrath will be enveloped by God's mercy in an eschatological embrace (*CD* II/2:227, 283).

In this dialectical fashion of predestination, Barth articulated a positive meaning of the church of the gospel, which is, in fact, the first and final determination of Israel. However, this direction is not supposed to be misunderstood as an ecclesiological model of integration without qualification. According to Barth, the gospel preexists even in the realm of the law. When this prehistory is enacted within the history of Israel, Israel participates, together with the church, in the perfect form of community, that is, the body of Christ. In other words, Israel is not dissolved into the church, but rather together with the church it has a universal mission.

The church of the coming person preexisted in Israel. Therefore "it does not alter Israel's special determination, but illumines and interprets it" (*CD* II/2:266). Barth described the relationship of Israel to the church in the sense of indissoluble unity: "As the crucifixion of Jesus is a divine benefit in its association with His resurrection, so also is Israel's history of suffering in its association with the pre-history of the Gospel enacted within it" (*CD* II/2:266). Israel's participation in Jesus Christ—regardless of whether they remain unbelieving Jews—does not necessarily mean the replacement or integration of Israel into the sphere of the church, but articulates Jesus Christ's embracing of unbelieving Jews as his natural environment. Israel is not only elected for rejection, but "the unity of the man who both passes and comes in the person of Him, who has suffered death for all and brought life to light for all" (*CD* II/2:267). In the case of the church preexisting in Israel, Barth positively confirmed Israel's election. Therefore the church lives on in Israel, and Israel lives on in the church for coexistence and pro-existence.

What is striking is Barth's reflection on the remnant for God's sake. In correspondence to the living God, Barth conceives of the remnant in connection with the representation, so that he has an inclusive understanding of the remnant. In Barth's interpretation of Romans 9–11, Elijah functions as a prototype of the remnant. Barth legitimizes St. Paul and his office of apostleship as the evidence that God has not thrown away

God's people (*CD* II/2:269). However, Elijah does not form one single exception. Where he stands, there are seven thousand who have not bowed their knees to Baal. These elected people form Elijah's invisible surroundings and represent the whole of Israel with this solitary prophet. These are remnants chosen by God's grace, rather than an irrelevant minority in Israel. Through recourse to the beginning of God's covenantal relation to Israel, God repeats and proves God's beginning with Israel. The new grounding of the covenant between God and humankind is an empirically perceivable sign of God's faithfulness to Israel. In the case of Abraham, election is a living order from the beginning (*CD* II/2:214).

This thesis provides a new chance for the whole of Israel. If God's action makes a new creation, the new covenant is proof of God's performing will upon the whole of Israel. This protological aspect carries the weight of content in eschatological correspondence. The whole of Israel is not sanctified through the rest, but the rest represents the whole Israel. What is represented authentically in the rest is the root, that is, Jesus Christ, the last-born, but, in fact, the firstborn brother. In this regard we speak of an immanent continuity between God and Israel that is grounded in God's mercy and is created in it. According to Barth, there is no election without the covenant, and vice versa. The theology of election is a theology of covenant for Barth. Correspondingly the doctrine of election is to be understood as the doctrine of God's will of covenant. All events of God's will are the event of God's will of covenant. Therefore the doctrine of election retains a theocentric character in matters of Israel as God's covenantal people.[18]

Like Luther, who saw an evangelical rejoicing of the law in the gospel,[19] Barth anchors the Torah as a category of the covenant in the promise. In this framework of Barth's covenantal theology, Judaism retains a theologically important place for Barth, where Judaism is not merely reduced into a Jewish religion of law. By placing Judaism primarily in the

---

18. In his *Gospel and Law* (1935), Barth argues, it is necessary to speak of covenant and promise. The Torah must be seen in connection with the reality of the covenant. The gospel then becomes the gospel when the Torah is hidden and included in it. Barth begins his theological foundation of God's covenant by determining the relationship between law and gospel with reference to Galatians 3:17. Anyone who speaks of the topic of the relation between gospel and law must, first of all, speak of the gospel. The law, according to Galatians 3:17, followed the promise, in other words, the law must follow the gospel. Cf. Barth, *Evangelium und Gesetz*, 5.

19. Cf. Luther, "How Christians Should Regard Moses (1525)" 135–48.

promise, Barth understands Israel as hearer of the promise so that Israel remains a people of hope.[20]

According to Barth, the concrete history of Jesus Christ is the history of the confirmation of Israel's permanent and complete covenant (Jer 31:31–34) and worldwide reconciliation (2 Cor 5:19–21), which implies God's election of Jesus Christ. For Barth, Jesus Christ, as the mirror of the fatherly heart of God (Luther), or as the mirror of the election (Calvin), becomes the ontological ground for God's election of Israel. Election as God's gracious election is God's yes to Israel and to all peoples in Jesus Christ. The eschaton of the history of Jesus Christ as the Jew, which presupposes the priority of the election of Israel, primarily reveals the electing God of Israel. The election of Jesus Christ as the Messiah of Israel and the Lord of the church and of the world includes the one community of God in the two forms: Israel and the church. Israel is God's chosen community, and the church exists as the ecumenical people of God from all nations in the framework of God's one and nonterminated covenant.

In superordering the election of Israel over the justification of the ungodly in a systematically dogmatic way, Barth paved the way for the paradigm shift from the Reformation principle of justification toward Israel's election.[21] At this juncture, we notice that Barth integrates the important Reformation understanding of the doctrine of election as the mystery of justification into the knowledge of God's faithfulness toward the election of Israel/Judaism. Understood this way, justification of the ungodly is a participation in God's election of Israel because God's covenant with Israel is not terminated. God becomes known only through God. In other words, the knowledge of God is identical with the knowledge of election. The covenant between God and humans is based on God's eternal will.

---

20. From this perspective, the doctrines of justification and sanctification can be understood as coming out of God's covenant with Israel. Israel's election is confirmed in Jesus Christ. At the same time, the permanence of Israel's covenant (*CD* IV/1:32) is preserved in Jesus Christ. Israel as the people of God's covenant is not replaced.

21. In Barth's paradigm shift, Israel/Judaism and the church exist as the two forms of the one elected community of God. Therefore Barth understood justification of the ungodly theologically and covanentally from the standpoint of God's faithful election of Israel. Justification is not supposed to end God's faithfulness in the election of Israel/Judaism, but a Christian teaching of justification is subordinated to God's election of Israel and extracted from this election.

The problem of the knowledge of God consists in God's covenantal relationship to humans and the superiority of God in this election.

God in the Transforming Act

Between the immanence and the transcendence of God, Barth finds the concept of the objectivity of God, which is the fundamental concept of his understanding of election (*CD* II/1:20). Barth's establishment of the first commandment as a theological axiom is the necessary consequence coming from the insight of the self-sanctification of God as the grounding structure of divine action and as the decisive way of divine objectivity.

Barth's fundamental thesis in his doctrine of God reads: "Alles in allem real verändernde Tatsache, dass Gott ist" (*KD* II/1:289; *CD* II/1:258). It indicates that the objectivity of God is really the transforming fact. That "God is" has its truth in a real revolution of all life-connections. There is no Being of God without this revolution. Knowledge of God's being is performed in accordance with this transformation. The concept of the revolution of God, which was a guiding principle in shaping the eschatology and political theology of Barth in the two editions of *Romans*, is integrated into his doctrine of God in *Church Dogmatics*. For this reason, in the act of revelation, God stands "in favor of the threatened innocent, the oppressed poor, widows, orphans and aliens." "God always takes His stand unconditionally and passionately . . . against the lofty and on behalf of the lowly; against those who already enjoy right and privilege and on behalf of those who are denied it and deprived of it" (*CD* II/1:386).

According to Barth, God's being is in becoming not in the sense of ontological correspondence, but is in becoming in the coming of God's kingdom in a transforming and eschatological sense. There is a dialectically organic relationship between God as *der ganz Andere* (the Wholly Other) and God as *der ganz Ändernde* (the Wholly Changing) in Barth's thought.[22] The doctrine of the Trinity stands in contrast to all other possible doctrines of God or concepts of revelation (*CD* I/1:301). Barth's hermeneutical approach to the Trinity is far from being critical, realistic,

---

22. "They should and must live with the fact that . . . materially changes, all things and everything in all things—the fact that God is." *CD* II/1: 258. For the term of God as the wholly Other (*der ganz Andere*), see R II:4, 11, 17, 25, 82, 274, 351. For the term of God as *der ganz und gar Änderende*, see *CD* IV/4:161.

and dialectical out of the veiling-unveiling structure and concept of God's revelation.

Jüngel does not take the objectifying and epistemologically grounded aspect of God into full account in dealing with Barth's conception of election and the Trinity.[23] When it comes to the Trinitarian doctrine of God, it is of special significance to recognize an antimythological dimension of the concept of God in Barth's theology.[24] Thus Jüngel's attempt at localizing ontologically Barth's talk about God goes against Barth's intention. Jüngel's thesis is that "God's being is ontologically localized."[25]

According to Barth, looking to God in Jesus Christ has to do with radical and real transformation. This is the event of altering and transforming the whole human situation and the history of the world. God as the New is this New (CD IV/3.2:711). Barth's concept of God, which had been shaped in a social and political life setting since his Safenwil period, cannot properly be understood without attention to the left-wing Hegelian concept of praxis, as well as without God's covenantal relationship with Israel.[26] The ontological localization of God's being in becoming must be discussed in relation to the postulate of the social concept of God's reality (God's being is in acts of transformation and revolution) as well as the Jewish idea of the becoming of the living God (in view of the particularity of God's covenantal relationship with Israel).

For Barth the root of the doctrine of the Trinity is anchored in the lordship of God in the Old-Testament sense. The lordship of God, which constitutes the root of the doctrine of the Trinity, must be understood in Barth's koinonial term of the threeness and the oneness of the Triunity

23. Cf. Jüngel, *God's Being Is in Becoming*.

24. Marquardt, *Theologie und Sozialismus*, 232: According to Marquardt, "Jüngel rightly remarks: 'Barth's dogmatics makes ontological statements all along the lines. But this dogmatics is not an ontology.'"

25. Jüngel, *God's Being Is in Becoming*, xxv. Against this direction, Hans-Joachim Kraus states that God's being, in the theology of Karl Barth, shares itself in the history of God's coming. Barth's idea of the becoming of God's objectivity is based primarily on the fundamental and categorical meaning of the Old Testament rather than the categories of Hegel's philosophy of history. Kraus, *Reich Gottes*, 102, 180.

26. Cf. Chung, *Karl Barth und die Hegelsche Linke*, 62. God's Being is in becoming in the coming of God's kingdom, which takes place in the three forms of the parousia of Jesus Christ (CD IV/3.§69. 4). Barth's concept of the revolution of God, which is associated with the real principle of transformation, would point to another dimension of God's radical transcendence, without losing its anti-ontological left-wing Hegelian dimension.

(*Dreieinigkeit Gottes*, *CD* I/1:§9.3).²⁷ Furthermore, Barth discussed God in divine communal relations in terms of the formulation of the one who loves in freedom (*CD* II/1:§28). As Barth writes, "God is not in abstracto Father, Son and Holy Ghost, the triune God. He is so with a definite purpose and reference; in virtue of the love and freedom in which in the bosom of His triune being He has foreordained Himself from and to all eternity" (*CD* II/2:79). The guiding principle for Barth's dogmatics is none other than that "God is" (*KD* II/1:288).

God's being must be understood in terms of God's being in love and freedom. As with the love of God, divine freedom "has its truth and reality in the inner Trinitarian life of the Father with the Son by the Holy Spirit" (*CD* II/1:317). In this light, God's being is in becoming, in the coming of God's kingdom, especially in view of the God of Israel. *Analogia relationis* is not merely ontological, but participatory, committed, and eschatological. The coming of God's kingdom, the knowledge of the new heaven and the new earth will be the final, universal, and definitive manifestation of God in Jesus Christ in whose death and resurrection this great transformation has already taken place. Christian community, with penultimate seriousness, participates in the act of God in Jesus Christ, not as an idle spectator, but in active obedience.

God's objectivity (*Gegenständlichkeit*) opens the new world to the knowledge of God. Barth's understanding of God as the transforming reality would be consonant with the Jewish understanding of God. The Being of God objectively carries out Godself in transformation of God's existence. Therefore "God exists" is not a neutral indicative-sentence, because God changes our situation and thus God is confessed as the reality of this change.²⁸

However, from the ontological perspective, Jüngel makes a critique of Gollwitzer's concept of God's existence as "God in and for Godself," because Gollwitzer stands in line with the classical concept of substance. Although Gollwitzer conceives of God's being as a personal being in terms of *analogia relationis*, Jüngel insists that "God in and for Godself" has to be formulated on the basis of the event of revelation. Revelation is God's self-interpretation. Jüngel does not reject that Gollwitzer is aware

---

27. The perichoretic fellowship is what Barth calls the "definite participation of each mode of being in the other modes of being" (*CD* I/1:370). What remains a mystery in dealing with the Trinity is due to *mysterium trinitatis* (*CD* I/1:368).

28. Gollwitzer, *Existenz Gottes im Bekenntnis des Glaubens*, 172.

of the possibility of speaking of Godself-relatedness in a Trinitarian way. Nevertheless, Gollwitzer's concept of "God in and for Godself" is proved concretely false when seen in terms of the correspondence of the relation *ad extra* and *ad intra*, namely, *analogia relationis*.[29]

It is certain that Gollwitzer draws the distinction between the essence and the will of God. However, his distinction does not "leave a gap in a metaphysical background to the being of God which is indifferent to God's historical acts of revelation."[30] According to Barth, "God does not will to be understood otherwise, than in the concreteness of life, in the determination of His will, which is as such a determination of His being" (*CD* II/2:79). What is at stake for Gollwitzer is rather to secure God's freedom with respect to God's work and giving *ad extra*. Even within Barth's reflection on God's Triunity, God remains free in God's revelation rather than becoming a prisoner of humans. God's freedom is the basis for distinguishing the essence of God from the will of God. Hence all our knowledge of God is incomprehensible and inadequate to us (*CD* I/1: 371).

Gollwitzer is concerned with distinguishing God's self-relatedness ("God in and for Godself" as the essence of God) in the immanent Trinity from God's personal being (God's appropriation as the will of God) in the economic Trinity. For Gollwitzer, the revelation of God is an announcing of God's will and living inauguration of fellowship. Revelation does not open up the possibility to establish itself over "God's being in and for Godself." In Gollwitzer's interpretation of Barth's correspondence between the immanent Trinity and the economic Trinity, he grounds himself on Barth's cardinal principle *esse sequitur operari*.[31]

In so doing, Gollwitzer runs counter to Jüngel's interpretive way of inserting an ontological location of God's being into Barth's conception of the Trinity. Gollwitzer's remark is right, in that Barth's theological approach of returning from the act of revelation to God in the immanent Trinity remains strongly christological, that is, oriented towards the act of revelation. God's act *ad extra* toward creatures is anchored in God's essence, which is God's eternal will. Nevertheless, it is not possible *per*

---

29. Jüngel, *God's Being Is in Becoming*, 106, 109.
30. Ibid., 6.
31. Gollwitzer, *Existenz Gottes im Bekenntnis des Glaubens*, 105.

analogiam to conceptualize the essence of God in human words,[32] because God remains God in the act of humiliation. Gollwitzer strongly affirms the ontological difference between God and creatures, but this difference must not be supplemented through an ontology of God. The analogy can be conceptualized as *analogia relationis* only on the basis of God's condescension into the human realm, not as the *analogia entis*.[33]

God *for us*, according to Gollwitzer, cannot be understood without reference to who God *in se* is. "God in and for Godself" means, for Gollwitzer, a biblical expression of the living God. In agreement with Miskotte, Gollwitzer states: "God exists"—God is the promising encouragement of awakening joy and shock and not a reclining indicative—calls for the performance of life. "God exists" means: "This event (today of Lk 4) and the existence of God among us are identical . . . .We bear witness to what is called in Christ Jesus . . . God exists—what does it mean finally? It means this: In the Jubilee year (Luke 4:19), it becomes obvious that we exist out of grace, certainly God exists so that we are blessed, so certainly God eternally is blessed in Godself."[34]

What is decisive in Gollwitzer's concept of God is to characterize YHWH in covenantal relationship with Israel and with the death and resurrection of Jesus Christ. "God in and for Godself" is God in covenant with Israel and Father of Jesus Christ who comes as self-sacrificing love to us. God, who acts in time (yet God is not subordinated to time), takes the way of promise to fulfillment, one that includes our past (the past of humanity) and our future (the future of humanity). Therefore God's way becomes central in what is in the doctrine of Trinity. Therefore the assertion of God's being in the New Testament is legitimate and necessary: God is love (1 John 4:16).[35] The will of God in relation to humanity is the kingdom of God.[36]

32. Ibid., 148.

33. Ibid., 106,148. 149. Therefore it is possible *per analogiam* to argue for a way of coming back only from God's will to the essence of God's will. That is, a theological way from God's historically announced will toward God's eternal will as the will of God's free love.

34. Ibid., 198.

35. Gollwitzer, "Wort 'Gott' in Christlicher Theologie," 107–8.

36. Gollwitzer, "Der Wille Gottes und die Gesellschaftliche Wirklichkeit," 274. For Barth, the reality and actuality that effects the resurrection of the crucified is "as the real ground of his life for the humans of all times the real ground of transformation of its situation" (*CD* IV/1:316).

There are two expressions describing God's objectivity in Barth's thinking. One is the primary objectivity that refers to Trinitarian knowledge. The ground of all objectivity and knowledge of God is to be sought in Godself. In the living relation of God to Godself as Father, Son, and the Holy Spirit, God becomes object to Godself. God *in se* is manifest and eternally actual in the Trinitarian relationship. This is the primary meaning of God's being in freedom and aseity (*CD* II/1:306). The objectivity of the Trinitarian life must be understood as God's deed, action, and decision.

Therefore God becomes objective to Godself. God speaks to Godself, chooses and differentiates from Godself. God's objectivity is grounded actually in God's will, election, and saying. God is predestinarian under the perspective of God's election. The concept of the objectivity of God is a concept of divine action, which is grounded in the liveliness of God. God objectifies Godself, so the liveliness of God is, as such, the objectivity of God.[37]

God's objectivity articulates God's intimacy and nearness to humans—but implies no identification with them. The independence of humans as covenant partner is grounded in the salvation of God's objectivity. God in the covenant becomes immediate to humans, and humans are capable of becoming God's covenant partner. The reality of humans, namely, the objectivity of humans, therefore, is grounded in the objectivity of God. God's liveliness (the primary objectivity) describes the secondary form of God's objectivity. This is the existence of the human nature of Jesus Christ, who stands in the innermost connection with God's election of grace. Before and after the epiphany of Jesus Christ, the existence of the human nature of Jesus Christ is the first sacrament, on the ground of *gratia unionis*, its union with the eternal Word of God. Christ's revelation is the secondary objectivity of God (*CD* II/1:53–54). In the union of the eternal Word of God with the man Jesus, covenant grace becomes explicit and manifest in the actual historical sense. The action in which God unites Godself with the man Jesus is God's secondary objectivity. The event of *gratia unionis*, that is, the life of Jesus from

---

37. *Fides quaerens intellectum* underlines Barth's understanding of God in a Trinitarian framework, in which we notice his radical understanding of God as objectivity in relation to the changing reality of the human situation. As Marquardt comments, "the *res* of objectivity of God has its intelligibility in God's choice, and its *veritas* in self-differentiation of God *in se*" (Marquardt, *Entdeckung des Judentums*, 168).

Christmas to Easter, is authentically the covenant event. Herein Barth accentuates Jesus Christ as the substance of all other elections.

For Barth, the election of Israel is in sacramental continuity with the human nature of Jesus Christ. The election of Israel, before, outside, and after the man Jesus, is also grace, not in the sense of direct *gratia unionis*, but in the sense of *gratia adoptionis*. Union is the basis of adoption: "God was present to Israel and is present to the Church *gratia adoptionis*," for the sake of Jesus Christ (*CD* II/1:485). Through Jesus Christ the adoption of Israel and the church takes place as the children of God. Therefore Israel is affirmed in a christological and messianic way, in light of the natural environment of Jesus Christ. In the understanding of Israel as the people of the covenant, Barth makes Israel belong to the natural environment of Jesus Christ.

As much as the historical environment is distinguished from the natural environment in Jesus Christ, Israel (as the people of God and also the people called Jews) is for Barth the natural environment for the election of Jesus Christ: the Word become Jewish flesh (*CD* IV/1:166, 171). God is concerned with "the existence of a man of Israel, an Israelite" (*CD* IV/1:167). The New Testament witness to Jesus as the Christ stands on the soil of the Old Testament without separation from it. The Jewish province of Jesus is the natural fact that gives meaning to Jesus's existence. The self of Jesus comes from Israel (*CD* III/2:215). Jesus as a Jew is the fulfillment of the meaning of the history of Israel. After the redeemer of the world has emerged from the middle of Israel, appeared as its Messiah, and fulfilled his mission, Jesus Christ, according to his Jewish flesh, retains the old Israel in his constitution as the natural people of the offspring of Abraham. Jesus Christ is a son of Abraham.

The covenant of God is fulfilled through God's faithfulness in the coming of the Son from the tribe of Abraham. Given this fact, Barth's understanding of Mary is located in the connection of nature and history. Because Mary is a direct recipient of grace, Barth proves the election of Israel and Mary (*KD* IV/2:48). The Jewish mother is the representative of Israel, and Israel, in its culmination of history, takes part in the event of salvation and election in a natural way. In the form of Mary, the historical meaning of the natural people of Israel becomes manifest. The natural and biological dimension of the Jewish hope should not be mystified in an anti-Semitic direction, nor should the tribe of Abraham be spiritualized in a Christian way.[38]

From the perspective of God's election, Barth saw God's faithfulness in the face of the unfaithfulness of God's people. Herein Barth was confronted with a particular manifestation or trace of God's providence (*CD* III/3:217). Therefore God's decree in the election of Israel is an eternal and unshakable one that could not change God's faithfulness. In it there is the necessity of the proof of God's existence in the enigmatic character of this people. God became flesh of our flesh in a member of Israel (*CD* III/3:221). They are a mirror of the election of God's grace and mercy, in which all people participate. In tracing God's election, providence, and covenant with the Jews, Barth affirmed the particularity of God's election for the Jews "in whom there is fullness of salvation for all men of all nations" (*CD* III/3:226).[39]

In Marquardt's interpretation of Barth's understanding of election, we read: "According to Barth, next to the particular elect in Israel, the whole people of Israel also remain elect . . . Thus, in relation to Israel we are not to speak of a *praedestinatio gemina*, but of a *praedestinatio dialectica*: not of *electio* and *reprobatio*, but of a double election."[40] Understood in this way, the doctrine of "the recapitulation of all things" (*apokatastasis panton*) becomes open for Barth: "To speak of an open number of men here instead of all men is not to impute any impotence or limitation to God's salvific design. It is God's will to save all men, as 1 Tim 2:4 and other scriptural passages clearly point out . . . The open number of the elect should not be made a closed number, as the classical doctrine of predestination tends to" (*CD* II/2:466). In connection with his doctrine

---

38. For Barth, Israel's perennial nature (*CD* IV/1:689) and survival as a people are characteristic of the *indelebilis* of Israel (R I:319). According to Barth, the history of the Jews, which is seen in light of divine rule (*gubernatione Dei*), is also a demonstration of God's existence. One is reminded of a remark from the personal physician to Frederick the Great: "The proof for God's existence, your majesty, are the Jews" (*CD* III/3:210).

39. "But in spite of the destruction and persecution and above all the assimilation and interconnection and intermingling with other nations the Jews are always still there, and always again there . . . not often loved or even assisted or protected from outside by the others, but quite the reverse; usually despised for some obscure reason, and kept apart, and even persecuted and oppressed by every possible spiritual and physical weapon, and frequently exterminated in part; yet always and everywhere surviving; again and again demonstrating its continued existence by the fact of it; again and again winning for itself an involuntary respect" (*CD* III/3:212).

40. Marquardt, *Entdeckung des Judentums*, 260.

of election, Barth was attacked and charged, on account of his language of the triumph of grace, with being on the verge of *apokatastasis*.[41] In Barth's statement we read: "The Church will then not preach an apokatastasis, nor will it preach a powerless grace of Jesus Christ or a human wickedness which is too powerful for it. But without any weakening of the contrast, and also without any arbitrary dualism, it will preach the overwhelming power of grace and the weakness of human wickedness in the face of it" (*CD* II/2:477).

Karl Barth and the Positivism of Revelation

In his prison letters, Bonhoeffer charged Barth with positivism of revelation, which deeply disturbed Barth himself.[42] According to Bonhoeffer, "secret or arcane discipline" must be kept and restored, "whereby the mysteries of the Christian faith are protected against profanation" (*LPP*: 286). In a 1944 letter (dated April 30), Bonhoeffer said that Barth was "the only one to have started along this line of thought," pointing to what a religionless/worldly Christianity would mean. However, he "did not carry it to completion, but arrived at a positivism of revelation which in the last analysis is essentially a restoration." In a religionless world, Christ is no longer an object of religion but the Lord of the world. Bonhoeffer, in a prison letter (May 5, 1944), argued that Barth replaced religion with "a positivist doctrine of revelation which says, in effect, 'Take it or leave it': virgin birth, Trinity, or anything else; each is an equally significant and necessary part of the whole, which must simply be swallowed as a whole or not at all" (*LPP*:286).

In his response to Bonhoeffer, Barth sensed "the enigmatic utterances of his letters."[43] The relationship between Barth and Bonhoeffer is complicated; Bonhoefer's discovery of dialectical theology, which he made in reading *The Word of God and the Word of Man* during the winter

---

41. Berkouwer, *Triumph of Grace*, 295. In Brunner's critique of Barth, "Barth goes far beyond all historical universalists. Scripture does not talk about universal reconciliation. On the contrary, it talks about judgment, and a double outcome of judgment: salvation or damnation. So the doctrine of universalism is the denial of judgment." Brunner, *Dogmatik*, 1:359; cf. Moltmann, *Coming of God*, 239.

42. For the study of the complicated relationship between Karl Barth and Bonhoeffer, see Andreas Pangritz's book, *Karl Barth in the Theology of Dietrich Bonhoeffer*.

43. Smith, *World Come of Age*, 90. Cf. Pangritz, *Karl Barth in the Theology of Dietrich Bonhoeffer*, 7.

of 1924/25, came to him "like a liberation,"[44] although he had critical reservations with Barth's excessive emphasis on the inaccessibility and free majesty of God. So in his doctoral dissertation, *Sanctorum Communio* and in the Habilitation dissertation, *Act and Being,* Bonhoeffer began to mobilize a Lutheran criticism of Barth's Reformed position on *non capax.*

While serving a German congregation in Barcelona in 1928, Bonhoeffer continued his conversation with Barth by studying the "Prolegomena" of the *Christian Dogmatics* (1927): "I am reading Barth's *Dogmatics* again. It is very much worth the effort."[45] Although Bonhoeffer does not reject Barth's theological way from above to below, it is of special significance for Bonhoeffer not to undercut a social and historical dimension to this vertical way from above.[46]

Bonhoeffer's concern is to call for an arcane discipline for the mysteries of the faith to protect them against profanation. However, Barth's concern is not to reserve the teaching of double predestination as a kind of arcane wisdom of theologians (*CD* II/2:18). The mystery of election, seen in light of the gospel, can "lay claim to . . . full publicity within the Church" (*CD* II/2:18) rather than keeping it quiet. Bonhoeffer was more concerned with renewing an arcane doctrine as well as deepening biblical worldliness. If Christ can become the Lord of the religionless as well (*LPP*:280), how and to what extent can God's election be related to the religionless world? Would Barth's attempt run into such a positivism that there would occur a thorough public profanization of the mysteries of the faith? Would the religionless world be considered enough in Barth's doctrine of election? Wouldn't the world, in Barth's theology, be left to its own devices? (*LPP*:286). As far as Jesus Christ as the Lord of the world is concerned, Bonhoeffers' thesis is that Christ and the world have come of age. This is "the claim of a world that has come of age by Jesus Christ"

---

44. *DBE*:52.

45. Dietrich Bonhoeffer in a letter to Walter Dress (March 13, 1928); cf. Pangritz, *Karl Barth in the Theology of Dietrich Bonhoeffer,* 24.

46. During his study at Union Theological Seminary in New York (1930/31), Bonhoeffer was regarded as "the most convinced disciple of Karl Barth" (*DBE*:117). Initially Bonhoeffer agreed with Barth's theological direction: "'Human speech' concerning God must correspond to God's way coming from above to what is below. In my thinking I must take note of this from above to the below" (*DBE*:12, 154).

(*LPP*:342), not on the basis of religion, but "on the basis of the gospel and in the light of Christ" in its "coming of age" (*LPP*:329).

According to Bonhoeffer, the church remains the church only when it exists for others (*LPP*:381). The church's service toward the world is grounded on the man for the others, namely, God in human form, the Crucified (*LPP*:381), rather than the exaltation of the Crucified One. Wouldn't Barth's emphasis on the exaltation of Christ and the triumph of grace lead implicitly to an ecclesiastical triumphalism, so that an eager effort becomes meaningful in converting the godless world to the Christian church?

For Barth, God's mystery is to be found in God's election of grace (*CD* II/2:24–25). It is good, joyful and hilarious news for us. The Holy Scripture speaks of God's grace of election as one single point, namely, the name of Jesus Christ, which means "the substance of all the preceding history of Israel and the hope of all the succeeding history of the Church" (*CD* II/2:53).

Barth's doctrine of predestination is less speculative and follows the biblical testimony in accordance with the gospel. However, Bonhoeffer discerns positivism of revelation when Barth speaks of full publicity by the church (*CD* II/2:18). Bonhoeffer seems to ask whether the mysteries of faith can be profaned when Barth speaks of full publicity by the church. This said, the positivism of revelation turns the mysteries of faith into a law, so that the world is left to its own devices. What interests Bonhoeffer is a religionless/worldly Christianity for the sake of the world come of age. According to Bonhoeffer, Christ as the Lord of the world stands for the world, which has come of age. The world must be understood on the basis of the gospel and in the light of Christ in its coming of age (*LPP*:329).

For Barth, "the kingdom of Christ is greater than the sphere of Israel and the Church" (*CD* II/2:571). Bonhoeffer's motif of the church for others remains central in Barth's theology. The exaltation of Christ "will inevitably become a proclamation to others" (*CD* II/2:429). Barth opens the closed circle of election toward the world and integrates the process of divine reconciliation into the world. In God's election and mission, divine reconciliation becomes a real event (*CD* II/2:461). Characterizing the community of Jesus Christ as being active for the world, Barth depicts the church in terms of the communion of the Holy Spirit (*CD* IV/3.2:856). In dealing with Jesus Christ as the true witness, Barth arranges the concept of vocation for concrete fellowship with God. If God's election looks forward to the future event of vocation, vocation looks backwards to election.

At this juncture, Christian ministry, mission, and vocation entail a strong eschatological dynamism in terms of Christian hope for Jesus Christ, who is to come. Alongside the eschatological perspective, the Holy Spirit is highlighted in terms of the future outpouring of Christ's Spirit on all flesh (Acts 2:17). In this expectation, the dividing wall between Jews and Gentiles, therefore, Christians and non-Christians, has finally been broken down (Eph 2:14). In light of God's "universal" reconciliation with the world, Barth rejects the conversion of people of other cultures into the Christian religion. Conversion is not the work of the Christian church at home or abroad: "This is the Work of God alone" (*CD* IV/3.2:876).

However, Pangritz distinguishes Bonhoeffer from Barth in the notion of the church for others: the former understands the church's service for the world simply as being for others, while the latter understands the existence of the church for others in light of the triumph of grace—an understanding not derived from a missionary consciousness or from an eagerness to convert the godless world. According to Pangritz's characterization, Bonhoeffer is a theologian of the world come of age, whereas Barth is a theologian of triumphant grace. It is so-called ecclesiastical triumphalism that would secretly govern Barth's doctrine of election in regard to Israel and the world.[47]

Barth refers to the coming of age with a different evaluation than Bonhoeffer. Although Barth does not underestimate modernity's demand for freedom, autonomy, and true rationality, a human coming of age would be exposed to the danger in which God would be dispensed with for the sake of human maturity. With regard to the theme of secularization, Barth contended: "Even in the sphere of Christendom there are many who belong sociologically, by name and baptism, but do not belong at all in practice, being blind and deaf heathen. There is a whole world which for various reasons is not yet or no longer attached to any religion, and certainly not to the Word of God, but obstinately boasts of its own sovereignty" (*CD* IV/3.1:119). The world regards itself as still or once again "come of age" and in so doing, it holds itself to be sovereign.

---

47. Pangritz, *Karl Barth in the Theology of Dietrich Bonhoeffer*, 124, 128.

In Barth's view, the notion of having come of age is characteristic of the delusion of modernity. Freedom is the highest goal for the sovereign, autonomous maturity of human beings, but this freedom is revealed as that of the bourgeois individual, who exalts himself or herself in search of freedom through a lordly grasp on nature and fellow humans, as well as through an increasing desire for possession. Barth's critique of modernity has a parallel in his critique of religion, idolatry, and the capitalistic desire for possessions.[48] Barth declares, "To exist privately is to be a robber" (*CD* IV/1:778). In his later self-correction, Barth states: "Thinking in terms of the humanity of God, we cannot at all reckon in a serious way with *real* 'outsiders', with a 'world come of age,' but only with a world which *regards* itself of age (and proves daily that it is precisely not that). Thus, the so-called 'outsiders' are really only 'insiders' who have not yet understood and apprehended themselves as such."[49]

Pangritz further criticizes Barth for not seriously contemplating both the Jewish No to Jesus Christ and Bonhoeffers' idea of the godlessness of a world come of age.[50] In his *Ethics*, Bonhoeffer argues that the atheists' godlessness is full of God's promise in contrast to the hopeless godlessness of the religious (E:103). Bonhoeffer's Christology for others is deeply connected with Jesus Christ's solidarity with the working class, an aspect later formulated as the theological perspective from below.[51] Furthermore, for Bonhoeffer, the Jew keeps open the question of Christ (E:89). The Jewish "No" to church is therefore positive and not negative because "Western history is, by God's will, indissolubly linked with the people of Israel, not only genetically but also in a genuine uninterrupted encounter . . . An expulsion of the Jews from the West must necessarily bring with it the expulsion of Christ. For Jesus Christ was a Jew" (E:89).[52]

48. *KD* [Nachlass], 365.
49. Barth, *Humanity of God*, 58.
50. Pangritz, *Karl Barth in the Theology of Dietrich Bonhoeffer*, 127.
51. As Bonhoeffer says, "The working class may distinguish between Jesus and his Church; he is not the guilty party. Jesus, yes; Christ, no! Jesus can then become the idealist, the socialist. What does it mean when the proletarian says, in his world of distrust: 'Jesus was a good man'? It means that nobody needs to mistrust him. The proletarian does not say, 'Jesus is God.' But when he says, 'Jesus is a good man,' he is saying more than the bourgeois says when he repeats, 'Jesus is God'" (Bonhoeffer, *Christ the Center*, 35).
52. At an earlier stage, however, Bonhoeffer would be careless with anti-Jewish overtones when he describes the final homecoming of Israel: "The church of Christ has never

Although Barth explicitly articulates his theological concern about Israel in terms of his formulation that "the bow of the one covenant arches over the whole" (*CD* II/2:200), his reflection on Israel for God's judgment in relation to the church as a reflection of God's mercy (*CD* II/2:210) is not consistent and consonant with the essentially christological approach of Barth's doctrine of election. Although Barth is able to eschew the theological tradition of supercessionism, he deals with the relationship between Israel and the church (in *CD* II/2) in terms of the relation between law and gospel, or judgment and grace, rather than first dealing with God's foundational covenant with Israel and then through it, the fulfillment of the Gentile world in the cross and resurrection. Unlike Barth's dialectic of election and rejection—in that Israel serves as an ongoing witness to God "in the perduringly negative form of a witness to unbelief and divine wrath"[53]—Bonhoeffer gives a perduringly positive role of Israel "in a genuine uninterrupted encounter." As an encounter between Western history and the people of Israel, the idea of the conversion of Israel becomes impossible for him. As Bonhoeffer says, "Western history is, by God's will, indissolubly linked with the people of Israel, not only genetically but also in a genuine uninterrupted encounter."[54]

This being the case, the dialectic of election and rejection of Israel for Bonhoeffer has to assume a dialectical predestination leading up to *apokatastasis*. In the statement of Bonhoeffer, we read: "It means that nothing is lost, that everything is taken up in Christ, although it is transformed, made transparent, clear, made free from the anguish of selfish desire. Christ restores all this as God originally intended it to be" (*LPP*:170).[55] Any statement about this eschatological doctrine "only

---

lost sight of the thought that the 'chosen people,' who nailed the redeemer of the world to the cross, must bear the curse for its action through a long history of suffering... But the history of the suffering of this people, loved and punished by God, stands under the sign of the final home-coming of the people of Israel to its God. And this home-coming happens in the conversion of Israel to Christ... The conversion of Israel, that is to be the end of the people's period of suffering" (Bonhoeffer, "Church and the Jewish Question," 226).

53. Marquardt, "Feinde um unsretwillen," 335.

54. Strangely enough, Haynes wants to discern the witness-people myth even in this important statement of Bonhoeffer, from which Haynes discloses Bonhoeffer's own deep-seated anti-Judaism.

55. Although Bonhoeffer, in his early phase, paid attention to the "inner necessity of the idea of *apokatastasis*" in light of a judgment of grace, instead of double election (*SC*: 286), he was hesitant to integrate "this final word of eschatological thinking" into "a self-

expresses a hope"; such statements "cannot be made part of a system" (SC:287). Like Barth, Bonhoeffer left open this eschatological perspective as "the sigh of theology whenever it has to speak of faith and unfaith, election and rejection" (AB:161).

In renewing a limitation in Barth's doctrine of Israel, Marquardt argues that Christians need this testimony of Bonhoeffer so that they may become aware of their "'unbelieving' sisters and brothers in the world."[56] Marquardt diagnoses that in Bonhoeffer's thought, Israel "testifies with its confession of God's transcendence in spite of Christ . . . to the eschatological proviso in the self of God that is not annulled even in the sending of Jesus Christ."[57] Bonhoeffer raises his charge of the positivism of revelation against Barth, and challenges the Confessing Church for the sake of a world come of age and its religionlessness. Thus he is confronted with a "church on the defensive" and its lack of "taking risks for others" (LPP:380–81).

However, Barth's theology of Israel and his so-called doctrine of lights in the world does not contradict Bonhoeffer's theology of Israel and world orientation. Barth's motif of "the church for others" in Bonhoeffer's fashion cannot be promptly and easily ignored. What is decisive in Barth's doctrine of election is to affirm, clarify, and develop the point that "the bow of the *one* covenant arches over the *whole*" (CD II/2: 200).

In accordance with Barth's intention, Bonhoeffer's uniqueness lies in integrating the actuality of revelation (including its priority) into the historical reality of God. In other words, the revelation of God is "not executed in the realm of ideas but in the realm of reality" (DBW:10, 436). In this light we need to understand Bonhoeffer's controversial statement that "there is no God who is 'there'" [Einen Gott, den "es gibt," gibt es nicht] (AB:115). It shows that God's being comes into all other realities to change and transform them materially; God's reality is not diminished in the historical sphere. We see here a parallel with Barth's keen statement that God is "the fact . . . that materially changes all things and everything in all things" (CD II/1:258).[58]

---

evident point of departure for a dogmatic train of thought" (SC:171 n. 29).

56. Marquardt, "Feinde um unsretwillen," 335.

57. Ibid.

58. Pangritz takes Barth's doctrine of the true words outside the church to be a correction of Bonhoeffer's charge of positivism of revelation. Pangritz, *Karl Barth in the Theology of Dietrich Bonhoeffer*, 132–47.

A Model of Correlation between the History of Israel and Jesus Christ

In the doctrine of reconciliation—when it comes to the service of the church (*CD* IV/3.2:§72.4)—Barth's description of the Jews is remarkably changed from his previous negative description. The entire history of Israel reveals itself as God's gift of covenant and grace. The history of Israel is the gift of God's honor and of human salvation. Barth takes into consideration the prophecy of the messianic history of Israel as the adequate prefiguration of the messianic prophecy of Jesus Christ. It is "comparable without reservation" (*CD* IV/3.1:65). In this regard, the entire history of Israel is present as mediating and representational history that shines for all people.

In dealing with the doctrine of reconciliation, Barth connects 2 Cor 5:19 with 2 Cor 5:17. God's reconciliation in Jesus Christ with the world must be seen in the material relation to the thesis that anyone who is in Jesus Christ is the new creation. Because the old world is passed in Jesus Christ, the new world has become in him. In the Barthian sense of reconciliation, we cannot separate the reconciliation in Jesus Christ from the apocalyptic theme of the passing old world and the coming new world. Hence, Barth has developed the reconciliation of the Messiah (2 Cor 5:19) as the grounding and revolutionary transformation of the situation of all humans and the entire world. So comes the provocative sentence of Barth: In Jesus Christ, God removed not merely sins but "their very root, the man who commits them" (*CD* IV/1:77).[59]

The inclusive aspect of the death of Jesus Christ characterizes reconciliation not in the partial change but in the comprehensive, total, and revolutionary exchange and transformation. Hence the situation of humans in their wholeness to God is reversed without reservation. In Barth's radical understanding of reconciliation, we are not supposed to ignore its christologically personal aspect for Barth. It is the situation of sinful humans in their totality that Jesus Christ makes his own. He has made himself sinner for us and entered into our place as sinners. In this connection Barth returned to Luther's christologically personal understanding of representation, as expressed in Luther's famous formulation of "happy exchange." For Luther, Christ not only as *persona privata*

---

59. In the event of his death and resurrection, Jesus Christ, "in his own person . . . has made an end of us as sinners and therefore of sin itself" (*CD* IV/1:253).

but also as *persona maxima* took over the person of all sinners. Christ is *maximus peccator*, and *peccator peccatorum*.⁶⁰ Along the lines of Luther's christologically personal aspect, according to Barth, if Jesus enters into solidarity with sinners, he is made a sinner for us.⁶¹

Besides, for Barth, reconciliation does not replace an eschatological consummation.⁶² According to Barth, the doctrine of reconciliation should not be discussed apart from the reconciliation of Israel's history in regard to the nonterminated covenant. Barth already locates the doctrine of election (*CD* II/2) prior to the doctrine of reconciliation, so that the former implicates the deep dimension of the doctrine of reconciliation. Next, the Christian doctrine of reconciliation should not be discussed apart from the eschatological theme of the passing old world and the coming new world of God. The character of Jesus's messianic fight ("Jesus is the victor") actualizes and deepens Blumhardt's eschatological message of hope. In it Barth discusses the hope of the coming of a new heaven and a new earth and the related expectation of the new pouring of the Holy Spirit upon all flesh. It is the promise of the Holy Spirit. The reconciled nature of creation is still moving towards its redemption and consummation (*CD* IV/3:336–37). The messianic ruling and definitiveness of Jesus Christ in all areas of the world is to be understood not in a static or totalitarian manner, but in a dynamic and teleological manner. Barth's christological eschatology integrates universal justice (justification) and

---

60. As Luther states, "in short, he has and bears all the sins of all in his body—not in the sense that he has committed them but in the sense that he took these sins, committed by us, upon his own body, in order to make satisfaction for them with his own blood" (*LW* 26:277).

61. Against Barth's doctrine of reconciliation Soelle unilaterally charges it with retaining an objectivistic understanding of representation. According to her, the representation, which is not in need of addition, is to be objectified as the past. However, she overlooks Barth's christologically personal aspect and, furthermore, does not understand that Barth's exclusive representation has an inclusive implication in itself, not the other way around. See Soelle, *Christ the Representative*, 88ff.

62. Pannenberg charges that Barth's concept of reconciliation becomes "inevitably totalitarian" as an act solely of God's sovereignty. In this evaluation, Pannenberg shares Soelle's critique of Barth's reconciliation as objectivist, and Wagner's critique of Barth's Christology as "theological liquidation." In contradiction, Barth's doctrine of christological reconciliation retains a pro-Israelite contour and shows the strong political implications of reconciliation as liberation from the eschatological perspective. Cf. Pannenberg, *Systematic Theology*, 2:431. Soelle, *Christ the Representative*, 88ff.

freedom (sanctification) of all humans into the process of fighting the history of Jesus Christ.[63]

Barth presents without reservation his unique and remarkable dogmatic systematization of Israel in relevance to his Christology by comparing Jesus with the entire history of Israel. In the connection with *munus propheticum Christi*, Barth interprets the prophecy of Jesus Christ through the mediation of the particularity of Israel to all people. This said, the particular history is reflected in the general (*CD* IV/3.1:64). However, Marquardt argues that Barth's model of Israel is still captive within the limitation of the old typological method. Through the method of typology, Barth intends to conceive of the specific historicity of Jesus Christ through the comparison of Jesus with the entire messianic history of Israel. Therefore, the history of Israel is understood as "the pre-history of Jesus Christ and its word His fore-word" (*CD* IV/3.1:66). At this juncture, the history of Israel and its prophecy cannot have any continuation, because they find their fulfillment only in Jesus Christ. Although the history of Judaism may be even a kind of proof of God, "as abstract recollections they have always a notably unsubstantial and unprofitable character, with no true or genuine prophecy" (*CD* IV IV/3.1:70).[64]

Barth's understanding of the resurrection is based on a covenantal theological framework. His understanding of resurrection is distinguished from the theological project of resurrection in the universal-historical, proleptic framework (Pannenberg) or from the promise-historical-adventist perspective (Moltmann).[65] Barth understands the reconciliation

---

63. Moltmann's messianic Christology, in which the crucified is already Lord yet still on the way to reigning over all, is not a way of overcoming Barth's eschatological concern in Christology. Rather, Barth's christological eschatology can be understood as an indispensable part of the history of the prophecy of Jesus Christ according to the glory of the mediator in *CD* IV/3.1:§69.

64. According to Marquardt, this typological method—in that the history of Israel is made into a type for the prophecy of Jesus Christ—can become a medium of anti-Judaism. Barth, like the whole tradition of Christianity, does not think of Judaism and the entire history of Jewish people as the configuration of Jesus Christ when Barth speaks of the entire history of Israel. Cf. Marquardt, *Das christliche Bekenntnis zu Jesus, dem Juden*, 2:225.

65. From the standpoint of the resurrection of the crucified Christ, Moltmann takes seriously the underside of history in contradiction to the universal-historical orientation of the dominant side of history. "Revelation as history" (Pannenberg) tends to understand world history as salvation history so that it ignores world history as a history of tragedy. As opposed to Moltmann and in contrast to liberation theology, Pannenberg

in terms of the nonterminated covenant of God with Israel and with the resurrection likewise in this context. Furthermore Barth understands covenant, reconciliation, and resurrection in terms of the emancipatory event of the Exodus. If the cross and resurrection are not separable from the exodus of Israel, the covenant, fulfilled in the reconciliation, is also not separable from the history of the exodus event, namely the history of the liberation of Israel. Therefore Barth understands the promise of universal liberation in terms of covenant and resurrection. In this regard, Barth does not ignore postbiblical Judaism after the resurrection of Jesus Christ.

Furthermore, Barth, in his *Ad Limina Apostolorum*, speaks of the history of Israel and present Judaism as "the primal form of the one God's revelation." The factual continuing existence of Judaism—whether believing or nonbelieving—is the single natural-world, historical proof of God's existence. At this juncture, Barth rejects a Roman Catholic attempt at putting Judaism at the same level as non-Christian religions.[66]

The history of Israel is "the true type," "an exact representation and adequate prefiguration" of the prophecy of the history of Jesus Christ (*CD* IV/3.1:66). This prefiguration of Israel points to its configuration with the presence of Jesus Christ. Barth established David as the central figure of the messianic history of Israel and also as the categorical actuality in relation to the history of Jesus Christ. Jesus Christ, in his correlation with the prophecy of the entire messianic history of Israel, is the actual prophecy of God for all humans.

Barth was less convinced about a universally oriented attempt to confirm and vindicate the truth of theology from without or of the eschatological openness of Christology. He views any attempt at verifying the truth of revelation from without as a false freedom. Rather, Barth takes his direction of verifying the continuous confirmation of the Christian faith, through the thinking and praxis necessitated by the demands of the theological subject matter and the encounter with history, society,

---

views the phenomenon of political religion in American Christendom positively. See Klappert, *Worauf wir hoffen*, 56.

66. Barth, *Ad Limina Apostolorum*, 39–40. From the perspective of "the primal form of the one God's revelation" in Barth, Klappert rather speaks of the configuration of the entire messianic history of Israel and Judaism. In the glory of the mediator and in Jesus Christ as the light of life that shines on all humans, the entire history of Israel is present as the light of the peoples (Isa 42:6). See Klappert, *Versöhnung und Befreiung*, 22.

politics, creation, and religions. For Barth, the theological *Sache* is the grounding correlation between the messianic prophecy of Jesus Christ and the prophecy of the entire messianic history of Israel—the place to meet and take seriously secular and creaturely realms. The fulfillment of the covenant and the coming of God's kingdom, which is in the form of the reconciliation of Christ, are also the anticipation of the coming of God's kingdom and salvation. God is and remains God of Israel; on the way to God's kingdom and creation, God's covenant and God's faithfulness to Israel should not be reversed by a universal-cosmic eschatology.[67]

In 1966 Barth stressed that beyond the question of interconfessional ecumenicity, our relationship with Judaism is the real, great ecumenical question. Judaism, in Barth's view, is to be theologically appreciated as the root of the church. Understood in this way, it would be fair to say that for Barth, Judaism, after the resurrection of Christ, can be regarded as the prophetic witness of the first Testament, namely, the Old Testament's original form of the one revelation of God. Therefore, dialogue with Judaism is the presupposition for the discovery of the true words within world occurrences and in creation.

It is therefore impossible for Barth that the church, in relation to the synagogue, would proclaim the true God against the false God of the synagogue and oppose this false God with respect to the triune God. The God whose work and word, whom the church witnesses to the world, is the God of Israel. According to Barth,

> "They are Israelites, and to them belong the adoption, the glory, the covenants, the giving of the law, the worship, and the promises; to them belong to the patriarchs, and from them, according to the flesh, comes the Messiah, who is over all, God blessed forever. Amen" (Rom 9:4–5). "For salvation is from the Jews" (John 4:22). "But if some of the branches were broken off, and you, a wild olive shoot, were grafted in their place to share the rich root of the olive tree, do not boast over the branches" (Rom 11:17–18).

---

67. Unlike Moltmann and Pannenberg, Marquardt characterizes Judaism as the Word of God that speaks to us in the life of the Jewish people. Different from Marquardt, however, Barth consciously does not provide one single example in his so-called doctrine of lights (*KD* IV/3:152–53), because he secures the freedom of the messianic prophecy of Jesus Christ and does not intend to block or limit our own freedom (by offering examples of words or lights from God in the secular and creaturely realms) for discovering the true words within world occurrences. Cf. Marquardt, *Das christliche Bekenntnis zu Jesus*, 2: 226, 71.

Barth regards these statements as asserting the priority of Israel over against the Gentile Christians. The guests in the house of Israel are all the Gentile Christians from all countries and from all time. Accepted into the election and calling of the Jews, the Gentile Christians live in communion and fellowship with the king of the Jews (CD IV/3.2:877).

When we take into consideration the correlation between Jesus Christ as the Jew and the entire messianic history of Israel (CD IV/3.1: 40–78), Barth's theology of Israel powerfully accentuates the permanence of Israel's covenant in which God in Jesus Christ remains eschatologically faithful. Jesus Christ would be no Jesus Christ without Israel.[68] In speaking of the permanence of Israel's covenant, Barth even had in mind today's Judaism of Israel as well. When Christians conceive of the church and synagogue as unconnected, everything is at stake. Where this separation occurs, something negative occurs to the Christian community.[69] In the place of separation and division, the whole reality of God's revelation is unfortunately denied. Furthermore, God's extraordinary revelation truly lives in this Jewish people today.[70] Although Barth portrays the Judaism of Israel as the great demonstration of the unworthiness of humans, nevertheless, Jewish history in the postresurrection of Jesus Christ and until the Holocaust is the subsequent witness of what happened in the man of Israel, Jesus, on the cross. According to Barth, Israel confirms its entire preceding history in the crucifixion of Jesus.

At the height of the Holocaust in July of 1944, Barth stated,

> What kind of picture is it that is raised to our eyes in the middle of today's contemporary occurrences just in the groundless and defenseless slaughtering of the Jewish people? Is it not that punished and tormented servant of God for the sake of others from the book of Isaiah? Is it not our crucified Lord Jesus Christ himself who becomes visible in the destiny of those countless Jews who are shot or finally murdered through poison gas? Like God has delivered up God's Son for us, it is what is once more carried out before us here in the destiny of his physical brothers and sisters. What should we now really say, if it has satisfied God to make this sign from this people in the middle of our time?[71]

68. Barth, *Dogmatik im Grundriss*, 86.
69. Ibid., 87.
70. Ibid., 88.
71. Barth, *Schweizer Stimme*, 318–19,

The Jewish people and Judaism for Barth—because of their election for our sake, not because of their sin—are substantially the negative witness to the wrath of God on the cross of Jesus Christ. As R. R. Geis states, Jewish people grasp and acknowledge their martyrdom as the consequence of election, as the testimony of God to an alienated and unredeemed world.[72] For Geis, the suffering is the "salt-covenant," or "corporal punishment of love" on the one hand, but on the other, the suffering is for God's sake. Unlike Geis, Barth does not actualize the suffering of Judaism as suffering for the unredeemed world, or for God's sake. Rather, Barth, in light of God's faithfulness in Jesus Christ to Israel, elaborates a dialectics between God's Yes and God's No, in which the former is profoundly hidden in the latter, while the latter is included in the former. For this reason, Barth decidedly rejects any Christian attempt at missionizing the Jews. In the words of Barth: "but the Jews, even the unbelieving Jew, so miraculously preserved . . . through the many calamities of his history . . . is the natural historical monument of the love and faithfulness of God, who in concrete form is the epitome of the man freely chosen and blessed by God, who as a living commentary on the Old Testament is the only convincing proof of God outside the Bible" (*CD* IV/3.2:877). In this regard, Barth calls for the abandonment of Jewish mission in the post-Holocaust era. The concept of Jewish mission is theologically impossible: "In relation to Synagogue, there can be no real question of 'mission' . . . Mission is not the witness which it owes to Israel" (*CD* IV/3.2:877).

According to Marquardt, Barth's doctrine of Israel can be understood as having two faces: a face looking backwards and a face looking forwards. Barth's failure to take seriously Jewish self-understanding continues to be a limitation of Barth's theology of Israel, and this is part of the face that looks backwards.[73] Marquardt's position is about introducing and integrating Jewish self-understanding as a further categorical dimension in the theological discussion. In view of Barth's doctrine of Israel, he asks whether election in Christ must lead necessarily to such silence about Israel's self-understanding of election.[74] Therefore he criticizes

---

72. Geis, *Gottes Minorität*, 203, 202, 26.
73. Marquardt, *Entdeckung des Judentums*, Vorwort.
74. Ibid., 130.

Barth's theology of Israel for how it often dismisses Jewish self-understanding as a *quantité négligeable*.⁷⁵

In a letter to Marquardt, Barth mentioned that Marquardt discovered and expounded his doctrine of Israel "with great skill and finesse, and historically and materially," to which Barth himself could have no objection. Furthermore, Barth confessed that he himself could never have introduced his doctrine of Israel in Marquardt's manner. So Barth praised the merits of Marquardt's contribution toward Barth's own doctrine of Israel, yet not without a certain anxiety.⁷⁶ Barth agreed that there is indeed a gap in his own theology of Israel, but not as an excuse, but as an explanation, he was not averse to accept the critique that Marquardt raised. Barth gave explanations for two things: 1) Biblical Israel is a significant concern; however, he did not have the intellectual energy to fully engage Jewish thinkers such as Baeck, Buber and Rosenzweig; and 2) Barth confessed himself not decidedly as a philo-Semite. He had to suppress his irrational inclination against the Jewish people on the basis of all his presuppositions. In some sense, Barth responded with the sigh of *Pfui!* to his allergic reaction against the Jews. This aspect could have had a retrogressive effect on his doctrine of Israel.⁷⁷

Barth also mentioned that Marquardt had noted "the beginnings of improvement" in him, "or at least a serious attempt at it," which Marquardt alluded to. In noting some indications in this direction, Barth referred to his continuing developments in several places: in his 1954 seminar that was a supplement to the declaration of "Christ—the Hope of the World," in the World Council of Churches meeting at Evanston, Illinois; in a summons in 1938 drawn up by W. Vischer dealing with Barth's debate with

75. Ibid., 296.

76. Marquardt explained his position regarding Barth's anxiety about the future direction of his theology of Israel in his emeritus lecture at the Free University of West Berlin (Feb 7, 1997). For Marquardt, the theological dimension does not appear in the divine definition of the Jewish people, but only in the affecting of his own Christian self-understanding through his practical and spiritual relationship with this people. Cf. Marquardt, "'Abirren' Zu Erscheinungsformen des Häretischen in meiner Theologie," 157.

77. Letter to Marquardt, September 5, 1967, in Barth, *Letters: 1961–1968*, 262. Barth's confession, in the letter to Marquardt, is unfortunately misused as evidence of suppressed anti-Semitism in the disguise of Barth's often-imputed philo-Semitism. Cf. Updike, *Gottesprogramm. Roger's Version*. (Hamburg: Reinbeck, 1988), 272. Against this assertion, Eberhard Busch apologetically undermines the weight of Barth's aversion in Barth's overall thought, because such aversion was general in Christian circles at the beginning of the twentieth century. Cf. Busch, *Unter dem Bogen des einen Bundes*, 12–13.

Brunner about whether salvation is or was of the Jews (John 4:22); in Barth's response to Vatican II's declaration about non-Christian religions in his book *Ad Limina Apostolorum*; and in his contribution to a panel discussion held in Chicago in 1962.[78]

In his text titled *The Hope of Israel,* Barth wrote, "We have to say first of the people which bases its hope on the same object, which is also the ground of our hope, namely in the coming Messiah . . . it [this hope] is based namely in the promises of God, which he has given his chosen people. If it can be claimed by a community at all that it lives by hope, then this is to be said precisely and first of Judaism. Israel is the people of hope."[79]

Barth's characterization of Israel as the people of messianic hope affirms the prophetic witness of the Christian community accompanying the witness of Judaism. Judaism is appreciated in its prophetic witness (the witness of the prophets) in the history of Israel, to which the Old Testament testifies. The prophet of the entire history of Israel, which is the light to the peoples, means that Israel is the prefiguration and configuration of Jesus Christ.

In his writing *Ad Limina Apostolorum*, Barth devoted himself to the serious study of the sixteen Latin texts in Vatican II, especially regarding matters of Israel and non-Christian religions. Barth asked on what grounds the Declaration could speak of the past and present history of Israel in the same breath as Hinduism, Buddhism, and Islam. According to Barth, the Old Testament presents the original form of the one revelation of God rather than a religion. In the existence of later and contemporary Judaism, we have the natural proof of God in world history. Instead of regarding the Jews as a separated people, Barth wondered if we shouldn't make a formal confession of guilt in view of anti-Semitism in the ancient, medieval, and modern church.[80]

In his dialogue with American rabbi Jakob Petuchowski, Barth also mentioned a possibility for dialogue: "There is an open way for the dialogue between Jewish theologians and Christian theologian like me.

---

78. Letter to Marquardt, in Barth, *Letters 1961–1968,* 262–63. Herein Barth also mentioned his severe criticism of the Zagorsk declaration and his commendation of the counterdeclaration. Marquardt included it in his essay "Christentum und Zionismus," see Marquradt, *Verwegenheiten,* 166.

79. Quoted in Busch, *Karl Barth: His Life,* 402.

80. Barth, *Ad Limina Apostolorum,* 36–37.

Namely, we have a real, broad level for dialogue, because we read the same Torah, the same prophets and the same scripture."[81]

In Jewish-Christian dialogue, the particular universal significance of Jesus Christ encourages the church to enrich and deepen the subject matter of the gospel as it encounters Jewish people. The Logos speaks the word of the faith of Israel, *dabar*, together with them. It is therefore of special significance to carry out exegetical work on some passages associated with "anti-Judaism" in the New Testament, which have been misused for legitimizing the church's anti-Judaism position. As far as God at Golgotha is no less than the God of Abraham, Isaac, and Jacob, a true dialogue cannot be done at the cost of delimiting or sacrificing its own position as a dialogue partner. Rather, Jewish-Christian relations should be pursued, renewed, and transformed in the face of the mystery of God in *dabar* as well as in the Logos, learning to hear the Word of God unfailingly. As far as Israel is a hearer of God's promise, Christians are encouraged to share and learn a common hearing from the promise of God. There is the rainbow of God's one covenant arching over Israel and the church. In a conversation with Rabbi Petuchowski, Barth stated:

> I shall consider the creation of the modern State of Israel in the context of the fulfillment of the Old Testament. A possible explanation is that it is another and new sign of the electing and providentially ruling grace and faithfulness of God to that seed of Abraham, a very visible sign, visible for every reader of the papers, the whole world—a sign which is not to be overlooked. After the horrors of Hitler's time the reappearance of Israel, now as a nation in the political realm, even as a state, may well be called a miracle for all that have eyes to see this evidence, and a scandal for all those who have not eyes to see. Remember the answer, mentioned yesterday, given to Frederick the Great, "The proof for God's existence, your majesty, are the Jews." And we could now add today, "your majesty, the State of Israel." The Jews have always owed their existence to the power of God alone and not to their own force or to the might of their history. And here we have another case of this kind of existence of Israel. God alone can help it to exist and it seems that he will do so.[82]

---

81. Barth,"Fragen von Rabbi Petuchowski, Antworten von Karl Barth," 18–24,

82. Barth, "Introduction to Theology: Questions to and Discussion with Dr. Karl Barth," *Criterion* no.1 (Winter 1963) 21–22.

In the interview of 1964 to 1968, we take note of Barth's continuity with his theology of Israel in his doctrine of election: the christological-eschatological participation of Gentile Christianity in the covenantal blessing of the Jews as God's people. Such an eschatological engrafting model of the church into God's covenant and promise with the Jews is compelling and central. Christians are those who look back first to the Messiah who has already come, rather than those who seek a Messiah in the future who has not yet come. On this christological basis, the Christian looks forward into the future in expectation and hope of the coming Messiah.[83]

If Barth speaks explicitly of the sending of Israel to the people of the world and its fulfillment in Jesus Christ, the world must be integrated into the realm of the eschatology of Israel. With respect to the christological embrace of the world into the ream of God's action with Israel, Barth articulates: "As Israel comes toward Jesus Christ and Jesus Christ comes from Israel onwards, the gospel issues—universally (!) just in this particularity (!)—the gospel of the covenant of grace and peace which is established, preserved, carried out and completed by God."[84] The object of theology is the particular Word of God who has become the flesh of Israel and thus is established as the redeemer of the world universally for all humans. This points to Barth's model of christological participation by way of the relation between particularity and universality.

---

83. Barth, *Gespräche, IV: 1964–1968*, 308.
84. Barth, *Einführung in die evangelische Theologie*, 31.

NINE   The Liberative Dimensions in Barth's Theology

Barth's Contribution for Liberation Theology

IN HIS *INTERVIEW*,[1] REMINISCENT OF MARTIN LUTHER'S *TABLE TALK*, we see Barth's lifelong interest in political issues. At the celebration of his eightieth birthday, Barth explained that the reader of *Church Dogmatics* needs to know that he comes from religious socialism. Barth recalled that he pursued something other than *Church Dogmatics* in Safenwil, namely, lectures on the workers movement, social justice, and trade unions. He became a member of the Swiss Socialist Party. While involved in these activities, Barth came to a particular discovery: the children of this world are often wiser than the children of light. "The socialists were among the most vivid listeners to my sermons, not because I preached socialism, but because they knew I was the same man who was also attempting to help them."[2]

In the 1960s, Barth made it an urgent task of the church to call for political decisions in the witness of faith regarding questions such as nuclear weapons, rapprochement with the communist nations, protest against the Vietnam war, and resistance to anti-Semitism: "A *practical* pacifism with the slogan 'War—never again!' is something that *today* really ought to force itself on the church. Especially in view of the development of nuclear weapons and the threat that all life might be destroyed."[3]

---

1. Barth, *Gespräche 1964–1968*. Cf. Hunsinger, "Conversational Theology."
2. Barth, *Gespräche 1964–1968*, 506.
3. Ibid.

The freedom of God calls for responsible human freedom. God acts and loves in God's eternal freedom. The authority of God is none other than the authority of freedom, as opposed to the authority of compulsion or coercion. In an explication of his so-called doctrine of lights, Barth wrote that the "lights and words of the world" were not based on his metaphysical speculation, but on his practical experience with the godless outside the church during his period at Safenwil. In other words, Barth's openness to world and religious pluralism in his so-called doctrine of lights is supposed to be discussed within his practical concern for the world rather than in metaphysical-speculative concern such as is seen and embodied typically in a traditional concept of *theologia naturalis* or the current theology of religions.

Barth's contribution to liberation theology can be seen in numerous ways.[4] Remaining faithful to the God who takes the side of the small, the marginalized, and the lowly, Barth committed himself to the priority of praxis and the church's option for the poor. For Barth, the church is fundamentally on the side of the victims of disorder and is to espouse their cause by keeping it over against those who represent the social disorder of the status quo (*CD* III/4:544). What guides Barth's theology is "the category of praxis" (*CD* II/2:548), and his goal is to pursue social progress or even socialism. It is inseparable from the decisive Word of the proclamation of God's kingdom as it has already come, is coming and is still to come (*CD* III/4:545). Barth's theology is "simply the theory of this praxis" in the light of the kingdom of God (*CD* II/2:548).

According to Barth, everything that is believed must be put into praxis. "Only the doer of the Word is its real hearer" (*CD* I/2:792). As Barth says in *Romans I*, there is "*no* ethics from the *ultimate* standpoint which we must adopt in Christ. There is *only the movement* of God to which, in every single moment, there must correspond on our part a quite definite recognition of both the situation and our necessary action following from it" (R I:392).[5]

---

4. Cf. Plonz, *Herrenlosen Gewalten*. Cf. Eicher, "Gottes Wahl," 21–36; see also Hunsinger, "Karl Barth and Liberation Theology," 42–59.

5. Gollwitzer rightly interprets this statement saying, "the entire theological work to come was a commentary on this Safenwil statement, and it served to determine the Christian and ecclesiastical activity which was 'necessary' on the basis of the gospel, and thus which was no longer simply congenial or arbitrary." Cf. Gollwitzer, "Kingdom of God and Socialism in the Theology of Karl Barth," 88.

From *Romans* onwards to his most mature work embodied in *Church Dogmatics*, Barth had attempted to deepen and actualize liberative dimensions such as God's relationality with the world in the coming kingdom and Jesus Christ as the partisan of the poor in christological, Trinitarian, ecclesiological, and covenantal terms. Barth has been committed to a revolutionary theology by way of transcending the status quo. This commitment becomes manifest and obvious in Barth's own orientation to the radical ideology-critique of all that exists.

During the Safenwil period, Barth had developed a unity between exegesis and social-historical criticism in which "the historical critics, it seems to me, need to be more critical!" (R II:x). Barth's discovery of the new world in the Bible integrated the world of the newspaper into interpretation of the Bible. An organic connection between the Bible and the world of the newspaper stood against the mechanical, technical, or manipulative mediation between the two worlds. As long as God is something completely different, as long as the new world in the Bible pointed to the world that renews and transforms the world of the newspaper, Barth recognized and established the significance of a social-transcendental connection in the interpretation of the Bible.

Later, in *Church Dogmatics*, Barth stated that all exegesis and hermeneutics simply represent "the life lived at this period, here or there, by the fraction of humanity concerned, and the awareness of life experienced by them." That is to say "their particular culture, civilization and technics, their historical past and present[,] . . . their national qualities, aspirations and disillusionments, their moral standards and customs, their political order and disorder, their retrogressive or progressive commercial relations and…their particular degree of religion or irreligion" (*CD* IV/3.1: 821).

These all influence and determine the interpretation of the Bible. For this task Barth introduced a new exegesis conditioned by contemporary time. Therefore Barth did not experience the essence of time in history or ontological historicity, but at the level of human transcendental social connections. This said, for Barth the interpretation of time and all its historical documentations can be done sociocritically, even in a decisively political manner under the social category of understanding.[6] Barth's notion of exegesis in connection with the social category of un-

---

6. Marquardt, *Theologie und Sozialismus*, 106.

derstanding becomes an indispensable part of characterizing his political and liberative theology. Therefore the timeless gospel that avoids contemporary events is not the pure gospel. When its testimony is intended to be evangelical in an abstract sense, it is actually false prophecy (*CD* III/4: 512).

As Barth states, "What 'there is' is not as such the command of God. But the core of the matter is that God gives his command, that he gives himself to be our Commander. God's command, God himself, gives himself to be known. And as he does so, he is heard. Man is made responsible" (*CD* II/2:548). Although Barth was averse to identifying himself with any 'ism,' his faithfulness to scripture led him to affirm the existence of the church with its political responsibility for the sake of the poor, the weak, and the oppressed.

Barth's grounding of ethics in the doctrine of the God who loves in freedom dialectically combines God as the transforming reality with a summons to discipleship in relation to the concrete political situation in the world. Barth's understanding of grace becomes obvious, in that grace that is not to be lived practically is not grace. There is no doubt that Barth stands in the European liberating tradition against capitalism, imperialism, anti-Judaism, and antisocialism as well. In Barth's sharp rejection of liberal theology or neo-Protestantism we witness his antibourgeois tendency against the absolutization of bourgeois culture in the social, political, economic, and scientific realms.

Barth's reflection on the relation between Christian community and civil community can be understood as continuous of what he expressed in the five theses of the Barmen Theological Declaration. The criterion for dealing with a political relation between two communities is the kingdom of God, which explicitly means the reign of Jesus Christ over the world to the glory of God the Father. When the church engages in the politics of God's kingdom, it must not exchange the kingdom of God for the ideal state of the natural law. In thesis 14 of "The Christian Community and the Civil Community" (1946), Barth utilizes *analogia relationis* to exhibit the kingly reign of Christ for all kingdoms of the world:

> The direction and line of Christian political differentiation, judging, choosing, wanting and campaign is related to parable-capacity and -neediness of the political essence . . . The justice of the state in Christian perspective is its existence as a *parable*, a correspondence, analogy to the kingdom of God which is believed in

the church and is proclaimed by the church ... It is in need of parable, just as it is capable of parable. So also through it the history is brought under way, which shapes civil community as the parable of kingdom of God and also has the execution of its justice toward the zeal and content."[7]

According to Barth, the existence of civil community should be formed and established as a parable in correspondence to the kingdom of God. The civil community is capable of becoming a parable reflecting the kingdom of God indirectly, as a mirror image. At this juncture, Barth also rejects both identification of the kingdom of God with the church, as well as absolute difference between them. The church's involvement in the political realm exemplifies, for the sake of illumination, its connection with God's order of salvation and grace, and stands against the darkening thereof. Christian political co-responsibility has the content and zeal of forming the civil community in accordance to the parable of the kingdom of God and the realization of its justice.

This political engagement on the part of the Christian community stands necessarily in the service of and the struggle for social justice. In choosing manifold socialistic possibilities (social liberalism, cooperativism, syndicalism, free-market economics, moderate or radical Marxism), the Christian community takes into account the maximum amount of social justice. The church must concentrate on the lower and lowest levels of human society (thesis 17). The categories of *Gleichnis* (parable) and of *Entsprechung* (correspondence) form a constructing principle in Barth's political ethics in an analogical yet extremely concrete fashion. In it the concept of parable strengthens the Christian community to stand in commitment to social justice based on more democracy and more social justice and to establish "a brotherly human society filled with salvation in communion with God."[8]

Barth's theological affinity for socialism becomes obvious and striking in the fourth thesis of *Darmstädter Wort* (1947). It reads: "We have been misled, as we overlooked that the economic materialism of Marxist doctrine has brought anew to the light an important element of the biblical truth (resurrection of the flesh!) which was largely left behind by the church, as we opposed un-biblically spiritualistic Christendom to it and

---

7. Barth, "Christian Community and the Civil Community," 284.
8. Gollwitzer, "Kingdom of God and Socialism in the Theology of Karl Barth," 97.

as we, in this false fighting front, failed to make the *Sache* of the poor in superior light of the gospel about God's coming kingdom as the *Sache* of the church."[9] Barth identified the doctrine of Marx with historical materialism, according to which the whole history of the human race at its core is the history of economics. Differentiated from the achievements of civilization, science, art, the state, morality, and religion, which are only phenomenal accompaniments of economic history, economics is conceptualized as the true historical reality (*CD* III/2:387).

According to Barth, historical materialism, as a prediction regarding the future course of human history, erects the economic and welfare social state in which there are no more exploiters and no more exploited. Morality in the form of hypocrisy in the bourgeois class state can become a target to overcome. This is the aim of Marxism, for which only economic material development becomes a driving force. This is the hope or eschatology which Marx and his followers pursue as the supreme good and as the appropriate driving motive for socialist action on the way to the future of the new classless community (*CD* III/2:388). Therefore historical materialism is a summons or an appeal to "openmindedness towards the economic meaning of history in general and the necessity of its critique in the light of the dominating class war: to faith in its necessarily approaching goal" (*CD* III/2:388).

Barth utilized Marx's denouncement of the church as "a relic of capitalism" in his construction of an energetic revision of theological anthropology in light of eschatology (*CD* III/2:390). According to Barth, the judgment and promise of God concerning the whole human being cannot be properly understood without material and economic reality. The church needs to make a point of attesting to the economic and material reality of society with the message of the resurrection of the dead instead of showing a culpable indifference towards the problem of contemporary economics (*CD* III/2:389). In Barth's theological framework, historical materialism can be accepted and structured as *per accidens*, not as *per essentiam* (*CD* III/2:387). In his meditation on the second petition of the Lord's Prayer, Barth takes the word of grace so seriously that the human is called to be a "co-fighter" with God. The creatures in their struggle fight against ungodly arrogance in following what the Creator fights against.

---

9. Klappert, *Versöhnung und Befreiung*, 228.

Given this fact, Barth's concept of parable and correspondence is oriented toward social praxis and egalitarian democracy in following the footsteps of the God of Israel, as friend and covenant comrade of human beings in the fight against the social, political, and cultural reality of nothingness.[10] Barth's reflection on nothingness does not seek a new ontology of chaos as the myth for seeking refuge in escapism or for minimizing the reality of evil. In contrast, it retains an ideology-critical function toward the reality of lordless powers in the unreconciled world as is visible in the Holocaust, nuclear weapons, and capitalism.

In a posthumously released fragment on the ethics of reconciliation, Barth deals with the rebellion of the lordless powers in regard to social, political, and cultural injustice. In this ethics, the kingdom of God stands as the order of the coexistence of humans with God, which, as such, includes in itself a form of co-existence by securing human rights, freedom, and peace in corresponding to God's kingdom. However, against this order there stands disorder that destroys human relation. In this contradiction the Christian community must be engaged—with the petition of the kingdom of God—for "struggle for the human justice."[11] Because Barth describes God's action as the revolution in the doctrine of reconciliation, the history of reconciliation is understood as the establishment of a new order that has an affinity for democratic socialism. The resistance against unrighteousness, the "revolt against the disorder" (*KD* IV/4 [Nachlass] §78.1) implies a counterrevolution or countermovement of Christians against the power and principalities of lordless violence. Christians call on God for their removal in the second petition. Barth's contribution to liberation theology can be found in his theology of God's act for the world, political-ethical resistance to the reality of lordless powers, and an affinity for social justice in light of God's kingdom.

---

10. In his book *The Destruction of Reason* (1954), Lukács referenced Barth's paragraph on nothingness in *CD* III/3 §50 (1953) in the face of the barbarism of militarism, the failure of the humanist enlightenment in Europe, and the consequent German idealistic philosophy that led to National Socialism. He sent his greetings to Barth via Hans-Joachim Iwand at the Christian Peace Conference in Prague: "If you see Mr. Barth, and he does not deny to welcome the greeting of an atheist, please greet him for me. I have no more desire to read German philosophers today. But his [*Church*] *Dogmatics* I read. It is the great spiritual movement of Germany." Georg Lukács, communicated by Hans-Joachim Iwand to Karl Barth, December 31, 1959. Cf. Winzeler, "Zäsur des Dialogs," 28.

11. *KD* IV/4 [Nachass] §78.

In her discussion of Barth and Franz Hinkelammert, Sabine Plonz makes an attempt at rereading the theology of Barth and its contextual character from the perspective of liberation theology. In her rereading, Plonz specifically utilizes Barth's analysis of lordless powers in his posthumous ethics of reconciliation in a critical and heuristic dialogue with Hinkelammert's liberation theology and its fetishism critique.[12]

According to Dannemann, the whole framework of the doctrine of reconciliation can be regarded as Barth's christological, Trinitarian, and anthropological actualization of the "revolution of God," in which there is explicit continuity between the two editions of *Romans* commentaries and *Church Dogmatics*.[13] The reconciliation is the transformation of the situation between humans and the world, that is, revolutionary, radical, total and universal transformation. God as wholly other means, in agreement with his grounding thesis—*esse sequitur operari*—God as *ganz und gar Ändernde* (God as the One who changes completely; *KD* IV/4:161), which means *alles in allem real verändernde Tatsache dass Gott ist* ("the fact that God is, materially changes all things and everything in all things" (*KD* II/1:289; *CD* II/1:258; IV/3.2:814, 1069; IV/4:65).

In speaking of Barth's concept of justification and justice, it is of special significance to see the event of justification in light of God who socially and materially changes and transforms the old situation of humanity, including all in all. For Barth, God "exists" under the historical-worldly concept of "fact" (*Tatsache*). God's reality, God's factual existence, occurs socially and materially by transforming human beings and the whole world, history, and nature. God exists really in the actual change of human beings who also are, in turn, called to change the reality of the world.

In a 1923 article, Barth proposed Christian ethics in terms of integrating Jewish chilliasm, expressing "freedom in love and love in freedom." This formulation became actual in the form of socialist hope for the future. In his doctrine of God in *Church Dogmatics* Barth integrates

---

12. Plonz, *Die herrenlosen Gewalten*, 319-37, 343-53.

13. Dannemann, *Theologie und Politik im Denken Barths*, 151. In light of the revolution of God, Barth deals with the judgment of God (namely the work of the self-abasement of the Son of God in *CD* IV/1), the existence of the kingly man (namely the work of the exalted Son of man in *CD* IV/2), the fighting-and-victory-history of Jesus Christ (namely the work of the prophecy of the Son of God and the Son of man in *CD* IV/3), and finally the divine turning of every human to faithfulness toward God in *CD* IV/4.

an ethical-socialistic, utopian-chilliastic concept of hope with his theological reflection on God. God's being is the one who loves in freedom. God's being is in act (*CD* II/1:§28). The event of justification is a way of demonstrating the real "fact" that God "exists." This idea aims at creating the new human being, who, in turn, bears witness to this God by engaging in the renewing and changing of the world.

In his "Socialist Speeches," Barth already took into account a dialectical relation between material base and infrastructure by relating this dialectical interaction to the relation between God's praxis and human praxis. The Christian is an active partner with God rather than a passive speculator. A serious interaction is grounded in the biblical-Jewish concept of the covenant. Thus justification is explicated like a moment from above to below, and also from below to above. Barth's teaching of justification, which aims at the creation of the new humanity, is grounded in his deliberation of God by "the fact that not only sheds new light on, but materially changes, all things and everything in all things—the fact that God is" (*CD* II/1:258).

Barth's deliberation on God cannot be conceived of without connection to the sphere of the public and the political. A theological-dogmatic reflection of God is embedded in practical and political realms. In Barth's concept of justification, the law exists as a necessary form of the gospel rather than remaining an accusing function against the sinner. Barth's interpretation of Jesus Christ as the true revolutionary in this line corresponds to the qualitative character of transformation of the situation between humans and the world in the event of reconciliation. Jesus Christ as the true revolutionary is the "partisan of the poor" (*CD* IV/2:180). In "the active life" (*CD* III/4:§55.3), which constitutes an ethics of the doctrine of creation, Barth already made his critical analysis of the capitalist economic-social order for the transformation of its society in anticipation of the kingdom of God. It is worthwhile to discuss Barth's critical attitude toward alienation and reification in capitalist society as well as in state socialism, especially if we are to review Barth's contribution to liberation theology in an ecumenical and global context.

Barth's Analysis of Alienation and Reification

Just as he had in his two editions of *Romans*, Barth, in *CD* IV, states that the need to overcome alienation has social-political implications. Barth defines the substance of alienation or reification in a threefold form: the alienation of humans from God, from fellows and from self: in other words, enmity against God, brother-murder, and self-destruction of humanity (CD IV/1:397–403, IV/2:409–10). Alienated humans seek their identity by desiring to become lords. In order to gain autonomy, the alienated human falls into the social-political consequence of autonomy. The autonomy of the superhuman plays out as with the great lords, thus destroying the individual and the society. Alienation occurs not only as activism but also as quietism. The apathetic person considers the renewal of human essence to be unnecessary. The false autonomy of the average person leads to antagonism between humans. They exercise the strange power of inhumanity in terms of oppression and exploitation of others, which begins with theft and murder and ends in regional and world wars (CD IV/2:436–37).

In the framework of reconciliation ethics, according to Barth human alienation from God is connected with human self-alienation, which destroys the whole of human relations. Instead of freedom, righteousness, and justice, which would correspond to the order of the kingdom of God, bondage, unrighteousness, and injustice dominate. Human dignity becomes basically problematic. Alienation consists of a human attempt for absolute and lordless existence. Human beings fall into a humanocentric myth that claims they are sovereign, autonomous, and self-righteous. Human capacities become lordless powers that have humans at each other's disposal in an absolutistic way. When the New Testament speaks of the lordless powers consciously in a mythological fashion, these powers are an expression of human alienation or sin.

In light of the kingdom of God, Barth does not mythologize the connection between alienation and injustice, or between sin and death. According to Plonz, this could be understood as Barth's critique of Weber. If "the disenchantment of the world" (through rationalization of the religious charisma in the process of its institutionalization) is understood as a definitive assertion for the present, the present would be regarded as a rationally structured reality clear of idol-faith. In misjudgment of the idols, people are vulnerable to injustice executed by the lordless powers.[14]

---

14. Plonz, *Die herrenlosen Gewalten*, 324.

For this reason, Barth defends himself against the mythologization of the rationality of biblical faith as is seen in the school of Bultmann.[15]

Rationality for Barth arises from its relation to *ratio* of God, to the rationality of covenant between God and humans, to the rationality of reconciliation history.[16] Barth does not find it meaningful to combine the rationality of capitalism with the rationality of human action in correspondence to the rationality of reconciliation. Moreover, wherever capital dominates and rules, the human becomes a thing. The *ratio* of God obviously contradicts the dominion of capital. Bureaucratic rationalism is as irrational as capitalist reality is. In the analysis of the modern, capitalist rationality Weber evaluates the capitalistic rationality positively, while Barth does so negatively. The irrationality of capitalism, which is characterized by alienation and reification, belongs to the marks of the unreconciled society for Barth.

Alienation and reification of human thinking and action leads to comprehensive bureaucratization of human existence (*CD* IV/2: 680–81). The meeting of the human being with fellows is carried out bureaucratically. Human relation becomes an abstract, anonymous relation. When it comes to bureaucratization of human existence, Barth depicts the misuse of human life as a thing. This thing, which builds the periphery of life, is food, goods, and life assistance in material, spiritual, technical, civilizing, and cultural arts. These are apparatuses and fittings on which human life and existence are dependent (*CD* IV/3.2:667). These things are integrated into human life by taking care of human social life. When humans stand under the care of these things, the process of reification becomes compelling and escalates, so that the alienation of the human being from God, co-fellows and from oneself is intensified. Human life falls into the service of lordless powers. When serving the things of the world (such as capital, institutions, state, and the like) they become idols for humans so that the human being becomes reduced to a thing in relation to other human beings. It leads to misuse and disregard of cohumans so that they become mere objects, namely, the instruments and materials for private interest and egotism. This is an inevitable process of compulsion to the thing (*Sachzwang*) in the capitalist society and the state-socialist society as well. The expression of reified thinking and action is an ideology that

---

15. *KD* IV/4 [Nachlass], 369.
16. *FQI*:39–68. *KD* I/1:139.

covers and hides the latent private interest. Alienated humans carry it out at the expense of their fellows. In capitalism as well as in state socialism, we notice the immanent tendency towards antagonism, oppression, and exploitation of others (*CD* IV/2:434–37).

Jesus Christ as the reconciler enters as the agent of change against this unreconciled society characterized by the rule and dominion of the lordless powers. Barth describes the history of the prophecy of Jesus Christ as the history of the fight against the rule of the lordless powers. The fight against the power and principalities of alienation and reification is God's fight that activates and mobilizes humans in this prophetic direction. Human co-praxis in the divine history of reconciliation, according to Barth, is defined as the engagement of humans in the movement of liberation coming from God.[17] The rule of lordless powers is not completely negated yet. Therefore the history of reconciliation is, according to Barth, located between the history of the fight for the total negation of alienation and reification, and God's advent.

According to Barth, the unreconciled society is a society of isolated, autonomous, private existence. Self-realization for private existence means realization of its egotism (*KD* III/2:274–76). "True Christianity cannot be a private Christianity, i.e., a rapacious Christianity. Inhumanity at once makes it a counterfeit Christianity. . . . It cuts at the very root of the confidence and comfort and joy, of the whole *parresia*, in which we should live as Christians, and of the witness which Christianity owes to the world" (*CD* IV/2:442). Barth mentions capitalism and state socialism as examples of un-reconciled society. In a capitalist society, alienation, reification, and bureaucratization of human existence are reflected and mirrored as symptoms of unreconciled society. Capital, not the human, is the measure of all things in capitalism.[18] In defining capital as the thing that dominates and rules human life in the capitalist society, Barth understands the rule of capital as the presupposition for a society of the isolated private existence. The fight for capital is a form of the fight for survival. In the nihilistic dynamics of capitalism, Barth discerns an undoubtedly demonic occurrence that consists of the earning and increasing of pos-

---

17. For Barth, justification as God's judgment of humanity comes as God's forgiveness. Sanctification as the telos of justification is the positive exaltation of humans to the status of freedom (*CD* IV/1:§3, IV/2:§66. 1. 2.); vocation as the telos of justification and sanctification is in its apex of human liberation (*CD* IV/3.2:§71. 6).

18. Barth, *Schweizer Stimme*, 422–23.

sessions. Defined as increasing possessions, capitalism has a natural disposition toward the accumulation of possessions. This accumulation marks the essence of capitalism. This becomes the self-perpetuating purpose of the capitalist society.

Capitalism as the earning and increasing of private possessions belongs to the autonomous individual, who has no responsibility for others. The capitalist economy is organized always as a private economy, as an economy for which the private property of the instrument of production—bound to the right of the freedom of the individual—is a principle of diamond solidity.

> It is here that the revolution of empty and inordinate desires take place: of the lust for a superabundance which is not the natural and beautiful abundance of life but the overflow of nothingness, which does not decorate anything but only pretends to do so, like a stage–prop instead of the real thing; of the lust for possessions which will not be used even perhaps for the purposes of luxury but are desired only as a security and pledge against future use, or perhaps only for the sake of the idea of possession . . . ; of the lust for an artificially extended area of power over men and things in the form of artificial instruments, as if it were not conceit or deception to regard the acquisition of the power of even the mightiest instrument as an increase of one's own real power over life. (CD III/4:538)

Furthermore, Barth understands capital as a possession to be expressed in the form of money. Money is precisely the power that orients humans toward alienation and reification. In capitalism, capital functions not only as the thing that rules human life. Capital also expresses itself as private possession in the form of money. In capitalist society, human laboring and economic activity do not stand in the service of satisfying human desires or necessities. Rather human laboring and economic activity concentrate on the earning of capital, and this earning becomes the real meaning and purpose of the labor process. The orientation of the labor process toward capital earning determines the relation between humans and social apparatuses in capitalism. According to Barth, the struggle for capital is a form of the struggle for existence. The use of capital is purely illusory, yet also dynamic. In its composition of both the trivial and dynamic, it is almost an unequivocally demonic process. This demonic process of capital "consists in the amassing and multiplying of possessions expressed in financial calculations (or miscalculations), i.e., the 'capital' which is in the hands of relatively few, who pull all the strings" (*CD* III/4: 531–32).

In Barth's understanding, capitalism epitomizes a nonfree and unreconciled society in which the apparatus in the form of capital dominates human life. In the process of the accumulation of capital, the human becomes reified to the status of a thing in the structure of the social apparatus. Interpersonal relations in capitalism appear as relations among things. In this way capital effects and propels the alienation and the reification of human thinking and action in the capitalist society. According to Barth, in the ruling process of capital, money can realize its value as capital in the socioeconomic arena. Therefore capital can be analyzed in relation to the social processes of labor.

Given this fact, Plonz discerns a parallel between Karl Barth and Marx concerning a fetishism critique in capitalism. According to Marx, the concept of fetishism is articulated in the combination of alienated production relations, religion, and ideology construction. Marx's theory of alienation and its continued development into the fetishism theory offers a basis for liberation theologians such as Hinkelammart to discuss a theological discourse on sin and injustice in light of the process of fetishism. In other words, this theory helps concretize bondage and alienation and reveal the rational reason of the dominion of lordless powers. According to Plonz, Barth's idea of commodity fetishism is relevant to Marx's theory of fetishism.[19] In Marx's view, capital fetishism governs commodity fetishism. Compulsion to consummation and acceleration exists and lives inherently in capital's desire for the utilization of all. The social relation of producers among themselves appears to them as the social relation of their products. Therefore the definite social relations of humans assume for them the fantastic form of relations between things.[20] Commodity fetishism is a social theoretical category of explaining the independent law under the reign of lordless powers.

Furthermore Marx's idea of money fetishism is relevant to Barth's confrontation with the lordless powers. Marx already, in his *Paris Manuscript*, had recognized the significance of money for understanding the reification process. He illustrates the omnipotence of money, for

---

19. *KD* IV/4 [Nachlass] §78.2.
20. Marx, *Kapital*, Bd.1, in *MEW* 23:86.

example, in his consideration of the doctrine of *creatio ex nihilo*.[21] With the domination of money, the principle of private property is established. Barth's critique of mammon is embedded within his critique of the lordless power of money.[22]

As we have already seen in Barth's definition of capital, capital as a possession is expressed in the form of money. Money has power that leads the capital-oriented human toward alienation and reification. For Barth, capital as self-increasing private property is not only the thing that dominates human life in capitalism; private property also rules, expressed in the form of money.[23] The capitalist form of the labor process can be spoken about at the point where the function of capital is spoken about in the labor process. In the analysis of the alienation and the reification in the capitalist labor process, Barth states that the laborer has different relations to capital than the employer. Work under the mode of competition will always be an inhuman activity: "So long as workers forget the fellow-humanity without which they cannot be men, and confound their vital claims with their empty and inordinate desires, their work necessarily stands under the sign of competition and therefore of conflict" (*CD* III/4: 541). Barth's idea of humanity is, at its root, anticapitalist: "Humanity, the characteristic and essential mode of man's being, is at its root fellow-humanity. Humanity which is not fellow-humanity is inhumanity" (*CD* III/4:117).

Humanity in the authentic sense is distorted through the privatization of human existence and the human desire to possess capital. The chief characteristic of capitalism is *Aneignung*, which implies a lifestyle in which humans search for material possessions in order to satisfy their own needs, pleasures, and power, and doing so leads to the exclusion of others. Economically speaking, *Aneignung* is egoism, that which is the root of privatization and constitutes the root of the struggle for existence in the capitalist society. Under the restless economic competition of

21. Lochman, *Encountering Marx*, 60–61. Under the rule of money, everything changed, Marx said: "No eunuch flatters his oppressive master more, nor seeks to entice him into the gratification of new appetites more seductively to his own profit, than does the industrial eunuch, the producer, entice the golden bird, surreptitiously sneaking the widow's mite from the pocket of his dear Christian neighbour. Every product is a bait, with which the other is caught and his money lured away from him; each need, real or imaginary, is a weakness which leads the bird into the trap."

22. Plonz, *Die herrenlosen Gewalten*, 329–30.

23. *KD* IV/4 [Nachlass], 380–82.

capitalism this desire for egotism is veiled, legitimized, and sanctioned through the institutions, laws, and statutes in the capitalist society. "As I live for me, I live necessarily against others."[24]

Under the rule of capitalist society, private property and the privatization of values and human relations are institutionalized and propel the pursuit of markets and products in other countries. In the capitalist society, argues Barth, occurs a necessary interrelation between foreign policy, the armaments industry, and industrial power in Western countries. "It is when interest-bearing capital rather than man is the object whose maintenance and increase are the meaning and goal of the political order that the mechanism is already set going which one day will send men to kill and to be killed"(*CD* III/4:459).

A consequence of the privatization of social relations is the corruption and alienation of the task and meaning of human labor, which is ordered and commanded by God. Barth discusses the organization of labor in terms of a contract between the employer and the employee for establishing conditions and wages. Under "the laborer," Barth understands the person participating in the labor process as one who is reliant on his or her labor capacity and income capacity in order to survive by possessing their time and labor power only as property. Therefore, they find themselves being economically dependent for their livelihood on the social class of the employers who offer the opportunities of work and reward. Employers have over the employee the "advantage of possessing the means of labor, the so-called means of production, i.e., the soil, raw materials, tools, machines and working capital" (*CD* III/4:541–42). They can bring the labor power into the labor process. Because employers are dependent on reception of the offered work by the laborers, they have no influence upon the purpose of their labor. What is produced determines what the labor offers, that is, the proprietor of capital, namely, the means of production. For the laborer, the expected wage (namely, money value) and not the labor itself becomes the meaning of labor.

On the basis of this mechanism, the laborer begins to think and act in a capitalist way. The measure of money value, namely, the capital expressed in the form of money, rules the participation of the laborer in the labor process. As the labor appears as money value, it stands in strange relation to the laborer.

---

24. Barth, *Ethik I*, 274.

They are competing for the necessities of life, for the higher or highest satisfaction of these necessities. The one aim is to be better off than the other simply for the sake of being better off than the other. By doing better, he hopes to secure easier and ampler access to that for which the other also strives. He does it for his own advantage, and therefore inevitably to the disadvantage of the other and at the cost of the partial or even perhaps the total exclusion of the other from that which both desire. (CD III/4:540)

The strange determination of the labor that is carried out through the dominion of capital is, according to Barth, the ground of alienation.

In the analysis of the legal form of the free labor contract between employer and employee, Barth perceives exploitation taking place in its economic content. At first sight, the labor contract is described as a free agreement between employer and employee. In fact, however, equality between contract partners does not exist. The employer as the owner of the capital (or means of production) has incomparable advantage over the employee by dictating the so-called free labor contract in accordance with his or her own interest and advantage (CD III/4:542). Behind the formal equality of the contract partners, the inequality of the relation is hidden. The economically stronger partner determines the money value of the weaker partner's labor. Because of this double standard, the labor contract becomes a mask used for covering inhumanity in the capitalist organization of the labor process: "This is social injustice in a form which is less blatant than simple competition, which is apparently grounded in co-ordination, which may even seem to be legitimate in view of its inclusion of free and reciprocal contracts, but which is even more oppressive and provoking in its ostensible show of justice, and can only make industrial peace the more radically impossible of attainment" (CD III/4:542). Where there is a fight for competition and survival, the class struggle really occurs. It simulates equality, corporality, interest collection, and willingness to take part in labor.

The relation between employers and employees is imprinted on capitalist society by inequality, the inequality that leads to the exploitation of the laborer by the employer. According to Barth, the labor process in the great and general sense of the Western world is based, by and large, on the principle of exploitation of the one by the other. Since the time of Marx, the awakening of the working class has been brought to "consciousness of its power," "its internationally directed self-defense and self-assistance both politically and in the form of trade unions and co-operative societies." A slogan against the exploitation of the weak by the strong had been erected in the passage of the years. In Barth's view, it could hardly be denied that "at least in the West, the modern industrial process does in fact rest on the principle of the exploitation of some by others" (*CD* III/4:542–43). For Barth the genuine value of labor cannot be mediated through mere money value or capital value but through the labor of the humans—seen as real co-workers in the labor process and in the seeking out of their life's desires and necessities. The profit motif of the owner of the means of production effects the oppression and exploitation of the human through the cohuman. As capital exploits and oppresses, the employee becomes the victim of the labor process under the dominion of capital.

Against the laborer the employer who participates in the labor process is at the disposal of the so-called means of production. The relation between employer and laborer is characterized by the class struggle. The class struggle is defined as the exploitation of the laborer practiced by the employer. In other words, it is defined as a component of economic reality rather than as a political program for the preservation of the class interest or for the laborer's economic fight against the employer. Class struggle, according to Barth, is primarily class struggle "from above" and secondarily class struggle "from below."[25] The modern industrial process is based in fact on the principle of the exploitation of some by others. Because of the means of production, the economically stronger can turn to their own advantage the labor contract with the economically weaker partner (*CD* III/4:542).

The proletarian "class egotism" is conceived of as a reaction to the bourgeoisie. Barth's thesis of class struggle "from above" comes from the fact that the employer has the initiative in the capitalist labor process and determines the relation between employer and laborer. Barth's concept of class struggle from above manifests itself as inhuman in a threefold sense: 1) as friend-to-enemy relation (concurrence/relation), 2) as tyranny-slave relation, and 3) as bureaucratization (instrumentalization) of the relation between employer and employee. The inhumanity of the

---

25. In the analysis of the relation between class rule and class struggle, Gollwitzer remains faithful to this ground principle of Barth: "Class struggle is always primarily the class struggle from above. Class struggle from below is answer, reaction, counter-violence." Gollwitzer, *Kapitalistische Revolution*, 72 (my translation).

class struggle destroys the humanity of labor and the humanity of those who take part in the labor process. The class struggle and the revolution against the empty and inordinate desires behind it are expressions of the revolution against nihilism. In capitalistic-nihilistic desire, the human is victimized by empty and inordinate desires (*CD* III/4:553). The alienation of employers from laborers becomes manifest in that employers justify their relation to laborers in terms of exploitation and class struggle without recognizing the reality of this relation. They legitimize the profit economy. Barth reports on the argument of the employers: 1) the right and private property of the means of production, which is bound to the freedom and right of the individual, is untouchable; 2) the employer is the best laborer, whose advantaged position in the labor process is based on his or her special competence; 3) without competition and struggle between humans, there is no economic and technical progress; 4) capitalism has evolved into a better form than have previous societies; and 5) the prophecy of the collapse of capitalism (for instance, Marx's theory of the increasing enrichment of fewer, and the developing proletarization of the middle classes, with the cumulative misery of the masses, and especially of the proletariat) has proved wrong (*CD* III/4:542–43).

Be this as it may, Barth asks: "Nevertheless, of what avail are all these arguments in face of the simple fact that this system does permit in practice and demand in principle that man should make another man and his work a means to his own ends, and therefore a mere instrument, and that this is inhuman and therefore constitutes an injustice?" (*CD* III/4:543). In this regard Barth critiques the arguments of the employer as pseudo-arguments, therefore, as the concealing of the economic reality. In these covering arguments, the alienation of the employer is also reflected. On the basis of interest that contributes to profit and on the basis of their bourgeois class egotism, they are not in a position to comprehend the inhumanity of their relation to the laborers. Because of self-deception with regard to their situation in the labor process, employers are also captive in the capitalist organization. A possible reform to overcome the alienation of the employer, argues Barth, would consist in the transition from a private and profit economy toward a cooperative organization of the labor process.[26]

---

26. Barth illustrates a case of the Zeiss group at Jena; see *CD* III/4:543.

In analyzing the alienation of the employer, Barth articulates the reality that the employer also becomes an instrument of capital by subordinating himself or herself to the process of reification. In the service of capitalism, the employer is like his or her fellows. At issue for Barth is not to discredit the employer as inhuman but to show that the domination of capital and capitalism is a form of an unreconciled society. In it harm is done against the employer as well as the laborer. Thus Barth's critique is aimed at the principle of capitalism. In the context of reconciliation ethics, Barth characterized the lordless powers negatively as on the one hand dark, ghostly, fleeing, of various kinds, and hard to name.[27] But on the other hand, Barth does not ignore the positive factor of lordless powers; in this reality there is no entreaty to human freedom, no overlooking, no forgetting, no denying. In the service of human liberation, the lordless powers are not only the support but the motor of the society, and they are the secret guarantee of human self-intelligibility, habit, custom, tradition, and institutions. They are the hidden wire pullers in the great and small enterprise, movement, production, and revolution. They are not only the potent but the real factors and agents of human progress, regress, and standstill in politics, economics, science, technology, and war; but they are also factors in the evolution and obstruction of the completely personal lives of individual humans. From this evaluation Barth views the lordless powers as dynamic, autonomous, technical, administering, powerful, purpose oriented, and revolutionary.[28]

To illustrate the rule of lordless powers, Barth illustrates four realms: The first is political absolutism, in which the idea of the imperial effects the demonization of the political. The fifth thesis of the Barmen Declaration documents a challenge to the national socialist subjection of human rights under state power. The second realm is mammon, namely, material property, possessions, and wealth.[29] The demonic lies in the detaching of exchange value from the use value of material wealth for living. The symbolic character of money as an allotted good enables its continued development into a treasure, through bank accounts and ever-increasing capital.[30] At this juncture, money becomes the embodiment

27. *KD* IV/4 [Nachlass], 367; Barth, *Christian Life*, 216.
28. Ibid., 368, 372.
29. Ibid., 378.
30. Ibid., 381.

of all values and a steering instrument of social development at both the national and international levels. Barth's theory of money is meant to reveal its fetish character that can destroy human life. Money, the flexible and powerful means, supposedly handled by humans, following in reality its own legality, can ground opinions and convictions in a thousand ways. It oppresses, affecting other humans like a brutal fact—now an economic upswing, now a business recession; now stopping and causing the crisis, now serving the peace but bringing cold war in midst of peace, preparing and giving rise to bloodshed. It creates paradise here, but, correspondingly, provisional hell here as well. Money is a lordless power that absolutely rules the individual, the human relationship, and humankind: "If they are only pseudo-objective realities, strangely enough they are still powerful realities which make a fine display of their lying objectivity."[31]

Third, the lordless powers turn a spiritual capacity into an ideology. In this area, Barth sees the possibility and reality of idol worship. The ideal that serves the living spiritual activity becomes the idol. Human thinking is subject to the ideological realm in which one moves.[32] The sign of ideologization is the development of "ism," the use of slogans and its expansion through political propaganda.

Fourth, *chthonic* forces, which arise from the dominion and subjugation of nature. On the one hand there is the inevitable scientific and technological change of the whole cosmos.[33] On the other hand, laws rule daily life: laws of fashion, sport, pleasure, obsession; laws for traffic in the destruction of nature and the killing of humans. Human will in bondage and enmity to life is the result of this dominion of the lordless powers.[34] In various realms such as politics, economics, human and natural science, technology, consumerism, and daily behavior, the lordless powers develop in every case their own effect. All these are expressions of the rule of capital and are forces of death.

At this juncture, Barth binds the liberation of the kingdom of God to an ideological critique in an investigation of reality. Christians pray "your kingdom come" as an indication that God resists human injustice and evil. This prayer is a summons for human righteousness and order, and

31. Ibid., 382
32. Ibid., 383–84.
33. Ibid., 389.
34. Ibid., 395.

as an eschatological prayer it tells us that "He [God] is the mystery that cannot be imprisoned in any system of human conceptuality but can be revealed and known only in parables. He is God acting concretely within human history."[35] "Where the command of God is heard it will always be a summons to counter-movement of this kind . . . The [Christian] community at least cannot participate in the great self-deception concerning the character of the situation . . . Work under the sign of this competition will always imply as such work in the form of a conflict in which one man encounters another with force and cunning, and there cannot fail to be innumerable prisoners, wounded and dead" (*CD* III/4:541).

Reconciliation for More Democracy and More Social Justice

Barth understood the reconciliation of society as the revolutionary transformation of the unreconciled society toward more democracy and social justice. The reconciled society is characterized by the removal of both alienation and the reification of human existence, which amounts to the cessation of the rule and domination of the lordless powers in the unreconciled society. The active life created by God and reinstated in the reconciliation of Jesus Christ implies a new definition and a change in humans' relation to God, to fellow humans, to the world, and the environment. This simultaneously subjective and objective orientation is the special and the new orientation of the active life (*CD* III/4:§55.3). The negation of human social alienation and of broader societal alienation implies the exclusion of antagonism between humans. The struggle for survival in the unreconciled society finds its end, and therefore the end of the oppression and exploitation of humans by humans also happens. Humans, who are no longer the instrument of a strange purpose, discover the genuine social character of human existence. Solidarity and communion become the principles of the human life of togetherness (*KD* IV/2:821).

Coordinating humanity's genuine desires with the necessities of life calls for a common way of living, with human dignity and equality. For Barth, the society would be reconciled when there exists a community of free humans, a community without paternalism; when exploitation and oppression of others are removed; when class differences and national

---

35. Ibid., 435–36.

borders, war, enforcement, and violence are eliminated; when a culture of the Spirit replaces the culture of the thing; when humans live with humanity rather than with reified objectivity, and with mutuality in place of universal resentment.

Although the democratic society is not identical with the kingdom of God, Barth implores Christianity to keep itself leftist over against the social disorder of class society. The church is to keep to the political left in opposition of the status quo of society; in other words, the church is to reside fundamentally on the side of the victims of disorder and to espouse their cause (*CD* III/4:544). As Barth stated, "the Christian community can and must also espouse various forms of social progress or even socialism—always the form most helpful in its specific time and place and in its specific situation. Yet her decisive word cannot consist in the proclamation of social progress or socialism. It can only consist in the proclamation of God's revolution against all "ungodliness and wickedness of men (Rom 1:18)" (*CD* III/4:545). For Barth, reform politics and revolution were not mutually exclusive. At this juncture, Barth's summons to countermovement was directed against the capitalist economic order and the totalitarian state socialism because "a call for counter-movement" is "on behalf of humanity and against its denial in any form, and therefore a call for the championing of the weak against every kind of encroachment on the part of the strong" (*CD* III/4:544).

With this reservation in mind, the idea of socialism, for Barth, retained a positive, worldly, relational zeal—the kind found in human politics; it remains an essential component of theological social teaching for Christian ethics, that is, for the struggle for the humanization of the human, for the service of Christian community and for Christian life, and for engagement for peace in the world. Barth is critical of the current existing model of democracy and socialism. When democracy loses social content, it becomes a formal democracy.

Likewise the communist state socialism came under Barth's critical view. In totalitarian state socialism, socialist class struggle is camouflaged in place of the open capitalist class struggle. Barth doubts whether in Marxist state socialism the exploitation has been brought to an end, whether there are no classes with opposing interests, no more class struggle. "It is doubtful . . . although the letter of the Marxist programme means that there can be no more exploiters and exploited, it does not settle the matter that there is no more private ownership of the means of production or free enterprises, or that the direction of the labour process has been transferred to the hands of the state" (*CD* III/4:544).

In state socialism there occurs a new form of oppression of human by human and a new power elite. Rather than the employer, the almighty party and its police and propaganda retain a central function. According to Barth, these powers are the lordless powers of state socialism. State socialism implies a new hypostatization of the state in the interest of the ruling and privileged minority, and a renewed establishment of the state dictatorship and social order without social democracy. For Barth, the labor movement (of the second and the third International) opposed proletarian class egotism to bourgeois class egotism. Class egotism, like all egotism, is an expression of human alienation. A false, egotistic, utilitarian character was smuggled into the workers' movement. As long as the human forgets fellow humanity and pursues empty and inordinate desires instead of genuine and vital claims, human work "will necessarily stand under the sign not merely of competition but of exploitation, of open class war, whether in its capitalistic or its socialistic guise" (*CD* III/4:545).

Instead of reconciliation with the whole, the exchange of an existing dominion and slavery for a new dominion and slavery had crept zealously into the politics of the workers' movement. This was a particularistic tendency leading to separation. Instead of the movement, the distinguished leader of labor movement (namely, the Social Democratic Party) took over the function and the power with which a new class system established itself (*CD* III/4:539–40).

Lenin's negative understanding of reconciliation indicates a far-reaching encapsulation of his political perspective: The irreconcilable fight against the class enemy becomes self-purpose. The existence of antagonistic particularity becomes a raison d'etre. In this way the proletarian class egotism is perpetuated into the independent establishment. It functions as the social basis of renewing legitimation of particularism and separation. It is no accident that Lenin's negative concept of reconciliation affected state socialism.[36]

---

36. Given this fact, Wielenga clarifies the difference between Barth and Lenin regarding the concept of reconciliation. Barth understands reconciliation and transformation as sanctification of the whole in the Hegelian sense, while Lenin, apart from the Hegelian tradition, understands reconciliation purely negatively as the antithesis to social change, as the freezing of class contradiction, and as the capitulation of the proletariat. See

According to Barth, state socialism, like capitalism, is a form of antagonistic and unreconciled society. During the East-West conflict in the cold war, Barth refused to take sides—because of his theological and political critique of both social systems, not because of his apolitical disinterestedness. Barth's conception of social democracy is the proposal toward a third way beyond both capitalism and totalitarian state socialism. This concept stands behind Barth's cooperation with the "free Germany movement."[37]

Democracy and socialism have an affinity to God's reconciliation with the world and the reconciled society. Basic values such as freedom, equality, and brotherhood; or freedom, justice, and solidarity have an affinity with God's zeal for reconciliation in history and its corresponding human-political zeal and purpose. In following the history of the prophecy of Jesus Christ, Christian community between the times of "already" and "not yet" is encouraged to pursue democracy and socialism as the inner worldly, relative confirmation of freedom and equality in view of God's kingdom. According to Barth, the concept of true work has as its aim the freedom of humanity for life, according to which he brings into critical view as "a kind of perpetual competition," systems such as the American Taylor or the Russian Stachanovite (CD III/4:550).

In defining the prophetic struggle for a social democracy or democratic socialism as corresponding to the reconciliation of God with the world and to the reconciled society, Barth also underpinned democracy and socialism as the countermovement against the capitalist as well as the state-socialist form of social alienation and reification. Democratic socialism for Barth is the concrete political zeal that is to be strived after and set in motion (KD III/4:524–26, 624–26). In this regard social-democratic civil community belongs to Barth's concept of the "righteous state," which contradicts and opposes all political, social, and economic tyranny and anarchy. Barth's utilization of the Reformation principle of the righteous state becomes manifest in his theological idea of social theory: society is to be always renewed (*Societas semper reformanda*) (KD III/4:592–626).

Barth's reform politics as a countermovement lies in 1) human engagement for establishing marks and characteristics of the reconciled society; 2) critiquing the alienation and reification of human existence

---

Wielenga, *Lenins Weg zur Revolution*, 18–22, 469–72.

37. Marquardt, *Theologie und Sozialismus*, 50–61.

in the capitalist as well as in the state-socialist order on behalf of the humanization of society, in which the Christian community always stands in engagement and solidarity with the weak and the poor; and 3) fighting for the reconciliation of the society: reform politics as the counter-movement has a relative meaning in view of the line and direction of the kingdom of God rather than being fixed into an absolute position. "The relativity of even the most radical attempt at reform in the guise of 'evolution' simply proves again that whatever can be done by men or said by Christians in the direction of such attempts can have only relative significance and force . . . Even the most well-meaning and rigorous attempts at counter-movement can arrest and modify but not entirely remove it" (*CD* III/4:545).

Barth's social theory can be characterized by the thesis that every social order in world history is in need of change and is capable of being transformed. This stance led to struggle for the reconciliation of society as the ongoing countermovement against political alienation and reification. For this reason, Barth was not very convinced of or sympathetic to the system-conforming reformism of social democracy in Western Europe. Barth's reform politics had the zeal to overcome the capitalist system and was in agreement with ideas of social revolution.[38]

Barth's conception of permanent reform politics did not intend to overthrow the social totality directly but to overcome elements of the social order that were responsible for causing alienation and reification in an unreconciled society. Barth's critique of the revolution model (in the case of Leninism) and of the system-conforming reform model (in the case of social democracy in Western Europe) makes clear that Barth's way of reform politics and countermovement (associated with his concept of democratic socialism) corrected the one-sided fixation of both models.[39]

---

38. From the perspective of Gollwitzer, the choice between reform and revolution has become an abstraction. They are no longer exclusive. Reform *or* revolution are no alternatives for socialists. Reform *instead of* revolution is a boon for capitalists. To be sure, reform *and* revolution is a socialist solution. In the theological existence between East and West, Gollwitzer remains faithful to his teacher, Barth, whose theological and social intention Gollwitzer has portrayed impressively in his book *Kingdom of God and Socialism in the Theology of Karl Barth*. See also Gollwitzer, *Kapitalistische Revolution*, 69.

39. Barth's concept of democracy is more in line with the political philosophy of Rousseau, to whom Barth himself refers in his "Christian Community and Civil Community" (thesis 28). Barth, however, is not in agreement with Rousseau's idea

According to Barth's socialism, in the transition from this dimension into the political form and reality, the Christian community affirms freedom as the basic right guaranteed to every citizen through the civil community. This freedom and its consequences in the political and legal spheres can be sought according to its own insight and choice and also independently. According to Barth, freedom is ensured in definite political and legal spheres, but not in politically and legally ordered and regulated spheres (family, education, art, science, faith).[40]

At a minimum, Barth's engagement in order to chart the line and direction that comes from the gospel points to more social justice and more democracy in political realms, witnessing them as parables of the kingdom of God. In the sense of a Christian line and direction, Barth's ideas of analogy, parable, and correspondence do not exclude historically the materialistic deliberation of history and its social critique, but mobilize them toward more democracy and more social justice, which are ongoing parables of and toward the permanent revolution of God.[41] In critically viewing pacifists as well as militarists, Barth considered the fashioning of the state for democracy, and of democracy for social democracy, to be the primary concern of Christian ethics:

> Pacifists and militarists are usually agreed in the fact that for them the fashioning of peace as the fashioning of the state for democracy, and of democracy for social democracy, is a secondary concern as compared with rearmament or disarmament. It is for this reason that Christian ethics must be opposed to both. Neither rearmament nor disarmament can be a first concern, but the restoration of an order of life which is meaningful and just. (CD III/4:459)

In anticipation of the coming kingdom of God, Barth encouraged Christian communities to engage in establishing marks of the kingdom

---

grounding democracy in terms of the social contract. According to Barth, the idea of democracy must be developed in terms of the sociality of God in correspondence to the sociality of humans.

40. In thesis 18 Barth states: "The church will not in all circumstances withdraw from and oppose what may be practically a dictatorship, that is, a partial and temporary limitation of these freedoms, but it will certainly withdraw from and oppose any out-and-out dictatorship such as the totalitarian state" (Barth, "Christian Community and Civil Community," 284).

41. Gollwitzer, *Kapitalistische Revolution*, 120.

of God, such as democracy and social justice in human society, instead of remaining idle spectators. Through establishing such marks, Barth intended to change the alienation and reification in the social order. Especially in view of the fighting and victorious history of the prophet Jesus Christ, whom he characterized as the revolutionary (*KD* IV/2:193, 195), Barth insisted that reconciliation had overcome the enmity between God and humans and had established peace and solidarity among humans. Therefore, humans are free in life, in contact, in solidarity, in fellowship with God, and, further, with the world beloved by God and with fellow humans (*KD* IV/3:285). This aims to remove the bureaucratization of the human existence (the power of human existence) as a reified objectivity that administers and dominates inhumanely between alienated humans. The alienation and reification of humans that enjoins human existence to comprehensive bureaucratization stands in conflict with the society of *communio sanctorum* given by God. A bureau is a place where the human is regarded under certain schemata and treated, absolved, and sick according to definite plans, principles, and regulations (*KD* III/2:302). According to Barth, "The Christian community stands in political realms . . . in engagement and struggle for social justice. And it will make choices at any rate in the choice between the various socialistic possibilities . . . from which it believes in each case to expect . . . the most measurement of social justice."[42]

Karl Barth from the Angle of Liberation Theology

From the perspective of liberation theology in Latin America, especially according to Gutiérrez, Barth is regarded as a theologian who can give impetus to "the eruption of the perspective of the poor into the modern problematics."[43] It is also of special significance to accept Barth's critique of religion and the relevance of theology to the social reality. Plonz, in her attempt at rereading Barth's contextual theology, clarifies the relevance of Barth to liberation theology in terms of Barth's reception of Feuerbach and his preference for social reality. According to Plonz, Hinkelammert's liberation theology also takes Feuerbach seriously in a threefold sense: in the affirmation of free humans, in the negation of human bondage, and

---

42. Ibid., see also thesis 17.
43. Gutiérrez, *Power of the Poor in History*, 65.

in the mediation of an ideal of freedom in the picture of free humans as the image of God.[44] Unlike in Barth, however, in the circle of liberation theology the preference for social reality becomes manifest and obvious in the recognition of the religiosity of the poor. For instance, the religion of the poor extols another God than the God of the ruling and powerful. It can be understood as an expression of cultural resistance against the dominating culture. The spirituality of the poor retains and develops a critical power in the area of economics as well as in other realms of life. From this perspective, Plonz argues that contextual, cultural, and religious situation plays no role in Barth.[45]

As Gutiérrez recognizes an antibourgeois and liberating aspect in Barth's theology, he perceives and locates the character of Barth's theology as a theology seen from the underside of history. According to Gutiérrez, Barth's experience with social and political reality amounts to a frank political militancy. On point of fact, Gutiérrez recommends Barth's resistance to the encapsulation of the Word of God into a bourgeois mentality in light of Barth's notion of God as one who takes sides with the poor against the powerful. Be that as it may, Barth would be hesitant to agree with the liberative thesis of "the Poor as *locus theologicus* of Christology," in which the poor are not a parable mirroring of the reality of kingdom of God but are (without an eschatological proviso) equated with it.[46]

In addition, Christology in the framework of liberation theology funds insensitivity to Jesus as a Jew. In it we hear that "Jesus has an experience of a different God."[47] Jesus is depicted as antagonistic in his reactions to the Jewish establishment, which Jesus intends to destroy: "the Yahweh of their cult against Jesus' *Abba*."[48] In this anti-Jewish overtone, Jesus becomes the total Liberator from the Jewish religion, which would imply the removal or expatriation of Judaism from a christological understanding of Jesus Christ. For Barth, however, Jesus as the "partisan of the poor" is born a Jew; and in Barth's understanding of Jesus Christ, in Christ's assumption of Jewish flesh, Israel is not to be abandoned or perishable but to be exalted and included.

---

44. Plonz, *Die Herrenlosen Gewalten*, 351–52.
45. Ibid., 349–50.
46. Sobrino, "Systematic Christology," 142.
47. Bravo, "Jesus of Nazareth, Christ the Liberator," 110.
48. Ibid., 118.

As we have already seen, Barth's profound insight about humanity in the first edition of *Romans*—that "humans under grace are what they will make out of themselves. They are free in God . . . They have the gift of activity of good will" (R I:169)—finds its echo in this liberative statement: "With deliberation not the word 'freedom,' but the dynamic word 'liberation'" (*KD* IV/3.2:760; *CD* IV/3.2:663) becomes characteristic of Christian existence. This liberation aspect gains prominence when it comes to Barth's critique of the lordless powers of political absolutism and economic mammonism. As Marquardt says, for Barth "theology which knows what it is about is theology of revolution, far from all fashionable trends and the decline into the 'journalism of revolution' . . . it is *necessary* theology of revolution, and does not need to become something else tomorrow, or the day after tomorrow. And it is then necessarily, as a theology of the One who takes the side of the poor, itself partisan, socially conscious, and class conscious."[49] Barth's encounter with liberation theology calls for a further dialogue regarding the unity between dogmatics and ethical praxis, the relation between Israel and theology, and the relation between the gospel and religious pluralism. Barth's dialogue with religious pluralism will be dealt with in the next chapter.

---

49. Marquardt, *Theologie und Sozialismus*, 296.

CONCLUSION   Karl Barth and an Unfinished Project for Religious Pluralism

SO FAR IN THIS BOOK I HAVE DISCUSSED BARTH'S THEOLOGY IN LIGHT of its connection with contemporary issues so that his theology of God's Word is revealed as being grounded in God's action for the world. In the Safenwil period, Barth's theological thinking of God and political engagement was deeply shaped by his pastoral, socialist life-setting. He understood God radically as a *totaliter aliter*—the One who breaks into human society, disrupting and transforming it in a completely different manner—rather than referring to the wholly transcendent divine principle. His confrontation with the Catholic teaching of *analogia entis* and *theologia naturalis* should be understood and interpreted from the perspective of his critique of its overemphasis on human ontological capacity to attain God's salvation apart from God's historical action in Jesus Christ, who becomes Jewish flesh and the partisan of the poor. Thus his confrontation with Catholic theology and neo-Lutheran theology during the period of National Socialism was politically motivated and biblically grounded, especially in a pro–Old Testament orientation. Barth's theology cannot be adequately understood without connection to its social-political aspirations and Israel, which is biblically based and legitimate. Barth's slogan "Beginning again at the beginning" points to his exegetical and practical orientation for God, who is the God of Israel and the Father of Jesus Christ. In fact, God's revelation in Jesus Christ means revolution, liberation, and the transformation of status quo in human society.

Barth has been read and is being discussed in different contexts and diverse perspectives; as a result, many labels and characterizations have been given to him, whether in positive appraisal or on a critical note.

In view of his diverse stages and different emphases which make up the direction of his theological development, it would be risky to narrow down his theology to a fixed thought-movement or a school of so-called Barthianism. Barth's theology (critical, dialogical, open to the world) is inherently related to the concrete contextuality of his life setting.

He once spoke of his desire not to be venerated but to be understood. Accordingly, Barth's theology is inherently a request for understanding and clarification because he himself calls for such a dialogue. Barth himself does not see even his *Church Dogmatics* as a conclusion, but "as the opening of a new conversation" about the question of the right course for theology.[1]

After Vatican II, Barth demonstrated a friendly attitude toward Catholic theology and remarkable openness to the reality of religious pluralism. Eberhard Busch reports on Barth's remarkable interest in the Second Vatican Council.[2] According to Busch, during the spring and summer of 1966 Barth made a serious study of the sixteen Latin texts that were "produced by the council and of at least some specimens of the abundant literature devoted to the council."[3] Barth took delight in the renewal movement of the Catholic Church before and after the council and hoped for this movement to continue. Although not overestimating the renewal movement in the Roman Catholic Church, Barth hoped for a renewal of the church in the sense of a conversion to Jesus Christ. Barth's visit to the Vatican (a six-day *peregrinatio ad limina apostolorum*) convinced him that "the church and theology over there are more on the move than I had imagined."[4]

Barth articulated five points regarding the astonishing renewal in Roman Catholicism after Vatican II: (1) The Bible has held a central place and comes as *the* witness to revelation. (2) There is a concentration on Jesus Christ. (3) The church essentially as the people of God. (4) Preaching and the Eucharist as the genuine function of worship (5) A necessary and proper opening of the church to other confessions, to

---

1. Cf. Busch, *Karl Barth: His Life*, 488.

2. Ibid., 478–85. Barth characterizes his dogmatics in terms of a biblical and confessional attitude. Barth's dogmatics is ecclesiastical in a universal sense, and therefore ecumenical. "Where dogmatics exists at all, it exists only with the will to be a Church dogmatics, a dogmatics of the ecumenical Church" (*CD* I/2:823. cf. 836–37).

3. Busch, *Karl Barth: His Life*, 481.

4. Ibid., 484.

world religions, and to the world.⁵ Given the results of Vatican II, Barth retracted his earlier position concerning the so-called *analogia entis* as the invention of the antichrist. He found it no longer necessary to discuss this theory because "we are in unity about what can be meant by it."⁶

In this openness we note that Barth's theology of christological concentration does not replace the mystery of God whose name is revealed to Israel. Rather Barth's Christology is characterized by a theocentric and irregular manner. Nevertheless, a theology of world religions remained a fragmentary and incomplete project for Barth. In this chapter, I shall explore the relevance of Barth's unfinished project for religious pluralism as the conclusion of my study of Barth, and especially in reference to Barth's deliberation on the mystery of God and East Asian readings of Barth.

Karl Barth and the Mystery of God

For Barth, christocentrism does not contradict or replace the mystery of God but complements it because humans are not meant to be the possessors of God's truth. The name Jesus Christ does not replace the name God of Israel, nor is it in competition. In his lecture at Elgersburg (October 3, 1922), "The Word of God as the Task of Ministry," Barth formulated a theological method: "We are, however, human and as such cannot speak of God. We should recognize both our ought and our cannot and thus by that recognition give just God the glory" (*ADT*:199; my translation). Barth believed that human beings are not capable of speaking of God despite making dogmatic, critical, and dialectical claims. Although Barth holds a critical reservation against any human way or method of speaking of God, he endorses a dialectical method without losing the incomprehensiveness of God. In this light, Barth elaborates the theocentric character of his dialectical theology in the following way: "The genuine dialectician knows that this center cannot be apprehended or beheld, and he will not if he can help it allow himself to be drawn into giving direct information about it" ("Word of God and the Task," 206).

---

5. Karl Barth, *Gespräche IV, 1964–1968*. Cf. Hunsinger, "Coversational Theology."

6. Ibid., 337. Later in Barth's life we see his yes to Brunner. "If he is still alive and it is possible, tell him again, 'commended to our God,' even by me. And tell him yes, that the time when I thought that I had to say 'No' to him is now long past, since we all live only by virtue of the fact that a great and merciful God says his gracious Yes to all of us" (Busch, *Karl Barth: His Life*, 476–77).

Hence the fact that God's speaking of Godself becomes possible in human language is based not on the dialectical way, but from the side of God. This said, for Barth God is not merely a transcendental being apart from history. Rather from all eternity, God has determined to turn to humanity. Therefore "theology means rational wrestling with mystery. But all rational wrestling with this mystery, the more serious it is, can lead only to its fresh and authentic interpretation and manifestation as a mystery. For this reason it is worth our while to engage in this rational wrestling with it" (*CD* I/1:368).

As Barth states, "In revelation God is always, not quantitatively (for gigantic or infinite does not make God), but qualitatively different from us, not spatially, but occupying a totally different place according to the mode of space."[7] This God challenges human attempts to degenerate God into human ideology in which God is reduced to one's own culturally conditioned system. This God wants a totally different society from the one we want. This God stands on the side of the oppressed poor, the threatened innocent, widows, orphans, and aliens (*CD* II/1:386).

For dogmatic relevance in regard to a definite political problem and task, we notice Barth's dogmatic awareness of sociopolitical issues; he expands his theological horizon to recognize from a theocentric, irregular perspective the strange voice of God outside the walls of Christianity. The mystery of God, according to Barth, is related to the possibility of God ("*Gott kann*" aspect), which plays a constitutive role in highlighting another aspect of church dogmatics, namely, irregular dogmatics. Barth states this aspect of irregular dogmatics in a rather provocative way: "God may speak to us through Russian Communism, a flute concerto, a blossoming shrub, or a dead dog" (*CD* I/1:55).

As in *Romans I*, Barth integrated people outside Christianity into his inclusive theology of God's kingdom. In *Romans II*, Barth made a distinction between the regular and the irregular in referring to the sciences as ordinary, regular, bourgeois possibilities of consideration in comparison with theology as extraordinary, and as an irregular, revolutionary act of daring. The theology of irregular and revolutionary acts places all human possibilities (even including theology itself) under the attack of God. Dogmatics, which Barth calls an act of daring, even runs the risk of losing its life under the attack of God. What dogmatics seeks, at best,

---

7. *UCR* 1:134.

are approximations of dogma, because God the mystery is the object of dogmatics. God is not at the disposal of human scientific rationality and language.[8]

As a definition of the term "irregular dogmatics," Barth would understand a reflection on the Word of God that is practiced "unmethodically, chaotically, as in guerrilla warfare, rather than as a regular soldier." This irregular dogmatics runs counter to the danger inherent in the regular scholastic practices of dogmaticizing, ossifying, and being stubborn. In such irregular dogmatics, the theological work and task can be practiced often infinitely more fruitful than in the achievement of dozens of the all-too-methodical systematician (*CDE*:15).

In the prolegomena of *Church Dogmatics* (1932), Barth states emphatically that such irregular dogmatics must not be any less scientific than other regular, scholastic dogmatics. Scholastic dogmatics should not try to regard itself as better dogmatics. It should not disdain listening to time and the voice of free dogmatics. The dogmatician must think and speak in a particular age and context. Therefore, "the historical account and the personal confession of faith in the name of contemporaries can only be means to this end" (*CD* I/1:281). For Barth, regular and scientific dogmatics does not remain merely a bourgeois, self-satisfied and self-satisfying science. Rather it is to be deepened and actualized in terms of the radical, transforming, and revolutionary character of irregular dogmatics in light of God's revolution and mystery. Therefore Barth validates social concepts in dogmatics in a historical-social manner and thus justifies social-political analysis in a dogmatic-systematic manner. At this point I notice a radicality in a postfoundational direction, which shapes and underscores Barth's theological consciousness for interrelating dogmatic discourse wtih secular and postmodern realms of otherness.

Accordingly, in the volume called *The Doctrine of the Word of God* within *Church Dogmatics*, Barth's irregular dogmatics deals with what can be described as the strange, strident, and even ominous voice of God coming from outside the sphere of Christianity. It is related to Barth's theocentric emphasis on the freedom of God. In emphasizing God's free-

---

8. In his *Göttingen Dogmatics*, Barth does not ignore an aspect of the irregular dogmatics: "The will to complete work will be better here than resting content with work only half done; however true it may be that much half-way done or one-quarter done work is actually more fruitful in terms of its inner value than much that is fully done." (ibid., 39).

dom, Barth allows that the outer sphere of the church, in turn, serves to enrich and deepen the theological discourse on the Word of God. Barth's turn to dogmatics does not dilute or dampen his political radicalism or the dimension of world-affirmation, because he regards sociopolitical and cultural consciousness to be important components in his *Church Dogmatics*. According to Barth, "an education in the arts and a familiarity with the thinking of the philosopher, psychologist, historian, aesthetician, etc., should be demanded of the dogmatician or the theologian" (*CD* 1/1:283).

Given this fact, Barth reconstructs a significant dimension of culture within his dogmatic theology. Theology is a specific activity of humanity. In other words, "the problem of theology and dogmatics can also be seen as wholly within the framework of the problem of culture" (*CD* 1/1:284). For Barth, God's Word is God's act, which means primarily its contingent contempraneity. In other words, Barth's theology of God's Word in action is deeply engaged in contemporary issues, that is, in the social, cultural, and political realms. In recalling Luther's manner of irregular dogmatics, Barth stated that dogmatics is an art among other arts and can be taught and learned like them. However, this art of dogmatics points to Holy Scripture as the decisive norm.

While Barth's regular dogmatics deals with God's reality within the church, and holds an ecclesiological aspect with an emphasis on the confessional and foundational dimension, his irregular dogmatics at the same time deals with the universality of God's reign over the world in Jesus Christ. Therefore Barth speaks of a tension between the particularity of Jesus Christ and the universality of God as follows: "The focal points and foundations themselves determine that in dogmatics strictly speaking there are no comprehensive views, no final conclusions and results. There is only the investigation and teaching which take place in the act of dogmatic work and which, strictly speaking, must continually begin again at the beginning in every point" (*CD* I/2:868). Barth's catchphrase "begin again at the beginning" reminds us that his theology always had to do with the concrete situations in which he did his theology. What is at issue is not a social, cultural priority, but the actuality of God, which moves human beings (as faith knows it), if faith can see the world in light of the life of God.

In continuity with this universality of God, yet with a theocentric emphasis, Barth stated: "The fundamental lack of principle in the dogmatic method is clear from the fact that it does not proceed from the centre but from the periphery of the circle or, metaphor apart, from the self-positing and self-authenticating Word of God (*CD* I/2:869)." According to Barth, as the event of God's work and activity, the Word of God does actually speak in all directions like the periphery of a circle. What is said in all directions can and must be heard and repeated. In the presentation and unfolding of dogmatic theology, Barth emphasizes a human spirituality of obedience and daring: obedience because the object alone can inspire; daring because human free decision making must come into play in every attempt at dogmatic work (*CD* I/2:870). In the presentation and unfolding of the speech of God as the mystery of God (*CD* I/1:162), Barth relates this aspect to "a penultimate 'de-assuring' of theology" (*CD* I/1:164–65). For him, the mystery of God denotes God's revelation in a hidden (i.e., a nonapparent) way. The mystery of God is the concealment of God in God's unveiling to human beings. God's veiling can be seen in God's unveiling. Like Luther, Barth repudiates human trespassing into direct knowledge of God as *speculatio majestatis* (*CD* I/1:173).[9]

As far as revelation is the incarnation of the Word of God, Barth takes the incarnation to be entry into the secularity of the world: "If God did not speak to us in secular form, He would not speak to us at all. To evade the secularity of His Word is to evade Christ" (*CD* I/1:168). For the sake of the mystery of God in the speech-act framework, Barth strikingly follows in the footsteps of Luther's *theologia crucis* as a principle of Luther's whole theology. At this point, Barth interprets Luther's idea of all creation as *larva Dei*, the indirectness of God's self-communication in a twofold manner: one due to the creatureliness, another due to the sinfulness of the creature. Barth cites Luther's statements with almost-unheard-of sharpness:

> Therefore must God's faithfulness and truth even become first a great lie ere it become the truth. For to the world 'tis a heresy. So seemeth it ever to ourselves as if God would leave us and not keep His Word and in our heart He looketh to become a liar . . . God cannot be God, He must first become a devil, and we cannot come up to heaven, we must first go down to hell, we cannot become God's children, we must first become the devil's children. For all

---

9. For Barth's reception of Luther's *theologia crucis* in favor of the speech of God as the mystery of God, see *CD* I/1:178–79.

that God saith and doth, the devil must have said and done (*Ps117 expounded*, 1530, WA, 311, p. 249, 1.21) (*CD* I/1:167–68).

Along these lines is the speaking and receiving of God's Word, an act of God in reality that contradicts and conceals God. In it God's revelation is God's miraculous act, "the tearings of an unterably thick veil, i.e., His mystery" (*CD* I/1:168). According to Barth, God veils Godself, and in so doing God unveils Godself. Hence we must not try to intrude into the mystery of God. For the sake of mystery and the freedom of God, Barth does not accept a direct identification of God *in se* (the immanent Trinity) with God *for us* (the economic Trinity). Therefore the *mysterium trinitatis* remains a mystery. Theology means rational wrestling with the mystery of God, the wrestling which leads only to its fresh and authentic interpretation and manifestation as a mystery (*CD* I/1:368). God does not make Godself a prisoner of human beings. God remains free in God's working and giving. Hence the Triunity of God is incomprehensible to us (*CD* I/1:371). Although, for Barth, Christology constitutes the basis and criterion for the understanding and interpretation of God's freedom and mystery in God's immanence, it does not imply Christian absolutism or ecclesiastical narrow-mindedness (*CD* II/1:320).

This aspect becomes more obvious and central later in Barth's reflection on extramural lights and words in the world. Barth's slogan "begin again at the beginning" also characterizes well the dynamic, critical, actual, analogical and inclusive manner of Barth's world-open theology. In other words, God who is made known in Jesus Christ remains profoundly unknown to us in the incomprehensible depths of divine mystery and freedom. God is the mystery of the world. This train of thought assumes Barth's theology of analogy, parable and correspondence. Human discourse of analogy is appropriate to express a parabolic similarity between God and the world; God's relation to the world is not as identity or dissimilarity. It is the incomprehensibility of theological *Sache* that stands against literalism and makes it possible to speak of God properly by way of analogy. Therefore theological description for Barth does not bring contrast between metaphor on the one hand and literal intratextuality on the other, as postliberal narrative theology does.[10] A dialectical and analogical relation between intratextual theology and extrascriptural cat-

---

10. Lindbeck, *Nature of Doctrine*, 118. For the difference between Barth and Lindbeck, see Hunsinger, "Truth as Self-Involving," 305–18.

egories goes along with interconnection of regular theology to irregular spheres in which the text stands for the world and the world becomes the sphere of God's speaking. A relation between text and the world is not based on one exclusively absorbing the other, but a theological *Sache* in the text brings biblical narratives and extrascriptural realms to organic connection with the world. Therefore, Barth's so-called hermeneutical actualism, beyond literalism and expressivism, points to the divine incomprehensibility that is given and known to us only through revelation.[11]

For Barth, *ratio veritatis* is more than the identification between *noetic ratio* and *ontic ratio*, because God in the *ratio veritatis* is the One who is more than can be conceived of. In the analogy of correspondence, we see that Barth relates his dogmatic work to the *verbum concrtetissimum*. The divine mystery can be formulated in terms of an analogy of faith that has its ground in the Word of God, i.e., Jesus Christ. In the concept of correspondence, divine mystery does not mean *via negativa* in the neo-Platonic sense but *via dialectica* with emphasis on God's gracious love for the world. It refers to *analogia fidei*, in which faith is understood as the unity of theoretical reason and practical obedience, namely, a praxis-determining factor that corresponds at the theoretical level to a social parable at the level of social praxis. The mystery of God, therefore, should be spoken of as the One who loves in freedom. This is characteristic of the being of God in act.

Karl Barth and Religious Pluralism

The recent shift of interest in ecumenical theology and interreligious dialogue points to the fact that Christianity is obliged to reflect on the pluralist demands of other religions. A term like "theology of religions"

---

11. As Hunsinger rightly says, "'Analogy' allowed the equally indispensable elements of reticence and predication to emerge in proper proportion with respect to such a referent. Reticence was required by the mystery, predication by the reality, of the event; imaginative response was an eminently appropriate and well-nigh unavoidable scriptural strategy for depicting a referent which, though real, was largely incomprehensible... The truth of the analogical predication, of course, depended on its having ultimately been guided and inspired by God. In, with, and under the human imaginative response to the biblical narratives, divine self-predication was believed to have been at work; and this belief itself could arise not as a rational inference about the text, but only as a response to the grace mediated through the text by the self-revealing God." (Hunsinger, "Beyond Literalism and Expressivism," 214–15).

implies the universal project of including and integrating all religions and ideologies into the mystery of God as the Great Integrator. Pluralism has now become the governing rule and ideology in welcoming, approving, and affirming all ideas and practices. In the light of pluralism as reflected in the literature of the theology of religions, Barth has undergone intense criticism for his conservative/evangelical attitude toward world religions, in which he appears to be the neo-orthodox and the exclusivist representative.[12]

According to Paul Knitter, Barth's understanding of religions, which is characterized by a conservative and evangelical model, becomes inappropriate in dealing with the reality of religious pluralism. For Knitter, Barth's verdict that religion is unbelief devalues the dignity and orientation of world religions. Along the lines of Knitter, John Hick deals with Barth's theology of Christianity and the World religions: "Such sublime bigotry could only be possible for one who had no real interest in or awareness of the wider religious life of mankind. For it is evident, when one witnesses worship within the great world faiths, including Christianity, that the same sort of thing is going on in earth."[13]

At any rate, the first article of the Barmen Declaration causes misunderstanding and even confusion about Barth's relevance to the reality of world religions, while capturing the christocentric direction of Barth's theology: "We repudiate the false teaching and truths as divine revelation alongside this one Word of God, as a source of her preaching."[14] Regarding himself a Barthian theologian, Hendrik Kraemer at the World Missionary Conference at Tambara in 1938 aroused a storm of indignation by his insistence that Christ alone is the way to salvation. Kraemer's purpose was to state "the fundamental position of the Christian church as a witness-bearing body in the modern world."[15] For Kraemer, Christianity as the religion of revelation holds the place of the normative uniqueness, relativizing truth claims of other religions. Because salvation is available and valid only through Jesus Christ in Christianity, the conversion model

---

12. Knitter, *No Other Name?* 80–96.
13. Hick, *God Has Many Names*, 90.
14. Leith, *Creeds of the Churches*, 520.
15. Kraemer, *Christian Message in a Non-Christian World*, v.

is at the center of Christian mission by "pursued[ing] the non-Christian world to surrender to Christ as the sole Lord of life."[16]

Claiming to be a follower of Barth, Kraemer proposed a model of conversion based on ecclesiocentrism in encounters with people of other faiths. Given this fact, it is allegedly said that the Barthian theology cannot endorse Christian communities in their endeavor to seek an interreligious dialogue with world religions such as Judaism, Islam, Hinduism, or Buddhism in a positive sense. The charge of evangelical exclusivism was brought against Barth in that his position confines salvation and truth only to the Christian church. In the "Copernican revolution" of the theology of religions, Barth's theology is illustrated as the best example of the old Ptolemaic system of geocentric thinking, in that the incarnate revelation of God in Jesus Christ stands at the center of the universe of world religions. The excessive emphasis on particularity of a "once-and-for all" Christ is inclined to be a basis for spreading intolerance, Christian imperialism, even "Christofascism."[17]

Given this charge against Barth, I am interested in presenting and clarifying Barth's concept of Christ and the world religions to speak out against misunderstanding of Barth's theology. When examining carefully Barth's theology with respect to religious others, confining Barth's position to any single quarter or spectrum (for instance, exclusivism, inclusivism, or pluralism) is difficult. As we have outlined in Barth's *Romans I* and *II*, Barth's inclusive, universal theology of God's kingdom had integrated and already transformed Troeltsch's question about the absoluteness of Christianity into his own theological framework rather than excluding it. In addition, Barth's openness to the mystery of God in freedom and majesty, which forms the central framework of his irregular dogmatics, enables him to reflect deeply on the horizon of the universal grace of God in the context of a pluralistic world.

Barth's theology of religion and world religions is located in *Church Dogmatics* I/2 (paragraph 17) and in *Church Dogmatics* IV/3 (paragraph 69) within the context of his so-called doctrine of lights. Part of *Church Dogmatics* I/2 Barth titled "the Revelation of God as the Abolition of Religions" (*CD* 1/2:280–361). An English translation of the German *Aufhebung der Religion* as "the abolition of religion" is very misleading,

---

16. Kraemer, *Why Christianity of All Religions?* 15.
17. Driver, *Christ in a Changing World*, 65.

unfortunately. A Hegelian sense of *Aufhebung* has two poles: negation (negative) and elevation (positive). Revelation as *Aufhebung* of the religion is highly dialectical in a Barthian fashion. Revelation as an exclusive way from God to the world remains fundamental in Barth's approach to people of other faiths. However, God's way to us does not destroy the parabolic character of religions in mirroring signs of God's kingdom. This refers to a positive pole of *Aufhebung*, in the sense of sublation. Religions are kept and reserved and transformed in light of God's coming kingdom, rather than totally denied, destroyed, and negated. Therefore Barth's intention is to affirm, first of all, the priority of revelation over religions without exhausting, ecclesiasticizing, and Christianizing other religions, because they will be given a parabolic character in pointing and witnessing to God's kingdom. So Christianity stands in coexistence with many various religions.

In addition, we read in the same context two different statements of Barth regarding religion: "Religion is unbelief, idolatry, self-righteousness . . . It is an affair of the godless man . . . the one great concern, of godless man" (*CD* I/2:7). Yet, at the same time, Barth argued: "But the religion and religions must be treated with a tolerance which is informed by the forbearance of Christ, which derives therefore from the knowledge that by grace God has reconciled to Himself godless man and his religion. It will see man carried, like an obstinate child in the arms of its mother, by what God has determined and done for his salvation in spite of his own opposition"(*CD* I/2:299). Therefore in light of the *assumptio carnis*, religion is related to revelation as Christ's human nature is related to the divine nature in the event of incarnation.

Barth's theology of religion in his early stage has a negative tone because of neo-Protestantism under the influence of religious consciousness or religious experience. As Barth noticed, neo-Protestant theology recommended "the nature and incidence of religion . . . as a norm and principle by which to explain the revelation of God" (*CD* 1/2:284). Where revelation is exchanged for or replaced by the concept of religion, theology has lost its object (*CD* I/2:294). However, in Barth's view, the world of religions becomes an object within the theological realm in light of divine revelation, not the other way round. In other words, religion needs to be set and reflected on within the sphere of divine revelation rather than taken as an independent area separated from it. Therefore Barth's christological doctrine of the *assumptio carnis* (assumption of the flesh) makes it possible to speak of revelation as the ground of elevating religion into the sphere of *assumptio carnis* (*CD* I/2:297). In God's revelation, God is present and at work in the world of human religions. In approaching the *assumptio carnis*, Barth refined the *extra Calvinisticum* in terms of *enhypostasis* and *anhypostasis* and moved in an inclusive and universal direction. As the incarnated Word is the eternal Son of God who became flesh (*enhypostasis*), so Jesus the human is none other than the eternal Son of God (*anhypostasis*) (*CD* I/2:163–64).

Although Barth later rejected the *extra Calvinisticum* as a disastrous speculation, his critical acceptance of the *extra Calvinisticum* provided a universal, inclusive basis for his Christology of *anhypostasis* and *enhypostasis*. From this we note a strong indication of the remaining majesty and freedom of divine Word in the state of incarnation. In addition, this is also a witness to the divine actuality as well as to the divine universality of the Word, which is deeply associated with the mystery of God in Barth's theocentric and irregular thought. The christological elevation of the world of religions into the unity of God does not remain a metaphysical establishment or a renewal of Thomas's dictum, but socially, materially, and politically transforms its structure and framework in its inherited and traditional form. The incarnation of the eternal Word is not merely restricted to the human Jesus, but includes the humanity of Jesus and that of all human beings. In Jesus Christ not merely one human, but the *humanum* of all humans is posited and exalted to unity with God (*CD* IV/2:49).

What is more relevant is to see a social and material transformation of religions in light of God as *ganz Ändernde*. If the *assumptio carnis* is seen through a relation between *anhypostasis* and *enhypostasis*, "it is the concrete possibility of the existence of a man which will be like the concrete possibility of the existence of all men and in the realization of which this man will be our Brother like ourselves" (*CD* IV/2:48). Furthermore, in the assumption of human flesh, God has implicitly assumed our *humanitas*. The church exists *anhypostatically* and *enhypostatically* in virtue of Jesus Christ. Barth's idea of *totus Christus* retains the comprehensive character of Christ's humanity's representing our *humanitas* in the collective sense (*CD* IV/2:59–60). Barth's affirmation of "the ontological connection" between God and human beings (*CD* IV/2:281) makes it possible and plausible to read the *assumptio carnis* in terms of the *assumptio humanum*, in that we see strikingly God's radical solidarity with the whole of humankind in God's elevating and taking up the whole of humankind, including the world of religions, into unity with God. In fact, the being of Jesus Christ includes all human beings (*CD* IV/2:280). This christological universalism leads to openness to the truth claims of other cultures and religions by integrating them *anhypostatically* and *enhypostatically* into Jesus Christ. However, Barth would be reluctant to accept without qualification the *extra Calvinisticum* since the doctrine is based on the *logos spermatikos*, a cardinal doctrine of natural theology. Thus considered, a Catholic approach combining Barth with Aquinas should pay more attention to the socially, materially, and culturally transforming horizon of Barth's theology.[18]

Explaining his so-called doctrine of lights, Barth affirmed that there would be ungodly *Mitbrüder* extended from the kingdom of God outside the walls of Christianity,[19] although he remained hesitant to give his full credit to Rahner's idea of anonymous Christianity. From the perspective of the *assumptio carnis*, Barth speaks of revelation as the *Aufhebung* of religion (*CD* I/2:297). When religion is seen in light of divine revelation, it is revealed as unbelief. Nevertheless, the Christian religion is the true religion because of divine justifying grace. However, a distinction between Christianity as the true religion and Christianity as a human religion of unbelief would be misleading since in Barth's discussion of religion as unbelief there is no distinction between Christian and non-Christian religion. "Therefore, the discussion cannot be understood as a primary polemic against the non-Christian religions, with a view to the ultimate assertion that the Christian religion is the true religion" (*CD* I/2:326). Besides, Barth's critique of religion is directed primarily at Christianity as a religion rather than at world religions. His critique of religion has to apply first and most acutely to ourselves (*CD* I/2:327). Christianity must be relativized "in favor of revelation, which means a crisis even for the religion of revelation" (*CD* I/2:331). Unfortunately, liberal theology had placed the concept of religion, instead of divine revelation, at the center of theology.

In keeping with the perspective of revelation, all religions, including the Christian religion, must be seen as unbelief falling under the judgment of revelation. As Barth states, it is only by the revelation of God

---

18. Dinoia, "Religion and the Religions," 248-49.
19. Barth, *Gespräche IV, 1964-1968*, 401.

in Jesus Christ that we can characterize religion as unbelief. Religion is both negated and exalted by revelation, because God is known to us only through God Godself. In contrast to an anthropological approach to God, divine revelation contradicts and negates religion. But from the standpoint of God (*von Gott her*), "in His revelation God is present in the world of human religion" (*CD* I/2:297). We discern that "in His revelation God actually entered a sphere in which His own reality and possibility are encompassed by a sea of more or less adequate . . . parallels and analogies in human realities and possibilities" (*CD* I/2:282). The reason why the Christian religion becomes the true religion of revelation is based on God's gracious work in the world of religions. However, Christianity as the true religion can be spoken of only by analogy with the justification of the sinner: "We can speak of 'true' religion only in the sense in which we speak of a 'justified sinner'" (*CD* I/2:325). Based on the central Reformation doctrine—*justificatio impii*—we need have no hesitation in saying that the Christian religion is the true religion (*CD* I/2:337).

However this may be, it does not mean for Barth that the Christian religion as such is the fulfilled nature of human religion, or that as the true religion Christianity is fundamentally superior to all other religions (*CD* I/2:298). For Barth, revelation is incommensurable with religions, and this is true of Christianity as a religion as well. Revelation as God's self-communication goes beyond all religious manifestations. Therefore there is no point of contact from the human side regarding a relation between revelation and religions. Since Barth applied his harsh criticism of religion as unbelief even to Christianity, a "better-than-thou" attitude becomes impossible.

In the name of Jesus Christ, which means Immanuel, the revelation of God in Jesus Christ provides the criterion for and the primary source of truth that makes it possible to consider Christianity as the true religion: "The religion of revelation is indeed bound up with the revelation of *God*: but the revelation of God is not bound up with *the religion* of revelation" (*CD* I/2:329; Italics mine). Therefore the Christian approach to the world of religions can be characterized by the forbearance of Christ, by great cautiousness and charity, and by a very marked tolerance. This is "a tolerance which is informed by the forbearance of Christ, which derives therefore from the knowledge that by Grace God has reconciled to Himself godless man and his religion" (*CD* I/2:299). Yet against the power of syncretism, Barth's recommendation of a Christian attitude toward non-Christian religions consists in spiritual poverty and the power of revelation within it (*CD* I/2:334).

Because of divine reconciliation with the world, the name of Jesus Christ is deeply connected with God's universal work in the world and the cosmos. It is like "an obstinate child in the arms of its mother, by what God has determined and done for his salvation in spite of his own opposition" (*CD* 1/2:299). In a theological consideration of religion, it is therefore meaningful and possible for Barth to adopt self-abasement of his own religion: in other words, to acknowledge the need for a strong forbearing tolerance (*CD* I/2:299). With this in mind, Barth boldly asks: "The Veda to the Indians, the Avesta to the Persians, the Tripitaka to the Buddhists, the Koran to its believers: are they not all 'bibles' in exactly the same way as the Old and New Testaments? Are not at any rate the elements and problems in the basic outlook of all religions the same as those of Christian doctrine: the world's beginning and end, the origin and nature of man, moral and religious law, sin and redemption?" (*CD* I/2:282). This theme is developed and refined in more detail in his doctrine of secular parables of the reign of God in *Church Dogmatics* IV/3:

> We recognize that the fact that Jesus Christ is the one Word of God does not mean that in the Bible, the Church and the world there are not other words which are quite notable in their way, other lights which are quite clear and other revelations which are quite real . . . Nor does it follow from our statement that every word spoken outside the circle of the Bible and the Church is a word of false prophecy and therefore valueless, empty and corrupt, that all the lights which rise and shine in this outer sphere are misleading and all the revelations are necessarily untrue. (*CD* IV/3.1:97)

Because the Christian religion becomes true only by virtue of the justifying grace of God, it would be absurd and misleading to speak of a superiority of Christianity over other religions. Barth in this regard was critical of the historical mistake of Christianity in its attempts to demonstrate its absolute superiority in terms of pious community, doctrine, liturgy, and political institution (*CD* I/2:333–37); or "in ecclesiastical institutions, theological systems, inner experiences, the moral transformations of individual believers or the wider effects of Christianity upon the world at large" (*CD* I/2:357). Christians should not "become Philistines or Christian iconoclasts in face of human greatness as it meets

[them] so strikingly in this very sphere of religion" (*CD* I/2:300). Just like in *Romans*, we hear a relativization of Christian religion in Barth's statement: "In the world of religions, the Christian religion is in a position of greater danger and defenselessness and impotence than any other religion. It has its justification either in the name of Jesus, or not at all" (*CD* I/2:356). According to Barth, the Christian religion is rooted in an act of divine revelation that is the name of Jesus Christ. It is not a product of "a missionary and cultic and theological and political and moral force" separated from the name of Jesus Christ (*CD* I/2:347).

Barth and Pure Land Buddhism

To articulate the significance of the name of Jesus Christ in interreligious dialogue, Barth paid special attention to Pure Land Buddhism. Jodo-Shinshu Buddhism as a religion stands close to the grace religion of the Reformation. What is Jodo-Shinshu Buddhism? Shinran (1173–1262) is regarded and revered as the founder of the school of the true teaching of the Pure Land (Jodo-Shinsu Buddhism), which is often referred to merely as Shin (or Pure Land) Buddhism. Shinran's uniqueness in the Buddhist tradition consists in his paradigm shift from self-awakening toward the other power of Amida Buddha. In shifting the paradigm, Shinran became a strong defender of the universal grace of the absolute other power in Amida Buddha.[20]

Before dealing with Shinran's doctrine, it is important first to understand his teacher, Genku Honen (1133–1212). Honen took the teaching of Buddhism to lie only in the three disciplines: percepts, concentration, and wisdom. During his formative period, he came to the awareness that the more he attempted to practice these three disciplines, the more he found himself failing in them. The decisive turning point for Honen occurred finally in 1175 when he read a commentary on the *Meditation Sutra*. "Whether walking or standing, sitting or lying, only repeat the name of Amida with all your heart. Never cease the practice of it even for a moment. This is the very work which unfailingly issues in salvation, for it is in accordance with the Original Vow of that Buddha."[21] This passage came upon Honen as a liberation, leading him to abandon other

---

20. See Chung, *Martin Luther and Buddhism*, 381–93.
21. Harper and Ishizuka, *Honen: The Buddhist Saint*, 187.

practices and instead focus on reciting the name of Amida. The exclusive practice of *nembutsu* (recitation of the name Buddha) itself thus became fundamental to Honen's teaching.

In keeping with Honen, Shinran was embedded in his own experiential perspective. According to Shinran, confirmation of rebirth in the Pure Land, and enlightenment in terms of the *nembutsu* and the true faith, are central to Sakyamuni's teaching. Shinran had practiced *nembutsu* for many years as a monk on Mount Hiei. Yet he did not feel nearer to the enlightenment. Finally he abandoned the *nembutsu* itself as a practice or means for attaining the enlightenment. He concluded that the more the impure mind tries to purify itself, the worse we are doomed to fail. Therefore the self-power (willpower) of the practitioner must be negated by the other-power of Amida. According to Shinran, human works such as meditation and the study of sutras can become meaningful only when they are done out of thankfulness for having been already liberated and enlightened by the power of Amida. If deliverance is completely dependent on the power of the Buddha's realized vows, Pure Land soteriology does not merely remain in Buddhist faith and the recitation of the *nembutsu*. It also retains an aspect of altruism because the pursuit of enlightenment finds its goal in working for the deliverance of all sentient beings from suffering (*dukkha*).

Here the *ordo salutis* is changed: the religious life is an expression of our gratitude for the Buddha's compassion. Then, the assurance of our final enlightenment through our faith/trust in the Buddha's vows is expressed as the recitation of the name of Amida Buddha. Furthermore, gratitude beyond recitation must also be expressed by a compassionate concern to share the teaching with others. Although ethical duty is not necessary for enlightenment, it can be a means by which the compassion of the Buddha becomes real and manifest in the world. Shinran's sensitivity to ethical responsibility and respect for other faiths became extraordinary and compelling. He accused Buddhist institutions and clergy of not representing and practicing Buddhist compassion and wisdom. Therefore Shinran criticized Buddhist institutions for being outwardly Buddhist but at the same time inwardly heathen. A paradigm shift from the egocentric character of religious effort to its altruistic nature marks Shinran's understanding of Buddhist soteriology on the basis of the universality of the Buddha's vow.

Let me conclude the universal teaching of salvation in Shinran by comparing it with a remark of his teacher, Honen. Honen said, "Even sinners will enter into life; how much more the righteous?" while Shinran said, "If the righteous enter into life, how much more in the case of sinners" (quoted in *CD* I/2:341)?

The difference between Honen and Shinran becomes clear. For Shinran, an evil person possesses the capacity to receive Amida's grace of salvation, that is, Buddha-nature. Contradicting the primal vow of Amida Buddha is the statement that if an evil person attains birth (rebirth in the pure land after death), so naturally a good person will attain it also. If a good person were to attain birth through self-power, this would run counter to Amida's primal vow. Therefore abandoning attachment to self-power and entrusting oneself wholeheartedly to other-power is necessary for one to enter the life of nirvana in the Pure Land. For this reason, Shinran argued that "even the virtuous man is born in the Pure Land, so without question is the man who is evil."[22] In his reading of Pure Land Buddhism, Barth noticed that there is "a wholly providential disposition" in the faith in Amida Buddha (*CD* I/2:340). But Barth does not discern the name of Jesus Christ in this Buddhism. If the name of Jesus Christ does not restrict God's universal activity in the world religions, if the world of religions is seen in light of God's reconciliation, if God speaks to us through Pure Land Buddhism as one of God's strange voices, should not Barth have evaluated more positively this Buddhism by way of a parable of God's kingdom?

Nevertheless I am interested in Barth's symptom-seeking approach to the name of Jesus Christ as it is implicitly present in Buddhism. To what extent does it become possible to make plausible an approach to seeking and finding a symptom of God's kingdom in Buddhism? What elements in Buddhism can be brought into dialogue with the Christian religion for the sake of signs and symptoms of God's kingdom? Although Barth does not give a clear account of this hermeneutical principle of encounter, in his doctrine of reconciliation he asks whether the radicality of salvation in the religions belongs to the true words of prophecy of Jesus Christ. In Barth's statement, we read: "We may think of the radicalness of the need of redemption or the fullness of what is meant by redemption if it is to meet this need" (*CD* IV/3.1:125). When we discern a radical

---

22. Keel, *Understanding Shinran*, 31.

human desire for redemption in other religions, when we meet a desire for grace or for complete redemption in other religions, we can hear from world religions true words of Jesus Christ. Revelation as *Aufhebung* of religion gives a messianic, parabolic character and dynamism to religions in light of the messianic *prophetia universalis* of Jesus Christ. Barth's approach to religion moves to describe religion from the inside, from the angle of revelation, instead of analyzing religious experience.

In Barth's quotation from Shinran's remark ("if the righteous enter into life, how much more in the case of sinners"), we perceive a radical human desire for redemption or grace. Unlike Honen (and his remark, "even sinners will enter into life, how much more the righteous"), Barth would prefer to see a radical justification by other-power in Shinran's Pure Land Buddhism in comparison with the Reformation principle of grace. Barth perceived that a forensic understanding of the grace principle in Shinran has a providential disposition. However, in this Buddhism Barth argued that there would be a default of critical resistance to cultic-ethical righteousness. An irreconcilable difference between the two religions comes in the name of Jesus Christ. The name Jesus Christ is different from the name Amida Buddha, but the former can be heard outside the sphere of the Christian church. To find the symptom of the name Jesus Christ in the world religions constitutes a Christian attitude based on self-criticism and radical openness toward religious others (*CD* I/2:342).

Reconciliation and a Doctrine of Lights

What sense would it make to speak of Barth in the context of religious pluralism? To what extent would Barth make a contribution to pluralistic claims in light of God's reconciliation? In his inquiry of secular parables of the truth (the so-called prophetic work of Jesus Christ, *CD* IV/3.1:38), Barth dialectically combined the Word of Jesus Christ (in accordance with the Barmen Declaration) and various claims to truth in a pluralistic society. According to Barth, we have no reason "not to accept the fact that such good words may also be spoken *extra muros ecclesiae*" (*CD* I/3.1:110). The centrality of Christ for Barth does not justify the intention of absolutizing Christian subjectivity or the Church and its tradition. Pluralism is nothing new for Barth, because the message of Jesus from the beginning entered a world full of a "multiplicity of religious, cultic and doctrinal systems" (*CD* IV/3.1:93).

When it comes to true words outside the church, Barth's approach is to relate, discuss, and actualize them in terms of secular parables; this theme had been basic to his previous reflection (in the Tambach lecture in 1919) on the eschatological relevance of world events and in his doctrine of irregular dogmatics (*CD* I/1:§7.2.). Jesus Christ as the one true Word of God makes these other words in the world true "so that the narrative is no mere metaphor but a disclosing yet also concealing revelation, self-representation and self-offering of the kingdom and the life, and therefore His own self-revelation"(*CD* IV/3.1:112). In the service of the Word of Jesus Christ, there are other words and lights pointing or witnessing to it. All the lights outside the circle of the Bible and the church are not meant to become words of false prophecy or of no value (*CD* IV/3.1:97). Does not Barth's reflection on this third sphere of witnessing to Jesus Christ (including words and signs and lights and revelations in the world of non-Christian religions) contradict a general picture of a neo-Orthodox or an exclusive Barth? Barth was more sincere than so-called Barthians in taking seriously modern neopagan, secular humanism and the extra-mural words of other religions and systems.

If there are such words and lights, namely parables of God's kingdom at a very different level in the secular world, Barth asks: "Should it not be grateful to receive it also from without, in very different human words, in a secular parable, even though it is grounded in and ruled by the biblical, prophetico-apostolic witness to this one Word?" (*CD* IV/3.1:115–16). What makes true the words spoken in the secular world is based on the revelation of the reconciliation of God with the world, which is effected in Jesus Christ. How do we encounter parables of God's kingdom "in the strange interruption of the secularism of life in the world"? (*CD* IV/3.1:117).

For clarification of this task, Barth wanted to talk about words *extra muros ecclesiae* not by recourse to the sorry hypothesis of a so-called natural theology, but by recourse to the universal dimension of Christology. In Barth's view, the way of natural theology is based on a knowledge of God supposedly "given in and with the natural force of reason or to be attained in its exercise." Natural theology, apart from and independent of the Bible and the church, can reach "only abstract impartations concerning God's existence as the Supreme Being and Ruler of all things, and man's responsibility towards Him" (*CD* IV/3.1:117). Consequently, natural theology has no capacity of dealing with parables of the reign of God in accordance with the testimony of Scripture. What Barth intended was to speak of the idea of secular parables by way of the universal reign of Jesus Christ. Without leaving the sure ground of Christology, Barth did not restrict the sovereignty of Jesus Christ revealed in his resurrection merely to the testimony of Scripture and the church. Barth's way was not meant to come back to a pristine *theologia naturalis* but was a counterproposal to the limitations of *theologia naturalis*, transforming its social and material dimension in its inherited and traditional form. In this regard Barth revised, renewed, and transformed the version of the ancient Platonic and patristic idea of a *logos spermatikos* for the sake of secular parables of God's kingdom. The Christian community must listen attentively to these alien witnesses to the truth as the strange voice of God, without excluding, replacing, or rivaling them.

For Barth, God cannot abandon or withdraw God's control from any secular sphere in a world reconciled with God in Jesus Christ, "even where from the human standpoint it seems to approximate most dangerously to the pure and absolute form of utter godlessness." "While man may deny God, according to the Word of reconciliation God does not deny man. Man may be hostile to the Gospel of God, but this Gospel is not hostile to him" (*CD* IV/3.1:119). Barth argued that no prometheanism could be effectively maintained against Jesus Christ. Through the death and resurrection of Jesus Christ, utter godlessness in all its forms has been destroyed once and for all. In light of the resurrection of Jesus Christ, even from the mouth of Balaam we recognize "the well-known voice of the Good Shepherd," which should not be ignored despite its sinister origin (*CD* IV/3.1:119). According to Barth, "our present contention is that what was and is possible for Him in the narrow sphere [namely, of the Bible and the church] is well within His powers in the wider [namely, in secular humanism and world religions]" (*CD* IV/3.1:118).

Thus considered, Barth's position implies inclusivism on a radical openness to forms of secularism or pluralistic claims to truth, even in spite of these claims' sinful origin. Profane words and lights are regarded as true in correspondence to the Word of reconciliation, because God is active also in other religions and cultures. However, Barth was hesitant to canonize or give a dogmatic status to such extraordinary ways and free communications of Jesus Christ (*CD* IV/3.1:133–34). If Barth canonizes or gives a dogmatic example of secular parables, it would be inevitable for him to run into relativistic syncretism in which there would occur an expropriation of God's covenant with Israel in a concrete, historical reality. Without leaving his sure ground of christological particularity, Barth maintained that the church had the task of examining closely whether these profane words and lights would be in agreement with Scripture or church tradition or dogma, and whether the fruits of those words outside Christianity would be good and their effect positive in the community. This is what Barth called a "supplementary and auxiliary" criterion, namely, "the fruits which such true words have borne and seem to bear in the outside world where they have their more or less strange and puzzling origin, i.e., in the secular world surrounding the community" (*CD* IV/3.1:127–28).

From this perspective, Barth's reading of Buddhism by way of symptom-seeking hermeneutics needs to be discussed and developed in connection with his examination of the profane words, as different from Scripture or church tradition or dogma. Furthermore, in affirmation of "dangerous modern expressions like "the revelation of creation" or "primal revelations" (*CD* IV/3.1:140), Barth assumed that the divine work of reconciliation did not negate the divine work of creation, or deprive it of meaning. There is no point in tearing asunder "the original connection between creaturely *esse* and creaturely *nosse*" (*CD* IV/3.1:139). Secular parables are not to be refused, but accepted as "free communications of the will of its Lord" (*CD* IV/3.1:130); this becomes a central motif in Barth's doctrine of true words *extra muros ecclesiae*. If pluralism means, by definition, other sources or norms of revelation outside, alongside, or apart from Jesus Christ, Barth argued, "there is not a single word in any of the prophets to indicate that this fact made any impression on them" (*CD* IV/3.1:93). The notion that a plurality of divine revelations in the Old Testament is not to make the action and speech of God in the history of Israel as "one of many to which validity might be ascribed." Likewise according to the New Testament, it is well known that "the multiplicity of religious, cultic and doctrinal systems [is] characteristic of the world to which they went with their message of Jesus of Nazareth" (*CD* IV/3.1:93).

According to Barth, in the face of the pure and absolute form of utter godlessness in its dangerous form, we Christians, on the basis of resurrection of Jesus Christ, must "be prepared at any time for true words even from what seem to be the darkest places"(*CD* IV/3.1:119). After all, when the hour of God comes in Jesus Christ by the power of the Holy Spirit, there is no refusal, rebellion, or resistance "on the part of non-Christians [that] will be strong enough to resist the fulfillment of the promise of the Spirit which is pronounced over them too . . . or to hinder the overthrow of their ignorance in the knowledge of Christ" (*CD* IV/3.1:355). Therefore the truth of Jesus Christ in its unity and totality is always implicitly present or heard in any of its manifestations as secular words. From this we would see Barth's robust confidence and hope of salvation for people *extra muros ecclesiae*.[23] Barth's tendency toward universal reconciliation can be seen in the following passages: "We are summoned to believe in Him, and in His victorious power, not in the invincibility of any non-Christian, anti-Christian or pseudo-Christian worldliness which confronts him. The more seriously and joyfully we believe in Him, the more we shall see such signs in the worldly sphere, and the more we shall be able to receive true words from it" (*CD* IV/3.1:122). "To be more explicit, there is no good reason why we should not be open to this possibility . . . of an *apokatastasis* or universal reconciliation" (*CD* IV/3.1:478). This refers to Barth's confession of hope about an open possibility of universal salvation due to Christ's reconciliation with the world. In this sense Jesus Christ is the hope even for those of other faiths (*CD* IV/3.1:355–56).

By transforming and establishing the dimension of natural theology socially, materially, and culturally through Christology, Barth gives some indication that true words may be heard even from "openly pagan" worldliness:

> We may think of the mystery of God, which we Christians so easily talk away in a proper concern for God's own cause. We may think of the peace of creation, or its very puzzling nature, and the consequent summons to gratitude . . . We may think of the resolute determination, perhaps, to attack these evils. We may think of the lack of fear in the face of death which Christians to their shame often display far less readily than non-Christians near and

---

23. As Barth states, "Hence no aversion, revolt, resistance or outrage on the part of non-Christian can alter the fact that he, too, exists in the world which God created good as the external basis of the covenant and therefore for this salvation, and which He has reconciled in Jesus Christ in the fulfillment of this covenant and in realizations of the election in which he, too, is elect" (*CD* IV/3.1:355).

far . . . Especially we may think of a humanity which does not ask or weigh too long with whom we are dealing in others, but in which we find a simple solidarity with them and unreservedly take up their case. (*CD* IV/3.1:125)

Given all these phenomena, Barth argued that their languages, however alien their forms may be, are the language of parables of the kingdom of heaven.

This said, wouldn't we see in this passage Judaism, socialism, and practical forms of humanness without faith and world religions next to the great light of Jesus Christ? For Barth, Jesus Christ as "partisan of the poor" is in solidarity with *massa perditionis* who belonged to the party of the godless assailed by the Pharisees (*CD* IV/3.2:587). The Word of God, which "swims against the stream" (*CD* IV/3.2:581), becomes visible in Jesus's table fellowship with publicans and sinners (*CD* IV/3.2:586). Barth asks whether Jesus "does not call men out of the *massa perditionis* to set them at God's side within the world" (*CD* IV/3.2:587). Jesus's solidarity with *ochlos* (in Korean: *minjung*) "can consist only in the attestation and proclamation" of God's free grace, which means Jesus Christ as "the saving coup d'état of God" (*CD* IV/3.2 620). Moving in this direction, Barth's reflection on words *extra muros ecclesiae* as free communications of God stands as a preference for a secularism of militant godless people, namely, in solidarity with the life of *massa perditionis*. This aspect constitutes a point of departure for dialogue with East Asian minjung theology.

According to Klappert, Barth includes Israel in the doctrine of lights because of Israel's guarding "the mystery of God, which we Christians so easily talk away." For Barth, the Jewish community is placed on the same level as other secular parables of God's kingdom.[24] Without doubt, argued Marquardt, prevalent among them (over other examples) is the socialist option.[25] Later Barth himself, in explication of his so-called doctrine of lights, affirmed that the children of this world are often wiser than the children of light.[26] There are *Mitbrüder* (brothers and sisters) in protest (socialist atheists), who are included in the inheritance of the promise and hope of the kingdom of God: "In the sphere of reverence

---

24. Klappert, *Israel und die Kirche*, 58–59; Klappert, *Versöhung und Befreiung*, 44–45.

25. Marquardt, *Theologie und Sozialismus*, 254.

26. Barth, *Gespräche IV,1964–1968*, 401.

before God, there must always be a place for reverence of human greatness" (*CD* I/2:301).

According to Barth, there is in the secular world a more distant periphery ("the express and unequivocal secularism of militant godlessness," [*CD* IV/3.1:121–22] and a closer periphery ("the mixed and relative secularism," [*CD* IV/3.1:120]) of the biblical-ecclesial sphere. From both of them "Jesus Christ can raise up extraordinary witnesses to speak true words of this very different order" (*CD* IV/3.1:118). Barth's preference for a secularism of militant godlessness over a mixed and relative secularism becomes obvious in the following statement:

> Yet we must continually ask ourselves whether this mixed and relative secularism might not be characterized by perhaps an even greater resistance to the Gospel for the very reason that it is used to being confronted by and having to come to terms with it, and is thus able the more strongly to consolidate itself against it, making certain concessions and accommodations no doubt, parading in large measure as a world of Christian culture, but closing its ears the more firmly against it, and under the sign of a horrified rejection of theoretical atheism cherishing the more radically and shamelessly a true atheism of practice. (*CD* IV/3.1:120).

Despite this critique, Barth's particular commitment to Jesus Christ does not block his radical openness to ungodly forms of radical secularism as well as to the world of religious others, in light of God's reconciliation. Christian uniqueness is sought in the context of plural forms of religious lights in the world religions, without falling victim to creeping secularization; or, without Christian ideologization of the different ways of religious others. Barth asks, "Why should it not be possible for God to raise up witnesses from this world of tarnished untruth . . . ?" (*CD* IV/3:1:121). "Neither the militant godlessness of the outer periphery of the community, nor the intricate heathenism of the inner, is an insurmountable barrier" to God (*CD* IV/3.1:121). Henceforth the nature of secular truth-claims to be genuine parables of God's kingdom can be revealed in that they have "their final origin and meaning in the awakening power of the universal prophecy of Jesus Christ Himself" (*CD* IV/3.1:128–29).

Because of the radical investigation of the question of true words outside the sphere of the church, Barth, in contrast to Zwingli, does not give explicit examples of them within the context of dogmatics. Barth restrains himself at the point where Zwingli had appealed explicitly that Hercules, Theseus, Socrates, Cicero, and others had attained their salvation in heaven (*CD* IV/3.1:135). Barth's hesitation to canonize or give dogmatic status to such extraordinary ways and free communications of Jesus Christ is not to forbid a dogmatician from identifying examples of true words in various contexts. Rather, because of the lordship of Jesus Christ and because of the radical character of this investigation, Barth did not want to equate the true Word of Jesus Christ with other extraordinary words, or to limit the individual's freedom of investigation regarding a relation between Jesus Christ and true words outside the sphere of the church in a particular context (*CD* IV/3.1:133). The dialectical tension between the Christian claim of uniqueness for Jesus Christ and the profound Christian openness to pluralism keeps Barth from falling into a gray zone of relativististic syncretism visible in the theology of religions project in writers such as Hicks, Knitter, and Panikkar. For Barth, the question of how to recognize the particularity in light of a universal Christology shaped a dialectical relation between regular dogmatics and the irregular dogmatics in terms of relativization, institution, and integration (*CD* IV/3.1:159). Barth's universalism cannot be properly understood without reference to the particularity of Jesus as a Jew. A Buddhist universalistic reading of Barth in terms of *Urfaktum Immanuel* (in the case of Katsumi Takizawa) needs to pay more attention to a particular historical concept of Christ based on the reality of the covenant between God and Israel.

Karl Barth, Katsumi Takizawa, and Asian Minjung Theology

Katsumi Takizawa (1909–1984) studied under the guidance of Karl Barth at Bonn in 1933 and took issue with the notion of the God-human relation in Barth's thought from a Buddhist perspective. Barth was impressed by his Japanese student, who wrote a challenging article against Bultmann but did not want to be baptized into the theology of Barth.[27] As Busch reports, Takizawa preoccupied himself with the name Jesus Christ in Barth's theology: "Since my [Takizawa's] fortunate encounter with Karl Barth in Bonn, the name of Jesus Christ has in a miraculous way become something from which I can no longer . . . detach myself."[28] Takizawa found in Barth's thought some important elements in affinity with Zen Buddhism and the school of Amida Buddhism. According to Takizawa,

27. See Takizawa, "Was hindert mich getauft zu werden," in Takizawa, *Das Heil im Heute*, 11–24.
28. Busch, *Karl Barth: His Life*, 203.

Barth's Christology, in keeping with the *Urfaktum* of human beings and of creation, corresponds to the universal *Sunyata* of Zen Buddhism. This *Urfaktum* means the true I-self of Zen Buddhism, which already existed from the foundation of the world.

According to Takizawa, the primary contact of God existed even before the appearance of the historical Jesus. Therefore the event of Jesus alone should not be regarded as the exclusive ground for the salvific relationship between God and human beings. For Takizawa, accepting Jesus Christ as the Son of God thus has relevance for Christians alone. If Christian theology restricts "God with us" merely to the historical Jesus, it remains arbitrary, especially to religious others.[29]

For Christians, the event of enlightenment has something to do with the name of Jesus Christ. However, the effect of the Truth happening in Christ relativizes the exclusive meaning of the historical Jesus. At that point, Takizawa was interested in the development of a Buddhist Christology beyond the classic dogmatic pattern of Christology in the Western church. His concern was to point to the Greater One to whom the whole person of Jesus bears witness.[30] At any rate, Takizawa portrays the Greater One—to whom Jesus bears witness all his earthly life—as the *Urfaktum* Immanuel (which means "God with us") as the crucial relation that has always existed, even before the historical Jesus. What we recognize in Jesus Christ is the performance and fulfillment of the *Urfaktum*, which is unknowable to us even through Jesus Christ. It is not restricted to the human Jesus. The God who was in Christ (2 Cor 5:19) was beforehand and eternally, is presented for today, and will remain the eternal God with us all.[31]

In altering Barth's theology to the point of relativizing the historical Jesus, Takizawa is in favor of the divine immediate, original relation to human beings outside the particularity of God's covenant with Israel. In Takizawa's reading of Barth, it is possible to discern a retrieval of a *theologia naturalis* from the perspective of *Urfaktum* Immanuel. Takizawa takes Barth's Trinitarian formulation ("God is beforehand in himself") as transcending the name of Jesus Christ. Takizawa's theocentric, monistic

---

29. Takizawa, "Was hindert mich getauft zu werden," 37.

30. Takizawa, *Reflexionen über die universale Grundlage*, 76–87.

31. See Marquardt's interpretation of Takizawa's Buddhist Christology in Marquardt, *Das christliche Bekenntnis*, 28–43.

reading of Barth may be compared to the Buddhist principle of *dharmakaya*, the Essence Body.

Zen Buddhism teaches about the fundamental situation of human beings, who do not exist apart from Buddha regardless of whether they know it or not. This is the Buddhist idea of so-called nonduality, namely, the principle of radical relationality and complementarity. Barth's word *theoanthropolgy* (meaning that no matter how hostile or alien human beings may be toward God, God does not deny human beings) corresponds with Takizawa's Buddhist reading of *Urfaktum* Immanuel. Takizawa's contribution is to radicalize the significance of Jesus Christ up to the point where the fundamental experience of every human being, even in other religions, becomes meaningful in the second Immanuel, found in Jodo-Shin Buddhism. With a Barthian orientation in mind, he paves the way for a christological foundation of religious pluralism in light of a Buddhist concept of *Urfaktum* Immanuel, namely *dharmakaya*.

With his letter to Takizawa on August 4, 1958, Karl Barth sent his first printed sheet, including the pages from 115 to 153, of *Church Dogmatics* IV/3. As we have already discussed, in Barth's so-called doctrine of lights, he spoke about the theme of truths in the world religions in the light of the messianic prophecy of Jesus Christ, which stands in correlation with the prophecy of the entire messianic history of Israel.

Barth was aware of Christian Europe's increasing "direct contact with the far more numerous non-Christian multitudes of the far West and East." Among these peoples, European forms of Christian faith had coexisted with many foreign religions since the sixteenth century (*CD* IV/3.1:19). In this context, Barth was suspicious of theological attempts to justify and verify the absoluteness of Christianity in either a universal-historical or an ecclesial-historical manner because in the face of the universal prophecy of Jesus Christ, Christendom stood on the same plane as other religions. God escapes every conceivable synthesis (capricious conjunction of Jesus Christ with something else) as the work of religious arrogance, whether the synthesis involve Mary, the church, individual history, or a presupposed human self-understanding.

In his 1972 study of Barth, Katsumi Takizawa furthermore represented his thesis that Barth had arrived at Takizawa's theological concern, so that the history of Christ can be understood in the framework of *Urfaktum* Immanuel.³² Barth's reflection on true words and lights in world history and in creation has paralleled his discovery of Judaism and socialism as having places in Christian theology. *Urfaktum* Immanuel in a Barthian sense (which presupposes the prophecy of the whole messianic history of Israel) is not separate from the historical fact of Immanuel in Jesus Christ in the messianic history. The true words and lights in creation, when seen in terms of the universal reconciliation of God in Jesus Christ with the world, constitute Barth's sensitivity to the theocentric dimension of irregular dogmatics. The reciprocal relation that Barth posits between the messianic history of Israel and the prophetic history of Christ, despite embracing Takizawa's interreligious interests, does not give full credit to Takizawa's universalizing the *Urfaktum* Immanuel symbolically in relation to the Buddhist idea of *Sunyata* as *Dharmakaya*.³³

Given this fact, for Barth, the name of Jesus Christ is not meant to be a universalized form of *Urfaktum* Immanuel or a Buddhist idea of *dharmakaya*. Rather this name refers to no less than Jesus as a historical Jew, and was expanded and universalized given his death on the cross and his life for the world in resurrection. In this regard, Barth did not give his accord to the pluralistic tendency of theology toward a gnostic short-circuiting of Jesus Christ's particularity. Universalism without particularism runs the risk of becoming anti-Judaic; so also particularism without universalism meets the pitfalls of a positivism of revelation or imperialistic exclusivism.

A reading of Buddhism by way of symptom-seeking hermeneutics does not lie in universalizing either Christianity or Buddhism, or in eradicating differences between them. Rather, a reading of religious others needs to be discussed in terms of its parabolic character in accordance with Scripture or church tradition or dogma. An attempt at mixing up or universalizing the differences of each religion from others does not help to improve or deepen Christian uniqueness or a Christian contribution in encounter with other religions. A recognition of the differences does

---

32. See Klappert, *Versöhnung und Befreiung*, 46.

33. Gollwitzer, in his letter to Takizawa, articulates Barth's concern in *CD* IV/3 saying that the church should understand the true words outside the walls of Christianity as those spoken by Jesus Christ himself outside the church. The words and lights outside have nothing to do with general revelation in the sense of natural theology, but with the universal prophecy and revelation of Jesus Christ. Gollwitzer, Letter to Takizawa on November 29, 1977, in Takizawa, *Heil im Heute*, 204-13.

not come from a Christian religious standpoint but from the mystery of God, who made a covenant with Israel, revealed Godself in Jesus Christ, and in him reconciled Godself with the world and with all of us. God's reign has already begun and is present to us through the Holy Spirit and finally will come as a consuming fire to reconcile all things to Godself. Barth's contribution in the pluralistic context lies not merely in the inclusive direction of his theology for interreligious dialogue but in his strong awareness of Jesus Christ as the source of a natural surrounding for Israel, and in his sensitivity to the modern political, economic, and ecological predicament.

Given descriptions of Barth's theology as political radicalism and as religious openness, Barth's theology of *extra muros ecclesiae* (outside the walls of the church) and *massa perditionis* (the lost public) demonstrates an affinity to Asian minjung theology. Minjung (the poor mass) is the Korean translation of *ochlos* in the Gospel of Mark. Minjung theology begins by taking seriously the social biography of Jesus in connection with the *ochlos*-minjung. The word of God according to minjung theology takes place always as a dynamic event in sociohistoriocal form rather than as confined to a confessional form or an ecclesial sphere. The word of God is alive in the minjung experience of *han* (culmulative oppressed feeling) and their oppressed discourse. Asian minjung theology denotes its interest in the praxis of emancipation and solidarity with *massa perditionis* in sociopolitical realms as well as in interreligious contexts. Wisdom of the world religions is appreciated as a free communication and speech event of God so that interreligious dialogue should be done for the sake of promoting religious peace and mutual cooperation, in accompaniment with the life reality of minjung.[34]

For Barth, Jesus Christ as the partisan of the poor is in solidarity with *massa perditionis*, who belonged to the party of the godless assailed by the Pharisees (*CD* IV/3.2:587). The word of God which "swims against the stream" (*CD* IV/3.2:581) becomes visible in Jesus's table fellowship with publicans and sinners (*CD* IV/3.2:586). Barth asks whether Jesus "does not call men out of the *massa perditionis* to set them at God's side within the world" (*CD* IV/3.2:587). Jesus's solidarity with the *ochlos* "can consist only in the attestation and proclamation" of God's free grace which means Jesus Christ as "the saving coup d'état of God" (*CD* IV/3.2:620).

---

34. Chung, "Asian Contextual Theology of Minjung and Beyond," 6–14.

Moving in this direction, Barth's reflection on words *extra muros ecclesiae* as free communications of God maintains a preference for the secularism of the militant godlessness of people, namely, in solidarity with life of *massa perditionis*. Thus, a kind of christological-preferential option for the poor still remains a central tenet in Barth's doctrine of reconciliation because Jesus Christ is a partisan of *ochlos*/minjung, the aspect of which is obscured in the circle of theology of religions.

Toward the World-open Theology of Barth

As Klappert reports on Barth's assertion of religions from Barth's interview of 1962 in the United States, religion represents human possibilities, which are given with the true nature—namely, given as a phenomenon of God's good creation of humans. Through the fall of human beings, the creaturely powers of humans (tradition, reason, religion, sexuality) have been alienated from God. So the creaturely powers would become powers, lords, and agents of violence that enslave and dominate humans. In and with the resurrection of Jesus Christ, humans are liberated from the bondage of these false gods, and therefore liberated as God's new creatures. The resurrection of Jesus Christ is the beginning of a new heaven and a new earth in the hope of the last parousia of Jesus Christ.[35]

Klappert provides Markus Barth's report in the Leuenberg conference of 1992, which reveals his father's plan that if time had allowed him, Barth wanted to preoccupy himself with the history of religion. In consideration of Barth's plan on the history of world religions, Klappert introduces Barth's planned proposals: 1) the relation between Christendom and Judaism; 2) the relation between Judaism and Islam; and 3) the relation between Buddhism and Hinduism. In examination of Markus Barth's authorized text on his father's plan of the history of world religions Busch wrote to Klappert on December 12, 1992 that Markus's text showed Barth's impression of the question about the non-Christian religions in the Second Vatican Council. Rather than the title of the general history of religion proposed by Markus Barth, Busch is certain of "the ecumenical theology of the Holy Spirit" in Barth's plan. In view of Barth's plan, Klappert speaks of a dialogical model of a neighbor relation with world religions in the framework of the ecumenical theology of the Holy

---

35. Klappert, *Versöhnung und Befreiung*, 47–48.

Spirit. This ecumenical theology is based on the axiomatic correlation between the messianic prophecy of Jesus Christ and the entire messianic history of Israel and has the presupposition in this relation. Barth, in his response to a Hindu conception of the hidden Christ, says, "The wind blows were it wills (John 3:8): Breakthrough (revelation) of the hidden Christ is always and everywhere possible: Inside and outside the church: even in the life and work and message of strangers (Melchizedek! [Gen 14:18–19, Heb 7:1–4]), heathens, atheists!"[36]

In his response to the Vatican documents in 1967–1968, Barth raised questions concerning the confession of guilt by the church with regard to Israel and non-Christian religions. He inquired as to whether in the mentioning of the Muslim religion such a guilt confession would remind people of the church's fatal role in the so-called crusades.[37] In the year 1968 Barth wrote a letter to H. Berkhof in which Barth reported his dialogue with an Islamic scholar, J. Bouman from Lebanon: "In the theological appreciation of the situation there [in Lebanon] . . . we were all but completely in agreement and also in the fact that a new understanding of the relation between Bible and Koran is an urgent task for us."[38] For this urgent task of understanding the relation between the Bible and the Koran, Barth was concerned with developing a world-open theology of the Holy Spirit in an ecumenical horizon. Jürgen Fangmeier reports Barth's last concern with the religions. If Barth had had time, he would have been intensively preoccupied with 1) Roman Catholicism, 2) the Eastern church, and 3) equally importantly the world religions. According to Fangmeir's report, Barth's approach to world religions does not lie in making the general basis for interreligious dialogue to be a conviction in which Jesus Christ should be exalted as the summit. Rather, Jesus Christ is the ground out from whom a completely new dialogue with world religions would be open.[39] Barth's possible model of interreligious dialogue with respect to Judaism and Islam would have been characterized by deepening and actualizing the universal prophecy of Jesus Christ in correlation with the messianic prophecy of the entire history of Israel. The

---

36. Barth, *Gespräche IV 1964–1968*, 565.
37. Barth, *Ad Limina apostolorum*, 39–40.
38. Klappert, *Versöhnung und Befreiung*, 49–50.
39. Barth, *Briefe 1961–1968*, 505.

messianic prophecy of Jesus Christ has already happened upon all flesh: the spirit is promised (*CD* IV/3.1:274-367).

Barth's dialogical model with Judaism and then other religions would not have given full credit to the theological circle highlighting relativistic pluralism at the cost of the particularity of Jesus Christ. Nor would Barth have joined the theological circle espousing the superiority and the absoluteness of Christianity for the sake of ecclesiological triumphalism. In his doctrine of true words and lights in world history and in creation, Barth was not convinced about exalting the absoluteness of Christianity over other religions, but rather about leading the Christian church to self-criticism with a humble attitude and radical openness toward religious others as "free communications of the will of its Lord" (*CD* IV/3.1:130).

For Barth, claims to religious truth within the created cosmos are placed in parallel relation to the Word of Jesus Christ, in which alone can mutual recognition and transformation be achieved hermeneutically and practically for interreligious dialogue.[40] Thereby the otherness outside Christianity is not subsumed into the Christian church but rather exists as a distinct partner witnessing to the work of God's reconciliation with the world and to the coming kingdom of God. The divine work of reconciliation does not negate the divine work of creation or deprive it of its meaning.

A strange, even uncomfortable, ominous voice stemming from outside the walls of Christianity serves as an inspiration for setting Christians free from the excessive project of the Enlightenment in the West, leading them to a humble attitude and radical openness toward God's coming future. If Christians were to lose God's other voice, Christian uniqueness would fall into the gray zone of a blind faith. A Christian theology of religions in favor of Christian uniqueness does not, in fact, stand in opposition to the reality of pluralism itself, because God is the One who accepts the world's pluralism and integrates all its variety and plurifor-

---

40. Marquardt, in his letter to me (December 15, 2001) mentioned Barth's practical concern about Christian-Hindu relations when it comes to the cosmic Christ. According to Marquardt, Barth's conception of parables of the kingdom of God encourages us hermeneutically to pay attention to the possibility of other religions for becoming parables of God. In this regard Barth's reflection of *assumptio carnis* and *hyper pollou* may become a christologically inclusive counterthesis, in a practical sense, to the natural theology. Cf. Chung, *Friedrich-Wilhelm Marquardt*, 243-49.

mity through God's universal grace in Jesus Christ into the unity with the coming kingdom of God.

Buddhist-Christian conversation is meaningful in so far as it gives rise to a common language in difference and improves a mutual enrichment and transformation without losing uniqueness or doing harm to other areas for potential dialogue. This hermeneutical process enables participants to witness their uniqueness, to interact with mutual humility and openness, and finally to enrich and renew each tradition in light of God's reconciliation in Jesus Christ with the world. Furthermore, Barth's theology of irregularity of divine speech act challenges a hermeneutic of fusion of horizon (H.-G. Gadamer) and demonstrates an ideology-critical suspicion of human language which can be distorted in the social and public sphere. Thus, Barth's notion of true lights and worlds as free communications of God would not contradict a hermeneutical project of the fusion of horizons between Christianity and other religions. Rather Barth's notion of true lights can become a basis for a postfoundational reading and encountering and recognizing religious others as the strange voice of God. Let me conclude this discussion of the world-open theology of Karl Barth in the midst of religious pluralism by quoting Eberhard Busch's report: "There may be a religious West, but there is not a Christian West," and "it could well be that one day true Christianity will be understood and lived better in Asia and in Africa than in our aged Europe."[41]

---

41. Busch, *Karl Barth: His Life*, 468.

BIBLIOGRAPHY

Primary Literature

Barth, Karl. *Ad Limina Apostolorum: An Appraisal of Vatican II.* Translated by Keith R. Crim. Richmond: John Knox, 1968.
———. *Against the Stream: Shorter Post-War Writings, 1946-1952.* Translated by R. G. Smith. New York: Philosophical Library, 1954.
———. *Anselm: Fides quaerens intellectum.* Translated by Ian W. Robertson. London: SCM, 1960.
———. "Antwort an D. Achelis und P. Drews." *ZTK* 19 (1909) 479-86.
———. *Antwort : Karl Barth zum siebzigsten Geburtstag am 10 Mai 1956.* Zurich: EVZ, 1956.
———. "Auf das Reich Gottes warten." In *Suchet Gott, so werdet ihr Leben!*, by Karl Barth and Eduard Thurneysen 175-90. Munich: Kaiser, 1928.
———. "Biblical Questions, Insights, and Vistas." In *The Word of God and the Word of Man*, 51-96. Translated by Douglas Horton. New York: Harper & Row, 1957.
———. *Briefe 1961-1968.* Edited by Jürgen Fangmeier und H. Stoevesandt. Zurich: TVZ, 1975.
———. *Christ and Adam: Man and Humanity in Romans 5.* Translated by T. A. Smail. Scottish Journal of Theology Occasional Papers 5. Edinburgh: Oliver and Boyd, 1956.
———. *Christengemeinde und Bürgergemeinde.* Theologische Studie 104. Zurich: TVZ, 1984.
———. "The Christian Community and the Civil Community." In *Karl Barth: Theologian of Freedom*, edited by Clifford J. Green, 265-95. Minneapolis: Fortress, 1991.
———. *The Christian Life. Church Dogmatics IV, Part 4, Lecture Fragments.* Translated by Geoffrey W. Bromiley. Grand Rapids: Eerdmans, 1981.
———. "The Christian's Place in Society." In *The Word of God and the Word of Man*, 272-327. Translated by Douglas Horton. New York: Harper, 1957.

———. *Die Christliche Dogmatik im Entwurf*. Edited by Gerhard Sauter. Gesamtausgabe, II. Akademische Werke. Zurich: TVZ, 1982.

———. "Die Christlichen Kirchen und die heutige Wirklichkeit." in *EvT* 47 (1946) 212–16.

———. "Church and Culture." In *Theology and Church: Shorter Writings, 1920–1928*, 334–54. Translated by Louise Pettibone Smith. The Preacher's Library. London: SCM, 1962.

———. "Church and Theology." In *Theology and Church: Shorter Writings, 1920–1928*, 286–306. Translated by Louise Pettibone Smith. The Preacher's Library. London: SCM, 1962.

———. *Church Dogmatics*. 4 vols. Translated and edited by Geoffrey W. Bromiley and G. T. Thomson. Edinburgh: T. & T. Clark, 1956–1969; 2004.

———. *Einführung in die evangelische Theologie*. Zurich: EVZ, 1962.

———. *The Epistle to the Romans*. Translated by Edwyn C. Hoskyns from the sixth German edition of *Der Römerbrief*. First German edition published in 1919. A Galaxy Book. London: Oxford University Press, 1968.

———. *Ethik I: Vorlesungen, Münster, Sommersemester 1928*. Edited by Dietrich Braun. Zurich: TVZ, 1973.

———. *Evangelium und Gesetz*. Theologische Existenz heute 32. Munich: Kaiser, 1935.

———. *Evangelical Theology: An Introduction*. Translated by Grover Foley. Grand Rapids: Eerdmans, 1963.

———. "Fate and Idea in Theology." In *The Way of Theology in Karl Barth: Essays and Comments*, 25–61. Edited by H. Martin Rumscheidt. Translated by George Hunsinger. Allison Park, PA: Pickwick, 1986.

———. *Final Testimonies*. Translated by Geoffrey W. Bromiley. Grand Rapids: Eerdmans, 1977.

———. "Fragen von Rabbi Petuchowski, Antworten von Karl Barth." *Criterion* 2 (1963) 18–24.

———. *From Rousseau to Ritschl*. London: SCM, 1959.

———. *Gespräche, IV: 1964–1968*. Edited by Eberhard Busch. Zurich: TVZ, 1997.

———. "Der Glaube an den persönlichen Gott." *ZTK* 24 (1914) 21–32, 65–95.

———. *Gottes Gnadenwahl*. Munich: Kaiser, 1936.

———. *The Göttingen Dogmatics: Instruction in the Christian Religion*. Translated by Geoffrey W. Bromiley. Grand Rapids: Eerdmans, 1991.

———. *"Der Götze wackelt": Zeitkritische Aufsätze, Reden und Briefe von 1930 bis 1960*. Edited by Karl Kupisch. Berlin: Vogt, 1961.

———. *The Holy Ghost and the Christian Life*. Translated by R. Birch Hoyle. London: Frederick Muller, 1938.

———. *How I Changed My Mind*. Edinburgh: The Saint Andrew Press, 1969.

———. *The Humanity of God*. Translated by John Newton Thomas. Atlanta: John Knox, 1960.

———. "Jesus Christ and the Movement for Social Justice." In *Karl Barth and Radical Politics*, edited and translated by George Hunsinger, 19–37. Philadelphia: Westminster, 1976.

———. *Das christliche Leben. Die Kirchliche Dogmatik* IV/4. Fragmente aus dem Nachlass, ed. H. A. Drewes and Eberhard Jüngel. *Gesamtausgabe* II. Zurich: TVZ, 1976.

———. *Letters, 1961–1968*. Translated by Geoffrey W. Bromiley. Edinburgh: T. & T. Clark, 1981.

———. "Ludwig Fuerbach." In *Theology and Church: Shorter Writings, 1920–1928*, 217–37. Translated by Louise Pettibone Smith. The Preacher's Library. London: SCM, 1962.

———. *Letzte Zeugnisse*. Zurich: EVZ, 1969.

———. "Liberal Theology: Some Alternatives." Translated by L. A. Garrard. *Hibbert Journal* 59 (1960–1961) 213–19.

———. "Moderne Theologie und Reichgottesarbeit." *ZTK* 19 (1909) 317–21.

———. "Not und Verheißung der christlichen Verkündigung." In Karl Barth, *Das Wort Gottes und die Theologie*, 99–124. Munich: Kaiser, 1924.

———. *Predigten 1913*. Edited by Nelly Barth and Gerhard Sauter. Zurich: TVZ, 1976.

———. *Predigten 1914*. Edited by Ursula Fähler and Jochen Fähler. Zurich: TVZ, 1974.

———. "The Principles of Dogmatics according to Wilhelm Hermann." In *Theology and Church*, 238–71. Translated by Louise Pettibone Smith. London: SCM, 1962.

———. "The Problem of Ethics Today." In *The Word of God and the Word of Man*, 136–82. Translated by Douglas Horton. New York: Harper, 1957.

———. *Protestant Theology in the Nineteenth Century: Its Background and History*. Translated by Brian Cozens and John Bowden. Valley Forge: Judson, 1976.

———. *Die protestantische Theologie im 19. Jahrhundert*. Zurich: TVZ, 1981.

———. *Reformation als Entscheidung*. Theologische Existenz Heute 3. Munich: Kaiser, 1933.

———. "The Righteousness of God." In *The Word of God and the Word of Man*, 9–28. Translated by Douglas Horton. New York: Harper & Row, 1957.

———. "Roman Catholicism: A Question to the Protestant Church." In *Theology and Church: Shorter Writings, 1920–1928*, translated by Louise Pettibone Smith, 307–33.

———. "The Strange New World within the Bible." In *The Word of God and the Word of Man*, 29–50. Translated by Douglas Horton. New York: Harper and Row, 1957.

———. *Eine Schweizer Stimme, 1938–1945*. Zurich: EVZ, 1945.

———. *Theology and Church: Shorter Writings, 1920–1928*. Translated by Louise Pettibone Smith. The Preacher's Library. London: SCM, 1962.

———. *The Theology of John Calvin*. Translated by Geoffrey W. Bromiley. Grand Rapids: Eerdmans, 1965.

———. *The Theology of Schleiermacher: Lectures at Göttingen, Winter Semester of 1923/24*. Translated by Geoffrey W. Bromiley. Grand Rapids: Eerdmans, 1982.

———. *Vorträge und kleinere Arbeiten.* Vols. 1 and 2. Edited by Hans-Anton Drewes und Hinrich Stoevesandt. Zurich: TVZ, 1990–1994.
———. "Das was nicht geschen soll." *Neuer Freier Aargauer: Sozialdemokratisches Tagblatt* (15 August 1919) 1–2.
———. *The Word of God and the Word of Man.* Translated by Douglas Horton. New York: Harper and Row, 1957.
———. "The Word of God and the Task of the Ministry." In *The Word of God and the Word of Man*, 183–217. Translated by Douglas Horton. New York: Harper, 1957.
———. *Das Wort Gottes und die Theologie.* Munich: Kaiser, 1924.
———. "Ein Wort an das aargauische Bürgertum." *Neuer Freier Aargauer: Sozialdemokratisches Tagblatt* 14/157 (10 July 1919) 1.
Barth, Karl, and Rudolf Bultmann. *Karl Barth-Rudolf Bultmann: Letters 1922–1966.* Edited by Bernard Gaspert. Translated and edited by Geoffrey W. Bromiley. Grand Rapids: Eerdmans. 1981.
Barth, Karl, and Eduard Thurneysen. *Karl Barth-Eduard Thurneysen: Briefwechsel, I. 1913–1921.* Zurich: TVZ, 1973.
———. *Karl Barth-Eduard Thurneysen: Briefwechsel, II. 1921–1930.* Zurich: TVZ, 1974.
———. *Suchet Gott, so werdet ihr Leben!* Munich: Kaiser, 1928.

Secondary Literature

Achelis, Ernst Christian. "Noch einmal: Moderne Theologie und Reichgottesarbeit." *ZTK* 19 (1909) 406–10.
Adorno, Theodor. *Negative Dialectics.* Translated by E. B. Ashton. New York: Seabury, 1973.
Adorno, Theodor, and Max Horkheimer. *Dialektik der Aufklärung.* Frankfurt: Fischer Taschenbuch, 1969.
Andreson, Carl, Adolf-Martin Ritter, et al. *Handbuch der Dogmen und Theologiegeschichte.* Vol. 1, *Die Lehrentwicklung im Rahmen der Katholizität.* Göttingen: Vandenhoeck & Ruprecht, 1988.
Anzinger, Herbert. *Glaube und kommunikative Praxis: Eine Studie zur "vordialektischen" Theologie Karl Barths.* Munich: Kaiser, 1991.
Aquinas, Thomas. *Summa Theologica.* Translated by the English Dominican Fathers. 21 vols. New York: Benziger Brothers, 1947.
Balthasar, Hans Urs von. *The Theology of Karl Barth.* Translated by John Drury. New York: Holt, Rinehart and Winston, 1971.
Barth, Heinrich. *Das Poblem des Ursprungs in der platonischen Philosophie.* Munich: Kaiser, 1921.
———. "Gotteserkenntnis." In *ADT* 1:22–55. Edited by Jürgen Moltmann. Munich: Kaiser, 1963.
Bandis, Andreas, and others. *Richte unsere Füsse auf den Weg des Friedens: Helmut Gollwitzer zum 70. Geburtstag.* Munich: Kaiser, 1979.

Beintker, Michael. *Die Dialektik in der 'dialektischen Theologie' Karl Barths*. Munich: Kaiser, 1987.

Berkouwer, G. C. *The Triumph of Grace in the Theology of Karl Barth*. Translated by Harry R. Boer. Grand Rapids: Eerdmans, 1956.

Bethge, Eberhard. *Dietrich Bonhoeffer: Man of Vision, Man of Courage*. Translated the by Edward Mosbacher et al. Edited by Edwin Robinson. New York: Harper & Row, 1970.

———, et al., editors. *Dietrich Bonhoeffer Werke*. 17 vols. Munich: Kaiser, 1986–1999.

Biemann, Asher, editor. *The Martin Buber Reader: Essential Writings*. New York: Plagrave Macmillan, 2002.

Blumhardt, Christoph. *Ansprachen, Predigten, Reden, Briefe: 1865–1917*. 3 vols. Neukirchen-Vluyn: Neukirchener, 1978.

Bock, Paul, editor and translator. *Signs of the Kingdom: A Ragaz Reader*. Grand Rapids: Eerdmans, 1984.

Böhm, Manfred. *Gottes Reich und Gesellschaftsveränderung: Traditionen einer befreienden Theologie im Spätwerk von Leonhard Ragaz*. Münster: Edition liberación, 1988.

Bonhoeffer, Dietrich. *Act and Being: Transcendental Philosophy and Ontology in Systematic Theology*. Edited by Wayne Whitson Floyd Jr. Translated by H. Martin Rumscheidt. DBW 2. Minneapolis: Fortress, 1996.

———. *Christ the Center*. Translated by Edwin H. Robertson. Harpers Ministers Paperback Library. San Francisco: Harper & Row, 1978.

———. "The Church and the Jewish Question." In *No Rusty Swords: Letters, Lectures and Notes 1928–1936, from the Collected Works*, 217–25. Translated by Edwin H. Robertson and John Bowden. London: Collins, 1966.

———. *Ethics*. Edited by Eberhard Bethge. Translated by Neville Horton Smith. The Library of Philosophy and Theology. New York: Macmillan, 1955.

———. *Life Together; Prayerbook of the Bible*. Edited by Geffrey B. Kelly. Translated by Daniel W. Bloesch and James H. Burtness. DBW 5. Minneapolis: Fortress, 1996.

———. *Letters and Papers from Prison*. Edited by Eberhard Bethge. Translated by Reginald H. Fuller, Frank Clarke, John Bowden, et al. New York: Macmillan, 1972.

———. *No Rusty Swords: Letters, Lectures and Notes 1928–1936, from the Collected Works*. Translated by Edwin H. Robertson and John Bowden. London: Collins, 1966.

———. *Sanctorum Communio: A Theological Study of the Sociology of the Church*. Edited by Clifford J. Green. Translated by Reinhard Krauss and Nancy Lukens. DBW 1. Minneapolis: Fortress, 1998.

Brakelman, Günter. *Die Soziale Frage des 19. Jahrhunderts*. Bielefeld: Luther, 1975.

Bravo, Carlos. "Jesus of Nazareth, Christ the Liberator." In *Systematic Thoelogy: Perspectives from Liberation Theology*, edited by Jon Sobrino and Ignacio Ellacuría, 106–23. Maryknoll, NY: Orbis, 1996.

Brunner, Emil. "Die Andere Aufgabe der Theologie." *Zwischen den Zeiten* 7 (1929) 255–76.

———. *Die Mystik und das Wort*. Tübingen: Mohr/Siebeck, 1924.

———. *Natur und Gnade*, Tübingen: Mohr/Siebeck, 1934.
Einführung und Dokumentation. Neukirchen-Vluyn: Neukirchener, 1983.
Buber, Martin. *Das dialogische Prinzip*. Heidelberg: Lambert Schneider, 1965.
———. *Das Problem des Menschen*. Heidelberg: Lambert Schneider, 1952.
———. "Spirit and Body of the Hasidic Movement." In *The Martin Buber Reader*, edited by Asher Biemann, 63–71. New York: Palgrave Macmillian, 2002.
———. "Three Theses of a Religious Socialism." In *The Martin Buber Reader: Essential Writings*, edited by Asher Biemann, 258–60. New York: Palgrave, Macmillan, 2002.
Bues, Eduard, and Markus Mattmüller. *Prophetischer Sozialismus: Blumhardt, Ragaz, Barth*. Freiburg Schweiz: Exodus, 1986.
Burgsmüller, Alfred, and Rudolf Weth, editors. *Die Barmer Theologische Erklärung:*
Busch, Eberhard. "The Covenant of Grace Fulfilled in Christ as the Foundation of the Indissoluble Solidarity of the Church with Israel: Barth's Position on the Jews during the Hitler Era." Translated by James Seyler and Arnold Neufeldt-Fast. Unpublished.
———. *Karl Barth: His Life from Letters and Autobiographical Texts*. Translated by John Bowden. Grand Rapids: Eerdmans, 1994. Reprint, Eugene, OR: Wipf and stock, 2005.
———, editor. *Reformationstag 1933: Dokumente der Begegnung Karl Barths mit dem Pfarrernnotbund in Berlin*. Zurich: TVZ, 1998.
———. *Unter dem Bogen des einen Bundes: Karl Barth und die Juden 1933-1945*. Neukirchen-Vluyn: Neukirchener, 1996.
Calvin, John. *Institutes of the Christian Religion*. Edited by John T. McNiell. Translated by Ford Lewis Battles et al. 2 vols. Philadelphia: Westminster, 1960.
Carr, Edward Hallet. *The Bolshevik Revolution, 1917–1923*, Vol. 3. A History of Soviet Russia. Harmondsworth: Penguin, 1988.
———. *German-Soviet Relations between the Two World Wars, 1919–1939*. Albert Shaw Lectures on Diplomatic History. London: Oxford University Press, 1952.
Chung, Paul S., editor. *Friedrich-Wilhelm Marquardt: Auschwitz and the God of Israel*. Seoul: Korean Presbyterian Publishing Company, 2004.
———. "Introduction: Asian Contextual Theology of Minjung and Beyond." In *Asian Contextual Theology for the Third Millennium: Theology of Minjung in Fourth-Eye Formation*, edited by Paul S. Chung, et al., 1–14. Princeton Theological Monograph Series 70. Eugene, OR: Pickwick, 2007.
———. *Karl Barth und die Hegelsche Linke*. Bern: Lang, 1994.
———. *Martin Luther and Buddhism: Aesthetics of Suffering*. Revised edition. Princeton Theological Monograph Series 80. Eugene, OR: Pickwick, 2008.
Chung, Paul S., et al., editors. *Asian Contextual Theology for the Third Millennium: Theology of Minjung in Fourth-Eye Formation*. Princeton Theological Monograph Series 70. Eugene, OR: Pickwick, 2007.
Cochrane, Arthur C. *The Church's Confession under Hitler*. Philadelphia: Westminster, 1962.

Cohen, Hermann. "Kant, 1896." In *Marxismus und Ethik*, edited by Hans-Jörg Sandkühler and Rafade de la Vega, 45–86. Suhrkamp Taschenbuch Wissenschaft 75. Frankfurt: Suhrkamp, 1974.

Dannemann, Ulrich. *Theologie und Politik im Denken Karl Barths*. Gesellschaft und Theologie: Abeteilung systematische Beiträge 22. Munich: Kaiser, 1977.

Diem, Hermann. "Karl Barth as Socialist." In *Karl Barth and Radical Politics*, edited and translated by George Hunsinger, 121–38. Philadelphia: Westminster, 1976.

Dinoia, J. A. "Religion and the Religions." In *The Cambridge Companion to Karl Barth*, edited by John Webster, 243–57. Cambridge Companions to Religion. Cambrdige: Cambridge University Press, 2000.

Drews, Paul. "Zum dritten Mal: Moderne Theologie und Reichgottesarbeit." *ZTK* 19 (1909) 475–79.

Driver, Tom F. *Christ in a Changing World: Toward an Ethical Christology*. New York: Crossroad, 1981.

Egger, Heinz. *Die Entstehung der Kommunistischen Partei und des Kommunistischen Jugendvandes der Schweiz*. Zurich: Genossenschaft Literaturvertrieb, 1952.

Eicher, Peter. "Gottes Wahl: Unsere Freiheit. Karl Barths Beitrag zur Theologie der Befreiung." In *Karl Barth, der Störenfried?*, edited by Friedrich-Wilhelm Marquardt, Dieter Schellong, and Michael Weinrich, 215–36. Einwürfe 3. Munich: Kaiser, 1986.

Engels, Friedrich. "Supplement to *Capital*, Vol. 3." In *Capital*, Vol. 3, 893–95. London: Lawrence & Wishart, 1977.

———. "Engels an Joseph Bloch (Sep. 21, 1890)." In MEW 37:462–65. Berlin: Dietz, 1986.

Evang, Martin. *Rudolf Bultmann in seiner Frühzeit*. BHT 74. Tübingen: Mohr/Siebeck, 1988.

Eyck, Erich. *A History of the Weimar Republic*. Vol. 1, *From the Collapse of the Empire to Hindenburg's Election*. Translated by Harlan P. Hanson and Robert G. L. Waite. New York: Wiley, 1962.

Feuerbach, Ludwig. *The Essence of Christianity*. Translated by George Eliot. Introductory essay by Karl Barth. Foreword by H. Richard Niebuhr. The Library of Religion and Culture. New York: Harper & Row, 1957.

———. *Das Wesen des Christentums*. Edited by W. Bolin and F. Jodl. Stuttgart: Reclam, 1959.

Figes, Orlando. *A People's Tragedy: The Russian Revolution 1891–1924*. New York: Penguin, 1996.

Fraenkel, Peter, translator. *Natural Theology: Comprising "Nature and Grace" by Professor Dr. Emil Brunner and the reply "No!" by Dr. Karl Barth*. London: Bles, 1946

Frei, Hans W. "The Doctrine of Revelation in the Thought of Karl Barth, 1909 to 1922: The Nature of Barth's Break with Liberalism." PhD diss., Yale University, 1956.

———. *Types of Christian Theology*. Edited by George Hunsinger and William C. Placher. New Haven: Yale University Press, 1992.

Frölich, Paul. *Rosa Luxemburg: Gedanke und Tat*. Berlin: Dietz, 1990.

Gay, Peter. *Weimar Culture: The Outsider as Insider*. New York: Harper and Row, 1968.

Geis, Robert Raphael. *Gottes Minorität; Beiträge z. jüd. Theologie u. z. Geschichte der Juden in Deutschland*. Munich: Kösel, 1971.
Geras, Norman. *The Legacy of Rosa Luxemburg*. London: NLB, 1976.
Glasse, John. "Barth zu Feuerbach." *EvT* 28 (1968) 459–95.
Gollwitzer, Helmut. *Befreiung zur Solidarität : Einführung in die Evangelische Theologie*. Munich: Kaiser, 1978.
———. *Die Existenz Gottes im Bekenntnis des Glaubens*, Munich: Kaiser, 1963.
———. *Die Kapitalistiche Revolution*. Munich: Kaiser, 1974.
———. "The Kingdom of God and Socialism in the Theology of Karl Barth." In *Karl Barth and Radical Politics*, edited and translated by George Hunsinger, 77–128. Philadelphia: Westminster, 1976.
———. *Krummes Holz-Aufrechter Gang: Zur Frage nach dem Sinn des Lebens*. Munich: Kaiser, 1970.
———. "Martin Bubers Bedeutung für die protestantische Theologie." In *Auch das Denken darf dienen: Aufsätze zu Theologie und Geistesgeschichte*. Vol. 2, 36–61. Munich: Kaiser, 1988.
———. *Der Mensch, du bist gefragt: Reflexionen zur Gotteslehre*. Edited by Peter Winzeler. Munich: Kaiser, 1988.
———. *Richte unsere Füsse auf den Weg des Friedens: Helmut Gollwitzer zum 70.Geburtstag*. Munich: Kaiser, 1979.
———. "Vom Nutzen und Grenzen soziologischer Theologiebetrachtung." *EvT* 33 (1973) 622–26.
———. "Der Wille Gottes und die Gesellschaftliche Wirklichkeit." In *Der Mensch, du bist gefragt: Reflexionen zur Gotteslehre*, 274–79. Munich: Kaiser, 1988.
———. "Das Wort 'Gott' in Christlicher Theologie," In *Der Mensch, du bist gefragt: Reflexionen zur Gotteslehre*, 86–111. Munich: Kaiser, 1988.
———. *Zuspruch und Anspruch: Predigten*. Munich: Kaiser, 1968.
Gorringe, Timothy J. *Karl Barth: Against Hegemony*. Christian Theology in Context. Oxford: Oxford University Press, 1999.
Green, Clifford J., editor. *Karl Barth: Theologian of Freedom*. Minneapolis: Fortress, 1991.
Gutteridge, Richard. *The German Evangelical Church and the Jews, 1879–1950*. New York: Harper and Row, 1976.
Gutiérrez, Gustavo. *The Power of the Poor in History: Selected Writings*. Translated by Robert R. Barr. London: SCM, 1983.
Greschat, Martin. *Das Zeitalter der Industriellen Revolution: das Christentum vor der Moderne*. Christentum und Gesellschaft Bd. 11. Stuttgart: Kohlhammer, 1980.
Groll, Wilfried. *Ernst Troeltsch und Karl Barth, Kontinuität im Widerspruch*. BevT: Abhandlungen 72. Munich: Kaiser, 1976.
Grundmann, Reiner. "Why Is Werner Sombart Not Part of the Core of Classical Sociology?: From Fame to (Near) Oblivion." *Journal of Classical Sociology* 1 (2001) 257–87.
Gudopp, Wolf-Dieter. *Martin Bubers dialogischer Anarchismus*. Bern: Lang, 1975.

Harms, Jens, editor. *Christiantum und Anarchismus: Beiträge zu einem ungeklärten Verhältnis*. Frankfurt: Athanaüm, 1988.

Harnack, Adolf von. *What Is Christianity?* Translated by Thomas Bailey Saunders. Harper Torchbooks. New York: Harper & Row, 1957.

Havelock, Harper C., and Ryugaku Ishizuka. *Honen: The Buddhist Saint*. 1925. Reprint, New York: Garland, 1981.

Haynes, Stephen R. *Reluctant Witnesses: Jews and the Christian Imagination*, Louisville: Westminster John Knox, 1995.

———. *Prospects for Post-Holocaust Theology*. American Academy of Religion Academy Series 77. Atlanta: Scholars, 1981.

Hennecke, Susanne, and Michael Weinrich, editors. *"Abirren": Niederländische und deutsche Beiträge von und für Friedrich-Wilhelm Marquardt*. Wittingen: Erev-Rav, 1998.

Heppe, Heinrich. *Die Dogmatik der evangelisch-reformierten Kirche. Dargestellt und aus den Quellen belegt*. Edited by Ernst Bizer. Neukirchen: Moers, 1935.

Herrmann, Wilhelm. *The Communion of the Christian with God*. 2d English edition. Translated by J. Sandys Stanyon. London: Williams and Norgate, 1909.

———. *Ethik*. Tübingen: Mohr/Siebeck, 1913.

———. *Gesammelte Schriften*. Edited by F. W. Schmidt. Tübingen: Mohr/Siebeck, 1923.

———. *Systematic Theology*. Translated by Nathaniel Micklem and Kenneth Sanders. London: Allen & Unwin, 1927.

———. "Warum bedarf unser Glaube geschichtlicher Tatsachen?" In *Gesammelte Schriften*, edited by F. W. Schmidt, 214–38. Tübingen: Mohr/Siebeck, 1923.

Heron, Alasdair I. C. *A Century of Protestant Theology*. Philadelphia: Westminster, 1980.

Hick, John. *God Has Many Names*. Philadelphia: Westminster, 1980.

Historische Kommission der Partei der Arbeit der Schweiz. *Zur Geschichte der kommunistischen Bewegung in der Schweiz*. Zurich: Die Komission, 1981.

Hood, Robert. *Contemporary Political Orders and Christ*. Pittsburgh Theological Monographs 14. Allison Park, PA: Pickwick, 1985.

Hunsinger, George. "Barth, Barmen and the Confessing Church Today." In *Disruptive Grace: Studies in the Theology of Karl Barth*, 60–88. Grand Rapids: Eerdmans, 2000.

———. "Beyond Literalism and Expressivism: Karl Barth's Hermeneutical Realism." In *Dusruptive Grace: Studies in the Theology of Karl Barth*, 210–25. Grand Rapids: Eerdmans, 2000.

———. "Conversational Theology: The Wit and Wisdom of Karl Barth." No pages. Accessed April 2, 2008. Online: http://libweb.ptsem.edu/collections/barth/articles/Hunsinger.aspx?menu=296&subText=468.

———. *Disruptive Grace: Studies in the Theology of Karl Barth*. Grand Rapids: Eerdmans, 2000.

———. *How to Read Karl Barth: The Shape of His Theology*. New York: Oxford University Press, 1991.

———, editor and translator. *Karl Barth and Radical Politics*. Philadelphia: Westminster, 1976.

———. "Karl Barth and Liberation Theology." In *Disruptive Grace: Studies in the Theology of Karl Barth*, 42–59. Grand Rapids: Eerdmans, 2000.

———. "Truth as Self-Involving: Barth and Lindbeck." In *Disruptive Grace: Studies in the Theology of Karl Barth*, 305–18. Grand Rapids: Eerdmans, 2000.

Iwand, Hans Joachim. *Nachgelassene Werke*. Bd. 1, *Glauben und Wissen*. Munich: Kaiser, 1962.

Jäger, Hans Ulrich. *Ethik und Eschatologie bei Leonhard Ragaz: Versuch einer Darstellung der Grundstrukturen und inneren Systematik von Leonhard Ragaz' theologischem Denken unter besonderer Berücksichtigung seiner Vorlesungsmanuskripte*. Zurich, Universität. Institut für Sozialethik. Veröffentlichungen 5. Zürich: TVZ, 1971.

Johnson, William Stacey. *The Mystery of God: Karl Barth and the Postmodern Foundations of Theology*. Columbia Series in Reformed Theology. Louisville: Westminster John Knox, 1997.

Jost, Hans Ulrich. *Linksradikalismus in der deutschen Schweiz 1914 bis 1918*. Bern: Staempfli, 1973.

Jüngel, Eberhard. *Barth-Studien*. Ökumenische Theologie 9. Zurich: Benzinger, 1982.

———. *God's Being Is in Becoming: The Trinitarian Being of God in the Theology of Karl Barth: A Paraphrase*. London: T. & T. Clark, 2001.

———. *God as the Mystery of the World: On the Foundation of the Theology of the Crucified One in the Dispute between Theism and Atheism*. Translated by Darrell L. Guder. Grand Rapids: Eerdmans, 1983.

———. *Gott als Geheimnis der Welt: Zur Begründung der Theologie des Gekreuzigten im Streit zwischen Theismus und Atheismus*. Tübingen: Mohr/ Siebeck, 1986.

———. *Karl Barth: A Theological Legacy*. Translated by Garrett E Paul. Philadelphia: Westminster, 1986.

———. "Von der Dialektik zur Analogie: Die Schule Kierkegaards und der Einspruch Petersons." In *Barth-Studien*, 127–79. Ökumenische Theologie 9. Zurich: Benzinger, 1982.

Kant, Immanuel. *Critique of Pure Reason*. Translated by Norman Kemp Smith. New York: St Martin's, 1965.

———. *Fundamental Principles of the Metaphysics of Morals*. Translated by Thomas K. Abbott. Indianapolis: Bobbs-Merrill, 1949.

Käsemann, Ernst. "Justification and Salvation History in the Epistle to the Romans." In *Perspectives on Paul*, 60–78. Translated by Margaret Kohl. London: SCM, 1971.

Keel, Hee-Sung. *Understanding Shinran: A Dialogical Approach*. Nanzan Studies in Asian Religions 6. Fremont, CA: Asian Humanities, 1995.

Kelly, Geffrey B., et al., editors. *Dietrich Bonhoeffer Works*. Translated by Daniel W. Bloesch and James H. Burtness. 7 vols. Minneapolis: Fortress, 1996–2001.

Kierkegaard. Søren. *On Authority and Revelation*. Translated by Walter Lowrie. Princeton: Princeton University Press, 1955.

———. *Training in Christianity*. Translated by Walter Lowrie. Princeton: Princeton University Press, 1952.

Klappert, Bertold. *Die Aufweckung des Gekreuzigten: Der Ansatz der Christologie Karl Barths im Zusammenhang der Christologie der Gegenwart*. Neukirchen-Vluyn: Neukirchener, 1971.

———. *Israel und die Kirche: Erwägungen zur Israellehre Karl Barths*. Theologische Existenz heute 207. Munich: Kaiser, 1980.

———. *Promissio und Bund: Gesetz und Evangelium bei Luther und Barth*. Forschungen zur systematischen und ökumenischen Theologie 34. Göttingen: Vandenhoeck und Ruprecht, 1976.

———. *Miterben der Verheissung*. Beiträge zum jüdisch-christlichen Dialog. Neukirchen-Vluyn: Neukirchener, 2000.

———. *Versöhnung und Befreiung: Versuche, Karl Barth kontextuel zu verstehen*. Neukirchen-Vluyn: Neukirchener, 1994.

———. *Worauf wir hoffen : das Kommen Gottes und der Weg Jesu Christi*, mit einer Antwort von Jürgen Moltmann. Guttersloh: Kaiser, 1997.

Knitter, Paul F. *No Other Name? A Critical Survey of Christian Attitudes toward the World Religions*. American Society of Missiology Series, 7. Maryknoll, NY: Orbis, 1985.

Kolakowski, Leszek. *Main Currents of Marxism: Its Origins, Growth and Dissolution*. Vol. 2, *The Golden Age*. Translated by P. S. Falla. Oxford: Oxford University Press, 1990.

Kraemer, Hendrik. *The Christian Message in a Non-Christian World*. New York: Harper & Brothers, 1938.

———. *Why Christianity of All Religions?* Translated by Hubert Hoskins. Foundations of the Christian Mission. London: Lutterworth, 1962.

Kraus, Hans-Joachim. *Reich Gottes, Reich der Freiheit: Grundriss systematiche Theologie*. Neukirchen-Vluyn : Neukirchener, 1975.

———. *Theologische Religionskritik*. Neukirchener Beiträge zur systematischen Theologie 2. Neukirchen-Vluyn: Neukirchener, 1982.

Kreck, Walter. *Die Zukunft des Gekommenen*. Munich: Kaiser, 1966.

Krupskaja, Nadeshda. *Eine Biographie*. Berlin: Dietz, 1986.

Küng, Hans. *Does God Exist?: An Answer for Today*. Translated by Edward Quinn. New York: Vintage, 1981.

Kupisch, Karl. *Zwischen Idealismus und Massendemokratie: Eine Geschichte der evangelischen Kirche in Deutschland von 1815–1945*. Berlin: Lettner, 1955.

———. *Karl Barth in Selbstzeugnissen und Bilddokumenten*. Rowohlts Monographien, 174. Hamburg: Rowohlt, 1971.

Kutter, Hermann. *Sie Müssen! Ein offenes Wort an die chrtistlcihe Gesellschaft*. Berlin: Hermann Walthersbuchhandlung, 1904.

———. *Das Unmittelbare. Eine Menschheitsfrage*. Jena: Diederichs, 1911.

———. *Wir Pfarrer*. Leipzig: Haessel, 1907.

Lapide, Pinchas, and Jürgen Moltmann. *Israel und Kirche: Ein gemeinsamer Weg? Ein Gespräch*. Kaiser Traktate 54. Munich: Kaiser, 1980.

Leith, John, editor. *Creeds of the Churches*. Atlanta: John Knox, 1983.

Lejeune, Robert, editor. *Christoph Blumhardt und seine Botschaft*. Erlenbach: Rotapfel, 1938.

Lenin, Vladmir Illich. *Letters from Afar*. New York: International, 1932.
———. *Works*, vols. 10, 24, 27, and 29. London: 1960–1970.
———. *The State and Revolution*, in K. Marx, F. Engels, V. Lenin: *On Historical Materialism: A Collection*. Moscow: Progress Publishers, 1972.
Lindbeck, George. *The Nature of Doctrine: Religion and Theology in a Postliberal Age*. Louisville: Westminster John Knox, 1984.
Link, Christian. *Die Welt als Gleichnis: Studien zum Problem der natürlichen Theologie*. BEvT 73. Munich: Kaiser, 1976.
———. *Schöpfung: Schöpfungstheologie in reformatorischer Tradition*. 2 vols. Handbuch systematischer Theologie 7. Gütersloh: Mohn, 1991.
Lochman, Jan M. *Encountering Marx: Bonds and Barriers between Christians and Marxists*. Philadelphia: Fortress, 1977.
Lowe, Walter. *Theology and Difference: The Wound of Reason*. The Indiana Series in the Philosophy of Religion. Bloomington: Indiana University Press, 1993.
Lukács, Georg. *The Destruction of Reason*. Translated by Peter Palmer. Atlantic Highlands, NJ: Humanities, 1981.
Lull, Timothy, editor. *Martin Luther's Basic Theological Writings*. Minneapolis: Fortress 1989.
Luther, Martin. *D. Martin Luthers Werke. Kritische Gesamtausgabe*. 61 vols. Weimar: Hermann Böhlaus Nachfolger, 1883–1983.
———. "How Christians Should Regard Moses (1525)." In *Luther's Basic Theological Writings*, edited by Timothy Lull, 135–48. Minneapolis: Fortress, 1989.
———. *Luther's Works*. Edited by Helmut T. Lehmann. Vols. 31–55. Philadelphia: Fortress, 1955–1986.
———. *Luther's Works*. Edited by Jaroslav Pelikan. Vols. 1–30. St. Louis: Concordia, 1955–1967.
Luxemburg, Rosa. *Kirche und Sozialismus*. Frankfurt: Stimme, 1974.
Lyotard, Jean-François. *The Postmodern Condition: A Report on Knowledge*. Theory and History of Literature vol. 10. Minneapolis: University of Minnesota Press, 1984.
Machovec, Milan. *Marxismus und dialektische Theologie*. Zürich: TVZ, 1965.
Malanowski, Wolfgang. *November-Revolution 1918: die Rolle der SPD*. Hamburg: Spiegel, 1969.
Marquardt, Friedrich-Wilhelm. "Der Aktuar. Aus Barths Pfarramt." In *Karl Barth, Der Störenfried?*, edited by Friedrich-Wilhelm Marquardt, Dieter Schellong, and Michael Weinrich, 93–139. Einwürfe 3. Munich: Kaiser, 1986.
———. *Der Christ in der Gesellschaft, 1919–1979: Geschichte, Analyse und aktuelle Bedeutung von Karl Barths Tambacher Vortrag*. Theologische Existenz heute 206. Munich: Kaiser, 1980.
———. *Das christliche Bekenntnis zu Jesus, dem Juden: Eine Christologie*. 2 vols. Munich: Kaiser, 1991.
———. "Erster Bericht über Karl Barths 'Sozialistisches Reden.'" In *Verwegenheiten: Theologische Stücke aus Berlin*, 470–88. Munich: Kaiser, 1981.

———. *Die Entdeckung des Judentums für die christliche Theologie: Israel im Denken Karl Barths*. Abhandlungen zum christlich-jüdischen Dialog 1. Munich: Kaiser, 1967.

———. "Exegese und Dogmatik in Karl Barths Theologie: Was meint: 'Kritischer müssten mir die Historish-Kritischen sein!'?" In *Verwegenheiten: Theologische Stücke aus Berlin*, 381–406. Munich: Kaiser, 1981.

———. "Der Götze wackelt. Der Generalangriff aus dem Römerbrief." In *Verwegenheiten: Theologische Stücke aus Berlin*, 407–23. Munich: Kaiser, 1981.

———. *Theologie und Sozialismus: Das Beispiel Karl Barths*, Munich: Kaiser, 1972.

———. "Religionskritik und Entmythologsierung: Über einen Beitrag Karl Barths zur Entmythologisierungsfrage." In *Verwegenheiten: Theologische Stücke aus Berlin*, 339–80. Munich: Kaiser, 1981.

———. *Verwegenheiten: Theologische Stücke aus Berlin*. Munich: Kaiser, 1981.

Marx, Karl. "Economic and Philosophical Manuscripts." In *Karl Marx: Selected Writings*, edited by David McLellan, 75–122. Oxford: Oxford University Press, 1988.

———. *Das Elend der Philosophie*. MEW 4. Berlin: Dietz, 1971.

———. *Frühe Schriften*. Werke, Schriften, Briefe. Bd. 1. Edited by Hans-Joachim Liber and Peter Furth. Stuttgart: Cotta, 1962.

———. *Das Kapital*. Bd.1. MEW 23. Berlin: Dietz, 1958.

Mattmüller, Markus. "Der Einfluss Christoph Blumhardts auf schweizerische Theologen des 20. Jahrhunderts." ZEE 12 (1968) 233–46.

———. *Leonhard Ragaz und der religiöse Sozialismus*. 2 vols. Basler Beiträge zur Geschichtswissenschaft 67, 110. Zurich: EVZ, 1968.

———. "Der Einfluss Christoph Blumhardts auf schweizerische Theologen des 20. Jahrhunderts." ZEE 12 (1968) 233–46.

McCormack, Bruce L. *Karl Barth's Critically Realistic Dialectical Theology: Its Genesis and Development, 1909–1936*. Oxford: Clarendon, 1995.

McLellan, David, editor. *Karl Marx: Selected Writings*. Oxford: Oxford University Press, 1988.

McNeill, John T. *The History and Character of Calvinism*. New York: Oxford University Press, 1954.

Mechels, Eberhard. *Analogie bei Erich Przywara und Karl Barth: Das Verhältnis von Offenbarungstheologie und Metaphysik*, Neukirchen-Vluyn: Neukirchener, 1974.

Moltmann, Jürgen, editor. *Anfänge der dialektischen Theologie*. 2 vols. Theologische Bücherei; Neudrucke und Berichte aus dem 20. Jahrhundert 17. Systematische Theologie. Munich: Kaiser, 1962–1963.

———. *The Coming of God: Christian Eschatology*. Translated by Margaret Kohl. Minneapolis: Fortress, 1996.

———. *The Crucified God: The Cross of Christ as the Foundation and Criticism of Christian Theology*. New York: Harper and Row, 1974.

———. *Experiences in Theology: Ways and Forms of Christian Theology*. Translated by Margaret Kohl. Minneapolis: Fortress, 2000.

———. *History and the Triune God: Contributions to Trinitarian Theology*. Translated by John Bowden. New York, Crossroad, 1992.

———. *The Trinity and the Kingdom: The Doctrine of God*. Translated by Margaret Kohl. San Francisco: Harper & Row, 1981.
Muller, David L. *An Introduction to the Theology of Albrecht Ritschl*. Philadelphia: Westminster, 1969.
Neuser, W. H. *Karl Barth in Münster, 1925–1930*. ThSt 130. Zurich: TVZ, 1985.
Ngien, Dennis. *The Suffering of God according to Martin Luther's* Theologia Crucis. American University Studies. Series VII, Theology and Religion 181. New York: Lang, 1995.
Niebuhr, H. Richard. *Christ and Culture*. New York: Harper & Row, 1951.
Overbeck, Franz. *Christentum und Kultur: Gedanken und Anmerkungen zur modernen Theologie*. Edited by Carl Albrecht Bernoulli. Basel: Benno Schwabe, 1919.
Otto, Rudolf. *The Idea of the Holy*. Translated by John W. Harvey. London: Oxford University Press, 1958.
Pangritz, Andreas. *Karl Barth in the Theology of Dietrich Bonhoeffer*. Translated by Barbara and Martin Rumscheidt. Grand Rapids: Eerdmans, 1989.
———. *Friedrich-Wilhelm Marquardt: Eine theologische-biographische Skizze von Andreas Pangritz*. Berlin: Aktion Sühnezeichen Friedensdienste, 2003.
Pannenberg, Wolfart. *Jesus—God and Man*. Translated by Lewis L. Wilkens and Duane A. Priebe. Philadelphia: Westminster, 1968.
———. *Systematic Theology*. 3 vols. Grand Rapids: Eerdmans, 1991–1998.
———. *Systematische Theologie*, Bd II. Göttingen: Vandenhoeck & Ruprecht, 1988.
Parsons, Talcott. *The Structure of Social Action: A Study in Social Theory with Special Reference to a Group of Recent European Writers*. 2d edition. Glencoe, IL: Free Press, 1949.
Peterson, Erik. "Was ist Theologie?" In *Theologische Traktate*, 9–43. Munich: Im Koesel, 1951.
Plonz, Sabine. *Die Herrenlosen Gewalten: Eine Relektüre Karl Barths in befreiungstheologischer Perspektive*. Mainz: Grünewald, 1995.
Przywara, Erich. *Analogia Entis: Metaphysik*. 3 vols. Schriften/Erich Przywara. Einsiedeln: Johannes, 1962.
———. *Was ist Gott: Eine Summula*. Nuremberg: Glock und Lutz, 1953.
Ragaz, Leonhard. "The Battle against Bolshevism." In *Signs of the Kingdom: A Ragaz Reader*, edited by Paul Bock, 43–46. Grand Rapids: Eerdmans, 1984.
———. *Die Bible, Eine Deutung*. Bd. 3, *Die Geschichte Israels*. Zurich: Diana, 1948.
———. *Der Kampf um das Reich Gottes in Blumhardt, Vater und Sohn, und weiter!* Erlenbach-Zurich: Rotapfel, 1925.
———. "Gospel and the Current Social Struggle." In *Signs of the Kingdom: A Ragaz Reader*, edited by Paul Bock, 3–15. Grand Rapids: Eerdmans, 1984.
———. *Mein Weg*. 2 vols. Zurich: Diana, 1952.
———. *Weltreich, Religion und Gottesherrschaft*. 2 vols. Erlenbach-Zürich: Rotapfel, 1922.
Rendtorff, Rolf. "Die jüdische Bibel und die antijüdische Auslegung." In *Auschwitz, Krise der christlichen Theologie*, edited by Rolf Rendtorff and Ekkehard Stegemann, 99–116. Abhandlungen zum christlich-jüdischen Dialog 10. Munich: Kaiser, 1980.

Rendtorff, Rolf, and Ekkehard Stegemann, editors. *Auschwitz, Krise der christlichen Theologie*. Abhandlungen zum christlich-jüdischen Dialog 10. Munich: Kaiser, 1980.

Rendtorff, Trutz, editor. *Die Realisierung der Freiheit*. Gütersloh: Mohn, 1975.

Robinson, James M., editor. *The Beginnings of Dialectic Theology*. Richmond: John Knox, 1968.

Rotelle, John E., editor. *The Works of St. Augustine: A Translation for the 21st Century*. Vol. 5, *The Trinity*, translated by Edmund Hill. New York: New City, 1991.

Rostig, Dittmar. *Bergpredigt und Politik: Zur Struktur und Funktion des Reiches Gottes bei Leonhard Ragaz*. European University Studies. Series XXIII, Theology 419. Frankfurt: Lang, 1991.

Rousseau. Jean-Jacques. *On the Social Contract, with Geneva Manuscript and "Political Economy."* Edited by Roger D. Masters. Translated by Judith R. Masters. New York: St. Martin's, 1978.

Ruschke, Werner. *Entstehung und Ausführung der Diastasentheologie in Karl Barths zweitem Römerbrief*. Neukirchener Beiträge zur systematischen Theologie; Bd. 5. Neukirchen-Vluyn: Neukirchener, 1987.

Sandkühler, Hans-Jörg, and Rafade de la Vega, editors. *Marxismus und Ethik*. Suhrkamp Taschenbuch Wissenschaft 75. Frankfurt: Suhrkamp, 1974.

Sauter, Gerhard. "Soziologische oder politische Barth-Interpretation?" *EvT* 35 (1975) 173–83.

——— . *Die Theologie des Reiches Gottes beim älteren und jungeren Blumhardt*. Studien zur Dogmengeschichte und systematischen Theologie; Bd. 14. Zurich: Zwingli, 1962.

Schellong, Dieter, "Barth Lessen." In *Karl Barth, Der Störenfried?*, edited by Friedrich-Wilhelm Marquardt, Dieter Schellong, and Michael Weinrich, 5–92. Einwürfe 3. Munich: Kaiser, 1986.

——— . "Karl Barth als Theologe der Neuzeit." In *Karl Barth und die Neuzeit*, by Karl Gerhard Steck and Dieter Schellong, 37–102. Theologische Existenz heute 173 Munich: Kaiser, 1973.

——— . "On Reading Karl Barth from the Left." In *Karl Barth and Radical Politics*, edited and translated by George Hunsinger, 139–45. Philadelphia: Westminster, 1976.

Schleiermacher, F. *Der Christliche Glaube*, Bd. 2. Ed. Hermann Peiter, Berlin, New York: de Gruyter, 1984.

Schimdt, Jacques. "Am Scheideweg." *Neuer Freier Aargauer. Sozialdemokratisches Tagblatt* 14/34 (11 February, 1919) 1–2.

Schmidt-Ammann, Paul. *Die Wahrheit über den Generalstreik von 1918: Seine Ursachen, seine Verlauf, seine Folgen*. Zurich: Morgarten, 1968.

Scholder, Klaus. *The Churches and the Third Reich*. Vol. 1, *Preliminary History and the Time of Illusion, 1918–1934*. Translated by John Bowden. London: SCM, 1989.

Schwoebel, Christoph, editor. *Karl Barth-Martin Rade: Ein Briefwechsel*. Gütersloh: Gütersloher Verlagshaus Gerd Mohn, 1981.

Smart, James D., translator. *Revolutionary Theology in the Making: Barth-Thurneysen Correspondence, 1914–1925*. Richmond: John Knox, 1964.

Smith, Ronald G., compiler. *World Come of Age: A Symposium on Dietrich Bonhoeffer*. Philadelphia: Fortress, 1967.

Sobrino, Jon. "Systematic Christology: Jesus Christ, the Absolute Mediator of the Reign of God." In *Systematic Theology: Perspectives from Liberation Theology*, edited by Igancio Ellacuría and Jon Sobrino, 124–45. Maryknoll, NY: Orbis, 1996.

Sobrino, Jon, and Ignacio Ellacuría, editors. *Systematic Theology: Perspectives from Liberation Theology*. Maryknoll, NY: Orbis, 1996.

Soelle, Dorothee. *Christ the Representative: An Essay in Theology after the "Death of God."* Translated by David Lewis. London: SCM, 1967.

Sombart. Werner. *Economic Life in the Modern Age*. Edtied by Nico Stehr and Reiner Grundmann. New Brunswick, NJ: Transaction, 2001.

———. *Die Gewerbliche Arbeiterfrage*. Sammlung Göschen 209. Berlin: G. J. Göschen, 1912.

———. *Der moderne Kapitalismus*. Bd. 3, Das Wirtschaftaleben im Zeitalter des Hochkapitalismus. Leipzig: Duncker & Humblot, 1927.

———. *A New Social Philosophy*. Translated and edited by Karl F. Geiser. Princeton: Princeton University Press, 1937.

———. *Sozialismus und soziale Bewegung im 19. Jahrhundert*. Jena: Fischer, 1896.

Sonderegger, Katherine. *That Jesus Christ Was Born a Jew: Karl Barth's "Doctrine of Israel."* University Park: Pennsylvania State University Press, 1992.

Sozialismus aus dem Glauben: Verhandlungen der Sozialistischen Tagung in Heppenheim. Zurich: Rotapfel, 1929.

Spieckermann, Ingrid. *Gotteserkenntnis: Ein Beitrag zur Grundfrage der neuen Theologie Karl Barths*. BEvT 97. Munich: Kaiser, 1985.

Steck, Karl Gerhard and Dieter Schellong. *Karl Barth und die Neuzeit*. Theologische Existenz heute 173 Munich: Kaiser, 1973.

Stendahl, Krister. *Paul among Jews and Gentiles and Other Essays*. Philadelphia: Fortress, 1976.

Steubing, Hans, et al., compilers. *Bekenntnisse der Kirche. Bekenntnistexte aus 20 Jahrhunderten*. Wuppertal: Brockhaus, 1985

Stoevesandt, Hinrich. "Von der Kirchenpolitik zur Kirche!: Zur Entstehungsgeschichte von Karl Barths Schrift 'Theologische Existenz heute!' im Juni 1933." ZTK 76 (1979) 118–38.

Takeuchi, Yoshinori, editor. *Buddhist Spirituality: Later China, Korea, Japan and the Modern World; An Encyclopedic History of the Religious Quest*. In association with James W. Heisig, Paul L. Swanson, and Joseph S. O'Leary. World Spirituality 9. New York: Crossroad, 1999.

Takizawa, Katsumi. *Das Heil im Heute: Texte einer japanischen Theologie*. Edited by Theo Sundermeier. Theologie der Ökumene 21. Göttingen: Vandenhoeck & Ruprecht, 1987.

———. *Reflexionen über die universale Grundlage von Buddhismus und Christentum*. Bern: Lang, 1980.

Tappert, Theodore G., editor and translator. *The Book of Concord: The Confessions of the Evangelical Lutheran Church*. Philadelphia: Fortress, 1959.
Thompson, Geoff, and Christian Mosert. *Karl Barth: A Future for Postmodern Theology?* Adelaide: Australian Theological Forum, 2000.
Thurneysen, Eduard. *Die neue Zeit: Predigten, 1913-1930*, Edited by Wolfgang Germ. Neukirchen-Vluyn: Neukirchner, 1982.
———. *Karl Barth: "Theologie und Sozialismus" in den Briefen seiner Frühzeit*. Zurich: TVZ, 1973.
———. "Sozialismus und Christentum." In *ADT* 2:221-46.
———. "Unsere rotten Brüder." *Die Glocke* 22 (1914) Nr.8.
Tillich, Paul. *Christianity and the Encounter of World Religions*. Fortress Texts in Modern Theology. Minneapolis: Fortress, 1994.
———. *Systematic Theology*. 3 vols. Chicago: University of Chicago Press, 1951-1963.
———. *Theology of Culture*. Edited by Robert C. Kimball. New York: Oxford University Press, 1959.
Torrance, T. F. *Karl Barth: An Introduction to His Early Theology, 1910-1931*. London: SCM, 1962.
———. *Karl Barth, Biblical and Evangelical Theologian*. Edinburgh: T. & T. Clark, 1990.
———. *Reality and Scientific Theology*. Theology and Science at the Frontiers of Knowledge 1. Edinburgh: Scottish Academic, 1985.
———. *Theological Science*. Oxford: Oxford University Press, 1969.
Troeltsch, Ernst. *The Absoluteness of Christianity and the History of Religions*. Translated by David Reid. Research in Theology. Richmond: John Knox, 1971.
———. *Christian Thought: Its History and Application*. London: University of London Press, 1923.
———. *Religion in History*. Edited by James Luther Adams and Walter F. Bense. Fortress Texts in Modern Theology. Minneapolis: Fortress, 1991.
———. *The Social Teachings of the Christian Churches*. 2 vols. Library of Theological Ethics. Translated by Olive Wyon. Louisville: Westminster/John Knox, 1992.
Trotsky, Leon. *Mein Leben: Versuch einer Autobiographie*. Berlin: Dietz, 1990.
Updike, John. *Das Gottesprogramm. Roger's Version*. Hamburg: Reinbeck, 1988.
Villa-Vincencio, Charles, editor. *On Reading Karl Barth in South Africa*. Grand Rapids: Eerdmans, 1988.
Vorländer, Karl. *Die neukantische Bewegung im Sozialismus*. Kantstudien 7. Berlin: Reuther & Reichard, 1902.
Wagner, Falk. "Theologische Gleichschaltung: Zur Christologie bei Barth." In *Die Realisierung der Freiheit. Beiträge zur Kritik der Theologie Karl Barths*, edited by Trutz Rendtorff, 10-43. Güttersloh: Mohn, 1975
Weber, Max. *The Protestant Ethic and the Spirit of Capitalism*. Translated by Talcott Parsons. New York: Scribner, 1958
Weber, Otto. *Grundlangen der Dogmatik*, vol. 2. Neukirchen-Vluyn: Neukirchener, 1987.

Webster, John, editor. *The Cambridge Companion to Karl Barth*. Edited by John Webster. Cambridge Companions to Religion. Cambridge: Cambridge University Press, 2000.

Weinrich, Michael. "Der Katze die Schelle umhängen: Konflikte Theologischer Zeitgenossenschaft: Anregungen aus der theoloigschen Biographie Karl Barths." In *Karl Barth, Der Störenfried?*, edited by Friedrich-Wilhelm Marquardt, Dieter Schellong, and Michael Weinrich, 140–214. Einwürfe 3. Munich: Kaiser, 1986.

Welch, Claude. *Protestant Thought in the Nineteenth Century*. 2 vols. New Haven: Yale University Press, 1985.

Welker, Michael. *Creation and Reality*. Translated by John F. Hoffmeyer. Minneapolis: Fortress, 1999.

Wielenga, Bastiaan. *Lenins Wege zur Revolution: Eine Konfrontation mit Sergej Bulgakov und Petr Struve im Interesse einer theologischen Besinnung*. Munich: Kaiser, 1971.

Winzeler, Peter. "Der Gott Israels als Freund und Bundesgenosse des Menschen im Kampf gegen das Nichtige." *Zeitschrift für Dialektische Theologie* 1 (1985) 2–73.

———. "'Tut um Gottes Willen etwas Tapferes!' Die Vorsehungslehre bei Ulrich Zwingli und Karl Barth." Unpublished manuscript. Habilitationsschrift. Free University of Berlin, Germany, 1985.

———. "Die verneinte Natur der bejahten Kreatur. Das Nichtige in Barths Nein! Zur Natürlichen Theologie am Beispiel der bejahten Güte der Geschlechterdifferenz." In *Vom Zentrum des Glaubens: Festschrift für Dietrich Braun zum 70*, edited by Klaus Bajor-Mau et al., 309–26. Religionswissenschaft und Theologien 8. Rheinfelden: Schäuble, 1998.

———. *Widerstehende Theologie: Karl Barth, 1920–35*. Reihe im Lehrhaus 1. Stuttgart: Alektor, 1982.

———. "Eine Zäsur des Dialogs. Zur Erinnerung an Karl Barth." *Neue Dialog* 1:3 (2001) 21–38.

Zahn-Harnack, Agnes von. *Adolf von Harnack*. Berlin: de Gruyter, 1951.

INDEX

Anti-Semitism, 22, 295, 296, 380, 415, 419
Amida, 466, 467, 475
Analogy of being (*analogia entis*), ix, 15, 16, 18, 19, 20, 21, 25, 26, 31, 32, 237, 261, 308–17, 320, 324, 326, 328, 329, 330, 338, 339, 340, 397, 449
    of faith (*analogia fidei*), 4, 5, 15, 16, 19, 20, 25, 26, 31, 32, 237, 269–76, 308–17, 320, 324, 328, 329, 330, 339, 340, 457
    of relation (*analogia relationis*), 5, 26, 32, 315–30, 340, 395, 396, 397, 422
Anarchism, 82, 83, 85
Aneignung, 433
Anhypostasis, ix, 11, 16–18, 26, 345–51, 371–72, 376, 461, 462
Apokatastasis panton, 400, 401
Assumptio carnis, 16, 17, 18, 267, 321, 346, 348, 370–76, 388, 460, 461

Das Nichtige, 320, 425
Die Hilfe, 66–69, 91, 113, 156, 173
Dharmakaya, 477, 478

Enhypostasis, ix, 11, 16–18, 26, 345–51, 371–72, 376, 461, 462
Extra Calvinisticum, ix, 16–18, 135, 139, 145, 198, 203, 217, 220, 226, 274, 278, 287, 308, 346, 348, 375, 461, 462

General Strike of 1918, 146–54

Honen, 465–68

Krisis, 2, 25, 209, 225

Logos spermatikos, 17, 18, 106, 347, 380, 462, 470

Lenin, 31, 65–67, 79, 80, 81, 89, 90, 91, 100, 134–46, 149, 176, 193, 442
Lukács, G, 425

Massa perditionis, 473, 479, 480
Minjung, 27, 473, 479

Neo-orthodoxy, x, 14–15
Nembutsu, 466
Neue Wege, 58, 64, 65, 72, 80, 81, 86, 104

Positivism of revelation, 13–15, 401–7
Praedestinatio dialectica, 125, 400
Praedestinatio gemina, 91, 125, 300, 311, 386, 400
Pure Land Buddhism, 27, 465–68

Realdialetik, 5
Regunum naturae, 178–82, 189
Regnum gloriae, 184, 190, 273
Regnum gratiae, 179, 182–83, 273
Religious Socialism, ix, 25, 26, 28, 29, 33, 49, 64, 69–86, 128, 341

Schöpfungsoffenbarung, 338
Shinran, 465–68
Socialist Speeches, 47–58, 69, 74–78,
    113, 141
Status exaltationis, 356, 363
Status exinanitionis, 356, 363
Sunyata, 476, 478

The Blumhardt movement, 154–61
The Communist Manifesto, 55, 97, 195
The Tambach lecture, ix, 5, 25, 128,
    162–91, 220, 257
The Treaty of Brest-Litovsk, 162, 192,
    193
Theologia naturalis, xi, 15–20, 23, 26,
    31, 32, 189, 297–308, 330–44,
    420, 449, 470, 476
Theologische Existenz Heute, 12, 288,
    289
Totaliter aliter, 9, 83, 86, 111, 121, 126,
    171, 181, 183, 197, 202, 216, 227,
    234, 239, 449

Urfaktum Immanuel, 475-478
Urgeschichte, 198–99
Ursprung, 2, 6, 35, 36, 62, 63, 116–24,
    132, 137, 143, 197, 198, 200, 209,
    279
USPD, 89, 163

Vestigia trinitatis, 273

Wort zur Lage, 290, 295, 296
Wort zur Sache, 290, 295, 296
Zimmerwald conference, 87, 90, 139,
    149, 152

www.ingramcontent.com/pod-product-compliance
Lightning Source LLC
Chambersburg PA
CBHW021230300426
44111CB00007B/487